THE COLLEGE PRESS NIV COMMENTARY

ROMANS

JACK COTTRELL
with Terry A. Chaney

New Testament Series Co-Editors:

Jack Cottrell, Ph.D. Tony Ash, Ph.D.
Cincinnati Bible Seminary Abilene Christian University

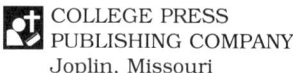
COLLEGE PRESS
PUBLISHING COMPANY
Joplin, Missouri

Copyright © 2005
College Press Publishing Company

Printed and Bound in the
United States of America
All Rights Reserved

Unless otherwise noted, Scripture quotations are taken from the HOLY BIBLE, NEW INTERNATIONAL VERSION®. NIV®. Copyright © 1973, 1978, 1984, by International Bible Society. Used by permission of Zondervan Publishing House. All rights reserved.

Library of Congress Cataloging-in-Publication Data

Note: This commentary has been previously published in 2 volumes, ISBN 0-89900-632-9 and ISBN 0-89900-647-7, with the following CIP data:

Cottrell, Jack.
    Romans/Jack Cottrell
      p.   cm. — (The College Press NIV commentary)
    Includes bibliographical references.
    ISBN 0-89900-247-1
    1. Bible. N.T. Romans—Commentaries.   I. Title.   II. Series.
BS2665.3 .C68 1996
227'.1077—dc21

                                                      96-46296

ABBREVIATIONS

AG   *Arndt and Gingrich, Greek lexicon, 1957 ed.*
ASV   *American Standard Version*
BAGD   *Arndt and Gingrich, Greek lexicon, 2 ed., 1979*
ESV   *English Standard Version*
GC   *God the Creator, by Jack Cottrell*
GRe   *God the Redeemer, by Jack Cottrell*
GRu   *God the Ruler, by Jack Cottrell*
JC, I   *Romans, Volume I, by Jack Cottrell*
JC, II   *Romans, Volume II, by Jack Cottrell*
KJII   *King James II (New Testament translation)*
KJV   *King James Version*
LB   *Living Bible*
lit.   *literally*
LXX   *Septuagint (Greek translation of the OT)*
MP   *McGarvey-Pendleton Romans commentary*
NAB   *New American Bible*
NASB   *New American Standard Bible*
NEB   *New English Bible*
NIV   *New International Version*
NRSV   *New Revised Standard Version*
NT   *New Testament*
OT   *Old Testament*
RomDeb   *The Romans Debate, by Karl Donfried*
RSV   *Revised Standard Version*
SH   *Sanday and Headlam Romans commentary*
TDNT   *Theological Dictionary of the NT, ed. Kittel*
TEV   *Today's English Version*

(For fuller titles and publishing information on books, see the bibliography.)

PREFACE

In 1996 and 1998 College Press published the two volumes of Jack Cottrell's commentary on Romans as part of *The College Press NIV Commentary* series. Immediately the volumes received deservedly high praise. As a writer Cottrell has the relatively unusual ability to present his ideas clearly and simply. Even when dealing with complex issues he can cut to the very marrow of the matter. He takes great care to wrestle with the text until the meaning of Paul's words — God's words — is accurately exposed. In the process of explaining the text, Cottrell also interacts with other writers assessing their positions, attacking their weaknesses and confirming their contributions to the understanding of the text. All the while he is concerned about theology: theology that comes directly from Romans to be sure; however, he is also concerned about the theology that comes to Romans from the rest of Scripture. Cottrell also writes from the unique perspective of one who has long been a part of the Restoration Movement.

In 2003 Dru Ashwell, executive editor of College Press & HeartSpring Publishing, approached me about the possibility of reducing the two-volume set to a single volume. The primary motivation behind this change is the desire to see greater distribution and use of what we consider to be a very important contribution from one of the Restoration Movement's most popular contemporary writers. The simple fact is more people are likely to benefit from a single volume on Romans than a double volume with its increased cost and depth of material. However, from the beginning we agreed that all the material ought to be included in the abridged version by way of an electronic copy. Thus we have the best of all possibilities: an abridged version of the commentary that also includes the original, unabridged version.

A quick comparison will show that the primary changes made to reduce the original version to a single volume include the following. We have omitted many quotations from other writers and commentaries. When Cottrell discusses alternative understandings and positions on the text, we have reduced them or omitted them entirely. Many other explanations and notes from the original have also been summarized or removed. *However*, here it is important to notice that where this new, abridged version departs from the original, there is a disk symbol [⚫] which directs one to the original two volumes. (For example, ⚫I:26 indicates page 26 of volume one in the original.) It is our collective

Preface to the Combined Volume

desire that everyone who uses this abridged volume might frequently consult the unabridged version for further information and might come to know fully the Gospel of Grace that is the Epistle to the Romans.

Terry Chaney

BIBLIOGRAPHY

The following bibliography includes commentaries, books, and articles cited in the text and notes of this work. Citations include a minimum of information; the reader must use this list for full titles and bibliographical data.

When commentaries are cited, only the author's name and page number are given. When other sources are cited, usually just the author's name and an abbreviated title (in **bold print** below) are given. Some sources are cited with an even more abbreviated reference (see list of abbreviations). As explained in the preface, the symbol ✺ indicates material contained in the electronic version of the original 2-volume commentary.

I. COMMENTARIES

Achtemeier, Paul J. *Romans*. Interpretation: A Bible Commentary for Teaching and Preaching. Atlanta: John Knox Press, 1985.

Barclay, William. *The Letter to the Romans*, 2 ed. The Daily Study Bible. Edinburgh: Saint Andrew Press, 1957.

Barrett, C.K. *A Commentary on the Epistle to the Romans*. Harper's New Testament Commentaries. New York: Harper & Row, 1957; reprint, Peabody, MA: Hendrickson, 1987.

Bartlett, C. Norman. *Right in Romans: Studies in the Epistle of Paul to the Romans*. Chicago: Moody Press, 1953.

Batey, Richard A. *The Letter of Paul to the Romans*. Austin: R.B. Sweet, 1969.

Black, Matthew. *Romans*, 2 ed. New Century Bible Commentary. Grand Rapids: Eerdmans, 1989.

Boice, James Montgomery. *Romans*, 4 vols. Grand Rapids: Baker, 1991ff.

Brokke, Harold J. *Saved by His Life*. Minneapolis: Bethany Fellowship, 1964.

Bruce, F.F. *The Epistle of Paul to the Romans*. Tyndale New Testament Commentaries. Grand Rapids: Eerdmans, 1963.

Brunner, Emil. *The Letter to the Romans: A Commentary*. Trans. by H.A. Kennedy. London: Lutterworth Press, 1959.

Calvin, John. *Commentaries on the Epistle of Paul the Apostle to the Romans*. Trans. by John Owen. Grand Rapids: Eerdmans, 1947 reprint.

Cottrell, Jack. *Romans*. 2 Vols. The College Press NIV Commentary. Joplin, MO: College Press, 1996.

Cranfield, C.E.B. *A Critical and Exegetical Commentary on the Epistle to the Romans.* 2 vols. The International Critical Commentary, new series. Edinburgh: T. & T. Clark, 1975 (1990 corrected printing).

Denney, James. "St. Paul's Epistle to the Romans." In *The Expositor's Greek Testament.* Ed. by W. Robertson Nicoll, II:555-725. New York: George H. Doran, n.d.

DeWelt, Don. *Romans Realized.* Joplin, MO: College Press, 1959.

Dodd, C.H. *The Epistle of Paul to the Romans.* New York: Harper & Brothers, 1932.

Dunn, James D.G. *Romans.* 2 vols. Volume 38 in Word Biblical Commentary. Dallas: Word Books, 1988.

Earle, Ralph. *Romans.* Vol. 3 of Word Meanings in the New Testament. Grand Rapids: Baker Book House, 1974.

Edwards, James R. *Romans.* New International Biblical Commentary. Peabody, MA: Hendrickson, 1992.

Erdman, Charles R. *The Epistle to the Romans: An Exposition.* Philadelphia: Westminster, 1925.

Fitzmyer, Joseph A. *Romans: A New Translation with Introduction and Commentary.* The Anchor Bible. New York: Doubleday, 1993.

Godet, Frederic L. *Commentary on the Epistle to the Romans.* Trans. by A. Cusin. Ed. by Talbot W. Chambers. Grand Rapids: Zondervan, 1956 reprint of 1883 ed.

Greathouse, William M. *Romans.* Vol. 6 of Beacon Bible Expositions. Kansas City, MO: Beacon Hill Press, 1975.

Grubbs, Isaiah Boone. *An Exegetical and Analytical Commentary on Paul's Epistle to the Romans.* Ed. by George A. Kingman. 6th ed. Nashville: Gospel Advocate, n.d.

Haldane, Robert. *An Exposition of the Epistle to the Romans.* MacDill AFB: MacDonald Publishing, 1958.

Harrison, Everett F. "Romans." In *The Expositor's Bible Commentary* 10:1-171. Ed. Frank E. Gaebelein. Grand Rapids: Zondervan, 1976.

Hendriksen, William. *Exposition of Paul's Epistle to the Romans.* 2 vols. New Testament Commentary. Grand Rapids: Baker, 1980-1981.

Hughes, R. Kent. *Romans: Righteousness from Heaven.* Preaching the Word. Wheaton, IL: Crossway Books, 1991.

Käsemann, Ernst. *Commentary on Romans.* Trans. by Geoffrey W. Bromiley. Grand Rapids: Eerdmans, 1980.

Lard, Moses E. *Commentary on Paul's Letter to Romans.* Cincinnati: Standard Publishing, n.d.

Lenski, R.C.H. *The Interpretation of St. Paul's Epistle to the Romans.* Columbus, OH: Wartburg Press, 1945.

Lipscomb, David. *Romans.* Vol. I in A Commentary on the New Testament Epistles. 2nd ed. Ed. by J. W. Shepherd. Nashville: Gospel Advocate, 1965.

Lloyd-Jones, D.M. *Romans: An Exposition of Chapters 3.20–4.25 – Atonement and Justification.* London: Banner of Truth Trust, 1970.

_____ . *Romans: An Exposition of Chapter 6 – The New Man.* Grand Rapids: Zondervan, 1973.

_____ . *Romans: An Exposition of Chapters 7.1–8.4 – The Law: Its Functions and Limits.* Grand Rapids: Zondervan, 1973.

_____ . *Romans: An Exposition of Chapter 9 – God's Sovereign Purpose.* Grand Rapids: Zondervan, 1991.

Luther, Martin. *Luther: Lectures on Romans.* Ed. & trans. by Wilhelm Pauck. The Library of Christian Classics. Vol. XV. Philadelphia: Westminster, 1961.

MacArthur, John, Jr. *Romans.* 2 vols. The MacArthur New Testament Commentary. Chicago: Moody, 1991, 1994.

McClain, Alva J. *Romans: The Gospel of God's Grace.* Ed. by Herman A. Hoyt. Chicago: Moody Press, 1973.

McGarvey, J.W., and Philip Y. Pendleton. *Thessalonians, Corinthians, Galatians, and Romans.* Cincinnati: Standard Publishing, n.d.

McGuiggan, Jim. *The Book of Romans.* Lubbock, TX: Montex Publishing Company, 1982.

Mitchell, John G., with Dick Bohrer. *Right with God: A Devotional Study of the Epistle to the Romans.* Portland, OR: Multnomah, 1990.

Moo, Douglas. *The Epistle to the Romans.* The New International Commentary on the New Testament. Grand Rapids: Eerdmans, 1996.

Morris, Leon. *The Epistle to the Romans.* Grand Rapids: Eerdmans, 1988.

Moser, K.C. *The Gist of Romans,* revised ed. Delight, AR: Gospel Light, 1958.

Moule, H.C.G. *The Epistle of Paul the Apostle to the Romans.* The Cambridge Bible for Schools and Colleges. Cambridge: The University Press, 1918.

Mounce, Robert H. *Romans.* Vol. 27 in The New American Commentary. Nashville: Broadman & Holman, 1995.

Murray, John. *The Epistle to the Romans.* 2 vols. New International Commentary. Grand Rapids: Eerdmans, 1959, 1965.

Newell, William R. *Lessons on the Epistle of Paul to the Romans.* N.p., 1925.

Newman, Barclay M., and Eugene A. Nida. *A Translator's Handbook on Paul's Letter to the Romans.* London: United Bible Societies, 1973.

Nygren, Anders. *Commentary on Romans*. Trans. by Carl C. Rasmussen. Philadelphia: Fortress Press, 1949.

Reese, Gareth L. *New Testament Epistles: A Critical and Exegetical Commentary on Paul's Epistle to the Romans*. Moberly, MO: Scripture Exposition Press, 1987.

Robertson, A.T. *The Epistles of Paul*. Vol. IV in Word Pictures in the New Testament. Nashville: Broadman, 1931.

Sanday, William, and Arthur C. Headlam. *A Critical and Exegetical Commentary on the Epistle to the Romans*. 2nd ed. The International Critical Commentary, old series. New York: Charles Scribner's Sons, n.d.

Schlatter, Adolf. *Romans: The Righteousness of God*. Trans. by Siegfried Schatzmann. Peabody, MA: Hendrickson, 1995.

Shedd, William G.T. *A Critical and Doctrinal Commentary on the Epistle of St. Paul to the Romans*. Grand Rapids: Zondervan, 1967 reprint of 1879 edition.

Shields, Bruce. *Romans*. Standard Bible Studies. Cincinnati: Standard Publishing, 1988.

Smith, Sherwood. *Thirteen Lessons on Romans*. Vol. 1 (1979); and *Thirteen Lessons on Romans*. Vol. 2 (1981). Joplin, MO: College Press.

Stedman, Ray C. *From Guilt to Glory, Volume I: Romans 1–8*. Waco: Word Books, 1978.

Stott, John. *Romans: God's Good News for the World*. Downers Grove, IL: InterVarsity, 1994.

Thomas, W.H. Griffith. *Romans: A Devotional Commentary*. 3 vols. London: Religious Tract Society, n.d.

Vanderlip, George. *Paul and Romans*. Valley Forge, PA: Judson Press, 1967.

Williams, William G. *An Exposition of the Epistle of Paul to the Romans*. Cincinnati: Jennings and Pye, 1902.

Wuest, Kenneth S. *Romans in the Greek New Testament for the English Reader*. Grand Rapids: Eerdmans, 1955.

II. MISCELLANEOUS BOOKS AND ARTICLES

Arndt, William F., and F. Wilbur Gingrich. *A Greek-English Lexicon of the New Testament and Other Early Christian Literature*. Chicago: University of Chicago Press, 1957.

Arndt, William F., and F. Wilbur Gingrich. *A Greek-English Lexicon of the New Testament and Other Early Christian Literature,* 2 ed., revised and augmented by F. Wilbur Gingrich and Frederick W. Danker from Walter Bauer's Fifth Edition, 1958. Chicago: University of Chicago Press, 1979.

Augustine, *The **Confessions** of St. Augustine*. Vol. XIV in The Works of Aurelius Augustine. Ed. by Marcus Dods. Trans. by J.G. Pilkington. Edinburgh: T. & T. Clark, 1876.

Balz, Horst. "ἀποκαραδοκία." *Exegetical Dictionary of the New Testament*. Ed. by Horst Balz and Gerhard Schneider, I:132-133. Grand Rapids: Eerdmans, 1990.

Bartchy, S. Scott. *MALLON CHRESAI: First Century **Slavery** and the Interpretation of 1 Corinthians 7:21*. Society of Biblical Literature Dissertation Series 11. Missoula: Scholars Press, 1973.

Beker, J.C. "The **Faithfulness** of God and the Priority of Israel in Paul's Letter to the Romans." *RomDeb*, 327-332.

Bilezikian, Gilbert. *Beyond Sex **Roles***. 2nd ed. Grand Rapids: Baker, 1990.

Boers, Hendrikus. *The **Justification** of the Gentiles: Paul's Letters to the Galatians and Romans*. Peabody, MA: Hendrickson, 1994.

Bornkamm, Günther. "The **Letter** to the Romans as Paul's Last Will and Testament." *RomDeb*, 16-28.

Boswell, John. *Christianity, Social Tolerance, and Homosexuality*. Chicago: University of Chicago Press, 1980.

Bruce, F.F. "The Romans **Debate**—Continued." *RomDeb*, 177-194.

Büchsel, Friedrich. "κρίνω [etc.]." *TDNT*, III:921-954.

Campbell, William S. "Romans III as a **Key** to the Structure and Thought of the Letter." *RomDeb*, 251-264.

Carson, D.A. *Exegetical **Fallacies***. Grand Rapids: Baker, 1984.

Coleridge, Samuel Taylor. *The **Table Talk** and Omniana of Samuel Taylor Coleridge*. London: Oxford University Press, 1917.

Cooper, John W. *Body, Soul, and Life Everlasting: Biblical Anthropology and the Monism-Dualism Debate*. Grand Rapids: Baker, 1989.

Corson, John. "**Faith** Alone Involves Obedience, Too!" *Christian Standard* (10/2/77), 5-6.

Cottrell, Jack. *Baptism: A Biblical Study*. Joplin, MO: College Press, 1989.

_____. "Baptism According to the **Reformed Tradition**." In *Baptism and the Remission of Sins*. Ed. by David W. Fletcher, 39-81. Joplin, MO: College Press, 1990.

_____. "The Biblical **Consensus**: Historical Backgrounds to Reformed Theology." In *Baptism and the Remission of Sins*. Ed. by David W. Fletcher, 17-38. Joplin, MO: College Press, 1990.

_____. "**Covenant** and Baptism in the Theology of Huldreich Zwingli." Unpublished doctoral dissertation. Princeton, NJ: Princeton Theological Seminary, 1971.

_____. "**Faith**, History, and the Resurrection Body of Jesus," *The Seminary Review* (Dec. 1982): 28:143-160.

_____. *Faith's **Fundamentals**: Seven Essentials of Christian Belief*. Cincinnati: Standard Publishing, 1995.

_____. ***Feminism** and the Bible: An Introduction to Feminism for Christians*. Joplin, MO: College Press, 1992.

_____. "**1 Timothy 2:12** and the Role of Women." Four parts. *Christian Standard* (January 10, 1993) 4-6; (January 17, 1993) 4-6; (January 24, 1993) 4-6; (January 31, 1993) 4-6.

_____. *Gender **Roles** and the Bible: Creation, the Fall, and Redemption*. Joplin, MO: College Press, 1994.

_____. *His **Truth***. 2nd ed. Joplin, MO: College Press, 1989.

_____. "**Priscilla**, Phoebe, and Company." *Christian Standard* (December 12, 1993) 4-5.

_____. "**Response** to My Critics." Three parts. *Christian Standard* (November 21, 1993) 5-6; (November 28, 1993) 4-6; (December 5, 1993) 4-6.

_____. *Thirteen Lessons on **Grace***. Joplin, MO: College Press, 1988.

_____. *Tough **Questions**, Biblical Answers*. Part Two. Joplin, MO: College Press, 1986.

_____. *What the Bible Says about God the Creator (**GC**)*. Joplin, MO: College Press, 1984.

_____. *What the Bible Says about God the Redeemer (**GRe**)*. Joplin, MO: College Press, 1987.

_____. *What the Bible Says about God the Ruler (**GRu**)*. Joplin, MO: College Press, 1984.

Delling, G. "λαμβάνω, etc." *TDNT*, IV:5-15.

_____. "ὑπερέχω, ὑπεροχή." *TDNT*, VIII:523-524.

_____. "τάσσω [etc.]." *TDNT*, VIII:27-32.

DeYoung, James B. "The **Meaning** of 'Nature' in Romans 1." *Journal of the Evangelical Theological Society* 31 (December 1988): 429-441.

Donfried, Karl P. "False **Presuppositions** in the Study of Romans." *RomDeb*, 102-125.

_____, ed. *The Romans **Debate***. Revised & expanded edition. Peabody, MA: Hendrickson, 1991.

_____. "A Short **Note** on Romans 16." *RomDeb*, 44-52.

Erickson, Millard J. *The Evangelical **Mind** and Heart*. Grand Rapids: Baker, 1993.

Fiensy, David A. *New Testament **Introduction***. The College Press NIV Commentary. Joplin, MO: College Press, 1994.

Foerster, Werner. "σώζω, etc." *TDNT*, VII:965-1024.

Forster, Roger T., and V. Paul Marston. *God's **Strategy** in Human History*. Wheaton, IL: Tyndale House, 1974.

Friedrich, Gerhard. "εὐαγγελίζομαι, etc." *TDNT*, II:707-737.

Fuller, Daniel P. *The **Unity** of the Bible: Unfolding God's Plan for Humanity*. Grand Rapids: Zondervan, 1992.

Fürst, Dieter. "**Confess**." In *The New International Dictionary of New Testament Theology*. Ed. by Colin Brown, I:344-348. Grand Rapids: Zondervan, 1975.

Gaertner, Dennis. *Acts*. The College Press NIV Commentary. Joplin, MO: College Press, 1993.

_____. "Romans: Gospel of God's **Fairness**." *Christian Standard*, part 1 (12/20/87), 14-16; and part 2 (12/27/87), 4-6.

Graber, Friedrich. "All, Many." *The New International Dictionary of New Testament Theology*. Ed. by Colin Brown, I:94-97. Grand Rapids: Zondervan, 1975.

Gromacki, Robert. *The **Virgin Birth**: Doctrine of Deity*. Nashville: Nelson, 1974.

Gundry, Robert H. *Sōma in Biblical Theology: With Emphasis on Pauline Anthropology*. Grand Rapids: Zondervan, 1987.

Harris, M.J. "**Prepositions** and Theology in the Greek New Testament." Appendix. *The New International Dictionary of New Testament Theology*. Ed. by Colin Brown, III:1171-1213. Grand Rapids: Zondervan, 1978.

Hobbs, A.I. "**Conversion**: What Is It, and How Produced?" In *The Old Faith Restated*. Ed. by J.H. Garrison, 254-274. St. Louis: Christian Publishing Company, 1891.

Hodges, Zane C. *Absolutely **Free***. Grand Rapids: Zondervan, 1989.

Hoekema, Anthony A. *The **Bible** and the Future*. Grand Rapids: Eerdmans, 1979.

Hübner, Hans. "ἄτιμος." In *Exegetical Dictionary of the New Testament*. Ed. by Horst Balz & Gerhard Schneider, I:177. Grand Rapids: Eerdmans, 1990.

Jervell, Jacob. "The **Letter** to Jerusalem." *RomDeb*, 53-64.

Jeremias, Joachim. *The Central **Message** of the New Testament*. London: SCM Press, 1965.

Jewett, Robert. "Following the **Argument** of Romans." *RomDeb*, 265-277.

Keil, C.F., and F. Delitzsch. *The Pentateuch*. Trans. by James Martin. Vol. 1 of Commentary on the Old Testament in Ten Volumes. Grand Rapids: Eerdmans, 1981.

Kittel, Gerhard, and Gerhard Friedrich, eds. *Theological Dictionary of the New Testament*. Trans. & ed. by Geoffrey W. Bromiley. 10 vols. Grand Rapid: Eerdmans, 1964-1976.

Klein, Günter. "Paul's **Purpose** in Writing the Epistle to the Romans." *RomDeb*, 29-43.

Köster, Helmut. "τέμνω [etc.]." *TDNT*, VIII:106-112.

Lamar, J.S. "The **Ground** of Man's Need of Salvation." In *The Old Faith Restated*. Ed. by J.H. Garrison. St. Louis: Christian Publishing Company, 1891. Pp. 98-119.

Lampe, Peter. "The Roman Christians of **Romans 16**." *RomDeb*, 216-230.

Lewis, C.S. *The **Abolition** of Man*. New York: Macmillan, 1947.

_____. *The Four **Loves***. London: Geoffrey Bles, 1960.

Luther, Martin. "Preface to the Complete Edition of Luther's **Latin Writings**." In Vol. 34: *Career of the Reformer IV*. Luther's Works (American Edition). Ed. by Lewis W. Spitz and Helmut T. Lehmann, 327-338. Philadelphia: Muhlenberg Press, 1960.

_____. "**Preface** to the Epistle of St. Paul to the Romans." In Vol. 35: *Word and Sacrament I*. Luther's Works (American Edition). Ed. by E. Theodore Bachmann and Helmut T. Lehmann, 365-380. Philadelphia: Muhlenberg Press, 1960.

MacArthur, John F. Jr. *The **Gospel** According to Jesus: What Does Jesus Mean When He Says, "Follow Me"?* Revised ed. Grand Rapids: Zondervan, 1994.

Maurer, Christian. "ὑπόδικος." *TDNT*, VIII:557-558.

_____. "πράσσω, etc." *TDNT*, VI:632-644.

Michaelis, W. "μάχαιρα." *TDNT*, IV:524-527.

Milligan, Robert. *Exposition and Defense of the **Scheme** of Redemption*. St. Louis: Bethany Press, n.d.

Moreland, J.P., and David Ciocchi, eds. *Christian **Perspectives** on Being Human: A Multidisciplinary Approach to Integration*. Grand Rapids: Baker, 1993.

Morris, Leon. *The Apostolic **Preaching** of the Cross*. 3 ed. Grand Rapids: Eerdmans, 1965.

Murray, John. *The **Imputation** of Adam's Sin*. Grand Rapids: Eerdmans, 1959.

Nash, Donald A. "A **Critique** of the New International Version of the New Testament." Cincinnati: Christian Restoration Association, n.d.

Oepke, Albrecht. "καθίστημι, etc." *TDNT*, III:444-447.

_____. "ζέω, ζεστός." *TDNT*, II:875-877.

Pentecost, J. Dwight. ***Things** to Come*. Findlay, OH: Dunham, 1958.

Pinnock, Clark H. "From **Augustine** to Arminius: A Pilgrimage in Theology." In *The Grace of God, the Will of Man: A Case for Arminianism*. Ed. by Clark H. Pinnock, 15-30. Grand Rapids: Zondervan, 1989.

Piper, John. *The **Justification** of God: An Exegetical and Theological Study of Romans 9:1-23*. 2nd ed. Grand Rapids: Baker, 1993.

Reese, Gareth L. *New Testament History: A Critical and Exegetical Commentary on the Book of **Acts***. 2nd ed. Joplin, MO: College Press, 1976.

Reicke, Bo. "προΐστημι." *TDNT*, VI:700-703.

Rengstorf, Karl Heinrich. "δοῦλος, etc." *TDNT*, II:261-280.

Ridderbos, Herman. ***Paul**: An Outline of His Theology*. Trans. by John R. de Witt. Grand Rapids: Eerdmans, 1975.

Rueda, Enrique. *The Homosexual **Network**: Private Lives and Public Policy*. Old Greenwich, CT: Devin Adair, 1982.

Ryrie, Charles C. *So Great **Salvation**: What It Means to Believe in Jesus Christ*. Wheaton, IL: Scripture Press/Victor Books, 1989.

Sanders, E.P. ***Paul** and Palestinian Judaism*. London: SCM, 1977.

Schaff, Philip. "**Preface**." In John Peter Lange, *Commentary on the Holy Scriptures: Romans*. Trans. by Philip Schaff. Grand Rapids: Zondervan reprint, n.d.

Schneider, Johannes. "παραβαίνω, παράβασις, etc." *TDNT*, V:736-744.

Schreiner, Thomas R. "Does Romans 9 Teach Individual **Election** unto Salvation?" In vol. 1 of *The Grace of God, the Bondage of the Will*. Ed. by Thomas R. Schreiner and Bruce A. Ware, 89-106. Grand Rapids: Baker, 1995.

Schrenk, Gottlob. "ἱερός, etc." *TDNT*, III:221-283.

Schüssler Fiorenza, Elisabeth. *In **Memory** of Her: A Feminist Theological Reconstruction of Christian Origins*. New York: Crossroad, 1987.

Shank, Robert. ***Elect** in the Son: A Study of the Doctrine of Election*. Springfield, MO: Westcott Publishers, 1970.

Sherlock, William. *A Discourse Concerning the Divine **Providence***. Pittsburgh: J.L. Read, 1848.

Spencer, Aida B. *Beyond the **Curse**: Women Called to Ministry*. Nashville: Thomas Nelson, 1985.

Spicq, Ceslas. *Theological **Lexicon** of the New Testament*. Trans. by James D. Ernest. 3 volumes. Peabody, MA: Hendrickson, 1994.

Stählin, Gustav. "φιλέω [etc.]." *TDNT*, IX:113-171.

_____. "σκάνδαλον, σκανδαλίζω." *TDNT*, VII:339-358.

Stendahl, Krister. ***Paul** among Jews and Gentiles and Other Essays*. Philadelphia: Fortress Press, 1976.

Stuhlmacher, Peter. "The **Purpose** of Romans." *RomDeb*, 231-242.

_____. "The **Theme** of Romans." *RomDeb*, 333-345.

Thielman, Frank. ***Paul** and the Law: A Contextual Approach*. Downers Grove, IL: InterVarsity, 1994.

Thiessen, Henry. ***Introduction*** *to the New Testament*. 2nd ed. Grand Rapids: Eerdmans, 1944.

Trench, Richard Chenevix. ***Synonyms*** *of the New Testament*. Grand Rapids: Eerdmans, 1958.

Tyndale, William. "A **Prologue** to the Epistle of Paul to the Romans." In *The New Testament, Translated by William Tyndale, 1534*. Ed. by N. Hardy Wallis, 293-318. Cambridge: University Press, 1938.

Unger, Merrill F. *Unger's Bible* ***Dictionary***. 3rd ed. Chicago: Moody Press, 1966.

Vincent, Marvin R. *The Epistles of Paul*. Vol. III in **Word Studies** in the New Testament. Grand Rapids: Eerdmans, 1973 reprint of 1887 edition.

Walters, James. "'**Phoebe**' and 'Junia(s)' — Rom. 16:1-2, 7." In Vol. 1 of *Essays on Women in Earliest Christianity*. Ed. by Carroll D. Osburn, 167-190. Joplin, MO: College Press, 1993.

Watson, Francis. "The Two Roman **Congregations**: Romans 14:1–15:13." *RomDeb*, 203-215.

Wesley, John. *Journal from October 14, 1735, to November 29, 1745*. Vol. I in The **Works** of John Wesley. Grand Rapids: Zondervan, reprint of 1872 ed.

Wedderburn, A.J.M. "The **Purpose** and Occasion of Romans Again." *RomDeb*, 195-202.

Wiefel, Wolfgang. "The Jewish **Community** in Ancient Rome and the Origins of Roman Christianity." *RomDeb*, 85-101.

Wiens, Delbert. "An **Exegesis** of Romans 5:12-21." *Journal of Church and Society* (Fall 1969): 5:42-54.

Weiss, K. "φέρω [etc.]." *TDNT*, IX:56-87.

Williams, Philip R. "Paul's **Purpose** in Writing Romans." *Bibliotheca Sacra* (January–March 1971): 128:62-67.

Wright, N.T. *The* ***Climax*** *of the Covenant: Christ and the Law in Pauline Theology*. Minneapolis: Fortress Press, 1993.

————————. "The **Messiah** and the People of God." Oxford University: D.Phil. dissertation, 1980.

Young, Richard. *Intermediate N.T.* ***Greek****: A Linguistic and Exegetical Approach*. Nashville: Broadman & Holman, 1994.

INTRODUCTION

I. ROMANS: ITS INFLUENCE AND IMPORTANCE

God's Word is a lamp to our feet and a light for our path (Ps 119:105), and no part of it shines more brilliantly than the book of Romans. The truth of God's Word sets us free (John 8:32), and Romans teaches us the most liberating of all truths. God's Word is sharp and piercing like a sword (Heb 4:12), and no blade penetrates more deeply into our hearts than Romans. Overall the book of Romans may be the most read and most influential book of the Bible, but sometimes it is the most neglected and most misunderstood book.

In 1 Cor 15:3-4 Paul sums up the gospel as these three truths: Christ died for our sins, was buried, and was raised up again on the third day. The reality of the historical facts of the Savior's death and resurrection is stressed over and over in the book of Acts. Romans, however, is an exposition of the *meaning* of these facts. In the language of 1 Cor 15:3, Romans focuses not on "Christ died," but on the next three words: "*for our sins*." Acts explains what salvation consists of and how we may receive it. Romans does the same, but carries the explanation to heights and depths that thrill and satisfy the soul, providing it with an experience that is at the same time intellectual, spiritual, and esthetic.[1]

The unparalleled ability of Romans to convict sinners and to motivate Christians is well attested. The comment of Sanday and Headlam (v) has often been noted: "If it is a historical fact that the spiritual revivals of Christendom have been usually associated with closer study of the Bible, this would be true in an eminent degree of the Epistle to the Romans." Leon Morris (1) concurs: "It is commonly agreed that the Epistle to the Romans is one of the greatest Christian writings. Its power has been demonstrated again and again at critical points in the history of the Christian church" (❧I:22-24).

Modern scholars and expositors seem unable to praise the letter to the Romans highly enough. "This is in every sense the greatest of the Epistles of Paul, if not the greatest book in the New Testament," declares Thiessen (*Introduction*, 219). Newell (375) says Romans is "probably the greatest book in the Bible." "If the apostle Paul had written nothing else, he would still be recognized as one of the outstanding Christian thinkers of all time on the basis of this letter alone," say Newman and Nida (1) (❧I:24-25).

Scholars praise Romans as the clearest statement of the *gospel* of salvation. Luther called it "the purest gospel" ("Preface," 365). Nygren agrees (3): "What the gospel is, what the content of the Christian faith is, one learns to know in the Epistle to the Romans as in no other place in the New Testament" (◐ I:25). Scholars also praise Romans for its unparalleled presentation of the essence of Christian *doctrine*. In his "Preface" to Romans (380) Luther says that in Romans we "find most abundantly the things that a Christian ought to know, namely, what is law, gospel, sin, punishment, grace, faith, righteousness, Christ, God, good works, love, hope, and the cross; and also how we are to conduct ourselves toward everyone." Thus, as Schaff says ("Preface," v), it seems that Paul "wanted in this one epistle to sum up briefly the whole Christian and evangelical doctrine" (◐ I:26).

Concerning its doctrinal content, MacArthur lists 49 significant questions about God and man that are answered by Romans, e.g., How can a person who has never heard the gospel be held spiritually responsible? How can a sinner be forgiven and justified by God? How are God's grace and God's law related? Why is there suffering? MacArthur (I:xi-xii) points out that these key words are used repeatedly in the epistle: God (154 times), law (77), Christ (66), sin (45), Lord (44), and faith (40).

Which of these assessments is correct? Is Romans the crowning presentation of the Christian *gospel*? Or is it the grandest statement of Christian *doctrine*? Actually, it is both. Romans is *the* theology of the New Testament; it is also *the* definitive statement of the gospel. In this epistle doctrine and gospel merge, and the result is a spiritual feast for Christians.

Boice (I:10) advises that "it is time to rediscover Romans." Actually, it is *always* time to "rediscover" Romans, and down through the history of Christianity individuals have been doing just this. The results have been earth-shaking. It can and does happen over and over, in the lives of individuals, in congregations, in the Church at large. F.F. Bruce (60) has well said, "There is no telling what may happen when people begin to study the Epistle to the Romans."

II. THE AUTHOR OF ROMANS

The epistle to the Romans was written by the Apostle Paul (1:1).[2] In the past a few critics challenged this, but without any real basis in fact (SH, lxxxvi-lxxxvii). Today, as Cranfield says, "no responsible criticism disputes its Pauline origin" (I:2) (◐ I:27).

A. Paul's Jewish Background

It is not necessary to go into the details of Paul's life, except for a few facts that are important in view of the content of the epistle, which relates especially to the distinction between law and grace. One relevant fact is Paul's Jewish background, which he proudly avowed: "I am an Israelite myself, a descendant of Abraham, from the tribe of Benjamin," a "Hebrew of Hebrews" (11:1; Phil 3:5; 2 Cor 11:22). Though born in Tarsus, he was reared in Jerusalem (Acts 22:3), the capital of Judaism.

Paul's education included strict and thorough religious training in the contents of the Old Testament — especially the Law (Torah) — at the feet of Gamaliel (Acts 22:3). Gamaliel was one of the most famous and most revered of all rabbis. His knowledge of the Law was so great that he was practically identified with it. "Under Gamaliel," says Paul, "I was thoroughly trained in the law of our fathers" (Acts 22:3).

Paul's zeal for God and commitment to his Law was total (Acts 22:3; Gal 1:14). He was a Pharisee (Acts 23:6; Phil 3:5), which he properly identified as "the strictest sect of our religion" (Acts 26:5). The glory of the Pharisees was the Law. Thus Paul not only knew the Law but also devoted himself to scrupulous obedience to its commandments (Acts 26:4-5; Phil 3:6).

This probably means that he was a legalist in the proper sense of that word, i.e., one who sought acceptance by God on the basis of his obedience to the Law. This is implied in the way he contrasted his pre-Christian life (Phil 3:6) and his Christian life (Phil 3:9). This is also the way Pharisees are generally pictured in the Gospels.

Paul's zeal for the Law was expressed perhaps most vehemently in his fanatical persecution of the earliest Christians, all converted Jews whom he no doubt regarded as traitors to God and his Law (Phil 3:6).

B. Paul's Conversion to Christianity

The second relevant fact about the Apostle Paul is his conversion. The details need not be recounted here. What is important is that the one who converted him to Christianity was no human preacher, but was Jesus himself (Gal 1:15-16). Also, the gospel he preached was not taught to him by a human teacher; he received it by direct revelation from Jesus (Gal 1:11-12). The result was that Paul's conversion, his change, his turnaround, was complete. Whereas before he was totally committed to the Mosaic Law as a way of life and salvation, once converted he was just as totally committed to the gospel of grace.

As a Christian Paul set himself in complete opposition to everything he had stood for as a Pharisee. He now understood the way of law to be futile (10:3). He saw that his former legalistic approach to salvation was, as Murray says, "the antithesis of grace and of justification by faith" (I:xiii). Thus when Paul presents the classic contrast between law and grace in Romans, he speaks as one who knew both sides of the issue from personal experience and from the best teachers available (❧ I:29).

C. Paul's Commission as the Apostle to the Gentiles

The last detail about Paul's life that is relevant here is his call and commission to be the Apostle to the Gentiles (Acts 26:17). His appointment as an *apostle* (1:1) invested him with the full authority of Jesus Christ and with the inspiration of the Holy Spirit so that his teachings are truly the Word of God (1 Cor 2:6-13; 1 Thess 2:13). When we read the book of Romans, we must understand it to be nothing less than this.

Also, Paul's appointment as the apostle *to the Gentiles* (1:5) completely governed his thoughts and deeds from that point on. As a Jew and a Pharisee, he had no doubt shared the typical Hebrew aversion to anything Gentile; and he had no doubt gloried in the Jews' exclusive position as God's chosen people. Thus when God revealed to him the mystery of the Gentiles — that it had been his plan all along to include Gentiles in the people of the Messiah (Eph 3:1-10), Paul was overwhelmed with awe and joy (❥I:30).

Throughout the Roman epistle, Paul writes with the full consciousness of his mission to the Gentiles and of the Gentiles in his audience. One point that he clarifies in the letter is the relation of the Gentiles to the Jews with respect to salvation.

III. TIME AND PLACE OF WRITING

(See ❥I:30-31.) While in Ephesus on his third missionary journey, "Paul decided to go to Jerusalem, passing through Macedonia and Achaia. 'After I have been there,' he said, 'I must visit Rome also'" (Acts 19:21). He shortly departed for Achaia (Greece) and arrived in Corinth, where he stayed for three months (Acts 20:1-3) (❥I:31).

It was in the midst of this final journey, during the three months Paul spent at Corinth, that he most likely wrote the letter to the Romans. He was apparently staying at the house of Gaius (16:23), one of his converts at Corinth (1 Cor 1:14). The letter was carried to Rome by Phoebe, a Christian from the church in nearby Cenchrea (16:1).

The exact date of the writing of Romans is calculated in relation to the overall chronology of Paul's life and work. There is no unanimity on this chronology, though the differences of opinion are minor. Everyone agrees that the Apostle's stay in Corinth must have been in late winter and/or early spring, since he planned to set out from there and arrive in Jerusalem by Pentecost. Most agree also that this would have been in the middle or late 50s. Thus Romans was probably written early in A.D. 56, 57, or 58.

IV. RECIPIENTS OF ROMANS: THE CHURCH IN ROME

Rome was the largest and most important city in the Roman Empire in Paul's day. Its population was probably over one million (Unger, *Dictionary*,

936). Of this number, it is estimated that forty to fifty thousand were Jews, with as many as fifteen identifiable synagogues (Dunn, I:xlvi; Edwards, 9).

How the church in Rome originated is not known. There is no real evidence that Peter founded it, contrary to a common tradition. Some say that Rom 15:20 shows this could not have been the case. Here Paul says that he does not intend to "be building on someone else's foundation." The fact that he did plan to visit Rome and work there implies that no apostle had been there yet (MacArthur, I:xviii; Moo, 4).

One very common speculation is that the Roman church was probably started by Jews and proselytes from Rome who were in the audience that heard Peter's sermon on the day of Pentecost (Acts 2:10) and who were among the converts baptized that day. Upon returning to Rome, they would have established the church there. If so, and this seems very likely, then the first Christians in Rome were converts from Judaism.

Another likely speculation is that Christians from other churches, perhaps some of Paul's own converts from his earlier work, were among those who started the Roman church and helped it to grow. Perhaps some of Paul's acquaintances named in Romans 16 were among this group. Such a scenario is highly probable, given the importance of Rome and the constant travel to and from that city.

Thus the church in Rome would have begun not as the result of some formal missionary effort, but by residents converted while traveling (e.g., Acts 2:10) and by Christians moving there from other places. Their own evangelistic efforts would certainly have focused on the synagogues of Rome, following the pattern of evangelism reflected in the book of Acts. This would have resulted in converts not only from Judaism but also from among Gentile "God-fearers" who were commonly attached to the synagogues (Dunn, I:xlvii-xlviii).

The epistle to the Romans is addressed "to all in Rome who are loved by God and called to be saints" (1:7) (❂I:33-34). These saints in Rome were almost certainly a mixture of Jewish and Gentile Christians, though there is no way to tell which group had the larger number. There appears to have been tension if not conflict among the two groups (❂I:34).

What is obvious is that in the epistle Paul addresses both groups, with some passages being specifically directed toward the Jewish Christians and some toward the Gentile Christians (see Moo, 9-10; Murray, I:xviii-xix). Some say the letter as a whole is directed mainly to the Jewish saints; others say it was mainly intended for the Gentiles.

Hendriksen is surely right, though, when he says that regarding the main point of Romans this whole question is really irrelevant, since it applies equally to both groups (I:23). *All* are sinners (3:9,23), *no one* will be saved by law (3:19-20), and *all* are equal recipients of the grace that is in Christ Jesus (3:24; 4:11-12). Hendriksen stresses Rom 10:12-13, "For there is no difference between Jew and Gentile — the same Lord is Lord of all and richly blesses all who call on him, for, 'Everyone who calls on the name of the Lord will be saved.'"

V. THE OCCASION OF THE WRITING

What were the circumstances that prompted Paul to write his epistle to the Romans? We are fortunate that Paul reveals his mind to us in certain statements of his desires and plans in chapters 1 and 15. These statements show us what occasioned the writing of Romans.

One main consideration was Paul's immediate travel plans. After preaching 20 years in the eastern and northeastern sections of the Mediterranean area, he was now planning a trip to Spain (15:15-24). But first he had to go to Jerusalem (15:25-31). His purpose for doing this was to deliver the funds he had been collecting from the Gentile churches "for the poor among the saints in Jerusalem" (15:26). He wanted to do this personally, to make sure that the funds were properly received (15:28). To this end he asked the Roman Christians to offer two specific prayers for him (15:30-31).

First, he knew that he still had many enemies in Jerusalem among the Jews especially, so he requested that the Roman Christians "pray that I may be rescued from the unbelievers in Judea" (15:31) (❂I:36).

Second, Paul was not really sure how the offering from the Gentile churches would be received by the Jewish saints in Jerusalem (❂I:36). He was anxious that it might be received in the proper spirit, so he asked the Romans to pray "that my service in Jerusalem may be acceptable to the saints there" (15:31).

Thus Paul was ultimately bound for Spain, after an initial trip to Jerusalem. But there was a third item in his itinerary: an intermediate stop in Rome itself (Acts 19:21; 23:11), a place he had never been. So he announced to the Christians in Rome that on his way to Spain he would stop and visit them (15:23,24,28). This was something he had longed to do for many years and had even made plans to do (1:11,13; 15:23), but had "often been hindered from coming to you" (15:22; cf. 1:13) (❂I:36).

Paul had several reasons for wanting to visit Rome, but mainly he just wanted to preach the gospel there. "I am obligated," he says, "both to Greeks and non-Greeks, both to the wise and the foolish. That is why I am so eager to preach the gospel also to you who are at Rome" (1:14-15). By this means or by some accompanying means he would be able to "impart to you some spiritual gift to make you strong" (1:11). This would also enable him to "have a harvest among you, just as I have had among the other Gentiles" (1:13) (❂I:37).

VI. THE PURPOSE OF ROMANS

The question of Paul's *purpose* for writing the epistle to the Romans is very controversial; there is much disagreement about it (see *RomDeb*). Everyone agrees on the facts described above relating to the *occasion* for the writing. The problem is that these facts have to be assessed in view of the contents of the main body of the letter, 1:18–15:13. The question is not just why he wrote a letter to the Roman church, but why he wrote this *specific* letter with this particular content. Why does he write "such a lengthy and involved discussion to a largely unknown congregation"? (Dunn, I:lv).

There are two basic approaches to this question. The older and more traditional approach is that the historical circumstances as described in the previous section were not particularly relevant with regard to Paul's decision to write the letter. Neither Paul's own plans nor the state of the Roman church presented him with a pressing need or occasion that required him to write. Thus, unlike his other letters, Romans is more or less nonoccasional. It is regarded rather as a kind of timeless theological essay on the essence of Christianity.

The more recent approaches to the purpose of Romans take the opposite view, that it is "a situational letter rather than a doctrinal treatise" (Jewett, "Argument," 265). Paul was not simply writing an essay detached from his circumstances, but was specifically addressing a particular situation that needed his attention at that time. Thus Romans is just as much an occasional letter as 1 Corinthians or Galatians.

Those who take the latter approach usually go in one of two directions. Some emphasize that Paul wrote the letter to fulfill certain needs of his own, relating to his trip either to Jerusalem or to Spain. Others say that Paul wrote mainly to meet the needs of the Roman church at that particular time.

It is possible, of course, that Paul had more than one purpose for writing Romans.

A. Romans Is a Doctrinal Essay

Now we shall go into a bit more detail concerning the possibilities outlined above. The first view is that Paul was not addressing a specific situation but was writing a timeless doctrinal essay. In its most extreme form this view says that Romans is a complete systematic theology, a compendium of Christian doctrine (❧I:38-39).

Most who take this nonoccasional view, however, say that it is an exaggeration to call Romans a full-blown systematic theology. It is a doctrinal essay, to be sure, but one that is more focused and limited in its scope.

Just what is the focus of this doctrinal essay? The most common view is that it has to do with the doctrines of salvation, i.e., that Romans is a summary or synopsis of Paul's *gospel* (❧I:39). Vincent summarizes this whole approach quite well when he says that Romans "is distinguished among the epistles by its systematic character. Its object is to present a comprehensive statement of the doctrine of salvation through Christ, not a complete system of christian doctrine" (*Word Studies*, III:x).

The idea that Romans is a kind of doctrinal essay focusing on the general doctrine of salvation is correct, in my opinion. However, I do not think it is wise to separate it too sharply from the occasion or circumstances discussed in the last section. It *is* an essay on salvation, but its purpose was definitely related to the circumstances at that time, as we shall see below.

B. Romans Was Occasioned by Paul's Immediate Needs

The second major approach to the purpose of Romans is that it was occasioned by the various circumstances relating to Paul's immediate plans in relation to his mission. In other words, it was designed to meet needs that Paul felt in his own life at the time.

The main idea here is that Paul determines to set forth in writing a "sermon" or a lengthy presentation of his gospel. He does this because he needs to introduce himself to people who are not familiar with him or with what he preaches. Or, he does this because his enemies are spreading false rumors about what he preaches, and are misrepresenting his gospel especially as to what he says about Jew-Gentile relations. Thus Romans is not just a presentation but also a defense of Paul's gospel (❂ I:41-42).

Why was it crucial for Paul at this particular time to write such a presentation and defense of his gospel? The answer is that it was necessary in order to facilitate his immediate plans. For one thing, he was on his way to Jerusalem with the offering for the poor saints, and was apprehensive about how this would turn out. Thus some contend that in this letter Paul was rehearsing what he was going to say in Jerusalem in defense of himself and in an effort to seal Jew-Gentile unity (❂ I:41).

Though this is a fairly common view today, some object to it or at least doubt that it could be the only purpose for Romans (Moo, 18). Thus other aspects of Paul's immediate plans must have elicited the letter. One of the most obvious is Paul's plan to visit Rome itself. Though he knew some of the Roman Christians, he had never been in Rome and would not know most of the people there. It must have seemed expedient, then, for him to write a kind of "letter of introduction" for himself, especially in view of the false rumors that were probably afoot (❂ I:41-42).

Those who hold this view usually take it a step further, and say that Paul laid out and defended his gospel to the Romans as a means of enlisting their support for his Spanish mission. In a real sense Rome was just a means to an end, both in Paul's itinerary and in his missionary strategy. He needed them as a kind of "base of operations" for what he hoped to accomplish in Spain (Stott, 33). Thus "if Rome was to be his base, the Romans would need to be assured of his message and theological position" (Morris, 17).

C. Romans Was Occasioned by Needs at Rome Itself

As we have just seen, those who believe the writing of Romans was motivated by the immediate circumstances sometimes locate those circumstances in Paul's own personal needs. Others who take the occasional approach, however, believe that the situation in Rome itself is what Paul is specifically addressing in this epistle (◉ I:42).

Whatever the nature of those problems or needs, Paul wrote to resolve them. Since all of Paul's other letters were "addressed to the specific situations of the churches or persons involved," says Donfried, we must begin with the assumption that Romans "was written by Paul to deal with a concrete situation in Rome" ("Presuppositions," 103).

1. The Need for Jew-Gentile Unity

What sorts of needs existed at Rome that would call forth from Paul's pen the most magnificent gospel tract ever written? Several possibilities are suggested, but the one most commonly held begins with the assumption that there was considerable tension in the Roman church between the Jewish Christians and the Gentile Christians. Thus the purpose of Paul's letter was to resolve this tension.

This view usually grows out of speculations concerning the development of the Roman church following Claudius's decree expelling the Jews from Rome. With Jewish Christians being forced to leave Rome, the Gentile Christians became the dominant force; and this situation prevailed even after the former returned to Rome. This led to conflict between the two factions. This scenario is supported by the various references to Jews and Gentiles (Greeks) in Romans, by the discussion of the weak (Jews?) and the strong (Gentiles?) in 14:1–15:13, and by several references to unity and division within the church (12:16; 15:5; 16:17-18) (◉ I:43-44).

2. The Need for an Apostolic Foundation

Another possible need being addressed by Paul is related to the circumstances of the origin of the church in Rome. It is inferred from 15:20 that no apostle was involved in its founding, nor as yet had even visited Rome. Thus Paul was concerned that the church did not have a solid apostolic foundation (see Eph 2:20), and he writes this epistle in order to provide that foundation. This is the view of Günter Klein ("Purpose," 39, 42), but Morris (11-12) gives reasons for doubting it.

3. The Need for Paul's Gospel

Another possibility (to which I subscribe) is that Paul did indeed recognize the need of the Roman church to hear his apostolic preaching and teaching, but not necessarily in a foundational sense. This view begins with Paul's sense of duty, based upon his special calling, to preach the gospel to everyone in the Gentile world (1:14), including those in Rome: "That is why I am so eager to preach the gospel also to you who are at Rome" (1:15).

But these people are already Christians. Why would Paul want to "preach the gospel" to *believers*? Here is a point that is often missed: the gospel is more than just the initial evangelistic witness given to unbelievers with a view to their conversion. It also includes the deeper meaning and implications of the basic facts of salvation, which are things about which even mature believers can never hear enough. That Paul wanted to preach the gospel to the Christians in Rome means that he wanted to go deeper into the meaning of Christ's saving work "for our sins," unfolding for them the full power of the gospel in the Christian life and at the same time clearing up common misunderstandings that may arise through incomplete knowledge.

Paul's desire, of course, was to do this in person, and he had often planned to travel to Rome for this very reason. Up to this point, however, God's providence had prevented it (1:13; 15:22). Now he is once again planning to go to Rome, after his trip to Jerusalem with the offering. But based on his past experience and the uncertainty about what would happen to him in Jerusalem (Acts 20:22-24), at this point he could not be certain that he would ever reach Rome in person (SH, xlii).

This led Paul to the conclusion that if he was ever going to preach the gospel in Rome, perhaps the only way he would be able to do so was *in writing*. Thus he takes the time, while staying in Corinth just before traveling to Jerusalem, to prepare a well-thought-out essay on the gospel as every Christian needs to hear it; and he sends it on to Rome in advance of his intended trip there.

According to this view, then, Romans is not just a basic presentation of the gospel, written in order to provide the Roman Christians with a missing apostolic foundation. And as Nygren (7) rightly notes, "it is a misunderstanding of Romans to see in it a typical example of Paul's missionary preaching." This is contrary to those who think Paul was just introducing himself to the Roman church, hoping to win their support for his mission to Spain by rehearsing the gospel as he usually preached it. Stuhlmacher rightly notes that how Paul "preached and taught as a missionary cannot be simply inferred from the outline of Romans" ("Purpose," 242).

According to this view, then, the primary purpose for Romans is not related to some need within Paul himself (e.g., his concern for defending himself; his missionary plans); nor is it related to some negative situation in the Roman church (e.g., Jew-Gentile disunity). It is motivated rather by Paul's loving concern for his fellow-Christians at Rome, and his desire to bless their hearts and lives with this written version of the deeper aspects of the gospel of grace (❥I:46).

D. Conclusion

We have surveyed the main reasons why Paul wrote the epistle to the Romans. It should be obvious that some of these reasons may overlap or be combined; so we need not focus narrowly upon just one of them (❂ I:46).

In my opinion, though, the dominant reason is the last one discussed above: Paul's desire to preach the gospel to the Romans, and his decision to do so in the form of an epistle. This is the factor that Paul stresses in the introductory section of the letter, where we would expect him to say what is closest to his heart. It seems inappropriate to give priority to ch. 15 on this matter, and to pass over what Paul himself chooses to mention first of all. Just because he tells the Romans about his plans in ch. 15 is no reason to assume that his purpose for writing to Rome is specifically or directly related to these plans.

We may conclude, then, that Romans is indeed an *occasional* letter, that it was occasioned by the need of the Roman Christians to hear Paul's gospel and by the circumstances that made it expedient for him to send it to them in written form at this particular time. Thus Romans is by design a clear presentation of the deeper implications of the gospel, written not for Paul's sake but for the sake of the church at Rome. The references to Paul's own plans and needs in ch. 15 are secondary.

At the same time, just because of the nature of the situation that caused Paul to write this epistle, the purpose for Romans includes the first view discussed above, namely, that it was intended to be a kind of doctrinal essay focusing on the meaning of salvation through the grace of our Lord Jesus Christ. As noted above, it is a systematic presentation of the *gospel*: not necessarily the gospel as proclaimed in an evangelistic situation, but the gospel as unfolded to mature Christians.

When this point is understood, we can see that the epistle to the Romans is intended not just for the saints in Rome in the middle of the first century A.D., but for all Christians in all ages. It is relevant for all since it deals with salvation from sin through God's grace (❂ I:47-48).

In most of the discussions of the purpose of Romans, a forgotten factor is the role of the Holy Spirit in the inspiration of Scripture. It is Paul himself who tells us that "all Scripture is God-breathed" (2 Tim 3:16). Whatever circumstances led Paul to compose his letter to the Romans, the choice to write and the message he wrote were not his alone. The Holy Spirit worked through Paul to produce this letter (see 2 Pet 1:20-21), and the Holy Spirit knows more than any man what is needed by every sinner and by every Christian seeking peace and power. In the final analysis it is the Spirit of God, and not just the Apostle Paul, who speaks to our hearts in the epistle to the Romans.

VII. THE THEME OF ROMANS

It is generally recognized that the content of the epistle is doctrinal in nature. Its main body is an essay or treatise with a strong doctrinal emphasis and seems to be built around a particular theme. The question now is, exactly what *is* the theme of Romans? Several answers have been proposed.

A. Justification by Faith

The Reformation established a way of looking at Romans that still has considerable support among Protestants, namely, that the main theme of the epistle is stated in 1:16-17. It can be summed up in the familiar phrase, "justification by faith," i.e., justification or righteousness before God comes through faith alone. However, many scholars today have rejected this traditional approach on the basis that too much of its subject matter simply does not relate to this subject, as Boers (78) says (❂ I:49).

B. The Righteousness of God

Those who are not satisfied with justification by faith as the theme for Romans sometimes opt for one that is very similar, namely, the righteousness of God (1:17).

Since the righteousness of God is integrally related to justification by faith, the two themes are sometimes confused. This is because one aspect of the theme of divine righteousness is that the righteousness of God is the basis for the personal justification of individual sinners (❂ I:50).

But most of those today who say that the righteousness of God is the theme of Romans are using the expression in a more comprehensive sense. For them it includes the idea of the divine righteousness as the basis for individual justification, to be sure. But in Romans, they say, the theme is more inclusive than this. It includes God's righteousness as the basis not only of his dealings with individual believers, but also of his dealings with mankind in general and especially with the Jewish nation in the context of redemptive history.

The question raised by the indiscriminate offer of justification by faith to both Jews and Gentiles is whether God is being fair with the Jews, in view of all the special treatment he has already bestowed upon them and the special promises he has given them. Does the gospel's "no partiality" principle bring God's righteousness and faithfulness into question? Paul seems to be dealing with this issue especially in Rom 9-11.

Thus according to this view the theme of Romans is not just the salvation of man but the defense of God, with perhaps the greater emphasis falling on the latter (❂ I:50).

C. The Equality of Jews and Gentiles

A third view is that the theme of Romans is the equality of Jews and Gentiles in God's plan of salvation. This is currently a popular view. It stems mainly from a certain reconstruction of the origin and development of the Roman church. It goes hand in hand with the idea that the letter is intended to deal with certain specific circumstances existing in Rome, especially the apparent disunity between Jewish and Gentile Christians. It recognizes that "the entire letter to the Romans is . . . permeated with Jew-Gentile issues" (Fiensy, *Introduction*, 230).

In its most general form this view says that the main emphasis of Romans is the universality of the gospel: there is just one way of salvation for Jews and Gentiles alike (❧I:51).

Interpreters differ as to the nature of the circumstances that led Paul to emphasize the theme of equality. Some say the Gentile Christians at Rome did not want to fully accept the Jewish Christians, so Romans is basically defending the right of the latter to full status in the Kingdom of God. On the other hand, some say the problem in Rome was the status of the Gentile Christians (❧I:52).

Either way the subject is approached, the main point is the same: the principal theme of Romans is to demonstrate the equality of Jews and Gentiles with regard to God's saving grace.

D. Sinners Are Saved by Grace, Not Law

All of the themes discussed above are certainly present in Romans, and all are important. All of them contribute significantly to the main theme. But I believe none of them as such is the main point Paul is communicating to us in the epistle. Rather than seeing 1:16-17 as the thesis statement for Paul's treatise, I see it more or less as the starting point leading up to the thesis, which is 3:28: "For we maintain that a man is justified by faith apart from observing the law."

In the most general sense Paul's thesis relates to the *gospel*, since his desire to preach the gospel in Rome (1:15) is what led him to compose the epistle as a written version of his gospel. But since the gospel is the good news about salvation, also in a general sense the theme of Romans is *salvation*. And the manner in which sinners are saved, whether Jews or Gentiles, is the same: justification by faith. (❧I:53).

But the theme of Romans is more precise than this. Yes, sinners are justified by faith, but this means they are *not* justified by works of law, which is the only alternative. It is just as important to include the negative statement in the theme as the positive one.

In actuality, then, the basic theme of Romans is the contrast between law and grace as ways of salvation. This contrast is seen especially in 3:28, which (literally translated) says, "For we maintain that a man is justified by faith apart from works of law." The contrast is stated succinctly in 6:14, "You are not under law, but under grace." *This* is the gospel, the good news of salvation. Certainly it is good news to know that God justifies us by faith in the saving work of Jesus Christ. But in a real sense it is also good news to know that we are *not* justified by law-keeping: a way of salvation which is not only futile but which sinners in their hearts *know* is futile, and which thus leads only to self-deception or to despair (❧I:53).

Thus Paul's theme is indeed that we are saved by grace, *not* by law. Law is not a viable option as a means of salvation; the only way for sinners to be counted righteous before God is by grace. Yes, we are justified by faith, but not by works of law. Yes, the righteousness of God figures prominently in our justification, but in contrast to the righteousness of man. Yes, Romans does emphasize full equality regarding this way of salvation; Jews and Gentiles are saved the same way. Both are saved by grace and justified by faith as provided by the righteousness of God, but in contrast with every false way.

This contrast between law and grace as competing ways of salvation is not a matter of OT versus NT nor Old Covenant versus New Covenant, as if law were the way to be saved prior to Christ and grace is the way to be saved now that Christ has come. Also, the contrast between law and grace — THIS IS VERY IMPORTANT — is not simply the Law of Moses versus the grace of Jesus Christ. No sinner has ever been saved nor can be saved by the law that applies to him, whether it be the Law of Moses for Jews under the Old Covenant, or some other comparable set of God's commandments for anyone else in any other time. Every sinner who has been saved since the time of Adam has been saved by grace and not by law, and this will always be the case.

The problem that Paul addresses in the book of Romans is not one that confronts Jews only, nor Gentiles only. It is not a problem faced only by those who are under the Mosaic Law, nor only by those to whom the Mosaic Law does not apply. The problem being addressed is this: *As a sinner, how can I be saved?* It is a problem faced by Jews and Gentiles alike, and the solution is the same for both.

Perhaps even more significantly, the problem addressed in Romans is not one confronted only by unbelieving sinners. It is a problem that believers often wrestle with as well (e.g., the Judaizers). When we state the problem thus — "As a sinner, how can I be saved?" — we can break it down into two separate problems. First is the unbeliever's problem: "How can I *become* saved?" The answer is: by grace through faith, not by works of law.[3] Second is the believer's continuing problem: "How can I *stay* saved?" And the answer is: by grace through faith, not by works of law.

This is why the epistle to the Romans has always been and always will be in a class by itself with regard to its impact on individuals and upon the church as a whole. Its basic theme is one that is always needed and always applicable, and one that will result in the highest praise to God the Redeemer once it is understood.

VIII. OUTLINE OF ROMANS

PROLOGUE — 1:1-17

I. **Epistolary Greeting** — 1:1-7
  A. **The Author Introduces Himself** — 1:1
    1. A Slave of Christ Jesus
    2. Called to Be an Apostle
    3. Set Apart for the Gospel of God
  B. **The Gospel and the Old Testament** — 1:2
  C. **The Subject of the Gospel Is Jesus** — 1:3-4
    1. The Two Natures of Jesus
    2. The Incarnation
    3. Messiahship
    4. The Two States of Jesus
    5. The Resurrection of Jesus
    6. The Son's Full Identity
  D. **Paul's Apostleship** — 1:5
    1. The Origin of Paul's Apostleship
    2. The Character of Paul's Apostleship
    3. The Focus of Paul's Apostleship
    4. The Purpose of Paul's Apostleship
    5. The Goal of Paul's Apostleship
  E. **The Recipients of Paul's Letter** — 1:6-7a
  F. **The Blessing** — 1:7b
II. **Personal Remarks** — 1:8-15
  A. **Paul's Prayers for the Romans** — 1:8-10
  B. **Paul's Desires Regarding Rome** — 1:11-13
  C. **Paul's Debt to the Romans** — 1:14-15
III. **Transitional Statement** — 1:16-17
  A. **The Glory of the Gospel** — 1:16a
  B. **The Power of the Gospel** — 1:16b
  C. **The Scope of the Gospel** — 1:16c
  D. **Faith and the Gospel** — 1:16c
    1. Faith Is a Condition for Salvation
    2. Faith Is Not the Only Condition
  E. **The Heart of the Gospel** — 1:17a
  F. **The Golden Text of the Gospel** — 1:17b

PART ONE: THE IMPOTENCE OF LAW AS A WAY OF SALVATION — 1:18–3:20

I. **The Sinfulness of the Gentiles** — 1:18-32
  A. **Universal Knowledge of God and His Law** — 1:18-20

Romans Outline

    B. Universal Rejection of the True God — 1:21-25
    C. The Utter Depths of Gentile Depravity — 1:26-32
  II. The Sinfulness of the Jews — 2:1-3:8
    A. Jews Are under the Wrath of God, No Less Than the Gentiles — 2:1-5
    B. God Will Be Partial to No One in the Judgment — 2:6-11
    C. Under Law, the Criterion of Judgment Is Obedience Alone — 2:12-16
    D. Jews Who Look to the Law for Salvation Are Condemned by Their Own Disobedience — 2:17-24
    E. True Jewishness Is Identified Not by Circumcision but by the Inward State of the Heart — 2:25-29
    F. Such Equal Treatment of Jews and Gentiles Does Not Nullify But Rather Magnifies God's Righteousness — 3:1-8
  III. Universal Sinfulness and Hopelessness Under Law — 3:9-20

PART TWO: THE ALL-SUFFICIENCY OF GRACE AS A WAY OF SALVATION — 3:21-5:21

  I. Grace as Justification by Christ's Blood through Faith — 3:21-31
    A. Righteousness through Faith Is Now Fully Revealed — 3:21-23
    B. Sinners Are Justified by the Blood of Christ — 3:24-26
    C. Sinners Are Justified by Faith Apart from Works of Law — 3:27-28
    D. The Way of Grace Is Available to All — 3:29-30
    E. Grace Lets Law Do Its Proper Work — 3:31
  II. Abraham: Paradigm of Grace — 4:1-25
    A. Abraham Was Justified by Faith Apart from Works — 4:1-5
    B. David Explains and Confirms Justification by Faith Apart from Works — 4:6-8
    C. Membership in Abraham's Family Is by Faith, Not by Circumcision — 4:9-12
    D. The Inheritance Promised to Abraham Comes by Faith, Not by Law — 4:13-17a
    E. Faith Means Giving Glory to God and Believing His Promises — 4:17b-22
    F. Those Who Believe like Abraham Are Justified like Abraham — 4:23-25
  III. Grace and Assurance — 5:1-21
    A. Assurance of Personal Salvation — 5:1-11
      1. Justification by Faith Is the Key to Assurance — 5:1-2
      2. Tribulations of Believers Do Not Nullify Assurance — 5:3-5
      3. Christ Died for Us While We Were Still Sinners — 5:6-8
      4. Our Hope Is Even More Secure Now That We Are His Friends — 5:9-11
    B. The All-Sufficiency of the Death of Christ — 5:12-21
      1. One Sin of One Man (Adam) Brought Sin and Death to All — 5:12-14
      2. Christ and His Sacrifice Are Greater Than Adam and His Sin — 5:15-17
      3. Christ's Cross Completely Cancels the Results of Adam's Sin — 5:18-19
      4. Grace Triumphs over Sin and Death — 5:20-21

PART THREE: THE ALL-SUFFICIENCY OF GRACE GIVES VICTORY OVER SIN — 6:1–8:39

I. Objections to Grace Based on a Fear of Antinomianism — 6:1–7:13
   A. Does Grace Make Sin Irrelevant? NO! — 6:1-14
   B. Does Freedom from Law Mean We Are Free to Sin? NO! — 6:15–7:6
      1. We Are Slaves to God — 6:15-23
      2. We Obey God from Our Hearts — 7:1-6
   C. Does Grace Mean That Law Is Bad? NO! — 7:7-13
II. Grace Gives Victory over Sin — 7:14–8:13
   A. The Christian Continues to Struggle against Sin — 7:14-25
      1. The Nature of the Struggle — 7:14-20
      2. The Source of the Struggle — 7:21-25
   B. Victory over Sin Comes through the Holy Spirit — 8:1-13
      1. God Frees Us from Sin's Penalty and Power — 8:1-4
      2. Sin and Death Are Defeated in Us through the Holy Spirit — 8:5-13
III. The Assurance of Final and Total Victory over the Fallen World — 8:14-39
   A. The Holy Spirit Marks Us as Sons and Heirs — 8:14-17
   B. The Redeemed Cosmos Is Our Inheritance — 8:18-25
   C. God Promises to Bring His Family through Earthly Trials — 8:26-30
   D. God's Gracious Love Gives Us Unshakable Assurance — 8:31-39

PART FOUR: THE FAITHFULNESS OF GOD IN HIS DEALINGS WITH THE JEWS — 9:1–11:36

I. THE PROBLEM OF ISRAEL: THE AGONY AND THE ECSTASY OF THE JEWISH NATION — 9:1-5
   A. Israel's Agony: They Are Accursed — 9:1-3
   B. Israel's Ecstasy: They Are Recipients of Unspeakably Glorious Privileges — 9:4-5
II. THE DISTINCTION BETWEEN ETHNIC AND SPIRITUAL ISRAEL — 9:6-29
   A. Israel's Situation and God's Faithfulness — 9:6-13
      1. God's Word Concerning Israel Has Not Failed — 9:6a
      2. The Key to the Puzzle: The Existence of Two Israels — 9:6b
      3. Ethnic Israel Exists by God's Sovereign Choice — 9:7-13
         a. The Choice of Isaac — 9:7-9
         b. The Choice of Jacob — 9:10-13
   B. God's Right to Choose and Use People without Saving Them — 9:14-18
      1. God's Righteousness Is Challenged — 9:14
      2. God's Sovereignty in Election for Service — 9:15-16
      3. God's Purposes Can Be Served by the Unsaved — 9:17-18
   C. God Used Ethnic Israel to Produce Spiritual Israel — 9:19-29
      1. The Objection — 9:19

Romans Outline

      2. Paul's Initial Rebuke of the Objector's Attitude — 9:20-21
      3. Beyond Ethnic Israel to Spiritual Israel — 9:22-24
         a. The Calvinist View
         b. Seeing Paul through Non-Calvinist Eyes
      4. Prophetic Confirmation of God's Purpose — 9:25-29
III. ISRAEL'S CHOICE OF LAW RATHER THAN GRACE — 9:30–10:21
    A. Personal Righteousness versus the Righteousness of God — 9:30–10:3
      1. The Reason for the Gentiles' Acceptance — 9:30
      2. The Reason for the Jews' Lostness — 9:31-33
      3. The Jews' Rejection of God's Righteousness — 10:1-3
    B. Christ Alone Is the Source of Saving Righteousness — 10:4-13
      1. An Either-Or Choice: Works-Righteousness or Faith in Christ — 10:4
      2. The Futility of Law-Righteousness — 10:5
      3. Saving Righteousness Comes through Trusting Christ's Works, Not Our Own — 10:6-10
      4. God's Righteousness Is Available Equally to Jews and Gentiles — 10:11-13
    C. The Jews Have Not Believed in Christ, and Their Unbelief Is Inexcusable — 10:14-21
      1. The Necessary Prerequisites to Saving Faith — 10:14-15
      2. Most Jews Have Not Believed the Gospel Message — 10:16
      3. The Jews' Problem Is Not Ignorance but Stubbornness of Will — 10:17-21
IV. THE SALVATION OF GOD'S TRUE ISRAEL — 11:1-32
    A. God's True Israel Is the Remnant Chosen by Grace — 11:1-6
      1. God Has Not Rejected His People — 11:1-2a
      2. God Had a Remnant of Believers in the OT — 11:2b-4
      3. Those under Grace Are God's New Covenant Israel — 11:5-6
    B. Unbelieving Israel Has Been Hardened — 11:7-10
    C. The Hardening of Unbelieving Israel Becomes a Blessing for Both the Gentiles and the Jews — 11:11-16
    D. The Olive Tree: A Metaphor of Judgment and Hope — 11:17-24
      1. Words of Warning to Gentile Christians — 11:17-22
      2. Words of Hope for Hardened Jews — 11:23-24
    E. God's Plan for Israel's Salvation — 11:25-32
      1. The Mystery of Israel's Salvation — 11:25-27
      2. God's Continuing Love for Israel — 11:28-29
      3. God's Ultimate Purpose Is Mercy — 11:30-32
V. DOXOLOGY: GOD'S WAY IS RIGHT — 11:33-36

PART FIVE: LIVING THE SANCTIFIED LIFE — 12:1–15:13

I. A CATALOGUE OF VIRTUES — 12:1–13:14
    A. Grace Demands a Transformed Life — 12:1-2

    B. Using the Gifts of Grace for Unselfish Service — 12:3-8
    C. Miscellaneous Moral Teaching — 12:9-16
    D. Personal Vengeance Is Forbidden — 12:17-21
    E. The Relation between Citizens and Government — 13:1-7
    F. The Relation between Love and Law — 13:8-10
    G. Walking in the Light — 13:11-14
II. **CHRISTIAN LIBERTY IN MATTERS OF OPINION —** 14:1–15:13
    A. Do Not Judge Others in Matters of Opinion — 14:1-12
        1. We Should Accept All Whom God Has Accepted — 14:1-3
        2. We Answer to Our Lord and Not to Each Other — 14:4-9
        3. Each of Us Will Be Judged by God — 14:10-12
    B. The Stewardship of Christian Liberty — 14:13-23
        1. We Must Sacrifice Our Liberty for the Sake of the Weak — 14:13-15
        2. Do Not Allow What You Consider Good to Be Spoken of as Evil — 14:16-18
        3. We Must Do Only Those Things Which Build Others Up — 14:19-21
        4. Each Christian Must Be True to His Own Convictions — 14:22-23
    C. Living in Unity and Hope — 15:1-13
        1. Selfless Service Produces a Unified Witness — 15:1-6
        2. Through Christ's Selfless Service, Jews and Gentiles Glorify God Together — 15:7-12
        3. A Prayer That All Believers May Abound in Hope — 15:13

PART SIX: PERSONAL MESSAGES FROM PAUL — 15:14–16:27

I. **PAUL'S MINISTRY AS THE APOSTLE TO THE GENTILES —** 15:14-33
    A. Reflections on His Past Service — 15:14-22
    B. His Plans for the Future — 15:23-29
    C. His Request for Prayer — 15:30-33
II. **PAUL AND HIS FELLOW WORKERS —** 16:1-24
    A. Commendation of Phoebe — 16:1-2
    B. Greetings to Individual Acquaintances — 16:3-16
    C. Warnings against False Teachers — 16:17-20
    D. Greetings from Paul's Companions — 16:21-24
III. **CONCLUDING DOXOLOGY —** 16:25-27

Notes

[1] See DeWelt, 13; Moser, iii. See the explanatory note at the beginning of the bibliography for my policy regarding citations in the text and in notes.

[2] Ordinarily, citations from the book of Romans will consist only of the chapter and verse numbers, without "Romans."

[3] How baptism fits into this answer is discussed in our comments on 1:17 and 6:1-5.

1:1-17 — PROLOGUE

I. 1:1-7 — EPISTOLARY GREETING

In the Greek this section is one long sentence. It has the same general form as a standard epistolary greeting of the time, but is much longer. A normal greeting would have been something like this: "From Paul, to the saints in Rome, greetings." (See Jas 1:1 for something close to this.) It is lengthy even for Paul, and is the longest greeting of all his epistles.

A. The Author Introduces Himself (1:1)

1:1 Paul, a servant of Christ Jesus, called to be an apostle and set apart for the gospel of God . . . . Here (see v. 5 also) Paul succinctly introduces himself to the Roman Christians by describing himself in three important ways. Perhaps he felt the need for this careful introduction because he had not yet been to Rome and was not known personally to many of the Christians there.

1. A Slave of Christ Jesus

Paul describes himself first of all as a slave of Christ Jesus. The NIV term "servant" is too weak. The Greek word, *doulos*, was almost always used of a true slave. The NASB term "bond-servant" is very close to this idea. "Bondslave" (e.g., 1 Pet 2:16, NASB) is redundant.

In the Greek world a slave was basically the property of an owner and had no say with regard to his circumstances (❧I:60). At the same time the OT Law presents the possibility of a person's entering such a state voluntarily. When the time came for a temporary slave to be set free, he could willingly choose to surrender himself back to his owner in a state of permanent servitude. Such a decision was usually based on love for the owner, or for family members that might be left behind if freedom were chosen (Exod 21:5-6; Deut 15:12-17).

Paul applies this term to himself here and elsewhere (Gal 1:10; Phil 1:1; Titus 1:1) (❧I:60). He was not a slave to any human master; in fact, he was a free-born Roman citizen (Acts 22:24-29). He tells us that he was rather a slave "of Christ Jesus." This is how he thought of his Christian existence first of all; this was the key to his self-identity.

This is true of Christians in general: being a Christian means being a slave of Jesus. This is a main implication of our confession that "Jesus is Lord" (10:9).

His Lordship is his ownership and authority over his property, his slaves. Thus in our confession we acknowledge that Jesus is our owner and that we are his property. We voluntarily surrender our wills to his and put ourselves at his disposal. We accept this as our natural state and commit ourselves to unconditional service solely for the glory of God (Phil 2:11).

Such acceptance of the role of a slave is of course the very antithesis of the sinful world's ideal of autonomy or total freedom from authority. This was true in the ancient Greek world, where such freedom was prized as the basis of personal dignity (❂I:61). Thus when we accept the basic role of "slave of Jesus Christ," we are no longer conforming ourselves to the pattern of this world (12:2)

Paul the slave served Christ Jesus willingly, from his heart. His compulsion was grounded in love, not fear (2 Cor 5:14). Not only did he say, "I am debtor" or "I am obligated" to preach (1:14), but he also declared "I am ready" or "I am eager" to preach the gospel (1:15). His heart was in it, and he would not have had it any other way. We may note that Paul also calls himself a "servant" (διάκονος, *diakonos*) of the gospel (Eph 3:7), and a "minister" (λειτουργός, *leitourgos*) of Christ (15:16). These terms do not have the connotation of compulsion or servitude, but focus on the fact that the servant is doing a specific work on behalf of someone else. The exact nature of Paul's work as a servant is given in the two other ways he describes himself in this verse.

2. Called to Be an Apostle

The second thing Paul says about himself is that he has been "called to be an apostle" (❂I:61-62). The calling to which Paul refers here is similar to the way God called men to serve him in OT times, e.g., Abraham (Gen 12:1); Moses (Exod 3:1-10); and Isaiah (Isa 6:1-13). It was a call to service, not a call to salvation. The latter concept is in view in 1:6-7, but not here in 1:1. It is very important to understand this distinction, as we shall see in our discussion of Rom 9-11.

The fact that Paul was called by Jesus Christ was the basis for his self-understanding as a slave of Jesus. The call placed upon him the inescapable obligation to do what his Lord commanded him. Also, this call was important to Paul as a basis for the divine authority of his ministry. He did not choose on his own to try to be an apostle; he was *called*! He was not appointed an apostle by any human agent; he was called *directly* by Jesus Christ! See Gal 1:1.

Paul says he was called to be "an apostle." This word comes from the very common verb ἀποστέλλω (*apostellō*), which means "to send (on a mission)." In the NT it often refers to sending someone on a spiritual mission; see Matt 10:5; John 17:18. The noun itself (ἀπόστολος, *apostolos*) is sometimes used in the NT in a generic sense and means simply "someone sent on a mission," i.e., an ambassador, a messenger, a representative, or even a missionary. See Acts 14:14; Rom 16:7; 2 Cor 8:23; Phil 2:25; Heb 3:1.

Most often, though, *apostolos* refers to those who were specially qualified and specially appointed to the highest human office of service to the church. Apostleship is named as the preeminent spiritual gift (1 Cor 12:28-29; Eph 4:11). It is applied to the original group of twelve men chosen by Jesus (Matt 10:2) and to the postresurrection group of twelve in which Matthias replaced Judas (Acts 1:26). This group is often referred to simply as "the twelve" (e.g., John 6:70-71) or as "the apostles" (e.g., 1 Cor 15:7; Gal 1:17).

What was special about those who were chosen for the office of apostle? First, they were chosen personally by Jesus Christ (John 6:70). This applies to Paul, too (Gal 1:1). Second, they had to be eyewitnesses of Jesus' ministry, especially of his resurrection (Acts 1:21-22). Paul stresses that he qualifies in this respect: "Am I not an apostle? Have I not seen Jesus our Lord?" (1 Cor 9:1; see 15:8). Third, they were endowed with the Holy Spirit (John 14:26; 15:26; 16:12-15; 20:22). Paul was conscious of his own special guidance by the Spirit (1 Cor 2:7-13; 7:40). Fourth, the apostles were given teaching and ruling authority over the whole church (John 20:23; Acts 2:42; 6:6; Eph 2:20; 3:5; 2 Pet 3:2). The Apostle Paul shared this authority (1 Thess 2:6; 1 Tim 2:7). Finally, apostles were given special miraculous powers as signs of their authority (Matt 10:1; Acts 2:43; 5:12; 8:18). The same was true of Paul (15:19; 2 Cor 12:12).

While Paul shared the basic apostolic qualifications with the twelve, in some ways his apostleship was unique. As far as we know, he was not an eyewitness of Jesus' entire ministry, from his baptism by John to his ascension (Acts 1:21-22), though he saw the risen Christ: "Last of all he appeared to me also" (1 Cor 15:8). Because of the unusual circumstances of his call, he refers to himself as "abnormally born" into the office of apostle (1 Cor 15:8). Also, Paul's ministry was unique in that he was specifically appointed to be the apostle to the Gentiles (see v. 5 below).

In no case, however, were Paul's office and apostleship inferior to that of the twelve (2 Cor 11:5; 12:11). As an apostle of Christ Jesus, he spoke with the full authority of Jesus himself. We need to keep this in mind as we read the book of Romans. It is part of "the apostles' teaching" (Acts 2:42); it is Scripture (2 Pet 3:16); it is "the word of God" (1 Thess 2:13).

3. Set Apart for the Gospel of God

Paul's three descriptions of himself move from the general to the specific: from "servant of Christ Jesus" to "an apostle," as the more specific form of servanthood, to "set apart for the gospel of God," as the specific focus of his apostleship.

The Greek term for "set apart" (ἀφορίζω, *aphorizō*) means "to separate, to set apart for a distinct destiny or role" (see Matt 25:32). Paul is saying that God singled him out and separated him from all other men and even from all the other apostles, giving him a special role. He uses the same word in Gal 1:15, saying that God set him apart even from his mother's womb (see Jer 1:5). In his omniscience God foreknew even before Paul was born that he would respond positively to his call on the Damascus road. The special role for which Paul was set apart was to preach "the gospel of God," the "good news" of God. (Even more specifically, he was to preach the gospel to the Gentiles; but he does not mention this until v. 5.)

In what sense is it the gospel *of God*? Possibly in the sense that the gospel message is *about* God, i.e., about what he has done to save us, especially in contrast with what we try to do to save ourselves (❂I:64). However, he probably means that it is *from* God, that God is its source. In saying this he is emphasizing the divine authority of his gospel message. It is not something he made up, nor did he receive it from any other man. It came from God himself (Gal 1:11-17) (❂I:64-65).

B. The Gospel and the Old Testament (1:2)

1:2 the gospel he promised beforehand through his prophets in the Holy Scriptures . . . . Here Paul's subject continues to be the gospel. His specific point is that the gospel concerning the saving work of Jesus is not some new and unexpected development in God's plan. Rather, it is something that God had already "promised beforehand" in the OT (❂I:65).

God gave his promises "through his prophets" (see 16:25-26). A prophet is basically a spokesman for someone else, one who speaks on behalf of another. God's prophets are those whom he chooses to speak for him, to deliver his own words (3:2) to others. In this sense all biblical authors are prophets since their writings are God-breathed (2 Tim 3:16). In this functional sense, men such as Moses and David and Samuel are prophets no less than Isaiah and Amos. In the early years of the church, before the NT writings were generally available, the OT prophets were a main source of the gospel (❂I:66).

Paul says the prophetic promises are recorded "in the Holy Scriptures" (❂ I:66). His point is that the prophetic promises concerning the gospel of Jesus Christ come to us through writings that are "the very words of God" (3:2), and thus are inspired and completely trustworthy. That Jesus died and was raised from the dead can be established by examining the NT records and other early testimony through purely scientific historical method. But the fact that "Christ died for our sins" and that "he was raised on the third day" *according to the Scriptures* (1 Cor 15:3-4) undergirds the gospel with fully divine authority.

Why does Paul emphasize the OT origin of his gospel at this point? As the book of Acts shows, the OT was often cited by the early Christians for apologetical purposes. I.e., fulfilled prophecy is a means of proving the divine origin both of the prophecy itself and of the work that fulfils it. Paul may have had this in mind here in 1:2.

It is more likely, though, that his purpose is polemical. There is no question that many Jews and even Jewish Christians had serious difficulty with the idea that anyone could be saved "apart from observing the law" (3:28), in particular the Law of Moses. However, the gospel of Jesus Christ, as known and preached by Paul in Romans, is that we are justified through faith apart from law-keeping of any kind. Thus it is important for him to show that this message is not some innovative heresy that he himself has concocted, but that it stands in continuity with what God has always taught through his inspired prophets. God has always had just one way of saving sinners, and Paul's presentation of that way is in perfect harmony with the Holy Scriptures of the OT. By stressing this point at the very beginning of the epistle, Paul seeks to deflect any criticism and skepticism that might be directed toward his teaching by Jewish readers.

Paul says that the gospel was *promised* in the OT. Does this mean that the gospel itself did not exist in OT times, and that salvation in those days came through some other means? No, not at all. God has always saved sinners by graciously forgiving their sins on the conditions of repentance and humble, believing acceptance of his forgiveness. The OT is filled with teaching concerning God's gracious nature and his promise of pardon (e.g., Exod 34:6; Ps 32:1-2; Isa 65:1-2; Hos 11:8-9; 14:1-3). Also, this forgiveness has always been based on the saving work of Jesus Christ, even when that work was only foreknown by God and not yet known by believing sinners (see 3:25).

OT saints knew and believed in God's saving grace, but they did not know specifically about Jesus of Nazareth and his role in the provision of the very grace that saved them. They had the gospel of Jesus Christ himself, but only in the form of promises to be fulfilled in the future (see Acts 13:32-35; Gal 3:18; Heb 11:8-13). They did not know who Jesus was, nor did they know exactly what he would be doing to save them. The prophets themselves — and even the angels — did not know these things (1 Pet 1:10-12). Our blessing is that we know not only the promises, but also the fulfillment. We know Jesus himself. We know the gospel in its fullness.

C. The Subject of the Gospel Is Jesus (1:3-4)

1:3-4 regarding his Son, who as to his human nature was a descendant of David, and who through the Spirit[1] of holiness was declared with power to be the Son of God by his resurrection from the dead: Jesus Christ our Lord. As we have noted above, the subject or substance of the gospel is Jesus. It is God's gospel "regarding his Son." These two verses are about the *identity* of his Son, or what is usually called the *person* of Christ. The main focus here is not on his work, which is brought out more fully in the body of the epistle.

1. The Two Natures of Jesus

Though this is not necessarily its main emphasis, this passage definitely affirms the two natures of Jesus, his humanity and his divinity. The latter is seen in the naming of Jesus as "his Son," i.e., the Son of God.

When applied to Jesus, this title has several connotations. Most significantly it refers to the unique relationship between Jesus and God the Father. Because of the supernatural circumstances of his virgin conception and birth, God himself designated Jesus as "the Son of the Most High" (Luke 1:31-32) and "the Son of God" (Luke 1:35). Twice the Father spoke from heaven and declared of Jesus, "This is my Son" (Matt 3:17; 17:5). In accordance with the Father's revelation, Peter confessed Jesus as "the Son of the living God" (Matt 16:16). When Jesus affirmed that he was the Son of God (Matt 26:63-66) and referred to God as "my Father" (John 5:17; 10:29), his Jewish enemies interpreted this as a claim to be equal with God (John 5:18), or a claim to actually *be* God (John 10:31-33). What is important is that Jesus did not attempt to refute this inference. Thus both the Jews' reaction to Jesus' claim to be God's Son, and Jesus' own response to this reaction (see the contexts), show that it is a title of deity. "Son of God" is a title regularly applied to Jesus by Paul (● I:69).

This text also emphasizes the humanity of Jesus, "who as to his human nature was a descendant of David" (literally, "from the seed of David"). The reference to the seed of David indicates that Jesus had not only divine but also human parentage. Both Joseph and Mary were descendants of David; Jesus was "from the seed of David" through his mother.

The Greek text says that Jesus was from the seed of David "according to the flesh." The NIV translation ("as to his human nature") is not literal but captures the meaning of the expression quite well. Paul's use of the term *flesh* (σάρξ, *sarx*) is notoriously complex (● I:69). Quite often it stands for human nature as such, in its entirety (e.g., 4:1; Eph 6:5; Phil 3:3-4; Heb 12:9). "Flesh and blood" is a fuller expression for the same thing (e.g., Gal 1:16; Eph 6:12; Heb 2:14). "All flesh" and "no flesh" refer to the human race in general (e.g., Mark 13:20; Luke 3:6; Rom 3:20; Gal 2:16). This seems to be the primary meaning in v. 3, just as the NIV understands it. The same expression and the same idea are found in 9:5, which says that Jesus came from Israel "according to the flesh." First Timothy 3:16 affirms that Jesus "was revealed in the flesh" (NASB). John 1:14 sums up this idea perfectly: "The Word became flesh"; the divine Logos became a human being (● I:70).

2. The Incarnation

It is best to understand *ginomai* here as "came into being" or "came into existence" (see John 1:3, NASB) (● I:70). The idea is that the Son of God came into existence from the seed of David as to his human nature. This is a reference to the incarnation, in which the eternal Logos "became flesh" (John 1:14, also *ginomai*), or became a human being. Prior to the incarnation, his human nature did not exist. The human person, Jesus of Nazareth, had a beginning. Jesus of Nazareth, indeed, Jesus the Christ, did not exist prior to his miraculous conception in the womb of Mary.

However, the divine person called the Logos *did* exist before the incarnation; indeed, he existed eternally along with God because he *was* God (John 1:1). But at a specific point in time the eternal Logos "made himself nothing" (Phil 2:7) and entered into an incomprehensible kind of unity with a real human being who began to exist at this same point in time, namely, Jesus of Nazareth.

3. Messiahship

Verse 3 says Jesus "was a descendant of David." Why *David* in particular? If the point is simply Jesus' human nature, why not "from the seed of Abraham"? Why not "born of Mary"? What is distinctive about his being from the seed of *David*? One thing at stake here is the uniqueness of Jesus. All Jews were known as sons of Abraham (John 8:33,37; Rom 11:1; 2 Cor 11:22). All Christians are Abraham's spiritual seed (4:13,16,18; Gal 3:29). But Jesus alone is the son or seed of David as the Bible uses that expression.

More specifically, what is at stake is Jesus' identity as the Messiah or Christ. The OT promised and the Jews universally believed that the Messiah would be a descendant of David. To say that Jesus was from the seed of David is to confess him to be the Messiah, the one promised and expected as the Savior of his people. As Jesus' contemporaries expressed it in John 7:42, "Does not the Scripture say that the Christ will come from David's family?" (literally, "from David's seed") (❂I:71).

The main emphasis of this identification is on Jesus' kingship and lordship. Most of the promises concerning David's seed echo 2 Sam 7:13, "I will establish the throne of his kingdom forever" (see Ps 132:11; Jer 23:5; Ezek 37:24). The angel who announced Christ's birth to Mary told her, "The Lord God will give him the throne of his father David" (Luke 1:32). David was to the Jews their "great king" (Matt 5:35), but God promised that the Messiah's kingdom would be even more glorious and that it would never end. Jesus as the Messiah is "great David's greater son."

4. The Two States of Jesus

When we get into the content of v. 4, a whole new perspective on Jesus Christ is opened up. Here we see that Paul is showing us not only the two *natures* of Christ, but also his two *states*, namely, the two stages of his messianic career. The first is his state of humiliation, which is the period of his earthly ministry from the point of his incarnation up to and including his death on the cross. It is likely that v. 3 is referring to this state, and that the term *flesh* connotes not only Jesus' humanity as such, but his human nature in its weak and not-yet-glorified state. These were truly "the days of his flesh" (Heb 5:7, NASB). This was the time when his "equality with God" was veiled by his humanness and his servanthood and his shameful death on a despicable cross (Phil 2:6-8). See 2 Cor 8:9.

But this is only his state "according to the flesh," and was followed by a state of the highest exaltation, to which v. 4 refers. The period of nothingness (Phil 2:7-8) is replaced by one of infinite and eternal glory (Phil 2:9-11): "Therefore also God highly exalted him, and bestowed on him the name which is above every name, that at the name of Jesus every knee should bow, of those who are in heaven, and on earth, and under the earth, and that every tongue should confess that Jesus Christ is Lord, to the glory of God the Father" (NASB). In the state of his exaltation Jesus is not just the Son of God, but is *the Son of God with power*.

The best understanding of "with power" takes it as modifying the title "Son of God," as in the NASB [1977 ed.]: Jesus "was declared the Son of God with power" (❖I:72-73). I.e., in his state of exaltation Jesus is not just the Son of God, but is the Son of God *with power*. This understanding follows the word order in the original text most closely. Also, v. 3 indicates that Jesus was already the Son of God in his state of humiliation; thus v. 4 must be pointing us to a new phase of his existence in which he is invested with unprecedented power. He has entered a new state or stage of his messianic career. In his unglorified state, "the days of his flesh," Jesus of Nazareth was the divine Son of God by virtue of the incarnation. But now as the result of his messianic work he has been exalted to a new state of power and glory. This comes specifically as the result of his work of death and resurrection, in which he confronted the archenemies death and Satan (Col 2:15; Heb 2:14-15; Rev 1:18) and decisively defeated them. Thus what was his *by nature* (because he was the incarnation of deity) has now become his *by right*. He has earned it; he has achieved it by his work.

5. The Resurrection of Jesus

Paul says that the transition point where Jesus crossed the line from humiliation to glory was his resurrection from the dead. By this specific act he was declared to be the Son of God with power. The word translated "by" is ἐκ (*ek*). It is no doubt intended here to have the causal meaning, "by means of, as the result of." As the result of his resurrection, Jesus is declared to be the Son of God with power.

A more serious issue is the meaning of the Greek word ὁρίζω (*horizō*), translated "declared" in the NIV. According to this understanding the resurrection is the act which reveals and affirms the fact that Jesus is the Son of God. By this act he is "seen to be" the Son of God (Morris, 47). This understanding would emphasize the apologetical function of the resurrection, which it certainly has (❖I:74). But the question is, is this the best meaning of the word *horizō* here?

Many believe this meaning is too weak, and suggest that the word actually bears something close to a causal connotation. (See Cranfield, I:61; Moo, 47-48.) The idea is that by his resurrection Jesus is appointed or constituted the Son of God with power; he is ordained or installed as the Son of God with power.

This latter understanding is the better one. It is closer to the actual meaning of the term (see Moo, 47-48). Also, it is more in keeping with the two-states understanding of vv. 3 and 4. It is similar to the concept in Acts 2:36, which says that God *made* the crucified and risen Jesus to be both Lord and Christ. The same word (*horizō*) is used in Acts 10:42 and Acts 17:31 to say that Jesus has been *appointed* judge of the world.

The point is that the resurrection of Jesus is the crucial transition point in his work as Messiah. It is the deathblow to his enemies, it gives him universal authority and dominion, and it enables him to perform his continuing work of priestly intercession (4:25; Heb 7:16).

Another thought in v. 4 is that Jesus was appointed to be the Son of God with power "through the Spirit of holiness" (see Moo, 49-50). This is sometimes taken to mean *Jesus'* spirit: either his human soul, in contrast with his physical nature ("flesh," v. 3), or his divine nature, in contrast with his human nature. It is much more likely, though, that it refers to the *Holy* Spirit. Why is this unusual wording, "the Spirit of holiness," used here? The probable answer is that Paul is using the Hebrew idiom, found in Ps 51:11 and Isa 63:10, thus reminding his readers again of his dependence on the OT (v. 2).

The main reason for taking this as a reference to the Holy Spirit is that the Spirit is often elsewhere described as the Spirit of life and the giver of life (e.g., John 6:63; Rom 8:2; 2 Cor 3:6), and especially as the one who raised Jesus' body from the dead: 8:11; 1 Tim 3:16; 1 Pet 3:18. Understanding v. 4 as a reference to the Holy Spirit fits this picture very consistently, since "the Spirit of holiness" is here said to be the agent of Christ's resurrection. The preposition "through" is κατά (*kata*); it is often translated simply "according to." It can be used in a causal sense, though, as seems to be the case here (Hendriksen, I:41).

6. The Son's Full Identity

As if to summarize his theological description of God's Son in vv. 3-4, Paul ends v. 4 with this full yet succinct identification: He is "Jesus Christ our Lord." These three appellations pull together all that has already been said.

"Jesus" is the proper name of the incarnate Son of God and calls attention to his human nature as one born in the line of David. It also points to his work as the Messiah, since it means "Yahweh is salvation" (*GRe*, 25-26).

The title "Christ" is the Greek equivalent of the Hebrew "Messiah." It means "the anointed one," i.e., the one appointed and anointed by God to perform the work of salvation, as promised in the OT Scriptures (v. 2) (❦I:75-76).

Jesus is also called "Lord" (κύριος, *kyrios*), a term applied to him often in

Romans. Its literal meaning is "owner," which applies in the most absolute sense to God's Son since in his divine nature he created all things (John 1:3). It is also a title that connotes the deity of Jesus, especially as used by an OT scholar such as Paul. Because he used the LXX extensively, Paul must have seen that *kyrios* was the Greek word used there to represent the Hebrew sacred name, Yahweh, over 6,150 times. Paul could not have used this word as his almost-exclusive title for Jesus without in his mind identifying Jesus as Yahweh. This is something he does explicitly in 10:9-13.

D. Paul's Apostleship (1:5)

1:5 Through him and for his name's sake, we received grace and apostleship to call people from among all the Gentiles to the obedience that comes from faith. In v. 1 Paul begins to introduce himself, especially as an apostle set apart to preach the gospel. His mention of the gospel leads him to describe it as being promised in the OT (v. 2) and as being about God's Son (v. 3a). His mention of God's Son leads him to speak in more detail of his glorious nature (vv. 3b-4). Now in v. 5 he returns to his self-introduction by further elaborating on his call to apostleship.

1. The Origin of Paul's Apostleship

He speaks first of the *origin* of his apostleship: it came "through him," namely, through Jesus Christ. This is a reference again to the call that was extended to him by the glorified Christ on the road to Damascus (Acts 9:3-6; 22:6-10; 26:13-18).

2. The Character of Paul's Apostleship

Next Paul speaks of the *character* of his apostleship: it came to him as a gift. This is the point of his statement, "we received grace and apostleship." (He says "we" only in the editorial sense, since he is talking only of himself.) The Greek word for "apostleship" is ἀποστολή (*apostolē*); it is used only here and in Acts 1:25; 1 Cor 9:2; Gal 2:8.

Why does he say that he received *grace* and apostleship? Here is where the concept of gift appears. The Greek word for "grace" (χάρις, *charis*) in its most general sense means "a gift that brings joy or gladness." It almost always includes the connotation of a gift; sometimes it is used even for the act of thanksgiving for a gift.

What does it mean in this verse? Some take it as a reference to the saving grace that Paul allegedly received on the Damascus road, along with but as distinct from his call to apostleship (e.g., Murray, I:13). In this sense v. 5 would be saying that Paul received from Jesus both saving grace and his apostolic calling. The more common view, and the one preferred here, is that the word *grace* refers to the apostleship itself. "Grace and apostleship" here means "the grace of apostleship" or "the gracious gift of apostleship."

This latter view is preferred for several reasons. For one thing, Paul's personal call by Jesus on the road to Damascus was specifically a call to the apostleship only. Jesus did not actually speak to him about salvation; he left that up to Ananias. Second, the gifts of service to which the word *grace* applies include the gift of apostleship (1 Cor 12:28; Eph 4:7,11; see Rom 12:3,6). Finally and most significantly, in many other places Paul speaks of his call to apostleship as an act of grace (15:15-16; 1 Cor 3:10; 15:10; Gal 1:15; 2:9; Eph 3:7-8).

3. The Focus of Paul's Apostleship

As an apostle Paul was told to work specifically "among all the Gentiles." The Greek word is ἔθνος (*ethnos*, most often used in the plural). In this context, it refers only to the *Gentile* nations, i.e., the nations that are distinct from the Jews.

Of course, Paul was not meant to preach *exclusively* to Gentiles. Jesus told him that he should declare his name "before the Gentiles and their kings and before the people of Israel" (Acts 9:15). Paul was very aware that the gospel was for "the Jew first" (1:16). Nevertheless it is clear that the *primary* focus of Paul's ministry was intended to be the Gentiles (Acts 22:21; 26:17).

4. The Purpose of Paul's Apostleship

In this verse Paul tells us the specific purpose of his apostleship, namely, "to call people from among all the Gentiles to the obedience that comes from faith." The words "to call" are not in the original, though the idea is certainly present (see 2 Thess 2:14). The concept of purpose is actually found in the Greek preposition εἰς (*eis*), which can mean "unto" in the sense of "for the purpose of" (Cranfield, I:66). Paul says he was given grace and apostleship *unto* — for the purpose of bringing about — "the obedience that comes from faith."

This is an extremely important idea, one that should give every Christian worker insight into the purpose of his or her ministry. The purpose or the immediate "goal of the gospel" is to produce the obedience that comes from faith. Paul elsewhere rejoices that through his ministry Christ has been able to produce "the obedience of the Gentiles by word and deed" (15:18, NASB). In 16:25-26 he declares that the mystery revealed in the gospel "has been made known to all the nations, leading to obedience of faith" (NASB). In 1:5 and 16:26 the Greek expression is exactly the same (though the NIV without good reason translates it differently in the two verses). It is εἰς ὑπακοὴν πίστεως (*eis hypakoēn pisteōs*), without any definite articles. It literally means "unto obedience of faith." Exactly what it means is a matter of much debate (❋I:79-81).

Some take it to mean "obedience *and* faith, or "believe *and* obey" (NEB, LB, TEV, NIV [16:26 only]). Another view is that it means "the obedience that is included in faith as part of its definition (Reese, *Acts*, 598-610). A third suggestion is that it means "the obedience that consists of faith" (Cranfield, I:66-67; Murray, I:13-14). "Obedience to the faith" is a fourth view (KJV, Moffatt, Phillips).

A final understanding is that it means "the obedience which results from faith." In my opinion, this is Paul's intended meaning; a wide range of commentators agree. Though it is not a strict translation, the NIV rendering is on target exegetically: "the obedience that comes from faith." According to this understanding "faith" is the subjective act of believing, and "obedience" is the whole scope of Christian good works.

This view is preferred mainly because of its contextual harmony with Romans as a whole. While faith in Jesus is stressed as the natural and necessary response to his saving work, the epistle makes it clear that this faith cannot stand alone. Paul shows in chs. 6–8 and 12–15 that the end result of the gospel is obedience or good works or sanctification. His point here in 1:5 is that he was called to be an apostle *not* just to lead the Gentiles to faith as an end in itself, but to lead them to the kind of faith that produces *obedience*.

Still, the emphasis in the expression "obedience of faith" is not on obedience as such but on faith. God wants obedience, yes; but he wants the obedience of *faith*, i.e., the obedience that comes from, results from, or is motivated by faith in Jesus Christ. Continuing daily obedience to God's commandments is expected and even necessary in some respects, but the *only* kind of obedience that satisfies God is the obedience that is the expression of faith. This is the intended outcome of Paul's gospel, just as it should be for us. The purpose of preaching the gospel is to bring about obedience, but only an obedience that springs from faith rather than from legalistic requirements. God wants obedience, but he wants the obedience of *faith* (❖I:82).

5. The Goal of Paul's Apostleship

In the Greek the last phrase of v. 5 is "for his name's sake." While the immediate purpose or goal of Paul's gospel was to bring about obedience of faith among the Gentiles, its *ultimate* goal was to bring honor and glory to the name of Christ. This is a general principle of the Christian life: everything we do should be done to the glory of God (1 Cor 10:31) and in the name of Jesus Christ (Col 3:17) (❖I:83).

E. The Recipients of Paul's Letter (1:6-7a)

1:6-7a And you also are among those who are called to belong to Jesus Christ. To all in Rome who are loved by God and called to be saints . . . . The first six verses are an expanded version of the first segment of an ordinary epistolary greeting, identifying the author. The seventh verse contains the other two segments, identifying the recipients and offering a blessing. But even before Paul gets to his formal acknowledgment of the recipients (v. 7a), he begins to address them as an add-on to his reference to the Gentiles in v. 5: "And you also are among those" Gentiles who have been called to the obedience of faith.

Verses 6 and 7 probably reflect the ethnic identity of the Roman church. Verse 6 definitely addresses Gentiles, but v. 7 seems to be more inclusive: "To all in Rome," i.e., *all* Christians, both Jewish and Gentile. The way the Gentiles are addressed in v. 6, though, seems to indicate that they made up a large part if not the main part of the church in Rome (see 1:13).

The recipients of the letter — and by extension all Christians of all times — are described in three ways in these verses. Verse 6 says that we are "called to belong to Jesus Christ." The word "called" is the same as in v. 1, "called to be an apostle," and the same as in v. 7, "called to be saints." The calling itself is not the same, though. In v. 1 the call is to a specific role of service, while vv. 6-7 speak about the calling of sinners to salvation.

That God calls sinners to salvation is a Bible teaching on which all agree (e.g., 8:30; 1 Thess 2:12; 5:24; 1 Pet 2:9; Jude 1). The disagreement comes as to the nature of the call. Some say the call is selective and efficacious. I.e., God gives it only to the elect, and it irresistibly causes the recipient to believe and to accept God's grace. This is the Calvinist doctrine of the "effectual call," and commentators of that persuasion read this idea into vv. 6 and 7 (e.g., Moo, 54; Murray, I:15; Morris, 38; MacArthur, I:28).

Others say that while God's call to sinners is gracious and powerful and necessary, it is nevertheless universal and resistible. This is the biblical view. God calls sinners through the gospel (2 Thess 2:14), which is his power unto salvation (1:16). The message of the cross draws *all* men to the Christ (John 12:32). Faith comes through the written Word (John 20:31) when that Word is faithfully preached (10:13-17). Sinners' hearts are hardened, and without the powerful message of the gospel none would turn to God (John 6:44-45; Heb 4:12). In this sense the gospel call is a *necessary* condition for salvation. The Calvinist error is to make it also a *sufficient* condition, which it is not. The sinner still has the free will either to answer the call or to resist it (Isa 65:1-7; Matt 23:37; Acts 7:51; Rev 22:17).

To say that we have been *called* to belong to Jesus and to be saints emphasizes God's gracious desire for our salvation (2 Pet 3:9) and his initiative and persistence in the whole salvation process. Because he cares, he calls — and calls, and calls, and calls.

We are called "to belong to Jesus Christ." The words "to belong to" are not in the original text; they represent the NIV's interpretation of the simple expression, "called of Jesus Christ" (a genitive connection; see the NASB). This could possibly mean "those who are called *by* Jesus Christ" (Cranfield, I:68), or it could be a possessive genitive, as the NIV has concluded (also Murray, I:15; Moo, 54; Morris, 52). Either way is grammatically and theologically correct. The latter possibility is consistent with the Lord-slave relationship (vv. 1,4). The gospel call is a call to yield ourselves to Christ's Lordship (ownership) and to become his loving and willing life-slaves.

The recipients of the letter (and thus all of us by extension) are also "loved by God." (For other texts that speak of Christians as "loved by God," see Col 3:12; 1 Thess 1:4; 2 Thess 2:13; Jude 1.) It is true that God loves all human beings both as his creatures and as sinners who need his salvation (John 3:16; Rom 5:8; Eph 2:4-5; 1 John 2:2; 4:9-10). This is contrary to many who are of a Calvinist persuasion who say that God's love is selective and directed only toward the elect (see *GRe*, 329-332, 381-383). On the other hand, God *does* have a special love for those who answer his call and open their hearts to receive it (John 14:21; Rom 5:5; 8:35). Because we belong to him in a special way, he loves us as a father loves his own children, as a husband loves his own wife, and as a shepherd loves his own sheep (*GRe*, 343-344).

The last description of those in Rome (and the rest of us) is that we are "called to be saints" (see 1 Cor 1:2). The words "to be" are not in the original text but express the idea accurately (see "called to be an apostle" in v. 1). The word "saints" means simply "holy ones," and the word "holy" means simply "separated" or "set apart" in a special relation to God. When used in the sense of saints it does not describe a distinctively high level of Christian maturity achieved by only a few. Rather, it describes the status of every Christian: we have been separated from the "dominion of darkness" (Col 1:13; 1 Pet 2:9) and from "the present evil age" (Gal 1:4), and we have been placed by God's grace within his kingdom (Col 1:13) and family (2 Cor 6:17-18). We *are* saints, and therefore we should live like saints (12:1-2).

F. The Blessing (1:7b)

1:7b We finally come to the third and last segment of the letter's greeting, namely, the blessing: **Grace and peace to you**. This is Paul's standard epistolary blessing. It is exactly the same in four of his other letters and very similar in the rest. These two important words together sum up the essence of the gospel and thus the essence of the message of Romans: "grace, therefore peace" (see 5:1). Because we are under his grace, we have peace with him and peace within.

The source of this grace and peace is specified; it is **from God our Father and from the Lord Jesus Christ**. Though the Father's loving and gracious heart desired from eternity past to bestow grace and peace upon his sinful creatures, it could not be done without the saving work performed by the incarnate Logos in the person of Jesus of Nazareth. Thus the Father and the Son together are the source of our grace and peace. Such a close linking of the Father and the Son is typical of Paul and is indicative of the deity of the Son (❂ I:86).

This brings Paul's lengthy epistolary greeting to an end. Our commentary on it is also lengthy, not just because the greeting itself is so long but also because it is so filled with doctrinal content. As MacArthur correctly notes, "The entire thrust of the sixteen chapters of Romans is distilled in the first seven verses" (I:3). Its content thrills our souls and whets our appetites for the rest of the letter.

II. 1:8-15 — PERSONAL REMARKS

In this section Paul briefly lays aside his apostolic persona (but not his apostolic authority) and addresses the saints in Rome on a personal level. He speaks not just as Paul the Apostle, but as Paul the man, Paul the fellow-Christian (❂ I:87).

A. Paul's Prayers for the Romans (1:8-10)

1:8 First, says Paul, I want to tell you what I have been praying for. (This is not the first in a series of things, since he does not go on to a "second" and "third." It is "first" in the sense of "before I go any further, before I get into the meat of this letter or into its formal teaching.") **I thank my God through Jesus Christ for all of you.**

Here Paul offers a prayer of thanksgiving. Some take it as a diplomatic gesture. I.e., by starting with this positive personal comment the author intends to "get on the good side" of the readers. This is probably reading too much into it, however. Such a statement of personal thanksgiving or blessing or concern normally followed the epistolary greeting in all letters of that time and culture (see Morris, 55, n. 97). This was Paul's own standard practice; similar remarks appear after the greetings in all his other letters except Galatians.

By referring to God as "*my* God" Paul reveals the close, intimate relationship he has with the Father. For him God was not just an academic subject but one whom he knew personally. He knew what it meant to speak to God as "Abba! Father!" and he says that we may do the same (8:15).

Paul offers his prayer "through Jesus Christ," who is the one and only mediator between our sinful selves and the holy God (John 14:6; 1 Tim 2:5; Heb 4:16). This is not just a formality, but a sincere acknowledgment that the atoning work of Jesus makes it possible for us to be accepted by God and allowed into his presence.

Paul says he thanks God "for all of you." This includes all the saints at Rome, from both Jewish and Gentile backgrounds (see v. 7). This means he was praying not only for the few that he knew personally, but also even for those whom he did not know. We are following Paul's example when we pray for people whom we have never met, whether it be friends' relatives or Christian workers in all parts of the world.

Paul says he thanks God **because your faith is being reported all over the world**. The specific reason for his thanksgiving has to do with the *faith* (πίστις, *pistis*) of the Christians at Rome. Why was this so? Was there something special about their faith? Bruce speaks of "the high and renowned quality of their faith" (75). Perhaps Paul means not just their faith, but their *faithfulness* (which is a valid connotation of *pistis*). This may be inferred from the fact that all people knew not only of the Romans' faith but also of their *obedience* (16:19). This is an indication of the principle that true faith always produces obedience (see 1:5).

On the other hand, many commentators deny that there was any special quality to the Romans' faith. It was just ordinary faith, like anyone else's.

If it was not an especially deep and strong faith, why would Paul give thanks for it? Some say it was appropriate to thank God for their faith since he was the author of it (Moo, 57), a suggestion motivated more by Calvinist beliefs than by the text. Actually Paul specifies exactly why he is thankful. He thanks God not for their faith as such, but for the fact that their faith "is being reported all over the world," i.e., the known world (and still perhaps hyperbole). Paul had traveled a lot, and everywhere he went people talked about the fact that there was a Christian church *even in Rome*.

1:9-10a God, whom I serve with my whole heart in preaching the gospel of his Son, is my witness how constantly I remember you in my prayers at all times . . . . "God is my witness" is a kind of oath, in which he calls upon God to bear witness to the truth of his statement. This is a frequent practice of Paul; see 9:1; 2 Cor 1:23; 11:31; Gal 1:20; Phil 1:8; 1 Thess 2:5,10. He calls upon God to be his witness especially when he is affirming things that others cannot establish for themselves, especially (as in this case) revelations of his own inner thoughts and feelings (Cranfield, I:75; Morris, 57). God is a true witness to these things because he knows all things, even the thoughts of our hearts, and he cannot lie (1 John 3:20; Titus 1:2).

Paul uses this oath so that he can communicate how serious he is about his concern and prayers for Rome. He wants them to have no doubt about this, especially in view of the fact that he had not yet been there, and also in view of the fact that his immediate plans are to go to Jerusalem, not Rome (15:25). The oath will help the cynics not to doubt his sincerity.

Paul cannot refrain from a parenthetical description of God as the one "whom I serve with my whole heart in preaching the gospel of his Son." The word for "serve" is λατρεύω (*latreuō*), which in secular use meant "to work for pay." In the NT it always has a religious sense, meaning either "worship" (either of the true God or of false gods), or "service rendered to God" (Matt 4:10; Phil 3:3; 2 Tim 1:3). The noun form is similar (9:4; 12:1).

"With my whole heart" translates ἐν τῷ πνεύματί μου (*en tō pneumati mou*), "in or with my spirit." The NIV captures the meaning of this phrase, since both "heart" and "spirit" are words referring to the inner part of our being, in contrast with the outward or physical part. To serve God in one's spirit is to serve him with deep, sincere motivation (see 6:17, lit., "you obeyed from the heart"). Paul is saying that his service to God is completely sincere and internally motivated.

Paul also reminds us that he serves God "in preaching the gospel of his Son." Though the word "preaching" is not in the original text, this is probably the right understanding. As we have seen, the whole focus of Paul's life and ministry is the gospel. His entire service to God is directed toward the end of proclaiming the gospel.

Paul calls upon God to bear witness to this fact in particular, "how constantly I remember you in my prayers at all times." "Constantly" in this case does not mean "without interruption," but *regularly*. He says that he always remembers or mentions the Roman church when he prays. He uses similar language in Eph 1:16, 1 Thess 1:2-3, and Phlm 4. Paul must have had an extensive prayer list, at least in his mind.

1:10b In the latter part of v. 10 Paul gets to his main point, mentioning the specific prayer that is on his mind: **and I pray that now at last by God's will the way may be opened for me to come to you**. That is, he prays that God will allow him to travel to Rome for a personal visit with the saints there. In view of v. 13, we can surely infer that he had no doubt prayed this prayer for many years (❷ I:91).

Whereas v. 8 is a prayer of thanksgiving, this is a prayer of petition. The Greek word is δέομαι (*deomai*), which means "desire, ask, beg, beseech," and is often used in the NT in that sense. The use of such a word shows that it is acceptable and appropriate for us to present our requests to God (Phil 4:6), contrary to the occasional suggestion that such an act is either futile or very arrogant and presumptuous. (See *GRu*, 361-367.)

Since Paul had planned and no doubt prayed to visit Rome for quite some time, he was obviously feeling a bit frustrated and maybe just a little bit impatient because this prayer had not yet been answered (1:13; 15:22). This seems to be indicated in the string of short Greek words that follow: εἴ πως (*ei pōs*) — "if in any way, if by any means, if somehow, if possibly" (the NIV does not translate these words); ἤδη (*ēdē*) — "now," after waiting all this time, after being denied so often; and ποτέ (*pote*) — "at some time, at last." I.e., "I pray that — somehow, sometime, NOW! — God may permit me to come to you." Here we see a touch of frustration, and a sense of urgency and eagerness, and perhaps even some uncertainty as to whether his present plan will be fulfilled (15:23-33; see Moo, 59, n. 29; Murray, I:21).

Balancing this outburst of restlessness is an acknowledgment of God's wisdom and control over the situation. He prays that he may visit Rome "by God's will." He knows it is not wrong for him to make specific plans, but he also knows that God in his sovereign providence will either permit him to carry out his plans or else will somehow intervene and prevent it (1:13). This is the nature of God's permissive will (see *GRu*, 313-317). See Acts 18:21; Rom 15:32; 1 Cor 4:19; 16:7; Heb 6:3; Jas 4:15.

Paul also knows that God can sovereignly intervene and providentially cause his trip to come about, overcoming all obstacles and circumstances, specifically in answer to his prayer. Thus he prays that by God's will "the way may be opened" for his visit. The fact is that God did answer this prayer (Acts 23:11), but certainly not in a manner that Paul would have preferred. He eventually went to Rome as a prisoner of the state (❂ I:92).

B. Paul's Desires Regarding Rome (1:11-13)

1:11 In this section Paul explains the reason for his persistent and heartfelt prayer to visit Rome. **I long to see you**, he says (15:23). This is a very intensive word and indicates very deep desire (see 2 Cor 5:2; Phil 1:8; 2:26; 1 Thess 3:6; 2 Tim 1:4). Of course Paul already knows many of the Roman Christians (16:3-15), but his desire is not limited to them.

Why is Paul so eager to see the Romans? He explains, **so that I may impart to you some spiritual gift to make you strong . . . .** Whatever the nature of this gift, it was something within Paul's power to pass along to the church, something that he himself could impart or share. Paul saw himself as the source of this gift, or at least the agent by whose action it could be imparted.

The word for "gift" is χάρισμα (*charisma*). In the NT this noun is used always for gifts that come ultimately from God. We may discern two main categories of gifts: the gift of salvation itself (5:15-16; 6:23); and gifts of ministry or service, i.e., gifts that endow the recipient with the right and ability to render special service to the church. This is the more frequent usage. These latter gifts may be miraculous or nonmiraculous.

The word for "spiritual" is πνευματικός (*pneumatikos*). This is the only text where it is specifically used with "gift" for the phrase "spiritual gifts"; but see 1 Cor 12:1 and 14:1, where the word "gift" seems to be understood. In what sense is a gift *spiritual?* On the one hand something may be called spiritual if empowered by or derived from the Holy Spirit (1 Cor 2:13; 15:44,46), just as a person may be called spiritual if led by the Holy Spirit (1 Cor 2:15; 14:37; Gal 6:1). Thus a "spiritual gift" would be a gift bestowed by the Holy Spirit. On the other hand something may be called spiritual because it is related to the spirit of man or to the spirit world, in contrast with the physical (Rom 15:27; 1 Cor 9:11; Eph 1:3; 6:12; 1 Pet 2:5). In this sense a "spiritual gift" would be something relating to the spiritual life of Christians.

Can we be sure of the exact nature of the gift Paul wished to bestow upon the Romans? Probably not. He himself does not specify what it was; he says only *some* gift (τι, *ti*, an indefinite Greek particle) (❂ I:94).

Some say that Paul wanted to bestow gifts of service upon the Romans, i.e., miraculous gifts such as prophecy and tongues (Lard, 35) (❂ I:94). Perhaps since no apostle had yet been to Rome (as far as we know), Paul felt the Roman church had the same need as the Samaritan church prior to the visit of Peter and John (Acts 8:14-19). If indeed gifts of ministry were what Paul had in mind here, he would have been thinking of miraculous gifts, since there is no indication that the laying on of apostles' hands was needed for the bestowing of nonmiraculous gifts.

The other main possibility is that Paul was referring to the general spiritual benefit that he could bestow upon the Romans as the result of his own work of "preaching, teaching, exhorting, comforting, praying, guiding, and disciplining" (MacArthur, I:43) (❂ I:94).

Though I do not rule out the view that miraculous gifts are what Paul has in mind, I think this latter suggestion is most likely the case. We need not state it in vague and general terms, however. I believe we can be quite specific about what Paul meant, namely, the gift he wanted to bestow upon the Romans was the gospel itself (1:15). In 1 Thess 2:8, using the same verb as here (μεταδίδωμι, *metadidōmi*), Paul says, "We were delighted to share with you . . . the gospel of God" (see v. 9). In 1 Cor 9:11 he refers to his preaching of the gospel as sowing "spiritual" things (see 1 Cor 9:14). The gospel is a spiritual gift in that it comes ultimately through the revelation and inspiration of the Holy Spirit, but Paul also calls it "*my* gospel" (2:16; 16:25; 2 Tim 2:8) since it was entrusted to him for preaching. It is also a spiritual gift in the sense that it builds up the spirit, as compared with a material gift such as the money he was taking to Jerusalem (15:27). Paul's preference was to bestow this gift of the gospel upon the Romans in person (1:13-15); but it was also possible, as a second choice, to do it by means of this epistle.

The reason why Paul wanted to give the Romans this gift was "to make you strong" (στηρίζω, *stērizō*), i.e., to strengthen you, to establish you upon a firm foundation, to confirm you in your faith. (See Luke 22:32; 1 Thess 3:2,13; 2 Thess 3:3; 1 Pet 5:10.) Of course, the purpose of miraculous spiritual gifts was to confirm faith and build up the church (1 Cor 14:3-5,26-33; Eph 4:11-14; Heb 2:4), so this would be consistent with the view that this was the nature of the gift. But it should be noted that the word *stērizō* is also used in Romans 16:25 to describe the effect of preaching the gospel: "Now to him who is able to establish you by my gospel." Thus in v. 11 Paul says he wants to go to Rome in order to bestow upon the Roman Christians a spiritual gift that will strengthen them, namely, the gospel of Jesus Christ.

1:12 that is, that you and I may be mutually encouraged by each other's faith. This verse presents an interesting addendum to the thought of v. 11. The expression translated "that is" suggests an amendment or modification of what Paul has just said. While not retracting his point about wanting to bestow some gift upon the Romans, he now graciously acknowledges that they would actually be able to give him encouragement as well: I can help you, but you can also help me.

This was not just a statement of formal courtesy or false piety or tactful diplomacy, as if he really did not mean it. No, Paul genuinely felt that he would be blessed by his visit to Rome. In 15:24 he speaks of going to Rome "to enjoy your company for a while." "Enjoy your company" is a loose way of translating a verb that means "to be filled full." He knew that his visit would fill empty places in his own life.

Such mutual encouragement made possible by Paul's visit would come, says Paul, "by each other's faith." The Romans would be able to know Paul in person, not just by reputation. They not only would be able to hear about Paul's faith through this letter or from others, but would be able to hear about it from Paul's own lips and, even better, to see firsthand how he lived his faith in his everyday life. Also, Paul would be able to observe firsthand how the Romans would mature in their faith through his own gospel preaching.

1:13 At this point some of the Romans might have been tempted to think, "Well, if Paul is really sincere, if he really wants to see us so badly, why has he not come before now?" Here Paul addresses this possible suspicion: **I do not want you to be unaware, brothers . . . .** (cf. 11:25; 1 Cor 10:1; 12:1-2; 2 Cor 1:8; 1 Thess 4:13). He uses this double negative for emphasis. Such an introduction means, "This is a really important point. Listen carefully. I want to make sure you understand this." He wanted no misunderstanding on this point about his desire to come to Rome.

He calls them "brothers," a term he used often to refer to his fellow Christians. Though he was a physical or racial brother only to the Jews (see 9:3), as a Christian he regarded all men of whatever background as his brothers if they were fellow Christians. Thus even the members of the (mainly) Gentile church at Rome are addressed as "brothers."

What was he so eager to have his brethren know? **. . . that I planned many times to come to you (but have been prevented from doing so until now) . . . .** He is not speaking here of simple desire to visit them, but of actual, concrete plans: not just once or twice, but often. That he had made such plans many times indicates the longstanding nature of his concern for Rome, contrary to any who might have doubted it.

So far, however, they had *not* been carried out, but it was not Paul's fault; he had "been prevented from doing so." (See 15:22.) In this parenthetical statement he does not say what prevented him from coming to Rome. The demands of preaching to the unchurched eastern Mediterranean area no doubt were a main factor (15:20-22; but see Acts 16:6-9; 1 Thess 2:18).

After this parenthesis about being hindered, Paul continues his thought about his plans by stating what he hoped to accomplish by coming to Rome. In v. 11 he said he wanted to impart some spiritual gift to the Romans in order to strengthen them. Here he says he had planned to come **in order that I might have a harvest among you . . . .** The NASB is more literal: "obtain some fruit."

The question here is the nature of the fruit Paul hoped to reap from among the Romans by his presence there. One possibility is that he is referring to converts he would win to Christ through his preaching (Stott, 57). Jesus calls the lost world a harvest field where fruit may be gathered (Matt 9:36-38; John 4:35-36). Paul refers to the first converts in an area as the "firstfruit" (16:5; 1 Cor 16:15).

The term *fruit* is also used in the NT in the sense of bearing or producing the fruit of mature character and holy conduct. This concept appears in the gospels (Matt 3:8,10; 7:16-20; 12:33) and in the concept of the "fruit of the Spirit" (Gal 5:22-23). See also Eph 5:9; Phil 1:11; Heb 12:11; 13:15; Jas 3:17-18.

The terminology of obtaining or producing fruit may also refer to the more general concept of cause and effect. I.e., whenever anything produces something as its effect, that is its *fruit*. For example, whenever our lips produce praise, that is their fruit (Heb 13:15). If discipline causes righteousness, that is its fruit (Heb 12:11). The fruit or effect of slavery to sin is shame and death, but the fruit of slavery to God is sanctification and eternal life (6:21-22).

This is the sense in which we talk about the "fruit of our labor," i.e., the good results of our labor, whatever those results may be (❧I:98). It is probable that here in 1:13 Paul is using the term *fruit* in this general sense of *results*. Thus he is saying that his desire and plans to go to Rome are for the purpose of winning converts as well as building up and strengthening the existing saints (Cranfield, I:82). He hopes first of all to preach the gospel "among you" in an evangelistic sense, thus directly reaping fruit and adding more Christians to the body there. But he also hopes to preach the deeper gospel truths that will lead to stronger faith and more mature character for the entire church, just as he has said in v. 11. And so Paul's preaching will "get fruit" in Rome indirectly, by causing the Christians there to achieve greater depths of holiness.

In these ways Paul will have fruit in Rome **just as I have had among the other Gentiles**. By the time Paul wrote Romans he had preached the gospel to a large portion of the Gentile world (15:19,23), with much fruit being produced. See Phil 1:5-6,10, where he says that the preaching of the gospel continues to produce the fruit of good works and maturity in the lives of Christians in Philippi. But somehow it would just not be fitting if he obtained fruit from all over the Gentile world but passed by its very capital and nerve center, Rome itself.

C. Paul's Debt to the Romans (1:14-15)

1:14 I am obligated both to Greeks and non-Greeks, both to the wise and the foolish. Paul has spoken frankly to the Romans about his prayers and desires for them; now in these two verses he reveals another aspect of his heart. Specifically, he unveils for us all the strong sense of obligation that drove him to burn himself out in service to Christ. For "I am obligated" the text says, literally, "I am a debtor." A debtor is someone who *owes* somebody something. It can be a debt of money (Matt 18:24) or a moral obligation of some other kind. In the latter sense we speak of a debt of gratitude (15:29) or of paying one's debt to society.

Here Paul is referring to his personal debt or moral obligation to preach the gospel to the Gentiles of the world, based on his calling as God's apostle to the Gentiles (1:1,5). Because of this, he says, "I am compelled to preach" (1 Cor 9:16). He was entrusted with the gospel as an inescapable stewardship. Preaching the gospel was a debt he owed to God, because God appointed him to do it.

Actually, though, in this text Paul says he is a debtor not to God but to the Gentiles themselves. His commission put him in debt to the latter as well. He *owed* it *to the Gentiles* to preach the gospel to them. How was this the case? Consider this scenario: a very wealthy man dies and bequeaths his estate to a distant relative. His lawyer is entrusted with the task of tracking down this relative and transferring the estate to him. In a real sense the lawyer owes it to the relative to make sure he receives the inheritance (see Stott, 59).

With reference to his debt, Paul says he is obligated "both to Greeks and non-Greeks, both to the wise and the foolish." There are two issues here. One, how extensive are these expressions? Do they encompass the whole world, or just the Gentiles? Second, is the second pair equivalent to or different from the first (❖ I:100)?

Some think the terms Paul uses are meant to encompass the whole world, but it is better to limit them to "the sum of Gentile mankind," as Cranfield says (I:83). It is true that Paul sometimes uses "Greeks" as a synonym for Gentiles (1:16; 2:9-10; 3:9; 10:12), but this is when he is contrasting them with Jews. Here the term has the more limited reference of the sophisticated, civilized, cultured Gentiles, those who were "Greek" by language and culture, whether they were born of Greek parentage or not (Barclay, 8). The word for "non-Greeks" is actually βάρβαρος (*barbaros*) or "barbarians," or the less civilized peoples who spoke strange languages that sounded like "bar-bar-bar" gibberish to sophisticated "Greek" ears.

"The wise and the foolish" also refers to Gentiles. Some see these categories as distinct from the previous ones (Cranfield, I:83-84; Morris, 65). It is more probable, though, that they are equivalent to the first pair and are just one way of explaining the difference between them (Hendriksen, I:54). Greeks are wise and learned, at least in their own eyes and with a worldly wisdom (1 Cor 1:19-20,26-27); barbarians are foolish and uneducated and without understanding.

1:15 In this verse Paul takes the general principle stated in v. 14 and applies it specifically to the Christians in Rome. Just because he has this overwhelming obligation to the Gentile world, **"That is why I am so eager to preach the gospel also to you who are at Rome."** The expression that begins this verse can be translated either "that is why," as in the NIV, or "as far as I am concerned, as for me, for my part," as in the NASB. Paul's point is that whether his circumstances or God's providence allows him to come to Rome or not, in his own heart and mind he is ready and eager to be there and to preach the gospel.

Since Paul was a debtor to all Gentiles everywhere, Rome was certainly included in this debt. Thus he wanted to preach the gospel "to you (ὑμῖν, *hymin*) who are at Rome." A question that arises here is whether *hymin* means "*to* you" or "*among* you." Some say the latter, because they think preaching the gospel is always an evangelistic effort. Thus they say Paul could not really preach the gospel to the Roman Christians; they had already heard it and accepted it. What he meant was that he was ready to preach the gospel to the unsaved in their midst or in their city (Godet, 90; Moo, 63; Watson, "Congregations," 213).

This limitation on εὐαγγελίζομαι (*euangelizomai*) is not justified, however. Its primary connotation is preaching the gospel to the lost, and Paul certainly did a lot of this (15:20) and no doubt planned to do it in Rome. But it also has the connotation of explaining the fuller content of the gospel to the church, "the on-going work of teaching and discipleship that builds on initial evangelization" (See Moo, 63) (❂ I:101-102).

One thing that seems clear from the content of this epistle is that the gospel of grace is often misunderstood and often requires a lot of follow-up clarification and explanation. Possibly under the influence of the Judaizers, the Romans were struggling with the role of works in relation to grace and faith. This explains the emphasis on justification by faith apart from works of law (3:28). God intends the gospel to produce obedience, but it must be the obedience *of faith* (1:5).

It is clear from this verse and from earlier statements by Paul that he wanted to preach the gospel to the believers in Rome in order to clarify and establish their faith in Christ's redeeming work. This gives us our best clue as to Paul's purpose for writing his epistle to the Romans. He is under divine obligation to preach the gospel to them. He wants to do so in person; but in case his present plans to go there do not work out, he decides to preach the gospel in the form of a letter. He cannot wait any longer to pay his debt to them.

III. 1:16-17 — TRANSITIONAL STATEMENT

Most Bible students regard this section as a statement of the *theme* of Romans. If this is so, it does not constitute a full statement of the theme, but is more of a preliminary or introductory statement, a transitional statement tying the prologue to the main body of the epistle (❖I:102-103).

As has been the case throughout the prologue, the main point of this section is *the gospel*. These verses deal with its glory, its power, its scope, its relation to faith, its heart, and its golden text.

A. The Glory of the Gospel (1:16a)

1:16 This verse opens with a transitional word, γάρ (*gar*), meaning "for, because" (omitted by the NIV). In v. 15 Paul has declared his eagerness to preach the gospel in Rome, and v. 16 gives the reason for this: I am eager to do this, because **I am not ashamed of the gospel . . . .** (❖I:103). By repudiating such shame, Paul is saying that he will never have to worry about having devoted his life to a false cause. He is confident that the gospel is everything it claims to be, and that he will never have to apologize or be sorry for believing it and preaching it.

Some (e.g., Bruce, 79) say the expression "I am not ashamed" is a literary device used for the purpose of emphasizing a positive point (like "I do not want you to be unaware" in v. 13). Thus Paul's real point would be that he considers it a great honor to preach the gospel; it is his pride and glory. There could hardly be any shame attached to something as glorious as the gospel (❖I:103-104).

At any rate, Paul says he is *not ashamed* of this gospel. He is ready to preach it anywhere, even and especially in Rome itself, the very center of human power and pomp and presumptuousness, the crossroads of worldly wealth and wisdom and sophistication. Though he had no confidence in his own powers (1 Cor 2:1-3), he had every confidence in the gospel itself, or rather in the One of whom it speaks: "I am not ashamed, because I know whom I have believed, and am convinced that he is able to guard what I have entrusted to him for that day" (2 Tim 1:12).

B. The Power of the Gospel (1:16b)

Paul's next statement gives the reason why he is not ashamed of the gospel: **because it is the power of God for the salvation of everyone who believes . . . .** "Because" translates the particle *gar*, used for the second time in the verse. Why is Paul not ashamed of the gospel? Because it is not foolish and weak as the world thinks, but is rather the instrument of omnipotence, the almighty power by which God saves sinners. In some cases weakness may indeed be a proper reason for shame, but not *power*, and certainly not the power *of God*.

"Power" translates δύναμις (*dynamis*), from which come English words such as "dynamic" and "dynamo" and "dynamite." It means power in the sense of the ability and competence to accomplish something. The perception that the gospel is weak and foolish is totally false and could not be further from the truth.

Specifically what is the power of the gospel able to accomplish? It is able to *save* those who believe. It is the power of God unto (*eis*) salvation. This recalls 1:4, which declares that the risen Jesus is now the Son of God *with power*. He is fully able to save us.

In what sense is the "gospel" God's power unto salvation? How does it save us? Here we must distinguish between the gospel as a verbal message proclaimed by a preacher, and the gospel as the actual reality of which that verbal message speaks. Strictly speaking it is not the message itself that saves, but the saving work of Christ of which the message informs us. The gospel is not just words that impact our minds, but works that impact our sinful situation and deliver us from it (see Nygren, 77) (❥I:105).

Salvation can be described both negatively and positively, in terms of what it saves us *from* and what it saves us *to*. It delivers us from all the perils and consequences of sin (Morris, 68), e.g., "from God's wrath" (5:9). It saves us to the blessed states of grace and glory (5:2). The salvation brought by the gospel is a process. With reference to the past, we have already been delivered from the penalty of sin into the state of justification. Regarding the present, we are being delivered from the power of sin by the process of sanctification. As to the future, we will be delivered from the presence of sin in the final glorification.

C. The Scope of the Gospel (1:16c)

Another point Paul addresses in this text is the *scope* of the gospel. He says it is God's power for the salvation of everyone who believes: **first for the Jew, then for the Gentile**. In terms of its intention and potential, the gospel's power is universal. God wants everyone to receive the salvation embodied in it.

This is not a concept of universal*ism*, though, as if every human being will be fully, finally, and unconditionally saved. The actual reception and application of the gospel is limited only to those who believe in it. The world is divided into two categories: those who believe in the gospel, and those who do not. The former are saved; the latter are not.

The Jew-Gentile distinction is no longer relevant where salvation is concerned (10:12; 1 Cor 12:13; Gal 3:28). The gospel is intended equally for everyone alike, whether Jew or Gentile.

Although Jews and Gentiles receive the same salvation in the same way, Paul says a certain priority applies to the Jews. God's gospel of salvation is for the Jew *first* (see 2:9-10). Some think this is indicative of a permanent priority and perpetual preference to be enjoyed by the Jews as God's chosen people.

Others more properly see the "Jew first" principle as a temporary though significant result of God's choice of the Israelite nation as the primary agent by which the Messiah was brought into the world. The Jews enjoyed a place of priority in the historical process by which God has accomplished his plan of redemption (Godet, 92; Hendriksen, I:61). Paul's specific point is that, as a natural result of their unique role in preparing for the Messiah (3:2; 9:4-5), the Jews were the first to hear the gospel message and the first to have the opportunity to accept it in faith (see Acts 2-9) Paul practiced this principle in his own ministry (Acts 13:46; 18:5-6; 19:8-9). In view of the outstanding service rendered to God by Israel as a nation, it was only proper that this opportunity for believing the gospel be extended to them first.

This fits into Paul's overall message in Romans in two ways. First, this emphasis on the divine courtesy extended to the Jews provides balance to Paul's frequent references to the Gentiles (e.g., 1:5,13-14). Second, it would help to plant respect for the Jewish Christians in the minds of the (probable) Gentile majority in the Roman church (❂ I:107).

D. Faith and the Gospel (1:16c)

The gospel is the power of God for salvation to "everyone who believes." The references to faith in these two verses are crucial for the theme of the letter as a whole and for the very nature of salvation by grace. (Paul has already referred to faith in vv. 5,8,12.) The Greek words for faith (noun, πίστις [*pistis*]; verb, πιστεύω [*pisteuō*]) mean "to rely on, to believe, to trust, to have confidence in."

Saving faith in Jesus, of which this verse speaks, has two main components. First, faith includes *assent*: acknowledging the truth of a statement, or granting the fact that a particular statement is true. This is a cognitive act, a judgment of the intellect based on sufficient evidence. In the Bible this aspect appears most clearly when the verb is used with the conjunction ὅτι (*hoti*), a combination translated "to believe that" (something is true). See John 8:24; 11:27,42; 13:19; 14:10; 16:27,30; 17:8,21; 20:31; Rom 6:8; 10:9; 1 Thess 4:14; Heb 11:6; Jas 2:19; 1 John 5:1,5.

The second component of saving faith is *trust*: acknowledging the trustworthiness of a person, entrusting yourself or something you value into another person's care, or surrendering yourself in some sense to that person. This is a volitional act, a decision of the will based on a combination of personal need and a confidence that the other person can meet that need. It is directed toward the person himself and not just toward statements about him. In biblical terminology this aspect of faith appears most clearly in the expressions "to believe in" (John 3:16,18,36; 6:29,40; 7:38; 9:35; 11:25-26; 14:1; Acts 10:43; Rom 10:14; Gal 2:16) and "to believe on" (Matt 27:42; John 3:15; Acts 9:42; 11:17; 16:31).

The faith of which Paul speaks here is not just a general faith in God (Heb 11:6) or a general trust in the beneficence of his providence. It is specifically faith in *the gospel*, faith in Jesus Christ as Savior, faith in his blood (3:25), faith in his resurrection (10:9).

1. Faith Is a Condition for Salvation

Two main points must be made concerning the relation between faith and the gospel as stated here. First, faith is presented as a *condition* for receiving the salvation provided by the gospel. This shows that salvation and grace itself are conditional.

This is contrary to the Augustinian (e.g., Calvinist, Lutheran) idea that salvation is given unconditionally only to those whom God unconditionally chooses to save. In this view faith is not a condition for salvation, but is itself one of the gifts bestowed unconditionally upon selected sinners. The preaching of the gospel is just the occasion in connection with which God bestows faith; it has no power to induce faith in the hearer.

This is contrary, though, to biblical testimony concerning the power of the word. As Paul clearly says in 10:17, "Faith comes from hearing the message" (see Heb 4:12; John 20:31). It exerts a drawing power upon all who hear it (John 12:32). As free-will beings, though, sinners may resist this power (Matt 23:37; Acts 7:51; 2 Pet 3:9). Thus the calling of the word is universal and resistible. This is the opposite of Augustinianism, which says God's call is selective and irresistible (❧ I:109-110).

But having said this, I must point out that v. 16 is not talking about *how gospel preaching produces faith* at all, but rather *how the gospel events produce salvation*. That gospel preaching produces faith is true, as Scripture teaches elsewhere, but this is not the point here. The "gospel" to which Paul refers here is not the message of the gospel as preached, but the reality of the saving events of which the gospel speaks, i.e., the death and resurrection of Christ. The "power of God" lies in these mighty works of the Son of God. And Paul's point is that these mighty works produce salvation itself, not that they produce faith.

How does Paul relate faith to the gospel in this verse? He says simply that the gospel produces salvation for "everyone who believes." I.e., the saving works of Jesus do not save all sinners; they save only those who accept them in faith. In other words, Paul is most decisively asserting that faith is a necessary condition for being saved. Salvation is *conditional*. This is not by any means contrary to the concept of salvation by grace. Grace is by its very nature unmerited, but this is not the same as unconditional. We should never speak of "unconditional grace." Some conditions for salvation would definitely be meritorious and would thus contradict grace; but some conditions are not meritorious and are not "works" in the Pauline sense. Faith is certainly a condition, but it is not a work in any meritorious sense (Eph 2:8-9) (see *GRe*, 389-399).

As a condition for salvation nothing could be more natural than faith, and more compatible with the nature of grace as a gift (4:16; 11:6). Since our salvation is accomplished by the work of someone else (Jesus), and since it is offered to us as a free gift, the only thing we can do is accept God's word that this is so, and hold out an empty hand to receive the gift. Faith is often identified with this empty hand.

In summary the gospel is both the saving *events* or redemptive works of Jesus, and the *message* that proclaims these saving works to us. The gospel events are the power of God that works salvation in our hearts, and the gospel message is the power of the word that produces faith in those events. The former cannot take place until the latter has occurred.

2. Faith Is Not the Only Condition

Now we turn to the second main point concerning the relation between faith and the gospel. We have seen that salvation is conditional, but now we must affirm that *faith is not the only condition*. We could say that faith is a *necessary* condition for salvation, but it is not a *sufficient* condition.

A large portion of Christendom, both Calvinist and non-Calvinist, will immediately reject this statement. After all, has not Protestantism always been identified with the principle of *sola fidei*, "by faith alone"?

Recently this position has been argued by those who reject what they call "lordship salvation." This view, represented notably by Zane C. Hodges and Charles C. Ryrie, asserts the following: "Faith is the one and only condition requisite for receiving eternal life. . . . There is no mention of repentance, of good works, of commitment to lordship. It is faith, and faith alone" (Erickson, *Mind*, 109).

This idea that faith is the only condition for salvation is incorrect and is based on false assumptions and faulty hermeneutics. Several things must be remembered. First, these two verses — Romans 1:16-17 — do not exhaust the content of the gospel but are a kind of introductory summary of its main points, a transitional statement leading into the fuller exposition of the gospel.

Second, as we saw under 1:5 above, we must not only *believe* the gospel but also *obey* it. "Obeying the gospel" is not the same as obeying the law, i.e., "works of law" (3:20,28). It is rather doing those things we are instructed to do in order to receive God's saving grace. When we examine the evangelistic preaching in the book of Acts, we see that the gospel as preached to sinners included not only the good news of salvation as such, but also the necessary instructions for receiving this salvation. The latter is also part of the good news and should never be thought of as incompatible with it, since God would never tell us to do something as a condition for receiving salvation that is in any way a violation of its gracious character.

Third, we must remember that all the conditions related to salvation do not have an *identical* relation to salvation. They are all necessary, by God's decree; but they are not necessary in the same sense. As an analogy, food or nourishment is a necessary condition for maintaining physical life, but the process of eating the food is also necessary as the occasion for receiving the food into our bodies. Or, to get light from the electricity flowing through the wiring in one's house, a light bulb is a necessary condition; but so are a lamp and a plug. In order to see a baseball game in person, it is necessary to have a ticket; but it is also necessary to go to the place where the game is played at the time it is played. In these illustrations the food, the bulb, and the ticket are the primary conditions for achieving the desired goals (life, light, game). However, the other considerations are no less necessary; as auxiliary conditions they simply play different roles in the process of achieving the goals.

In spite of their historical commitment to the *sola fidei* principle, most Protestants actually acknowledge that this is so. For example, except for those who are radically committed to the "faith and nothing else" view, such as those who oppose "lordship salvation," almost all Protestants realize that *repentance* is a necessary condition for salvation. They appeal to a universally accepted principle of hermeneutics, namely, that *all* the Bible says about a given subject must be considered before we can draw final conclusions about that subject. That is, we must not take texts such as John 3:16, Acts 16:31, Rom 1:16-17, and Eph 2:8-9 in isolation from other texts that speak of the essentiality of repentance and submission to Christ's lordship (e.g., Luke 6:46-49; Acts 2:38; Rom 10:9-10).

A good example of this approach is Millard Erickson (*Mind*, 120). He asks why such men as Zane Hodges ("faith and nothing else," anti-lordship salvation) and John MacArthur (faith *plus* repentance and submission to Christ's lordship as conditions) can come to such different views. The problem, says Erickson, stems in part from the fact that "the Bible gives different formulas for conversion, different responses to the query, 'What must I do to be saved?'" Hodges emphasizes only those that specify faith. But how are we to regard those texts that specify repentance, and do not even mention faith?

The best answer, says Erickson, is that the two sets of passages must be combined and integrated in order to have the complete picture of the conditions for salvation. I.e., "both faith and repentance are necessary to salvation. In those biblical passages where only one is mentioned explicitly, the other is implicit. Repentance and faith would then be complementary aspects of a whole — conversion."

If Erickson is right, and I believe he is, then this shows that faith is not the only condition for salvation; and Rom 1:16-17 cannot be used to defend a radical "faith and nothing else" view of salvation. But I and many others will insist that Erickson has not gone far enough. He is methodologically correct to insist that we must apply the proper hermeneutical principle to this question, but he errs in limiting its application only to repentance. In view of the many passages that also include *baptism* as part of the gospel instructions on how to be saved (e.g., Acts 2:38; 8:36; 22:16; Col 2:12; 1 Pet 3:21), we cannot honestly exclude it from the list of conditions for salvation. There is no valid reason why Erickson should not treat baptism in exactly the same way he has treated repentance.

The hermeneutical principle that requires us to include repentance in the list also requires us to include baptism. To criticize the likes of Zane Hodges for excluding repentance from the list of conditions and then to exclude baptism is seriously inconsistent.

It is likewise incorrect to cite the Reformation principle of *sola fidei* and to appeal to the great reformer Martin Luther in an effort to limit the conditions for salvation to faith alone. Luther was certainly committed to *sola fidei*, but this in no way prevented him from acknowledging repentance and baptism as part of the salvation process. In fact, no one has affirmed more forcefully than Luther that the act of baptism is the time when and place where God bestows saving grace upon the sinner (see "Consensus," 31-34).

Since the main content of the gospel is the saving work of Jesus Christ, it is understandable that the primary condition for receiving salvation is faith in the Savior and his saving work (3:25; 10:9). We can accept Jesus as Savior only through faith; thus faith is the only *means* by which the gift of saving grace can be received. But faith in Jesus as Savior cannot be separated from a specific attitude toward the sins from which he saves us and a determination to avoid sin in the future. This necessarily involves repentance and submission to Christ as Lord. What faith is to Christ as *Savior*, repentance is to Christ as *Lord*. And for reasons known for sure only to God, he has specified that baptism is the time/place where he chooses initially to bestow the forgiveness of sins and the gift of the Holy Spirit (Acts 2:38; see below on 6:1-4) (*Baptism*, 18-22).

Following the analogy of the ball game as mentioned above, faith is the ticket that secures admittance to the game. At least, faith is the front side of the ticket; a ticket always has two sides, and the other side of this one is repentance. But the ticket will do the baseball fan no good unless he goes to the place where the game is to be played. Baptism is equivalent to going to the stadium, since this is where God says the action will take place.

We do agree, though, that faith is the only *means* and the key condition for salvation. It is not only necessary in the beginning for the very reception of salvation (Col 2:12), but is also necessary as an ongoing state of mind that continues to cling to and rest upon the gospel promises throughout the Christian life. This may be why Paul says the gospel is God's power unto salvation for "everyone who *believes*" (present tense).

E. The Heart of the Gospel (1:17a)

1:17 In v. 16 Paul says the gospel is God's power unto salvation. In v. 17 he answers the question as to *why* this is so. For the third time in this section he uses the particle γάρ (*gar*), meaning "for" or "because." The gospel is God's power unto salvation, **For in the gospel a righteousness from God is revealed, a righteousness that is by faith from first to last . . . .** That is, the source of the gospel's saving power is "the righteousness of God." This is the heart of the gospel.

The Greek text does not literally say, "in the gospel." The text says "in it." But since the antecedent of "it" (v. 17) is "the gospel" in v. 16, the NIV just spells it out: "in the gospel." In any case the gospel is what reveals the righteousness of God, and this is why it has the power to save sinners.

This righteousness of God is *revealed* in the gospel, says Paul. The word *reveal* refers here to divine activity; it means "to disclose, to uncover, to unveil, to make known." Interpreters agree that this righteousness of God is revealed not just in the gospel as it is preached, but primarily in the gospel as it is enacted by Jesus Christ on the stage of history itself. That is, the very deeds of which the gospel speaks are the revelation of this divine righteousness that brings salvation (❂ I:115-116).

Certainly, whatever gives the gospel its power should be considered the heart of the gospel, and that is identified here as "the righteousness of God." To understand what this means, we must define the term *righteousness* (see *GRe*, ch 4, especially 189-196) (❂ I:116). Though many today try to deny it, the biblical usage of this term demonstrates its meaning to be "conformity to the proper and relevant standard or norm" (*GRe*, 191-196; Cranfield, I:93-94). The proper norm for human righteousness is the law of God; thus when applied to human beings righteousness means conforming to God's law or satisfying the requirements of his law (*GRe*, 196-201).

What, then, is the righteousness *of God*? And in what sense is it revealed in the gospel? This latter point is important, since whatever our understanding of the righteousness of God, it must strike the sinner as *good news*. It is after all the heart of the gospel. In this connection it is important also to identify the intended contrast. The gospel reveals the righteousness of God, as opposed to — what? The answer is, as opposed to the righteousness of man, or human righteousness achieved through conformity to the law of God. This contrast is the main point of Romans. It is the contrast between law and grace as ways or methods of being accepted by God. Paul's point is that we are not under law (as a way of salvation), but under grace (6:14). We are justified by faith in God's righteousness, not by works of law or personal conformity to God's law (3:28). The choice is between personal righteousness and God's righteousness (10:3). Those who have any hope of heaven are trusting in God's righteousness and not their own (Phil 3:9). Since most of us are aware of the fact that our own personal righteousness falls far short of the required norm (Isa 64:6; Rom 3:23), the revelation of the righteousness of God as an alternative way of salvation is surely gospel — good news.

But if righteousness means conformity to a norm, how can this apply to God? What is the "norm" to which he must conform? Certainly there is no law or standard apart from God with which his actions must be compared. That is true; thus the norm to which his actions must conform is *his own nature*. In the most basic sense, to say that God is righteous means that his actions are always true to his nature. Contrary to the idea that righteousness is always a relational term, i.e., faithfulness to a relationship, the ultimate essence of divine righteousness is God's faithfulness to *himself*, to his own nature and to his own word. That God is righteous means he will never act in a way that is contrary to his nature and his word. In this sense righteousness is an attribute of God's nature, and the term is used in this sense quite often in the Bible, especially in the OT (*GRe*, 210-215).

Is this the "righteousness of God" of which Paul speaks here in v. 17? One thing that makes this a problem is the fact that such righteousness includes the idea that God must be true to his *holy* nature, which means that he must encounter sin with wrath and retribution. This concept of wrath and vengeance and retributive justice is already amply revealed in God's *law*; in what sense could it now be revealed in the *gospel*? Indeed, how could it be revealed in the gospel at all, if the gospel is supposed to be *good* news? How can the prospect of being righteously punished with God's eternal wrath be considered "good news" to the sinner?

As we saw earlier in the introduction, this is exactly how Martin Luther as a Catholic monk had been taught to understand this phrase, "the righteousness of God," as used in 1:17. As a result he was angry with God and was completely unable to understand either the gospel or the book of Romans. Then he began to see that in this and other NT contexts this phrase refers not to righteousness as an attribute of God's nature as such, but to righteousness as something established by God and bestowed upon sinners as a saving gift. This new understanding transformed Luther's whole approach to the gospel and led to the Reformation ("Latin Writings," 336-337).

Luther was right, and most Protestants have followed his thinking on this subject (see Cranfield, I:97-98). The righteousness of God revealed in the gospel is the gift of righteousness that God gives to sinners, on the basis of which he accepts them as righteous, i.e., as conforming to the norm of his law, or as having satisfied the requirements of his law. It is given to us in the form of a "robe of righteousness" (Isa 61:10), and we wear it as a covering that hides our own "filthy rags" (Isa 64:6). Paul speaks of this as "the righteousness that comes from God" (Phil 3:9), and as something that becomes ours in the same sense that our sins became Christ's as he was dying for us (2 Cor 5:21). The NIV translation of 1:17, "righteousness *from* God," reflects this idea.

Specifically what is this righteousness of God, this gift of God's grace that is revealed in the gospel? We know that God *imparts* a righteous character to us through the gift of the Holy Spirit received in Christian baptism, so that we actually become more and more righteous, more and more holy as we mature in our faith. But it is generally agreed that "the righteousness of God" in 1:17 is *not* this *imparted* righteousness, but is rather an *imputed* righteousness, i.e., a righteousness established by someone else (Jesus Christ) and set down to our account and counted as our own. It results not in a righteous *character*; this comes from the Holy Spirit's working in us. It results rather in a righteous *status*. This righteous status is the state of being justified. Justification is thus not equivalent to the righteousness of God, but is the result of it.

But again, specifically what *is* this righteousness of God that is imputed to our account, on the basis of which we are justified? It begins with the righteousness of God in the first sense above, i.e., righteousness as the attribute of God that requires him to be true to his nature in everything he does. Thus even in the salvation of sinners he must be righteous, that is, he must be true to his nature as a just and holy God. He must be true to his law; he must be sure that the requirements of his law are satisfied. But how can God save sinners and at the same time uphold the integrity of the very law they have sinned against?

This is the heart of the reason why the Logos became flesh; this is the centerpiece of the work of Christ; this is the heart of the gospel. Jesus came as our substitute in reference to the law; he came to uphold the integrity of the divine law by *satisfying the requirements of the law in our place*. To most Protestants this means that Jesus kept all the law's commandments on our behalf; then this "active righteousness" is imputed to us so that we may be counted righteous, i.e., counted as having never sinned. But this is a serious error. Jesus did keep all the law's commandments (2 Cor 5:21; Heb 4:15), but this was something required of him just as it is of any other human being. It was something he had to do for himself; it provided no "extra merit" that can be shared with others. It was also a necessary prerequisite for his atoning sacrifice.

In what sense, then, did Jesus satisfy the requirements of the law in our place, so that God can save us and at the same time be true to his nature as a holy God (i.e., be righteous)? We must remember that law has two components: commandments we are obligated to obey, and penalties we must pay if we disobey. If we do not satisfy its requirements for obedience, we must satisfy its requirements for penalty. Either way righteousness is preserved and the integrity of the law is upheld. Here, then, is the key to understanding "the righteousness of God" in v. 17: Jesus came to establish God's righteousness by *satisfying the law's requirement for penalty* in our place. His suffering and death (his "passive righteousness") were not necessary for his own sake; thus they constitute a kind of "extra merit" that can be shared with those who need it. This is how God can "justify the wicked" (4:5), or count him as righteous: he transfers Christ's payment of the law's penalty to the sinner's account. This is how the sinner is justified, or counted righteous: he is counted as having already paid the penalty for his sins. In other words, I am *justified* not because God treats me "just if I'd" never sinned, but because he treats me "just if I'd" already paid my penalty.

No wonder "the righteousness of God" is the heart of the gospel! It is no less than the substitutionary atonement provided by the Son of God through his death on the cross. This is the sense in which the cross is the greatest demonstration of the righteousness of God that can ever be made (3:25-26). The "robe of righteousness" bestowed upon sinners is in reality the very blood of Christ that has paid the debt of penalty for our sins (1 Pet 1:18-19). "My hope is built on nothing less than Jesus' blood and [Jesus'] righteousness."

Though the good news of the righteousness of God is its central concept, it is not the sole content of the gospel. The gospel speaks also of the resurrection of Jesus, and of the saving gifts of justification and the Spirit's indwelling, and of the gracious conditions for receiving these gifts — especially faith. Verse 17 reaffirms the conditional nature of salvation and the essentiality of faith. This gift of God's righteousness, says Paul, "is by faith from first to last." The NIV paraphrases considerably here. The first part of v. 17 is translated more literally by the NASB: "For in it the righteousness of God is revealed from faith to faith." This last expression, "from faith to faith," is notoriously difficult (❁ I:120-121). But whatever its exact meaning may be, it does not add anything significant to the phrase "everyone who believes" in v. 16.

F. The Golden Text of the Gospel (1:17b)

Having given his preliminary and very condensed statement of his thesis, i.e., that the gospel of the righteousness of God is able to save everyone who believes it, Paul then cites a passage from the OT as a kind of proof text: **just as it is written: "The righteous will live by faith."** This is a quotation from Hab 2:4 (quoted also in Gal 3:11 and Heb 10:38). By citing this verse Paul again shows the continuity between his gospel and the OT (see v. 2). The strong connecting word καθώς (*kathōs*), "just as," emphasizes this sameness; and the formula "it is written" reminds his readers that he is quoting authoritative Scripture.

By citing this passage here in the transitional statement of his theme, Paul shows us that it contains the kernel or essence of the gospel. We may call it the "golden text" of the gospel. Nygren says, "The whole message of this epistle is contained in 1:17, particularly in the prophetic quotation" from Habakkuk. "On that scriptural text the apostle constructs his letter" (81) (❁ I:121-122).

The original statement in Hab 2:4 refers to living by faith in God's wise purposes and providence, in the face of the imminent captivity of God's people by the Babylonians. When Paul cites this passage here, however, he lifts it to a higher plane. He presents it as a *promise* to those who believe, and not as an admonition to live faithfully. He is not just telling us that we ought to conduct our lives according to faith. Rather, he is giving a basic summary of the gospel. Thus it is a *promise*: the righteous person will be preserved alive by faith. But in the context of the NT gospel, "preserved alive" means much more than it did for the trembling Habakkuk in the face of the Babylonian threat. It refers to spiritual or eternal life: the righteous will receive eternal life by faith (❁ I:122).

The main hermeneutical problem for this quotation is whether "by faith" is intended to modify the subject ("the righteous one") or the verb ("will live"). The word order in the Greek text favors the former: the one who is righteous by faith will live. (This is also the word order in the text of Hab 2:4.) Several English translations render it thus, e.g., the NEB, the RSV, and TEV. This seems to be most consistent with the immediate context and with the constant emphasis of the epistle (Nygren, 86; Cranfield, I:102). When understood thus, it is clear that "will live" means "will be saved." It also makes the implied contrast more clear: the one who is righteous by faith will live, not the one who tries to be righteous through his own works (3:28; 10:3). This view is defended by Lard (45-46) and Morris (71-72).

Many take it the other way, though: the righteous will live by faith (thus the NASB and the NIV). This view is defended by Murray (I:33) and Hendriksen (I:64-65, n. 31). Now, if Paul's main point is that the righteous should conduct their lives by faith, then this translation would be the more natural. But if he means (and I think he does) that the righteous *will live eternally* — be saved — by faith, then the former way is better.

Conclusion

The focus of Paul's apostleship and the focus of the epistle to the Romans is the gospel, the good news of God. Why is the good news so *good*? Surely if we are told that we can be saved rather than lost, this is good. But the news is even better than this. It involves not just a contrast between sin and damnation on the one hand, and salvation on the other. It is also a contrast between two entirely different ways of salvation, two ways of being right with God or of entering heaven. One is the true way that will really save us; the other is a false way that actually leads to despair and death. These two ways are *law* and *grace*. The good news — the very best news of all — is that we can be saved by grace through faith, apart from works of law (3:28). This is the gospel (❥I:123-124).

Here I want to call attention to one of the most serious errors committed by many Christians in their attempt to understand the gospel of grace. They correctly see that the gospel can be understood only as contrasted with law. The problem is that they *limit* "law" to *the Law of Moses*, and thus see the gospel as standing in contrast only with the Law of Moses. As I see it, *there is no greater hindrance to a proper understanding of the gospel of grace than this*. The actual contrast is not just between the gospel of Jesus Christ and some particular law code, especially the Law of Moses, but between grace as a method or system of salvation (on the one hand) and law as a method or system of salvation (on the other hand). The law system is not limited to depending on the Law of Moses for salvation; it is something that may be (futilely) pursued wherever human beings have any awareness at all of God's moral law, whether this be through a special revelation such as the Law of Moses or the Pauline epistles, or whether it be only through the general revelation written on the heart (2:14-15).

This contrast between grace and law as ways of salvation has been present ever since God began presenting the good news of forgiveness of sins, as far back as Eden (Gen 3:15). Everyone who has had access to God's special revelation has had the choice between law and grace. Those who lived under the Law of Moses knew the grace of God (3:21), though certainly not as fully as those who know Jesus himself. Anyone under the Law of Moses who was saved — indeed, any sinner anywhere, anytime who has been saved — was saved by grace through faith in God's promises, not by law-keeping of any sort.

As we shall see in the next section, every person who lives and has a mature rational awareness of himself and of the world knows God's law to some extent. Unless such a person comes into contact with God's special (biblical) revelation, *law* is the only system of relating to God that he will ever know. Also, many of those who do have special revelation and its message of grace (many Christians!) do not really understand it, and they still labor under the misconception that their ability to obey God's commandments is the determiner of their salvation or damnation. But Paul makes it very clear that "no one will be declared righteous in his sight by observing the law" in any form (3:20). *This is why the good news is so good!* It tells us, even those of us who want to be saved and are already struggling to be saved by our works, that the one true, effective, conscience-clearing, peace-giving, fear-banishing way of salvation is *grace*, which means putting your complete trust in the work of Jesus Christ rather than in your own works as the way of being accepted as righteous by God.

No wonder it is the *gospel* (*good* news), and no wonder Paul was so excited about it! No wonder it is dynamite! God has given us an alternative to law as a way of salvation — an alternative to law, which is a way of *human* power, or rather, human *weakness*; a way in which it is *theoretically* possible to be right with God, but which in fact will never work because it is nullified by the presence of even a single sin; a way which in fact leads only to despair or else to self-deception and false confidence.

But the gospel gives us an *alternative* to this, a way of salvation that depends not on man's weakness but on God's power, a way that depends not on human righteousness but on God's righteousness, a way that depends not on our ability to keep God's commandments but on Christ's ability to pay our penalty for us, a way that *will* lead to salvation for everyone who believes. Is this not good news?

NOTES

[1] Please consult NIV original text for their footnotes here and throughout.

1:18–3:20 – PART ONE
THE IMPOTENCE OF
LAW AS A WAY OF SALVATION

We come now to the first main section of the book, 1:18 through 3:20 (✺I:127). When we move from the transitional statement in 1:16-17 to the first verse of this section, we certainly must be surprised if not shocked. After building up our excitement and expectation with a reference to God's *good news*, the Apostle immediately drops us into the black abyss of the wrath of God! This is surely a surprising way to begin to talk about the *gospel*! Why does Paul do it this way?

First, it is a general principle that one must understand the seriousness of his predicament before he can appreciate the need and availability of its solution. In this case, we must know that we are sinners under the righteous wrath of God before we can know and appreciate God's saving grace.

Thus before Paul explains the gospel of grace in more detail, he focuses on the sinfulness and helplessness of the entire human race. But this is secondary to and supportive of the main point, which is *the impotence of law as a way of salvation*. We must not forget that the main theme of Romans involves the contrast between grace and law as ways of salvation: sinners can be saved only by grace, not by works of law. Paul will establish the reality and the glory of salvation by grace in the second main section (3:21-5:21), but first he must show that there is absolutely no possibility that anyone may be saved by the alternative, law. Thus in this first main section everything is designed to establish this point, that by works of law no flesh will be justified in his sight (3:20). Black's heading is on target: "The Failure of Law" (39).

One point must be clearly understood: strictly speaking, it is possible to be right with God by means of law, works of law, or the law system. The universe as originally created was a law system through and through; everything existed within the general framework of God's laws, both physical and moral. Man as created was "right with God" in terms of the system of law. How does this system work? How may one be right with God in terms of law? The rules are very simple. They are stated in terms of the two aspects of law as explained earlier: commandments and penalty. Here is how the law system operates:

> KEEP THE COMMANDMENTS, AND
> (THEREFORE) ESCAPE THE PENALTY.
>
> BREAK THE COMMANDMENTS, AND
> (THEREFORE) SUFFER THE PENALTY.

So why is 3:20 true? Why is the law impotent to save? Because *no one* has kept the commandments — all have sinned (3:9-18). A person is counted as "keeping the commandments" only if he does so perfectly; even one sin makes him liable for the penalty (Jas 2:10; Gal 3:10). In 1:18–3:20 Paul does show that all have sinned, but he does this in order to show that no one can ever be right with God by means of the law system. Thus the only way anyone will ever be saved is by the alternative provided by God, which is grace.

The main subject of this first main section, then, is *law* as such (not just the Law of Moses). Since the very essence of sin is transgression of the law, or lawlessness (1 John 3:4), we cannot even know what sin is, nor can we understand ourselves as sinners, until we see ourselves in our true relation to God's law. This is the reason why the preaching of the law must precede the preaching of the gospel. This has strong implications for our methodology of evangelism in general, and our concept of child nurture in particular. Before a person (such as a child) is ready to accept Christ as Savior, he must understand that he has broken God's commandments and stands under the penalty of God's law.

Even more important is the fact that we must see that the law system cannot make us sinners right with God, so that we will know that "grace through faith" is the only possible *way* of salvation. We must see the impotence of law for salvation before grace as such can mean anything to us.

In this section and elsewhere, Paul uses the term *law* (νόμος, *nomos*) in several distinct ways. Sometimes it does mean specifically the Law of Moses, e.g., 2:12-14,17-18,20,23,25-27; 3:21b; 4:16b; 5:13,20. But at other times it means the universal moral law or the general will of God for all people, e.g., 2:14d-15; 3:19-21a,28,31; 4:13-15. Sometimes it means law as a principle or as a system of relating to God, in contrast with grace, e.g., 3:27; 6:14-15.

This section presupposes that God's law as the basic framework for existence is a reality with which everyone must deal. God's universal moral law, his righteous commandments, are everywhere and demand a response from everyone who is conceptually mature enough to understand what this means. Within the framework of law we face an inescapable choice or set of options. When confronted by God's law we must *either* keep it perfectly and thus receive the blessings it promises, *or* we must break it and incur the penalty it prescribes.

Obviously any rational person should choose the first option. The awful reality, though, is that *everyone* has chosen the second option. No one has kept God's law perfectly; all are lawbreakers and thus have incurred the penalty of eternal death in the lake of fire. Here within the framework of law the first choice is no longer an option, and payment of the penalty is no longer avoidable. Thus anyone who is still counting on his record as a law-keeper (i.e., his own righteousness) for salvation is either deceiving himself with a false self-righteousness or is heading into hopeless despair.

Consistent with his holy and righteous wrath, God *could* send every human being to hell. We have all broken the commandments and all deserve the penalty. But here is where the gospel comes into the picture. Consistent with his loving and righteous grace, God has given us another choice or another set of options. Since payment of sin's penalty is now inescapable, this second set of options has to do with how this penalty will be paid. Now, because of grace, we may choose *either* to stay within the framework of law and pay the penalty ourselves, *or* we may trust someone else to pay this penalty on our behalf. This latter choice is the grace option, and it requires us to renounce the impotent and damning law system and to place ourselves under the shelter of the grace system, which is the same as accepting the gift of God's righteousness, which is believing that the blood of Christ has already paid the penalty for our sins.

The message of Romans is simply this: Within the law system ("Keep the commandments and escape the penalty, or break the commandments and suffer the penalty"), the first option is closed. All have broken the commandments and are under its penalty; thus no one can be right with God in terms of law. This is the message of 1:18-3:20. However, in his boundless love God has provided another choice for us, the choice of grace itself. This is the point of 3:21-5:21: our only hope is grace.

This first main section of Romans is thus necessary to show us that there is no hope for salvation as long as we remain in a law-relationship with God. Paul makes this point by showing us that all have sinned, which renders law impotent as a way of salvation.

Why is it necessary for Paul to take so long to make this point? Why can't he just say, as he does in 3:23, that "all have sinned"? The reason is because not everyone is willing to accept this statement at face value. Many insist that at least a few people, or a few groups of people, have not really sinned in the technical sense of that word, or at least will not be held responsible for their sins, or perhaps will be treated as exceptions to the general rule. This section is necessary because some are sure to lobby for such exceptions. Paul takes the time to show that there are *no exceptions* to the rule that all have sinned, and therefore law cannot save anyone but can only condemn. We can imagine this conversation between Paul and such a lobbyist: "Sure, Paul, we agree. No one will be saved by law since all have sinned. But surely there are some exceptions to this rule." "All right," says Paul. "Just what exceptions did you have in mind?" The objector smiles and replies, "Why, just two small groups: the *Gentiles* and the *Jews*!" (❂I:131).

I. 1:18-32 — THE SINFULNESS OF THE GENTILES

Paul's first point in this section is to show that the Gentiles have no basis for claiming to be exempt from the law's penalty. That the main subject of this passage is the Gentiles can hardly be denied. Most commentators prefer to say that the passage refers to the Gentiles primarily or mainly, but not exclusively. There is good reason for this, as we shall see.

The main problem raised about the Gentiles is this: why should they need grace, if they have never had access to law? The Jews, not the Gentiles, were chosen by God to receive the revelation of his great Law through Moses. If the Gentiles do not have this Law, how can they be considered as sinners? Surely God must excuse them on the basis of their ignorance. After all, does not God himself say that "where there is no law there is no transgression" (4:15)?

This is the same view that many people have today about the so-called "heathen," or pagans who have never heard the gospel. I.e., surely God has no basis for condemning them, if they have never seen or heard of the Bible. Surely God will not hold them accountable for what they have had no opportunity to know. So surely these modern-day Gentiles will not be lost. Some even question the need for missionary activity on such grounds.

This is the very issue Paul is addressing in this passage. What makes this category of people distinct is the fact that they have had no access to special revelation; their knowledge of God has been derived from *general revelation only*.

These two basic kinds of revelation are usually distinguished. *Special* revelation is that which God gives to specific people in specific times and places, either through deeds or words. All word revelation falls into this category; when God speaks to mankind in human language, he speaks into a particular place and time, usually through a spokesman or prophet. Much of such revelation has been written down for us in the Bible; all biblical revelation is special revelation. *General* revelation, on the other hand, is revelation that is given to all human beings in general, via means that make it universally available, such as the phenomena of creation and providence (Ps 19:1-6; Acts 14:17; Rom 1:19-20).

Paul's point in this passage is that even though the Gentiles may not have access to the special revelation of God's law, they know enough about God and his law through general revelation to be held accountable. They have broken the law they have, and are therefore without excuse and thus are under the wrath of God.

What is said in this passage actually does apply to all people, since general revelation by its very nature is known to all — even to Jews and others who have access to special revelation. But the specific issue with which Paul is dealing is the status of those who have been exposed to general revelation *only*. This would include most of the people who lived in pre-Christian times, and it would include anyone living today who has not yet come into contact with biblical revelation (❥I:133).

A. Universal Knowledge of God and His Law (1:18-20)

In order to show that the Gentiles, individually and as a group, will be justly judged and condemned within the framework of law, Paul must first show that they do indeed know God and his law, and have indeed broken it. This is the point of 1:18-32, and the universal knowledge of God and his law are the subject of vv. 18-20.

The NIV fails to translate the connecting γάρ, *gar*, "for, because," at the beginning of v. 18. This word shows that Paul is introducing the reason why only the righteous by faith will live, namely, because there is no other viable option. The only other way to eternal life is through perfect obedience to God's law, and no one will qualify on this basis. Even the Gentiles have sinned and are under God's wrath, so even the Gentiles need to hear the gospel of righteousness by faith.

In other words, this section shows the universal need, not just for salvation as such, but for the specific *way* of salvation that is the heart of the gospel (1:16-17).

1:18 The wrath of God is being revealed from heaven against all the godlessness and wickedness of men who suppress the truth by their wickedness . . . . Paul gets right to the point: The Gentiles are under the wrath of God. God's wrath is a fearsome reality (see *GRe*, 275-319). We must never weaken its force by separating it from the nature and will of God, as some try to do. Such a view is a serious departure from the teaching of Scripture, where wrath is not an impersonal process but the deliberate penal judgment of the personal God. To say that this wrath is being revealed "from heaven" is a way of repeating for emphasis the fact that it is the wrath of the personal and holy God.

God's wrath should not be compared with frivolous, impetuous, capricious human anger. It is rather the inevitable retributive response of the eternally holy God against anything that violates his own being. It is the "consuming fire" aspect of his nature (Heb 12:29).

Paul says the wrath of God "is being revealed" (present tense). This is the same word as was used in v. 17 for the righteousness of God. As in that case, the revelation is given not necessarily in the form of a verbally communicated message but in the reality of the punitive events themselves. Exactly what are these events that reveal to us the wrath of God (❂I:134-135)?

The wrath of God is being revealed throughout history, especially upon the Gentile or pagan world "in the events of history" (Moo, 101) (❂I:135). This includes the retributive penalties imposed by human governments (12:19; 13:4), the accusations of conscience (2:15), the pain of childbirth (Gen 3:16), the necessity for toil as the result of a sin-cursed environment (Gen 3:17-19; Rom 8:20-22), and the inescapable penalty of death itself (Gen 2:17; 3:19; Rom 1:32; 5:12; 8:10). Most significantly, the context itself suggests that the most obvious revelation of God's wrath is his judicial action of "giving over" the Gentiles to the bitter consequences of their sinful desires and depraved lifestyles (1:24,26,28).

Paul says this wrath of God is being revealed "against all the godlessness and wickedness of men." The word "all" makes the reference universal; there are no exceptions. God's wrath is against all the sins of all people, even those of the Gentiles.

The word translated "godlessness" is ἀσέβεια (*asebeia*). Words from this word group refer to ungodliness: opposition to and rejection of God. The other word, "wickedness," translates ἀδικία (*adikia*). This is from the word group having to do with righteousness or justice, which as we saw earlier means conformity to the appropriate norm. Human righteousness thus means conformity to God's law. With the negating alpha (as here) the meaning would be *un*righteousness, wickedness, or actions that are contrary to God's law (❶ I:136). *Asebeia* thus refers to sin as a direct attack on or rejection of God himself; *adikia* refers to sin as a violation of God's law (1 John 3:4).

The verses that follow depict the abandonment of the true God as one kind of sin, as distinct from all the immoral and evil deeds that sinners commit among and against one another. And it seems clear that Paul is saying that the former in some way leads to the latter.

The last part of v. 18 says that God's wrath is directed against "men who suppress the truth by their wickedness." What truth? The verses that follow show conclusively that Paul is referring to truth about God himself (see vv. 19-20,25) and about his law or will for all mankind.

The verb translated "suppress" is κατέχω (*katechō*). This combines the ordinary verb *echo*, "to have, to hold (to)," with the prefix for "down" (*kata*). This prefix adds an emphasis which can be interpreted variously, but which in this case obviously means "to hold *down*, to suppress." God's wrath is directed against those who suppress his truth.

To say that the Gentiles suppress the truth means that they do *have* the truth and even know that it is true. In other words, the very act of suppressing the truth is evidence that they know it and are therefore without excuse and are no exception to the need for grace. The problem is that they deliberately reject it; they refuse to accept it and acknowledge it as truth. To some this may appear to be a genuine ignorance of the things of God, but Paul is saying it is only an apparent ignorance and not a real one. The knowledge is there, but suppressed.

They suppress the truth "by their wickedness." This is the word *adikia* again, as used earlier in the verse and translated "unrighteousness" in the NASB. At issue is whether the preposition ἐν (*en*) should be translated "in" or "by." If the former, then the point is that the Gentiles are comfortably ensconced in their wicked lifestyle and want to preserve it and therefore suppress all thoughts of

God so as not to feel guilty. If the latter, then the point is that they suppress the truth by means of their wicked living; by their evil deeds they openly renounce the validity of God's claims on their lives. Both ideas are true, but it is difficult to tell which one Paul specifically had in mind when he wrote. Perhaps he was thinking of both.

1:19 since what may be known about God is plain to them . . . . This verse begins with "since" or "because," giving the reason for the preceding statement. God's wrath is being revealed *because* all people do know God (19-20) but have deliberately rejected him (21-25). Verses 19-20 are mainly establishing the fact that the Gentiles do have the truth (as v. 18 implies). Specifically, they have it through the *general revelation* that comes to all people through their awareness of the created universe. (See *GC*, 319-353.)

Paul refers to "what may be known about God" in this way (❶I:138). The NASB says, "that which *is* known." This is its meaning in all other NT occurrences, and its most common meaning elsewhere (❶I:138). This is no doubt Paul's intended meaning here, contrary to the NIV. In this context his point is not about what *may* be known, but about what *is* known (vv. 20-21).

The object of this knowledge is God himself. This explains the content of "the truth" of which v. 18 speaks. What the Gentiles know about God "is plain to them," says Paul. The word for "plain" is φανερός (*phaneros*), which means "manifest, evident, clear, plain, open, visible, easily seen." This is why this truth is known: it cannot be missed.

Another point of debate is the phrase ἐν αὐτοῖς (*en autois*), translated "to them" in the NIV. This is possible, since the preposition *en* can mean "to." However, *autois* without any preposition also means "to them," and it is used thus and translated thus in the latter part of this same verse. I take it as unlikely that Paul would use the two different expressions to mean the same thing so close together, contrary to the NIV. Another possibility is that *en autois* means "within them," as in the NASB. This would refer to a revelation planted within the heart and known from within (as in 2:14-15), but the context is against this connotation here. The best translation is "among them, in their midst," which is most consistent with v. 20. The first part of v. 19 thus says, "Because that which is known about God is plain to be seen in the very midst of them." ("Them," of course, refers especially to the Gentiles.)

Why is it so plain? **. . . because God has made it plain to them**. It is a matter of God's "deliberate self-disclosure," as Cranfield says (I:114). I.e., the Gentiles know this truth about God because he chose to make himself known. Their knowledge is neither an accidental discovery nor a cleverly devised speculation.

1:20 For since the creation of the world God's invisible qualities—his eternal power and divine nature—have been clearly seen, being understood from what has been made, so that men are without excuse. Verse 20 begins with

Paul's favorite explanatory word, "for" (*gar*). How can we say that God has made truth about himself plain even to the Gentiles? Because, "since the creation of the world" certain truths about God have been clearly known through created things themselves. This has been the case ever since God originally created the world as recorded in Gen 1. From that time to the very present God has been revealing himself, and thus something about him has been and is known.

What is the *content* of this knowledge? Verse 19 is very general, but now v. 20 gets more specific: "God's invisible qualities" are known. This does not mean that God also has visible qualities; everything about the nature of God is invisible to his creatures. He cannot be perceived by our sight or senses (John 1:18; Col 1:15; 1 Tim 1:17; Heb 11:27; see *GC*, 229-233). Why is this fact about God mentioned here? It is a way of emphasizing the reality of the knowledge, expressed in the term "clearly seen" later in the verse. It is a play on words, as well as a conceptual paradox: how can "invisible things" be "clearly seen"? Cranfield (I:114) calls this an intentional oxymoron.

What specific qualities are known? "His eternal power and divine nature." It is not surprising that power should be mentioned, since God's omnipotence is the divine attribute most clearly expressed in the act and product of creation (see *GC*, 292-305). But why does Paul speak of *eternal* power. The word for "eternal" (ἀΐδιος, *aidios*) is rare, occurring only here and in Jude 6. There is no question that God is eternal, probably in more than one sense (see *GC*, 250-264). This includes the idea that he is everlasting, along with all his attributes. The question arises here, though, as to how God's eternity or everlastingness can be "clearly seen" by means of created things. One possibility is that Paul is assuming here a basic form of what is called the cosmological argument for the existence of God (see *GC*, 424-433). The created universe consists only of contingent things, i.e., things that have a beginning and are perishable. From their existence we infer that their cause must be a Creator who is *not* contingent, and who is therefore eternal and imperishable. Paul later refers to this basic distinction between the immortal, imperishable Creator and mortal, perishable creatures (1:22,24) as part of the knowledge for which all men are responsible.

The invisible qualities of God known through created things also include his "divine nature." The Greek word is θειότης (*theiotēs*). This is the sum of all the characteristics or perfections of deity, in other words, all the attributes we usually associate with God (❂I:140-141). This means that other qualities of God's nature besides his power are clearly seen from the created world. These include his glory (Ps 19:1) and his goodness (Acts 14:17), as well as his righteous judgment (1:32). See *GC*, 339.

Having spoken of the content of the Gentiles' knowledge, the text then emphasizes the *reality* of it. These things, Paul says, "have been clearly seen." The tense of the verb is actually present: "*are* clearly seen." Herein lies the paradox, that the invisible things of God are nevertheless seen by all. How is this the case? Paul is obviously speaking of "seeing" in a nonphysical sense. That is, the invisible things of God "are clearly seen by the eye of man's mind" (DeWelt, 28), or what Eph 1:18 calls "the eyes of your heart." The idea is that what we physically see in the created universe leads the eyes of our hearts to see these invisible divine qualities. In this way all people, including the Gentiles, have true knowledge of the true God.

Next Paul identifies the *source* of this knowledge: God's invisible qualities are "being understood from what has been made." "Being understood" is the verb νοέω (*noeō*), which specifically refers to mental seeing, the activity of the mind. To say that these things "are understood" just reinforces the fact that the knowledge is real. "Are clearly seen" is the main verb; "being understood" is a participle modifying it, explaining *how* these things are clearly seen. The answer is: "from what has been made," that is, the things made by God in the activity of creation, the created visible universe.

How are the phenomena of creation a source of true knowledge of God? On a common-sense level, when we view the wonders of nature we just instinctively infer a powerful Creator as their source. When such data are formally analyzed by the mind, the results are what are called the cosmological and the teleological arguments for the existence of God (on the latter see *GC*, 433-440). These arguments assume some basic reasoning power, which all human beings have by virtue of being created in God's image. This implies that we should be able to draw some true conclusions about God based on general revelation only (see Dunn, I:56-57). Such "natural theology" is not a product of speculative reason, but rather of God's own revelation as thought through by analytical reason.

We agree with Moo, though, that "this knowledge is both limited and impure" (123). It is impure because some things present in nature (such as human disease and death) are the result of sin and do not reflect the glory of God (8:18-23). It is limited in scope because some truths about God are not revealed in natural phenomena (e.g., the fact of the Trinity). Even the cosmological and teleological arguments are limited as to what kind of Creator can be inferred from the creation (see *GC*, 430-432, 438). Most significantly, general revelation does not give any information about *the gospel*, i.e., about salvation and about God as Redeemer. This information comes only through special or biblical revelation and thus is not available to the Gentiles unless someone takes it to them (10:13-17).

This leads to the last point Paul makes about the Gentiles' knowledge in v. 20, namely, its *result*. Their knowledge of God is sufficient "so that men are without excuse." "Men" is not in the text, which has only the pronoun "they," whose antecedent is the men who suppress the truth in v. 18. The main reference is to the Gentiles, but the state of being without excuse applies to all sinners, as 3:19-20 shows: "every mouth . . . the whole world . . . no one."

"Without excuse" translates ἀναπολόγητος (*anapologētos*), used only here and in 2:1. It is from the same root as the word that means "apology" in the sense of "apologetics, defense." As 1 Pet 3:15 says, the Christian can and should have an apology or defense for his hope, but Paul declares that the sinner has no defense or excuse for his sin. Why not? Because general revelation gives every person enough knowledge to be judged by (see vv. 21,32). No one, not even the most remote Gentile, will be able to plead ignorance on the judgment day (see 3:19; Matt 22:12). To be without excuse assumes each individual's free will and personal responsibility for his actions. It also assumes adequate knowledge of the standard by which our actions will be measured, which is Paul's point here.

Some take the end of v. 20 to be a statement of purpose: "so that they may be without excuse" (ASV), as if the very purpose of general revelation is to condemn (Mur I:40). Most, however, rightly take it as referring to the *result* of general revelation: "so that as a result they *are* without excuse (as in the NIV). I agree with Lenski (100), that to understand this in terms of purpose "would be monstrous."

Either way, the Gentiles are without excuse. Their godless and wicked behavior (v. 18) is inexcusable in view of what they know about God (vv. 19-20), and God is justified in pouring out his wrath upon them. The next section, vv. 21-25, will make this even more clear.

B. Universal Rejection of the True God (1:21-25)

To answer the objection that the Gentiles are an exception to the need for grace, Paul is showing that they stand condemned under the law. First he shows that they do have true knowledge of the true God (vv. 19-20). Now he is showing that they have refused to accept this truth and have rejected the God who gave it to them (vv. 21-25). Verses 21-23 are an explanation of how they have suppressed the truth (v. 18), as are vv. 25 and 28.

1:21 This verse begins the explanation of why "men are without excuse": **For although they knew God**, they did not respond as such knowledge requires. This participial phrase sums up the point of vv. 19-20 and reaffirms the reality of the Gentiles' knowledge of God. This does not mean that they know him intimately, in some saving sense. The idea may be better conveyed thus: "For although they knew *about* God."

Despite their knowledge, **they neither glorified him as God nor gave thanks to him . . . .** These two responses — to glorify God and give him thanks — are the most basic of all human obligations toward the Creator. They are the fundamental precepts of God's law for mankind, and Paul's implication is that they are known to all people through general revelation alone.

What does it mean to glorify God as God? The Bible often speaks of the "glory" of God (*GC*, 446-452), a term that is meant to sum up his collective greatness. God's glory is his infinite significance, the totality of his perfections, the fullness of his deity compressed into a single concept. Most specifically, his glory is his greatness as it is manifested and as it shines forth for all to see. To "glorify" God means simply to recognize, acknowledge, and bow down before this displayed glory in the spirit of worship, and to live the kind of life that causes others to do the same.

It is often observed that to glorify God is man's highest good (his *summum bonum*) and his highest obligation. It combines into one concept the requirements of the first commandment, "You shall have no other gods before me" (Exod 20:3); the greatest commandment, "Love the Lord your God with all your heart and with all your soul and with all your mind" (Matt 22:37); and the highest goal of life, "Seek first his kingdom and his righteousness" (Matt 6:33). In this last passage "kingdom" should be understood in its basic sense of *kingship* or *lordship*; our highest goal must be to honor God's lordship over all things. If glorifying God is man's highest obligation, then refusing to glorify God is man's worst sin.

The second response required by the knowledge of God received through the creation is to give him thanks. This is the only reasonable result of recognizing that this world is the product of an Almighty Creator, and that he stands behind all its bounty (Matt 5:45; Acts 14:17). Giving him thanks is simply acknowledging that he, rather than blind fortune or human merit, is the source of all life and blessings and happiness.

Taken together, these two basic obligations mirror God's twofold purpose for creating the universe in the first place, namely, to glorify himself and to share his goodness. See *GC*, 120-128.

Paul's main point, of course, is that even the Gentiles are responsible for obeying these two fundamental laws; but they have not done so. Instead of acting righteously upon the knowledge of God available to them, **. . . their thinking became futile and their foolish hearts were darkened**. The point is that they set their minds against God, and thus removed from the master plan or master program of all possible human knowledge the key element that makes sense of everything else. Their thinking is no longer the proper use of reason and logic, but is διαλογισμός (*dialogismos*), a term that is used often in the NT and almost always in the negative sense of evil, devious, useless thinking. Instead of true thinking it is mere speculation and self-serving rationalization.

Paul calls such thinking "futile," vain, empty, worthless, pointless. The Greek word here is from the same word group which in the LXX is sometimes used for idols (e.g., Lev 17:7; 2 Chr 11:15), i.e., they are empty nothings. The same is true of all godless thinking: it amounts to nothing; it reaches no valid conclusions.

Paul also says "their foolish hearts were darkened." In biblical language the heart is not just the emotional side of man, but the whole inner being encompassing all inner, spiritual activity such as thinking and willing. The "heart" is the source of thinking, and when the heart becomes "foolish" its thinking becomes futile. The word for "foolish" is also one of the sins listed in v. 31, where the NIV translates it as "senseless." It means void of understanding, or as Lard says, just plain stupid (55).

Their foolish hearts were "darkened." Since God is light (1 John 1:5), any heart that excludes God is literally in the dark. The light of God is purity, glory, and truth; when God is rejected, there is only the darkness of ignorance and evil and eventually the outer darkness of hell (Matt 8:12; 22:13; Jude 13). See Eph 4:17-18.

1:22 This and the next verse continue the indictment of the Gentiles. **Although they claimed to be wise, they became fools . . . .** Wisdom is knowing how to make the right choices and decisions based on available knowledge. Basically, it is knowing how to live. Those who reject God always think they are wise, and that their rejection of God is the highest evidence of that fact. They always think they are wiser than believers. They consider believers to be naive, gullible, foolish, illogical, and full of wishful thinking. They consider themselves to be sophisticated, unbiased, very intelligent, and guided by critical thinking. It is the nature of worldly wisdom to confuse real foolishness with real wisdom, and vice versa (1 Cor 1:18–2:8).

"They became fools" translates a verb from the Greek word family from which our word "moron" is derived. Thus they became foolish and moronic; they became "silly," says Lenski (104). They "made fools of themselves" (NEB). This applies especially to their moral reasoning, which can never be separated from how one thinks of God (❂I:147).

1:23 This verse explains more specifically *how* the Gentiles became fools. They did it when they . . . **exchanged the glory of the immortal God for images made to look like mortal man and birds and animals and reptiles**. People often measure their wisdom by the kind of deals or trades they make. Paul says the Gentiles have made a swap or an exchange, but it is not a very clever one. In fact, it is the worst possible exchange anyone could possibly make.

What have the Gentiles done? They have traded the real thing for the phony and useless. They have traded the true God for impotent idols. "The glory of the immortal God" is what they know through general revelation. As true God, he has always been and he always will be who he is, and therefore we can put absolute trust and confidence in him and his promises. Nothing is more valuable and precious than this. It is like the "pearl of great price": it is worth everything else to acquire and it must never be surrendered at any cost.

Yet this is what the Gentiles have exchanged — and for what? For images of men and birds and animals and reptiles! Not even *actual* men and birds and animals and reptiles, but just *images* of them. The Greek phrase is "the likeness of an image," or a likeness patterned after the form of these things. This refers to the grossest form of idolatry, the worship of manufactured statues of mere creatures.

Four kinds of idols are mentioned. Some are patterned after the *human* form, a common characteristic of pagan religions. The Greek gods of Olympus were pictured thus, as were some of the Egyptian deities. Rulers such as the Pharaohs and the Caesars were often given divine status. The other idols Paul mentions are patterned after three kinds of animals (see Acts 10:12): *birds*, such as the Egyptian gods Horus (a falcon) and Thoth (an ibis); *animals* (specifically quadrupeds), such as the bull (which was widely worshiped) and Egyptian deities such as Anubis (a jackal), Bastet (a cat), and Khnum (a ram); and *reptiles*. This last category is general enough to include the serpent (also widely worshiped) and the crocodile (Sobek in Egypt).

The characteristic shared by all these categories is *mortality*; they are all corruptible and perishable. This is true not just of the idols or statues, but of the things themselves after which the idols are patterned. Man himself is mortal or perishable; only God has inherent immortality (1 Tim 6:16; see *GC*, 245-250). If God so willed, he could annihilate every human being, body and spirit. To reject the one true and immortal God and to worship any mortal thing is the epitome of stupidity. Isaiah 44:9-20 underscores the irony of such idolatry, in which a man cuts down a tree, burns part of it to cook his food and keep himself warm, then makes an idol out of the rest of it and falls down and worships it. (See Isa 46:6-7.) No wonder Paul says, "They became fools"; no wonder they are under God's wrath (v. 18).

1:24 Paul now speaks of *how* this wrath is being revealed from heaven against the ungodly and unrighteous Gentiles. **Therefore God gave them over in the sinful desires of their hearts . . . .** "Therefore" means that what has just been described in vv. 21-23 is *why* God has acted in wrath toward them.

Exactly what has befallen the Gentiles as the result of their rejection of God? Paul says "God gave them over" to the sinful lifestyle they were intent on pursuing (see vv. 26,28). The Greek word (παραδίδωμι, *paradidōmi*) is quite common and is used for all sorts of activities, including some works of God (e.g., Exod 23:31; Lev 26:25; Deut 7:23; Acts 7:42; Rom 4:25).

How does God "give someone over" to do evil? The basic answer is that in the working of his providence "he ceases to restrain them from evil or protect them against it." In other words, "he lets them alone to do as they please without hindrance from him in the matter of sin" (Lard, 57). In his permissive will he allows them to plunge headlong into what their evil hearts desire.

This suggests that God often providentially restrains people from going as far into sin as they would and could. But there comes a time when God withdraws his restraint, in whatever way he judges appropriate. This is probably the concept reflected in Ps 78:29 and Ps 106:14-15, and in Hos 4:17, "Ephraim is joined to idols; leave him alone!" This is God's answer to the defiant sinners who mock him and challenge him to strike them dead if he is really there. God just turns his back on them. What could be more frightening than this? See 2 Thess 2:6-7.

Most commentators agree, though, that this "giving over" is not just a shrug of indifference by God; he is not just adopting a passive attitude while ceasing to do anything at all. In Murray's words, God's giving over "cannot be reduced to the notion of non-interference with the natural consequences of sin" (I:44). It is rather a deliberate, purposeful act by God.

On the other hand, we must not go to the opposite extreme and think that somehow God is *causing* the Gentiles to fall deeper into their sin. God does not cause anyone to do evil. Thus it is, as Lenski says (108), more than permission but less than causation.

Why does God do this at all? Some say the purpose of this "giving over" is ultimately redemptive. There is no indication of this in the text, though. The giving over is presented as a purely punitive act, an act of divine retribution, a penalty that is deserved (see v. 27, "the due penalty"). It is a judicial act, but it is not the final judgment. It does not cancel the missionary imperative, but rather intensifies it.

Paul continues his thought by saying that God gave the Gentiles over "in the sinful desires of their hearts." This is not what he gave them over *to*; this is what was *already* existing in their hearts. "Finding them living in lust," God ceased to restrain them (MP, 304). See Eph 4:19.

The word translated "sinful desires" basically means "strong desire," whether for something good (Luke 22:15; Phil 1:23; 1 Thess 2:17), or for something evil. It can be used for evil desire of any kind (1 Tim 6:9), but often connotes sexual lust in particular (e.g., 1 Thess 4:5; 2 Tim 3:6; 1 Pet 4:3). Using the word in its verbal form, this is what Jesus equates with committing adultery in the heart (Matt 5:28). The context of 1:24 shows that Paul is using the word here in the sense of sexual lust.

What, then, did God give the Gentiles over *to*? Because of their idolatry, and in their lustful condition, God gave them over **to sexual impurity for the degrading of their bodies with one another**. The desires are already there; the punitive action is that God withdraws his restraints and lets them act out their fantasies in a sexually impure lifestyle. The word is ἀκαθαρσία (*akatharsia*), which means impurity or uncleanness, and which is often used with the specific connotation of sexual impurity (see 2 Cor 12:21; Gal 5:19; Col 3:5). This is probably the case here, given the references to lust, to the misuse of the body, and to homosexuality. Thus the NIV properly translates it as "sexual impurity." This is not a condemnation of sex as such, but of sex out of control, outside the restraints of God's law.

Such unbridled, unrestrained sex is a degradation of the body, says Paul (see 1 Cor 6:18). The word translated "degrading" is ἀτιμάζω (*atimazō*), meaning "to dishonor, to debase, to disgrace, to degrade." It is the opposite of τιμάω (*timaō*), which means "to honor, to give honor to." When God is not honored as Creator (vv. 21,23), there is no longer any reason to respect and honor one's body as a creation of God and as a gift from God.

We may recall here that this "handing over" to sexual impurity is a punitive act. Some may wonder how allowing someone to do what his heart desires is a penalty. But let us not forget that God hands the Gentiles over not just to their sins but also to the consequences of their sins (see vv. 24b,27b), to which degraded and abused bodies are a witness. As MacArthur (I:100) points out, these consequences range from the grossly physical, such as venereal disease, to spiritual ones such as "loneliness, frustration, meaninglessness, anxiety, and despair." Sinners usually do not think much about such consequences until it is too late.

Worshiping false gods always corrupts morality, but the opposite is also true: corrupt morality leads to idolatry. Why are people so anxious to exchange the truth of God for idols and false gods? Because they have evil lusts they want to act out and justify, with no sense of guilt and fear of punishment. But they cannot do this under the eye of the true God! What is the solution? Get a new god (❧ I:152).

1:25 They exchanged the truth of God for a lie, and worshiped and served created things rather than the Creator—who is forever praised. Amen. Before Paul continues his emphasis on the depths of sin to which God has delivered the Gentiles, he again returns to their rejection of the true God. At this point the reader might be wondering, are these people really so bad that they deserve being rejected by God as v. 24 describes? Paul stops to remind us that, yes, they really *are* this bad; they do deserve to be rejected by God because they first rejected him (❧ I:153).

"The truth of God" is variously interpreted as "the true God" (NEB), truth *from* God (Lard, 58), and truth *about* God (NRSV). All of these concepts fit the context, but Paul probably had the last one in mind specifically. The Gentiles exchanged the truth about God they knew from general revelation, the truth "that God was the creator and thus the natural object of worship" (DeWelt, 30).

This truth was exchanged for a lie. Some note that the Greek has the definite article, "*the* lie" (Morris, 90). All sin is a lie, but idolatry is the supreme lie, the basic lie that leads to all other lies. In Isa 44:20 an idol itself is called a lie. On the other hand, the existence of the true God is the supreme truth (see Heb 11:6).

In the end the Gentiles not only *suppress* the truth (v. 18), but *exchange* it for a lie. Actually one is not possible without the other. The rejection of truth leaves a vacuum which will inevitably be filled by the most convenient lie.

Paul then summarizes the practical nature of this exchange, saying the Gentiles "worshiped and served created things rather than the Creator." This repeats the idea of v. 23. The word for "worshiped" (σεβάζομαι, *sebazomai*) is used only here in the NT, but it and other words in the same word family (see *asebeia* in v. 18) all refer to the worship and adoration of God, which of course should be reserved for the true God. The word for "served" (see 1:9) refers to external religious service and worship practices.

According to God's original plan for man and the rest of creation, man was supposed to worship and serve God alone while ruling over and subduing the whole world (Gen 1:26-28). Idolatry constitutes an upheaval and reversal of this creation order. Man, the intended lord of creation, deliberately makes himself religiously subservient to some created thing and thereby becomes a slave to the material world in general.

To worship and serve any created thing rather than the Creator is again the epitome of stupidity (see Isa 44:9-20 again). The importance of acknowledging God as the transcendent Creator cannot be overemphasized. It is absolutely fundamental to everything else; it is the primary truth in the biblical worldview. To realize the distinction between the creature (including oneself) and the Creator is the basis of all piety and morality. By denying the Creator his rightful place, idolatry strikes at the very root and foundation of truth.

In the face of such impiety Paul cannot suppress words of worship for the Creator, "who is forever praised." The word "praised" is literally "blessed," in the sense that he is worthy of praise, or worthy of having good things said about him. As we sometimes sing, "Blessed be the name of the Lord." God is thus worthy to be praised *forever*, says Paul, in spite of man's attempts to deny him.

To this he adds an "amen" for emphasis. The English "amen" is a transliteration of the Greek word, which is a transliteration of the Hebrew word signifying solemn agreement or confirmation. Its basic meaning has to do with truth. As Paul uses it here, it is equivalent to "It's the truth!"

It is important that we pause here and remind ourselves that although Paul is primarily concerned with the Gentiles in this passage, everything he says applies just as validly to those who know God and his law through special revelation also.

C. The Utter Depths of Gentile Depravity (1:26-32)

In this section Paul continues to show why the Gentiles are without excuse. He catalogs the horrible depths to which sinners sink when God abandons them to their wicked lifestyles. He stresses that even as they do these things, they know in their hearts that they are doing wrong and that they deserve the final penalty of death (v. 32).

Paul is not affirming that every individual Gentile is guilty of all the sins cataloged here. He is rather showing just how far darkened hearts can and often do go when they reject the light available to them. Not all cultures and not all individuals will fall this far, but many have and many will (Gen 6:5; 18:20; Ps 2:1-3). Tragically, as we read our newspapers and newsmagazines, and as we watch the daily news broadcasts, we cannot avoid the conclusion that many segments of our own modern culture are frighteningly close to the ugly picture Paul draws for us here.

1:26 Here the cause-and-effect relation between idolatry and God's punitive response is affirmed again. **Because of this**, i.e., because of their rejection of the Creator (v. 25), **God gave them over to shameful lusts**. This sums up v. 24. "Lusts" here is equivalent to "sinful desires" there. In other Greek literature this word (πάθος, *pathos*) does not always refer to lustful sexual passion, but it does in its three NT occurrences (here; Col 3:5; 1 Thess 4:5). The use of the modifier "shameful" makes this clear here. This word, actually a noun (ἀτιμία, *atimia*) is equivalent to the verb translated "degrading" in v. 24. It means "dishonor, contempt, shame, disgrace." Thus Paul is saying God gave them over to act out their dark passions in the most shameful and dishonorable ways.

As a prime example of these "shameful lusts" Paul specifically names homosexuality. The fact that he singles this out for condemnation, and the fact that he spells it out so thoroughly, indicate that this is the most shameful of the sexual lusts that run wild when God is rejected. MacArthur calls it "the most degrading and repulsive of all passions" (I:104). (We should note that what Paul is describing here are homosexual acts and practices, not necessarily homosexual inclination or the homosexual condition in itself. A person may exist with recognized homosexual tendencies, but not be guilty of sin unless he allows this condition to lead him into homosexual lusts and practices.)

Paul includes both female and male homosexuality in these "shameful lusts." **Even their women exchanged natural relations for unnatural ones**. This is the only specific biblical reference to lesbianism. Paul says "*Even* their women" are guilty of this sin. The Greek particles linking vv. 26 and 27 (τε . . . τε, *te . . . te*) mean "not only . . . but also" or "both . . . and." This puts the females and the males on the same base level, says Lenski (113).

Contrary to the NIV, neither here nor in v. 27 does Paul use the Greek words for "women" and "men," since these words can also mean "wives" and "husbands." Instead he chooses the terms "females" and "males." This is probably because the kind of sex he is talking about has no relation to what God intended for human beings in the husband-wife relationship; indeed it is the very antithesis of it. Also, the terms "women" and "men" have a distinctively human connotation, but those who engage in homosexual acts have succumbed to raw animal passion.

The *exchanging* of natural for unnatural sex echoes the earlier references to exchanging truth about God for false deities (vv. 23,25). Except for the omission of the prefix *meta* in v. 23, the same verb is used in all three verses. This shows that homosexuality is as unnatural and as worthy of condemnation as idolatry. It also illustrates the principle stressed earlier, that substitute gods and degenerate morality go together.

The term χρῆσις (*chrēsis*), translated "relations" in the NIV, is used in the NT only here and in v. 27. Its general meaning is "use" or "function" (as the NASB has it). But in secular Greek it was often a euphemism for sexual intercourse (see the NRSV). This is no doubt how Paul uses it here, as the NIV implies in rendering it "relations." The references to sexual sin in vv. 24,26a, and the clear reference to the equivalent male homosexuality in v. 27, make this conclusive. In straightforward terms, v. 26b reads, "Their females exchanged natural sex for unnatural sex."

The term "natural" (φυσικός, *physikos*) must be understood here and in v. 27 as meaning "according to God's created order" (see Stott, 78). "Unnatural" is literally "against nature" (παρὰ φύσις, *para physis*) and means what is contrary to the natural order of things as God intended them and created them in the beginning. This is the only meaning consistent with the present context. The main subject of this whole section is the Gentiles' knowledge of God as Creator and the knowledge of his basic ordinances for his human creatures. Thus the context requires us to understand natural sex as sex according to "God's creative intent" (Moo, 115; see Cranfield, I:125-126). When one gives up the Creator (v. 25), he likewise gives up the creation ordinances, which include the husband-wife relationship as the intended context for sex. Also, we must remember that this verse says that lesbian sex is unnatural sex, and unnatural sex is the essence of the "shameful lusts" to which God has delivered the Gentiles in his punitive wrath. "When these factors are considered, it is clear that Paul depicts homosexual activity as a violation of God's created order, another indication of the departure from true knowledge and worship of God" (Moo, 115).

It is very important to emphasize these connotations for "natural" and "unnatural," because contemporary pro-homosexual interpreters attempt to give these terms entirely different meanings here. They insist that Paul uses these words to refer to what is natural and unnatural for *particular individuals*, not for human beings in general. They say that heterosexual sex is what is natural for most human beings, i.e., it is their felt inclination. For these and these alone, homosexual sex is unnatural and therefore wrong. However, for some human beings homosexual sex is their felt inclination; therefore it is natural for them and is not wrong. Paul is not talking about this "natural" homosexuality at all—or so it is claimed.

As we have emphasized, the context of 1:26-27 simply will not allow this interpretation. Also, Paul does not say the women exchanged what was natural *for them* for what was against *their own* nature. The terms "natural" and "unnatural" are not limited or qualified in any way. See the discussion and refutation of Boswell's view in Stott (77-78) and in DeYoung, "Meaning."

1:27 In the same way the men also abandoned natural relations with women and were inflamed with lust for one another. This verse is an impassioned denunciation of male homosexuality. This sin is clearly named and condemned in other places in the Bible, but in none as emphatically as here. The word ὁμοίως (*homoiōs*) at the beginning of the verse, translated "in the same way," indicates an equivalence between female and male homosexuality; before God one is as bad as the other.

Expanding on his description of homosexual males ("gays"), Paul says they "were inflamed with lust for one another." They "burned in their desire" (NASB); they "were consumed with passion" (NRSV). Both Greek words in this expression are used only here in the NT. "Lust" is a specific form of the "sinful desires" of v. 24, and is equivalent to the "shameful lusts" in v. 26. To be *inflamed* with such lust is to be dominated and driven by an uncontrolled and all-consuming desire for homosexual contact. MacArthur correctly remarks (I:105), "There is a burning level of lust among homosexuals that beggars description and is rarely known among heterosexuals." Anyone who can stand to read descriptions of sexual practices in the homosexual subculture will readily agree with this statement. This does not mean that everyone with homosexual tendencies gives way to them; but when this does occur, it is like a forest fire out of control.

Men committed indecent acts with other men . . . ; literally, "males . . . with males." The catalog of "indecent acts" engaged in by male homosexuals is shocking and disgusting; they need not be named here. The Greek word for this expression is used in the NT only here and in Rev 16:15; cognates are found in 1 Cor 7:36; 12:23; 13:5. These words are often used to refer to the indecent and shameful exposure of the genitals (Dunn 1:65).

As a result of these indecent acts, they **. . . received in themselves the due penalty for their perversion**. This is a difficult clause, but its point is that homosexuals who indulge their wild passions get what they deserve; they reap what they sow; they suffer the deserved consequences of their perversion. This is not a reference to the final judgment, but to the infliction of divine wrath that comes in the form of historical circumstances.

The word "received" is an emphatic form of a common word and often means, as here, "to receive back, to receive in return," i.e., to receive as the fitting result of their actions. Cranfield says it "emphasizes the deservedness of the punishment" (I:127). This verb's object, "the due penalty," also clearly refers to deserved punishment. Gays deservedly receive the recompense due to them as specified by the Creator's law.

How may we understand this "due penalty" or recompense? Some think the sexual perversion itself is its own penalty, or at least is the just penalty for their rejection of God (Cranfield, I:126-127; Morris, 93). It seems more likely, though, that Paul is referring to some punitive consequences distinct from the homosexual acts as such, consequences they experience "in themselves" or "in their own persons" (NASB) as a form of the very wrath of God (v. 18).

There is scarcely any sin that subjects its perpetrators to more severe "deserved penalties" than male homosexuality. Is AIDS an example of this? Assuredly so. MacArthur is correct (I:107): "The appalling physical consequences of homosexuality are visible evidence of God's righteous condemnation. Unnatural vice brings its own perverted reward. AIDS is frightening evidence of that fatal promise." This is not to say that God deliberately created the HIV virus as a specific penalty for male homosexuals. As it exists under the curse (8:18-22), the world is full of all sorts of bacteria, viruses, and ailments that are a threat to all of us under certain conditions. The fact is, though, that certain practices, especially sinful practices, openly invite these maladies to strike us down. Licentious, promiscuous sex has always reaped the deserved harvest of sexually transmitted diseases; AIDS is just the latest version of this and male homosexuals are especially vulnerable to it.

We should understand, then, that AIDS is just one — albeit a fatal one — of many serious health consequences homosexuals have always received back as a due penalty for their perversion. Long before AIDS entered the picture, homosexual practices focusing on the anus and excrement have kept gay men in a constant state of health crisis. Lenski correctly comments (116-117) that the homosexuals' "recompense is the vicious effect of the unnatural sexual vices upon men's own bodies and their minds, corrupting, destroying, disintegrating.... It is noteworthy that in the Scriptures as in human experience sexual sins, and not only the worst form of these, carry a special curse; they not only disgrace, they wreck; their punishment is direct, wretched, severe." This is why Paul treats this sin separately and does not just include it in the listing in vv. 29-31.

Paul speaks of the due penalty for their "perversion." The word refers to wandering or roaming; figuratively it refers to wandering from the path of truth and morality. "Perversion" or "deviancy" captures the meaning very well in this context (❖ I:160).

1:28 Furthermore, since they did not think it worthwhile to retain the knowledge of God, he gave them over to a depraved mind, to do what ought not to be done. "Furthermore" translates the simple word καί (*kai*), "and." This verse reiterates what has been said thus far in vv. 18-27. It repeats the cause-and-effect principle resulting in God's giving the Gentiles over to unrestrained sin. As vv. 18,21,23 and 25 have already stressed, they have dismissed the true God from their worldview. This is portrayed as a deliberate decision to the effect that the whole idea of a transcendent Creator-God is not "worthwhile," or is worthless. The word is δοκιμάζω (*dokimazō*), which means "to test, to examine, to judge, to approve, to deem worthy, to see fit." This is stated as a negative: they did not approve of the truth about God; they did not think it worthy or fit to hold on to; they weighed the idea of God in the balances and found it wanting. Remember: "They became fools" (v. 22).

God's response to such presumptuous folly is that he gave *them* over "to a depraved mind" in return. The word for "depraved" is ἀδόκιμος (*adokimos*), which means "useless, failing the test, disqualified, worthless" (see 1 Cor 9:27; 2 Cor 13:5-7). This is a play on words and a matter of extreme irony (compare *dokimazō* and *adokimos*). They judged God to be a worthless idea, so God gave them over to their own worthless speculations. The mind that judges God to be worthless is itself worthless.

The last part of the verse, "to do what ought not to be done," again shows that faulty speculations about God directly affect moral theory and behavior. As Cranfield says, "The *adokimos nous* is a mind so debilitated and corrupted as to be a quite untrustworthy guide in moral decisions" (I:128). The fact is that the reality of the transcendent Creator-God is the starting point and the *sine qua non* for all valid ethics. Without him, there is no basis either for absolute ethical obligation or for absolute ethical norms (*GC*, 163-171). Without God, the only consistent ethic is some version of "might makes right."

"Ought (not) to be done" refers to how human beings act according to their nature as human beings. *Not* to do these things regarded as proper is to contradict one's own humanity.

1:29-31 They have become filled with every kind of wickedness, evil, greed and depravity. They are full of envy, murder, strife, deceit and malice. They are gossips, slanderers, God-haters, insolent, arrogant and boastful; they invent ways of doing evil; they disobey their parents; they are senseless, faithless, heartless, ruthless. This list of sins is not meant to be complete, nor is every sinner guilty of all the vices listed. Those listed are not meticulously chosen and organized so as to form the basis for a handbook on ethics. The terms sometimes overlap. They are not meant to offer any new teaching about right and wrong, but are representative of what Dunn calls the "conventional morality" already widely recognized (I:67). In this context the list is meant to make an overall impression regarding the sinfulness and guilt of the Gentile world, as much as it is intended to give us moral instruction. Such a list — a "catalog of vices" — was not uncommon even in the secular literature of the time; and several such lists appear elsewhere in the NT, though none is as extensive as this one (❂ I:162).

What follows here are brief comments setting forth the essence of each sin:

Wickedness (ἀδικία, *adikia*). The list begins with a very general term that may be like a heading over the rest, as the modifier "every kind of" may suggest. This is the term used twice in v. 18. It is a general term for unrighteousness or transgression of God's law.

Evil (πονηρία, *ponēria*). This is another general term, often occurring in contrast with "good." It is used often of Satan and his demons. It describes the inner nature of a person who delights in acting in ways that oppose God and goodness, and who puts his evil desires into practice.

Greed (πλεονεξία, *pleonexia*). This word is more specific than the first two, but is not as specific as "covetousness," which is often how it is translated. Covetousness is usually directed toward something specific (Exod 20:17), but greed is the insatiable desire to accumulate more and more things in general, without regard for the rights and needs of others. Col 3:5 says that this sin is idolatry, because acquisition of things becomes one's god.

Depravity (κακία, *kakia*). This is another very general term, difficult to distinguish from wickedness and evil. Barclay says it is "the most general Greek word for badness. . . . It is the degeneracy out of which all sins grow and in which all sins flourish" (27-28).

Envy (φθόνος, *phthonos*). As covetousness is directed toward a specific object, so envy is directed toward a specific person. It means not just wanting what another person has, but also resenting that person for having it. It is an attitude of ill-will and jealousy that leads to division and strife and even murder. (See the next few sins.)

Murder (φόνος, *phonos*), killing, the unlawful taking of someone's life. We should remember the NT teaching that hate and groundless anger are also forms of murder (Matt 5:21-22; 1 John 3:15).

Strife (ἔρις, *eris*), contention, rivalry, wrangling. This refers to someone who has a quarrelsome disposition, someone who is always looking for an argument or a fight.

Deceit (δόλος, *dolos*), guile, treachery, cunning, hypocrisy. Its absence in Nathaniel was so remarkable that Jesus commented on it (John 1:47), which indicates how difficult it must be to avoid this sin.

Malice (κακοηθεία, *kakoētheia*). This is another general term, translated variously as malignity, malevolence, spite, meanness, evil-naturedness (● I:164).

Gossips (ψιθυριστής, *psithyristēs*), literally, "whisperers," or those who whisper gossip into someone's ear behind another's back. They are talebearers, rumormongers, "whisperers-behind-doors" (Phillips) who spread their slanders secretly.

Slanderers (κατάλαλος, *katalalos*), literally, those who speak against others. Phillips translates it "stabbers-in-the-back." This is the same idea as the previous word, except the gossip or slander is open and public, not secret.

God-haters (θεοστυγής, *theostygēs*). This word usually means "hateful to God" and thus does not seem to fit in a list of sins (● I:164). Most interpreters just assume that Paul gives the word a new twist here, hence, "God-haters." This certainly fits the context as a whole.

Insolent (ὑβριστής, *hybristēs*). The person guilty of this sin is one who has a very high and arrogant opinion of himself, coupled with a very low and contemptuous opinion of others. It is "a lofty sense of superiority out of which the insolent person treats all others as beneath him" (Morris, 97-98). It is the attitude of a bully that leads him to use and abuse others, and run roughshod over the weak.

Arrogant (ὑπερήφανος, *hyperēphanos*), proud, haughty. This is the opposite of humble. It refers to a person who in his own mind sees himself as being far above others and as having no need of God. This is similar to the previous vice, but without the mean spirit toward others.

Boastful (ἀλαζών, *alazōn*). This refers to a person who brags about himself, often going beyond the truth in an effort to impress others.

They invent ways of doing evil, literally, "inventors of evil." Barclay says, "This phrase describes the man who . . . is not content with the usual, ordinary ways of sinning, but . . . seeks some new thrill in some new sin" (31).

They disobey their parents. In view of biblical teaching, (e.g., Exod 20:12; Eph 6:2) we should not be surprised to see Paul include this in a list of vices. It shows how important family integrity and submission to authority are in God's plan for mankind (❧ I:165).

Senseless (ἀσύνετος, *asynetos*), foolish (see v. 21). This refers not to one who *lacks* intelligence, but to one who refuses to use his God-given mind in a common-sense, God-honoring way. "It refers to those who act stupidly" in reference to God and morality (Morris, 98).

Faithless (ἀσύνθετος, *asynthetos*), unreliable, disloyal, dishonest, untrustworthy, treacherous. This is a person who will not keep his word or meet his obligations, a covenant breaker.

Heartless (ἄστοργος, *astorgos*). This is an unfortunate translation, a much too general term for a specific vice. A person who is *astorgos* is one who lacks "natural family affection, love for family members," especially the love that ties parents and children together. When it is absent the results are such things as abortion, infanticide, child abuse, fratricide, and matricide.

Ruthless (ἀνελεήμων, *aneleēmōn*), merciless, pitiless, callous, unfeeling toward others. This is a person who simply does not care when others are in need or are suffering. Morris perceptively remarks, "It is significant that, in an epistle that will stress God's mercy throughout, the list of vices should be rounded off with 'merciless'. This is the very depth of evil" (99).

1:32 This brings us back to the main point of this section, and it carries the description of Gentile depravity to its final depths. First, Paul specifically affirms the fact that the Gentiles have enough knowledge of God's law to be judged and condemned by: **Although they know God's righteous decree that those who do such things deserve death . . . .** The subject of this clause is the relative pronoun οἵτινες (*hoitines*), "the ones who," i.e., "These sinners I have just been naming are the very ones who know these things are contrary to God's law."

The knowledge Paul attributes to the Gentiles here is twofold. First, they know that such things as he has just mentioned are wrong. Second, they know that those who do such things "deserve death." In other words, they know not only the *commandments* of the moral law, but also its *penalty*. They are indeed without excuse.

The "righteous decree" of God refers specifically to the part about the penalty. God has ordained that those who commit these sins deserve to die. The word is δικαίωμα (*dikaiōma*, from the *dik-* word family, denoting righteousness), which means a decree or ordinance that is righteous and just. It is a righteous decree because those who sin are worthy of death; they deserve it. Also, the Gentiles' knowledge of this decree is not just abstract; they know it as *God's* righteous ordinance (❧ I:166).

This knowledge includes an inherent awareness that physical death as such is a righteous divine penalty for such sins, a fact affirmed in the Bible (5:12; 8:10). It also includes a similar awareness that there will be a final judgment before the Creator and Law-giver, where all will have to answer for these sins and be justly condemned to *eternal* death for committing them. The concept of such a final judgment and divine retribution is widespread in pagan religions. See Cranfield, I:134.

The question is, whence comes all this knowledge in the Gentile mind? The Gentiles (by definition) have had no access to some specially revealed form of God's moral law, such as the Law of Moses. Nor can we suppose that Paul is talking about an "unperished tradition" kept intact in every heart in every generation since Adam and Noah (contra Lard, 67). The only revelation Paul is assuming in this section is the general revelation that is available to the consciousness from the phenomena of creation. Can such revelation yield the kind of knowledge of which v. 32 speaks?

No, not by itself. But there is another aspect of general revelation not mentioned in this section but brought out later in 2:14-15. In these verses Paul speaks of the work of the law written in the heart, and of the conscience. From these two internal sources (inherent in every person by virtue of our being created in God's image), combined with the knowledge of the Creator derived from external general revelation, comes the knowledge to which 1:32 refers. The very *sense* of right and wrong, and the conviction that wrong deserves a penalty, "is ineradicably embedded in the human conscience" (Lenski, 124). The *content* of the moral law, i.e., the knowledge that specific acts are wrong, also comes from within. The knowledge that these things are wrong *before God* and will be judged by him comes from the knowledge of the Creator known from his visible creation.

Thus Paul makes his case that the Gentiles are without excuse, and are no exception to the general rule that no one will be accepted by God according to the terms of law. Verse 32 just adds the capstone to his argument.

Paul ends this verse and this section about the Gentiles by adding one more comment on the depth of their depravity: **they not only continue to do these very things but also approve of those who practice them**. Here Paul indicates that there is something worse than committing the sins named here. Some have said that Paul means this: that *approving of* and *applauding* such sins is at least as bad as, if not worse than, actually *doing* them. This is because the latter may be the result of circumstantial pressures and spur-of-the-moment passions, while the former comes from a deep-seated and dispassionate commitment to evil. (See Cranfield, I:133-135; Moo, 122.) The other approach, reflected in most translations and favored here, is that what is worse than just committing these sins is *both* committing them *and* encouraging others to commit them as well.

Either way Paul makes it clear that applauding and encouraging indulgence in sin is a serious aspect of the depravity of the Gentile world. The word means "to be pleased along with, to consent with, to give approval to, to applaud." Paul uses this very word to describe his participation in Stephen's death, though he did not throw any stones (Acts 22:20; see Acts 8:1) (❂I:168).

CONCLUSION

Though 1:18-32 applies particularly to the Gentiles (or those who have general revelation only), the fact is that every point made in this passage applies even more emphatically to those who have special revelation also. As far as the rejection of God and abandonment to wickedness are concerned, those in the latter group can reject both the general and the special revelation, and can be given over to depravity the same as the Gentiles. This has happened to many individuals in this group, but not to the group as a whole as in the case of the Gentiles.

Insofar as 1:18-32 is a description of the Gentile world as such, it is not just a description of the Greco-Roman world as Paul observed it in his time. It is a Holy Spirit-inspired description of the condition of the pagan world from the Fall up until now. It has just as much application today as it had in Paul's day, and the bottom line is still the same: they are without excuse.

The implications of this are extremely relevant for missions. Still today, many people try to find some way to excuse the many pagan idolaters (the "heathen," the unevangelized) remaining in the world. One view is that they do not know God so they cannot be held responsible. Paul specifically refutes this view. A second approach is that pagans *do* know God, and at least some have honored and served him well enough to be saved. Paul specifically refutes this false idea also. A third view grants that all pagans are condemned by the law of general revelation, but says that God will save them anyway if (and because) they have never had the opportunity to hear about Jesus and the way of grace.

This last view in effect misses the whole point of this passage. Whether individuals have or have not heard the gospel is not the issue. Whether they will be saved or lost depends not on what they have *not* heard, but on what they *have* heard. They will be judged according to the light they have, not the light they do not have. Paul's whole point is that they do have the light of God's moral law through general revelation; therefore they are without excuse if they do not keep it. The fact is, they *have not* kept it but have rejected God and have become thoroughly sinful. Thus they are under God's wrath (v. 18), not his grace.

The missionary imperative could not be made more plain than it is in Romans 1:18-32. We deceive ourselves if we hold out false hope for the unevangelized based on their nonhearing of the gospel (❉I:170).

II. 2:1–3:8 — THE SINFULNESS OF THE JEWS

Introduction

The overall subject of the first main section of Romans is the impotence of law as a way of salvation. No one can be right with God in terms of the system of law; there is no hope for salvation as long as one remains in a law-relationship with God. This is not inherently the case; a person *can* be right with God through law, as long as he does not break the law at any point. The problem, though, is that *all have sinned*; thus by works of law *no one* will in fact be justified before God (3:20). As a consequence the only possible way for anyone to be saved is through the alternative God has provided: the way of grace, the gift of righteousness made possible through the death of his Son.

Thus the main theme of this section is *law* — not just the Law of Moses, but the Creator's will and commandments in whatever form they have been made available to his creatures. In this subsection of Romans (2:1–3:8), the term "law" does primarily refer to the Law of Moses, but not exclusively so.

In 1:18-32 Paul shows that the Gentiles are not an exception to the fact that all stand condemned by God's law. The point of 2:1–3:8 is to show that the same is true for the Jews. This is in contrast with the Jews' own conviction (at that time) that they surely cannot stand condemned by the law, because as a nation they have their own very special relationship with God that will shield them from the divine wrath in the day of judgment. In this subsection, then, Paul has the objective of showing that this is a false idea, thus "deflating Jewish presumption" (Dunn, I:77). With reference to wrath and condemnation, salvation and eternal life, the Jews are *not* special; within the context of law God treats everyone alike.

1. Who Is Being Addressed in 2:1-16?

Some believe that Paul is addressing here all people of good moral character, including most Jews and also the more pious Gentiles of the Roman world (❉I:171-172). However, I agree with those who see all of chapter 2 as specifically dealing with the Jews from the very beginning. This is because the attitudes condemned in 2:1-16 (hypocritical judgmentalism toward the Gentiles; belief in divine partiality) were "peculiarly characteristic of the Jew," as Murray puts it. Also, the Jews were uniquely the objects of God's "kindness, tolerance and patience" (v. 4). Most significantly, throughout this section Paul refers consistently to only two categories of people (not three) as constituting the whole of mankind: Jews and Greeks (i.e., Gentiles). It is true that Jews are not addressed by name until v. 17, but this is a matter of tactics on Paul's part. By not explicitly naming the Jews as his target in the first several verses, he can possibly avoid putting them on the defensive and perhaps secure their agreement before they realize he is talking about them.

In the section on the Gentiles (1:18-32), we saw that the most significant distinction between Gentiles and Jews in this context is that the former are those who have been exposed to general revelation only, while the latter have knowledge of special revelation also. With regard to applicability to the present time, the Gentiles are equivalent to anyone today who has no knowledge of biblical revelation, and the Jews are equivalent to anyone who does have such knowledge.

It is important to keep this in mind as we go through this subsection, so that we will not miss its timeliness and relevance for the church in the Christian era. What is said in this passage applies to all who have access to special revelation, whether it be the OT or the NT or both. It applies to anyone who expects divine partiality or any kind of special privilege because of his external relationship to this revelation. This is true especially of those within the general context of Christendom who consider their knowledge of the Bible, their knowledge about Jesus Christ, their membership in a local church, their baptism, or their Christian heritage in general to be their sure ticket to heaven.

Exactly what is Paul's main point here regarding the Jews? It is well known, of course, that God had chosen the Jews from among all the peoples of the earth and had placed them in a special covenant relationship with himself ever since the time of Abraham. This special relationship is a major theme of the entire OT; it is not a matter of dispute. The problem is that the Jews had drawn some false and fatal conclusions from these facts. They developed the idea that somehow they, the Jews, would be in a special category and would receive special treatment on Judgment Day. From their covenant privileges they concluded that they would not be judged by the same criteria as the Gentiles. Dunn calls this "Jewish overconfidence in God's favor for and obligation to Israel," and an "assurance of a favored status based on and protected by God's election" (I:90).

Rabbinic writings reflect this attitude. These include quotes such as the following: "Circumcised men do not descend into Gehenna." "At the last Abraham will sit at the entrance to Gehenna and will not let any circumcised man of Israel go down there." "Circumcision will deliver Israel from Gehenna" (cited in Cranfield, I:172, n. 1). "All Israelites have a share in the world to come" (cited in Sanders, *Paul*, 147).

Paul's main point regarding the Jews, then, is to show that they will *not* be treated in any special way in the final judgment. They will have no special privileges, no advantages, just from the fact that they are Jews. God will show them no partiality.

The reason this is so is that *the Jews are sinners, too*, no less than the Gentiles; and under God's law all sinners are treated alike. That is, under the law system every Gentile who has sinned and every Jew who has sinned will be condemned to hell. And since all Jews are sinners, the law condemns them all. The bottom line, then, is that Jews no less than Gentiles stand in need of the gospel of grace; they need the righteousness that comes through faith in Jesus Christ. They are not an exception.

2. Does Romans 2 Teach Justification by Works?

A second general question with which we must deal before turning to the text has to do with the very nature of salvation. The issue in brief is whether or not Romans 2 teaches that a sinner can be justified by his own works. Unfortunately many interpreters have wrongly drawn this conclusion from certain statements in the text, and this conclusion has the effect of derailing the proper understanding of Romans and of the concept of grace from the very beginning. Thus it is extremely important to grasp the overall perspective from which Paul is speaking in this chapter. (The commentaries I especially recommend on this point are Lard and Moo.)

The problem arises when we attempt to interpret vv. 6-10,13, and 26. Verse 6 says God will repay every man according to his works. Verses 7 and 10 say God will give eternal life to those who persist in doing good. Verse 13 says that the doers of the law will be justified. Verse 26 suggests that Gentiles who keep the law will be saved.

The reason this is such a problem is that this seems to teach justification by works, in contradiction with the whole point of Romans and the whole concept of grace, namely, that we are justified by faith apart from works of law (3:28). In fact, it apparently contradicts the very point Paul wants to make in this first main section itself, namely, that by works of law no human being will be justified in God's sight (3:20). Someone with a low view of Scripture might feel comfortable affirming that Paul simply contradicts himself, but even apart from inspiration it is inconceivable that a man of Paul's obvious intelligence would have failed to recognize an outright inconsistency within a single section of an essay that is so tightly reasoned. Thus there must be another explanation (❥I:175-176).

I believe the best solution to the problem is as follows. In the texts in question (vv. 6-10,13,26) Paul is not talking about the judgment of Christians under grace, but about the conditions that prevail within the sphere or system of *law*, or about how a person is judged for either justification or condemnation under the provisions of God's law. As already explained, the subject of this whole section is law, and especially its inability to save sinners.

As we also saw earlier, the principles of law are this: "Keep the commandments, and therefore escape the penalty; break the commandments, and therefore suffer the penalty." Within the context of law, anyone who does not keep its commandments will be condemned. Likewise, anyone who perseveres in good works, who is a doer of the law, who keeps its commandments, *will be justified*. This is a statement of fact. Any Jew or Gentile who completely obeys the law available to him will be justified.

But as a matter of fact — and this is Paul's whole point in this section — there is no one at all in this category; everyone has sinned. As a formal principle it is true that the doers of the law will be justified. But in view of the universality of sin, it is only theoretically or hypothetically true. Not one single Jew and not one single Gentile will in fact be accepted by God in the final judgment because of his good works or his obedience to law. Thus vv. 7,10,13,26 should not be taken as referring to any actual state of affairs.

The actual state of things is given in 3:20, that by works of law no one will be justified, since the law judges everyone to be a sinner (❧ I:177-178).

It is important to remember that, *under law*, there is no way to be saved other than perfect obedience. This is contrary to the Jews' false confidence in their special status within God's great historical plan of salvation. They confused their election for *service* with election for *salvation*. They did not understand that their personal sins negated the value of law as a way of salvation. They could claim salvation by law only if they obeyed it perfectly, which they did not: "Jews and Gentiles alike are all under sin" (3:9).

A corollary of this is that once actual sin enters the picture, whether in the life of an individual or in the history of mankind, the only way to be accepted by God is through his plan of grace, i.e., through trusting God's promise to forgive our sins based upon his righteousness and not our own. Anyone who is ever saved — Jew or Gentile, in OT times or NT times, under the Law of Moses or in the Christian Church — will be saved in this manner, because the only alternatives are nonexistent perfect obedience (law) and the gospel reality of righteousness through faith (grace). See Moo, 156.

3. The Outline of This Section

In this subsection Paul's thought flows as follows.

2:1-5. First, the Jews are under the wrath of God, no less than the Gentiles. Thus they have no basis for passing judgment on the Gentiles and gloating over their fate.

2:6-11. Second, God will be partial to no one in the judgment. He will treat all alike, whether Jews or Gentiles. The principles of judgment as required by law will be applied to both in exactly the same way.

Romans Part One

2:12-16. Third, under law, the criterion of judgment is obedience alone, not whether or how one possesses the law or knows the law. It is especially important for the Jews to know that mere possession of the law is no indication of special treatment in the judgment.

2:17-24. Fourth, Jews who look to the law for salvation are in fact condemned by their disobedience to that law. They have broken the very law they glory in and rely upon.

2:25-29. Fifth, true Jewishness is identified not by circumcision but by the inward state of the heart. Thus the Jews' reliance upon physical circumcision as the sure measure of salvation is futile.

3:1-8. Finally, such equal treatment of Jews and Gentiles does not nullify but rather magnifies God's righteousness. Those who rail at God because of this equal treatment before the law have misunderstood God's purpose for Israel and deserve to be condemned for their blasphemy.

4. The Style of Writing

A final word here has to do with Paul's writing style in certain parts of this subsection, a style known as *diatribe*. This was a common method of teaching used by writers and instructors in Paul's time. To write in this style the author engages in a dialogue with an imaginary opponent or questioner, and the writing is addressed directly to this questioner (second person instead of third person) (❂I:179).

A. Jews Are under the Wrath of God, No Less Than the Gentiles (2:1-5)

2:1 You, therefore, have no excuse, you who pass judgment on someone else . . . . Using the second person ("you") of the diatribe style, Paul specifically addresses the Jews in the person of an anonymous representative, "O man" (not translated in the NIV). One can imagine this typical Jew, standing slightly behind and to one side of Paul, looking over the Apostle's shoulder as the latter continues to heap the blazing coals of God's wrath upon the heads of the Gentiles in 1:18-32. Under his breath he excitedly roots Paul on against these Gentile scum: "Go get 'em, Paul! Lay it on 'em! That's right! Amen!"

Then abruptly Paul stops speaking of the Gentiles, slowly turns toward his fellow Israelite, gets right up in his face, and says, in effect, "You like that, don't you? 'Get those Gentiles,' right? They really are wicked, aren't they? They deserve the wrath of God, don't they? Well, my brother, have I got news for you! You are no better than the Gentiles! When you point your finger at them, you have three fingers pointing back at yourself. As Nathan said to David, 'You are the man!'" (2 Sam 12:7) (❂I:180).

The word translated "no excuse" is the same one applied to the Gentiles in

1:20. As there, it means "without excuse, without defense" in the face of accusation. Since both Jews and Greeks are without excuse before the law, every mouth is thus silenced, and the whole world stands guilty before God (3:19).

In the words "you who pass judgment," the NIV smooths out an awkward Greek phrase that reads more literally, "O man — you *judging* man — every single one of you." The word for "pass judgment" (κρίνω, *krinō*) can refer to the act of judging as such, but it often has the stronger negative meaning of "condemn." The context shows the latter is intended here; it is no different in meaning from the intensified word (κατακρίνω, *katakrinō*) translated "condemning" that follows: **for at whatever point you judge the other, you are condemning yourself . . . .** "The other" refers to the Gentiles.

How can it be said that the "judging man" condemns himself? **. . . because you who pass judgment do the same things**. This assumes the principle, "Like sins deserve like condemnation" (Lard, 72), something the Jews seem to have forgotten. To say the Jews do "the same things" as the Gentiles does not mean that all Jews committed all the sins named in 1:18-32. By Paul's day idolatry was quite uncommon among the Jews, and homosexuality was always an abomination. Some think Paul is referring mostly to the fairly general and hard-to-avoid sins named in 1:29-31. In any case, the Jews are clearly guilty of the very sorts of things for which they condemned the Gentiles; thus they condemn themselves.

The problem is not just that the Jews were passing judgment as such, but they were doing so *hypocritically*. Even if there is some sense in which condemning someone else is legitimate (e.g., such as condemning his "fruit" [Matt 7:16], or deeds, in the light of the Word of God), it is never right to do so when we are guilty of the very same sins. See Matt 7:1-5.

2:2 Now we know that God's judgment against those who do such things is based on truth. Here Paul sets forth a general principle acceptable to both himself and the judging Jew: "we know," you and I, about the judging business, that the only judge whose judgment really counts is *God*, because his judgment is based on truth.

The word for "judgment" is κρίμα (*krima*), which connotes a negative judgment, a sentence of condemnation. God is a judge who will not hesitate to condemn those who practice "such things," i.e., the kind of sins named in chapter 1.

The point is that it does not matter who is committing these sins. God is an equal opportunity judge. His judgment is not based on race, sex, education, marriage status, or any other such incidental. It is "based on truth" or objective facts, not on subjective feelings, personal preferences, or favoritism.

Judgment involves three things: deeds to be judged, a standard by which to judge them, and a judge. Judgment *based on truth* involves a full, complete, objective knowledge of the relevant deeds; an objective, achievable standard known by or knowable to all; and a completely informed, totally fair judge. The final judgment includes all of these. (1) The judge will be God, specifically God the Son, Jesus Christ (2:16). He can and will judge according to truth because he knows all things, including the very thoughts of our hearts (2:16), and because he is righteous and thus meticulously fair (2:5). (2) The standard by which he will judge is his own law, which is known to all through either general or special revelation (2:12-15). (3) The deeds to be judged are our own, as exhaustively observed and infallibly remembered by the omniscient God, who will compare them objectively with the righteous standard and then reward us accordingly (2:6).

This point was intended especially to awaken the Jews to the reality of their situation. They literally expected God on Judgment Day to suspend this "judgment based on truth" and to usher them into heaven simply because they were Jews. So Paul wanted them to know that "in judgment it is not nationality or privilege that matters, but deeds" (Morris, 111).

Ideally it should be a comfort to anyone to know that on the Judgment Day we are going to receive a "fair trial." The ultimate stated goal of human judicial systems is a fair, objective trial based on the facts. The only problem with this, though, is that those who are *guilty* do not really want a verdict "based on truth." They know they are without excuse, thus they always seek to invoke some sort of special status or special circumstances that will allow them to escape their just judgment.

In God's judicial system, though, *as long as we are going by the rules of law*, there is no special status; there are no exceptions. Every deed is compared with the objective law by the righteous judge. Those who have broken the law at any point are condemned, be they Gentiles or Jews, those under general revelation only or those under special revelation also, church members or nonmembers.

The whole point of the gospel, of course, is that God himself has provided another, totally different system of judgment, one that is based not on the truth of the *law* but rather on the truth of *grace*. God has provided his own "exception" to judgment and condemnation according to law. One receives this exception-status not through Gentileness or Jewishness as such, but only through repentant faith in God's promise of forgiveness.

2:3 In v. 1 Paul affirmed that the judging Jew condemns himself; now in v. 3 he can repeat this point with emphasis, based on the principle enunciated in v. 2. The NIV changes the word order a bit. The verse actually begins as the NASB puts it, "And do you suppose this, O man." But the NIV begins it thus: **So when you, a mere man, pass judgment on them and yet do the same things . . . .** (❂ I:183).

"Pass judgment" is again *krinō*, as in v. 1, and means "condemn." The verse literally says, "When you condemn the ones who practice such things and (then) do the same things (yourself)." The repetition of these thoughts, already set forth in v. 1, is meant to help the Jews honestly see the naked truth about themselves: you *are* condemning the Gentiles, and you *are* doing the same things for which you condemn them.

The punch line is this: you who are doing these things, **do you think you will escape God's judgment?** "Do you think" is λογίζομαι (*logizomai*). It means "to suppose, to reckon, to consider, to conclude, to draw a conclusion based on a careful consideration of the facts." Actually, the Jews had drawn a conclusion that was *not* based on truth or facts, for this is exactly what they thought: that because of their special status as God's people, they were going to escape God's wrath and condemnation (*krima*).

Thus by asking this question Paul challenges them to *rethink* their status before God. He challenges them to rethink this presumptuous conclusion that they will escape God's judgment, that God will be partial to them just because they are Jews. The wording is emphatic: "Do you think that *you* — you of all people, you who commit these same damning sins — will escape God's wrath?" Yes, they did think it; but no, it would not happen.

2:4. One might think that the Jews through their presumptuousness were showing contempt only for God's wrath and judgment. But Paul says it is much worse than this: **Or do you show contempt for the riches of his kindness, tolerance and patience . . . ?** They not only refused to take God's sternness and severity seriously; they also took for granted his kindness (11:22).

Exactly what were the Jews taking for granted? The "kindness" or goodness of God, represented here by two related words, χρηστότης (*chrēstotēs*) (11:22) and χρηστός (*chrēstos*). This kindness of God is expressed especially in his "tolerance" (ἀνοχή, *anochē*) and "patience" (μακροθυμία, *makrothymia*), concepts not significantly different in this context. The essence of God's patience is delay and restraint in the execution of his wrath, the holding back of his righteous judgment. OT history is full of examples of divine kindness and patience toward Israel as a nation. Thus they were thinking lightly not just of one or two isolated cases, but of the "riches," the wealth of God's kindness.

Israel seems thus to have missed the point of God's efforts: **not realizing that God's kindness leads you toward repentance[.]** The purpose of such patience, of course, "is not to excuse sin but to stimulate repentance" (Moo, 133). See 2 Pet 3:9. The Jews, however, continued to misinterpret it as God's indifference toward their sin. What was in fact intended to lead them to repentance was taken as proof that they would not be punished for their sin.

"Repentance" (μετάνοια, *metanoia*) is a change of mind toward God and especially toward one's own sin. It is the sinner's admission of the awfulness of his rebellion against God and of the heinousness of his sin. Repentance comes when one opens his eyes to the seriousness of sin in general, and begins to despise his own sin in particular (❶I:185).

2:5 This verse is directly related to v. 4; the paragraph break should come after v. 5 and not before it as in the NIV. The only issue is whether v. 5 is a continuation of the question in v. 4 (so Phillips; see Lard, 76), or whether it is a statement following up on v. 4 (as in the NIV and elsewhere). Either way the point is the same: "Your sinful heart is hardened, and you will experience God's wrath." **But because of your stubbornness and your unrepentant heart, you are storing up wrath against yourself . . . .**

The Jews' sinfulness is described as "stubbornness," an attitude within Israel that had tried God's patience from the beginning (Exod 33:3,5; 34:9; Deut 9:13,27; Ezek 3:7). Such a condition may not be as openly odious as some of the sins attributed to the Gentiles in chapter 1, but in God's sight it is no less abominable (❖ I:186).

As a direct result of ("because of") this sinfulness of heart, the Jews are described as "storing up wrath against yourself." The word for "storing up" means "to treasure, to heap up, to lay up treasure." Since we usually associate treasure and laying up treasure with something very valuable and desirable (see Matt 6:19-20), it is a note of tragic irony that some choose to lay up the "treasure" of God's wrath. Perhaps by using this word Paul intends to highlight the foolishness of repudiating the *riches* of God's kindness (v. 4) and opting instead for the *treasure* of his wrath.

Paul says this "treasure" is being stored up **for the day of God's wrath, when his righteous judgment will be revealed.** "The day of God's wrath" is the general eschatological day of judgment, not the intermediate judgment of A.D. 70, when Jerusalem and the temple were destroyed. This is seen in the fact that in this context the "day of wrath" involves the Gentiles as well as the Jews (vv. 8-9,12,16). Revelation 6:17 describes it as "the great day of their wrath."

This "day of wrath" is also called a "day of revelation" (ἀποκάλυψις, *apokalypsis*). This word is often associated with the end times and Christ's second coming (8:19; 1 Cor 1:7; 2 Thess 1:7; 1 Pet 1:7,13; 4:13). Many things will be revealed or totally uncovered on that day, but here Paul specifies that the thing to be revealed is God's "righteous judgment." This is a judgment that will be entirely fair and just, one that is "based on truth" (v. 2).

B. God Will Be Partial to No One in the Judgment (2:6-11)

The transition from v. 5 to v. 6, from the first paragraph to the second paragraph of this section, seems to be this. In the first paragraph Paul declares that the Jews are under the wrath of God no less than the Gentiles. Now he is assuming that the Jews will respond to that point something like this: "Now wait a minute! How can we be under the same judgment as the Gentiles? You say we have sinned like the Gentiles. But even if that is so, remember: we are *Jews*. We are in a special category. God will not treat us as he treats others in the final judgment." In this paragraph Paul responds thus: "Yes, you *will* be treated just like all others. No, you will *not* be given a special dispensation on Judgment Day, and here's why!"

In this paragraph Paul directly addresses the root of Jewish arrogance, i.e., their assumption that they would be shown partiality on the last day. As mentioned in the introduction to this section, they confused their election to *service* with election to *salvation*. With regard to the former, God did show partiality toward Israel as a nation when he chose them, through Abraham, Isaac, and Jacob, to prepare the way for the coming of the Messiah. As means to this end God did bestow upon Israel as a nation many special blessings, including access to his special revelation (3:2), which included the knowledge of his grace.

Beginning with these facts the Jews then made an unwarranted step to a false conclusion, namely, that God would be partial to each individual Jew with regard to personal salvation. Paul attacks this false reasoning. Israel's election for service, with its attendant temporal blessings (3:2; 9:4-5), will have no direct effect on how God will treat individual Jews on the Judgment Day. On that day they will be treated in the same way as the Gentiles, with no exceptions, no concessions, no partiality. The same principles of judgment will be applied equally to all. The very nature of God demands it. God is righteous and fair, and it is contrary to his nature to show partiality. Thus God will be partial to no one in the judgment.

It is especially important to remember that in this section the main point is how individuals will be judged *under law*, not under grace. Thus — *this is very important* — we must not read this paragraph as including those who have put their trust in God's mercy or in the blood of Christ. What Paul says here applies only to those who are trusting the law (i.e., their obedience to law) to save them. His point is that in the final judgment, all those who are living within the sphere of law will be treated in the same way. For the purpose of deciding between salvation and condemnation, the rules of law will be applied in the very same way to both Gentiles and Jews.

2:6 God "will give to each person according to what he has done." This is a principle of judgment that God has always followed in handing out earthly blessings and punishments, and it will also be applied in the final judgment. It even applies in a qualified way to believers who are saved solely by grace through faith in the atoning work of Christ. For them, judgment according to works will provide evidence of the presence of their faith and thus will demonstrate God's impartiality even within the sphere of grace. Also, judgment according to works will determine the degree of rewards given to individual believers.

But under the system of law this principle applies in an unqualified way. Regarding the verdict for salvation or condemnation, this is the only thing to be considered. The righteous judge will compare each person's works with the law-standard available to him. Any deviation from the standard will result in condemnation. There is nothing else to be taken into account. There will be no balance-scale judgment to see if one's good works outweigh his sins (Jas 2:10). There will be no appeal to alleviating circumstances, nor casting of oneself upon the "mercy of the court." There will be no speculation about what a person would or might have done if only he could have heard the gospel. There will be no appeal to the blood of Christ; that is available only under the system of grace. Here the only consideration is *law*.

For some questionable reason the NIV has decided not to translate the word ἔργον (*ergon*; pl., *erga*) as "work" or "works" here or anywhere else in Romans 1-3 (see 2:7,15; 3:20,27-28). "According to what he has done" should read "according to his works." "Works" are whatever a person does in response to God's law, whether in obedience or in disobedience. Acts of righteousness are works; acts of unrighteousness (sins) are works. "Works" also includes outward deeds as well as inward attitudes, desires, and decisions (which only God can see, 2:16).

As Paul uses the terms, one thing that "works" does not include is *faith* (3:27-28; 4:5; 11:6; Gal 2:16; Eph 2:8-9). Thus it is a mistake to try to interpret "works" in 2:6 as including Christian faith and the works that grow out of faith, and thus to think that in vv. 7 and 10 Paul is referring to Christians. In this section Paul is not talking about Christians, or even about OT believers. This is contrary to the view of many, including Cranfield (I:151-152). Paul's point in 2:6 is that on Judgment Day, when God renders his verdict upon an individual according to the rules of law, the only thing he will take into account is that person's works.

The word "give" is too weak as a translation for the verb in this verse, which is ἀποδίδωμι, (*apodidōmi*). "Render" is also ambiguous. The word means "to pay; to repay; to give someone his due; to give someone what he deserves, whether a reward or a punishment."

When this principle is applied according to the terms of law, theoretically there are two outcomes: for those who have not broken the law, eternal life; for those who have broken it, eternal punishment. As we saw in the introduction to this section, there is in reality no one in the first category, which is Paul's main point (3:20). Everyone in fact falls into the second category, that of lawbreakers. Now, some object to such a "theoretical" or "hypothetical" understanding of this verse and of other verses in Romans 2, on the basis that Paul does not use hypothetical or conditional language in 2:6. He uses the simple, straightforward future indicative: God *will repay* each one according to his works.

This objection misses the point. The *principle* is not hypothetical. This *is* how God will actually render judgment, namely, according to works. Paul is not saying, "*If* God judges according to works," but that he *will* so judge. The only thing that is hypothetical is the outcome, i.e., whether anyone will be in the specific categories. This does not affect the certainty and the actuality of the judgment according to the principle, as stated in the plain, simple future indicative.

The future tense does refer to the final judgment, not to any temporal or intermediate ones. The emphasis on "each person" pointedly includes both

Gentiles and Jews. Wherever law is the applicable system of judgment, it will be applied to all who are under law, with no special deals for anyone.

2:7 The next four verses are a concise statement of the law system, or the principles by which God judges those who are under law rather than under grace. I have summarized these principles thus: "Keep the commandments, and therefore escape the penalty; break the commandments, and therefore suffer the penalty." Here they are stated in slightly more detail.

The purpose in these verses is to explain exactly *how* God will repay each person according to his works (v. 6), as dictated by the rules of law. **To those who by persistence in doing good seek glory, honor and immortality, he will give eternal life.** This is equivalent to "Keep the commandments, and therefore escape the penalty" in my summary above. "Persistence in doing good" is literally "persistence in good work." "Work" is singular; the expression means "good conduct, good behavior, commandment keeping." This refers not just to an "honest effort" to do good, but to actual sinless perfection (contra DeWelt, 36). This includes right inner attitudes as well as right external acts. It is the equivalent of "doing good" in v. 10.

Under law, such good work is the means of seeking "glory, honor and immortality." These are the rewards of heaven. "Glory" refers to living in the light and reflection of God's own glory, as the result of dwelling in the very personal presence of God (Rev 21:3; 22:4-5). "Honor" refers to God's own blessing and commendation for faithfulness, similar to Jesus' words, "Well done, good and faithful servant!" (Matt 25:21). "Immortality" is the state of incorruption, in which our bodies and spirits will never again be ravaged and destroyed by sin, disease, and death (21:4). (For creatures this immortality is acquired as a gift of God, and is not inherent as it is with God; see 1:23.)

To the one who seeks these things through his blameless conduct, God "will give eternal life." Actually there is no word in v. 7 for "will give"; this verb is rightly carried over from v. 6. As we have seen, this word refers not to the giving of a free and unearned gift of grace, but to the payment of what is due. This is the basis on which rewards are bestowed in the law system. To the person who persists in good work without breaking any of God's commandments, eternal life in heaven is what is due; it is the deserved reward.

This is the "hypothetical" element in this section. I.e., this is how it *would* happen *if* there were anyone who has persisted in good work to the point of perfection; but in fact no one has done so or will do so. Thus eternal life will in fact not be awarded to anyone on the basis of his good work.

2:8 But for those who are self-seeking and who reject the truth and follow evil, there will be wrath and anger. This is equivalent to the second half of my summary of the law system, "Break the commandments, and therefore suffer the penalty."

Commandment-breakers are described with three expressions. First, they are "self-seeking." To be selfish or self-seeking means to pursue our own desires and agendas rather than those God has planned for us. It means laying up treasures on earth — seeking earthly fulfilment (Matt 6:19), rather than seeking the heavenly treasures of glory, honor, and immortality (2:7; Matt 6:20).

Commandment-breakers are also described as those who "reject the truth and follow evil." "Evil" is ἀδικία, (*adikia*), "wickedness, unrighteousness" (1:18,29). More literally the expression reads "those who *disobey* truth and *obey* evil." These are simply two sides of the same coin; to do one is to do the other. The language is practically the same as that used to describe the Gentiles in 1:18, "men who suppress the truth by their wickedness [*adikia*]."

It does not matter whether this truth is known through general revelation or special revelation (2:12); those who suppress and disobey it will receive "wrath and anger." These two words are objects of "will give" in v. 6. In this context both terms refer to the eschatological pouring out of God's wrath after the final judgment. The word translated "wrath" (ὀργή, *orgē*) refers more to God's constant and controlled indignation toward sin, while the word for "anger" (θυμός, *thymos*) refers more to a passionate and destructive outburst of rage. Except for here (which is clearly eschatological in reference) this latter word is used for God's wrath only in Revelation (14:10,19; 15:1,7; 16:1,19; 19:15). At all times God is like a smoldering volcano, but in the end the volcano will erupt. "Our God is a consuming fire" (Heb 12:29).

This is the second of the two alternatives or the two potential outcomes when judgment is according to law. In reality it will be the only outcome, since all *are* commandment-breakers, but that is not Paul's point here. In this paragraph he is simply describing for us how judgment according to law will be conducted.

2:9 In the next two verses Paul repeats the essence of the law system, with the parts reversed. The beginning of v. 9 is equivalent to v. 8: **There will be trouble and distress for every human being who does evil . . . .** When God pours out his wrath and anger in the final judgment, the result for the condemned will be "trouble" (θλίψις, *thlipsis*) and "distress" (στενοχωρία, *stenochōria*). This is what they will experience for eternity.

This will be the result of God's judgment upon "every human being who does evil." Literally it says "upon every soul of man." The word "soul" is used here not in the metaphysical sense of the heart or spirit or inner man, as if only the soul (and not the body) suffers. Here "soul" means "person, individual," thus "every human being" (NIV), every single person among humankind "who does evil," who produces or brings about evil.

One new idea is added in this repetition of the thought of v. 8, namely, **first for the Jew, then for the Gentile . . . .** Here for the first time in this chapter Paul actually mentions the Jews, and he does so in a way that drives home his main point: the righteous judgment of God falls equally on both Jews and Gentiles. This is enough to expose the fallacy of the myth of divine partiality toward the Jews, but Paul goes even further. Not only does God apply the principle of judgment equally to the two groups; he will actually pour out his wrath on the "Jew first." This is an application of Jesus' principle, "From everyone who has been given much, much will be demanded; and from the one who has been entrusted with much, much more will be asked" (Luke 12:48).

2:10 but glory, honor and peace for everyone who does good . . . . This much of the verse is not different in substance from v. 7; it again sets forth the first principle of law-judgment, "Keep the commandments and therefore escape the penalty." The aspects of the heavenly reward are slightly different. Glory and honor are the same as v. 7, but here "peace" is substituted for "immortality." This is not significant; neither list is a complete menu of the blessings of eternal life. Each is no more than representative of the riches to be bestowed on "everyone who does good."

This last phrase can be rendered "everyone who works good or produces good." Again, since we are working here within the law system, this means "everyone who does good all the time and never produces evil." It is the same as "persistence in doing good" in v. 7.

Again the phrase is added, **first for the Jew, then for the Gentile**. The blessings of eternal life are given "first or chiefly to the Jew" because he, "through his superior advantages, hath made greater progress in virtue" (DeWelt, 34). This is not at all the same as favoritism with regard to the terms of judgment. The Jew has no "priority of privilege" (Dunn, I:93).

The point of these last four verses is to explain how the law system is completely impartial and favors neither the Jew nor the Gentile. "First for the Jew" does not mean "for the Jew on a different and more favorable basis." The basis for both is their works (v. 6), considered equally. "Paul's whole point here is that the terms of judgment are precisely the *same* for *everyone*." This undermines the Jews' belief "that God's judgment of Israel will be on different terms from his judgment of the nations as a whole" (Dunn, I:88).

2:11 For God does not show favoritism (❧I:194). This is the main point of the paragraph. The justice of the law is truly blindfolded; who the person is makes no difference. Only his works will be examined. This is simply a negative restatement of the principle set forth in v. 6 (❧I:194).

While the principle applies to everyone, in this context it is a message Paul directs especially toward the Jews. God cannot be partial because his judgment is based on truth (v. 2), and because it is righteous (v. 5). A judgment that shows partiality would not be righteous. Therefore you, O Jew, cannot expect special treatment on Judgment Day. You will be no exception to the conclusion stated in 3:20.

C. Under Law, the Criterion of Judgment Is Obedience Alone (2:12-16)

The next three paragraphs address two specific reasons why the Jews believed God would be partial to them in the last judgment: their possession of the Law of Moses, and the fact that they were circumcised. This paragraph (vv. 12-16) makes a very specific point about the former, namely, that the criterion of judgment within the law system is *obedience* to the law, not just possession of it or knowledge of it. Mere possession of the Law of Moses was no indication that the Jews would receive special consideration. As Cranfield sums it up, "Knowledge of the law does not in itself constitute any defence against the judgment of God" (I:139, 153).

This paragraph not only dissolves this basis for false confidence on the part of the Jews, but also defuses all possible complaints from the Gentiles that they are at a disadvantage in relation to the law since the Law of Moses was given only to the Jews. As Moo states the point, "In these verses Paul defends the equality of all people before God's judgment seat against the charge that the Jews' possession of the law gives to them a decisive advantage" (144-145).

In other words, the fact that the Jews had a specially revealed form of God's law does not negate the general principle of judgment stated in v. 11, "God does not show favoritism."

2:12 All who sin apart from the law will also perish apart from the law, and all who sin under the law will be judged by the law. Two things in this verse are quite clear. First, "law" means the Law of Moses, given to the Jews by special revelation. Second, those who are "apart from the law" are the Gentiles, and those "under the law" are the Jews (❂I:195-196).

What does the reference to people who "sin apart from the law" mean? How is it possible for a person to sin if there is no law to be broken (1 John 3:4)? Does not 4:15 say, "Where there is no law there is no transgression"? Yes, and that is the main reason why "law" in this verse must refer to the Law of Moses, and by inference to the moral law of God in any other *specially revealed* form, unwritten (as to Adam, Noah, and Abraham) or written (as in the NT). Thus in this reference Paul must be talking about people who have no access to specially revealed law, but do in fact have knowledge of God's law through general revelation, i.e., the Gentiles. The Gentiles do not need the Law of Moses in order to be judged according to law (as 1:18-32 has already shown).

In this context the main point is that the possession of or knowledge of the Law of *Moses* will make no difference as far as judgment according to law is concerned. "All who sin" will be condemned. The verb here is actually a past tense (aorist), "all who sinned or who have sinned." It is past tense from the perspective of Judgment Day, when one's past life will be considered as a whole. It means "all who have sinned, *period*, will perish," even if there has been just one sin (Jas 2:10; Gal 3:10). This is the rule when judgment is conducted according to law, and it will be applied to Jew and Gentile alike.

When judged even apart from the Law of Moses, the Gentiles "will perish." This verb means "to perish, to die, to be ruined, to be destroyed, to be lost." It is often used to refer to the eternal condemnation of the wicked, as it does here (see Matt 10:28; John 3:15-16; 10:28; 1 Cor 1:18; 2 Cor 4:3; 2 Thess 2:10; 2 Pet 3:9).

The second part of the verse refers specifically to the Jews, who sin under (within) the Law of Moses, with full knowledge of the specially revealed law of God. Thus they will be "judged by the law" of Moses. The word "judged" is too weak to translate κρίνω (*krinō*), which here means "condemned" and is no different in meaning from "will perish." (See 2:1,3; 3:7; 2 Thess 2:12.) Thus whether in possession of the Law of Moses or not, anyone who sins will receive the verdict of condemnation. (This is in contrast with the verdict of justification in v. 13.)

Here again is the tragic irony of the Jews' situation. The very law in which they trusted as a kind of charm guaranteeing their salvation (Morris, 122) will be the instrument of their condemnation because they have sinned against it. (The charge that they *have* sinned against it is made in detail in the next paragraph, vv. 17-24.)

2:13 For it is not those who hear the law who are righteous in God's sight, but it is those who obey the law who will be declared righteous. As this verse is examined we must remember two things. First, it relates only to the law system; it is a principle of judgment according to law. It is basically equivalent to vv. 7 and 10. "Keep the commandments, and therefore escape the penalty."

Second, whether there is anyone in this category is beside the point at this stage of Paul's argument. There does not need to be anyone in it for the principle to be true. As the statement of a principle it is like the sign that warns, "Trespassers will be prosecuted" — if anyone dares. Or it is like Jonah's message to Nineveh, "Forty more days and Nineveh will be destroyed" — unless they repent (Jonah 3:4). Such statements are straightforward, but they contain unspoken conditions (see Jer 18:7-10). That is the case here: those who obey the law will be declared righteous — if anyone does. Thus those are wrong who say this principle cannot be hypothetical because the verb is a simple future indicative.

The use of the concept of righteousness here focuses our attention squarely upon the thematic statement in 1:17. There Paul sums up the *grace* system of salvation, that a righteousness of God is revealed in the gospel, and that those who receive that righteousness by faith will live eternally. But here in 2:13 Paul is explaining the *law* system of being accepted as righteous by God, namely, by works rather than by faith. An understanding of this aspect of the law system is crucial for an understanding of Paul's main point in this section and in Romans as a whole. Under law the *only* way to be accepted as righteous is through obedience — perfect obedience — to the law's commandments. But all have sinned; therefore no one will in fact be saved by law. Thus the gospel alternative is our only hope.

Thus far we have seen several words relating to righteousness, but this is the first time the key term δικαιόω (*dikaioō*) has appeared. This is a legal term that refers to a judge's decision in a courtroom trial. It is the opposite of "condemned" (see v. 12) and is usually translated "justified," although some recent translations think this word is too theological and render it instead as "acquitted," "counted righteous," "put right," or "declared righteous" (NIV). The issue is this: if our relationship with God is based on law alone, then when we think of ourselves as standing before God as judge (whether now or at the second coming), how is it possible for him to regard us as righteous? How is it possible to hear the judge say, "Not guilty!" or "No penalty for you!"?

Paul's answer is stated in both negative and positive terms. First, contrary to the Jews' assumption, one cannot be accepted as righteous before God merely by *hearing* the law. By this he means "not those who *only* hear the law," as if having the law in one's possession or even in one's mind would be enough to be counted righteous. This applies not only to the Jews but to anyone who has access to special revelation of the Creator's will for his creatures. The word "hear" in this context means "hear" in the barest sense of the term, i.e., in the sense of having some knowledge content register in the consciousness and possibly retained in the memory, but without ever acting upon that content.

Paul next states the principle in a positive way: "It is those who obey the law who will be declared righteous." As vv. 14-15 show, he means "law" in whatever form it is available to anyone; for the Jews this would be the Law of Moses. "Those who obey the law" is literally "the doers of the law" (see Jas 1:22-25). "Doing" the law, doing God's will, doing sin, doing righteousness, doing the truth, doing good, doing evil — these are common ways of speaking in Scripture. Here "doing the law" is equivalent to obedience or good works (❂ I:199).

2:14 (Indeed, when Gentiles, who do not have the law, do by nature things required by the law . . . .) Like the NIV, many take vv. 14-15 to be a parenthesis, with the main flow of Paul's thought being resumed again in v. 16, which will conclude the paragraph. The thought developed in the parenthesis is called for by the apparent implications for the Gentiles of the principles stated in vv. 12-13. It is easy to see how these verses apply to the Jews, but when applied to the Gentiles, one might question the *fairness* of God's judgment. Is it fair to condemn the Gentiles for breaking the law if they do not even *have* the law (v. 12)? This question has already been answered in 1:18-32, but Paul answers it again here with more detail.

What the apostle is doing in these two verses is explaining the meaning of *anomōs* ("apart from the law") in v. 12. This is the category of the "Gentiles," he says, a word he has not used since 1:13. In between he has used "Greek" as its equivalent (1:16; 2:9-10), which the NIV translates as "Gentiles" anyway. These Gentiles, he says, are the ones "who do not have the law," namely, the Law of Moses, or by extension *any* specially revealed form of God's law. He repeats this fact later in the verse.

Nevertheless these very same Gentiles, who do not have the Law of Moses, sometimes "do by nature things required by the law." Literally Paul says "when" the Gentiles do these things. Thus he does not mean they do things of the law perfectly, or that they do *all* of the things required by the law. He means there are times when the Gentiles acknowledge the moral duties revealed in Moses' law, and there are times when they even live up to them (see Dunn, I:98; Hendriksen, I:97; Moo, 149-150).

Paul says the Gentiles do these things "by nature," i.e., through some kind of built-in, created instinct. That is, men's nature *as created* includes an innate awareness of the moral law of God. This is not the same as the knowledge of God himself, which registers upon our consciousness from observing created things outside ourselves (1:18-21). It is something that is already inside us as a universal moral consciousness, in the form of "a natural, in-born capacity" (Moo, 150). There will be more on this in the next verse.

As a result of this "innate awareness of God's moral demands" (Moo, 151), there is a sense in which **they [the Gentiles] are a law for themselves, even though they do not have the law . . .** in a specially revealed form. This means that their innate knowledge of God's law has basically the same content as the moral law revealed in the Law of Moses. That they are a "law for themselves" does not mean that the Gentiles are free to make up whatever law code they fancy, with God accepting that as the standard by which he will judge them. This is a quite common idea, but it is a serious mistake (Stott, 86). Rather, they are a law in themselves in that their inner being bears at least the remnants of God's moral law as it was imprinted upon human nature in the very beginning. See v. 15 (❖ I:200).

2:15 This verse is a further explanation of how the Gentiles, while not having access to the Law of Moses, still have a form of God's law. Specifically, it expands on the concept that the Gentiles are a law for themselves, **since they show that the requirements of the law are written on their hearts . . . .** They show or demonstrate this in their general agreement on basic moral principles, in their occasional obedience to these principles, and in their sense of guilt and hostility toward God when they disobey them.

"The requirements of the law" literally reads "the work of the law." A better rendering is "conduct," or "the conduct that the law demands" (Moo, 151) (❖ I:201).

The work of the law is "written on their hearts." This is the bottom line as to how the Gentiles have access to the law of God and how they can be justly condemned for breaking it. But what does it mean?

Some, perhaps out of an aversion to the very thought of innate knowledge of any kind, equate "written on the heart" with the generation-to-generation transmission of the moral knowledge revealed by God to Adam in the beginning. We can rule this out, however, since the language here — "by nature," "written on the heart" — seems calculated specifically to exclude the mechanics of tradition. It points unequivocally to something innate in each individual, to something "inwardly revealed" in the form of "inward, natural promptings" (MP, 312) (❷ I:201-202).

The best understanding of how the required conduct of the law is "written on their hearts" is derived from the NT teaching on the *image of God*. Parallel passages in Eph 4:23-24 and Col 3:9-10 speak about Christian sanctification as the process that renews the image of God within us. In the context the contrast is between the Gentiles' pre-Christian moral depravity and the new way of life required of Christians. The latter is described as putting on a new self, "which is being renewed in knowledge in the image of its Creator" (Col 3:10), language that clearly alludes to the original creation in God's image (Gen 1:26-27).

Analyzing these parallel texts gives us this scenario: 1) The original creation in God's image involved *knowledge* (Col 3:10), specifically a knowledge of "true righteousness and holiness" (Eph 4:24). Since the image of God is part of our very nature as human beings, we may conclude that this moral knowledge was part of mankind's original, created nature. 2) The Fall into sin resulted in a corruption of the image of God in an unspecified manner and degree. The innate moral consciousness remains intact enough to render everyone "without excuse," but it is corrupted to the point that it cannot be completely trusted and needs to be "recreated." 3) Part of Christian salvation consists in this very thing, i.e., the recreation of the inner image of God and thus the reconstruction of the inner moral compass. This is done not from within but from the outside, through the inspired teaching of apostles and prophets (2 Tim 3:16-17), such as Paul is providing to the Ephesians and Colossians in these very letters. This is the fulfilment of Jer 31:33: the law is *re*written on the minds and hearts of willing Christians through the Spirit-inspired words of the New Covenant revelation (❷ I:203).

Now we turn to the next part of v. 15, which focuses on another innate aspect of human nature, the conscience: **their consciences also bearing witness . . . .** The most important thing to know about the conscience is that it is *not* the same as "the work of the law written on the heart." The conscience itself has no content; it is not in itself a source of knowledge about right and wrong. It is rather an ability, a function (Murray, I:75). Specifically, conscience is the function of comparing our deeds with an accepted standard of morality, and of prodding us with a sense of guilt when a deed does not conform to the standard.

Whether the conscience functions properly or not depends on the accuracy of the standard with which it compares our deeds. To the degree to which the image of God remains intact within any individual, the conscience will work as intended by God. To the degree that the law-content written on the heart has been corrupted, the conscience will malfunction (❁I:203-204).

It is extremely important to remember this: wherever the knowledge of God's law has been corrupted, suppressed, exchanged, or in any way violated, the conscience will continue to function but will not produce trustworthy results. Until one has submitted to the saving work of Jesus Christ and the Holy Spirit, and has allowed the truth of biblical revelation to reinform his original moral database, the conscience will at times, perhaps most of the time, yield false results. "Always let your conscience be your guide" is bad theology. Actually, the conscience itself *needs* a guide or standard, and the only sure guide for sinners is the objective Word of God, the Bible.

The last part of v. 15 (**. . . and their thoughts now accusing, now even defending them.**) in my opinion is not different from the working of the conscience but is a clarification of how it works (❁I:204). The functioning conscience results in an inner dialogue, forcing the mind to verbalize thoughts such as "This must be OK" or "You know that's wrong, don't you?" Our thoughts either accuse us or defend us in reference to our deeds. These are technical legal terms that suggest a courtroom trial where the individual is the defendant and his own conscience-driven thoughts are both the prosecuting attorney and the defense lawyer.

It is important to see that this accusing and defending happens with reference to individual deeds, not to anyone's life as a whole. Thus Paul is not saying that in the day of judgment there may be some Gentile whose conscience will excuse him altogether so that he is saved. All Paul is saying is that sometimes in this life, when a Gentile does by nature what the law requires in a certain situation, his conscience will excuse him regarding that one decision.

When this inner moral consciousness (the inwardly written law plus the conscience) is combined with the knowledge of God learned through the created universe (1:18-21), the result is that even the Gentiles know that this law is the law of the Creator-God and that they are guilty before God when they break it and are worthy of the wrath God has ordained for such lawbreakers (see 1:32). (See *GC*, 329-336.)

2:16 This will take place on the day when God will judge men's secrets through Jesus Christ, as my gospel declares. It is clear that this verse concludes the paragraph, but its exact connection with the preceding text is uncertain. The words "this will take place" are not in the original, where the beginning words are "on which day God will judge." The idea is that some action mentioned in the preceding verse or verses will take place on the day of judgment. What action does Paul have in mind?

It is best to see v. 16 as an inclusive reference to all the main verbs pointing to Judgment Day in vv. 1-15: "will be revealed," v. 5; "will be judged," v. 12; "will be declared righteous" v. 13; and maybe "accusing" and "defending," v. 15 (see Hendriksen, I:96) (◉I:205).

We should think of v. 15 as ending in a dash — with v. 16 bringing the preceding thoughts to a climax and wrapping them up in a neat package. This effect is achieved when we add the word "all" to the NIV's added phrase, thus: "All this will take place . . . ."

This "day when God will judge" is the same as "the day of God's wrath" (v. 5). In v. 16 the word "judge" (*krinō*) seems to have its more general meaning of "pass judgment on." God will judge not just external and public deeds but also "men's secrets" — the hidden things of men's hearts as well as deeds done in private. The omniscience of God makes this possible (1 Sam 16:7; 1 John 3:20). Jesus stressed this point especially in reference to the hypocrisy of the Jewish leaders (Matt 6:4,6,18; 23:25-28), an application that is relevant to the thought in the next paragraph (2:17-24).

Paul adds a Christological note at this point: the judgment will take place "through Jesus Christ" (see 1:3-4). This means that Jesus is involved not only in the gospel of salvation through grace, but also in the process of judgment according to law. For other references to Jesus as judge, see Matt 25:31-33; John 5:22,27; Acts 10:42; 17:31; 1 Cor 4:5; 2 Cor 5:10; 2 Tim 4:1; Rev 22:12.

The words "as my gospel declares" (literally, "according to my gospel") are a bit of a problem for exegetes. Exactly what does this phrase modify (◉I:206)? Probably the best understanding is this: "My gospel declares that the judge will be Christ Jesus" (see Cranfield, I:163). "This last alternative does most justice to the somewhat unexpected reference to the gospel," says Moo (155). That Jesus will be the judge is good news because it points to the fact that there is a judgment beyond that of law, a judgment according to the grace established by the judge himself in his atoning death and victorious resurrection.

D. Jews Who Look to the Law for Salvation Are Condemned by Their Own Disobedience (2:17-24)

No one will be saved by his relationship to the law of God. Gentiles will not be saved by their *ignorance* of the law, because in fact they have knowledge of it. Jews will not be saved by their *possession* of the Law of *Moses*, because the only way to be saved by any law is through perfect obedience to it. There are no exceptions. God does not show favoritism, even to the Jews, when it comes to the final judgment.

In the previous paragraph Paul made the point that only doers of the law, not merely hearers or possessers, can be saved by the law system. Where does this leave the Jew? If he can no longer count on his privileged position as possessor of the law to secure his salvation, then his only hope (under law) is to obey it perfectly.

It seems that some Jews believed they were actually sinless before the law (Luke 18:9-14), including Paul (Saul) when he was a Pharisee (Phil 3:5-6). But Paul's point in this paragraph is that this is a lie. The Jews in fact are *not* "doers of the law," but are guilty of breaking the very law they glory in. The law they regard as a ticket to heaven shines like a spotlight upon their sin (3:20), thus dissolving their final hope before the law.

The first thing Paul does in this paragraph is dissect the nature of the Jews' hope in the law, the grounds for their law-based confidence as the specially chosen stewards of the Mosaic revelation (vv. 17-20). Then in the second half of the paragraph he rips off their mask of hypocrisy and exposes their own sinfulness (vv. 21-24). This latter segment is to the Jews what 1:29-31 was to the Gentiles.

2:17 Paul returns now to the diatribe style, which he suspended in vv. 6-16, and speaks directly to the Jews in the person of their anonymous representative: **Now you, if you call yourself a Jew . . . .** The Jews have been Paul's main target all along in chapter 2, but this is the first time he addresses them specifically as Jews. By Paul's time this had been their own favored self-designation for several generations, replacing "Israelite" and "Hebrew." It was "a name accepted with pride" (Dunn, I:109) (❂I:207-208).

Paul is not saying it is wrong for the Jews to call themselves Jews. In fact, most of the things he ascribes to the Jews in vv. 17-20 are not wrong in themselves. Almost all the claims and roles described here are things the Jews were *supposed* to do and be. The irony is that all these genuine privileges and prerogatives were trivialized by the Jews' false self-righteousness and hypocrisy.

Verse 17 includes two further descriptions of the Jewish self-confidence: **if you rely on the law and brag about your relationship to God . . . .** The first of these is the only inappropriate one in the whole list, and it skews all the rest. Relying on (resting upon, resting their hopes upon) the law was the Jew's root problem. "The Jew *rested upon* . . . the mere fact of having the law, as a ground of safety" (Lard, 90). Instead of relying upon their role as recipients of the Mosaic Law, they should have relied upon the mercy of God (2:4).

The Jews also bragged or boasted about their relationship to God. The Greek expression says simply "you are boasting in God." The problem with the Jews was that their boasting in God was selfish and exclusive, as if they alone had a claim upon God (3:27,29). It was a kind of name-dropping, a "self-centred boasting in him as a basis for one's own self-importance" (Cranfield, I:164).

2:18 if you know his will . . . . Even those who have only general revelation know God's will to a degree, but possessing his special revelation makes this knowledge more explicit and more complete. Certainly as possessors of the Law of Moses, the Jews knew God's will more thoroughly than anyone else up to the time of the New Covenant revelation. This is something they could rightly rejoice in.

The next clause, **and approve of what is superior**, also appears in Phil 1:10.

Each of the two key words has two nuances, which leads to differences in interpretation. One view is that the clause means, "You know how to discern what differs *from* God's will, you know how to tell right from wrong." This is the basis for the NEB's "You are aware of moral distinctions." Another view is that it means, "You know how to discern the superior elements *within* God's will, the things that matter, the essentials" (Cranfield, I:166; Phil 1:10, NIV). The last view is the one the NIV gives here in 2:18, "You approve of what is superior" (see also KJV, NASB). Either of these meanings is acceptable.

Both of these things — knowing God's will and discerning the essentials — are possible **because you are instructed by the law** . . . . This is the law's proper function, and the Jews would have been much better off if they had left it at that. Also, both of these things are commendable, as long as they are not considered to be a replacement for obedience. The error "lies not in knowing God's will, but in regarding this knowledge, by itself, as a mark of superiority, and ground of acceptance with God" (Lard, 91).

2:19 In this verse and the next Paul lists four basically similar things the Jews considered themselves to be. Because you know the Law of Moses so well, he says, . . . **you are convinced that you are a guide for the blind, a light for those who are in the dark** . . . . In Scripture both blindness and darkness are used figuratively to represent ignorance, especially ignorance of spiritual things. Both are dispelled by knowledge of the truth, which comes from the Word of God (Ps 119:105; John 17:17; Rom 2:20).

It was Israel's great privilege and responsibility to be "a light for the Gentiles" and "to open eyes that are blind" (Isa 42:6-7; 49:6). They were not commissioned to do this through worldwide missionary activity, but were meant to accomplish this indirectly through their faithful preparation for the coming Messiah, who himself would be the direct source of light and sight to the world (Luke 2:32; 4:18). The problem was that the Jews refused to accept their secondary role in this plan, and regarded themselves as the ultimate and final source of truth.

2:20. The Jew also considered himself to be **an instructor of the foolish, a teacher of infants** . . . . These are slightly different ways of saying the same thing, and, like the two roles in 2:19, are in themselves commendable. An "instructor" is an educator, a teacher; the verb form often refers to correction and chastisement. "The *foolish* strictly are the unintelligent (NEB, 'stupid'), those lacking the ability to think things out," says Morris. This is not talking about IQ as such, but "perception in spiritual things" (133). Someone can be MENSA material or a scientific genius, and still be foolish in his thinking about God and morality.

The word for "infants" means literally just that: infants, babies. It is often used figuratively for the spiritually immature, as in the case of new converts or those who have lagged behind in spiritual growth. The NT uses it of immature

Christians (1 Cor 3:1; Eph 4:4; Heb 5:13). The Jews of course regarded all Gentiles as foolish, and as spiritual infants or simple-minded children. Thus it is probable that Paul means in both these expressions that the Jews considered themselves to be proper teachers of the Gentiles, especially those who might be new converts to Judaism.

All of these elements of Jewish self-confidence were grounded in one thing: the law. You are convinced you can do these things, says Paul, **because you have in the law the embodiment of knowledge and truth** . . . . Indeed, the law possessed by the Jews — not just the Pentateuch but the entire OT — was an embodiment or repository of inspired knowledge and truth, and was therefore "useful for teaching, rebuking, correcting, and training in righteousness" (2 Tim 3:16). The Jews' mistake was the arrogant assumption that their Scriptures were the only source of knowledge and truth (contra 1:18-25,28,32) as well as the final source (rejecting the Christian revelation).

2:21 Verse 17 begins with the conditional word, "if," with all of vv. 17-20 depending on it. The expected matching "then" is not explicit at the beginning of v. 21 but is only implied: "If this is how you see yourself as a Jew, then why don't you *act* as a real Jew should act?" **. . . you, then, who teach others, do you not teach yourself?** This is the beginning of a series of "accusatory rhetorical questions" (Cranfield, I:167) dropped like bombshells into the midst of the smug Jewish complacency. They are based on the moral law as represented by the Ten Commandments.

Phillips renders this first question thus: "But, prepared as you are to instruct others, do you ever teach yourself anything?" The implied answer is "No, you are *not* teaching yourself." You are not "practicing what you preach." Cf. Ps 50:16-20; Matt 23:3; Gal 6:13.

From here to the end of v. 22 Paul gives several examples of "practicing what you preach against." None of these accusations implies that all Jews do all of these things all of the time. They are simply meant to drive home the point that every Jew has broken the law at some point, thus erasing all distinctions between Jews and Gentiles in reference to the judgment.

You who preach against stealing, do you steal? We usually associate *preaching* (κηρύσσω, *kēryssō*) with preaching the gospel, and this is indeed how the word is used most of the time in the NT. On a few occasions, though, it means simply "proclaiming a message" (see Gal 5:11; 1 Pet 3:19; Rev 5:2). To a Jew who gloried in the law (2:23), what greater message could there be than the law? This question, like the others in this series, is meant to stimulate the Jew's slumbering conscience.

2:22 You who say that people should not commit adultery, do you commit adultery? As Jesus showed in his Sermon on the Mount (Matt 5:17-48), the Jews tended to look at a commandment with a very narrow tunnel vision, seeing it as prohibiting a single act. One obeys "Do not murder," for example, as long as he avoids actually killing someone. But Jesus says that rash anger and demeaning words also violate this commandment (Matt 5:21-22). The same is true of the seventh commandment, "Do not commit adultery." To the Jews this commandment was obeyed as long as one avoided physical sexual contact with someone else's spouse. But Jesus says adultery can be committed in the heart, through lusting after someone who is not your spouse (Matt 5:27-30). In that light Paul's question may not be so easily answered, and few could really answer "Of course not!"

The next question is the most difficult to understand: **You who abhor idols, do you rob temples?** The first part is easy; the monotheistic Jews took the first two of the ten commandments seriously and in principle hated idolatry.

But what does Paul mean when he accuses the Jews of robbing temples (ἱεροσυλέω, *hierosyleō*)? Several views have been suggested, and it is difficult to be dogmatic about any one of them. Some see this word as referring to the literal theft of idols from pagan temples (see Acts 19:37), especially those made of precious metals, which could be melted down and sold for gain. This practice is specifically forbidden in Deut 7:25. Also, throughout OT history the Jews were constantly being seduced by the idolatrous practices of their pagan neighbors, so Paul could also be referring to the theft of idols for personal worship. (See Schrenk, "ἱερός," 255-256.) If the robbing of pagan temples is Paul's point, the latter purpose would seem to be what he has in mind, since stealing as such has already been mentioned, and since it would contrast better with "abhorring idols."

Another suggestion is that Paul is talking about some kind of practice that robs the temple of the true God rather than temples of pagan gods. One such possibility is the misappropriation of tithes brought to the temple for the service of God and used instead for personal purposes (see Stott, 91), or perhaps the withholding of one's own tithes, which Mal 3:8 describes as stealing from God. One problem with this view is how this could be parallel to idolatry, but perhaps the equation of greed with idolatry in Col 3:5 answers this.

A third view takes the word to mean "commit sacrilege" against the true God in some general, unspecified sense, without any literal temple theft being involved (Cranfield, I:169-170). In this sense it could be a reference to the next two verses, which accuse the Jews of bringing dishonor upon God by their hypocritical disobedience. The contrast then would be something like this: "You make a big deal of defending God's honor by attacking the reality of all false pagan gods, then turn around and bring shame upon his name by your sin."

The three sins of stealing, adultery, and sacrilege are only a few examples of Jewish hypocrisy; others could no doubt have been cited. Paul's purpose in mentioning these three was to lead the Jews to examine their lives on all matters of the law, and ultimately to realize that they were sinners no less than the Gentiles.

2:23 Some take this verse as a statement: "While you take pride in the law, you dishonour God by breaking it" (NEB). Others (like the NIV) take it as a question, the last in the series beginning in v. 21: **You who brag about the law, do you dishonor God by breaking the law?** Either way, along with the proof text cited in v. 24, it sums up the point of this paragraph and exposes the tragic contradiction in the Jews' relationship with the law.

Just as the Jews boasted (bragged) about their relation to God (v. 17), so they boasted about their relation to his law. (This is the same word that was used in v. 17; see the discussion there.) Again, the law of God no less than God himself is something believers ought to boast about, in the sense of giving it honor and taking pride in it and rejoicing in its truth and guidance. The whole of Ps 119 is a testimony to this, e.g., "Oh, how I love your law! I meditate on it all day long" (v. 97). The Jews' boasting, however, was self-centered. In Cranfield's words, they sought to use the law as a means of putting God in their debt, and regarded their knowledge of it as making them better than their fellow men (I:170).

In any case all their positive claims regarding the law were negated by their transgression of it. Their sin brought disrepute not only to the law but also to God himself, since the law cannot be separated from the Lawgiver.

2:24 As it is written: "God's name is blasphemed among the Gentiles because of you." This verse explains how lawbreaking dishonors God. Not only is it a personal insult against God on the part of the sinner himself, but it also causes others (here, the Gentiles) to blaspheme God and make fun of him.

In ancient cultures one's *name* was the embodiment of the whole person; in Scripture the name of God stands for everything that God is. Thus to blaspheme God's name is to blaspheme God himself. "Blaspheme" means to speak against or say something bad about; to blaspheme God is to speak against him, to mock or ridicule him, to curse him or rail against him.

"As it is written" indicates Paul is referring to OT Scripture. He seems to be thinking of two texts, Isa 52:5 and Ezek 36:20-23. In each case Israel is enduring the shame of exile, and their Gentile conquerors are pictured as mocking the allegedly great and powerful God whom the Jews bragged about and trusted in, but who could not deliver them from this humiliation. "Some God!" they sneered. "All day long my name is constantly blasphemed," says the Lord (Isa 52:5).

The kind of thing to which Paul is referring is not quite this dramatic, but it is just as damaging to God's "reputation." The Jews portrayed themselves as "the people of the law." Being the recipients and guardians of God's law gave them a bad case of spiritual pride and a sense of superiority over the Gentiles. This also made them and their law and their God very vulnerable to criticism and ridicule when they sinned against the very law they gloried in.

The bottom line of this paragraph is that the Jews can forget about appeal-

Romans Part One

ing to the law in any way as the basis for their hope on the day of judgment. Under law nothing but obedience counts, and in this department the Jews' record is no better than that of the Gentiles.

E. True Jewishness Is Identified Not by Circumcision but by the Inward State of the Heart (2:25-29)

Thus far in chapter 2 Paul has shown that the Jews are not excused from God's wrath simply because of their possession of and knowledge of the law. Now in vv. 25-29 he pictures the Jews as retreating to their final stronghold, their final line of defense: circumcision. Circumcision was their concrete, physical evidence that they were children of Abraham and were thus protected by the covenant that God had made with Abraham *and his descendants* (Gen 17:1-14) (❧ I:215).

Paul's purpose in this paragraph, then, is to do with circumcision what he has already done with the law, namely, show that it is no basis for special treatment on Judgment Day.

Paul accomplishes this in two steps. First (vv. 25-27), continuing in the diatribe style, he shows that circumcision does not take precedence over the law's more fundamental requirement, obedience itself. When God renders his final judgment for those under law (not under grace), he will divide them into two groups. But, contrary to the Jews' expectation, those two groups will *not* be the circumcised and the uncircumcised (equivalent to the Jews and the Gentiles). Rather, God will say, "All those who have *obeyed* the law as you have known it — circumcised or not — come over here. All who have *disobeyed* the law — circumcised or not — go over there." Thus under law uncircumcised persons could conceivably be saved and circumcised persons lost.

Second (vv. 28-29), Paul abandons the diatribe style and brings all of chapter 2 to a climax. For the first and only time in this first main section of Romans (1:18–3:20), he steps outside the sphere of law and sets forth a basic principle of grace salvation, i.e., true Jewishness is identified not by circumcision but by the inward state of the heart. Physical Jewishness, marked by physical circumcision, is not the measure of salvation; spiritual circumcision is.

2:25 Circumcision has value if you observe the law . . . . To his anonymous Jewish dialogue partner Paul succinctly sums up the circumstances under which physical circumcision will profit or be of value on Judgment Day. He says in effect, "To be sure, your circumcision does identify you with the family of Abraham, the chosen people, which gives you certain advantages and reasons to rejoice on an earthly level (3:1-2; 9:4-5). And there is even a sense in which your physical circumcision can help to usher you into heaven. You will remember that circumcision was incorporated into Moses' Law; therefore your reception of circumcision identifies you with that law and obligates you to keep the whole law (Gal 5:3). Because of this, circumcision viewed as a saving act cannot be separated from obedience to the entire law as the ground of your salvation. Thus we are back to the principle set forth in 2:13 — the doer of the (whole) law will be justified. Thus circumcision can save you 'if you observe the law,' i.e., if it is part of a life of complete and total obedience to the law."

We must be very careful *not* to read into v. 25a any reference to Christian faith or salvation by grace. The false covenant theology created in Reformed circles in the sixteenth century has caused some interpreters to transform "observe the law" into "believe in and live by the gospel" (e.g., Murray, I:85-86). But this misses the whole point. In vv. 25-27 Paul is still talking about the conditions of salvation under law, not grace; and the saving efficacy of law is clearly conditional upon perfect obedience: "*if* you observe the law." As in the earlier parts of this chapter, though, such an accomplishment is treated only as hypothetical. (See Moo, 168.)

The other side of this coin, which represents reality, is then given: **but if you break the law, you have become as though you had not been circumcised.** "If you break the law" must be seen in light of Gal 3:10 and Gal 5:3, and thus understood as meaning "if you break the law *even once*" (see Jas 2:10). As a law-truster, if you break just a single commandment, you will be under the curse of God's wrath. Your circumcision will be irrelevant; you will be in exactly the same boat as an uncircumcised person (a Gentile) when he breaks *his* law.

2:26 If those who are not circumcised keep the law's requirements, will they not be regarded as though they were circumcised? Here Paul continues to show the irrelevance of circumcision by showing how it affects the uncircumcised person, the Gentile. In what sense might such a person "keep the law's requirements"? Some say Paul is talking about Gentile Christians and their humble faith and faithful obedience to God under grace (Cranfield, I:173; Murray; I:86). This is a serious mistake, however. As in the previous verse Paul is still talking about final salvation or condemnation on the day of judgment, as determined by the principles of law. *If* a Gentile keeps *all* the righteous ordinances of the law, he will be saved even though he has not been circumcised. This is a conditional statement which never becomes actualized, though, because of the universality of sin.

Paul does not make this statement in order to give the Gentile hope under the law. He says it to the Jews, in order to doubly emphasize the irrelevance of circumcision under the judgment of the law.

The whole point is to show the Jews that, as sinners, it is futile to trust their physical Jewishness as their key to salvation. Physical descent from Abraham, membership in the Abrahamic covenant, physical circumcision, possession of the specially revealed Mosaic Law — all will be of no avail under law without a perfect record of personal righteousness, which they did not have.

2:27 In the beginning of this verse Paul mentions again the hypothetical Gentile who keeps the law: **The one who is not circumcised physically and yet**

obeys the law . . . . That the category is empty is shown by 1:18-32; 3:9. This does not affect Paul's point, though, since the mere possibility that a Gentile could ever sit in judgment on a Jew was an abomination to the Jewish mind. Yet this is exactly what Paul says could happen, in principle: that the obedient Gentile **will condemn you who, even though you have the written code and circumcision, are a lawbreaker** (❂1:218).

The verb κρίνω (*krinō*) probably does have its stronger meaning of "condemn" in this verse, as the NIV says. The obedient Gentile will condemn the disobedient Jews not as a judge as such, but "as a witness for the prosecution" (Cranfield, I:174). It is "probably the indirect judging of comparison. On the day of judgment, the Gentile, with his poor advantages, will condemn, by his superior conduct the lawlessness of the Jew" (MP, 316). In fact, as Lard notes (97-98), this will be true even when a Gentile is not perfectly righteous and therefore not saved, but at the same time is relatively more righteous than certain Jews.

2:28 The point of this main section of Romans is that no one can be saved when judged according to the rules of law. The Jews were willing to accept this as true for everyone except themselves. "This does not apply to us," they thought. Why not? "Because we are *Jews*. We are special. We are Abraham's children. We are circumcised. We have, not just any law, but the Law of Moses. God does not treat us as he treats other people."

In one sense, and on one level, all of this is true. On the physical level God used this one nation of mankind for the greatest mission imaginable: He used them to prepare for the coming of the Messiah, and even to supply his human nature (9:5). Just to *be* a Jew was to be involved in this mission, however marginally.

As I have indicated earlier, the Jews' critical error was to assume that this privileged status with regard to service also gave them a privileged status with regard to salvation. They assumed that their mere physical identity as Jews, marked by circumcision, was all they needed to be right with God. Romans 2 specifically refutes this idea. We may picture the Jew crying out in desperation, "If Jews are not special, who is? If my circumcision doesn't please God, what does?"

Even though Paul is not quite ready to get into this sort of question in detail, he does pause in these two verses to give us a foretaste of the message of grace. The person who is truly accepted by God, he says, is right with him on a different level — not the flesh, but the spirit. The things that make him special to God are not on the outside, such as physical birth as a Jew, physical circumcision, and mere outward obedience to the law's commands. Rather, they are on the inside, where God alone can see them.

This has always been true, in OT times as well as now in NT times. Paul states this truth specifically for NT times in Phil 3:3, "For it is we who are the circumcision, we who worship by the Spirit of God, who glory in Christ Jesus, and who put no confidence in the flesh . . . ." But since in 2:28-29 Paul is still basically addressing Jews, he makes this point using the terminology of Jewishness. In these verses the word *Jew* is a metaphor for saved persons of all ages. Not all Jews (by birth) are *real* Jews (9:6). Not all circumcised people have had the circumcision that really counts.

A man is not a Jew if he is only one outwardly, nor is circumcision merely outward and physical. This verse is the negative side of Paul's point; it states what true Jewishness is not. It is not based on external circumstances, such as physical birth to Jewish parents. Likewise, the circumcision that counts for eternity is not the outward circumcision of the male genitals.

2:29 No, a man is a Jew if he is one inwardly . . . . Here is the positive description of true Jewishness. "Inwardly" is literally "in secret," which is a way of describing either actions or states of the heart which only God can see (Matt 6:4,6; Mark 4:22; 1 Cor 14:25; 1 Pet 3:4). In this case it refers to the latter, as the following statement explains: **and circumcision is circumcision of the heart, by the Spirit, not by the written code.**

"The heart" refers to the soul or spirit, the inner man. "By the Spirit" probably refers to the Holy Spirit (as in the NIV), not the human spirit. There is no reason for Paul to mention the human spirit as the locus of this spiritual circumcision since he has already specified this as the heart, which is the same as the human spirit. Circumcision "by the written code" (literally, "by the letter") means physical circumcision in obedience to the commands of the law.

The distinction between external circumcision as the sign of membership in the covenant people, and inward circumcision as that which makes the individual acceptable to God, is found both in the Law of Moses and in the prophets (Deut 10:16; Lev 26:41; Jer 4:4; 9:25-26; Ezek 44:7; see Acts 7:51). There was no inherent connection between the outward and the inward forms of circumcision. Physical circumcision was a prominent and familiar phenomenon in Jewish experience; thus Moses and the prophets found it to be a convenient and appropriate analogy for the inward change God required for acceptance by him. The relation between the two is purely illustrative, and referring to this inward change as "circumcision" is situational and incidental (❂I:221).

True circumcision in the Messianic age, in fulfillment of Deut 30:6, includes the working of the Holy Spirit upon our hearts. Since Paul is speaking from the perspective of the Messianic age, he describes this inner circumcision as it takes place now, not as it occurred in the OT era. How does the working of the Spirit make the inner circumcision different in the NT age? On the one hand, it does *not* change the requirement for the individual to circumcise his own heart (as in Deut 10:16; Jer 4:4) by surrendering his own will to God in faith and repentance. The Holy Spirit has always been indirectly involved in this human decision as he prods the heart through the inspired Word of God, but the individual must still make the decision for himself. This is nothing new for our time.

On the other hand, the Holy Spirit does add a new element to this spiritual circumcision, a work of salvation unique to the Messianic age. We call it the new birth (John 3:3,5), regeneration (Titus 3:5), and resurrection from spiritual death (Col 2:12-13). This is an inward change worked directly upon our hearts (see Col 2:11), helping us to cut our ties with sin and to obey God's will from the heart out. (This will be discussed further under chapter 6 below.)

Such a man's praise is not from men, but from God. The true Jew's praise is not from men, because other human beings cannot see the heart, where the true circumcision occurs. Sometimes in our fallible evaluations of others based on externals, we praise or think highly of some individuals whose hearts warrant otherwise. Also, sometimes we ignore or think little of someone whose heart makes him a force for God. It is a comfort to know that the infallible God, who is greater than our hearts and knows all things (1 John 3:20), is able to discern and praise the true Jew, both now and in the final judgment (2:16) (❖ I:222-224).

F. Such Equal Treatment of Jews and Gentiles Does Not Nullify But Rather Magnifies God's Righteousness (3:1-8)

This paragraph answers anticipated misunderstandings and objections especially from Jewish readers, objections growing out of the things said about the Jews in chapter 2, especially in vv. 25-29. Here Paul returns to a modified diatribe style, posing questions and disposing of them with answers that are emphatic and to the point. They are questions Paul (a former Pharisee) knows are bound to arise, or which perhaps have already been "flung at him" in earlier face-to-face discussions with his former brethren (Stott, 95).

The discussion begins with a question about the role of the Jews in God's plan (vv. 1-2), then quickly moves on to the issue of the character of God himself (vv. 3-4). The thought is that what Paul says about the Jews in chapter 2 seems to nullify the apparent Jewish privilege and exclusiveness enjoyed since Abraham's day, and this in turn calls into question the truthfulness and faithfulness of God. Paul's response leads to a series of somewhat frivolous questions which may be interpreted as one last desperate attempt at Jewish self-justification (vv. 5-8).

Paul deals with these issues very briefly, knowing that he will return to them in more detail in chapters 9-11.

3:1 What advantage, then, is there in being a Jew, or what value is there in circumcision? The protester's thought is this: "If being a Jew gives us no advantage over the Gentiles on Judgment Day, then what's the big deal about being a Jew at all? Is he just now changing his mind about the Jews? Is he going back on his word? What's the use of being a Jew, then?"

3:2 Paul's answer is brief: **Much in every way! First of all, they have been entrusted with the very words of God.** The Jews' basic problem was the assumption that their election to God's service gave them a kind of automatic pass to heaven. Chapter 2 shows that this was false. But here Paul explains that even though this was not the case, there were many great and glorious privileges shared by every person born into Abraham's covenant family, whether he will ultimately be saved or not. The Jews' advantage is "much in many a way" (Lard, 101).

How are we to understand "first of all"? Ordinarily the word "first" (πρῶτον, *prōton*) indicates the first of a series of events or the first item in a longer list, leading us to expect other items to follow. This suggests that Paul does intend to present a longer series of advantages, but decides not to list them at this point. He waits instead until 9:4-5.

The one advantage mentioned here is that the Jews "have been entrusted with the very words of God." It is important in this context to stress this point, even if reference to the others can be delayed until later. This is because of what Paul has just said about the Law of Moses in chapter 2, namely, that mere possession of this specially revealed law was no basis for any Jew's personal salvation. Does this mean that the Jews' possession of God's special revelation was a trivial and inconsequential thing? No! On the contrary, it is a unique and glorious privilege, and one that is appropriately emphasized at this juncture.

What are the "very words of God" with which the Jews were entrusted? The Greek term is λόγιον, (*logion*), used here in the plural with the definite article. (See also Acts 7:38; Heb 5:12; 1 Pet 4:11.) In classical Greek this term was used for divine utterances, or oracles supposedly spoken by the gods through their inspired messengers. This is surely the sense in which Paul is using it here to represent the inspired utterances of the true God. It is variously translated as "the oracles of God" (KJV, NEB, NASB, NRSV), "the words of God" (NAB), and "God's messages" (Phillips). It is basically equivalent to *ho logos tou theou*, "the word of God," and occurs in this sense often in the LXX, especially in Ps 119. The NIV translation is excellent. It is proper to understand it as referring to the entire written OT, the "Holy Scriptures" (1:2) as possessed by the Jews.

That *ta logia tou theou* is referring to the written OT is shown by Paul's assertion that these oracles were "entrusted" into the care of the Jews. Murray rightly says, "It is as Scripture that these oracles were committed to the Jews; only in this form could the *Jews* be said to have been *entrusted* with them" (I:93). They were the guardians or custodians of God's special revelation in written form.

Being the chosen stewards of the oracles of God gave the Jews a privilege and an advantage that far surpassed anything enjoyed by the Gentiles, who knew the Creator and his law through general revelation only. (See Deut 4:8;

Ps 147:19-20.) Because they had his special revelation also, the Jews knew God not just as Creator, Lawgiver, and Judge, but also as a loving Savior. They knew not only his law, but also his grace; and they had the blessed opportunity to believe in his promise of forgiveness.

Of special importance is the fact that the Jews knew God's intention to send a Messiah, a Redeemer. They possessed the many predictive prophecies of his coming, and they nurtured the hope for his appearing. Thus those who happened to be living at the time of his coming would be the first to know him and to have the opportunity to believe in him and receive his salvation (1:16). Who could ask for greater advantages than these?

3:3 But [w]hat if some did not have faith? Will their lack of faith nullify God's faithfulness? These questions reflect the fact that many if not most Jews did not in fact put their saving faith in God's gracious promises in Old Covenant times, and did not believe in their Messiah when he came. Some did have faith (and thus were true Jews in terms of 2:29), but most did not (❖I:227).

The point is that the Jews through their stewardship of the *logia* of God had God's covenant promises all along, but many of them habitually, generation after generation, refused to put their heart's trust in these promises. Then when the prophecies and promises of the Messiah were fulfilled in Jesus Christ, many of Paul's Jewish contemporaries refused to believe in him.

This reality of Jewish unbelief raises the question or possible objection concerning God's faithfulness. Does the unbelief of some Jews mean that God's covenant purposes have failed? Does God's condemnation of the Jews who do not believe (strongly implied in the preceding chapters, especially in 1:5,16; 2:28-29) mean that he is breaking his promise to them and thus proving to be unfaithful?

The word for God's "faithfulness" is πίστις (*pistis*), which in reference to human beings can mean either faith or faithfulness. Since there is no legitimate sense in which God can be said to have faith, it is properly understood here as faithfulness. The word for "nullify" has the meaning of "make ineffective, render powerless" (see 3:31; 4:14; 6:6).

The wording of Paul's question indicates that he expects a negative answer: "The unbelief of some Jews does not mean that God is unfaithful, does it?" Thus even before he gives his strong negative reply in v. 4, he shows what the answer will be.

3:4 Is God unfaithful? Not at all! This is Paul's first use of the strong negative expression, μὴ γένοιτο, (*mē genoito*), literally, "May it not be!" It is usually translated with a strong English colloquialism, as in the NIV. This is an emphatic "No!" answer to the preceding question.

Let God be true, and every man a liar. We take this to mean, "Let it become evident or obvious that God is always true" (Lard, 102), or "Let God be recognized as true." God is always reliable, faithful, and true to his word. He always keeps his promises, both for blessing and condemnation. Because of his very nature he cannot lie (Titus 1:2).

The NIV connects this clause to the next with the simple copulative, "and." This does not properly reflect the stated contrast. Instead it should read "though" (NASB), "although" (NRSV), "even though," or "even if." The idea is that we should always acknowledge that God is true, even if every human being turns out to be a liar (see Ps 116:11).

Paul then quotes the second half of Ps 51:4, following the Septuagint: **As it is written: "So that you may be proved right when you speak and prevail when you judge."** In the Psalm this statement follows David's confession of his sin with Bathsheba. He is saying that the purpose of his confession is to prove that the sentence of condemnation God pronounced upon him (2 Sam 12:9-14) is justified (Hendriksen, I:111-112; Moo, 187, n. 50).

The word for "proved true" is δικαιόω (*dikaioō*), usually translated "justified" (NASB) and a key word in the doctrine of salvation. Its use in this verse helps establish its precise meaning as "declared righteous" rather than "made righteous," since we cannot *make* God righteous though we can acknowledge and declare him to be righteous (see the parallel in Luke 7:29). "When you speak" is literally "in your words." In the Psalm David is saying that God cannot be faulted for his words of condemnation against him. Paul gives the statement a more general application, saying that *whenever* God speaks, he will be proved right and his words will be found true.

The last line in the verse is difficult. It is likely that neither the NIV nor the NASB get it quite right. The verb should be understood in the Middle voice as meaning both that God always prevails when he brings suit against another, as in the case of David; and he always prevails when someone brings suit against him, as his Jewish accusers are doing in this paragraph. As Bruce says (96), God always wins his case when he enters into judgment (❧I:229-230).

Paul's principal and specific application is that God's promises to Israel will be fulfilled even if every individual Jew is unfaithful to God. Even if every Jew rejects God and is condemned to hell, God will still be faithful and his covenant will be fulfilled. This is so because God's covenant purpose for Israel did not guarantee the salvation of individual Jews. The basic covenant promise was not to individuals as such, but to Israel as a *nation*. The promise was not that all Jews would be saved, but that through the nation the *Messiah* would come. God promised to bless and preserve the nation as a nation *until* the Messiah came, but not beyond that. (See *GRe*, 391-395.) This is exactly what he did, and thus he was true to his word and covenant in every way.

3:5 Beginning in this verse Paul sets forth and replies to several anticipated objections to or false inferences from his point in 3:3-4, speaking from the standpoint of the Jewish objectors. Here is the first objection: **But if our unrighteousness brings out God's righteousness more clearly, what shall we say?**

That God is unjust in bringing his wrath on us? "Our unrighteousness" is the Jews' unbelief (v. 3), though the point would apply in principle to the sin and unbelief of all men (see 1:18). "God's righteousness" in this case is not the gift of righteousness of which 1:17 speaks, but God's own righteous character in contrast with the unrighteous character of sinners. To say that God is righteous means that his deeds are always consistent with his nature and his words (*GRe*, 194-196). This includes much more than his faithfulness to his covenant promises, and is not limited to his promises to bless and deliver his people. It also means God is true to his holy nature and to the ensuing necessity for punishing unbelievers.

The objector suggests that our unrighteousness "brings out more clearly" God's righteousness. This is an implication from v. 4a, "Let God be true, and every man a liar." The idea is that every sin of man forms a dark background upon which the corresponding divine virtue shines forth in contrasting brilliance and glory. This is definitely true, but "what shall we say" about it? That is, what conclusions might we draw from this? The false inference suggested by the Jewish objector is this: "If our sin magnifies God's righteousness, this is to his advantage and glory, and thus he really ought to reward us rather than condemn us. And if this is so, then God's condemnation of us is really unjust."

This question seems to reflect the Jews' refusal to come to grips with the point Paul made in chapter 2, that sinful Jews cannot be saved simply by being Jews, contrary to their misguided assumptions. It is another futile effort to avoid God's judgment, and one that has no merit whatsoever. This is shown by the way Paul words the question. He again uses the particle *mē*, anticipating a negative answer: "We really can't say that God is unrighteous when he inflicts wrath, can we?" This reflects the fact that all sinners know in their hearts that they really do deserve God's wrath.

(I am using a human argument.) Paul is here making it clear that he is not speaking for himself or for the Holy Spirit, and that he regards the question as the product of faulty human thinking.

3:6 Paul then gives his standard emphatic reply, **Certainly not!** (*mē genoito*), and words a brief reason for this answer: **If that were so, how could God judge the world?** What is his point here? One possibility is that he is stating a *reductio ad absurdum* argument. That is, if we grant the objection in the case of the Jews, we would have to grant it in the case of everybody ("the world"), since everyone else's sins also cause God's righteousness to stand out all the more. But this is absurd because we know there *will* be a judgment and that the wicked will be condemned. (See Lard, 104.)

A better understanding is that Paul is saying the question is absurd simply because "to impugn God's justice is to undercut his competence to judge" (Stott, 97). An unjust God is simply not worthy of judging the world. This is why the fact "that God who shall judge the world is just is a fundamental certainty of all theological thinking" (Cranfield, I:185). Abraham sums up this intuition: "Will not the Judge of all the earth do right?" (Gen 18:25; see Job 34:17). Indeed, if God were not just and righteous, why would he even *want* to judge the world? Thus the objection is worthless.

3:7 But the objector persists: **Someone might argue, "If my falsehood enhances God's truthfulness and so increases his glory, why am I still condemned as a sinner?"** This is basically a restatement of the objection in v. 5, as if the debater just refuses to give up on this point, i.e., "How can it be fair for a man to be blamed for his falsehood, when it has actually redounded to God's glory?" (Cranfield, I:185).

3:8 Verse 8 asks another question: **Why not say . . . "Let us do evil that good may result"?** It is best (❂I:232) to take this as Paul's own question, in which he states the logical yet absurd outcome of both v. 5 and v. 7. Thus the objection in v. 7 does have a response, and this is it (Cranfield, I:187). The force of the question is this: "Well, if that [v. 7] is the case, then we might just as well say, 'Let us do evil that good may result' — which we all know is absolutely ridiculous." Again, the question begins with the particle *mē*, which implies a negative answer.

This question is basically a statement of the principle that "the end justifies the means." This verse is a repudiation of that principle.

Paul notes parenthetically that he himself was being accused of teaching this lie: **as we are being slanderously reported as saying and as some claim that we say . . . .** A clear presentation of the gospel of grace sounds so radical to most people that they may indeed assume it implies a kind of indifference to obedience. Here Paul calls this accusation slander or blasphemy. In chapter 6 he discusses this inference in more detail and clearly shows it is not validly derived from the gospel.

Their condemnation is deserved. Of whom is Paul speaking? Perhaps those (the "some") who are slandering him, but more likely those who are pressing the absurd objection voiced in vv. 5 and 7 (Murray, I:98). It is not enough that Paul ridicules their view by showing its logical yet absurd end; now he turns his indignation upon the objectors themselves.

This is a fitting conclusion to this subsection (2:1-3:8). In chapter 2 Paul declares that the Jews are without excuse before God. They assumed their possession and knowledge of the Law of Moses, plus their physical descent from Abraham marked by circumcision, would be sufficient to save them in the final judgment. Paul says no: God will not be partial to the Jews. Anyone counting on law as his mode of salvation can be saved only by perfect obedience, and the Jews are *sinners* like everyone else. Therefore under law they stand *condemned* like everyone else. Their convoluted arguments (3:1-7) do nothing to alter this judgment. If anything, such twisted thinking only serves to demonstrate the fact that their condemnation is quite deserved. As Dunn paraphrases this last statement, "They deserve what's coming to them" (I:137).

III. 3:9-20 — UNIVERSAL SINFULNESS AND HOPELESSNESS UNDER LAW

Paul's main point in the first main section of Romans is to show that no one can be saved by law or law-keeping. Only a perfect person can hope to be accepted by God under the law system. The sad fact is that no such person exists. Every person is a law-breaker and is thus without hope under law.

In the first two main points of this section Paul has dealt with the two alleged exceptions to this rule: the Gentiles, or those without special revelation (1:18-32); and the Jews, or those who do have special revelation (2:1-3:8). Now in this final point (3:9-20) he pulls all of this together and draws his intended conclusion. He reaffirms the reality of universal sinfulness (v. 9), provides OT confirmation of it (vv. 10-18), and stresses the impotence of law as the result of it (vv. 19-20).

3:9 What shall we conclude then? Literally, "What then?" The NIV rightly takes this short phrase as introducing the conclusion of this section. **Are we any better? Not at all!** This brief passage of three Greek words is very difficult and is open to several interpretations (❂I:234-235). The most likely meaning is something like this: "Do we Jews have any advantage, then, in comparison with the Gentiles? No!" As the next sentence shows, in this whole section Paul has been using the two categories of Jews and Gentiles as inclusive of the entire human race. Of these two groups, Paul naturally identifies himself with the former. Also, a comparison seems to be in view, i.e., between the two groups. Thus: "Are we Jews any better off than the Gentiles?"

This query is stimulated by 3:1-2, where Paul affirms that the Jews have a great advantage over the Gentiles, especially in their possession of the oracles of God. Just so no one will misunderstand, Paul asks this question in v. 9 so that he can reemphasize the point made in chapter 2. That is, no matter what privileges the Jews may have enjoyed in relation to their unique role as the people through whom the Messiah would come, in reference to sin and judgment and their standing before God, they have no advantage whatsoever.

Paul's next sentence shows that this is the main point: **We have already made the charge that Jews and Gentiles alike are all under sin.** With reference to sin and guilt the Jews are on the same level as the Gentiles. Paul has already made this charge against the Gentiles in 1:18-32 and against the Jews in 2:1-29.

"Made the charge" is a legal term that refers to the act of filing charges against someone, or accusing them before a court of law. He has charged both Jews and Greeks (used in the sense of non-Jews, or Gentiles) of being "under sin." To be "under sin" is more than just committing sins; it is more than just being a sinner. It means to be under the power and dominion of sin. Sin is thus represented as a slave master; see 6:16-22.

The main point of this summary statement is the emphasis on *universality*. Paul says "*both* Jews and Gentiles are *all* under sin," with no exceptions. The significance of this universality of sin is seen in 3:19-20.

3:10 In v. 9 Paul says he has "made the charge" that all are under sin. Now in vv. 10-18 he offers proof of this charge in the form of citations from Scripture: **As it is written**. These words introduce a "quotation-chain" (Hendriksen, I:121) of fourteen short and sharp statements from several places in the OT (❂I:236). Paul applies them to all people in general. It is especially significant that he applies them to the *Jews* as well as to the Gentiles (❂I:236).

"There is no one righteous, not even one . . . ." (From Eccl 7:20; see Ps 14:1.) Here the word "righteous" (δίκαιος, *dikaios*) is used in its basic sense of "conforming to a norm." The norm to which every human being must conform is the law of God, in whatever form it is available and relevant to him. This text says that *no one* is righteous; no one has conformed to this norm; everyone has broken God's law; everyone has sinned (3:23). No one is righteous in an absolute sense, which is the only way one could be saved by law keeping. Thus the need for the gift of righteousness revealed and offered in the gospel (1:17).

3:11 "there is no one who understands . . . ." (From Ps 14:2; 53:2.) No creature can have infinite knowledge and know all possible truth about God. However, God gives every human being sufficient knowledge of himself and his law, even through general revelation (1:18-21; 2:14-15). This is the kind of understanding to which this texts refers. The problem is a hardness of heart (Eph 4:18) that tends to suppress the truth in favor of foolish and futile speculations (1:18,21), and exchange truth for lies (1:25). This is a universal problem; everyone is guilty of it to some degree.

There is **"no one who seeks God."** (From Ps 14:2; 53:2.) Since "seeking for God" presupposes a state of separation from God, it is something only sinners need to do. But the sinner's guilt causes him to run away from God (v. 12) and attempt to hide from him (Gen 3:8; Rev 6:15-17). In the light of 1:21-25, we understand that even the many false religions of the world are not efforts to *seek* God, but efforts to *escape* from him (MacArthur, I:184).

3:12 "All have turned away" from God. (From Ps 14:3; 53:3.) As previously mentioned, it is characteristic of sinners to turn *from* God rather than toward him. The verb (ἐκκλίνω, *ekklinō*) means to avoid or to deliberately turn away, not just to accidentally lose one's way (Morris, 167). See 16:17; 1 Pet 3:11. "We all, like sheep, have gone astray, each of us has turned to his own way" (Isa 53:6).

"they have together become worthless . . . ." (From Ps 14:3; 53:3.) As sinners, all have become unprofitable or useless. The Greek word translates a Hebrew word used to describe milk that has turned sour and thus cannot be used for its intended purpose. Likewise sinners have lost their usefulness and cannot fulfill their intended purpose of bringing glory to God.

"**there is no one who does good, not even one . . . .**" (From Ps 14:1,3; 53:1,3.) "Good" here refers to acts of obedience to God and acts of kindness toward one's fellow men. This does not mean that no one *ever* does acts of goodness; it means that no one *always* does them. The universality of this indictment is underscored by the addition of "not even one."

3:13 "Their throats are open graves . . . ." (From Ps 5:9.) Paul now begins to cite OT verses that refer to specific representative sins as illustrations of the universal sinfulness of man. This citation is the first of four that focus on "the sinfulness of human speech" (Moo, 203). A grave contains the rotting and putrid remains of a corpse; when it is opened, it emits a horrible stench. The sinner's throat (λάρυγξ, *larynx*) is like this grave. When he opens it to speak, all sorts of ugly, rotten, obscene words pour forth (see Eph 4:29). This follows Jesus' specific teaching in Matt 12:34: "Out of the overflow of the heart the mouth speaks" (see Matt 12:35; 15:18-20). Nothing reveals the state of the heart more consistently than how a person talks. A rotten heart produces rotten speech.

"**their tongues practice deceit.**" (From Ps 5:9.) This reads "They smoothed their tongues" in the Hebrew, says Robertson (345). That is, their speech is filled with smooth, oily talk, "the deceptive flatteries of those who intend evil" (Moo, 204). In Scripture the tongue is commonly linked with speech and especially with lying and evil talk (see Prov 6:17; 12:19; Micah 6:12; Jas 1:26; 3:1-12).

"**The poison of vipers is on their lips.**" (From Ps 140:3.) Understanding this to refer to the Egyptian cobra, Robertson says, "The poison of the asp lies in a bag under the lips" (345). This vivid analogy refers to those who use their words to destroy others, e.g., through lies, false accusations, slander, or gossip. Such words are like the poisonous venom of a snake.

3:14 "Their mouths are full of cursing and bitterness." (From Ps 10:7.) To curse someone is to verbally call for harm to befall him. It usually springs from a heart that is full of bitterness or hostility or anger toward that person. The sinner's heart is "full of" such bitter curses, i.e., it is not just an exception but is typical of his lifestyle in general (❷ I:238).

3:15 "Their feet are swift to shed blood . . . ." (From Isa 59:7.) This and the next two citations stress sinners' evil deeds, even to the point of shedding blood in violent assault and murder. Here the focus shifts from the organs of speech to the feet, the means of mobility by which a person is able to put his purposes into action. Being "swift" to shed blood suggests that such evil is carried out with eagerness and perverse delight.

3:16 "ruin and misery mark their ways . . . ." (From Isa 59:7.) This highlights the depravity of the sinner's heart by describing the wreckage he leaves in his wake. He pursues his selfish desires and purposes with no concern for others and without caring how he may be harming them (❂I:239). "Ruin" describes the shattered wreckage itself; "misery" refers to the pain and suffering experienced by those over whom the sinner has run roughshod.

3:17 "and the way of peace they do not know." (From Isa 59:8.) In line with the previous citations, Paul seems to be talking about peace and harmony among men, or human beings getting along with each other. Living in peace is something sinners do not know how to do, says Paul.

3:18 "There is no fear of God before their eyes." (From Ps 36:1.) The "fear of God" in the sense of reverence and awe toward the Creator should be the most fundamental attitude of the human heart. The "fear of God" in the sense of terror and dread before the Lawgiver and Judge should be the most immediate effect of sin upon the sinner's heart. But this citation says the sinner is characteristically devoid of both. (On the fear of God, see *GC*, 443-467.)

To say that there is no fear of God before a man's eyes, as Cranfield points out, "is a figurative way of saying that the fear of God has no part in directing his life, that God is left out of his reckoning, that he is a practical, whether or not he is a theoretical, atheist" (I:195).

This picture of mankind's depravity is very dark and somber indeed. Two cautions must be noted, however: 1) this passage does not mean that all people are *equally* guilty of the vices named here, and 2) there is no support here for the doctrine of *total* depravity (❂I:240).

3:19 Now we know that whatever the law says, it says to those who are under the law . . . . This verse and the next are crucial, since they draw the conclusion toward which the whole first section has been pointing. Also, a right understanding of this first half of v. 19 is crucial for a proper understanding of the two verses as a whole.

"We know" does not specify a particular group; it is simply a way of introducing an item of common knowledge, a generally accepted principle. It is equivalent to "everybody knows." In this context it means "Everyone who is spiritually informed knows."

What is it that everybody knows? That whatever "the law" says is relevant only to those who are subject to that law. This is a general principle and applies to every sort of jurisdiction, large or small.

What law or jurisdiction does Paul have in mind here? Many will immediately think of the Law of Moses, since Paul is especially concerned to demonstrate the sinfulness of the Jews. But most commentators take him to mean the OT in general, since he has just quoted from the wisdom literature and the prophets. Indeed, the same phrase (without the definite article) is used in 2:12 to refer to the special revelation given to the Jews.

In my opinion, though, the term "law" in this verse and the next has an even broader scope than this. Because of the absolute, universal language used in these two verses, I believe it refers to God's law in a very general sense, including (1) the demands and judgments of the OT as it speaks to the Jews; (2) the requirements of the "work of the law" written on the hearts of all, including the Gentiles; and (3) the requirements for holy living revealed in the NT Scriptures. This view is supported by the contrasting phrase in 3:21, "apart from law." There "law" cannot be equated with either the Mosaic Law or the OT as such, since it is distinguished from "the Law and the Prophets" (i.e., the OT).

What, then, does it mean to be "under the law"? The phrase is actually ἐν νόμῳ, (*en nomō*, see 2:12), which means "in the law, within the law, within the sphere of the law." A similar phrase is ὑπο νόμον, (*hypo nomon*), literally "under the law" (6:14-15; 1 Cor 9:20; Gal 3:23; 4:4-5,21; 5:18). Only the context of each passage can determine if *nomos* means the OT law specifically or God's law more generally. Here, as we have seen, it means the latter. To be "within the sphere of God's law" in 3:19 basically means first of all to be subject to its commands and penalties. But more significantly it means to be under the *system* of law as a standard of judgment and a means of being right with God.

What group of people is meant, then, by "those who are under the law"? Since most interpreters say "law" here means the OT, they say Paul is referring only to the Jews. Murray (I:106-107) and Hendriksen (I:124) agree that "law" means the OT, but they declare that it applies to both Jews *and* Gentiles. This application is correct, but "law" here is God's law in any form (in the heart, in the OT, in the NT). Thus "those who are under the law" are indeed both Jews and Gentiles, or all people in general.

Thus "whatever the law says" is addressed to all. Exactly what does the law say to us? It is taken for granted that it speaks God's will in the form of commandments. It has been established that the law also says that commandment-breakers are worthy of death (1:32). Those who break the commandments will suffer the penalty of the law; those who keep the commandments will escape that penalty (2:7-10). In this immediate context Paul refers to the point made by the series of quotations in vv. 10-18, i.e., the law of God says that everyone – EVERYONE – is a sinner.

This is relevant to the Jews, to be sure, since they considered themselves as exceptions to the rule that no one can be saved by law. But they are not the only ones who need convincing on this point. The whole world has the tendency to view salvation in terms of making oneself acceptable to God by one's own efforts (*GRe*, ch. 3). Thus this passage speaks out "against every attempt at self-salvation" (Stott, 104).

. . . so that every mouth may be silenced and the whole world held accountable to God. The word for "so that" is ἵνα (*hina*), which expresses purpose but also result. The reason why God's law stresses the reality of universal sinfulness is "so that every mouth may be silenced." The word for "silenced" evokes a courtroom scene in which the accused defendant is unable to respond to the charges brought against him (Cranfield I:196-197). See Ps 63:11; 107:42.

"*Every* mouth" means every individual, whether Jew or Gentile. Paul has already shown that the Gentiles (those with general revelation only) are "without excuse" (1:20), and that the Jews (those with special revelation also) are also "without excuse" (2:1). I.e., every mouth is *silenced*. The same universal language is used in the next clause: the "whole world," without exception.

"Held accountable" translates ὑπόδικος, (*hypodikos*), used only here in the NT. "Accountable" is really too weak a translation, since it does not necessarily imply guilt. But *hypodikos* refers to someone who *has* done something wrong and has been brought before the court to answer for his guilt. (See Maurer, "ὑπόδικος," 557-558.)

The law reveals that all are accountable "to God" or guilty "before God" (dative case). In God's court, he is both the accuser (the One wronged) and the judge (Moo, 205).

All in all, Paul represents all humanity as sinners under the law who are standing in a hopelessly terrifying situation. Why does he make this point? In order to show the universal need for grace, for the gift of God's righteousness.

3:20 Therefore no one will be declared righteous in his sight by observing the law . . . . Here Paul draws the conclusion toward which this whole section has been pointing: the impotence of the law as a way of being right with God. The word "therefore" (διότι, *dioti*) refers back not just to v. 19 but to the whole section, 1:18–3:19. "Therefore," given what has been established in this section as a whole, it is plain that "no one will be declared righteous in his sight by observing the law." The only way to be saved by law-keeping is through perfect obedience, but all have sinned.

The universal language in v. 19 is continued; "no one" leaves room for no exceptions. The Greek actually says "no flesh," a Hebraic way of saying "no human being."

"Declared righteous" is from δικαιόω (*dikaioō*), which is the word usually translated "justified" (see 2:13; 3:4). It is a courtroom term and thus follows naturally upon the previous verse. It refers to the judge's decision to drop the charges, and his declaration that the accused person may go free without suffering any penalty. In other words, it means to be declared righteous before the law. It does not mean "to make righteous," nor does it necessarily imply that the person *is* righteous. It simply means that the person is considered and declared to be right with the law.

"Observing the law" is a poor translation of the important expression "works of law" (ἔργων νόμου, *ergōn nomou*). The word "law" should not be capitalized here, as if it means the Mosaic Law. As in the previous verse it means God's law in general, in all its forms. "Works of law" is also used in 3:28, another key verse in Romans. There is no article before either "works" or "law" in either verse. This expression refers to *all* responses to whatever commandments of God's law apply to any given person. Efforts to limit this phrase to the works required by the Law of Moses only, or to OT commandments only (as in Dunn, I:154-159), are seriously misguided and are a grave hindrance to a right understanding of Paul's main point in Romans and of grace in general. The same is true of efforts to limit this phrase to works done from wrong motives (as in Barrett, 70).

Paul's point is that *no one* will be declared right with God on the basis of his obedience to God's commands. This would require absolute perfection, which no one has achieved or will achieve. (See Moo, 209-210; Cranfield, I:198.) The universal fact of sin absolutely rules out the law system as a way of justification. In theory such justification is possible, as 2:13 declares; but in reality it never occurs, as this verse affirms.

"Will be declared righteous [justified]" is future tense but does not refer just to some specific future event such as the final judgment. It is stated rather as a general principle. Because of sin no one will *ever* be justified before God on the basis of his own righteousness or works. Once sin enters a person's life, henceforward that door will be closed forever. See Murray, I:107.

. . . rather, through the law we become conscious of sin. "Rather" is not a good translation of the transitional word γάρ (*gar*), which means "for" or "because." The latter well suits Paul's meaning here. No one will be justified by works of law because the law reveals all of us to be sinners. The very law by which many assume they will be vindicated will actually be the instrument of their condemnation.

The point is that we need to use God's law for something that it can do rather than try to use it for something it can never do, which is to make any sinner right with God. It has other proper functions, to be sure, but one thing the law can do is show us how sinful we are and thus how much we need God's gift of righteousness through grace.

All in all the contents of this first main section of Romans are anything but *gospel*. From beginning (1:18) to end (3:20), the message is one long dirge of sin, wrath, and judgment. The essence of this section is as Hendriksen sums it up: "Man is doomed, doomed, doomed. His condition is one of thorough hopelessness and despair. And the law, with its demand of nothing less than moral and spiritual *perfection* . . . creates in him a dreadful, mortifying sense of sin; hence, a presentiment of doom, total and everlasting" (I:125).

"Good news"? Hardly. But the fact is that self-righteous, complacent people must be convinced of their desperate and hopeless plight under law before they can acknowledge their need for grace. Thus this section is a necessary prelude to the one that follows, which presents us with the way of *grace* as God's marvelous and powerful alternative to the impotent and futile way of law.

3:21–5:21 – PART TWO
THE ALL-SUFFICIENCY OF
GRACE AS A WAY OF SALVATION

The first main section of Romans demonstrates the seriousness of the human predicament under law. A person *could* be saved under the law system *if* he obeyed God's law perfectly. But 1:18–3:20 shows conclusively that all have sinned; therefore no one can be justified by obedience to law. For those who remain under law, the holy side of God's nature, the "consuming fire" of his wrath (Heb 12:29), will prevail in the end.

But God is not only a consuming fire; he is also love (1 John 4:8); and out of his boundless love he has provided another way or system of salvation, the way of *grace*. Whereas the rules of the law system allow for the justification only of the sinless, the grace system allows God to justify the wicked (4:5). Indeed, it is the *only* way a sinner can be justified.

The purpose of this second main section of Romans (3:21–5:21) is thus to set forth the essence of grace as a way of salvation, a way provided by the love of God as an alternative to law. Saving grace is the free, unmerited gift of salvation to sinners who have no claim on it and who in fact deserve its opposite. It is "favor bestowed when wrath is owed" (*GRe*, 375-377).

In reference to salvation from sin the term "grace" is used in several ways. First, grace is an attribute of the divine nature. It is the way God's love responds to sin. (Just as wrath is how God's *holiness* responds to sin.) It is his willingness and desire to accept us in spite of our sin. It is his readiness to forgive (Ps 86:5) and his desire to "graciously give us all things" (8:32) — the very things we have forfeited through our sin. In his love he wants us back, even though we have sinned against him. This is the heart of God's nature as a gracious God.

Second, the term "grace" is used for the gift of salvation itself. The content of this gift of grace is actually a "double cure," which is God's remedy for the "double trouble" caused by sin. Sin affects the sinner externally or objectively, causing the legal problem of guilt and subjecting him to the penalty of the law. It also affects the sinner internally or subjectively, causing the heart to become evil, weak, depraved, and spiritually sick. The gift of grace includes justification or forgiveness of sins to resolve the former; it includes regeneration and sanctification to overcome the latter. The former is accomplished through the power of the redeeming blood of Christ; the latter is effected through the power of the indwelling Holy Spirit. In general this section of Romans deals with the former, while the next section (6:1-8:39) deals with the latter.

Finally the term "grace" is used for the system of salvation given by God as the alternative to law. "You are not under law [as a way of salvation], but under grace [as a way of salvation]" (6:14). The contrast between law and grace is striking; they are in fact opposites. In the introduction to 1:18–3:20 the rules of the law system were stated thus:

> KEEP THE COMMANDMENTS, AND
> (THEREFORE) ESCAPE THE PENALTY.
>
> BREAK THE COMMANDMENTS, AND
> (THEREFORE) SUFFER THE PENALTY.

But the rules of the grace system, i.e., the way to be "right with God" in terms of grace, may be stated as follows:

> KEEP THE COMMANDMENTS, BUT SUFFER THE PENALTY.
>
> BREAK THE COMMANDMENTS, BUT ESCAPE THE PENALTY.

Whereas the rules of the law system are set forth in 2:7-10, the rules of the grace system are stated succinctly in 2 Cor 5:21, "God made him who had no sin to be sin for us, so that in him we might become the righteousness of God."

Under the law system a person is treated with utter fairness; he gets exactly what he deserves. But the grace system is just the opposite. It is neither fair nor just; under grace a person gets the very opposite of what he deserves. The first half of the grace formula, of course, applies only to Jesus Christ, since he is the only one who will ever keep the commandments with sinless perfection. He "had no sin." But at the same time he suffered the penalty; it was God's plan for him "to be sin for us," and in our place to suffer the divine wrath we deserve because of our sin. This was the exact opposite of what he deserved.

This is what makes the second half of the grace formula possible, namely, the part that applies to us. Under the grace system we who have broken the commandments also receive the very opposite of what we deserve. Through our faith in Jesus "the righteousness of God" — Jesus' payment of the penalty for sin in our place — is counted as our own, enabling us to escape the penalty we deserve.

This grace system, God's wonderful alternative to law, is the main focus of this section of Romans, with special attention being given to the first part of the double cure, or justification. The rest of chapter 3 (vv. 21-31) is the actual explanation of grace as a way of salvation. Chapter 4 provides OT confirmation, with Abraham being set forth as a paradigm of grace. Chapter 5 deals with the most immediate practical result of a right understanding of grace, namely, assurance of salvation. The first part (vv. 1-11) explains the relation between justification by faith and assurance; the latter part (vv. 12-21) emphasizes the all-sufficiency of the death of Christ as the source of saving grace.

I. 3:21-31 — GRACE AS JUSTIFICATION BY CHRIST'S BLOOD THROUGH FAITH

Paul has just declared that the whole world has sinned and stands guilty before God (3:19). The fact of guilt raises the problem of justification. How can sinners be justified, or brought back into a right relationship with God and his law? Can a person work himself back into a proper relation with this law? Perhaps with a little extra effort, we can go "above and beyond the call of duty" and do enough good works to make up for our sins. Is this possible? No! In the parable of the unprofitable servant (Luke 17:7-10) Jesus teaches that every good work we can possibly do is already owed to God (required by his law) and therefore cannot be used to pay the debt incurred by our sin. There is no such thing as extra merit; this is why works of law cannot justify sinners.

What, then, can we do? How *can* we be justified, be counted righteous, be accepted by God, escape the wrath and condemnation we deserve? Does any provision of the law allow a sinner to go unpunished? Can we remain under law and still be justified? No! If we are to be justified, we must leave the framework of law and enter the sphere of grace. This subsection of Romans shows us what this means by explaining that sinners can be justified by the blood of Jesus Christ through their faith in him. We can be justified only by faith apart from works of law (3:28).

In establishing this point the Apostle Paul produces what Morris declares to be "possibly the most important single paragraph ever written" (173), i.e., 3:21-26 (❂ I:250).

A. Righteousness through Faith Is Now Fully Revealed (3:21-23)

3:21 Paul's first words in this section emphasize the contrast between the two ways of salvation: **But now a righteousness from God, apart from law, has been made known . . . .** Under law, salvation is based on perfect human righteousness. Herein lies the impotence of the law system; 1:18–3:20 has shown man's righteousness indeed to be "filthy rags" (Isa 64:6) and futile for justification. But under grace, salvation is based on the righteousness *of God*, the meaning of which was discussed fully under 1:17 above. Here, as in 1:17, it does not mean God's own personal righteousness, the attribute of his nature that requires him always to be faithful to himself. It is rather the gift of righteousness that God gives to sinners, on the basis of which he accepts them as righteous. Specifically, it is Christ's satisfaction of the law's requirement that sinners be punished, which he accomplished in our place, as our substitute. This righteousness is bestowed upon us as a gift. The NIV reflects this interpretation when it translates the simple genitive "of God" as "from God."

The gift of God's righteousness is directly related to justification. These words have the same Greek root (*dikai-*). "Righteousness" is δικαιοσύνη (*dikaiosynē*), and "justification" is δικαίωσις (*dikaiōsis*). "To justify" means to count righteous or declare righteous (see 2:13, and 3:24 below). To say that the righteousness of God has been made known is to say that the means by which God justifies sinners has been manifested.

In what way has this righteousness been "made known"? This is the same idea as 1:17, namely, that the righteousness of God has now been *revealed* in the gospel. This refers not just to the spoken message of the gospel, but primarily to the saving events upon which that message is based. "Made known" is perfect tense, referring to the decisive past events of the death and resurrection of Jesus Christ. See 3:26.

A key part of this sentence is the phrase "apart from law." "Apart from" is χωρίς (*chōris*), a preposition indicating distinct separation from something. "Law" is the law system or the law of God in general, not specifically the Law of Moses. Thus the phrase means "without relation to the law system, without any connection to law." See 3:28

Exactly what does this prepositional phrase modify? Some say it modifies the verb, "made known." I.e., while law can manifest God's righteousness in the sense of his personal purity and integrity, only the gospel can make known his righteousness in the sense of his gift to sinners. Thus it is revealed "apart from law." The other possibility is that it modifies "righteousness of God." I.e., the kind of divine righteousness on the basis of which sinners are justified is not a righteousness measured by law but one that is defined and established outside the law system. It can be understood only in relation to a totally different way of salvation, the way of grace. While both views are possible, the latter is preferred. (See Morris, 174; Murray, I:109-110.) This righteousness that is apart from law is God's gracious alternative to the unattainable righteousness that comes by works of law (3:20).

Paul says this righteousness of God that is apart from law has been made known "now." The main question here is whether this "now" has a logical or a temporal, chronological sense. If the former, it is just a rhetorical device meaning something like "on the other hand." If the latter, it is setting up a contrast between what was known in the OT era and what has been manifested "now," in this NT age, through the work of the Messiah. The divine grace-righteousness has been revealed here and now, in our time, in our day. See 3:26; Gal 4:4. This latter meaning seems to be the intended sense.

This does not mean that this way of salvation is only now just beginning, and is only now for the first time being applied. It does not mean that people were saved only by law up to this point, and that Christ introduced grace as a new and different way of salvation. Salvation through grace, by means of the gift of the righteousness of Christ, has always been the only possible way sinners could be saved and have been saved. If Adam was saved, he was saved thus, "apart from law." Paul's primary example of this way of salvation is Abraham (ch. 4), who predated even Moses. What has happened "now" is that this grace-righteousness has been *manifested* as never before in the substitutionary death of Jesus Christ. This is not the first knowledge of grace itself, but the first clear knowledge of the *basis* for it in the blood of Christ. (See Murray, I:108-109; Morris, 173.)

This does not mean that there was no knowledge of justification by faith and sacrificial sin-bearing prior to Christ's coming. Thus to preclude a possible misunderstanding Paul says this was something **to which the Law and the prophets testify.** See 1:2; 4:1-25. "Law" here means the Pentateuch; "the Law and the prophets" together represent the entire OT (❧I:253).

3:22 Here Paul further clarifies the nature of the righteousness that is apart from law: **This righteousness from God comes through faith in Jesus Christ to all who believe.** Here again the implied contrast is between law and grace as systems of salvation. Grace-righteousness is not given to sinners by works of law (v. 20), but "through faith in Jesus Christ." This is the same thought expressed in v. 28, that "a man is justified by faith apart from works of the Law" (NASB) (❧I:253).

As noted under 1:16, the faith by which sinners receive the gift of righteousness is not just a general faith in God's existence and providential care, but is a specific faith in the person and work of the Savior, Jesus Christ. In OT times, since Jesus was not yet known, the object of saving faith was God's gracious promise to forgive sins. Now that the Redeemer himself has come and has purchased us with his own blood (Acts 20:28), we cannot be saved unless our faith is specifically directed toward him.

The role of faith is asserted twice: "through faith . . . to all who believe." When Paul says "through [διά, *dia*] faith," he is designating faith as the necessary *means* by which the gift of God's righteousness is received by sinners. As such, faith is never to be understood as a meritorious act, or as something we do that in some way deserves to be rewarded by God. The source and basis of grace-righteousness is not our faith but the one toward whom it is directed, namely, Jesus Christ.

"To all who believe" is not just a repetition for emphasis. The stress here is not on the word "believe" but on "all." Perhaps the point once again is to erase all distinctions between Jews and Gentiles and to show that they have equal access to the gospel (1:16).

The rest of v. 22, **There is no difference**, goes better with v. 23 and along with that verse forms a parenthesis that sums up a main conclusion of 1:18–3:20. The NIV does not translate the particle γάρ (*gar*), meaning "for" or "because." This little word introduces the *reason* why the righteousness of God is available to everyone on the same terms, namely, because "there is no difference" in their starting point or their status before God: all have sinned.

3:23 for all have sinned and fall short of the glory of God . . . . This verse also begins with γάρ (*gar*), "for," explaining why there is no difference among human beings as to the manner of their salvation. *None* can be saved by law through works; *all* must be saved by grace through faith — because all have sinned, and grace through faith is the only possible way for sinners to be saved. Once a person has sinned even once, he has forfeited all possibility of salvation by law-righteousness (Jas 2:10).

Because the language is the same as 5:12, some say this is a reference to Adam's sin and to the idea that all sinned in Adam (e.g., Shedd, 76-77). Whether this is so or not, the main emphasis must be upon the personal sins of all people of accountable age. Following this closely upon the first main section (1:18-3:20), this verse surely refers to the "all" described in 3:9-20.

"Fall short" is a good translation of the second verb (ὑστερέω, *hystereō*). It means "to lack, to be deficient in, to come short of, to be wanting, to fall behind." It is present tense, which suggests that it refers to a condition and not to action (Murray, I:112). I.e., once a person has sinned, he is in the condition or state of being destitute of the glory of God.

The difficult part of this verse is determining what is meant by "the glory of God" in this context (on the glory of God, see *GC*, 446-452). It may mean the honor and praise God would give us if we lived perfectly before him. By sinning we become unworthy of such praise. It may also mean the glory of God's presence in the future eschatological kingdom, from which sinners are excluded. Or it may mean the reflected glory of God that creatures made in his image are supposed to display by imitating his perfect moral character. This glory is bedimmed by sin, as a light bulb controlled by a rheostat becomes dimmer and dimmer when turned down. Salvation reverses this process and in the last day completely restores us to this image and glory of God. I have a slight preference for the last view. This goes well with the context. Paul's point is that the fact of sin disqualifies us from being acceptable to God on the basis of our own personal righteousness; thus we stand in dire need of the righteousness that comes from God through faith (❖I:255).

B. Sinners Are Justified by the Blood of Christ (3:24-26)

These three verses, says Godet (149), form "the most important passage in the whole Epistle." Arguably, it is the most important in the whole Bible.

3:24 and are justified freely by his grace . . . . The Greek text here is difficult (❖I:256). Many take vv. 22b-23 as a parenthesis and connect the participle, "justified," back to "all who believe" in v. 22a (e.g., Murray, I:114; Hendriksen, I:129). This yields the quite valid thought that all who believe are thus justified freely by his grace. This is probably the way it should be understood. Because of the intervening parenthesis the participle can be translated as a main verb, thus: "Those who believe are justified freely by his grace."

Thus in this unusual way v. 24 introduces one of the most important of all doctrines, justification by grace. The verb has appeared already three times in Romans (2:13; 3:4,20), but this is its first use for the act of God by which sinners are saved through Christ's blood.

As stated under 3:21 above, justification and righteousness are closely related. "To justify" means "to declare righteous." It does not mean "to make righteous," contrary to the traditional Roman Catholic view. These two distinct definitions of justification are one of the key differences between Catholics and Protestants.

Justification is a legal or judicial term; it has to do with one's relation to the law (see 2:13). It is best understood as the declaration made by a judge once his final decision as to guilt or innocence has been made. When he justifies a defendant, the judge declares that he is in a right standing with the law. Some say it is equivalent to the judge declaring the defendant "not guilty"; I prefer to say it means that the judge declares, "No penalty for you!"

That this is the true meaning of justification is seen by the way the Bible uses it in legal contexts, and especially in contrast with condemnation (see Deut 25:1; Prov 17:15; Rom 8:33-34). When a judge condemns someone, that does not *make* the latter unrighteous or guilty; it is simply a *pronouncement* that he is guilty. Likewise when a judge justifies someone, this does not *make* him righteous; it only *declares* his righteousness, as in the literal rendering of Luke 7:29.

If anyone could live a perfect life before God, God would justify him on the basis of his own works of personal righteousness (2:13). Such a person would merit or deserve to be justified, and his justification would not be a salvation event (❊ I:257).

However, because all have sinned, this will never happen (3:20). Thus God has provided an alternative to justification by law; he offers to justify sinners "freely by his grace." That it is done "freely" means it is a free gift, totally undeserved, unmerited, and unearned. (See the use of this word in Matt 10:8; 2 Cor 11:7; 2 Thess 3:8; Rev 21:6; 22:17.) That it is "by his grace" is the very same idea repeated for emphasis. It is the very opposite of justification in accordance with law.

We are talking now about justification as a salvation concept, because it is the justification of *sinners*. The God who saves sinners is, indeed he must be, a God who "justifies the wicked" (4:5). Perhaps we have read this verse so often that we forget what a shocking concept this is. Think about it: God the all-knowing and all-holy Judge looks the wicked sinner square in the eye and *justifies* him, declares him righteous, acquits him, pardons him, sets him free, cries "No penalty for you"!

This raises the question of the *basis* for the justification of sinners. How is it possible for the truly righteous God to declare sinners to be righteous? Here is the grace element: only on the basis of the gift of righteousness which he freely

Romans Part Two

gives to those who put their faith in Jesus. As we saw under 1:17 above, the specific content of this gift of righteousness is Jesus' satisfaction of God's law's requirement for penalty in our place. Jesus paid the penalty of eternal condemnation for us — a point that is elaborated in vv. 24b-26; and on this basis God releases us from this penalty and sets us free.

This is the heart of the concept of imputation. "To impute" (λογίζομαι, *logizomai* [used 11 times in ch. 4] and ἐλλογέω, *ellogeō*) is basically a word used in the context of commerce and bookkeeping. It means to apply an amount of money or something equivalent to someone's account (see Phlm 18), either as a charge or as a credit. Our situation as sinners is that we owe God the debt of eternal punishment; but God applies Christ's righteousness (his payment of the penalty in our place) to our account. This is "the righteousness of God" that comes to us as a gift (1:17; 3:21-22); on the basis of this imputed righteousness he justifies us, declaring, "No penalty for you!" Such justification is the same as forgiveness; see 4:6-8 (❋ I:258)

The second half of v. 24 begins Paul's detailed explanation of the death of Jesus as the basis for the sinner's justification: we are justified **through the redemption that came by Christ Jesus.** This and the next two verses tell us more about the basic meaning of the death of Jesus than any other NT passage. They are absolutely fundamental for a proper understanding of the cross.

That which "came by Christ Jesus," and specifically by his cross, is called "redemption" (❋ I:259). The basic idea of redemption is to set something or someone free from some kind of bondage, slavery, captivity, or obligation. Under the OT law, consecrated property, the firstborn, and slaves could be redeemed or "bought back" (see Exod 13:11-13; Lev 25:47-49; 27:11-19; Num 18:14-16). In NT times the terms were used for the act of ransoming slaves, prisoners of war, and condemned criminals.

What is the price by which sinners are redeemed from their sin? It is stated most vividly in 1 Pet 1:18-19, "It was not with perishable things such as silver or gold that you were redeemed . . . , but with the precious blood of Christ." Because the Son of Man came "to give his life as a ransom for many" (Matt 20:28), "we have redemption through his blood" (Eph 1:7). See Acts 20:28; 1 Cor 6:20; Rev 5:9. The blood of Christ pays the debt of eternal punishment that we owe to God himself; to pay this debt Jesus suffered the equivalent of eternity in hell for the whole human race.

3:25 Paul states this same truth in v. 25, where he uses another word parallel in significance to redemption: **God presented him as a sacrifice of atonement . . . .** The word translated "sacrifice of atonement" is ἱλαστήριον (*hilastērion*), which is also used in Heb 9:5. This term and its equivalent, ἱλασμός (*hilasmos*, 1 John 2:2; 4:10) stand for one of the most important concepts in the Bible.

Unfortunately, there is no unanimity as to the meaning of *hilasterion*.

Because it is used often in the LXX and in Heb 9:5 to refer to the lid of the ark of the covenant, i.e., the "mercy-seat," many find that meaning figuratively here in 3:25. Just as the mercy-seat was the place where the atoning blood of sin-offerings was sprinkled in OT times, so also is Jesus in a sense the place where the final atonement has been made for all times.

While this view presents no doctrinal problems and is very close to Paul's meaning here, it does not seem to capture the full significance of the term (Moo, 232-234). Consistent with its use in nonbiblical Greek, Paul more likely intends it to mean the atoning sacrifice itself, in the sense of a *propitiation*.

The key element in the concept of propitiation is the averting of wrath. To say that Jesus is a propitiation means that he offered himself as a sacrifice that turns God's wrath away from deserving sinners by accepting that wrath upon himself in our place. Thus he is a "wrath-removing sacrifice" (Hendriksen, I:132), a "wrath-averting sacrifice" (Moo, 236). Any interpretation of this concept that excludes the removal of the divine wrath from the purpose of the cross has missed its point and must be rejected. (See Morris, *Preaching*, chs. 5 and 6, for the most detailed explanation of why this is so.) The substitution of the ambiguous "sacrifice of atonement" for "propitiation" in the NIV and elsewhere is to be regretted (❂ I:260-261).

The word translated "presented" has more than one connotation, but the context favors the meaning, "to set forth, to display publicly." Verse 21 asserts that the righteousness of God has been "made known"; vv. 25b-26 say the cross is God's public demonstration of his righteousness. "Presented" in 25a fits this pattern, and refers to the openly historical event of the cross as explained by the gospel.

God presented Jesus as a propitiation **through faith in his blood.** As in v. 22, faith is a necessary condition for the actual application of the results of Christ's propitiatory sacrifice to the individual sinner. These results are not automatically and unconditionally applied to all sinners with a resulting universal salvation. But neither are the conditions meritorious in nature and thus inconsistent with grace (4:16; 11:6).

A point of dispute is the placement of "in [ἐν, *en*] his blood." The word order favors the view that this phrase modifies faith, i.e., "through faith in his blood" (NIV). See Lard, 118; Hendriksen, 1:132 (❂ I:262).

The fact that Jesus is a propitiation through faith in his blood implies that his blood, i.e., his substitutionary death on the cross, is what actually accomplishes the propitiation. It does so in the same way that it accomplishes redemption: it satisfies the penal wrath of God in the place of the sinners who actually deserve it. To have saving faith means we specifically believe that Christ's death on the cross is the basis for our forgiveness, even if we do not understand all the details about how this is so.

He did this to demonstrate his justice . . . . I.e., God presented Jesus as a propitiation for this purpose, to "demonstrate his justice." Some take the word "demonstrate" in the sense of "show forth, set forth, reveal publicly." This would make it similar to "presented" in 25a. Others say it means to demonstrate in the sense of "prove." Either view is possible; in fact, it is difficult to separate them in this context.

The cross as a propitiation specifically demonstrates God's "justice." The Greek term (δικαιοσύνη, *dikaiosynē*) is the same one used in 1:17; 3:5; and 3:21-22. In each of these instances it is translated "righteousness." The reason the NIV translates it "justice" in 3:25 is that its connotation here is different from 3:21-22. In the latter passage (and in 1:17) it refers to God's gift of justifying righteousness; here (as in 3:5) it means God's own righteous character, his inner integrity that requires him to be completely true to himself in all ways.

In this context it is clear that the aspect of his nature to which his righteousness requires him to be true is his perfect holiness. God's holiness in turn requires him to uphold the full integrity of his law, and this requires him to punish those who violate that law by their sin. This specific attribute of God is often called his *retributive justice*. Thus the translation "justice."

Why is such a demonstration needed? Because it would seem that God, in justifying sinners, is not being true to his law's requirement that sin must be punished. (See especially Exod 23:7; Deut 25:1; Prov 17:15.) But when Jesus is set forth *as a propitiation*, it is clear that God *is* punishing sins after all, albeit in the person of his only-begotten Son, who suffers the penalty in our place.

Such a demonstration was especially important **because in his forbearance he had left the sins committed beforehand unpunished . . . .** God's "forbearance" is his patience and longsuffering, which in essence means "delay and restraint in the execution of wrath." (See *GRe*, 357-361.) Paul's point is that God's failure to consistently punish sin throughout the OT era may have raised questions about his integrity. How could he claim to be a righteous and holy God, and at the same time forgive sins and leave them unpunished?

"Sins committed beforehand" does not refer to the sins an individual commits prior to his baptism, but to sins committed and forgiven prior to the cross. The only basis upon which sins may be forgiven is the propitiatory sacrifice of Jesus Christ, and it was upon this basis that God forgave sins even in the OT era, even before the historical event of the atonement had occurred. It was absolutely certain that the cross would occur (Acts 2:23); thus God freely dispensed its benefits before the fact.

The problem was not God's ability to forgive pre-cross sins as such, but the appearance this gave as to God's violating his own righteousness or justice in doing so. But, says Paul, any doubts concerning the integrity of God's justice that were thus raised are completely dispelled by the actual event of the cross, which was a public event presented before the whole world.

There is no basis in this text for denying that OT believers were fully forgiven even before the cross. Indeed, Paul's main paradigm for justification, i.e., forgiveness, is Abraham; see ch. 4 (❧I:264).

3:26 Whereas v. 25 relates the demonstration of propitiation to sins committed prior to the cross, v. 26 makes the same point as a general principle that applies especially to the Christian era. **He did it**, i.e., he set Jesus forth as a propitiation, **to demonstrate his justice at the present time, so as to be just and the one who justifies those who have faith in Jesus.** What has God done in this "present time"? He "sent his Son" (Gal 4:4) to establish and demonstrate the basis for the forgiveness he freely bestows in every era.

The latter part of v. 26 is a purpose statement, and expresses in no uncertain terms the ultimate purpose of the death of Jesus, i.e., so that God can be both *just* and *justifier*. This shows that the cross was not merely a *demonstration* of the fact that the forgiving God is just (as the RSV and NRSV imply), but was necessary in order that God might *be* just, even while he is justifying sinners (see Lard, 121). Because the cross in its nature and meaning was an act of redemption and propitiation, God is able to forgive righteously. Because Jesus on the cross was paying our debt of eternal punishment and bearing the full force of the wrath of God in our place, God is able to fully cancel our punishment and declare, "No penalty for you!" without compromising his nature as a holy God who must punish sin. (See *GRe*, 450-455.) Such justification "at the present time" is offered only to those "who have faith in Jesus" (see 3:22) (❧I:265).

C. Sinners Are Justified by Faith Apart from Works of Law (3:27-28)

In the rest of this chapter Paul returns to the question-and-answer format used in 3:1-9. What he has been saying since 3:9, and what he says here, is applicable to Jews and to the Mosaic Law, but it is also intended to apply to all people and to the law of God as such.

From 3:27 through the end of ch. 4, the main theme is *faith* as the means of appropriating the benefits of the atonement affirmed in vv. 24-26. From the human side this is the key difference between law and grace: the *means* of justification is *faith*, not works of law (3:28). This antithesis is not intended to set faith apart from every other human act, but rather to set it apart from works as the means of justification within the law system.

3:27 Where, then, is boasting? It is excluded. The word "then" (οὖν, *oun*) introduces a conclusion drawn from vv. 24-26, namely, that the grace system excludes boasting. (On the meaning of "boasting," see 2:17.) Unlike the law system, the way of grace is not consistent with boasting since the total package of salvation from beginning to end was conceived in the mind of God and made possible only through the work of Jesus, and is offered to sinners in the form of a free gift. (See Eph 2:8-10.)

"Excluded" is aorist tense: "it has been excluded" once for all. **On what prin-**

ciple? On that of observing the law? No, but on that of faith. Justification through the law system would permit boasting, but such justification is not possible since all have sinned. The grace alternative excludes boasting since the only meritorious works that produce salvation within this system are done by God himself through Jesus Christ. The only thing sinners can do is react to and respond to these divine works, and passively receive the benefits generated by them. The defining element in this unmeritorious response is faith (❧ I:266).

The latter part of v. 27 reads literally, "Through what law [νόμος, *nomos*]? of works? No, but through a law [*nomos*] of faith." The exact sense of *nomos* here is debated. The best understanding is that Paul here is using the word in a general sense, with a connotation that has not yet appeared in the epistle. The NIV translation, "principle," adequately reflects this understanding (❧ I:267). This is basically the way I have been using "system of salvation." His words "of works" (NIV, "observing the law") refer to the law system as such, and his words "a law of faith" refer to the grace system as such. We may paraphrase v. 27 thus: "Where, then, is boasting? It has been excluded. Through what system of salvation? The law system, in which one is justified by works? No, on the contrary, through the grace system, in which one is justified by faith."

3:28 For we maintain that a man is justified by faith apart from observing the law. It is tempting to translate λογίζομαι (*logizomai*) as "conclude" here (KJV; Lipscomb, 78; Wuest, 63), but "maintain, hold, deem" is probably better. It is the same word that is translated "reckon, count, impute" throughout ch. 4. The word "for" (*gar*) shows this statement is not a conclusion from v. 27, but is rather the basis for it (Lard, 123). The plural "we" probably refers to Paul and his Christian readers, and thus by implication to all believers: "we Christians" (Moo, 250; Morris, 187; Cranfield, I:220-221). "A man" refers to *any* man or *any* person, i.e., anybody who is actually justified. "Observing the law" is literally "works of law" and should be translated such, contrary to the NIV's unacceptable paraphrase (see 3:20).

This verse says nothing that has not already been said, especially in 1:16-17; 3:21-22; but it says it more succinctly and thus sums up the main thesis of the epistle. Anybody who is actually justified is justified only under the grace system, not under the law system. "Faith" is a kind of shorthand for the grace system as a whole, and "works of law" (like "works" in v. 27) is shorthand for the law system as a whole.

It is extremely important that we understand this verse aright since it is one of the main passages used to support the widely held "faith only" doctrine of salvation. It is recognized that this contrast between "faith" and "works of law" creates two categories. Then it is assumed that the *only* thing in the first category is faith, and faith alone. *Everything* else — every other possible human act, thought, attitude, or state of mind — goes into the second category as a "work of law." Thus under the grace system the sole condition for justification is faith (see 1:16 above).

The consistent result of this view is to exclude even *repentance* as a condition for justification, a position held by those who oppose what is called "Lordship salvation." Many who hold the "faith-only" view object to such an exclusion and argue that both faith and repentance are necessary conditions for justification, contrary to their "faith-only" interpretation of 3:28. Both groups then proceed to exclude *baptism* as a condition for justification. To avoid antinomianism it is usually added that the faith which, alone, justifies us is not *completely* alone, in the sense that it will naturally produce good works, even if these works are not directly involved in justification (Bruce, 109).

How may we respond to this view? The key point is a right understanding of the expression "works of law." It should be carefully noted that in this verse the only things specifically set apart from faith are whatever is meant by "works of law." But does this verse imply that *everything* that is not faith is automatically included in this category? The answer is no, as will now be explained.

Briefly, "works of law" here does *not* mean works of obedience to the Law of Moses; it does *not* mean perfect obedience to all commandments; it does *not* mean obedience done from legalistic motives (❥I:268-269). What, then, does it mean? Law itself, as said above, means God's commandments or law in general, and not just one limited version of it (such as the Law of Moses). It is composed especially of the moral law, which applies equally to all people in all ages, even though it is revealed in different forms and under different covenants. "Works of law," then, must mean any response to any such law, without restriction in terms of dispensation, form, or motive.

The preposition "apart from" is χώρις (*chōris*), a term which emphasizes separation: "apart from, without, separated from, without relation to, without regard to." "Apart from works of law" thus means "without regard to one's response to the law, apart from a consideration of how one responds to the law." But one may respond to law either positively or negatively, either in obedience or in disobedience. In 3:28 Paul has in mind *both* kinds of response: "Apart from a consideration of one's obedience and disobedience to law."

We know that "works of law" is intended to have this all-inclusive meaning here because of the parallel with "apart from works" in 4:6. In the latter passage Paul cites David in Ps 32:1-2 as evidence that a man is justified (reckoned righteous) "apart from works." But what "works" does David mention in these verses? Only transgressions and sins! To be justified apart from works thus includes the idea of being justified apart from a consideration of our sinful deeds. The similarity of meaning between 3:28 and 4:6 thus requires us to include sinful works in our understanding of "works of law" in 3:28. (This is why we cannot simply equate "works of law" with "perfect obedience to all the law requires." This is also why the NIV translation, "observing the law," is wrong; it refers only to a positive response to the law.)

On the other hand "works of law" cannot be expanded to mean "anything a person does." Even if faith is excepted, this is too broad because not everything a sinner does is a response to law. God gives his human creatures law in his role as Creator and Lord, and we as creatures respond to this law either by obeying it or disobeying it (i.e., in "works of law"). But once we have disobeyed it, God then begins to relate to sinful mankind in a wholly new role: that of Redeemer. As Redeemer he works out our salvation; as Redeemer he offers it to sinners with instructions on how to receive it. Such redemptive instruction is *not* "law," and our response to this instruction *cannot* be called "works of law."

Thus "works of law" cannot be broadened to include "anything a person does" besides faith. We cannot posit two categories of human acts, where faith alone is one category, with everything else constituting a second category called "works of law." Sinners are instructed, yea, *required* to do other things that cannot be labeled "works of law," because they are not responses to the law given by God as Creator to man as creature. The most obvious example of this is repentance, and an equally clear example is baptism. Both repentance and baptism are the sinner's response to God as Redeemer, not the creature's response to God as Creator. They are neither "works" nor "works of law," any more than saving faith is. (See the discussion of "obedience to the faith" under 1:5 above.)

This does not mean that we are justified *by* repentance and baptism, in the way that we are justified *by* faith. As discussed above, faith alone is the sole *means* by which justification is received. It does mean, though, that "faith" in 3:28 (as in 3:27) is an abbreviated way of referring to the grace system as a whole, and that repentance and baptism are legitimately understood within the grace system as conditions for receiving justification that are fully compatible with faith. They are not "works of law" any more than faith is.

D. The Way of Grace Is Available to All (3:29-30)

3:29 In vv. 29-30 Paul returns to a continuing theme of the epistle, that God's grace makes no distinctions among sinners; it is equally needed by all and equally available to all on the same conditions (see 1:16; 3:22). No one group has an advantage over any other; especially, the Jews have no advantage over the Gentiles. **Is God the God of Jews only?** This is the question Paul addressed at length in ch. 2. It reflects the mistaken Jewish attitude that their privilege of service implied a unique access to God and his salvation. But has not Paul clearly shown that the Jews do not have a monopoly on God? **Is he not the God of Gentiles too? Yes, of Gentiles too . . . .**

The general principle of v. 28 is given a specific application here. Under grace sinners are justified apart from their response to any given version of God's law, and this applies especially to the Law of Moses. God did not give the Law of Moses as an exclusive means by which Jews alone could be justified.

That was not its purpose. If it had been, then he could have simply left that law in place and continued to ignore the Gentiles (Acts 17:30). But God is God of all men, including the Gentiles; and now in the fullness of time (Gal 4:4) he has made it clear that he has always intended to include the Gentiles as full partners in salvation by grace (Eph 2:11-3:12).

3:30 Indeed, he *must* be the God of both Jews and Gentiles, **since there is only one God** . . . . The existence of only one God was a basic OT revelation (Exod 20:3; Deut 6:4), and a basic Jewish belief. By arguing thus, "Paul takes one of the most basic of Jewish beliefs, monotheism, and turns it against Judaism" (Moo, 251). I.e., he turns it against their false exclusivism.

. . . who [the one God] will justify the circumcised by faith and the uncircumcised through that same faith. Here Paul calls attention to the other main symbol of Jewish exclusivism, circumcision, and declares that within the grace system it makes no difference whatever (see 2:25-29). Both the circumcised (the Jews) and the uncircumcised (the Gentiles) are justified in the same way, i.e., by a common faith in a common Redeemer. Now that Christ has come, the Gentiles are specifically said to have *the (same) faith* as the Jews (πίστις [*pistis*] with the definite article).

Though two different prepositions are used for "by (ἐκ, *ek*) faith" and "through (διά, *dia*) faith," no significant difference in meaning is intended.

E. Grace Lets Law Do Its Proper Work (3:31)

3:31 (❄ I:272) After Paul has emphatically rejected the ability of law to justify (3:20), and has declared that justification can be received only apart from law (3:21,27-28), some are no doubt thinking that law must be rather obsolete. Paul voices this concern in the question, **Do we, then, nullify the law by this faith?**

This is not just a reference to the Mosaic Law or to the OT as a whole. The contrast throughout this section has been between grace on the one hand and law in general on the other hand, and it is no different here.

The question is, does grace abolish law, or render it ineffective and purposeless? Does it set the law aside so that it has no relevance to the Christian? Does faith "nullify the law"? (On the word "nullify" [καταργέω, *katargeō*], see 3:3.) **Not at all! Rather,** by it **we uphold the law.** A right understanding of grace and justification by faith actually establishes and confirms the law. How does it do this? By setting law free from a burden it is not able to bear and was never intended to bear, namely, function as a means of justifying sinners. When we stop trying to use the law and its commandments in such an impossible way, we can then let it perform its proper functions.

One such function is that it serves to show us our sin (3:20) and thus shows us our need for justification by faith. Also, it properly functions as a norm or standard for holy living. Even under grace, we have an absolute obligation to obey God's law (see I:273.)

II. 4:1-25 — ABRAHAM: PARADIGM OF GRACE

This next section of Romans (the entire fourth chapter) is a presentation of Abraham as a paradigm or pattern for grace. Paul seems to have several purposes in mind here. Most generally he uses Abraham's example to explain what it means to be justified by faith apart from works of law (3:28). More specifically, this appeal to Abraham provides OT confirmation for Paul's teaching. Perhaps Paul's most specific purpose in this section is to make it easier for the Jews to accept the gospel of grace (❂ I:274).

An appeal to the life of Abraham is ideally suited for these purposes. He is indeed an object lesson of the main truth that Paul is explaining in these chapters, i.e., that God's way of saving sinners is by grace, which means that we are justified by faith apart from works of law. Paul sees Gen 15:6 as a summary statement of this truth, and Romans 4 is basically an exposition of this verse.

With regard to the Jews, their supremely high regard for Abraham makes an appeal to his life a perfect means for correcting their legalism and exclusivism. Showing that Abraham was in fact accepted by God on the basis of grace, i.e., that he was justified by faith apart from works of law, will be a major step for Paul in breaking down Jewish resistance to the gospel.

In keeping with the thesis statement in 3:28, the major theme throughout this section is the contrast between law and grace as ways of salvation. The categories of law and grace are represented by the following concepts:

LAW	*GRACE*
works (vv. 2,4,6)	faith (vv. 3,5,9,11-14,16-20,24)
boasting (v. 2)	glorifying God (v. 20)
wages (v. 4)	imputation (vv. 3-6,8-11,22-24)
obligation/debt (v. 4)	gift/grace (vv. 4,16)
sin (vv. 5,7,8,15)	imputed righteousness (vv. 3,5,6,9,11,13,22)
law (vv. 13-16)	promise (vv. 13,14,16,20,21)
wrath (v. 15)	forgiveness (vv. 7-8)

While the contrast between the corresponding items is not as precise in every case as this chart might suggest, viewing the two lists together makes it clear that Rom 4 is indeed showing us the difference between these two possible ways of relating to God.

The law-grace distinction can be seen in the way faith is set over against a series of opposite concepts as Paul's argument progresses through 4:22. He first contrasts faith and works (4:1-8), then faith and circumcision (4:9-12), then faith and law (4:13-22). In this chapter it is important to see that "law" (except v. 16) is not limited to the Mosaic Law but refers to God's law in general and especially to law as a way of salvation (❧I:275-276).

A. Abraham Was Justified by Faith Apart from Works (4:1-5)

4:1 Paul begins this section on Abraham with a question: **What then shall we say that Abraham, our forefather, discovered in this matter?** How does he fit into this picture? Regarding this matter of justification, what did he find to be the case?

A major exegetical issue in this verse has to do with a phrase not even translated by the NIV, namely, κατὰ σάρκα (*kata sarka*), "according to the flesh." This phrase occurs at the end of the verse. The question is whether it modifies the verb "discovered," or the noun "forefather."

Some take it to modify the verb, i.e., "What was Abraham able to accomplish by his own human works?" The answer, of course, would be "Nothing!" (❧I:276-277). Others see this phrase as modifying "forefather." The question would then be, "What was the case regarding Abraham, our forefather according to the flesh, our physical ancestor?" (See 1:3; 9:3,5.) Either view is acceptable, but the word order favors the latter.

Why would Paul describe Abraham thus? Along with the possessive pronoun "our," this suggests that he is referring to Abraham as the "forefather of us Jews." The "our" is natural because of Paul's own identity as a Jew and thus as a physical descendant of Abraham. The main reason for referring to Abraham this way here in v. 1 is that it helps to set up a contrast that is important later in the chapter, namely, the contrast between Abraham's role as the physical ancestor of the Jews only, and his role as the spiritual ancestor of all believers, whether they be Jews or Gentiles (4:11-12,16). Paul's question thus means, "What shall we say with regard to Abraham, the illustrious ancestor of us Jewish people? How was he justified? By works, or by faith?"

4:2 In response to the question in v. 1, Paul considers the possibility that Abraham may have been justified by his works. **If, in fact, Abraham was justified by works, he had something to boast about . . . .** This assumes that if *any* person *were* justified by his works, then he would have reason to boast — a principle suggested also by Eph 2:9. In the Jews' opinion, Abraham was such a person (❧I:278). If this was the case, then Paul's main thesis in 3:28 would be false; and boasting would not be excluded after all, contrary to 3:27.

Well, says Paul, in the eyes of some this may be the case, **but not before God.** The reader must be careful not to misunderstand this very terse statement. E.g., he is not saying that Abraham could boast before *man*, but not before *God*. What, then, is the point? "But not before God" is simply a denial of the whole hypothesis that Abraham was justified by works. Contrary to

Jewish perspective, the way God sees it, Abraham did not find or discover justification by works (❋I:278).

4:3 What, then, is the answer to the question in v. 1? What did Abraham find to be the case with regard to justification? Paul passes by all human opinions and goes straight to "the very words of God" (3:2): **What does the Scripture say?** *Was* Abraham justified by works? No! How do we know? Because Scripture says: **"Abraham believed God, and it was credited to him as righteousness."** This statement, taken directly from Gen 15:6, is equivalent to saying that Abraham was justified by faith; this verse is quoted with the same meaning in Gal 3:6 and Jas 2:23.

The nature of Abraham's faith is explained later in the chapter (4:17-22), with an emphasis on the way he believed God's promises (4:21). Obviously the promises given to Abraham could not refer specifically to his future seed, Jesus Christ, and to his saving work. Nonetheless God gave him several promises of staggering import, all of which ultimately culminated in Christ's redeeming activity (Acts 13:32-33; Heb 11:8-13). First, God promised Abraham that he would be the father of a "great nation" with numberless offspring (Gen 12:2; 13:16; 15:5; 17:2-6; 18:18; 22:17). Second, he promised him and his offspring possession of the land of Canaan (Gen 12:2,7; 13:14-17; 15:7,18-21; 17:8; 22:17). Third and most significantly, God promised Abraham that "all peoples on earth will be blessed through you" (Gen 12:3; 18:18; 22:18) — a reference, of course, to the messianic purpose for which God called Abraham in the first place.

The point is that with regard to all these promises, Abraham humbly believed that God could and would keep his word. Consequently he surrendered himself to God and rendered to him the obedience of faith (1:5).

The statement quoted by Paul from Gen 15:6 occurs specifically upon one of the occasions when God promised Abraham numberless offspring (Gen 15:5). We must not conclude, however, that this was the only time when Abraham believed, nor that it was the only or even first time when "it was credited to him as righteousness." James 2:23 also quotes Gen 15:6, but applies it to the occasion when Abraham offered Isaac as a sacrifice, an event which occurred much later (Gen 22:1-18). This implies that Abraham's faith and the resulting justification were present from the day he was first called (Gen 12:1) and to the end of his life.

The word translated "it was credited" is a very important word that stands for an even more important concept, often called the doctrine of imputation. The term is λογίζομαι (*logizomai*), and it is used a total of 11 times in this chapter. Its meaning here seems to be rooted in the way it was used by Greeks in the field of business or commerce. (See 2:3 for another main connotation of the same word.) It was a technical term used to describe the procedure of entering a credit or a debit to someone's account. It is properly translated "to credit [NIV], to set down to one's account, to impute, to reckon, to count as, to regard as." It was credited or counted to Abraham "as righteousness." The righteous character of God and thus the righteous requirements of his law must be fully satisfied before a person can be saved (3:26). In this sense righteousness, or the satisfaction of the requirements of God's law (see 1:17), is the very basis for salvation. Theoretically one may satisfy the law's commandments through perfect obedience and thereby be saved on the basis of one's own personal righteousness, but universal sin makes this impossible. This is why God must credit or impute something else to sinners as the righteousness by which they are saved.

Exactly what is reckoned to Abraham, or credited to his account? In this verse (as in vv. 22-24) the passive verb has no specific subject, and is simply translated "it was credited." What is the "it"? Verses 5 and 9 specifically say that Abraham's *faith* was credited as righteousness. Faith is thus presented as a form of righteousness that stands over against perfectly righteous character and behavior, i.e., works (vv. 4-5). This does not mean, however, that faith itself is a meritorious act that is equal to a life of perfect obedience, thus making a person *worthy* of salvation. Again, in vv. 4-5 Paul makes it clear that when God credits faith as righteousness, this is a gift of grace and is something quite distinct from a merited or deserved reward for works.

In fact, strictly speaking, it is not faith itself that is credited to a sinner's account, but the ultimate *object* of his faith, namely, the atoning blood of Jesus Christ that satisfies the law's requirement for penalty in our place (see above, 1:17; 3:21-26). This and this alone is the righteousness that saves, and this is the righteousness that is credited to us. This is the significance of the language of 4:6 and 4:11, which says that *righteousness itself* is credited to believers. I.e., what is credited to us is not something we *do*, but something we *receive* as a gift. To say that Abraham's or anybody else's *faith* is credited as righteousness is shorthand for this basic gospel truth.

Of course, since Abraham lived about 2000 years before Christ, his faith in the Redeemer's blood was only indirect and not direct. Nevertheless God credited the full effects of the atonement to Abraham's account, since the cross and the resurrection of Jesus were the ultimate outcome of the promises that were the object of his faith.

The result of God's crediting Abraham's faith — or the ultimate object of it — to his account was that he was fully justified. "Faith credited as righteousness" is the same as *justification by faith*, or full forgiveness of sins. The idea that OT saints received only an "IOU" instead of full forgiveness, and that they were held in a limbo-like state instead of being taken directly to paradise when they died, is without foundation of the Bible. All of Romans 4, especially vv. 3-8, shows that Abraham and other OT saints were justified in the fullest sense of the word. Their sins were not just "rolled back" until Christ actually died, but were fully forgiven in view of the certainty of that future event.

4:4 Verses 4 and 5 show that salvation by law and salvation by grace are opposite to one another and are mutually exclusive (see 3:28). Verse 4 describes what it would be like to be justified by works of law, as some thought Abraham was (4:2a). It does so by setting forth a basic principle of economics, namely, the relation between work and wages: **Now when a man works, his wages are not credited to him as a gift, but as an obligation.** When anyone contracts to do a certain job and then completes that job, on what basis does he request his wages? Does he ask his employer to give it to him as a *gift*? Of course not! The wage is something that is owed to him; he has worked for it and he deserves it. From the employer's point of view he is obligated to pay the wage; it is a *debt* that he owes to the worker.

The implied parallel is clear. "When a man works" refers to anyone who is seeking to relate to God under the system of law. This is like working for wages, says Paul. Under law a person will receive from God exactly what he deserves or what he has earned by his works. The wages or reward, whatever that may be, is bestowed by God as a matter of debt or obligation, not as a gift. The word for "gift" is χάρις (*charis*), or *grace*. Thus when a man approaches God on the basis of law, he shuts himself off from grace. What is credited to his account, to be received on the day of judgment, is credited not according to grace but according to debt (❂ I:282).

4:5 However, to the man who does not work but trusts God who justifies the wicked, his faith is credited as righteousness Just as justification by works excludes grace, so does justification by grace exclude works. Who will be justified? "The man who does not work but trusts God." (❂ I:283)

"The man who does not work" is best understood as "the man who does not look upon his works as a means of laying hold of justification," or "the man who does not trust his works or depend upon them for his standing before God" (see MacArthur, I:239; Moo, 264). It means "the man who has renounced the law system, in which works are rewarded in terms of wages earned." As Morris (198) says, the contrast between v. 4 and v. 5 is not between one who works and one who does not work at all, but between one who trusts in his works and one who trusts in God.

The most striking part of this verse is the description of God as one "who justifies the wicked." In the OT God demanded that human judges in human courts of law should always condemn and never acquit (justify) such wicked persons (Deut 25:1; Prov 17:15; 24:24; Isa 5:23). God himself declares, "I will not justify the wicked" (Exod 23:7, KJV). Romans 1:18 pictures him as directing his wrath toward all human wickedness. But here in 4:5, he is pictured as the one who *justifies* the wicked!

How can this be? How can the righteous God justify the wicked? He cannot, within the parameters and constraints of *law*. Human courts are ordained to operate according to the principles of law, and God's own holy nature is bound by these principles. But here in 4:5 the perspective is not law but *grace*, and the principles of grace are the very opposite of law! Thus whereas the holy God who is a consuming fire (Heb 12:29) must *condemn* the wicked, the same God who is also loving and gracious can also *justify* the wicked! Because of his grace Christ died for all the wicked (5:6), and the wicked who put their faith in his saving death will be justified. This description of God thus epitomizes the very essence of grace.

In this context "the wicked" of course includes Abraham along with everyone else. All are sinners, and when we ask God to justify or forgive us, we must believe that he is a God who justifies the wicked, since that is exactly what we are asking and expecting him to do! Also, when we approach God and ask him to justify us, we are in effect asking him to justify us apart from our works — our *sinful* works. That is to say, the God who justifies the wicked *is* a God who justifies by faith apart from works. Paul explains this in vv. 6-8 by citing the testimony of David.

B. David Explains and Confirms Justification by Faith Apart from Works (4:6-8)

In the midst of his discussion of Abraham as a paradigm of salvation by grace, Paul inserts another relevant biblical quotation, this one from Ps 32:1-2a. This citation from the writing of David serves as further evidence of the unity between OT Scripture and Paul's teaching. It also provides crucial insight into the meaning of Paul's basic theme, that we are justified by faith apart from works of law (3:28). Also, in case there is any doubt, the quotation from David serves to generalize the assertion made concerning Abraham in 15:6 as quoted in 4:3, showing that it applies to all believers.

4:6 Paul introduces David's prophetic word thus: **David says the same thing when he speaks of the blessedness of the man to whom God credits righteousness apart from works . . . .** "Says the same thing" is the NIV's translation of the conjunctive phrase καθάπερ καί (*kathaper kai*), "just as also." This links the two OT quotes (Gen 15:6 and Ps 32:1-2a) closely together in meaning.

We must never try to understand "justification by faith apart from works" without a consideration of the meaning of these words of David. This is evident from the very way Paul describes David's testimony. Of whom is the Psalmist speaking? Of "the man to whom God credits righteousness apart from works." This language is directly tied in with the "righteousness of God" of which Paul speaks in his thematic statement in 1:17, and of which "the Law and the Prophets testify" (3:21). It refers to the gift of God's righteousness established by Jesus in his atoning sacrifice and received by sinners through faith (3:22-25). It echoes 4:3. "Credits righteousness" is the same as "justifies." "Apart from works" (χωρὶς ἔργων, *chōris ergōn*) is the same as "apart from works of law" (*chōris ergōn nomou*) in 3:28.

What does it mean to say that God credits righteousness apart from works, and why is this a blessing? Before answering these questions we must examine the content of the quotation from David.

4:7-8 Blessed are they whose transgressions are forgiven, whose sins are covered. Blessed is the man whose sin the Lord will never count against him. This is an almost exact quotation from Ps 32:1-2a (LXX), a Psalm attributed to David both by the OT text and by Paul (4:6). Each segment of the quote begins with the adjective μακάριος (*makarios*), just as the beatitudes do (Matt 5:3-11). It means "happy, fortunate, content"; in a theistic context it is properly translated "blessed, favored." (❁ I:285)

What is the nature of the blessing of which David speaks? Three separate expressions are used, all of which basically refer to the same thing: the way a person's sins are regarded by God under the grace system. Under grace, our "transgressions are forgiven"; our "sins are covered" and will never be counted against us. Two different words are used for sin. One (v. 7a) is ἀνομία (*anomia*), from *nomos* ("law") with a negating alpha, thus "lawlessness, transgression of the law" (see 6:19; 1 John 3:4). The other term (vv. 7b-8) is the common ἁμαρτία (*hamartia*, used 48 times in Romans), which refers to missing the mark or falling short of the standard (see 3:23). The connotations are similar if not the same.

The blessing of grace is that the engraced person's sins are *forgiven*. This is the common word ἀφίημι (*aphiēmi*) (❁ I:286). When used in the religious sense of forgiveness, it means "to release from the debt of punishment owed to God because of sin." A person whose sins are forgiven is a person for whom the debt of eternal punishment has been left behind.

Another way of saying this is that our sins have been *covered*. See Ps 85:2 for the parallel use of forgiveness and covering with respect to sin. To say that our sins are covered means that God himself has blotted them out of his own sight (Heb 8:12). When he looks at us in Jesus Christ, our sins are hidden from him in the sense that he does not hold them against us.

This is indeed the third way of expressing this blessing: for the man who is under grace, the Lord will never count his sins against him (v. 8). We are sinners, without question; but the gracious God will not make us pay for our sins. The term is λογίζομαι (*logizomai*) again, i.e., God will not reckon our sins against us; he will not enter them into our own personal accounts as debts for which we must render payment to God in the form of eternal punishment in hell. The emphatic certainty of this blessing is underscored by the use of a double negative, οὐ μή (*ou mē*): the Lord will by no means, he will not ever, he "will never" (NIV) hold our sins against us.

To say that such a person is blessed implies that he *knows* that his sins are forgiven and covered. Who can deny that this is indeed the greatest blessing we could ever desire or imagine? The knowledge that the gracious God has released us from the debt of punishment and will not hold our sins against us should fill us with eternal awe and amazement, with the greatest heights and depths of gratitude and love, and with "inexpressible and glorious joy" (1 Pet 1:8).

These two verses specifically assert the second half of the grace formula or grace principle (see the introduction to Part Two above): "Break the commandments, but escape the penalty." But we should never forget that the reason why God is able to bestow such an immeasurable blessing upon us, of course, is because of what Jesus has done for us through his work of propitiation on the cross. Instead of reckoning our sins to our account, God has reckoned or imputed them to Jesus Christ; he has put them down to Jesus' account, and Jesus has paid the deserved debt of punishment in full, in our place. This righteous payment of sin's punishment, rather than the sin itself, is then credited to our account; this is the righteousness of which v. 4:6b speaks. This is what it means to say that "God credits righteousness apart from works."

In a real sense this section (4:6-8) is the culmination of the explanation of justification by grace that was begun in 3:21. It casts vital and crucial light on the whole discussion and especially on the thesis statement in 3:28. It helps us to understand the meaning of justification as such, and it is crucial for our understanding of "justification by faith apart from works of law."

Our study of this section thus far (3:21–4:8) has yielded three important conclusions. In brief, (1) *justification of the wicked* is the same as *forgiveness of sins*; (2) justification is the same as the imputation of righteousness; and (3) "works of law" in 3:28 includes all responses to the Creator's law-commands, both obedient and sinful (❧ I:287-289).

C. Membership in Abraham's Family Is by Faith, Not by Circumcision (4:9-12)

Having established that Abraham is the OT paradigm for justification by faith by citing Gen 15:6, and having clarified what this means in a general way by citing Ps 32:1-2a, Paul now applies this specifically to the Jew-Gentile debate. In vv. 1-8 he shows that we are justified by faith alone, apart from a consideration of works. Now in vv. 9-12 he establishes from the Abrahamic paradigm that a person is justified by faith, apart from a consideration of whether he has been circumcised or not.

This is the second time Paul has discussed circumcision. In 2:25-29 he showed that the Jews who were attempting to be saved by law would be judged by their obedience or disobedience to the entire law, not just by their possession of circumcision. Here he shows that under grace those who share the Abrahamic blessing of justification are those who share his faith, not his circumcision. This is a direct attack on Jewish exclusivism, which linked circumcision to salvation and limited salvation to those who were circumcised (Acts 15:1).

Paul makes his point by observing that the announcement of Abraham's justification by faith (Gen 15:6) occurred many years before circumcision was introduced (Gen 17:9-14). Thus, as Bruce notes, there was no way that the Jews could argue that the faith principle was valid only for Abraham's circumcised offspring (111-112) (❂ I:289).

4:9 Is this blessedness (the forgiveness of which David speaks) **only for the circumcised, or also for the uncircumcised?** I.e., is it available only to the Jews, or is it for the Gentiles also? Cranfield says that the rabbis of Paul's day generally assumed that Israelites alone were forgiven (❂ I:234-235). But Paul here uses the example of Abraham to show that this assumption is false. His argument continues to be based on the parallel between Gen 15:6 and Ps 32:1-2a. In 4:6-8 he uses the latter text to explain the *meaning* of the former; here he cites Gen 15:6 again to establish the *scope* of the Psalms passage. **We have been saying** (4:3) **that Abraham's faith was credited to him as righteousness.** More specifically, as noted above, the implicit object of his faith (the righteousness of God in Christ) was credited to his account and counted as his own.

4:10 How is this relevant to the Jew-Gentile issue? Paul gets to this point by asking two questions: **Under what circumstances was it credited? Was it after he was circumcised, or before?** If Abraham had already been circumcised when his faith was taken for righteousness, then the Jews might try to argue that the blessing of forgiveness is only for them. But if this happened prior to the introduction of circumcision, then there is no way that this blessing can be limited only to those who are circumcised. The OT record is very clear. **It was not after, but before!** Thus as far as the conditions for justification are concerned, "circumcision was no factor at all" (Murray, I:137).

4:11 This does not mean that there was no relation at all between Abraham's faith and his circumcision. In the first part of v. 11 Paul comments on the introduction of circumcision into the covenant relationship thus: **And he received the sign of circumcision, a seal of the righteousness that he had by faith while he was still uncircumcised.** Abraham received this sign about 14 years or more after the specific recognition of his faith (cf. Gen 16:16 and 17:1). This shows that the circumcision was not a condition for his justification.

Why then was circumcision given? Paul uses two words that relate to its purpose or function: *sign* and *seal*. The former term comes directly from Gen 17:11, where God said to Abraham that circumcision "will be the sign of the covenant between me and you." This is no doubt the only reason why Paul here calls it "the sign [consisting] of circumcision." This was its commonly known purpose; it was "the sign of the covenant," or the sign of belonging to the covenant family consisting of Abraham's earthly descendants through Isaac and Jacob. It had this meaning not only for Abraham but for all who received it. Paul does not mean that circumcision was given as a sign of Abraham's faith or of his justification. Nor could it have served such a purpose for anyone else, since it was applied in infancy before faith could be present, and was applied to every male infant whether he grew up to become a believer or not (Gen 17:12).

But Paul does say that Abraham's own circumcision functioned as "a seal of the righteousness that he had by faith" even before he was circumcised. A seal (such as a signet ring or its impression) serves as a mark of ownership or identification. Thus by extension it can mean "a confirmation, an attestation, an authentication, a guarantee" (see 1 Cor 9:2). This latter meaning is the point here. By giving Abraham the sign of circumcision, God was providing him with an "outward and visible authentication, ratification and guarantee, of the righteousness by faith which was already his while he was still uncircumcised" (Cranfield, I:236). As such it served as a source of assurance to Abraham that God had truly accepted him and counted him righteous because of his faith.

The point that Paul makes from this is that it shows that Abraham was already justified before he received circumcision, since a seal does not confer that which it ratifies, but assumes that it already exists. "*This proves that circumcision has nothing to do with being declared righteous*," in the sense of being a necessary condition for it (Hendriksen, I:150).

It is commonly taught that what is said here of circumcision applies equally to Christian baptism, and to the "sacraments" in general. Indeed, in Christian literature baptism is constantly called "a sign and a seal." The NT itself never uses this language for baptism, though; calling it such is purely an inference from the supposed parallel between baptism and circumcision. Assuming such a parallel, commentators and theologians constantly use this passage as a foundation for their doctrine of the "sacraments" in general. They use it especially in an attempt to establish that a person must already be justified (forgiven) before he is baptized, and more generally to argue that there can be no connection between salvation and "externals" of any kind.

Two comments are pertinent. First, as far as its general meaning was concerned, *not even circumcision* was "a sign and a seal" pertaining to salvation. It was indeed a sign of covenant membership for all who received it, but there was no necessary relationship between covenant membership and salvation. Also, it was a seal of "righteousness by faith" *only* for Abraham. It was never intended to have this latter meaning for anyone else. Thus even if there were a parallel between baptism and circumcision in general, the concept of the seal would not be a part of it.

Second, the idea that baptism is the NT counterpart to OT circumcision must itself be rejected as a false doctrine (see under 2:29 above). It has neither a sound exegetical basis nor a solid theological rationale. It is an inference drawn from the faulty concept of covenant unity, which itself was created by Huldreich Zwingli in 1525 in the midst of his controversy with the Anabaptists regarding infant baptism (❧I:292, n. 50). The bottom line is that Romans 4:11 has nothing whatsoever to say about the meaning of Christian baptism. Nor does it warrant any general conclusion about the relation between salvation and "externals" as such.

In this text the main question is this: is the blessing of forgiveness for Jews only or for Gentiles also (v. 9a)? Paul sets the stage for his answer in vv. 9b-11a by showing that Abraham received forgiveness "by faith while he was still uncircumcised" (v. 11a). The answer is given in vv. 11b-12, where the Apostle affirms that Abraham is the spiritual father of all believers, whether they are circumcised or not. The NIV begins this answer with **So then**, indicating simple result. The Greek is better rendered in terms of purpose, however. See the NASB, "that he might be"; or the NRSV, "The purpose was." I.e., Abraham was credited as righteous prior to his circumcision *so that* he might be **. . . the father of all who believe but have not been circumcised, in order that righteousness might be credited to them.** This of course refers to the Gentiles, and it clearly shows that Gentiles may receive justification through faith no less than Jews.

There is no question that Abraham was the father or founder of the Jewish nation (4:1), and that being able to claim him as one's ancestor was a great privilege. Here, however, Paul is speaking of Abraham's *spiritual* fatherhood, which is determined not by physical descent but by imitation of Abraham's faith (Gal 3:7,29). He is "the father of all who believe," which was God's ultimate purpose for him from the beginning (Gen 12:3). All Christians have the privilege of calling Abraham "our father" and of inheriting the salvation promised through him (4:13-17; Gal 3).

4:12 This applies to the Jews also, both the true believers under the Old Covenant and Jewish Christians under the New Covenant. **And he is also the father of the circumcised who not only are circumcised but who also walk in the footsteps of the faith that our father Abraham had before he was circumcised.** Jews have the privilege of being children of Abraham in two senses. First, all are descended from him physically, an involuntary circumstance marked by circumcision. No promise of eternal salvation is attached to this relationship. Second, any individual Jew may choose to "walk in the footsteps of the faith" of Abraham. This choice is unrelated to circumcision as such; and this choice alone is the way of salvation, even for Jews.

The bottom line is that membership in Abraham's larger and permanent spiritual family is by faith in the blood of the Redeemer, not by blood relationship as marked by circumcision.

D. The Inheritance Promised to Abraham Comes by Faith, Not by Law (4:13-17a)

The salvation of sinners comes not in accordance with works done in response to law, but on the condition of faith in God's grace. This contrast between law and grace, between works and faith, has been Paul's overriding theme thus far (3:20-22,28; 4:2-5), and it continues to be so in this section. In chapter 4 the theme develops thus: we are justified by faith: apart from works (vv. 1-8); apart from circumcision (vv. 9-12); and apart from law (vv. 13-17a). These are not different points, but different aspects of the same point.

4:13 It was not through law that Abraham and his offspring received the promise that he would be heir of the world, but through the righteousness that comes by faith. The NIV fails to translate the connecting particle *gar*, "for," which connects this section with the previous one. The flow of thought is this: Abraham is "the father of all who believe" (4:11), *because* the blessing that God promised to give through him comes "not through law" but through faith.

The promise did not come "through law." To what law does this refer? Some say it must refer to the Mosaic Law, since "law" in vv. 14-16 seems to refer to this. This would certainly make sense, given the fact that the Mosaic Law did not even exist until over four centuries later (Gal 3:17-18). The form of this argument would thus be the same as the argument about circumcision in 4:9-12. Since the promise preceded circumcision by 14+ years, it cannot be dependent on circumcision; and since the promise preceded the Mosaic Law by 400+ years, it cannot be dependent upon the Law, either.

Others say the "law" in v. 13 refers to any and every form of law, including the Law of Moses but not limited thereto. This is not contrary to the context, since νόμος (*nomos*) in vv. 14-15 is better understood in this same general sense, and since this has been Paul's main connotation for it in the preceding context. The promise did not and does not come through obedience to whatever form of law one possesses, i.e., through law-keeping.

The focus here is on the concept of promise, which is a natural corollary of grace and faith. Grace focuses not on what man can do (i.e., works), but on what God has done and promises to do, and on what he promises to give to sinners as a result. All the sinner can do — and must do — is believe God's promises and accept his gifts.

The full scope of God's promises to Abraham was laid out under 4:3 above. He was promised possession of the land, numberless offspring, and the role of being a source of blessing for all nations. The OT text does not use the exact terminology used here — that Abraham "would be the heir of the world." This is probably a summary of the three main promises as they are now understood in the light of NT revelation. "The world" is first of all Abraham's innumerable family of spiritual children, drawn from "all peoples on earth" (Gen 12:3; see 18:18; 22:18). It probably also includes the new earth inherited by them (Matt 5:5; 2 Pet 3:13), of which the gift of Canaan (later Israel) was a symbolic type. To say that "he" (Abraham) would be the heir of the world means that he would inherit this spiritual family, and through them would inherit the (new) world itself.

The "offspring" (σπέρμα, *sperma*, "seed") of Abraham here refers to all believers, as v. 16 shows. In Gal 3:16 Paul says that technically the *one* seed and heir of Abraham is Jesus Christ, but all who put their trust in Christ are joined to him and thereby become Abraham's seed and heirs as well (Gal 3:26-29).

The NIV says that Abraham and his offspring "received" this promise. The Greek text actually has no verb. The thought is probably that the promise *will be fulfilled* to Abraham and his offspring. How? By faith, not by law. This contrast is Paul's main point. "Not through law" stands first in the verse for emphasis, and the connecting adversative ἀλλά (*alla*, "but") expresses a very strong contrast. Abraham's family is still growing today; and any individual can have a share of their abundant inheritance "through the righteousness that comes by faith," *not* by works of law.

4:14 For if those who live by law are heirs, faith has no value and the promise is worthless . . . . This and v. 15 explain why the inheritance comes "not through law." Genesis 15:6 is taken as the foundational principle, as establishing that justification is by faith. Once we accept this truth, we *must* grant that it cannot be by law, because the law principle (law as a way of salvation) is incompatible with the grace-faith system.

The NIV translation "those who live by law" is unfortunate. The Greek phrase is οἱ ἐκ νόμου (*hoi ek nomou*), "those of law." Everyone, even those who are saved by grace through faith, should *live* by law. That is, we should always obey the precepts of God's law. But those who are "of law" in this verse are those who are *depending* or *relying* on their law-keeping as the basis for their claim to the Abrahamic inheritance. This includes law-depending Jews but is not limited thereto. "Law" is not just the Mosaic law, but the code of commandments available to and applicable to any given person at any given time.

The two ways of salvation are incompatible, says Paul. If the inheritance comes "by law," i.e., by works, then faith would have no valid role in the process. The verb is κενόω (*kenoō*), "to empty." Faith would be emptied of its value; it would be irrelevant and ineffective (see 1 Cor 15:14). Also, the promise would be worthless; it would be nullified. Those who choose law as their way of relating to God thereby cancel his promise, since the two cannot coexist (Gal 3:18). Faith and promise go together, and they belong to an order that is distinct from law and works, namely, the order of grace. (See Stott, 131.)

4:15 because law brings wrath. The problem is not just the basic incompatibility of law on the one hand and faith and promise on the other. The more immediate problem is the fact that all are sinners (3:23), and under law sinners have forfeited the promise and are "heirs" only of wrath (see 6:23). When sinners remain under law, the only outcome is wrath.

How does law produce wrath? By definition law includes both commandments to obey and penalties for those who disobey. The commandments of the law are the very measure of sin (1 John 3:4). **And where there is no law there is no transgression** because there would be no standard by which any particular act could be judged right or wrong. But since there is law, there is also such a thing as sin. And since there is sin, the *penalties* of the law (i.e., wrath) must be applied. In this sense law cannot help but inflict wrath upon sinners; it is its very nature to do so.

"Where there is no law there is no transgression" is a general principle that may be applied either universally or particularly. Its universal application is theoretical only, i.e., *if* there were no law at all, then there would be no such thing as transgression or sin. But law does exist; therefore transgression also exists. The only practical application of this principle is in reference to particular cases, individuals, and laws. In cases where God has given us no commandments regarding a particular activity or behavior, either specifically or in terms of general principles, then that behavior cannot be called sinful. This is the category we call "matters of opinion."

Also, though law does exist, some individuals are unable (by reason of immaturity or mental handicap) to *understand* its true origin and nature as commandments of God bearing the penalty of eternal wrath. In this case "where there is no law" means "where there is no ability to know the law." This applies to those who have not reached what we call "the age of accountability." Furthermore, this principle may apply in the case of mature individuals who are involuntarily ignorant of a particular law of God. For example, those who are exposed to general revelation only will not be held responsible for obeying commandments that can be known only through special revelation. Thus this principle warrants the conclusion that God will finally judge all people in terms of their conscientious response to available light (❂ I:298).

4:16 Paul now draws his general conclusion from the preceding discussion: **Therefore, the promise comes by faith . . . .** Literally it reads, "on account of this — of faith." I.e., in light of what we have just seen, the promised inheritance can be received only through faith, not by law. Ἐκ πίστεως (*Ek pisteōs*), "of faith," is set in contrast with ἐκ νόμου (*ek nomou*), "of law" (v. 14).

It is "of faith" **so that it may be by grace . . . .** Given the reality of sin, law can only *enforce* the penalty of God's wrath; it cannot deliver us from it. Deliverance can come only in the form of forgiveness, forgiveness is possible only as a free gift of grace, and grace can be received only through faith in God's promise. Grace and faith are naturally compatible. Faith is the key that fits the lock that opens the treasure-house of grace.

Because the promise comes by grace through faith, it **. . . may be guaranteed to all Abraham's offspring . . .** i.e., to his spiritual children, or those who follow his example of faith. God's concern is to make the promise firm or secure to them all. The issue is not the objective believability of the promise, since God's power and truthfulness are a firm basis for this. The point rather is the subjective apprehension of the promise, the inner assurance that we are indeed safe and secure in "the bosom of Abraham," that "our transgressions are forgiven" and our "sins are covered" (4:7). Such assurance is possible only when we understand that the promised forgiveness is received by grace through faith. (See 5:1-11.)

This assurance comes **not only to those who are of the law but also to those who are of the faith of Abraham** — i.e., not only to Jews, but also to Gentiles. These descriptions of the two groups are quite condensed compared with vv. 11b-12, and present some difficulties. *Ek tou nomou*, "of the law," refers here to the Law of Moses, whereas the other references to law in this section seem to refer to law in general. Taken thus, the first part of this statement refers to the Jews, but by implication only to Jews who are believers. Then the second part of the statement refers specifically to those who are not of the Jewish law but who are only of the faith of Abraham, i.e., Gentile believers. The way of grace thus makes it possible for both categories to be included in the one redeemed family of Abraham: **He is the father of us all.** See 4:11b-12; Gal 3:29.

4:17a As it is written: "I have made you a father of many nations." Some take this to be a parenthesis. The quote is from Gen 17:5, and serves to reinforce the references in v. 16 to "*all* Abraham's offspring" and "father of us *all*."

E. Faith Means Giving Glory to God and Believing His Promises (4:17b-22)

In this section the focus changes from the *fact* of Abraham's justifying faith to its *nature*. Though Abraham's circumstances were different from ours, we can learn important lessons from him as to the kind of faith God expects from us today.

4:17b He is our father in the sight of God, in whom he believed.... If the first part of this verse is a parenthesis, then this clause connects directly with "the father of us all" at the end of v. 16. The NIV makes this connection simply by repeating the thought, "He is our father," though these words do not occur in the Greek text of v. 17. The idea is that in the sight of God Abraham the believer is the spiritual father of all subsequent believers; this is how God sees him (Cranfield, I:243).

Though Paul's wording here may seem a bit awkward, he puts it the way he does in order to focus our attention upon the object of Abraham's faith, namely, God himself. Having then named God as the one "in whom he believed," Paul then utters one of the most basic yet most profound descriptions of God in Scripture: He is **the God who gives life to the dead and calls things that are not as though they were.** This refers to resurrection from the dead and creation from nothing: the two masterworks in the repertoire of divine omnipotence. By his "incomparably great power" God raised Jesus from the dead (Eph 1:19-20).

As the focus of his faith, Abraham believed that God could miraculously restore both his and Sarah's reproductive powers, a kind of figurative "resurrection from the dead" (4:19; Heb 11:11-12). He also believed that God had the power to raise Isaac from the dead if necessary, had the commanded sacrifice been completed (Heb 11:19). This sets the example for us, who are called on to believe that God raised Jesus from the dead (4:24), and to believe that he raises us from spiritual death in baptism (6:4; Col 2:12) and will raise us up from physical death on the last day (8:11,23).

The second part of the description is more difficult. Literally it says God calls the not-being-things as being-things. Or, he addresses things that do not exist as though they exist. Many take this to be a reference to God's unique power to create *ex nihilo*, "from nothing" (see *GC*, 97-117); the wording seems to support this view (❂ I:300-301).

The general language is probably used, however, so that the concept of God's omnipotent, creative call can be applied specifically to Abraham's situation. As the object of Abraham's faith, God is surely the one who names or speaks "of things in the remotest futurity . . . , with as much certainty as if they existed" (DeWelt, 66). When God said to Abraham, "I have made you a father of many nations" (Gen 17:5), he spoke of the future, as-yet-unborn legions of believers as though they already existed (MP, 328). Thus Abraham's faith required him to believe that God controlled the future, and that he could and would bring into existence things which then existed for him only in the form of promises (Heb 11:10,13-16). This is an example for us today, since we also must believe that God can and will one day call into being our not-yet-existing redeemed bodies and their eternal home in the new heavens and new earth.

Thus this verse declares God to be sovereign over the two things that baffle human beings most: death and nothingness (Stott, 133). To believe that God is the master of these mysteries is to believe he can do anything. Abraham so believed, and thus rested his hope in God's promises.

4:18 Against all hope, Abraham in hope believed and so became the father of many nations, just as it had been said to him, "So shall your offspring be." This is Paul's first reference to hope (ἐλπίς, *elpis*) in Romans. Hope is closely related to faith. Indeed, it overlaps that part of our faith that is directed toward the future (8:24-25). In the same way it is closely related to assurance of salvation. Hope as such is the "expectation of something desirable" (Hendriksen, I:159). The biblical connotation does not involve the element of uncertainty or "wishful thinking" often attached to it in American vernacular. In Scripture, hope is the *confident* expectation of our future possession of all that God has promised us.

Abraham's hope was focused especially on the promise of countless descendants as recorded in Gen 15:5. After calling his attention to the multitude of stars in the heavens, God said to him, "So shall your offspring be." At this time Abraham was between 75 and 86 years old (Gen 12:4; 16:16), and was already very conscious of the fact that he was still childless (Gen 15:2-3). But God reassured him, and Abraham believed (Gen 15:6). At least thirteen years later, when he was 99 and Sarah was around 90 (Gen 17:1,17), God again promised that he would be "the father of many nations" (Gen 17:4); and he instituted circumcision as the sign of this covenant (Gen 17:10-14). Abraham demonstrated his faith in the promise by immediately ordering circumcision for himself and every male in his household (Gen 17:23-27).

Under such circumstances Abraham's hope surely transcended all expectation based on natural processes (his own "works"); it was surely grounded in his faith that God could raise the dead and bring something out of nothing. Paul says it thus, that Abraham believed "against all hope," yet "in hope." The word for "against" (παρά, *para*) can also mean "beyond." This difficult statement may thus be understood in two ways (see Cranfield, I:245-246). If *para* means "against," this says that Abraham from the beginning had been filled with true hope even though all along it meant going against all natural expectations. If *para* means "beyond," the idea is that in the beginning (Gen 12:1-3) Abraham's hope involved his and Sarah's natural ability to have children; but God delayed the birth of Isaac so long that they simply went beyond that point. Either way, Abraham continued to have hope, but ultimately he knew that its fulfillment rested completely in the hands of the omnipotent and faithful God. He knew that without God, he would be without hope (Eph 2:12); but he knew that God's promise is always a sufficient basis for hope.

4:19 Without weakening in his faith . . . . What makes this difficult to understand are the episodes recorded in Genesis that seem to reflect a weak faith on Abraham's part. To avoid an imagined danger in Egypt, he lied about his relationship with Sarah instead of trusting God (12:10-20). When Sarah appeared barren, he followed her suggestion and sought to beget offspring through her maidservant Hagar instead of waiting on the Lord (16:1-5). When God promised him a son by Sarah at ages 100 and 90 respectively, he laughed (17:17).

These episodes do not contradict Paul's statement, though. These are relatively minor incidents compared with Abraham's overall record of strong faith. Some people have a weak faith as such (14:1), but Abraham had only momentary lapses from which he always recovered. The Egypt event was early in his covenant relationship with God. Prior to the Hagar event God had not specifically named Sarah as the mother of his heir. Fuller says Abraham's laughter was "a laughter of faith and not mockery" (*Unity*, 307). When the greatest test of all came — the command to sacrifice Isaac, he did not hesitate (Gen 22:1-10).

. . . he faced the fact that his body was as good as dead—since he was about a hundred years old—and that Sarah's womb was also dead. "Faced the fact" is κατανοέω (*katanoeō*), "to consider, to contemplate." (❋I:303) The idea is that he was fully aware of his and Sarah's inability to have children; he took this into account but still continued to believe. (See Cranfield, I:247.)

Describing the lack of childbearing ability in terms of death highlights God's role in the birth of Isaac as a kind of resurrection from the dead (4:17,24). In this regard Abraham's body was "as good as dead" (see Heb 11:12), and Sarah's womb was dead. Even before they left Haran Sarah was declared barren (Gen 11:30). When the promise included her specifically she was 90 years old (Gen 17:17) and definitely "past the age of childbearing" (Gen 18:11; Heb 11:11).

Because of these factors the conception and birth of Isaac were undoubtedly the working of God's supernatural power. In view of the fact that he later fathered six sons by another wife, Keturah (Gen 25:1-2), we can assume that "the procreative power granted by God to Abraham was not confined to the birth of Isaac alone but remained with him afterward" (Moo, 284, n. 75).

4:20 In spite of the state of procreative "deadness," **[y]et he did not waver through unbelief regarding the promise of God, but was strengthened in his faith . . . .** This helps explain the fact that Abraham did not "weaken" in his faith, i.e., he did not waver to the point of unbelief (❧ I:304). This is not to deny that he sometimes had to struggle with his faith, but a struggling faith is not the same as unbelief.

That Abraham "was strengthened in his faith" means he was strengthened with reference to his faith; his faith itself was strengthened. How was it strengthened? Up to the time of Sarah's actual pregnancy and Isaac's birth (Gen 21:1-2), the only thing he had as a basis for his faith was the bare promise of God, which the Lord kept graciously renewing to him. But the repetition of the promise was enough; he continued to walk by faith, not by sight. "Abraham had nothing going for him except the promise of God. But for the man of faith that was enough" (Morris, 212).

What follows in the rest of v. 20 and in v. 21 is an excellent two-part summary of the essence of Abraham's justifying faith, and it presents a pattern that all believers can and must follow. The first aspect of Abraham's faith was that **he gave glory to God . . . .** The "glory" of God is his collective greatness, his total perfection, his manifested majesty (see 1:21). It cannot be increased; it can only be acknowledged and honored. We "give" glory to God by honoring him and by calling attention to everything that makes him great. The very essence of justifying faith is that it gives glory to God, since it is faith *in God* and in what *he* has done and promises to do, rather than a reliance upon ourselves and what we are able to achieve. Faith by its very nature puts ourselves in the background and turns the spotlight upon God.

4:21 This verse sets forth the second aspect of Abraham's faith: **being fully persuaded that God had power to do what he had promised.** The verb means "to be fully persuaded, fully convinced, fully assured." Toward what was this total confidence directed? Nothing less than the *promises of God*. Everything rested on whether or not God could keep his promises; Abraham believed that he could. He believed in the promises because he believed in the power, the "wonder-working power" of God, the power that is able to raise the dead and create from nothing (4:17).

Stott rightly points out that trusting in a person's promises requires believing he has not only the *power* to keep them, but also the *will* to do so. I.e., "behind all promises lies the character of the person who makes them" (134). Though it is not explicitly stated in this verse, it is implied that Abraham was fully persuaded not only that God *could* keep his promises because of his power, but also that he *would* keep them because of his faithfulness.

The essence of justifying faith still follows the pattern of Abraham. God promises to save us by his grace through the work of Jesus Christ. We are called on to trust completely in this promise, believing in the loving intention of God and the forgiving power of the cross. This is not easy to do, just as it is not easy for a drowning person to relax and let a lifeguard hold on to him and pull him to shore. Instinctively the drowning person wants to grab and hold on, while thrashing and kicking and straining; but this only hinders and may even thwart the attempt to save him. If he really wants to be saved, he must relax and trust himself to the expertise and ability of the lifeguard. Likewise if we want to be saved, we must truly believe in God's saving grace, which requires us to let go of our works and to rest in the certainty of his promises. Such faith enables us to stop anxiously examining our personal "workometer" in order to make guesses as to our salvation status. It enables us instead simply to fix our eyes upon Jesus, the author and perfecter of our faith (Heb 12:2).

4:22 This is why "it was credited to him as righteousness." Most of the verses in this section have explored the meaning of Gen 15:6a, "Abraham believed God." Having shown us in stunning fashion the main aspects of the patriarch's faith, Paul here closes this section by simply quoting Gen 15:6b again: "It was credited to him as righteousness."

The words "This is why" indicate that there is a cause-and-effect relation between the two parts of Gen 15:6. Because Abraham's faith was this kind of faith, he was fully justified before God.

F. Those Who Believe like Abraham Are Justified like Abraham (4:23-25)

4:23-24 The heading over this main section (ch. 4) calls Abraham the "paradigm of grace." Throughout the entire chapter we have been applying his example to all believers who follow him and especially to Christians today. In this last brief section of the chapter we see that such a parallel is intended. God wants us to know that those who believe like Abraham are justified like Abraham. In fact, says Paul, the key words in Gen 15:6 were included in the Bible specifically for our sakes. **The words "it was credited to him" were written not for him alone, but also for us** . . . . The whole account of Abraham and the record of his strong faith were written not just to honor him but to benefit us believers today.

"Not for him *alone*" suggests that it is appropriate for such a great man to be honored. It is fitting that he should live on in the memories of his children, both physical and spiritual, and that his life of faith should be held up as an example worthy of praise.

But we must not forget its intended application to our lives today. Indeed, the NT tells us that everything recorded in the OT, including good and bad behavior, has been recorded for our sakes, for us to learn both what pleases God and what angers him. (See 15:4; 1 Cor 9:10; 10:11; 2 Tim 3:16.) The example of Abraham is special, though, because it illuminates so clearly the essence of grace, the heart of which is justification by faith. The key words of Gen 15:6, "it was credited to him as righteousness," mean simply that he was *justified* — by his faith. This sets the pattern for those today **to whom God will credit righteousness**, i.e., whom God will justify. And of whom is this blessed category comprised? **. . . us who believe in him who raised Jesus our Lord from the dead . . . .**

The reference to crediting righteousness (i.e., justifying) has a future ring to it. Paul says literally that believers are "about to be" credited as righteous. Some see this as pointing ahead to the final judgment, where God will once and for all declare us righteous through the blood of Christ. Another possibility is that "about to be" points to what was in the future from the perspective of Abraham himself. In any case there is no reason to take this as implying that believers are not yet justified. Paul in other places makes it clear that our justification is a past event (4:7; 5:1; 1 Cor 6:11; Titus 3:7) and a present reality (3:24; 5:9). Indeed, the very example of Abraham confirms this: "it was credited" is past tense (4:3, 9-10,22).

The act of faith is here called believing "upon" (ἐπί, *epi*), which is not just bare intellectual assent to facts but also a surrender of the will and a commitment of the self to the *person* who is the object of faith, in this case God the Father. The focus is on faith in God the Father because of the prominence of the theme of resurrection from the dead (4:17,19) and because Scripture predominantly describes the resurrection of Jesus as the work of the Father.

It is clear that justifying faith must include faith in the resurrection of Jesus from the dead (10:9), in addition to faith in the atoning power of his death (3:25). Abraham's faith is most appropriately paradigmatic for the former since it was truly a faith that God is able to raise the dead (4:17,19). Our faith is no different, except we now know that this holy resurrection power is ultimately displayed in the raising of Jesus (Eph 1:18-20; Col 2:12). In this light it is significant that the final fulfilment of God's promise to Abraham was when he raised Jesus from the dead (Acts 13:32-34).

4:25 Paul fittingly closes this chapter with a brief summary of the gospel facts that make salvation by grace possible and that are at the very heart of justifying faith: the death and resurrection of Jesus (see 1 Cor 15:1-4): **He was delivered over to death for our sins and was raised to life for our justification.** The words "to death" are not in the Greek text, but this is no doubt the meaning. The term for "delivered over" is παραδίδωμι (*paradidōmi*), the same word used for God's act of delivering rebellious sinners over to the consequences of their sins in 1:24,26,28. Here the reference is to the One who was delivered over to the cross in their place, and ours. The One who so delivered him is the Father (Acts 2:23; Rom 8:32; see Rom 3:25).

He was "raised to life" refers to the resurrection of Jesus ("to life" is not in the original). The word for justification is the noun δικαίωσις (*dikaiōsis*), used only here and in 5:18. Usually the verb δικαιόω (*dikaioō*, "to justify") is used. Either way the concept is equivalent both to the expression "crediting of righteousness" (used throughout the chapter) and to the terminology of forgiveness (4:7-8).

The most difficult problem of interpretation in this verse comes from the double use of the preposition "for" (διά, *dia*). The concept is causal: "on account of, because of" (see NASB). The problem is whether the object of each of these two uses of *dia* is the *cause* or the *effect* of the action it modifies. If it is the cause, the phrase is said to be retrospective, or looking to the past. This seems to be the most natural way to understand the first clause: he was delivered up as the result of our sins. Our sins are the cause, and his death is the effect. But if the object of *dia* is the effect, the phrase is said to be prospective, or looking to the future. This seems most natural for the second clause: he was raised up in order to bring about our justification. His resurrection is the cause; our justification is the effect.

The reason this is problematic is that it seems Paul would not use *dia* here in parallel clauses in such different senses. Some take this view, while others argue for consistency and interpret both uses of *dia* in the same way. If both uses are retrospective, this would require us to say that in some way the resurrection was the result of our justification, as the cross was the result of our sins. On the other hand if both are prospective, it would require us to say that Jesus' death was the cause of something relating to our sins, such as their covering or atonement (❁ I:309).

In considering all these possibilities, the weakest concept is the idea that somehow Jesus was raised because we had already been justified, or that his resurrection was somehow the result of our justification. When we rule this idea out, that leaves us with just two options: either *dia* means different things in the two clauses, or both clauses have a prospective reference.

Though it is most natural to say that Jesus was delivered up on account of the fact of our sins (retrospective), it also makes sense to say that he was delivered up because of the need to atone for our sins (prospective). I do not know how to choose between these two meanings here; perhaps both are intended.

Regarding the second clause, to say that it is prospective is the better choice; but this still leaves us with the question, in what way does the resurrection of Jesus bring about our justification? It is much easier to see how Jesus *died* for our justification, but here Paul says he was *raised* for it. What does this mean?

Bruce (119) says Jesus was raised "to guarantee" our justification. But in what sense would this be the case? One possibility is that his resurrection demonstrates the validity of his claims and proves that the apostolic teaching about the meaning of the cross is true. Anyone could make lofty claims about his impending death (see Mark 10:45; John 12:32); but if his dead body turned to dust in his grave, we would be inclined to disregard his claims. But in the case of Jesus his resurrection confirms his claims and guarantees the justifying power of his blood; thus we know that our faith in his blood is not in vain. This is the faith that justifies, and because of his resurrection we have a firm basis for it. As Murray says, "Only as the living Lord can he be the object of faith" (I:156).

This is similar to Hendriksen's suggestion (I:161) that Jesus was raised in order to *assure* us that in God's sight we are indeed justified. "The Father, by raising Jesus from the dead, assures us that the atoning sacrifice has been accepted; hence, our sins are forgiven."

One other possibility is that Jesus' resurrection brings about our justification by enabling him to complete the full process of atonement. According to the OT pattern, the High Priest not only offered the sacrifice but also sprinkled its blood on the altar in the Most Holy Place (Lev 16). Likewise, to accomplish our justification, Jesus our Great High Priest not only had to offer himself as a sacrifice by shedding his blood on the cross; he also had to enter heaven itself "once for all by his own blood" and "appear for us in God's presence" (Heb 9:12,24; see Heb 6:19-20; 10:19-22). Therefore it was necessary for him to be raised from the dead so that he could ascend bodily into heaven and complete the work of atonement on which our justification is based.

III. 5:1-21 – GRACE AND ASSURANCE

How does Romans 5 relate to the overall development of Paul's argument in this epistle? In my opinion it should be regarded as the conclusion of the discussion that began at 3:21. The main subject continues to be the presentation of grace as the only effective way of salvation. In 3:21-31 Paul explains the essence of grace as the free gift of God's righteousness to sinners, a righteousness established by the propitiatory sacrifice of Jesus Christ and received by faith apart from works of law. In ch. 4 he shows that being counted righteous (i.e., being justified) by faith has always been God's way of saving sinners, citing especially the example of Abraham. Now in ch. 5 the Apostle sets forth one of the most important immediate results of justification by faith, namely, assurance of salvation.

Romans Part Two

In one way or another almost all commentators describe ch. 5 this way. They use a variety of terms but say the same thing, i.e., that this chapter presents the results, fruits, benefits, blessings, effects, or consequences of justification by faith. Though these benefits may be enumerated in various ways (e.g., peace, hope, joy), they all may be summed up in one word: *assurance*.

A. Assurance of Personal Salvation (5:1-11)

The first half of Romans 5 shows how justification by faith yields a genuine sense of assurance of personal salvation, a conviction of being at peace with God and accepted by God (❖I:311). This sense of personal assurance is the privilege of every Christian, and we cannot overemphasize the blessedness of it. Unfortunately, many Christians do not have such assurance, mainly because they do not understand its proper basis. What is that proper basis? It is the knowledge that we are justified by our faith in the atoning blood of Jesus Christ. That is the point of 5:1-11.

1. Justification by Faith Is the Key to Assurance (5:1-2)

5:1 Therefore, since we have been justified through faith, we have peace with God through our Lord Jesus Christ . . . . "Therefore" introduces the practical conclusion to be drawn from the presentation of grace in 3:21–4:25. "Since we have been justified through faith" sums up the main point of that passage and states the heart of grace. The verb is aorist (past) tense, indicating that justification is an event that has already occurred in the experience of Paul's Christian readers. This past act, however, produces a continuing state of *being* justified, so that the Christian is a justified person, a forgiven person. "Through faith" indicates the means by which we first *became* justified, and also the means by which we *remain* justified.

The main point here is the cause-and-effect relationship between justification and peace: because we have been justified, "we have peace with God." This refers to an objective state of peace, a cessation of hostilities and an end of enmity between God and the sinner. God's righteous love initiates a process of reconciliation (5:10-11), leading to this state of peace in which we are no longer God's enemies but are his friends. The key element in this process of reconciliation, of course, is "the death of his Son" (5:10); thus Paul says our peace with God comes "through our Lord Jesus Christ."

This peace is an objective state, not a subjective feeling; but we may rightly infer that peace as a subjective state of mind is the natural consequence of being at peace with God and knowing it.

This latter point — *knowing it* — is crucial for attaining subjective peace. Christians truly *are* justified and truly *are* at peace with God; but confusion about how faith, works, and justification are related often keeps them from understanding this and thus from having true inner peace. Only when we understand that we are justified by faith apart from works of law (3:28) can we have this inner peace, which is a basic element of assurance of salvation (❂ I:313).

5:2 Verse 2 continues the thought by speaking of Jesus as the one **through whom we have gained access by faith into this grace in which we now stand.** The work of Jesus is always the cause of our salvation, the meritorious ground or basis which makes it possible. "By faith" is simply the means by which we personally receive the gift of grace made available through his work.

Because of the demonstrative pronoun, "this grace" must refer specifically to something named in the preceding verse. Paul is most certainly referring to the state of justification, though he may also mean the state of peace with God. Most likely "this grace" includes both, since they are inseparable.

In any case Paul describes "this grace" as a state or sphere that is *entered* and in which one *stands*. The idea of entering grace is seen in the phrase "we have gained access." This is not the best translation; such language suggests personal accomplishment ("gained") rather than a free gift. The word for "access" is better rendered "entry" or "introduction" (NASB); this is consistent with the preposition "into" (*eis*) before "grace." The idea is that at a certain point of time we *entered* into the state of grace; we were introduced into it by Jesus Christ (❂ I:314).

Paul also says grace is a *state* "in which we now stand," within which we securely rest. The idea seems to be that of a continuing, abiding existence within the state of grace and suggests that our position in grace is firm and secure, rather than tentative and precarious. The point is that grace is like a room into which we enter by the door of Jesus Christ, a room which becomes our refuge and in which we continue to dwell (❂ I:314).

Verse 2 concludes with these words: **And we rejoice in the hope of the glory of God.** This affirmation is parallel to "we have peace with God" in v. 1. "Peace" is our present relationship with God; "hope of glory" (Col 1:27) points to our future heavenly inheritance.

"The glory of God" (see 3:23) in this verse is surely a reference to the final, eschatological revelation of God's majesty and splendor. Our hope is not only that we will one day *behold* his glory, but that in a limited sense we will actually *participate* in it or *partake* of it. The latter will be true in the sense that we will have a glorified body like the glorified human body of Christ, and in the sense that we will actually dwell in the beneficent radiance of God's glorious presence.

Paul says that we who are justified by faith and have peace with God have *hope* of this glory. As noted earlier (4:18), in the Bible the Christian's hope is a confident expectation of our future possession of all the elements of salvation not yet received (Cranfield, I:260; Stott, 140). Its object is not simply what we *want* to happen, but what God has *promised* will happen (see 2 Tim 1:12).

As such, biblical hope is the heart and core of the Christian's assurance of salvation. Assurance includes first of all the subjective peace of mind that comes from knowing we are at peace with God now that we are justified by faith. We are sure of our *present* relationship with God. But here we see that our assurance also includes a blessed confidence about the *future*. We have neither anxiety nor terror as we look ahead to the day of judgment, because we know that the same justifying blood of Christ that brought us into this present relationship with God will continue to cover us and will be our passage into future glory.

No wonder "we rejoice"! The same or similar words are translated "brag" or "boast" in earlier texts (2:17,23; 3:27; 4:2), but "rejoice" is proper and preferred in this context (as in 5:3,11). It is a stronger concept than ordinary rejoicing. This "exceeding great joy" rests upon the *hope* described above; it is the natural product and companion of assurance.

2. Tribulations of Believers Do Not Nullify Assurance (5:3-5)

In this fallen world everyone suffers the general ravages of sin, sickness, and death; but Christians often suffer even more in the form of persecution from Satan and from the unbelieving world. When this happens we are strongly tempted to doubt our salvation and to question the very love of God. Thoughts like these form in our hearts: "If God really loves me, why does he let these things happen to me? It seems as if God has abandoned me; he must be punishing me for my sin. Maybe there is no God, and heaven is a myth."

This seems to be the kind of potential situation Paul is addressing in these verses. He has stressed the reality of our peace and hope that are based on the knowledge that we are justified by faith in Christ's blood. But he knows that the hope of future glory is sometimes hidden by the dark clouds of present suffering. So he reminds us that within the broad scope of God's sovereignty and love, not even tribulations can nullify our assurance of salvation. In fact, they actually strengthen it.

5:3-4 Not only so, but we also rejoice in our sufferings . . . . "Sufferings" (afflictions, hardships) is a strong term and refers to the experiences of life that press down upon us and crush us both physically and mentally. Here they include the kinds of suffering shared by all people (e.g., hunger, war, disease, death), as well as persecutions directed specifically toward Christians. The latter are not just end-time tribulations, but include the constant hostility and ongoing opposition of the unbelieving world.

Here Paul makes the unlikely assertion that we *rejoice* in such suffering. In v. 2 he says we rejoice in our hope, which makes perfectly good sense. But now he says we also rejoice in the very things that would seem to negate and bedim that hope. In fact, he says that in an indirect way, such sufferings even *increase* our hope!

This does not mean that we should deliberately seek such suffering, like masochists; nor does it necessarily mean that God is purposefully causing us to suffer, contrary to a popular idea. It is rather a recognition of the fact that, now that suffering is present in the world and is inevitable for Christians, God is able to *use* it in such a way that it actually adds to our assurance (8:28). Thus the Bible consistently describes the afflictions of Christians as positive experiences that produce joy and blessing.

Paul does not go into great detail in explaining *how* tribulations produce hope. (He reflects further on these ideas in 8:28-39 (see below).) He mentions only three steps: **because we know that suffering produces perseverance; perseverance, character; and character, hope.** First, suffering produces perseverance. This word means patient endurance, steadfastness, the ability to bear and to bear up under whatever comes along. Sufferings do not in and of themselves automatically produce endurance. Rather, when we enter into such sufferings while holding onto the hand of God, he himself works endurance within us through them and for them.

Second, perseverance works character. The word here belongs to a word group that refers to the process of testing or trying or proving something, and also to the state of having been tested or proved and thus of being approved. The NASB more appropriately translates it here as "proven character." The idea is that sufferings are like a test which, when endured by the strength which God supplies, results in a quality of life and character that has been tempered and purified and demonstrated to be pleasing to God. (See Zech 13:9.)

Finally, proven character produces hope. This assumes that we as Christians are consciously aware that we have stood up under the trial of our sufferings, and that God has been with us and has not allowed us to be defeated by them. This gives us even more confidence in God, and the sense that nothing, not even the worst tribulations, can separate us from the grace of God and prevent us from entering eternal life. Thus our hope is strengthened and confirmed.

5:5 Here Paul stresses that no matter how severe our present trials may be, our hope is still secure because we know for a fact that God loves us. **And hope does not disappoint us . . . .** The word for "disappoint" is more properly translated "does not cause us to be ashamed." We will not be personally disappointed, nor will we have to feel humiliation and shame in the face of mocking and ridicule from the enemies of Christ.

. . . because God has poured out his love into our hearts . . . . Our hope is certain because it is grounded upon the reality of the love of God. "Into our hearts" refers to the soul or spirit (as distinct from the body), which includes the "conscious inner life" of the person (Schlatter, 122). Thus Paul is talking about how the love of God becomes present within our inner life and in a sense present to our consciousness. It becomes present within us by being "poured out" into our hearts. The imagery of "pouring out" represents the concept of *abundance*.

God's love is poured out into our hearts **by the Holy Spirit, whom he has given us.** This refers to the gift consisting of the Holy Spirit, who himself was poured out from heaven on Pentecost (Acts 2:17-18,33) and who is poured out into the heart of each individual believer in the act of baptism (Acts 2:38; Titus 3:5-6). Here "given us" refers to the latter event.

The main question now is, *how* does the Holy Spirit pour God's love into our hearts? (❃I:319) First, as the divine author of Scripture, the Holy Spirit pours out the *knowledge* of God's love into our hearts through the biblical testimony to the atoning sacrifice of Christ, which is the greatest possible demonstration of God's love (John 3:16; 15:13; Rom 5:8; 1 John 4:8-10) (❃I:319). Second, the Holy Spirit pours the love of God into our hearts as the agent by which the blessings of redemption are applied to us in the initial moment of our salvation (❃I:319-320). Third, the Holy Spirit pours the love of God into our hearts by strengthening our inner conviction of the certainty of God's love for us personally. Most commentators tend to ignore the first two points above and to focus entirely upon this subjective experience.

Certainly we cannot deny that the Holy Spirit strengthens and sharpens our awareness of and faith in God's love as a part of his sanctifying work in our hearts. But we must be careful not to separate this from the first two points above, as if some purely subjective experience of God's love were the basis for our hope. However important this inward strengthening of the Spirit may be, our hope is not based on this subjective experience as such. The fact is that this subjective experience presupposes and supplements several prior *objective* realities: the atoning death of Christ, the Spirit's inspiration of Scripture, our hearing and obeying of the gospel, and our reception of the Holy Spirit himself in Christian baptism.

3. Christ Died for Us While We Were Still Sinners (5:6-8)

The next six verses are an exposition of the point stated above, that assurance of salvation is ultimately based on the assurance that God really loves us. Here Paul explains how we can know for sure that God loves us, and he explains how this knowledge is the way to assurance.

One key element in Paul's argument is the distinction or contrast between *what we were* before we turned to God for salvation, and *what we are now*, in the present state of grace. The main point is this: if, while we were God's *enemies*, he loved us so much that he was willing to die for us, how can we think that he loves us any less now that we are his *friends*?

The other key element in the argument is the comparison between the first and second transitions in the process of our salvation. The first one, already accomplished, is the transition *from wrath to grace*. The second, which is yet to come, is the transition *from grace to glory*. Which of these transitions is the more difficult, the more radical, the less likely and less expected? The first one, by far. Yet, because of his love and by the power of the cross, God has brought us through this first transition, through faith. The main point now is this: if we have already experienced the first transition, which was infinitely unlikely and even impossible from the standpoint of human expectation, how much more can we confidently expect God to bring us through the second transition as well? We came through the first one by faith apart from works of law; are we now trying to make the second one somehow more difficult than the first?

In this present section (5:6-8) Paul focuses on what we *were*, prior to the first transition. His point is that no matter how miserable and hopeless our condition was then, God still loved us so much that Christ died for us.

5:6 You see, at just the right time, when we were still powerless, Christ died for the ungodly (❂ I:321). The love of God has been poured out into our hearts, and we have hope, *because* we have heard the gospel of the cross.

As Godet says (191), this verse "describes the miserable condition in which we were at the time when divine love was extended to us." First, we were ἀσθενής (*asthenēs*), "powerless, weak, helpless, without strength." Here this means not the finiteness of the creature, but the helplessness of the sinner. It refers to "that helpless weakness of sin which so incapacitated us as to render us incapable of goodness" (MP, 332). Also, we were totally helpless to do anything about it; we were unable to save ourselves.

Second, we were ἀσεβής (*asebēs*), "wicked, ungodly" (see 1:18; 4:5). This means that we were in a state of opposition to God and his law, and were totally undeserving of his loving forgiveness. It means that we were standing in his wrath, since the wrath of God is against all the wickedness (*asebeia*) of men (1:18).

These adjectives describe the condition of the whole fallen human race, and the plight of each individual in our unsaved state as God viewed us in his foreknowledge from the perspective of eternity past. ("We" refers to all human beings.) Even then he loved us so much that he planned the atonement (Rev 13:8); and "at just the right time" in history (see Gal 4:4), Christ came and died for us. This explains how God is able to justify the wicked (*asebēs*), as 4:5 declares. As the saying goes, "Love will find a way."

In the expression "Christ died for the ungodly," the word "for" is ὑπέρ (*hyper*, v. 8 also). It means "for" in the sense of "on behalf of, for the sake of." Though some question this, it can also mean more precisely "in the place of, instead of." In other words, it can have the connotation of substitution; and when used here for the death of Christ it connotes the substitutionary atonement.

5:7 Very rarely will anyone die for a righteous man, though for a good man someone might possibly dare to die. While the underlying Greek words for "righteous" and "good" can be understood as referring to a just and good *cause* or a just and good *man*, the latter seems the better choice, since the comparison is with Christ dying for *people* rather than a cause.

Another issue is whether the "righteous man" and the "good man" are basically the same, or whether there is a significant distinction between them (❂ I:323). The former view is to be preferred; the two clauses are best understood as saying the same thing in different ways. The first says it negatively: scarcely ever will anyone die for a righteous man. The second says it positively: well, maybe — possibly, perhaps — someone could be found who would do this. And if this is such a rarity, it goes without saying that we might as well give up trying to find anyone willing to die for a wicked and unjust person!

But is this not the very point Paul is making? There is indeed someone who was willing to die for the weak and the wicked, namely, Jesus our Lord! Thus the contrast here is not between the righteous man and the good man, but between the (hypothetical) good and righteous man of v. 7, and the weak and ungodly persons of v. 6. The latter are the very ones for whom Christ died! And if it is so difficult to find someone who is willing to die for a good man, then how much more *amazing* it is that he died for weak and ungodly sinners! In view of this contrast, the love of God is magnified even more, as Paul now states:

5:8 But God demonstrates his own love for us in this: While we were still sinners, Christ died for us. He died "for" us (*hyper*, see v. 6) while we were weak, ungodly sinners. This was our condition in the mind of God when he determined to give his only-begotten Son to be the propitiation for our sins. What more could he do to show us that he really and truly loves us? This actually *proves* it, says Paul. The word for "demonstrates" has the connotation of proof. That Christ died for our sins, while we were sinners, is proof of his love (❂ I:324).

4. Our Hope Is Even More Secure Now That We Are His Friends (5:9-11)

In this paragraph Paul brings into full view the contrast between what we were and what we are, and the relative ease of the remaining transition from grace to glory as compared with the already-accomplished transition from wrath to grace. Actually Paul's point here is that there are *three* stages in the Christian's spiritual journey, marked by the two transitions. In these verses they are named thus: (1) enemies; (2) justified and reconciled; (3) saved. The point is that if God's love has brought us from the first to the second stage, it will all the more surely bring us from the second to the third.

A more complete chart of these stages and transitions, based on this entire section (5:1-11) follows:

PAST	PRESENT	FUTURE
Powerless (v. 6)	Justified (vv. 1,9)	Glory of God (v. 2)
Ungodly (6)	Peace with God (1)	Saved from wrath (9)
Sinners (8)	Standing in grace (2)	(Fully) saved (10)
Enemies of God (10)	Rejoicing in hope (2,11)	
	Rejoicing in suffering (3)	
	God's love in our hearts (5)	
	Holy Spirit within us (5)	
	Under Christ's blood (9)	
	Reconciled to God (10,11)	

The key words in this paragraph are "much more." We may think of this passage as teaching us the "much more" of Christian assurance. We know that God has already brought us from wrath to grace through the greatest possible demonstration of his love, even though we were his enemies at the time. Therefore, now that we are his friends, we can have *much more* confidence that his love and Christ's blood will suffice to take us on to glory.

Verses 9 and 10 are parallel in form, both making this same point in different ways. Verse 9 emphasizes justification and thus our changed legal standing before God; verse 10 focuses on reconciliation and thus our changed personal relationship with God (Hendriksen, I:174). Each is an argument from the greater to the lesser, i.e., "When one has done *the most* for his *enemies*, he does not refuse to do *the least* for his *friends*" (Godet, 194).

5:9 Since we have now been justified by his blood, how much more shall we be saved from God's wrath through him! The opening words of this verse in the Greek are "Therefore much more." The word "therefore" shows that Paul is drawing a conclusion from the fact stated in v. 8, which is the "greater" element in his argument, v. 9 being the "lesser." The words "much more" are put here for emphasis.

The word "now" points to the present stage of our spiritual odyssey, as compared both with the past stage ("sinners," v. 8) and the future stage ("saved," v. 9b). Where are we, *now*? In 5:2 Paul says we are "standing in grace," which he here says includes being "justified." This is an aorist participle, referring to the past act in which God declared us righteous, resulting in the continuing state of being justified (see 5:1).

"By his blood" refers of course to the blood poured out on Calvary when Christ put himself in our place and suffered the eternal wrath of God for us. It is the efficacious basis for our justification. God counts us as righteous because he accepts Christ's payment of our penalty in our place. We stand in justification because we are now standing under his blood, which is over us as a shield from God's wrath. Standing in grace thus includes standing under the blood. See 3:24-26.

Our future state is described as being saved from God's wrath. Here "saved" is future tense and refers to our final salvation on the day of judgment. "God's wrath" is the sentence of condemnation at the final judgment and eternal consignment to the lake of fire. This is the ultimate outpouring of divine wrath. As Christians justified by Christ's blood, we know that this is not our destiny (❂ I:326).

Paul continues to remind us that this is all because of Jesus Christ. We became and remain justified "by his blood," and we shall be saved from wrath "through him!" "There is therefore now no condemnation for those who are in Christ Jesus" (8:1), i.e., under his blood.

5:10 For if, when we were God's enemies, we were reconciled to him through the death of his Son, how much more, having been reconciled, shall we be saved through his life! Here the form of the argument is exactly the same as v. 9, with the focus being on reconciliation rather than justification. The past-present-future theme is clearly stated: enemies, reconciled, saved. That the greater transition gives us assurance of the yet-to-come lesser one is emphasized by the repeated words, "much more."

The transition from being God's enemy to being in a state of reconciliation with him is as radical a transition as can be imagined. The worst possible situation a creature can be in is to be an enemy of God. This relationship of enmity includes, of course, the sinner's hostility toward and hatred of God (8:7; Col 1:21), which must be removed in the process of reconciliation. But it also includes God's hostility toward and hatred of the sinner (11:28), which must also be removed in this process (❂ I:327).

Paul's point is that, even while we were in this state of mutual hostility, God took the initiative to eliminate the enmity and bring about reconciliation between the warring parties. This means that the infinite and all-conquering love of God co-existed within his nature alongside his own enmity toward us in a kind of tension. (On this concept of tension within God's nature see *GRe*, 313-314, 372-375, 408.) But in accordance with his eternal wisdom, his love was able to find a way for him to give full expression to his righteous wrath and enmity, while at the same time offering reconciliation to repentant sinners. This "way" of course was "through the death of his Son," which was a propitiatory sacrifice that allowed God to pour out his wrath upon Jesus instead of upon us. Thus through the death of Jesus God's wrath is satisfied and his own enmity is set aside. This is the first step to reconciliation.

The second step is to confront sinners with the reality of what God has done, and to persuade them to give up their own enmity toward him and allow him to cancel his enmity toward them personally (5:11; 2 Cor 5:20). Only when this takes place does the reconciled state actually begin. At that point the "peace with God" of which 5:1 speaks begins to exist.

Now comes the argument from the greater to the lesser: "If God has done so much for his enemies, what will he not do for his friends?" (Erdman, 63-64). Being his friends, how *much more* can we now count on him to take us on to the final state of glory! God is no longer against us; he is *for* us (8:31), imperfect though we are. He surely will not abandon us now.

Again Paul refers to this future stage as "being saved," i.e., receiving the full and final salvation of heaven. "Through his life" refers to Christ's risen and glorified life as he exists at the right hand of the Father in his ongoing intercessory ministry (Mounce, 138). See 4:25; 8:34. This will come to a climax on the day of judgment, when Christ the Judge will himself intercede for us and continue to cover our sins with his blood and usher us into eternal life (❂ I:328-329).

5:11 Not only is this so, but we also rejoice in God through our Lord Jesus Christ, through whom we have now received reconciliation. "This" refers to "shall be saved" in vv. 9 and 10, namely, our future salvation. Paul is reminding us that our salvation is not just future; it has already begun. We have already received the reconciliation and possess it *now* as the result of being justified *now* (5:9).

Thus even now our lives are filled with *rejoicing in God*. This is the same word used in vv. 2 and 3, where the NIV also translates it "rejoice." In 2:17, where the word probably has the connotation of bragging or boasting in God, Paul reproves the Jews for joyfully boasting in God in reference to his Law, or more specifically in reference to their own prideful use of that Law. Here in 5:11 Paul shows us how to rightfully boast or rejoice in God, namely, in reference to his *grace*. We are constantly overwhelmed with "jubilant exultation" (Cranfield, I:268) as we think about what God has done for us through Jesus Christ.

Finally we must call attention to the way Paul has exalted Jesus Christ throughout this passage as the one who has made grace and assurance possible. Ten times in these 11 verses the saving role of Jesus is thrust before our consciousness: "through our Lord Jesus Christ . . . through whom . . . Christ died . . . Christ died . . . by his blood . . . through him . . . through the death of his Son . . . through his life . . . through our Lord Jesus Christ . . . through whom." He, and not ourselves — what he has done, not what we have done or are doing — is the source and basis for our assurance of salvation.

B. The All-Sufficiency of the Death of Christ (5:12-21)

This section, which serves as the conclusion to the second main section of Romans (3:21-5:21), has a reputation for difficulty (❂ I:330). To be sure, there are some genuine exegetical problems here; but once four key questions are answered, the overall meaning of the passage becomes quite clear.

The first question is this: *What is the purpose of this passage in relation to the epistle as a whole?* This passage is best understood as continuing the theme of assurance that began with 5:1. In 5:1-11 Paul assures us that we can put all our hope and confidence in *one saving act* (the cross) of *one man* (Jesus Christ). We have pointed out how in those 11 verses the apostle makes 10 references to the saving efficacy of Christ and his cross. In light of this someone might begin to wonder, "Isn't this expecting an awfully lot from just one man?" (❷ I:330)

In order to show that this is not as far-fetched as we might at first think, Paul calls attention to the man whose one act has already been demonstrated to have a universal effect upon the human race, namely, Adam. Then he uses this by way of comparison and contrast to show that the "one righteous act" of the one man, Jesus, will surely be just as efficacious and universal as the "one sinful act" of the one man, Adam — and even "much more" (5:15,17). His argument moves from the lesser to the greater. If we can accept the fact that the one sin of a mere man has brought sin and death upon the whole world, then we can surely believe that the atoning death of the Son of God has brought salvation upon the whole world. The purpose of the passage, then, is to increase our confidence in the all-sufficiency of the death of Christ.

The second preliminary question is this: *Does this paragraph teach the doctrine of original sin?* It is not wrong to raise this question. Indeed, we cannot read Paul's many references to Adam and to the universal consequences of his one sin without wondering about it. Adam's sin brought death, judgment, and condemnation upon all; by his one sin all were made sinners. Does this mean that every child is conceived and born sinful, and born condemned to death and eternal punishment? Is this the main doctrine Paul wants to establish in this passage?

The fact is that at least since the time of Augustine (early fifth century), many in Christendom have used these verses to construct this very doctrine. Because the concept of original sin has had such a profound and far-reaching impact upon Christian thought as a whole, Barclay has rightly said that no passage in the NT "has had such an influence on theology as this passage" (77). The doctrine of original sin basically teaches that, in addition to physical death, Adam's first sin brought severe spiritual consequences upon all his natural descendants. The term itself refers not to that first sin but to the spiritual state in which children are conceived and born as the result of it.

Now the question is this: does 5:12-21 actually teach some form of original sin? Without doubt Paul is here affirming that Adam's sin did bring serious consequences upon all his offspring. Our understanding of the exact nature of these consequences depends upon how we interpret the terms "death," "judgment," "condemnation," and "made sinners" as used in the text. Many have tried to limit them all to physical death only, thus denying that 5:12-21 teaches any sort of original sin. Others believe that these terms, both in themselves and as compared with the blessings received from Christ, must refer to something much more serious than physical death by itself. Thus they conclude that this text does indeed teach original sin.

The biggest problem with this whole approach is that it implicitly assumes that Paul's main subject here is Adam and his sin and its consequences. But that is not the case. Paul did not write this passage just to teach a doctrine of original sin. Yes, he does declare that Adam's sin brought all these terrible things upon the human race, but that is not his main point. His main subject is *Jesus and his cross* and the universal, all-sufficient consequences of that saving event. His purpose is not to emphasize what happened to the race as the result of Adam's sin, but to emphasize what has happened to it as the result of Christ's saving work.

The fact is that it really does not matter which view of "original sin" one holds. Did Adam's sin bring only physical death upon us? Or did it also bring spiritual depravity — partial or total? Did it also make us guilty sinners, condemned to eternal punishment in hell? In the final analysis it does not matter what content anyone feels compelled to pour into the concept of "original sin," because Paul's main point is this: *whatever the whole human race got (or would have got) from Adam has been completely canceled out for the whole human race by the gracious atoning work of Jesus Christ.* Make the Adamic legacy as dire as you want: physical death, total depravity, genuine guilt and condemnation to hell. The whole point of the passage is that Christ's "one act of righteousness" (5:18) has completely intercepted, nullified, negated, canceled, and counteracted *whatever* was destined to be ours because of Adam. All the potential spiritual consequences of Adam's sin are intercepted even before they can be applied. The only consequence that actually takes effect is physical death, and it is countered with the promise of resurrection to eternal life. (See my brief survey of the history of this interpretation: I:332-333.)

What does this mean? It means that there is no doctrine of original sin taught in 5:12-21. No child is actually conceived and born under the curse of Adam's sin. If anything, this passage teaches a doctrine of *original grace*: every child is born under the grace of God, born saved, "born free" from all spiritual effects of Adam's sin, and born with the guarantee of ultimate freedom from all physical effects of that sin by means of the resurrection unto glory. God began to apply this "original grace" to the first generation of Adam's own children, in the same way that the results of the cross were applied retrospectively to believing adults in the pre-Christian era (3:25).

We are now ready for the third question: *What is the scope of the words MANY and ALL as they are used in 5:12-21?* These terms appear at crucial points in the text. "Death came to all men" (5:12). By Adam's trespass "many died," but Christ's grace overflowed "to the many" (5:15). Through Adam came "condemnation for all men," but through Christ came justification of life "for all men" (5:18). In Adam "the many were made sinners," but in Christ "the many will be made righteous" (5:19). Exactly who are meant to be included in these terms?

What is at stake here is this: if the answer given to the second question above is correct, as it so obviously seems to be, why do so many still believe and teach a doctrine of original sin? The answer lies in how they interpret "many" and "all" in the verses cited above.

Most interpreters, even those who hold to original sin, generally agree that there is no difference in scope between the two terms themselves. I.e., "many" and "all" refer to the same group of people. The term "many" is not intended to be set in contrast with "all," but rather in contrast with "one." Even though Adam is just one man, his one sin had consequences that extend to *the many* (i.e., more than one). Even though Christ is just one man, his one act likewise applies to *the many*. The term "all" is then used to convey the connotation of totality, but is not meant to be broader in scope than "the many." I am in total agreement with this.

Wherein lies the problem, then? It lies in the way these two terms are applied to Adam on the one hand and to Christ on the other hand. The most commonly held idea seems to be that when these terms are used in relation to Adam's sin, they are completely universal in scope; but when they are used in relation to the work of Christ, they are more limited and restricted in scope and do not really mean "all." Adam did indeed inflict the entire race with the consequences of his sin, but the atoning work of Christ canceled out these consequences only for the smaller group of those who are actually saved. "Original sin," however understood, thus remains intact for the rest of mankind.

One way of saying this is that Christ's one righteous act is *able* to cancel original sin for everyone, that it has the power or potential to do so; but in fact it does so only for those who consciously *receive* the gift of grace through faith (5:17).

More often, however, especially for those who hold to the classical Augustinian doctrine of original sin, the distinction between Adam's "all" and Christ's "all" is stated thus: the consequences of Adam's act extended to all who were in him or belonged to him when he sinned—which includes the whole race; but the consequences of Christ's act extended only to "all" who were in him or belonged to him when he died—which includes only the elect.

In my judgment all such approaches to 5:12-21 are false; all attempts to reduce the "many" and "all" when used of Christ to anything less than their scope when used of Adam must be rejected. The reason should be obvious: such a discrepancy in the numbers would negate the whole purpose of the Adam-Christ comparison! The question of assurance is this: can I have confidence that Christ's work is sufficient for taking away all my sins — and those of the whole world as well? Paul's answer is "Yes! You *can* have such assurance! Look at what has already been done as the result of his work: his one righteous act has *already* counteracted *everything* brought upon *everyone* by Adam. This is the stepping-stone for our confidence that his work is capable of 'much more'

(5:15,17), i.e., it is capable of taking away all the consequences of our personal sins as well."

Thus to maintain the basic theme of assurance, we must insist that the terms "many" and "all" when used of Christ are at least as broad in scope as when used of Adam. Adam's sin brought sin, death, judgment, and condemnation upon *every* member of the human race; likewise Christ's atoning act brought righteousness, justification, and life upon *every* member of the human race. The failure to acknowledge this is the greatest hindrance to a proper understanding of this passage; it is also the single most influential reason why many still believe this passage teaches a doctrine of original sin.

This leads to the fourth and final preliminary question: *Does this passage teach universal salvation, then?* Some believe that Paul's use of "all" and the inclusive "many" do indeed suggest universalism (e.g., Käsemann, 157; Dunn, I:285, 297). Many of those who limit the "all" to whom Christ's work applies in 5:12-21 do so because they think that to do otherwise is to embrace such universalism.

The answer to the question, however, is NO! Romans 5:12-21 does not teach universal salvation, and taking the "all" and "many" who receive Christ's grace to refer to the whole human race does *not* entail such universalism. Why not? Because the primary focus of the passage as a whole and of these words specifically is how the work of Christ counteracts and cancels in their entirety the consequences of *the one sin of Adam* for every single individual. This is not a matter of possibility or potentiality; it is not just something Christ is able to do, or something that is offered to all and accepted by some. No, this is a reality; it is an accomplished fact; it has been done and will be done for the entire race; it is a sure thing.

However, Paul here absolutely does *not* say the same thing about the consequences for all *our own personal sins*. This is another matter altogether. As Romans has already made perfectly clear, the guilt and penalty for our personal sins are removed only through personal faith. The language of possibility and potentiality and "offered" applies to our personal sins, and 5:12-21 certainly implies that Christ's sacrifice is sufficient to take care of these also; indeed, this is the ultimate conclusion to which Paul's argument leads. But the universal language in the text applies only to what we have all received from *Adam's* sin.

In other words, from a practical point of view, this passage addresses the question of the spiritual state of infants when they are conceived and born. Do infants "inherit" anything from Adam, or is anything imposed upon them as the result of Adam's sin alone? Quite obviously so, particularly physical death. Paul affirms in 5:12 that death comes to all men as the result of sin, but this cannot mean personal sins since even infants sometimes die. Therefore death must come upon all because of Adam's sin. This is Paul's point in 5:13-14, where "those who did not sin by breaking a commandment" must refer to infants. (This is the force of the word καί [*kai*], "even," in v. 14.) It is likely that the language used in other verses (judgment, condemnation, made sinners) means that Adam's sin brought serious spiritual consequences upon infants as well.

The point of the passage, though, is that Christ's one atoning act cancels out *all* of these consequences for *all* infants. Because of Jesus Christ no infant is born sinful, depraved, or condemned. All do face the inevitability of physical death, but insofar as such death derives from Adam's sin, it too will one day be canceled out in the final resurrection from the dead. Every single baby is thus conceived and born in a redeemed or saved state (original grace!). The gifts of righteousness and justification and life are received universally and automatically by every infant as the means of salvation from Adam's sin. This is the only "universalism" in 5:12-21.

At the same time in this passage Paul alludes to the fact that babies grow up and reach the age of accountability and commit personal sins ("many trespasses," v. 16) (❖ I:337). When a child reaches the age of accountability and begins to become responsible for his personal sins, he forfeits the original grace under which he has been living since conception. He comes under the wrath of God and bears the full consequences of the sins that he is now committing by his own choice. He has even forfeited the redemptive resurrection gained through the cancellation of the death derived from Adam. If he dies in his own sins, he will be raised from the dead, but not redemptively in a glorified body like that of Christ.

The only way to escape the consequences of one's personal sins is by conscious choice and personal faith. Since everyone does not so choose and believe, there is no universal salvation.

Thus the spiritual odyssey of the individual has four possible stages: (1) *"Original sin,"* even if this is understood to involve only the penalty of physical death as the result of Adam's sin. Many understand it to include much more, of course. The main point about this stage is that (except for physical death) it is theoretical or potential only; it is never actually experienced because it is intercepted and canceled for everyone by the all-sufficient work of Christ. Thus no one ever actually passes through this stage, and children are certainly not born in it.

(2) *"Original grace,"* which is the stage we enter when we first come into existence and under which we stay until we reach the age of accountability, thanks to the work of the Second Adam. All infants and young children are here, as are those whose mental abilities never develop beyond those of young children. This is a state of salvation and it is universal; thus the concept of "universal salvation" applies here.

(3) *"Personal sin,"* the stage all enter when they reach the age of accountability and lose the original grace under which they were born. Those in this stage are the lost, the unsaved. If they die here they will be condemned forever to hell.

(4) *"Personal grace,"* a term we might use for the position occupied by all believers, or those who have personally repented and believed God's gracious promises. This is a state of salvation, but it is not universal. It is available to all, but is entered only through personal choice (❧I:338-339).

1. One Sin of One Man (Adam) Brought Sin and Death to All (5:12-14)

5:12 Therefore . . . . This first word in the verse indicates that Paul is about to draw a conclusion from something that serves as a premise or basis for it. Opinions vary widely as to what this premise is, but it probably includes both what precedes in this chapter plus what immediately follows. At the end of v. 12 Paul seems to break off his main argument until he can lay down some related truths; then he picks it up again in v. 18, with 18a reiterating v. 12 and 18b stating the long-awaited conclusion. The progression of the main thought, then, is this: "Therefore, in view of what has just been said about the saving power of the death of Christ (5:1-11), and also because we know that an example of such vicarious power already exists in the person of Adam (5:12-14), we may safely conclude that the one righteous act of the one man Jesus Christ is definitely sufficient to bring salvation to all people."

. . . just as sin entered the world through one man . . . . The "one man," of course is Adam (v. 14), who along with Eve was responsible for introducing sin into the world (Gen 3:1-7). Since Adam was the head of his wife and in a real sense the head of the whole human family, he alone is singled out as the responsible party and also as a kind of pattern for Jesus (v. 14). The word for "sin" is ἁμαρτία (*hamartia*), which in this case refers not to a specific act but to the very principle or power of evil and lawlessness that enters like an invading force and takes root in the hearts of its willing victims (Godet, 204; Moo, 319). "The world" (as in John 3:16) is the world of mankind, the sphere of human beings; sin had already entered the world of angels through the sin of Satan (1 John 3:8).

The main point of this statement is the phrase, "through one man," which is in the emphatic position in the Greek. To make his point that just one man (Jesus) is the source of all salvation, Paul is reminding us that just one man (and a lesser one at that) is the source of all sin.

. . . and death through sin . . . . This statement is highly condensed. Several words carry over from the first clause, so that the entire thought is thus: "And (just as) death (entered the world [of human beings]) through sin." In this case "sin" (*hamartia* again) seems to refer to the first specific sinful act of Adam, his disobedience to the command about the tree of knowledge of good and evil (Gen 2:16-17). Just as this one man was the channel through which sin entered, his one sin was the channel through which human death entered.

To what specific kind of death is Paul referring here? Many rightly understand the Bible to distinguish three kinds of death: physical, spiritual, and eternal (Godet, 205). Physical death of course is the death of the body; spiritual death is equivalent to the soul's condition of sinfulness and depravity (Eph 2:1,5; Col 2:13); eternal death is condemnation to hell or the lake of fire (Rev 20:6,14) (❂ I:341).

In my judgment, Paul's primary concern in 5:12 is with physical death; this is clear from 5:13-14, where physical death is obviously in view (Godet, 205; Smith, I:85). Whether Paul considers anything else to be imposed upon the human race as a result of Adam's one sin must be determined by a consideration of 5:15-19. But at this point, to focus on spiritual death misses the main point of 5:13-14, where physical death even among babies is cited as evidence for the point about the "one man" in v. 12.

Paul is not just saying that death is the result of sin in general, and he is especially not saying that each individual's death is the result of his own sin. No, his whole point in 5:12-21 rests on the fact that the deaths of all individual human beings are the penal consequence of one sin of *one man*, Adam: "The many died by the trespass of the one man" (5:15a; Smith, I:85).

. . . and in this way death came to all men, because all sinned . . . . Up to this point, based on 5:12a alone, there is no reason to extend the sin of Adam and the resulting death beyond their entry point, namely, Adam himself. But 5:12b shows that there is more to it than this — much more. This part of the verse reveals the universal consequences of Adam's one sin. "In this way," i.e., through the one sin of the one man, "death came to all men." The word for "came" means "went through," "spread," or "permeated." Paul is saying that death "made its way to each individual member of the race . . . like a father's inheritance divided among his children" (Sanday and Headlam, 133).

If Paul had ended his thought here and gone directly to v. 13, the task of exegetes and theologians would no doubt have been considerably lighter. But this was not to be. Led by the Spirit, Paul added, "because all sinned," or "because all have sinned." Thus sin, like death, is universalized: all die; likewise all sinned. Adam sinned, but everyone else sinned as well (❂ I:342).

But in what sense is it true that "all sinned"? I.e., how is the sin of all somehow the cause of the death of all, especially since the death of all has already been stated to be the result of the *one* sin of the *one* man, Adam?

Proposed answers fall into two categories. One approach is that the statement "all sinned" must be taken as referring to each individual's personal sins, as in 3:23. In this case each person dies because of his own sins. But how is Adam's sin involved? One view is that when we sin personally we are *imitating* Adam's sin; thus Adam's sin is still indirectly responsible for every person's death. Another view is that Adam's sin imposes a corrupt nature on all his descendants, which causes them all to sin and thus incur death. Again, the relation between Adam's sin and our death is indirect.

In my judgment neither version of this view is acceptable. Once Adam is made only the indirect cause of death, rather than the direct cause, the main point of the passage — the analogy between Adam and Christ — breaks down. The "one man Adam vs. one man Jesus" theme (5:15-19) loses its punch (Morris, 232). Also, neither form of this approach can explain the death of infants, who have not sinned personally. (See Murray, I:183-184, for these and other arguments against this view.)

The other approach to "all sinned" is to posit some kind of union between Adam and his descendants, the result being that when he sinned, we all somehow sinned in or with him. Thus "all sinned" does not refer to the subsequent personal sins of each individual, but to a kind of collective sinning of all in Adam's one act of disobedience in the Garden of Eden.

One version of this latter approach is to see all mankind as existing within Adam when he sinned, so that his sin literally was the sin of us all; thus we all are equally accountable for it and are punished for it. An analogy is the relation between Abraham and Levi in Heb 7:9-10. When Abraham paid tithes to Melchizedek (Heb 7:1-2), Levi also "paid tithes, for he was still in the loins of his father" when Abraham tithed. In this same sense we were all in Adam's loins when he sinned; thus we also sinned.

The other version of this second approach is to treat Adam as acting as a representative for the whole race in his test regarding the tree (Lard, 167-168; Smith, I:87). Thus Adam is called the "federal head" of all mankind (MP, 334). The analogy here is the relation between Christ on the cross and the whole human race. We were not in him when he died; but he died representatively for all (2 Cor 5:14), and the consequences of his death are imputed to others.

In my judgment this second approach is the better one, either according to its second version or as a combination of the two. (See Stott, 151-154.) "All sinned" does not refer to our personal sins, but to the one sin of Adam in which we all participated in some form, and for which we all suffer the penal consequences. We can offer no explanation for such an arrangement other than divine appointment (❧ I:344).

It is wrong, though, to conclude (as many do) that this understanding of "because all sinned" leads to the doctrine of original sin. I have explained in the introduction to this section why this is not the case.

5:13 Verse 12 introduces an intended comparison between Adam and Christ that is not completed. Only the "just as" portion (the *protasis*) is given; the "so also" part (the *apodosis*) is not stated. In 5:18-19 Paul will come back to the comparison and present it in two different ways. But before then, in 5:13-17 (sometimes treated as a parenthesis, as in the KJV), he pauses in order to verify and clarify what he says in 5:12.

In v. 12 two crucial points are made: one, that death is the result of sin; and two, that the death of all is the result of the sin of one man, Adam. Paul does not try to prove the first point, but 5:13-14 seems designed to prove the second point (Godet, 209; MP, 334; Murray, I:187). The proof lies in the fact that some people die even though they have never sinned personally, including babies, young children, and some with mental handicaps. Thus if sin is indeed the cause of death, the fact that such people sometimes die proves that the one representative sin of Adam must be that cause.

. . . for before the law was given, sin was in the world. But sin is not taken into account when there is no law. This and v. 14 are very difficult, and in my opinion can be understood only as an extremely condensed argument, some parts of which are assumed. We may wonder why Paul even brings up the Adam-to-Moses period, if his main proof is going to be infants. The answer seems to be that in the minds of his Jewish audience especially, the general nature of this period as a whole ought to prove Paul's point. This would seem to be the case based upon the combination of two factors: first, "where there is no law there is no transgression" (4:15); and second, the Law (Here "Law" must be understood as the Mosaic Law, in view of 5:14.) was not given until the time of Moses. Thus even though in the pre-Mosaic period people did things that were sinful, they could not be held accountable for them because there was no law. But the whole population in this period died anyway; therefore they must have died because of Adam's sin.

This train of thought would seem perfectly valid to many, especially to those who put such strong emphasis on the Law of Moses. So this is where Paul *begins* his argument, even though it is not where he ends it.

That "sin was in the world" before Moses' Law was given is indisputable (Gen 6:5,11; 8:21; 18:20; Exod 9:27). It is also indisputable that "sin is not taken into account when there is no law," as Paul had already said in 4:15. The word for "taken into account" (used here and in Phlm 18) is an accounting term and means "to enter into the ledger or into the account of someone." This is the concept of imputation, though in this case Paul is talking about imputing one's own sins to one's own account. He says this does not occur when no law exists by which sins can be identified as violations of God's will. In such a case God does not impute sinful acts to a person's account and therefore does not punish him. But since people between Adam and Moses did suffer the penalty of death (v. 14a), they could only have died because of Adam's sin.

This reasoning would be sound except for one thing: there *was* law between Adam and Moses! True, the Law of Moses was not yet given, but Paul has already argued that law is revealed and known through general revelation (1:18-32; 2:14-15); and he has already declared that Gentiles or pagans are "without excuse" (1:20) when they go against this general revelation. Indeed, Paul named a whole list of specific sins (1:24-31) committed by pagans; and he specifically said that those who commit these sins *know* God's decree, that those who do so are worthy of death (1:32)! Also, we have every reason to believe that God instructed Adam and Eve regarding his moral law; it is ludicrous to assume that the only law they were given was the one about the trees (Gen 2:16-17). What they knew of God's moral law would thus have been handed down from generation to generation, supplemented by occasional special revelation (e.g., Gen 4:9; 6:13; 7:1; 9:1-7). Otherwise, how could Noah have functioned as "a preacher of righteousness" (2 Pet 2:5)? The fact that God destroyed the human race (except for Noah's family) because of their wickedness shows that they had law and were being held accountable for it. The same is true of Sodom and Gomorrah. Thus the idea that "there was no positive commandment" in the pre-Mosaic period except for Gen 2:16-17 is quite false.

But if this reasoning is not sound, why does Paul bring it up? Because the argument would no doubt have occurred especially to Paul's Jewish audience, and he brings it up to get it out of the way. Thus I am suggesting that between v. 13 and v. 14 Paul is assuming that his readers will remember what he has already said very plainly in 1:18-32 and 2:14-15, and will draw their own conclusions as to the invalidity of the argument. This unspoken caveat then sets the stage for Paul's own argument in v. 14.

The thought of 5:13-14a may be paraphrased thus: "We have said that all die because of Adam's sin. But what gives us any reason to think this? Let's consider first of all a common assumption. Some who agree that Adam *must* be the source of human death base this conclusion on the fact that people died between Adam and Moses, before the Law was given; and we know God does not hold people accountable for their sins where is no law. Thus (so this argument goes) since people died then, they must have died because of Adam's sin.

"Now, at first glance this argument seems sound, but I'm sorry to say that it does not hold together. Why not? Mainly because it assumes that there was *no law* in this period between Adam and Moses; but this is not true. You will remember my clear teaching that there *was* law during this period, and people knew that by breaking this law they deserved God's wrath. So if we are going to show that all die because of Adam's sin, we must find another argument."

5:14 "Let's stay with the period between Adam and Moses. In this era (as in all other times, of course), death came to all human beings, *even* over those not old enough to commit personal sins like the sin of Adam. The fact that infants sometimes die is all the proof we need for the truth that all die because of Adam's sins."

Nevertheless introduces Paul's own valid argument, in contrast with the abbreviated invalid argument from v. 13.

. . . death reigned from the time of Adam to the time of Moses . . . . This is clearly a reference to physical death, which is personified as a tyrant having everyone under its power in the period in question (and in all other times as well; see v. 17). To depict death as a reigning monarch emphasizes its universal scope, its oppressive domination, and its inescapable certainty.

. . . even over those who did not sin by breaking a command, as did Adam . . . . This is the key point of the whole argument in vv. 13-14; this is what proves the fact that Adam's sin brought death upon us all: death reigned, *even* over this group. The word "even" (*kai*) is important, because it focuses the argument on a group that is more narrow than the general population of the earth (contra Godet, 212; Moo, 333). This group is described as "those who did not sin by breaking a command."

Who are in this group? It depends on what Paul means by the expression, "did not sin by breaking a command." The word "command" is not in the original; this participial phrase literally reads "the ones who did not sin after the likeness of Adam's transgression." The word for "transgression," παράβασις (*parabasis*), literally means "stepping over a boundary, a deviation from the prescribed path or norm, a trespass, a transgression." In the NT it refers to breaking God's law, a transgression of his law. Here in 5:14, the group singled out by Paul did not sin according to the likeness of the *parabasis* of Adam. I.e., they did not transgress God's law in the same way that Adam did.

Most interpreters take this statement to mean that the *law* which Adam transgressed was crucially different from the law transgressed by those who lived between Adam and Moses. I.e., it was of such a nature that he could be held responsible for breaking it, whereas the latter group could not. The law Adam transgressed (Gen 2:16-17) is variously described as a direct command, an express command, an explicit command, an expressly revealed ordinance, a positive prohibition, a clear and definite divine commandment, a prohibition known to be a commandment of God. It is implied that no other command of this nature was given by God until the Law of Moses. Some add that the command to Adam was accompanied by a death sentence, and in this way was different from any laws between Adam and Moses (MP, 334-335; Moo, 331). Thus it is concluded (by most interpreters) that the expression "those who did not sin by breaking a command" refers to *everyone* who lived between Adam and Moses, and not just to a special group such as infants.

The reasons I cannot accept this view are as follows. First, there *were* explicit commands and prohibitions (other than the command regarding the trees) between Adam and Moses, available in the beginning and sporadically thereafter by means of special revelation, and passed along as tradition to future generations. Also, the definitions usually given to *parabasis* in this context are much too narrow. It means transgression of the law, to be sure; but limiting such law only to that given through special revelation is indefensible. For example, in light of the emphasis Paul gives to general revelation in 1:18-32 and 2:14-15, the principle set forth in 4:15 (using *parabasis*) surely cannot be limited to specially revealed law. We should also remember that the laws known through general revelation also carry the death sentence and that this is known by those who break them (1:32).

Finally, the main difference between Adam's sin and the sins committed by the specific group in 5:14 was not a difference in the *kind* of law they transgressed, but rather in the *way* the law was transgressed. Adam's sin was indeed a voluntary, conscious, deliberate decision to disobey a command of God. But so were most sins committed by most people even before the Law of Moses came. It does not matter whether the law being transgressed was specially revealed or written on the heart; anyone deliberately breaking either kind of law was guilty of *parabasis* and thus was "without excuse" (1:20; 2:1). I.e., *all* lawbreakers during this period committed *personal* sins worthy of death.

But there is one *way* of sinning that is "not like the transgression of Adam" (ESV), i.e., not a voluntary, deliberate, personal sin. What is it? None other than the sin which everyone committed *representatively* in Adam in the Garden of Eden (5:12). This is the *only* kind of sin some people have committed, and *even they* sometimes die. Who are in this group? Infants, small children, and some with mental handicaps. These are the ones to whom Paul refers here in the "even" clause.

I am aware that many declare that Paul cannot be talking about infants here, but rather must be talking about adult sinners, or at least that he cannot be talking about infants only (Lard, 172). But it seems to me that this misses the whole point of Paul's argument, and severely weakens his case that Adam's sin is the cause of the death of all. Paul has made it clear that even sinners against general revelation are worthy of death and know it (1:32). Genesis makes it clear that the bulk of those who died in the Flood and in the cities of the plain deserved to die because of their own sin. Thus *only* a group (such as infants) who have committed no *personal* sins and who sometimes die anyway can truly prove Paul's point that the real cause of human death is the one representative sin of Adam.

Having established his point about Adam, Paul briefly points us back in the direction his original thought was beginning to take in v. 12, i.e., a comparison between Adam and Christ. He does this by stating that Adam **was . . . a pattern of the one to come.** "The one to come" refers to Christ, who was yet to come from Adam's perspective. The word "pattern" is τύπος (*typos*) or "type." Moo (334, n. 85) explains that this word originally meant "the impression made by striking something," and that it came to mean "a form, pattern, or example." In the NT it refers to "those OT persons, institutions, or events that are seen to have a divinely intended function of prefiguring the eschatological age inaugurated by Christ." See Cranfield, I:283.

In what sense does Adam prefigure Christ? Only in this one point, namely, that just as Adam was only one man yet performed a single act that affected the entire world, so also was Jesus Christ just one man whose one act likewise affected the whole human race.

2. Christ and His Sacrifice Are Greater than Adam and His Sin (5:15-17)

The main point in 5:12-21 is the one positive comparison between Adam and Christ, as just described. In this sense Adam is a type of Christ. But before

Paul actually states this comparison (5:18-19), he pauses once again, this time to make it clear that in most ways Adam and Christ are very *different*. Even though the positive comparison he is about to draw is very important, so are the *contrasts* between Adam's one sinful act and Christ's one saving act.

5:15 But the gift is not like the trespass . . . . This statement is a heading over 5:15-17, telling us that the subject is the contrast between the negative results of Adam's sin and the positive results of Christ's cross. The word for "trespass" is παράπτωμα (*paraptōma*), "a false step, straying from the path, departing from the norm." There is little difference between this and *parabasis* as used in 5:14. The word for "gift" is χάρισμα (*charisma*, closely related to χάρις [*charis*], "grace"). It refers to the gracious result that flows unto all from the one saving act of Christ, in contrast with the devastating result that comes upon all from Adam's trespass. What is this gift, this gracious result? Most likely it is the "gift of righteousness" (5:17), the imputed righteousness of Christ that results in justification (5:16,18) and life (5:17-18).

The rest of this verse is the first of three different ways Paul expresses this contrast. Adam's side of it is stated thus: **For if the many died by the trespass of the one man . . . .** This point has already been made in 5:12 and proved in 5:13-14. The word "many" (see 5:19) is equivalent in scope to "all men" in 5:12 and 5:18. Here it is used in contrast with "one," i.e., even though Adam was only *one* man, what he did had consequences for *many* men (denoting all others as a totality). The word "died" is aorist (past) tense, pointing back to the first sin of Adam as the time when all came under the sentence of death (Lard, 177).

The other side of the contrast is stated thus: **how much more did God's grace and the gift that came by the grace of the one man, Jesus Christ, overflow to the many!** The words "much more" indicate that this is an argument from the lesser (Adam) to the greater (Christ). Some say this expression has a *quantitative* meaning, indicating the superiority of the power and effects of Christ's cross as contrasted with the power and effects of Adam's sin. It describes "the infinitely superior effectiveness" of Christ's act (Cranfield, I:284).

The quantitative superiority of Christ's cross is suggested by the word translated "overflow." God's grace and the gift that comes by it overflowed or abounded to the many (see v. 17). This means first of all that God's gracious gift reached out to embrace *all* who have been affected by Adam's sin, and has completely canceled and nullified the total consequences of Adam's sin for the entire human race. Second, the overflowing "much more" of Christ's cross means that the saved state into which it brings us is a state far better than what was lost in Adam. But most importantly, the overflowing "much more" means that the one saving act of Christ not only saves the entire race from whatever consequences have come upon us because of Adam's sin; it also is able to save the entire race from the consequences of their own *personal* sins, and does in fact cancel all such consequences for those who personally accept the free gift of grace through faith. The saving work of Christ does not *actually* and in fact set the whole human race free from the effects of their personal sins; this would be universalism. Its application to personal sins is conditional and therefore limited. But the point is that the ability of Christ's cross to counteract mankind's personal sins means that its effectiveness extends far beyond the scope of Adam's sin (❥ I:352).

But some see another sense to the words "much more," called the *logical* sense, where the point is not the quantitative contrast between the two acts of the two men, but rather the *superior degree of certainty* we can have with regard to the efficacy of Christ's act, once we understand the nature and efficacy of the one act of Adam. This approach to "much more" presupposes the quantitative superiority of Christ over Adam (❥ I:353).

My inclination is to see both meanings, the quantitative and the logical, in Paul's reference to "much more." The former is surely emphasized as part of the contrast between Adam and Christ in 5:15-17, especially in the references to overflowing (v. 15), "many trespasses" (v. 16), and abundance (v. 17). The latter is even more appropriate, given the assurance theme that permeates this whole chapter. In view of what we know about Adam, we have all the more reason to put our total trust in the all-sufficiency of Christ's one saving act.

"God's grace" here probably refers to grace as an attribute of his nature. His loving grace overflowed to us in his decision to come to us in the person of "the one man, Jesus Christ," whose death provided for us the gift of righteousness and life.

Because of the widespread resistance to this fact, it is necessary to repeat here that "the many" to whom God's gracious gift has come are *the same* as "the many" who died from Adam's sin, and the same as the "all men" in 5:12 and 5:18. I.e., the term includes the whole human race, and it refers primarily to the complete cancellation of the effects of Adam's sin for all men. Any limitations we may place on "the many" (e.g., believers only, those who are "in Christ" only) begin to apply only when we get past this universal application to Adam's sin and are talking about individuals' personal sins.

5:16 Again, the gift of God is not like the result of the one man's sin . . . . This repeats the heading of v. 15 and introduces the second version of the contrast between Adam and Christ. Again the emphasis is on the infinite superiority of Christ's work. His saving act is much more efficacious than Adam's sin since it not only nullifies the universal results of that one sin but also is able to cancel the consequences of the personal sins of the many. It takes away the former unconditionally for all; it takes away the latter conditionally for believers.

"The one man's sin" is better translated "the one who sinned" (NASB). The gift again seems to be the gift of Christ's righteousness, on which our justification is based.

The judgment followed one sin and brought condemnation, but the gift

followed many trespasses and brought justification. One contrast here is between "one sin" and "many trespasses." The judgment unto condemnation results from the single sin of one man; but the gift unto justification applies not only to this one sin but to many personal sins as well (and thus is quantitatively superior).

Another contrast is between the results of each man's act. On the one hand, Adam's sin brought "judgment" unto "condemnation." This refers to the sentence of punishment, not only as pronounced but also as carried out. On the other hand, the free gift that comes from Christ, the gift of imputed righteousness (v. 17b), is unto "justification" (δικαίωμα, *dikaiōma*). This Greek word is used ten times in the NT, but it means "justification" only here (❂ I:354).

The key question concerning this verse is, what does Paul mean by "condemnation" and "justification"? He says Adam's sin brought condemnation, and Christ's cross cancelled the condemnation by bringing justification. Up to this point the apostle has mentioned only *death* as the result of Adam's sin, and contextually there has been no reason to think that he means anything more than *physical* death. But the language of this verse raises the question of whether something more serious must be added to the Adamic legacy.

Some are quick to answer *no*, nothing more than physical death is in view, even with these new terms. The "condemnation" means only the sentence of physical death, they say; and the "justification" means only the temporary suspension of this sentence allowing some time to live on the earth, then in the end resurrection from the dead (DeWelt, 78). We can agree that physical death is a judicial penalty and can rightly be called "condemnation." When *katakrima* is used in 8:1, however, it hardly seems limited to physical death, and is usually taken to refer to eternal punishment. Even the word *krima* ("judgment") is often used in this sense. Thus we are persuaded to think that by using the word "condemnation" Paul is telling us here that the death imposed upon all men because of Adam's sin is not just physical death, but includes eternal death also (see 6:23).

This conclusion seems all the more warranted when we realize that this condemnation received from Adam is counteracted with the "justification" received from Christ. In other contexts justification involves so much more than resurrection from the dead. Thus I believe we are wrong to limit it to that in this context. Here we should give it the meaning it has in other places, especially here in Romans, namely, the cancellation of eternal punishment in hell.

Indeed, this is exactly how almost everyone understands these two terms when they are applied to the "many trespasses" (personal sins) in this verse. Thus how can we give them a more limited meaning when applying them to Adam's sin and its consequences?

But when we interpret condemnation as eternal death in hell and justification as the cancellation of this eternal punishment, are we not opening the door to the doctrine of original sin? Not at all. But is this not the Augustinian view? No, it is not. True, the Augustinian doctrine of original sin says the condemnation of eternal death in hell comes upon all as the result of Adam's sin; but it omits the most important part of Paul's teaching, namely, that the original grace of Jesus Christ *justifies* all men insofar as Adam's sin is concerned. I.e., it completely cancels out this condemnation, so that in its eternal element it is never even applied.

5:17 For if, by the trespass of the one man, death reigned through that one man . . . . These words begin a third way of expressing the contrast between Adam and Christ, another way of explaining how the gift is not like the trespass. They add nothing to what has already been expressed in vv. 12-16. To say that death *reigns* emphasizes "the powerful and destructive sway it exercises over the affairs of human beings" (Hendriksen, I:181). The aorist tense again indicates the past point in time when death *began* to reign, i.e., when Adam sinned.

. . . how much more will those who receive God's abundant provision of grace and of the gift of righteousness reign in life through the one man, Jesus Christ. The word translated "abundant provision" (the noun form of the verb "overflow" in v. 15) points again to the fact that the benefits of Christ's cross extend far beyond the scope of Adam's sin and are able to offset the "many trespasses" (personal sins) of v. 16. This suggests that the phrase "much more" may again be emphasizing the quantitative superiority of Christ's work. There is no doubt, though, that "much more" has a logical force here and is stressing the glorious certainty or assurance we can have with regard to Christ's gift of grace. I.e., if the weaker cause (Adam's sin) can have universal effects, surely the more powerful cause (Christ's cross) can have even greater and wider effects (Godet, 220-223).

Many interpreters seriously misunderstand the identity of "those who receive" here in v. 17b. They say that this expression refers only to adults or those old enough to personally make a conscious decision to accept the promise of grace. They see this as parallel to "many trespasses" in v. 16b. Since that phrase means personal sin, "those who receive" is taken to mean those who personally believe. Some see another dimension of death being introduced at this point, too. In addition to the *physical* death (only) which came to all through Adam's sin, they see these verses as referring to *spiritual* death, which comes only as the result of personal sins (DeWelt, 82-83; Smith, I:85-86).

A principal reason why many take this view is their understanding of the verb λαμβάνω (*lambanō*, "receive"). Again and again we hear that this verb "is active, and not passive," and therefore that it must refer to a personal, conscious decision (❧ I:357).

Now, we can agree that personal, conscious, voluntary, active choice is a condition for receiving grace for those who have committed personal sins. We can also agree that such persons are included in the discussion at least in vv. 16-

17. But I believe it is a serious mistake to think that these are the only ones Paul has in view in these verses, and I believe it is contrary to fact to say that *lambanō* must refer only to the active, voluntary reception of grace.

Throughout these verses (15-17) where Adam and Christ are set in contrast to one another, the scope of those affected by both men is the same in all three verses. Adam's sin affected *all*, and so does the cross insofar as it cancels the results of Adam's sin for *all*. To deny this jeopardizes the main point of this whole passage, the *all*-sufficiency of Christ's cross. The reference to personal sins in this immediate text is *in addition to* the Adamic sin, but not instead of it. Also, as v. 16 indicates, it is likely that spiritual death (including eternal death) has been brought into the picture here, but there is no textual basis for regarding it as the result of personal sins only.

The key question, though, is whether *lambanō* necessarily means an active, conscious act. This seems to be a myth (❖ I:358). A survey of the many NT verses using this word shows that it can indeed refer to the passive reception of something, apart from a deliberate act of acceptance by the recipient (e.g., Luke 20:47; Acts 1:8; Rom 13:2; Jas 3:1; 1 Pet 4:10). The bottom line is that there is nothing in the word *lambanō* that requires us to limit "those who receive" to conscious, willing adults; the word is no less able to describe the passive reception of "original grace" by *all* those affected by Adam's sin, even in infancy or before.

We conclude, then, that the primary reference in v. 17b (as in 15b and 16b) is to the universal application of grace to all mankind to counteract the results of Adam's sin, with the added assurance that this grace is abundant enough to erase the effects of our personal sins as well.

In vv. 15-16 Paul has spoken of the "gift" that comes to all through Christ; here he identifies its content as "righteousness." This is the "righteousness of God" (1:17; 3:21) established by Christ's atoning death and received by sinners through grace. Thus it is not something different from the "abundant provision of grace," but explains what this grace consists of. Receiving this gift of righteousness is the event of justification.

Those who receive the gift will "reign in life" through the power of this one man, Jesus. Rather than being slaves of the tyrant death, they themselves will reign in abundant life. "Reign" is future tense and refers to the yet-to-come resurrection of the body at the end time and to the gift of eternal life to be lived in the very presence of God (❖ I:358).

3. Christ's Cross Completely Cancels the Results of Adam's Sin (5:18-19)

Having established the fact that Christ's one act is different from Adam's sin in many ways, Paul returns to the main point he began with in v. 12. He now focuses on the one respect in which the two are equal, namely, the breadth or scope of the effects of the one act of each. *Just as* Adam's sin had a universal effect, *so also* did the cross of Christ. This point is intended to reinforce our assurance that the cross is worthy of our trust. We need not doubt its all-encompassing and all-sufficient power.

Paul now makes explicit the one positive comparison he had in mind when he said that Adam was a type or pattern for Christ. He presents this comparison in two distinct ways.

5:18 Consequently, just as the result of one trespass was condemnation for all men . . . . This begins the first version of the comparison and basically sums up the content of v. 12, where Paul began to make this very argument before breaking it off for the parenthesis of vv. 13-17. No new concepts are introduced here.

The language is extremely condensed. A verb must be supplied as in the NIV: "the result . . . was." Also, I agree with the NIV's translation of "one trespass" rather than "the trespass of the one."

The word for "condemnation" is *katakrima* again (see v. 16). While physical death is no doubt included in the condemnation that comes from Adam, I believe that such a strong word as *katakrima* cannot be limited to that alone but must also include eternal condemnation (see 6:23; 8:1). This is all the more likely when we see that its opposite is *justification* (v. 18b). See the discussion under 5:16, above.

Through Adam's one sin this condemnation came upon "all men," the whole human race. Whether it was physical death only or both physical and spiritual/eternal death is largely irrelevant, since it has been totally nullified for "all men" by the cross, as the rest of the verse shows.

. . . so also the result of one act of righteousness was justification that brings life for all men. This is the long-delayed completion of the thought begun in v. 12. The word for "act of righteousness" is δικαίωμα (*dikaiōma*), the same word used for "justification" in 5:16. Sometimes it means "ordinance" of the law (2:26; 8:4), but "righteous act" is also a valid meaning (Rev 15:4; 19:8). The latter is appropriate here, since it is being contrasted with the one (sinful) act of Adam.

What is this "one act of righteousness"? No doubt it means the atoning death of Jesus on the cross. Many try to expand this "one act" so that it includes Jesus' entire sinless life (e.g., Hendriksen, I:182; Cranfield, I:289). But Christ's life as a whole hardly qualifies as "one act." More importantly, the comparison here is between *one* sinful act and *one* righteous act. To say that the latter includes the whole life of Christ compromises the comparison and forfeits the whole point of this passage (Dunn, I:283).

The result of this one righteous act is to offset the condemnation that came through Adam's sin. This result is called "justification that brings life," or literally "justification of life." "Justification" is δικαίωσις (*dikaiōsis*), used also in 4:25. What does this include? Those who see the condemnation as physical death only must and do limit this justification to the gift of physical life only (❋I:361).

As I have said in the discussion of 5:16 above, this is an unacceptable limitation to the concept of justification. Although seldom represented by a noun, the event and the state of justification are very often represented by the verb *dikaioō*. In these other contexts it implicitly involves the cancellation of the full penalty of sin, especially condemnation to hell. In my opinion limiting it to the cancellation of physical death alone gives it an unnatural sense. Thus I take it here to imply that Adam's sin brought full condemnation upon the entire race, but that Christ's cross brought full justification upon all men in that it releases all (in infancy) from Adamic condemnation and brings to all *eternal* life in the sense of release from the penalty of hell and entrance into heaven.

When Paul says the one righteous act of Christ results in justification of life *for all men*, he means exactly that and nothing less. In the introduction to this section I have discussed the common view that this "all" is somehow less than the "all" affected by Adam's sin. This view must be emphatically rejected. Christ's original grace cancels any potential state of original sin *for all men*. If this is not the case, then the point and purpose of 5:12-21 as a whole are completely negated.

5:19 For just as through the disobedience of the one man the many were made sinners . . . . This verse affirms the parallel between Adam and Christ in a different way, keeping the symmetrical form of v. 18. The word "for" may mean that Paul is here explaining why it is possible or appropriate for all to receive condemnation as the result of one man's sin. The reason is that, by this one man's sin, the many were "made sinners." This recalls the point at the end of 5:12, "because all sinned" in Adam. His sin was the sin of all; when he disobeyed God's command, all became sinners. Thus it is appropriate that all should be condemned for that one sin. ("The many" is universal in scope and equivalent to "all men" in v. 18a.)

The difficult question here is the meaning of "made" (:362). Does it mean merely "counted as" or "declared to be something," or does it mean "actually made to be something"? Another question is whether God or Adam is the subject of the action.

Whether the subject is God or Adam, in my opinion the second meaning of the verb is preferred, i.e., *made* and not just declared. This seems to be how the word is used in other contexts, even in classical Greek (see Godet, 225-226). In the NT it is most commonly used for appointing or ordaining someone to a particular position or office (❋I:362). As the result of Adam's sin, the many were actually "made to be" sinners; they were placed in the position of being sinners. This means that in their solidarity with Adam all men actually became sinners; that's why it was appropriate to *treat* them as sinners by condemning them (5:18).

One point must be kept in mind, namely, that whatever nuance we give to "made sinners," it must be parallel to the meaning we give to "made righteous" in 19b.

. . . so also through the obedience of the one man the many will be made righteous. The obedience of Jesus is set over against the disobedience of Adam. Some err again by expanding this obedience so that it "covers his whole life, not just his passion and death" (Cranfield, I:290). But again this destroys the parallel with the *one* act of Adam's disobedience. The obedience here is the one act of righteousness, the one supreme act of obedience, the cross (Phil 2:8; Heb 5:8).

The key question here is the meaning of "made righteous." The issue is whether it refers to a simple forensic declaration equivalent to justification, or whether it refers to a change in the sinner's nature or status by which he is actually made righteous. Our answer must take into account the parallel with "made sinners" in v. 19a, as well as the meaning of *kathistēmi* as discussed there.

Many take "made righteous" in the former sense alone (❂I:363-364). Others, however, see something of the latter sense in the expression (❂I:364). In my opinion, even if forensic righteousness is involved, the meaning of *kathistēmi* and the meaning of "made sinners," as discussed above, seem to require something of this second sense. I.e., as the result of Christ's one act of obedience, all are actually made righteous and become righteous.

The fact that this is future tense ("*will* be made righteous") may simply reflect the fact that this is an ongoing process and will continue to apply to people in the future (Murray, I:206). Or it may mean that this "making righteous" is something that will be consummated at the final judgment, when the redeemed will finally be completely sanctified (Godet, 226) (❂I:364).

4. Grace Triumphs over Sin and Death (5:20-21)

This brief paragraph makes a fitting conclusion not just to this section (5:12-21) but to Part Two as a whole. Indeed, it draws together the main elements of the entire letter thus far: law, sin, and death versus grace, righteousness, and life.

5:20 The law was added so that the trespass might increase. This is most likely a reference to the Mosaic Law. Why does Paul bring it up at this point? He is probably answering a question that must have been in the minds of his Jewish audience, i.e., how does the Law relate to all of this? To the devout Jew the Law was regarded as the solution to everything. Surely it must have some part in the resolution of the problem that began with Adam. But Paul has for all practical purposes jumped directly from Adam to Christ. Where is the place for Moses? (See Moo, 346.)

Paul's answer to such questions is not what the Jews wanted to hear. He says "the law was added." The word for "added" is not at all complimentary; the concept is closer to "temporarily tacked on." In its other NT use (Gal 2:4) it has a negative connotation ("sneaked in," NASB). That idea is somewhat harsh for this context, but the word is still unfavorable enough to suggest that the Law was definitely a secondary part of God's plan, and not an end in itself. It implies that the Law came in through the servants' door, as opposed to making a grand entrance. See Morris, 241; Moo, 346-347.

But that's not all. The Law was added, says Paul, "so that the trespass might increase." Thus in a sense the Law, rather than being a part of the solution, is a part of the problem! But this is not meant to be altogether negative. We must remember that it was God himself who added the Law (see Gal 3:19), and the increase of sin was at least part of the very reason why he added it in the first place. ("So that" is ἵνα [*hina*], indicating purpose.) And God would not have done this unless he had some ultimately good purpose in mind.

The Law certainly was not given to prevent sin; it was too late for that. Nor was it intended to save anyone from sin; it was too weak for that (Morris, 241). But it could cause sin to increase. Certainly sins were already present in abundance, because law in other forms was already present, including the law written on the heart. And certainly the giving of the Law of Moses added to the already-present ocean of sins. It did so by increasing the very number of laws that could be broken, and by provoking specific sins (7:7-8).

But this is not exactly the point here. The Law (indeed, any law) does make sins more numerous, but that is not what Paul names here as God's purpose for adding the Law. He says the Law was added so that *the trespass* (singular) might increase. "Trespass" is παράπτωμα (*paraptōma*), a word used several times in the previous verses for the *one sin* of Adam (vv. 15,17,18). Thus it seems likely that Paul is not talking here about the quantitative increase of sins in general, but some kind of increase in the sin of Adam.

In what sense could the Law cause "the trespass" to increase, and why would God purposely cause this to happen? (See Moo, 347-349, for a discussion of main answers to these questions.) The best answer is that the Law served to increase man's *awareness* of the power and seriousness of sin and of the sinful condition brought upon the world by Adam's trespass. By objectively embodying God's standard for righteousness, and by unmistakably identifying sinful behavior, the Law served to magnify the reality of sin and to intensify man's sense of hopelessness as he struggles against it. "The law causes sin to stand out in all its heinousness and ramifications."

But why did God *want* to thus increase the trespass? What possible good could come from this? The answer lies in the rest of the verse: **But where sin increased, grace increased all the more . . . .** God is always ready to bestow the gift of his grace, but (apart from the cancellation of the Adamic sin) this gift must be willingly accepted. Thus the only thing that prevents the increase of grace is man's denial of his need for it and his refusal to accept it. But when confronted with the law in any form, man can no longer deny that he is a sinner. So by increasing man's sense or consciousness of sin, the Law increases his sense of need for God's grace, thereby causing grace to be more readily received and thus to increase.

Actually this applies to any law from God, not just the Mosaic Law. But here Paul seems to be speaking especially of the latter. In what special sense has the Law of Moses caused sin and therefore grace to increase? The answer relates to God's messianic purpose for Israel as a whole. The Law of Moses magnified the reality and seriousness of sin within Israel as such. The chosen people's manifold violations of the law aspect of the covenant are recorded in detail in the OT. Thus the consciousness of sin increased not only for the Israelites themselves, but it increases also for all who read about them (1 Cor 10:6-11). Indeed, one of the clearest lessons we learn from the OT is the sinfulness of mankind and how we deserve to be condemned for our sins. Reading about Israel is like looking at ourselves in a mirror, and we do not like what we see.

But at the very place "where sin increased," namely, in Israel, God caused grace to increase *all the more*. Among the very people where the Law caused the trespass of Adam to explode like an atomic bomb, the grace of God exploded like the more powerful hydrogen bomb. This explosion of grace came in the person and work of Jesus the Messiah, which was the reason for Israel's existence in the first place. Thus the Law itself had a large part in Israel's purpose of preparation for the coming of the Savior. By increasing the consciousness of sin, it increased the sense of need for grace, and thereby caused at least some Israelites to welcome the Messiah all the more. This is one way the law, even the Law of Moses, should still function today.

5:21 so that, just as sin reigned in death . . . . "So that" introduces another purpose statement. It tells the reason why God wanted grace to increase, i.e., to be accepted by more and more sinners. The train of thought in vv. 20-21 is this: God added the Law so that the awareness of sin might increase (20a). He wants the awareness of sin to increase so that grace may be all the more accepted and increased (20b). And he wants grace to increase so that it might defeat sin and death and reign triumphantly in the end (21).

This thought is stated in the form of one last comparison. "Just as sin reigned in death" sums up the point about Adam in 5:12-19. Paul has said twice (vv. 14,17) that *death* reigned through Adam's sin. But here he identifies the true tyrant, sin itself. Sin not only rules the sinner's heart in a state of spiritual death (Eph 2:1,5; Col 2:13); it also tyrannizes man's physical existence by causing it to be permeated with the inescapable canker of bodily death. The aorist (past) tense is used in reference to the sin of Adam, at which time sin "established its reign" (Dunn, I:287).

. . . so also grace might reign through righteousness to bring eternal life through Jesus Christ our Lord. The reign of sin and death is not the final word.

Adam is not the victor; Jesus is. Sin reigned in death, and still does to some degree; but grace will ultimately reign in life, and already does to some degree. Grace reigns through righteousness, the righteousness of God which is the content of the gospel (1:17) and which was established by Christ's incomparable atoning sacrifice wherein he paid the penalty for our sins. When this gift of imputed righteousness is bestowed upon the believing sinner, sin and death become defeated enemies and grace reigns triumphant unto eternal life, all because of the all-sufficient redemptive work of Jesus Christ our Lord.

This statement appropriately brings the second main section of Romans to an end (❂ I:368).

6:1–8:39 – PART THREE
THE ALL-SUFFICIENCY OF GRACE GIVES VICTORY OVER SIN

Chapter 6 begins a new unit of the book of Romans. Whereas 1:18–3:20 and 3:21–5:21 present law and grace as contrasting ways of salvation, chs. 6–8 form a new, self-contained section that continues the theme of grace from a different perspective than the previous section (❧I:369).

INTRODUCTION
A. The Major Theme of This Section (❧I:369.)

Paul's explanation of grace as justification by faith in the previous section raises some questions. If we are justified by grace through faith apart from works (3:28), then what about law? What about sin? What about obedience? Is God's law irrelevant under grace? Are good works optional? Does it no longer matter whether we sin or not?

In answer to such questions Paul in effect reminds us that grace is a *double cure*. It not only takes away the guilt of sin through the imputed righteousness established by the blood of Christ; it also takes away the power of sin by healing the spiritual sickness that permeates both our souls and our bodies. In other words, grace includes not only *justification* but also *sanctification*, which begins with the decisive act called regeneration or the new birth and continues through the power of the indwelling Holy Spirit. In the present section Paul's focus is on this "other side" of grace, which brings not an external change in our legal status but an internal change in our nature and character. Now that the penalty of sin has been removed through justification, we are free to focus on being rid of sin itself: serving God, keeping his law, and doing good works.

B. The Doctrinal Content of This Section

The main theme of these chapters is how the grace of God gives us victory over sin. At this point it will be helpful to summarize their basic doctrinal content before setting forth the verse-by-verse exegesis upon which it is based.

1. Key Concepts

Several key concepts form the backbone of this section. The first is *law* (νόμος, *nomos*), which is used in three major ways. Primarily it refers to the preceptive will of God, the law-code that defines right and wrong conduct, the totality of commandments and prohibitions that apply to human beings in any given time or place. At times the Law of Moses may be specifically in view. However, the Law of Moses as one specific law code is simply representative of God's laws as such, in whatever form it is available and known (❋ I:371).

Second, sometimes in this section "law" means "order, pattern, system, governing principle, rule of life," especially in the sense of an all-encompassing world order or life paradigm (7:21; 8:2; see 3:27). Third, the term *law* sometimes refers to an indwelling, compelling force, or a dominating power that seeks to control the individual, either for good or for evil (7:23,25). Finally, Paul uses the term *law* to describe the system of salvation by works in contrast with the system of grace (6:14-15).

The second key concept is *sin* (ἁμαρτία, *hamartia*). This word is used over three dozen times in these three chapters, almost always in the singular in the sense of an active, alien force that seduces us, draws us to itself as into a black hole, permeates us, and makes us its captive. As such sin is not our actions nor the inert product of our actions, but a personified power that acts upon us. The key point of this whole section is that this enemy has been defeated, and thus "sin shall not be your master" (6:14).

Our relation to sin progresses through four stages. (1) At first sin is only potential (7:9). Because of original grace (5:12-19) we come into the world in a state of purity and innocence, but sin is still a possibility because of our free will. (2) Then, when we fall into disobedience, sin becomes imperial; it rules over us (6:6,14). (3) In conversion sin is conquered but is still residual and must be consciously resisted (6:12-13; 7:17,20). (4) In the end when we are free from this corrupted body (6:6; 7:24-25; 8:23), sin will finally be nil to us. We will be in the blessed state where all the effects of sin are completely removed from our being and our environment.

A third key concept is *death*, which appears in these chapters in a number of terms and forms, as follows: (1) Physical death as such, considered as an event (7:2,3; 8:10,36,38) or as an enemy to be conquered (6:9; see 5:14,17). (2) The physical death of Jesus Christ, considered as an event (6:10; 8:34), as an instrument of salvation (6:3,5), or as the state from which he was raised (6:4,9; 7:4; 8:11). (3) The spiritual death of the sinner, considered as the event of his first "fall" into sin, or as the state in which he subsequently exists (7:9-13; see Eph 2:1,5). (4) The soteriological death of the sinner's "old [spiritually dead] self" (6:6), his death "to sin" (6:2,11) and "to law" (7:4,6). This is a constitutive part of the event of regeneration or new birth and is an extremely important concept. It is an event that takes place in our own history, not in the first century and not in some transhistorical sphere. (5) The death of sins (8:13), which is a constitutive part of the ongoing sanctification process. (6) Eternal death, the ultimate penalty for sin (6:16,21,23; 7:5,24; 8:2,6,13).

A correlative concept is *resurrection*, which is threefold. First is Christ's resurrection from the dead, the event by which he conquered death and in whose saving power we participate. Second is the sinner's spiritual resurrection to new life. This follows upon his death to sin and is the climactic conclusion of the regeneration event. Third is the resurrection of the body in the end-time, which is the final stage in our victory over sin. Closely related, of course, is the concept of *life*. Those who have been raised from the dead are alive; they have "newness of life" (6:4, NASB) or "eternal life" (6:23) in two stages, spiritual and physical.

A final set of concepts that permeate this section are *slavery* and *freedom*. The sinner is pictured as a slave to law (7:1-5), sin (6:17,19-20; 7:14; 23; 25), and death (7:24; 8:2). Redemption is described as being set free from these (6:6,14, 18,22; 7:6; 8:2), but also as becoming enslaved to a new set of masters: God (6:22), obedience (6:16), and righteousness (6:18-19).

2. Anthropological Dualism: Body and Spirit

Scripture in general and Paul especially describe the individual human being as a twofold creature composed of a physical body or flesh, and a spiritual entity known variously as the spirit, the soul, the heart, and the inner man. Both body and spirit are created by God and are inherently good (Gen 1:31). There is no natural antithesis or antagonism between body and spirit. Both together form the whole human being; an individual is not complete without both. The body without the spirit is dead (Jas 2:26), and the spirit without the body is naked (2 Cor 5:3).

This view of man, known as anthropological dualism, is presupposed and asserted throughout this section of Romans (❂I:373). It is a key for understanding these chapters. It is crucial for a proper view of what sin has done to us and how we are saved from its effects. It is crucial for understanding both the nature of our present struggle against sin, and the content and significance of our hope. In brief, we are saved in two stages. In conversion only the spirit or inner man is changed, through the act of dying and rising again in baptism. The body is still under the curse of death and remains a stronghold from which sin continues to assault the spirit. The result is a serious struggle between the renewed spirit and the sin-weakened flesh. Victory is ours to win, however, because of the new life bestowed upon our spirits and because of the assisting power of the Holy Spirit. We are able to control our resisting bodies even as we look forward in hope to the time when these bodies also will be set free from sin in the day of resurrection and cosmic renewal.

In my exegesis of this passage I have found it necessary to go against the conventional understanding of the term *sarx* or "flesh." The common explanation is that this term, here and in other places in Paul, refers to the whole man (body and spirit) as controlled by sin in its preconversion, sinful state. It is seen as the "old man" that dies in conversion but still exerts a drawing power upon us from its grave. I have had to conclude, however, that the "flesh" is the physical body, not the entire person. It is true that the flesh is described in very negative terms both here and in other places in the NT. But that is not because the body is inherently sinful and antagonistic to the spirit, but only because it has not yet been redeemed and is still under the influence of sin and death.

3. The Stages of the Spiritual Life

Here I will briefly describe the main stages through which a believer passes on his way to eternal life, as set forth in Romans 6–8.

Conception to Accountability

In 5:12-19 we saw that Christ's atoning death redeemed us all from the consequences of Adam's sin. Even though a child is still subject to physical death with all its mortal preliminaries (such as defects and disease), he has the guarantee of redemptive resurrection in the last day. More importantly, no spiritual consequences actually reach the child directly from Adam. Every infant is conceived and born free from guilt, condemnation, and depravity. This is the time when one is spiritually alive (7:9). Sin is only potentially present as a possible choice of the free will.

The Sinner's Life under Law

When a young person becomes aware of God's law as *God's* law, and breaks it, he experiences his own personal fall and becomes a sinner (7:7-11). Both soul and body come under the power of sin. From this point on, he is living "under law" (6:14) and "in the flesh" (7:5).

Though the law in itself is good (7:12), to the sinner it becomes an occasion for sin (7:7-13). Because of the weakness of his spirit and the power of sin working in his flesh, the sinner looks upon the law as his enemy and is unable to obey it (8:7-8). Yet, paradoxically, he becomes a slave to law because he regards it as his only means of salvation. He is in an impossible situation: seeking salvation through flawed obedience to a law which cannot save him (8:3). Such is the futility of works-righteousness, or life "under law" (6:14).

Personified as an enslaving tyrant, sin as a dominating power invades the life of the fallen sinner and rules with an imperial presence over both spirit and body. The person literally becomes a slave to sin (6:12-20; 8:15). The same is true of death, which also takes control of the entire person (7:9-13). In the grip of sin the spirit dies in its ability to respond positively to the law. The body, already subject to physical death, becomes permeated by the seeds of spiritual death (7:5) and thus becomes "flesh" in the negative sense.

The second aspect of the sinner's "double trouble" is now in full bloom. He is "in the flesh" (7:5; 8:8) or controlled by its evil desires (6:12). He is existing and conducting his life "according to the flesh" (8:4-9,12-13).

The Conversion Event: Saving Grace Applied

When the spiritually dead person hears the gospel, accepts it as true, and puts his trust in the saving work of Jesus, he then submits to Christian baptism (6:3). At this specific point in time (baptism) he comes under the grace of God, not just for justification but also for regeneration or renewal.

The latter involves two distinct acts of God. The first is the *death* of the sinner's "old self" (6:6-8). This is a death to law (7:4,6) and a death to sin (6:2,4,11). The second is a *resurrection* of the believer into a state of new life (6:4-5,11).

The conversion event is also described in terms of slavery. The submissive believer is set free from slavery to sin (6:17-18,22). He is also set free from slavery to law, both as a way of salvation (6:14) and as an occasion for sin (7:3-6). Grace does not free us from slavery altogether, though; it simply provides us with new masters: God, obedience, and righteousness (6:17-18,22; 7:6).

A crucial point is how conversion affects the two aspects of our dual nature. At this point the whole person in principle dies and rises again, but in reality the spiritual death-to-sin and the resurrection to new life affect only the spirit. The body itself continues to be permeated with the power of sin and death (7:17-25; 8:10). Nevertheless the conversion experience includes God's promise that the body also will one day be redeemed through resurrection (6:5-8; 8:10-11).

The Believer's Life under Grace

The believer's life under grace is summed up in three words: power, struggle, and victory. As already suggested, the regeneration event (death-resurrection) gives the believer the power to conquer sin and to submit to God's law. Though the body is as yet unredeemed, we can reign over it (6:12-13; 8:12-13). This God-restored ability is the basis for strong exhortations to stop sinning (6:12-13,19). A desire to obey the law from the heart is also present (6:17; 7:15,22,25).

However, the presence of the "flesh" is the source of continuing conflict and struggle. The unredeemed body is still under the power, not just of physical death, but of spiritual death as well. "The law of sin and death" which once pervaded our entire nature is still residual in the believer's body (7:17-21,23,25). As such it exerts a drawing power upon the soul, pulling it back toward sin and spiritual bondage (7:23-24). Struggling against the "flesh" is the most basic form of spiritual warfare: the redeemed inner man versus the unredeemed body (7:23-25). The "flesh" is the *body itself* as inhabited by and controlled by this "law of sin and death," and as it exerts its drawing and seducing power over the inner man. Left alone, the redeemed believer would still be in a state of constant struggle, with the distinct possibility that the flesh might once more overcome the spirit (8:13).

Even in the presence of struggle we are assured of victory, however. We have already experienced victory over the guilt of our sin, through the blood of Jesus Christ (8:1,3,30,33-34). And now we are promised victory over *sin itself*, through the power of the Holy Spirit (8:2). In baptism (Acts 2:38) the Spirit of the Living God enters and indwells us (8:9,11). The purpose of his presence is to ensure our victory in this present struggle (8:4-9,14). He enables us to "put to death the misdeeds of the body" (8:13).

The Believer's Final and Total Victory over the Fallen World

The assurance of our final victory is our adoption into the family of God (8:14,16). The Holy Spirit is the mark of our sonship to God the Father (8:15-16). The risen Christ is the firstborn Son in this family, and our brother and fellow heir (8:17,29).

As of now we have only a small portion of our inheritance (8:23), but one day we will inherit a new cosmos (8:19-21) as the eternal home of our new, glorified bodies (8:11,23). Then our sonship will be complete (8:19), and the tyrant sin will be conquered forever and completely *nil* in our person and in our environment. This is our hope (8:24-25).

This hope is firm. Nothing outside ourselves can prevent us from receiving this inheritance. The Holy Spirit helps us in our struggles (8:13,26-27), and God's providence is completely in control (8:28). In accordance with his foreknowledge God has already predestined us to glory (8:18,29-30). Our assurance rests on nothing less than the power of the blood of Jesus Christ (8:31-34) and the security of his love (8:35-39).

C. The Outline of This Section

The material in these three chapters falls into three major parts. In the first part (6:1-7:13), Paul names three objections to grace based on a fear of antinomianism, and responds decisively to each. In the second part (7:14-8:13), Paul makes it clear that, rather than encouraging sin, grace provides the means for victory over sin. In the final part (8:14-39), Paul lays down the basis for our assurance of final salvation, despite our involvement in the continuing outward tension between the old creation and the new creation (❂ I:377-378).

I. 6:1-7:13 — OBJECTIONS TO GRACE BASED ON A FEAR OF ANTINOMIANISM

The rejection of law as a means of righteousness and salvation, and the presentation of grace as the only way of salvation, are bound to cause people to wonder whether law and obedience have any relevance at all in the Christian life. I.e., does grace lead to antinomianism? In its most general sense an antinomian is one who believes that we are not bound by law and have no obligation to obey it; hence there is no reason not to sin. In the Christian context the radical nature of grace — especially justification by faith apart from works of law (3:28) — may cause it to be mistaken for antinomianism by those whose knowledge of it is incomplete or perverted (◐ I:378).

A problem perhaps even more serious than antinomianism, though, is the fear that grace *will lead* to antinomianism if it is as radical as Paul seems to make it and if it is preached and embraced in this full radicalness. Thus the legalistic mind tends to resist grace and to raise this specter of antinomianism as a way of blocking its progress. Paul knows that his explanation of justification by faith is likely to be twisted into an antinomian doctrine; thus in this section he takes the initiative and refutes such a charge as part of his continuing presentation of grace.

How grace affects our relation to law, and the continuing role of the law in the Christian life, are main questions answered in this section. It is true that grace sets us free from law (not just the Mosaic Law, but *all* law) in some crucial ways. Mainly it sets us free from law as a way of salvation, something it cannot accomplish anyway. As corollaries grace sets us free from the condemnation of the law, and it frees us from legalistic motives for obedience. *But* — and here is the main point — it does *not* release us from our obligation to *obey* God's laws, in whatever form they are available to us and apply to us. Under grace we are all the more slaves to God and owe him our complete obedience, with the goal of achieving full personal righteousness and holiness (6:15-22).

But some, especially Jews, may argue that law is our only sure safeguard and weapon against sin. If we set aside the law, are we not opening the floodgates of sin? No, says Paul, we are not; anyone who thinks this has not yet grasped the full scope of grace. The fact is that grace is not just the only way to be justified and accepted by God; it is also the only source of victory over sin itself. Grace is what *enables* us to obey God's commandments. The first part of the double cure of grace is indeed justification through imputed righteousness (3:21–5:21), but the second part is regeneration and sanctification through imparted righteousness. Grace sets us free not only from sin's penalty, but also from its power. Because of law, we still *ought* to obey; but because of grace, we *can* obey.

A. Does Grace Make Sin Irrelevant? NO! (6:1-14)

The question with which this section begins suggests that grace must somehow negate our obligation to obey God's commandments. In responding to the question Paul unequivocally denies that this is the case — "By no means!" But then he shifts the discussion in a different and more relevant direction. Not only does grace *not* negate our *obligation* to obey God's laws; in fact it specifically gives us the *ability* to obey. This is the main point of this section. The first part (1-11) is mainly indicative, asserting the fact that grace has changed us and given us the power not to sin; the last part (12-14) is mainly imperative, commanding us not to sin (❂I:380).

6:1 What shall we say, then? Each of the three objections discussed in this section begins with the same form. First is a general interrogative: "What shall we say, then?" (6:1; 7:7) or "What then?" (6:15). Then comes the specific objection in the form of a question, followed by the emphatic denial, μὴ γένοιτο (*me genoito*; see 3:4 above) (❂I:380).

Shall we go on sinning so that grace may increase? In the phrase "go on sinning" the word for sin is a noun; literally it reads "remain in sin," i.e., in the sphere of sin. This expression is stronger than merely "continue to commit sins"; it means "continue in the state of sin or under the control of sin" (Moo, 355; Dunn, I:306). Thus, given the nature of grace, should we not just remain where we are without making any changes in our sinful lifestyles and sinful habits? Or to use the language of 6:2, should we not just continue to "live in" sin?

6:2 By no means! This is Paul's usual emphatic negative. **We died to sin; how can we live in it any longer?** This is the answer to the objection in a nutshell; it sums up the entire answer of vv. 3-14 (❂I:381).

In "died to sin" the verb is a simple aorist (past) tense, indicating a specific past event in our personal history. Speaking as Christians, at some point in the past we actually *died* to sin. Prior to that point we were dead *in* our sins (Eph 2:1), but at that point we died *to* sin. Here "sin" is singular. It refers to sin as a controlling power and as an enslaving tyrant. In relation to the power of sin, we died. See Col 2:20; 3:3.

This does not mean that something *within* us died, such as sin itself or the seed of sin or the power of sin. No, *we ourselves* died. I.e., the person we used to be, the one who was dominated by sin and the flesh — this "old man" (6:6) died. Something happened to us that was so radical that it can only be called an act of dying. It was an act of saving grace, performed upon us by the power of God. It was part of the event called regeneration; along with the immediately following act of resurrection it transformed us into new beings. This means that as Christians we have passed from under the control of sin and into the control of righteousness.

As Stott (170) points out, this does not mean that the Christian is in a state of death as far as sin's temptations and allurements are concerned, as if he were immune to them in the same sense that a corpse is totally beyond the ability to respond to physical stimuli (contra Lenski, 389-390). In this whole section it is clear that sin's drawing power still plagues Christians and must be consciously resisted. But because we have died to sin we are now resisting it from the outside rather than being overwhelmed by it within its own domain.

Our death to sin is a fact, and Paul uses this fact as the crux of his response to the objection in v. 1. Shall we as Christians continue to live in sin? How *could* we, since we have *died* to sin and have left its sphere? If you think otherwise, says Paul, you just don't get it. You don't yet understand what grace is all about. Grace is a *double* cure — not just forgiveness, but also a change in your very nature and character. For one who has died to sin to continue to live in it is a true contradiction of terms.

It is not a physical (metaphysical) contradiction, because it is actually possible for a believer to yield himself up again to sin's power; otherwise the exhortations *not* to do so (6:12-13) would be unnecessary and empty. It is rather a "moral contradiction" (Bruce, 136), a "moral incongruity" (Stott, 169). Literally Paul does not ask "How *can* we" (contra the NIV), but "How *shall* we" (future tense, NASB). Perhaps the sense of it is best expressed as "How *could* we?" (Phillips).

Paul does not ask how we could continue *to sin*, as if regeneration immediately makes us completely perfect and beyond sinning. He asks how we could continue to *live in sin* as a lifestyle, sinning habitually and perpetually (MacArthur, I:317) "We die to sin in so far that righteousness becomes the rule of life, and sin the painful, mortifying, humiliating, heart-breaking exception" (MP, 342).

6:3 Or don't you know what happened to you in your baptism? Literally Paul says "or are you ignorant" of this. His question has the tone of a mild rebuke, implying that you *should* know this, but just in case you do not I will explain it. In this instance his question has to do with baptism. Without a doubt all of Paul's Christian readers would have remembered the time and event of their immersion, since this was a part of the basic presentation of the gospel and of becoming a Christian. However, they may not have understood the deeper spiritual significance of this act; this is what Paul now explains. (See Cottrell, *Baptism*, ch. 7.)

Don't you know **that all of us who were baptized into Christ Jesus were baptized into his death?** "All of us who were baptized" means all Christians; in the NT there is no such thing as an unbaptized Christian. "Baptized" refers to water baptism and everything the NT includes in it (❂I:383).

It is "baptism into Christ Jesus." That Paul does not dwell on this point shows that it was a basic truth that any Christian would already know. To be baptized into Christ means to be baptized *for the purpose of* entering into a specific relationship with him, or into a living union with him. This is the significance of the preposition *eis*, "into." See Gal 3:27.

This union with Christ is not effected by the ritual itself, either by the water or by the act. It is accomplished by the grace and power of the living God alone. That it happens in the act of baptism is simply a matter of God's free and sovereign choice; he has appropriately designated this event as the occasion for the beginning of this saving union with the Redeemer. It is not wrong to say that the external ritual of water baptism *symbolizes* or has a metaphorical con-

Romans Part Three

nection with this saving union. What is wrong is to separate the symbol from the reality as if the temporal connection between them is irrelevant.

All of the above is part of what Paul assumes his Christian audience already knows. In the latter part of the verse he begins to talk about the point of which they may be ignorant, the point that he wants to stress in reply to the question in v. 1. Don't you know, he asks, that you were baptized into the *death* of Christ? If you were baptized "into Christ" as such, don't you realize that this means you were baptized into a union with Christ *in his death*? Ordinarily when we think about coming into contact with the death of Christ and its benefits, we think of the atoning and justifying power of his blood, and we think of the fact that baptism is for the forgiveness of sins (Acts 2:38), or justification. But here Paul primarily has something else in mind. He is letting us know that our union with Christ's death in our baptism had a result that is crucial for our victory over sin itself. This result is explained in the next verse.

6:4 We were therefore buried with him through baptism into death . . . . Here Paul continues to make his point by drawing a conclusion from his preceding statement, as indicated by "therefore." The main point of this conclusion is the phrase "into death." First of all, whose death does Paul mean? He has already said we are baptized into *Christ's* death (6:3). The phrase "buried with him" basically repeats this. Therefore we must conclude that "into death" means something else, namely, *our own* death to sin. When we were baptized into Christ's death (or buried with him through baptism), we were actually baptized/buried *into our own death* as well. According to v. 2, "we died to sin." This is the main point of this whole section and the main reason why grace does not imply antinomianism. The rest of this section (vv. 3-14) is meant to explain this death to sin. The introduction of the subject of baptism ("or don't you know") leads us to expect some specific reference to this death in connection with baptism. But if the phrase "into death" here in v. 4 does not refer to our personal death to sin, then this passage does not connect it with baptism at all, and there would seem to be no good reason even to bring up the subject of baptism. Also, everything in the following context presupposes such a reference to our own death to sin. Therefore I vigorously disagree with those who see "into death" as referring to Christ's death only. It may include that, but the main reference is to our own personal death to sin.

The implication is that in some true and significant sense, the death of Jesus has a death-dealing power in reference to sin. When we became united with Christ's death in baptism, our old sinful self was put to death — not by our own willpower, but by the power of his holy cross. It is as if, in his death, Jesus became a flame that is capable of destroying everything having to do with sin and death. When we are baptized into his death (buried with him in baptism), we touch this flame; and it consumes the "old man" of sin, and sets us ablaze with a holy fire that continues to purge the residual sin from our lives (❂ I:385).

Why does Paul say that "we were buried with him"? Obviously in the experience of most people, including Christ, death precedes burial and is distinct from it. Burial is simply the natural sequel to death. It is often assumed that this same distinction and sequence apply to the sinner's death to sin and his burial with Christ. It is assumed that the actual death to sin occurs prior to baptism, usually when faith and/or repentance begins. This is followed by baptism as a ritual burial of the corpse.

I see an entirely different picture here, however. Paul says nothing about dying *first*, and *then* being buried in baptism. Rather, he says very clearly and pointedly that we were buried with him *through baptism, into death*. The death and the burial are not separated by time. The only sequential relationship here is that the burial precedes the death as cause precedes effect. Also, both the death and the burial occur *through baptism*. There is no significant difference between the burial and the death. To be "buried with him through baptism" is just another way of saying "baptized into his death."

Then why does Paul adjust the image in v. 4a and speak of burial at all, rather than just death as such? For two reasons. First, his main point is that by being baptized into Christ's death, we have been baptized into our own death; and it would be awkward and ambiguous to repeat "baptized into his death" in v. 4. By switching to the image of burial he can make this point in a much more smooth and unambiguous way. Second, the image of burial is naturally suggested by the reference to baptism, which as an act of immersion into water is a perfect physical symbol of the deaths and resurrections (Christ's and ours) that are represented and occurring there. It is tragic that so many would rob baptism of this, its most central symbolism. I agree with all those who understand that baptism is immersion, and who declare that only in this form can its connection with the realities of death, burial, and resurrection — both Christ's and ours — have any meaning at all.

It is necessary at this point to raise the question as to *exactly when* the sinner's death to sin occurs. Paul says very clearly that we were "buried with him *through baptism* into (our) death." However, it seems that most interpreters are determined to locate it at some other point in time, *anywhere* but in baptism itself. Some say that believers literally died with Jesus on the cross; others say this death to sin occurs at the moment of faith and/or repentance (❂I:386-387).

Paul's language is clear, though. He says we were *baptized* into Christ's death, and that we were buried with him into death *through baptism*. The words "through baptism" belie all notions of postreality symbolism. They connect our baptism and our death to sin together as cause and effect. This does not mean that the water or the physical act as such produces this spiritual effect. Only the spiritual working of God himself, which he graciously performs in conjunction with the physical act, can cause us to die to sin and rise again.

Paul says that we are baptized into Christ's death, and that through baptism we are buried with him into our own death to sin. This means that God has so worked it that in some manner the death of Jesus Christ with all its saving benefits is literally present to the believing sinner and actually touches him in the act of baptism; and this union produces our death to sin.

Are we saying, then, that baptism is both the *occasion* and the *means* by which the believing sinner is regenerated? In reality, it is impossible to separate occasion and means. We can say that baptism is both if we remember one thing, namely, that the one act of baptism (Eph 4:5) is a dual event in which physical and spiritual acts are taking place simultaneously. While the believing sinner's body is being immersed into water by a human agent, God himself is working the works of salvation upon the sinner's spirit, including justification and regeneration. Physical immersion is the *occasion*, and the simultaneous working of God is the *means* of producing these effects. Thus in a general way we can say yes, baptism is a means of salvation in the sense that the total event includes not just the physical immersion but also the efficacious works of God.

In what sense, then, is faith itself (and perhaps repentance also) a *means* of salvation? Colossians 2:12 (NASB *only*) brings all these elements together: "Having been buried with Him in baptism, in which you were also raised up with Him through faith in the working of God, who raised Him from the dead." "Buried with him" and "raised up with him" are saving acts that effect justification and regeneration. "In baptism" (physical immersion) indicates the time, place, or occasion when these saving acts take place. "The working of God" is the *active* means that brings about these saving acts, and "through faith" is the *passive* means by which we receive their results.

Without a doubt our death to sin is one of the most important events in our lives, and Paul here makes it the keystone of his reply to the first antinomian objection to grace (6:2). Yet in a real sense this death is not the main event but is itself a means to an even greater end: resurrection. This is seen in the rest of v. 4, which is introduced by the word ἵνα (*hina*), indicating purpose and translated **in order that**. We were buried with Christ through baptism into our death to sin so that, **just as Christ was raised from the dead through the glory of the Father, we too may live a new life.** The death of our old man simply prepares the way for our new life.

The resurrection of Jesus is introduced here not just as an analogy of our own spiritual resurrection, but, like his death, as an essential part of his saving work with which we come into contact in baptism. The resurrection of Jesus Christ represents and generates infinite life-giving power (Eph 1:18-23; Heb 7:16), a power that produces in us the ability to walk in newness of life. "From the dead" is literally "from among the dead," but the sense is "from the state of death." That Jesus was raised "through the glory of the Father" probably means "through the Father's gloriously displayed power." (See under 1:21.)

The main idea here is "in order that . . . we too may live a new life." This is a very condensed statement. Paul does not specifically say that we were "raised from the dead" just as Christ was raised. It is definitely assumed, however, since he mentions it later (6:11,13) and elsewhere (Eph 2:5-6; Col 2:12-13). The word "too" connects his resurrection and ours.

That this resurrection also occurs in baptism, as the counterpart to burial, is implied in this verse and specifically stated in Col 2:12 (NASB only). As we will see below, there is a future aspect of our resurrection with Christ, but that must not be allowed to obscure the all-important spiritual resurrection that occurs in our baptism.

The ultimate purpose and goal of both our death to sin and our resurrection with Christ is the actual living of a new life. The NIV translation "may live a new life" is too sanitized. The Greek literally reads "might walk in newness of life" (NASB). The emphasis is on *life*. Prior to our conversion we were *dead* in our trespasses and sins (Eph 2:1,5), and our whole existence was under the pall of death. But in baptism all this was changed. Now the power that controls us is life, not death. Our existence is characterized by life rather than death.

This is indeed a *newness* of life — a new kind of life that transcends even that innocent state of life in which we were born and in which we existed until we sinned (7:9). It is life derived from Christ's own glorified existence, life transmitted to us by the Spirit of life (8:2), life that is in continuity with our ultimate eschatological and eternal life (6:23).

We do not just "live" this life; we *walk* in it. This word (περιπατέω, *peripateō*) is one of Paul's favorite expressions for one's behavior or daily conduct, good or bad. He uses it over 30 times in this sense, no doubt under the influence of a similar idiom in the OT (Dunn, I:315-316).

To "walk in newness of life" means to live a holy life, a life of obedience to God's laws. This is the whole purpose of our death to sin and resurrection with Christ. Rather than the antinomian inference that grace encourages sinning, it does just the opposite. By design and in effect it separates us from sin and sets us on the road of righteousness. The verb "to walk" is subjunctive, hence the translation "might walk." Death to sin and resurrection to life create the possibility and ability of walking in the new, holy life; but we must take the responsibility of applying this new life-power to our daily conduct. "Shall we remain in sin?" is the objection. Paul replies, "How *could* you? You have died to sin and been made alive in Jesus Christ! So *walk* in the possibilities and the power of your new life! *Just do it!*"

6:5 If we have been united with him like this in his death, we will certainly also be united with him in his resurrection. This verse basically restates the point of vv. 3-4, namely, that we died with Christ so that we might be raised up with him into a new life. If we have done the former, we must do the latter. We cannot die to sin and live in it at the same time (v. 2).

It is generally agreed that "united with" (from συμφύω [*symphyō*]) is a better reading than "planted together" (from συμφυτεύω [*symphyteuō*]; see KJV). The word is commonly used for the joining of two things that proceed to grow together as a unity, as in the fusing together of a broken bone or in the grafting of a branch into a tree. The latter image is especially appropriate in view of John 15:1-8 and Rom 11:17-24. When we are "grafted into" Christ, his life flows into us and we continue to grow with him into spiritual maturity.

The phrase "like this" in the NIV is a poor translation of "in the likeness of" (❂ I:391), i.e., "we are united with him in the likeness of his death."

What is the meaning of "the likeness of his death"? It is not the cross itself, nor the death of Christ itself. In view of the context it most probably is the act of baptism (Lard, 202; MP, 344), considered as the place where we become united with Christ in his death. On the spiritual side of the baptismal event, of course, we did not become united merely with the *likeness* of Christ's death, but with his death itself. But on the physical level, baptism (immersion) is indeed a symbolic *likeness* of that death.

The latter part of the verse is strictly parallel with the former part, as the words "certainly also" indicate. It is necessary to supply some words here, since the original says only "certainly also we shall be . . . of the resurrection." The NIV rightly adds "united with him." The parallelism suggests that we should also add "in the likeness of." Thus the thought is, "We will certainly also be united with him in the likeness of his resurrection."

The main point is that in our relation to Christ we cannot separate death and resurrection. If we have become united with Christ's *death* in the baptismal event that is the likeness of his death, then we also have become united with Christ's *resurrection* in that same event, which is also the likeness of his resurrection. In union with Christ there can be no death without resurrection. Thus how could we continue to live the old life of sin?

6:6 For we know that our old self was crucified with him . . . . "We know" can refer to what already is or should be known by all believers, or it can refer to something new that is about to be told. Here it is probably the latter. Following his general statements that we have been united with Christ's death, Paul is about to explain in more detail *how* this frees us from sin.

First of all, when we died with Christ, "our old self was crucified with him." What is "our old self"? Literally it says "our old man (ἄνθρωπος, *anthrōpos*)"; see also Eph 4:22; Col 3:9. This phrase is generally taken to mean the person we used to be in our fallen, unbelieving state — not a part of our being, but our whole being under the influence of sin. It is our former self, our "old man" in contrast with our "new man" (Eph 4:22,24) (❂ I:392).

I agree with this explanation for the most part, with the following qualification. I believe that here the "old man" refers only to the soul or spirit, which is the center and seat of selfhood or personhood in the human being. Thus the "old self" that has been crucified with Christ is our fallen spirit that was dead in its trespasses and sins (Eph 2:1). In other words, in terms of the anthropological dualism discussed in the introduction to this main section, in baptism the *inner* man, or spirit, experiences death and resurrection with Christ; but the *outer* man, or body, does not. On the "inner man," see Rom 7:22; 2 Cor 4:16; Eph 3:16; 1 Pet 3:4.

Thus here in 6:6 the "old man" is the "inner man" as it once existed under the control of sin. But it no longer exists as the "old man." That old man died; indeed, it was *crucified with Christ*. What does this mean? This is not a new idea; it is the same as our *death to sin* (6:2) that happened when we were baptized into Christ's death (6:3), and the same as our burial with him into death (6:4). Thus our crucifixion with Christ did not take place on Golgotha's cross, as if we were somehow literally yet mystically present there. We were not transported back in history; rather, the living Christ has become present in *our* history, specifically in the event of our baptism. The power of the cross was there applied to our fallen soul, putting it to death as to its sin-ridden existence.

Lenski reminds us that crucifixion is "a violent, accursed death." Thus when our old man died, he "was literally murdered in our baptism, he did not die willingly but was slain as one cursed of God, the passive implying God as the agent" (400). That this should occur in baptism is appropriate, since, as Morris reminds us (246-247), in the first century the Greek word for "baptize" itself "evoked associations of violence." In its basic meaning of "immerse," the word was used of "people being drowned, or of ships being sunk." Thus it makes sense for Jesus to call his crucifixion a baptism (Mark 10:38; Luke 12:50), and for Paul to call our baptism a crucifixion. Thus the baptismal ceremony is not just "gentleness and inspiration; it means death, death to a whole way of life," as Morris says.

Why was our old self crucified? **. . . so that the body of sin might be done away with . . . .** What is this "body of sin"? A common view equates it with the "old man" in the first part of the verse; and since the "old man" is usually taken to mean "the whole man, as controlled by sin," that is how the "body of sin" is understood as well (Cranfield, I:309). Many interpret Paul's use of the term "flesh" in the same way; thus all three expressions are taken as equivalent.

I think, however, that they cannot be the same, since the reason for the crucifixion of the "old man" is the destruction of the "body of sin." These are two different things. Thus I have concluded, based on the way Paul uses the terms "body" and "flesh" in the entire passage, that the "body of sin" here in 6:6 refers only to the physical body. It does not denote the body as such, as if it were inherently sinful. Rather, it is the body *of sin*, the body as it has become infected by and controlled by sin (JC, I:394). DeWelt calls it "the body . . . which sin has seized" (88) (❷ I:394).

The old man is crucified so that this body of sin "might be *done away with*." What does this mean? The Greek word is καταργέω (*katargeō*, see 3:3). It can have the strong sense of "abolish, destroy." Those who equate "body of sin" with "old man" may easily give it this sense here. If the "old man" is crucified, it dies and is "destroyed" (as in the KJV, RSV, NRSV). It is "done away with" (as in the NASB and later editions of the NIV). But if "body of sin" means the physical body, how would this apply? It is literally destroyed only when it dies. This may possibly be what Paul means, but this would not be very relevant to our baptismal death to sin and would do little to quench the fears of antinomianism.

It is much better to take *katargeō* here in its weaker sense of "put out of action, make ineffective, render powerless." The object of the action is not destroyed or done away with, but is defeated and disabled so that it loses its power. In this sense Satan himself was "rendered powerless" by the death of Christ (Heb 2:14). This is the sense that applies in 6:6. In fact, older editions of the NIV translated it "rendered powerless" here.

That is the whole point. The "old man" (the soul as corrupted by sin) is crucified with Christ, and by his resurrection is transformed into a new man, so that the lusts and temptations and weaknesses that still characterize our sin-ridden body can be resisted and suppressed and controlled, rather than being allowed to control. Thus in baptism not only does the soul itself undergo healing from the sin that has infected it, but also by that very fact it gains power over the not-yet-redeemed "body of sin."

It is true that the "body of sin" continues to be a beachhead or staging point for temptations and lusts of all kinds. However, it no longer has the willing partner of a fallen spirit, and it cannot dominate and rule the "new man" raised up in the latter's place. A tension remains between the redeemed spirit and the unredeemed body, to be sure (7:14-25), but we have all that is needed for a sure victory over sin.

That is the point of the rest of the verse, which is another purpose clause. The old man was crucified with the purpose that the body of sin should be rendered powerless; the body of sin is rendered powerless with the purpose **that we should no longer be slaves to sin . . . .** Sin (through our bodies especially) continues to assault and attack us, but we are no longer its slaves. "No longer" implies that we once were slaves of sin, but that has changed — *we* have changed, or have *been* changed.

This does not mean that we will never again sin. The power of sin that remains in our bodies still seeks to enslave us, and our raised-to-new-life spirits are not yet restored to full strength. Thus the threat of sin still lurks, and sometimes sin becomes the "heart-breaking exception" (MP, 342). But as Hendriksen says, "There is a vast difference between (a) committing a sin and (b) constantly living and delighting in sin" (I:198). Being delivered from slavery to sin means being set free from the latter.

6:7 because anyone who has died has been freed from sin. (❧I:396) One question raised here has to do with the meaning of "freed." This is a problem because the word is not literally "freed, set free" (as in 6:18), but rather the word regularly translated "justified" (δικαιόω, *dikaioō*) elsewhere. For this reason many say that justification is Paul's point here: the believing sinner who has died to sin has been set free from the penalty or condemnation of sin; sin no longer has any legal claims upon him. The problem with this is that justification is not Paul's subject in this paragraph. He is dealing not with the guilt of sin but with the power of sin (Käsemann, 170). The answer to the problem may lie in the combination of *dikaioō* and *apo* — "justified from" — is a broader concept that includes both justification and sanctification: freed from both the guilt and power of sin. Dying with Christ sets us free from that power (❯ I:396).

6:8 This verse basically repeats the point of 6:5, that union with Christ in his death necessarily involves union with him in his resurrection. **Now if we died with Christ, we believe that we will also live with him.** "Died with Christ" is the same as "baptized into his death" (v. 3), "buried with him" (v. 4), "united with him in his death" (v. 5), and "crucified with him" (v. 6). It happened in baptism.

"We believe" expresses not just Paul's faith but the faith of all Christians. This does not mean that everyone understands and consciously believes this truth; it means rather that it is a necessary part of the content of the Christian faith. If we believe that we died with Christ in baptism — and we do, then we should also believe that we shall live with him as well. The one implies the other.

"Believe that" expresses the *assent* aspect of faith (see 1:16), or the acceptance of the truth of the content of God's inspired word. See Cranfield, I:312.

We believe that "we will also live with him." Because the death and resurrection of Jesus are inseparable, with the same certainty our death with him implies our resurrection with him. But what does the future tense imply? Some see a reference to our bodily resurrection at Christ's return, "an actually glorified existence in the future" (MP, 345). While this is our ultimate hope and faith, and while it is implicitly included in the baptismal symbolism, the main reference here is to our present renewed spiritual life (6:11) that began with our resurrection with Christ in baptism (Morris, 254; Cranfield, I:312-313).

The future tense emphasizes the *certainty* of our newness of life (6:5). At this present time, our resurrection life is our holy living and obedience to God's laws. So how can the Christian "go on sinning" (6:1) (❯ I:397)?

6:9 To undergird the reality of the new life we now enjoy, Paul here goes into a bit more detail about its parallel and source, the resurrection existence of Jesus Christ. **For we know that since Christ was raised from the dead, he cannot die again . . . .** "We know" reflects the common Christian understanding of Christ's resurrection. If we already know this is true about Jesus, then we can have the same confidence regarding ourselves. I.e., what happened to Jesus is the basis for what has happened to us and therefore for our *assurance* that it has happened. We have confidence that God has raised us from the dead, because we know he raised up Jesus (Col 2:12).

"He cannot die again" distinguishes Christ's resurrection from all miraculous resurrections that brought other people back to life, such as Lazarus and Dorcas. Christ's resurrection was in a category by itself. It was not just a partial and temporary victory over death, but one that was total, decisive, and permanent. In his raised and glorified human nature he is the first-fruits of the eschatological resurrection itself and the first representative of the redeemed world of the new heavens and new earth. He is living a *new kind of life*, one that is beyond the reach of sin and death. . . . **death no longer has mastery over him.** It did once, for that brief time when he took our sins upon himself and allowed himself to be overwhelmed by death in our place. But in his resurrection Jesus won the decisive victory over sin and death, and we are even now sharing in that victory.

6:10 The death he died, he died to sin once for all . . . . This reinforces the point about Jesus' complete victory over death and the endless power of his new life. "Died to sin" means that he died in relation to sin; his death had something to do with sin (❂ I:398).

In what sense did Jesus die in relation to sin? Paul has already affirmed that he died to bear the guilt and penalty of our sin (3:24-26). But here he seems to refer to something else, i.e., that in some way Christ died to deliver a death-blow to sin and to destroy its power (Murray, I:224-225). See Eph 4:8; Heb 2:14-15. Sin the usurper (5:21) has been dethroned by the instrument of the cross. This is why our union with Christ in his death is the death of our own sin (6:4). The blood he shed in his victorious battle with sin is the instrument of our sanctification (Heb 10:10; 13:12); it sweeps aside "acts that lead to death, so that we may serve the living God" (Heb 9:14).

Jesus' death to sin was "once for all." This idea is emphasized in the book of Hebrews (e.g., 7:27; 8:28), where the point is the true efficacy of Christ's sacrifice, as opposed to the nonefficacy of the sacrifices under the Old Covenant. The latter had to be repeated often; but Christ's one act of death (5:18) was infinite in power and does not need to be repeated. In 6:10, though, the contrast is different. Here Christ's death is compared with his own resurrection. His encounter with sin was a one-time event, not an ongoing, never-ending mission. Sin has no power where Christ is concerned. It is a usurper in his universe. Jesus entered this fallen world where sin rules, fought sin on its own turf (so to speak), won the battle through the unlikely weapon of the cross, then arose and ascended into heaven (Eph 4:8). That's it; that's the end of it; he did it once and it was over. The descent so eloquently described in Phil 2:7-8 will never be repeated. "It is finished," he said as he died (John 19:30).

. . . but the life he lives, he lives to God. Here is the contrast: a one-time encounter with sin and death, but an ongoing and eternal reign in *life* through the power of God and in the presence of God the Father (Phil 2:9-11). "I was dead, and behold I am alive for ever and ever!" (Rev 1:18). His present state is characterized by *life*, the eternal life that comes only from God, in whom life is everlastingly inherent (John 5:26).

That Jesus lives "to God" must mean more than "for the benefit of, to the glory of, God" (Moo, 379). *Everything* Jesus did, including and especially his death, was for God's benefit and glory. This is why the main idea in living "to God" must refer to the new kind of life that he lives in his resurrected and glorified state at the very right hand of God the Father.

6:11 In the same way, count yourselves dead to sin but alive to God in Christ Jesus. This verse is closely associated with v. 10, contrary to the paragraph division in the NIV. It is important to understand the nature of *Christ's* death and resurrection, because we too have been put to death and raised again with him. Our death to sin and resurrection to newness of life draw their meaning and power from his own. Thus "in the same way" refers to what has just been said in vv. 9-10 especially, though it also sums up the entire didactic section in vv. 2-10.

"Count yourselves" is an imperative, an exhortation — the first in the epistle, as Morris notes (256). Nevertheless it is not parallel to the imperatives in vv. 12-13, which form the behavioral application of the factual data laid down in vv. 2-11. Verse 11 is an exhortation to accept these data as true. The verb is λογίζομαι (*logizomai*), which was used throughout ch. 4 in the sense of "declared, reckoned, imputed." This verse (6:11) is not talking about God's imputing something to us, though. We ourselves are the subject of the verb; Paul says emphatically, "*You* count *yourselves* dead to sin but alive to God." In other words, "I have been stating this as a fact over and over (vv. 2-10); now it is time for you to put yourselves into the picture. You must not only accept this death and resurrection as true in an abstract sense; you must consider it to be true of yourselves *personally*."

We are "dead to sin," in some ways just like Jesus. His encounter with sin was a once-for-all victory; when it was over, it was *over*. He left it behind him. Likewise we must realize that we too have died to our old life; we have left it behind us. We have moved on to something better; we are "alive to God" (Col 3:1-4). Just as the risen Christ now has a new kind of existence based upon and enveloped by the glory and power of God, so we also have a new existence, a newness of life in which everything is from God and for God. In this new life we look upon sin as our hated and defeated enemy, we look upon God's law with loving reverence, and we regard obedience to his law not only as our duty but also as our delight. All this is true only "in Christ Jesus," only because he too has died to sin and for our sins and has been raised again, and only because we have been crucified and raised up with him in our baptism.

With all this being true, why should we even *want* to remain in sin, much less think that it is somehow our obligation under grace (6:1)? The very thought

Romans Part Three

is ridiculous. "For the Christian to choose to sin is the spiritual equivalent of digging up a corpse for fellowship," says Mounce (153).

6:12 Therefore. Here is the significant transition from the *indicative* to the *imperative* part of this section. The former (vv. 2-11) sets forth the facts of our death and resurrection with Christ; the latter (vv. 12-13) exhorts us to live lives that are consistent with these facts.

. . . do not let sin reign in your mortal body so that you obey its evil desires. The focal point of these exhortations has to do with the *body*. Many see the "mortal body" here as equivalent to their interpretation of "old self" and "body of sin" in v. 6, i.e., as the entire fallen self. I disagree with this view and see "mortal body" as referring specifically to the physical body, just as I do "the body of sin" in v. 6. It is called the *mortal* body because it has not yet been redeemed (8:23) and thus is still under the curse of death (8:10; see 1 Cor 15:53-54).

We all have two choices. We can reign over sin, or we can let sin reign over us (v. 14). Here Paul speaks of this choice in terms of the body-spirit dualism. In the unregenerate sinner, sin reigns over the whole person, body and spirit. Through regeneration (dying and rising with Christ) the spirit is set free from the corruption and power of sin, but the body remains unredeemed. The exhortation, "Do not let sin reign in your mortal body," implies that sin is still present there. Our unredeemed bodies are thus a kind of weak point, a vantage point from which sin still opposes us and fights against us and tries to conquer us (Godet, 250; Hendriksen, I:201).

Sin launches its attack in the form of "evil desires" that press upon us, demanding us to fulfill them and obey them. The word for "evil desires" (ἐπιθυμία, *epithymia*) can mean strong desire of any kind, good or bad (see 1:24). Here the context justifies the translation "evil desires" or "lusts" (NASB). Most bodily desires are not evil in themselves, but only become so when they are not kept within the boundaries of God's laws. The very point of sin is to let these desires flow unchecked and unrestrained, as if we were no more than animals.

The very fact that we are exhorted to prevent this shows that if we do not take charge of ourselves and our bodies, and if we do not make a deliberate effort to resist sin, then it is possible for sin to regain dominion over us and reign in our bodies. If it were not possible, this exhortation would be a sham.

At the same time, the very fact that we are exhorted not to let sin reign shows that we *can* do this. Unlike animals, we are spirit as well as body and thus are more than bodily desires. And unlike unregenerate sinners, our spirits have been infused with new life and new power by which we can and must rule over these bodily desires and keep them within their God-imposed boundaries. Thus we are not helpless; *we are able* to prevent sin from reigning in and through our bodies. This is the point of this exhortation.

The central truth stated in 6:6 is the basis for this ability and this responsibility. Our "old man" (the fallen "inner man" or spirit) was crucified with Christ in baptism for this very purpose — that the body of sin (mortal body) might be rendered powerless to rule over us, so that we should no longer be slaves to sin. Thus contrary to all antinomian hopes and fears, grace does not give us an excuse to go on sinning, but instead makes it possible, even *morally necessary* to stop sinning.

6:13 The first part of this verse goes with v. 12; it continues the negative exhortation begun there concerning the body: **Do not offer the parts of your body to sin, as instruments of wickedness . . . .** "Of your body" is not in the Greek text, but this is the correct sense. The word for "parts" (μέλος, *melos*) means "limb, organ, body part, member." It refers to the physical body, in continuity with v. 12.

The image here is of someone presenting the assets under his control into the service of a monarch. "Offer" means "to place at the disposal of, to present for use in the service of." The word for "instruments" often means "weapons," and many take that as the meaning here (see Hendriksen, I:202-203). "Sin" is pictured as a tyrant or dictator who wants to use our own bodily members as instruments or weapons by which it can rule over us. "Wickedness," or unrighteousness, is the use to which our members are put when we let sin control us.

The rest of the verse contains a two-part positive exhortation about presenting everything in our control into the service of God the true King rather than sin the usurper. **. . . but rather offer yourselves to God, as those who have been brought from death to life; and offer the parts of your body to him as instruments of righteousness.** In the first part of the verse "offer" is present tense: "do not go on offering your members into the service of sin," in answer to the question in 6:1. Here in the latter part of the verse "offer" is aorist tense, reflecting "deliberate and decisive commitment" (Dunn, I:338). I.e., make up your mind and begin to do it *now*!

In my judgment these two positive imperatives reflect the spirit-body dualism. "Offer *yourselves*" refers to the spirit or inner man, the seat of selfhood, the "command center" for the whole person. This inner self is the part of us that has already "been brought from death to life" (vv. 2-11). Therefore we can and must present our whole inner being for service unto God — mind, will, emotions, desires, motives, passions, love. Only a person still dead in his transgressions and sins will continue to place these faculties into the service of sin and self.

The two parts of the positive exhortation are joined with the simple conjunction καί, (*kai*, "and"), indicating two separate ideas. The second part, "offer the parts of your *body*," refers to the physical body as distinct from the soul or spirit. The verb is not repeated in the Greek; it occurs once and has two objects: offer *yourselves* and *your parts*. "Of your body" is properly inferred from the word for "parts, members" (*melos*). Here the contrast with v. 13a is precise. Instead of presenting your bodily members to King Sin for unrighteous purposes, present them to God as instruments or weapons to be used for the cause of righteousness in daily obedience to his will (❷ I:404).

6:14 For sin shall not be your master . . . . Some take this future tense as an imperative; others see it as a promise. It is no doubt a promise; and since it is a divine promise, it is no doubt certain. More importantly, this promise cannot be limited to the final state; it is meant to apply to Christians *now*. Christians already, even now, have been set free from sin's dominion (6:18), and this freedom will continue until it is culminated and finalized in the end. This does not mean that Christians will never commit any sins; it means that sin will not be their controlling power. Nor is the promise unconditional; it assumes that we will fulfill the imperatives of vv. 12-13.

. . . because you are not under law, but under grace. This seems to give the *reason* why sin shall not be our master. If we were under law, sin would definitely lord it over us in every way. But because we are under grace, sin will not be our master in any sense.

Paul here contrasts law and grace as opposing ways of salvation. In 3:21-5:21 he has explained the first and primary benefit of grace, i.e., freedom from sin's *penalty* (in justification). Now (6:1-8:30) he develops the second benefit of grace, i.e., freedom from sin's *power* (in regeneration and sanctification). His point is that law cannot set us free from sin's penalty or power. It cannot justify a person once even a single sin has been committed, nor can it give sinners the strength necessary to obey its own commands. Thus as a way of salvation, law is a total failure (JC, I:421, n. 21). It leaves the sinner's life under the power of sin, and it cannot divert him from the inevitable destiny of (eternal) death. Indeed, it is "the law of sin and death" (8:2).

But the blessed grace of God does what the law cannot. Its double cure sets us free from both the penalty and power of sin. This is why sin shall not be the master of those under grace. Living under the prospect of the penalty of eternal condemnation is itself a form of bondage to sin, but the grace of Jesus Christ has set us free from that (8:1; Heb 2:14-15). Living under the tyranny of sin considered as an enslaving power is also a form of bondage, but the grace of Jesus Christ has set us free from that also, as this whole chapter shows.

Here the word "law" is not limited to the Law of Moses, contrary to the assumption of many (e.g., Dunn, I:339; Moo, 387-388). It refers to law in any form, i.e., to the law code applicable in any individual's circumstances. The point is that Christians, or believers in any age, are not under obligation to obey *any* law code as a way of salvation.

Limiting *nomos* here to the Mosaic Law makes the verse meaningless to most people, since most have never been under the Law of Moses and do not even know what it is. In fact most sinners are *neither* under the Law of Moses *nor* under grace, and the choice between the Mosaic Law and grace is unintelligible to them. But if "law" here means law in general, when properly explained this choice will be clear to anyone.

B. Does Freedom from Law Mean We Are Free to Sin? NO! (6:15–7:6)

The reference to freedom from law in v. 14 again raises the specter of antinomianism. If we are not under law, then are we not free from all obligation to obey any commands of God? This is basically the same question raised in v. 1, but at that point Paul did not deal with the issue of obligation as such. Instead in 6:2-14 he established the even more basic point of our *ability* to obey. Now he turns specifically to the question of *obligation*.

The spirit of antinomianism says we have two choices. We can choose *autonomy* and be a law unto ourselves, thus having the absolute freedom of self-determination. Or we can choose to submit ourselves as slaves to the *authority* of another. Only a fool would choose the latter. Why make yourself someone else's slave, when you can be your own boss?

Over against this fiction, Paul makes it clear that this choice between autonomy and authority does not really exist. *We are slaves* and always will be, whether we are under law or grace. The only choice we have is which master we will serve: God or sin. When we accept God's offer of grace, we are no longer slaves to law and sin; but we are still slaves: "slaves to God" (6:22). Grace does not diminish our obligation to obey his commands a single iota.

We must resist the continuing temptation to limit "law" to the Law of Moses. In this context the law/grace contrast does not refer to the transition from the Old Covenant age to the New Covenant age, but to each individual's personal conversion experience in either age (❖I:407-408). "Law" in this section refers to whatever form of law is available and applicable to any given individual in any given time.

The main point, though, is that our personal transition from law to grace changes our relationship to law in significant ways, but not in every way. Because of grace we are no longer under law as a way of salvation, but we are still under law as a way of life. Even though by grace we are not under the law's penalties, we are still under its commands. Though saved by grace we are still creatures and must still obey the Creator, but grace changes our motives for obedience. Our sinful impulses are no longer held in check merely by external restraints such as the threat of eternal punishment. Rather, we are impelled to obey by our internal desire to please God and to show him our loving gratitude for his grace.

The content of this section falls into two main paragraphs. The first (6:15-23) shows what freedom from law does *not* mean. I.e., it does not mean autonomy or antinomianism. The second paragraph (7:1-6) shows what freedom from law *does* mean, i.e., freedom from external, legalistic motives and freedom to serve God from the heart (❖I:408).

1. We Are Slaves to God (6:15-23)

6:15 What then? Shall we sin because we are not under law but under grace? By no means! This verse has the same form as 6:1: a brief opening question, an objection worded as a question, and an emphatic denial. While the objection is basically the same as 6:1 in that it voices the fear that grace will lead to antinomianism, there is a slight difference. In 6:1 the problem is that the availability and abundance of forgiveness would seem to make converts indifferent toward the abandonment of sin. Why not just sin all the more, since grace will surely cover it all? In 6:15 the problem is that the absence of law as a moral restraint would seem to leave the convert with no reason not to sin. Without law to restrain behavior, won't we just keep right on sinning? In fact, without law how can any specific act even be called a sin?

So, "shall we sin because we are not under law but under grace?" Paul's answer is the emphatic and decisive μὴ γένοιτο (*mē genoito*), "By no means!" Anyone who thinks this does not yet understand the meaning of freedom from law. The transition from law to grace does not leave us free to sin, as if there were no longer any law at all by which sin is defined and restrained. Accepting grace means the abandonment of the law system as a way of salvation, but it does not separate us from law altogether. Under grace the commands of the law are still operative as a binding norm, identifying the limits and requirements of accepted behavior.

I stress again that "law" must not be limited here to the Law of Moses. The point is not the end of the era of the Mosaic Law and the beginning of the era of grace. Trying to be saved by law was not just a problem for Jews under the Old Covenant; it is a danger faced by all people, no matter what form of law they possess. All sinners are "under law" even where the Law of Moses is totally unknown. Countless people today who have only an intellectual acquaintance with Jesus Christ and the NT Scriptures are "under law" because they believe that living according to NT ethical principles (such as the Sermon on the Mount) will save them.

On the other hand, coming under grace is a possibility for anyone who hears the promise of God's forgiveness known through special revelation. The Law of Moses was binding upon all Jews who lived under the Old Covenant dispensation, yet some were "under law" and some were "under grace." The former were those who believed their obedience to the Law of Moses was their ticket to heaven. The latter were those who trusted in God's promises rather than in their own goodness, but who nevertheless continued to obey the statutes of the Mosaic Law as the norm God had assigned to them. Anyone today who ceases to trust in his own righteousness as the basis for his acceptance by God, and who receives Christ as his Savior according to the terms specified in the NT, is no longer under law but under grace. But he is still bound to obey the moral statutes of the entire Bible and the religious statutes of the NT.

6:16 Don't you know that when you offer yourselves to someone to obey him as slaves, you are slaves to the one whom you obey . . . ? Slavery was commonplace in the Roman Empire of the first century. In large urban areas nearly half of the population were either slaves or freed slaves, therefore the first recipients of Paul's letter would have been very much at home with this metaphor. They would have readily understood ("Don't you know . . . ?") the principle the Apostle is enunciating here. It is based on the fact that in that culture many people entered into slavery voluntarily, often to pay off a debt. The principle is this: when you make a decision to obey someone, you become that person's slave.

Paul applies this principle to the individual's spiritual life. We are all slaves who serve a master, but we do have a choice as to whom we will serve. The concept of choice is seen in the expression, "offer yourselves" (see 6:13). This shows that the individual's free will is involved in both his sin and his conversion.

According to Paul your free-will choice determines **whether you are slaves to sin, which leads to death, or to obedience, which leads to righteousness[.]** These are the only two alternatives. We cannot serve both at the same time (Luke 16:13), and we cannot decline to choose (see Josh 24:15).

One choice is to be a slave of sin. Here Paul continues the image of sin as a personified power or tyrant that wants to reign over us (5:21; 6:12-14). When we decide to live a life of sin, we become its slave, for "everyone who sins is a slave to sin" (John 8:34). The result of serving as sin's slave is *death*. This is not the redemptive death of the "old self" (6:6), the death *to* sin discussed in 6:1-14. It is rather the death that comes *from* sin, the devastating effect of sinning and the divine curse upon sin. This includes spiritual death (Eph 2:1), or the present state of moral corruption that hardens the sinner toward God. It includes physical death, which is a triumph for sin since the sinner has no promise of redemptive resurrection. It includes especially the final curse of eternal death (6:23; Rev 20:14).

The other choice is to be a slave of obedience itself. Later Paul speaks of being slaves to righteousness (v. 18) and slaves to God (v. 22). These are not three choices, but are three ways of describing the same choice. Obedience is the means by which we live as slaves to God, and righteousness is its outcome.

Being a "slave to obedience" is an unusual expression. In effect it says that as Christians we are *obeying obedience*. This is precisely what we do throughout our Christian lives. But why this awkward expression? For one thing, it emphasizes the fact that we still have the *obligation* to obey God's law, even under grace. We are still slaves (to God), and this is "a dramatic way of emphasizing that obedience is the very essence of slavery" (Stott, 183). For another thing, it shows us that slavery to sin does not deserve to be called obedience; service to God is the only true obedience (❂I:411).

I think it is best to take righteousness here in the moral sense. It is true that the concept of forensic or imputed righteousness (justification) dominated in chapters 1–5, but in chapter 6 the focus has shifted to sanctification or personal righteousness. This is clear in 6:13, where righteousness is contrasted with wickedness; see also 6:18-20. Also, when we see that "leads to death" probably includes the sinner's present state of spiritual death or moral corruption, moral righteousness corresponds very well with it. Also, a serious problem with taking righteousness here in the forensic sense (justification) is that it makes justification the result of obedience, which is works-righteousness, contrary to Paul's whole point in 3:21–5:21. This can be avoided only if "obedience" here is the initial obedience to the gospel, but we have seen that is not the case. Being *slaves* of obedience is not a one-time act but a lifelong state.

It is probable (❂I:412) that "obedience" refers to specific acts of obedience and "righteousness" to the spiritual state of our souls that is being brought about by such acts. This reference to righteousness (as conformity to God's law) helps Paul make his point that being under grace does not make obedience to the law irrelevant.

Paul's main point here is to remind us that we have already made our choice as to whom we will serve. We have not renounced slavery; we have simply chosen a new master: God. Rather than being free from moral restraint, contrary to the objection in 6:15, we have placed ourselves even more firmly under it (❂I:412).

6:17 Now, given the two alternatives in v. 16b, where do we as Christians stand? Here is Paul's answer: **But thanks be to God that, though you used to be slaves to sin** in your pre-Christian life, **you wholeheartedly obeyed the form of teaching to which you were entrusted.** This refers to our conversion experience, when we made the choice to stop being slaves of sin and to surrender ourselves to God instead. "You obeyed" is aorist tense and refers to our initial obedience to the gospel when we offered ourselves (v. 16) as lifelong slaves to Jesus as Lord.

This initial obedience (which involved faith, repentance, and baptism) was done "wholeheartedly," or literally, "from the heart." This shows that our decision to surrender to God was our own choice and was not coerced or irresistibly imposed upon us. It also means that we gave ourselves to God "sincerely and earnestly" (Lard, 213). A slave's service is usually outward only, with the heart being in rebellion; but when we entered God's service the very first thing we surrendered to him was our heart. See 1 Pet 1:22.

The rest of this verse is extremely difficult. What is "the form of teaching," and in what sense were we "entrusted" or delivered to it? Many possibilities have been suggested, and it is difficult to discern a clearly preferable answer (❂I:413). "Teaching" refers to the whole scope of biblical and apostolic teaching (Acts 2:42). It includes all biblical truth, and is therefore the "sound doctrine" of the biblical worldview. To say that Christians have "wholeheartedly obeyed" this form of teaching means that we have begun to allow it to mold our beliefs and our behavior. Such is the essence of our slavery to God, and it is a lifelong process.

Why does Paul say we were "entrusted" to this form of doctrine? Would it not make more sense to say it was entrusted to us? The word is παραδίδωμι (*paradidōmi*), which in other places is used for the handing over or passing on of divinely revealed truth (1 Cor 11:2,23; 15:3; 2 Pet 2:21; Jude 3). But here the thought is different: we were handed over to this form of teaching. Some believe the concept comes from the world of slavery, the specific image being the occasion when a slave changes ownership and is "delivered over" to a new master (Cranfield, I:324; Dunn, I:343-344). This thought is appropriate in the context, but it should be supplemented by the following idea as well. When we became God's slaves, he delivered us over to the body of doctrine which he has revealed through his apostles and prophets, and instructed us to conform ourselves to it. This is our job as his slaves, and is in accord with the references to "righteousness" in vv. 16 and 18. By shaping our minds and deeds to the pattern or mold of sound doctrine, we achieve the righteousness that is characteristic of slaves to God.

6:18 You have been set free from sin and have become slaves to righteousness. This completes the thought begun in v. 17. We were once slaves to sin, but in conversion we were set free from it. This is the same event as dying to sin (6:2,11), but here it is described in terms of slavery. Under both images the action is something done to us: "our old self was crucified" (6:6, passive), and we "have been set free" (passive). This shows that, even though we have the freedom to choose the one to whom we offer ourselves as slaves (v. 16), we cannot be delivered from slavery to sin without the liberating power of God. As sinners we make the decision that we want to change masters, but God alone gives us the power to do so when he kills our old self and gives new life to our spirits in baptism. This breaks sin's power over us.

As regenerated Christians we are now "slaves to righteousness." This is the same as the second option named in v. 16, "slaves to obedience, which leads to righteousness." It is similar to v. 17b, that we have committed ourselves to obeying the form of teaching to which the Liberator has delivered us. We have acknowledged our obligation to conform our thoughts and deeds to the Lord's teaching, i.e., to become righteous. Conforming our lives to God's will has become our goal and our passion, and our feet have been set upon that road by the power of God. This is a slavery to which we willingly and joyfully submit.

6:19 I put this in human terms because you are weak in your natural selves. Here Paul explains that, when he uses the metaphor of slavery, he is using (what was then) a common, everyday human relationship to help us understand our spiritual condition. Why is this necessary? In literal translation, "Because of the weakness of your flesh."

What does this mean? One possibility is that "the weakness of our flesh" makes it difficult for us to understand spiritual things; thus an analogy from daily life, even if the parallel is not always exact, will help us to grasp their meaning. This weakness could be just creaturely finitude, in which case "flesh" would mean our (morally neutral) human nature (4:1; 9:3,5; see 1:3). Or, it could be a spiritual dullness, in which case "flesh" would mean our unredeemed bodily natures which still exert a negative influence upon our thinking processes. In either case the weakness is a difficulty of understanding.

Another possibility is that "the weakness of our flesh" refers to our sinful desires (6:12) and impulses toward autonomy; thus it is necessary to use this harsh and graphic slave analogy as a way of helping us curb these lusts and impulses (Käsemann, 182). By describing us as slaves Paul is able to stress our "total obligation and total accountability" to God, even under grace (Cranfield, I:321). In this way he accomplishes his contextual purpose of addressing antinomian fears and tendencies.

In any case Paul continues to use the slave analogy in the next few verses: **Just as you used to offer the parts of your body in slavery to impurity and to ever-increasing wickedness, so now offer them in slavery to righteousness leading to holiness.** This is a "before and after" description of our lives, as indicated by the word "now." I.e., both before and after that point of time in which we died to sin, when our old man was crucified with Jesus (6:2,6), our status was and is that of a slave. In our role as a slave we offer the parts of our body to a master (see 6:13,16). "The parts of your body" is literally "your parts" or "your members," but as in 6:13 the phrase "of your body" is implied. As in that verse and in 6:16, the implication is that each individual has the responsible freedom to choose the master to whom he will submit himself as a slave.

Before our conversion it was simply a fact that we offered our bodies to impurity (or uncleanness) and wickedness (literally, "lawlessness"). These words are just two ways of describing *all* sins. All sins are impure in that they contradict the purity of the holy character of God, and all sins are lawlessness in that they are disobedience to the law of God. This is just a more intense way of saying we were "slaves to sin" (6:16,20).

"Ever-increasing wickedness" is literally "lawlessness unto lawlessness." The idea is that when we yield our bodies to sin, this simply leads to more and more sin, specifically to a state characterized by lawlessness. This expression, which brings to mind the scenario of depravity described in 1:18-32, helps to make Paul's main point, that living under grace does not lead to lawlessness. Contrary to the objection in 6:15, and paradoxically, *living under law* leads to lawlessness, while *living under grace* honors God's law by leading to righteousness and holiness. This latter point is made in the last part of the verse.

The end of the verse is the only imperative in this section; everything else is stated as a matter of fact: we were once slaves to sin, but we have changed masters and are now slaves to righteousness. Given these facts, we are exhorted to live lives that are consistent with this new master-slave relationship, by presenting the parts of our bodies in slavery to righteousness. The words of comparison, "just as," encourage us to be as diligent in our slavery to righteousness as we once were in our slavery to impurity.

The imagery in this verse (slavery) is different, but the point is the same as 6:13. The implication is that our as-yet-unredeemed bodies will not easily give up their slavery to impurity; we must make a deliberate effort to conform them to the demands of righteousness.

Slavery to lawlessness and slavery to righteousness are exact opposites. As we have seen, righteousness as such means conformity to the relevant norm; the norm to which human beings must conform is the law of God. Thus the essence of moral righteousness is "satisfying the requirements of the law." Before conversion we fought the law; now we are committed to conforming our entire lives to it. Jesus has already satisfied the law's requirement for *penalty*, in our place; this is our justification. Now it is our responsibility to satisfy the law's requirement for *obedience*, which is our (progressive) sanctification.

Slavery to righteousness leads to holiness, says Paul. The latter word is ἁγιοσμός (*hagiosmos*), and there is some debate as to whether it means holiness (sanctification) as a process or as a state. It is probably the latter. The *process* of (progressive) sanctification, which simply means becoming more and more holy, is the same as obedience (v. 16) and the same as offering our bodies in slavery to righteousness. The final result of this process will be a *state* of complete sanctification or perfect holiness, which will occur when our bodies themselves are redeemed in the last day (8:23). See 6:22.

6:20 When you were slaves to sin, you were free from the control of righteousness. This statement continues to emphasize the before-and-after contrast of v. 19. The NIV does not translate the initial particle, *gar*, "for, because"; and thus the connection with v. 19 is obscured. Also, this statement is very condensed; it must be supplemented by an unstated conclusion. The entire thought seems to be this: "Just as you were once fully devoted to sinning, so must you now live as slaves to righteousness instead. For when you were slaves to sin, you were free with respect to righteousness; but now that you are slaves of righteousness, you must keep yourselves free from sin."

"Free with respect to righteousness" does not mean that as sinners we were free from the obligation to be righteous. It means we were free from the desire and from an inner sense of responsibility to be such. This is not a happy freedom, but one that is insidious and deadly.

6:21 What benefit did you reap at that time from the things you are now ashamed of? Those things result in death! The NIV omits the word "therefore," which actually begins the thought contained in vv. 21-22. This shows that these verses are drawing a conclusion from something in the preceding context. They seem to be expanding the thought concerning the respective consequences of slavery to sin and slavery to righteousness stated in v. 19. There it was said that slavery to impurity and lawlessness results in further lawlessness (see the NASB, not the NIV), while slavery to righteousness leads to holiness or sanctification. Now, says v. 21, in view of that, what are the relative benefits of these two forms of slavery?

The word translated "benefit" in vv. 21-22 is καρπός (*karpos*), or "fruit." This is likely intended in the positive sense of "benefit, advantage, profit." I.e., what good and beneficial result is produced by these respective forms of slavery (❂ I:418)?

The acts and habits of impurity and lawlessness, which characterized our life of slavery to sin, are things of which we are now ashamed. Shame is not the same as the feeling of guilt or the sense of regret with respect to sin. It is more a feeling of inner pain and humiliation and disgrace that causes us to wonder how we could ever have done those things which seem so repulsive and hateful to us now. Such a feeling of shame with reference to our former sins is a necessary aspect of repentance and sanctification. To be without shame is to be under sin's dominion.

The question is, what good fruit did we reap from such a life of sin? The implied answer is, none! Its only immediate result was more and more sin, as v. 19 says; and its final result (τέλος, *telos*) is death. Sin produces death in every form, but especially it results in the eternal death that follows the final judgment (see 6:16).

6:22 But now that you have been set free from sin and have become slaves to God, the benefit you reap leads to holiness, and the result is eternal life. The verbs in the first part of this verse are aorist participles, referring to the decisive past event of conversion when we as slaves were transferred from one master to another. The thought is the same as that of v. 18, with one variation. Verse 18 says we became slaves to righteousness; here we "have become slaves to God." The difference is not significant; in truth these are two ways of saying the same thing. In this context it has been appropriate to speak of slavery to obedience (v. 16) and to righteousness because the alternative is stated as slavery to sin, impurity, and lawlessness (❂ I:419).

Being "set free from sin" is not just freedom from its penalty, which is justification, but also freedom from its power over us. The latter is the point here.

The latter part of the verse states the contrast with v. 21. Whereas our slavery to sin gave us no benefits at all, as slaves to God we have fruit unto holiness or sanctification. This is the same idea as v. 19b. The fruit that we reap from being slaves of righteousness is first of all a life of obedience and virtuous character, which Paul calls the "fruit of the Spirit" (Gal 5:22-23; see Matt 5:17). This ultimately results in the complete sanctification or perfect holiness of which v. 19b speaks, and finally culminates in eternal life. The life of holiness which we have now begun will by God's Spirit progress to a state of moral perfection that will never end.

6:23 For the wages of sin is death, but the gift of God is eternal life . . . .

This often-quoted verse concludes this section on the Christian's slavery to God, adding little that is new (❂ I:420).

Death is described as the "wages of sin." In NT times the term here translated "wages" often meant "a soldier's pay," and some see that special meaning here. They believe it corresponds well with the word for "instruments" in v. 13, which often meant weapons of warfare. On the other hand, the term was also used for the allowance or pocket money given a slave by his master. Either of these special meanings could be intended, but more likely the word simply means wages in the general sense of compensation justly earned and deserved for labor performed (❂ I:420).

The main point here is the sharp contrast between the *nature* of the rewards bestowed respectively upon the slave of sin and the slave of God. The former receives *wages*, the latter a *gift*. These two terms characterize the two distinct ways a person can relate to God, and also the two systems of salvation, law and grace. Under law a person relates to God in terms of wages; i.e., he receives what he actually deserves for his works. But every man has sinned (3:23), and what a sinner deserves is death. Under grace, however, a person relates to God in terms of a gift; i.e., his reward is not what he deserves but what God desires to give him. And even though we have all sinned and deserve death, God desires to give us eternal life (❂ I:421).

Paul makes it clear that this free gift is possible only **in Christ Jesus our Lord.** Though eternal life is free to us, it is not free to God. It was paid for through the blood of Jesus. Thus this chapter ends with the same praise to the Redeemer with which chapter 5 began and ended (5:1,21).

2. We Obey God from Our Hearts (7:1-6)

Paul has already established that we are free from the law *as a way of salvation*, and nothing could be more meaningful than this. Now, in this brief paragraph, Paul makes the further point that grace frees us from the law by *changing our motivation* for obedience. Like a widow who remarries, we are still "under a husband," namely, Jesus Christ; but our obedience to him is from a willing and eager heart, not from the external constraint of legalistic motives (❂ I:421).

7:1 Do you not know, brothers . . . ? Who are these "brothers" (❂ I:421-422)? They are Paul's fellow Christians in general. He has already addressed the entire church at Rome by this title of affection (see 1:13). In 9:3 he does use the term for Jews specifically, but qualifies it with the phrase "those of my own race."

. . . for I am speaking to men who know the law . . . . What Paul says here about the law is true of all law. Most of the initial recipients of Romans, whether Jews or Gentiles, would have known the Law of Moses. They would also have been quite familiar with Roman law. Those living in other times and cultures will know other law codes, both divine and human. But the principle Paul states in this verse is true of all law, as is the specific example given in vv. 2-3. Thus here he simply means, "Now, brothers, I'm sure you all know how law works."

Specifically, you know **that the law has authority over a man only as long as he lives[.]** "Have authority over" is κυριεύω (*kyrieuō*), the same word used in 6:9 of death and in 6:14 of sin. The idea is not authority as such, but rather power or dominion or control (❂ I:419).

What does it mean to be ruled or controlled by law, as far as one's relation to God is concerned? It means to regard God's law as the dominant spiritual category in one's life. God is viewed primarily as the Lawgiver, and law is the whip in his hand by which he keeps us in line. Obeying the law, i.e., not sinning, becomes the only key to peace, and fear of hell becomes our primary motivation not to sin. Law thus dominates a person when he regards his destiny as being determined by his response to the commandments of a law code (❂ I:422-423).

The principle Paul enunciates here, though, gives hope to those who are thus controlled by law. It is true of any law that its power and authority apply to a person only as long as he is alive. When a person dies, he is no longer within the sphere of the law. In v. 4 Paul will declare that we have indeed died, alluding to our death to sin discussed in 6:1-14; and this death to sin was a death to the law. We are no longer "under law" in the sense that it is no longer in control of our lives.

7:2 In vv. 2-3 Paul's intention is simply to illustrate the principle stated in v. 1. His point is not to give instructions about marriage and remarriage; nor is he constructing an allegory in which every detail is intended to be matched with some spiritual reality. He is simply showing that death sets one free from law.

For example, by law a married woman is bound to her husband as long as he is alive; but if her husband dies, she is released from the law of marriage. The word "married" literally means "under a husband" and is used only here in the NT. Paul probably chose this word because he is still talking about what it means to be "under law" and "under grace" (6:14). To be under law is like being "under" or married to one kind of husband, while being under grace is like being "under" or married to another kind of husband.

The point is that just about any law code, human or divine, has specific laws and regulations concerning marriage. Since the main person in Paul's illustration is a wife, he speaks here literally of "the law of the husband." A wife is bound by whatever the law says about her relationship to her husband as long as they are both alive. But if death occurs, such law is no longer relevant. The wife is no longer bound by it; she has been released from "the law of the husband" (❂ I:424).

So then, if she marries another man while her husband is still alive, she is called an adulteress. But if her husband dies, she is released from that law and is not an adulteress, even though she marries another man. (See ❂ I:424.) Paul does not intend to set forth a comprehensive Christian view of marriage and divorce here. He is concerned only with pointing out how death affects the marriage.

As long as a woman has one husband, she cannot marry another man without becoming an adulteress; this would be bigamy. But if the husband dies, she can marry another man without committing adultery, since death makes all laws concerning adultery and bigamy irrelevant.

7:4 Having stated his principle in v. 1, and having illustrated it in vv. 2-3, Paul now draws his conclusion from the principle: **So, my brothers, you also died to the law through the body of Christ....** Just as death within a marriage cancels the law governing that marriage, so does the death of our "old self" bring an end to the law's dominion over us. "You also died" is definitely a reference to the death to sin emphasized in 6:1-14; here Paul is adding the fact that our death to sin was also our death to law.

It is significant that Paul says *we* died, not the law. If he were talking just about the Law of Moses (which he is not), he could have said that "the law died," because in a real sense this is true of the Mosaic law (Eph 2:15). The point, however, is not the cessation of the law, but a change within the sinner himself, the cessation of the sinner's wrong attitude toward the law and his wrong use of the law.

"Died" is passive, i.e., "put to death" or "made to die" (NASB). This indicates that the change within us was not something we could muster from our own inner strength, but was something that required the working of God.

In what sense have we been put to death with reference to law? Certainly we are not under the law as a system of salvation, and we are dead to the penalty of the law. This is true because of "the body of Christ," in that "he himself bore our sins in his body on the tree" (1 Pet 2:24). Thus our objective relationship with the law has been changed by virtue of Christ's propitiatory sacrifice.

But this is not the whole story, nor even the main point here. When we truly come to understand these *objective* changes in our relationship to the law, the result is a *subjective* change in our attitude toward it. The law no longer controls our concept of our relation to God and to salvation. We are no longer in bondage to the idea that our acceptance with God is determined by our performance as measured by the law (❖I:425).

Like a wife who remarries after her husband dies, we who are put to death with reference to the law immediately enter into a new "marriage," as it were, with Jesus Christ. You died, **that you might belong to another, to him who was raised from the dead, in order that we might bear fruit to God.** Whether we think of our relationship with Jesus in terms of marriage is not the point here. Some take it this way, and the Bible elsewhere makes ample use of the marriage metaphor as an appropriate way to picture the relation between God and his people (Dunn, I:362).

The main point is that we have come to "belong to" Christ, as the one "who was raised from the dead." Paul refers to Jesus in resurrection terms to remind us that in our union with him we also were raised from the dead (6:4-6). This gave us a whole new perspective on the law. We are like a wife who used to be bound only by duty to a mean and miserly husband, but who is now willingly and joyfully united to a new, loving, generous husband and cannot do too much to please him. Even so, instead of producing dead works from a dead heart as driven by the law's threats, we as Christians are now alive in our spirits so that we may bear the fruit of good thoughts, words, and deeds, motivated only by a love for our Lord and a desire to please him.

Some see the reference to "fruit" as a continuation of the marriage metaphor, since in the Bible children are often called "fruit" (see Smith, I:96). Others see it simply as a reference to people as trees and their works as fruit (Matt 7:16-20). The Christian bears good fruit to God through his willing obedience to God's commands. When we were dead in sin we produced bad fruit; even our works that looked good on the outside were like shiny apples filled with worms and rottenness within, since they sprang from legalistic and selfish motives. But under grace the fruit we present to God is the "obedience of faith" (1:5) motivated by love (John 14:15), which is sweet and pleasing to his taste.

7:5 For when we were controlled by the sinful nature, the sinful passions aroused by the law were at work in our bodies, so that we bore fruit for death (❄ I:426).

"Controlled by the sinful nature" is literally the simple phrase "in the flesh." This expression is used in different senses in various texts. Sometimes it means life in this present world, in this present body (2 Cor 10:3; Gal 2:20). In 2:28 it refers in a neutral sense to the physical nature as distinct from the spirit. Many think that "flesh" means the pre-Christian "sinful nature," as here in the NIV.

I disagree. In the introduction to this section I have stated my conclusion that *sarx* in this context is not some generalized sinful nature but is rather the physical body, especially viewed as sin-weakened and unredeemed and thus as a source of evil desires (6:12) and "sinful passions." Thus to be "in the flesh" means to be governed by our bodily desires in such a way that they are the center of our lives and are promiscuously indulged without regard for moral boundaries. This was our pre-Christian state, says Paul. Instead of controlling our bodies, our bodies controlled us. The NIV properly translates the preposition "in" (ἐν, *en*) as "controlled by."

The reference to "sinful passions" (literally, "the passions of sins") confirms this interpretation. The word for "passions" (πάθημα, *pathēma*) often means "suffering," but can mean strong desires and emotional feelings in general, as here. The word does not necessarily have a negative connotation; but here (and in Gal 5:24) it does, as indicated by the qualifier, "passions *of sins*." Paul says these sinful passions "were at work in our bodies," literally, "in our members" (see 6:13,19). Thus to be "controlled by the flesh" means to allow sinful passions to have free reign in the members of our bodies. Such passions include those that are directly associated with the body, such as sexual lust, gluttony, and slothfulness.

At the time when we were controlled by these things, we "bore fruit for death." In other words, their consequence for our lives was death in every sense (6:21,23). This is in contrast with bearing fruit for God in v. 4.

A key question here is, what does it mean to say these sinful passions were "aroused by the law"? This is important because it is a description of our condition "under law" (6:14), before we "died to the law" (7:4). The Greek text says simply that the sinful passions worked in our members "through the law." Some take this to mean only that the law *reveals* certain passions to be sinful (Lard, 225; see 3:20; 7:7). Others take it to mean that the law in some sense *stimulates* or excites these passions, as in the NIV's "aroused by" (Cranfield, I:337; Moo, 420). The latter is probably the intended sense (see 7:7-13).

This does not mean that the law is *supposed* to stimulate sin, and in the pure heart it does not do so. But in our fallen, sin-weakened condition, this is exactly what it did. Very often, to the sinful heart, just knowing something is wrong or against the law makes the doing of it all the more attractive. This is part of the power that sin *as lawlessness* has over us; it implants within us the spirit of rebellion against God's law, so that the law itself becomes the stimulus for doing the very thing it forbids.

7:6 This verse goes beyond a mere contrast with v. 5, and affirms that we have died to the law in a general sense. **But now, by dying to what once bound us, we have been released from the law . . . .** The definitive turning point in our lives was the moment of our death: our death to sin (6:2) and to the law (7:4). Here Paul is thinking especially of the latter. In our pre-Christian life the law bound us by inciting us to sin, by imposing its penalty upon us, by limiting us to a futile effort to save ourselves by our own obedience, and thus by restricting us to legalistic motives even when we tried to obey. But by dying with Christ we were set free from the law in all these senses.

In the rest of this verse Paul focuses on one specific result of our being freed from the law, namely, **so that we serve in the new way of the Spirit, and not in the old way of the written code.** The word for "serve" is δουλεύω (*douleuō*), which means "to serve as a slave, to obey." Though released from the law in some ways, we are still slaves and still owe to God an absolute obedience to his commandments. Thus freedom from the law is not freedom from obedience, but freedom from a negative, legalistic attitude toward obedience and toward the law as such.

This change is described as a transition from "oldness" to "newness." Formerly we served "in the old way of the written code," or literally, "in oldness of (the) letter." This means that we regarded the law as a cold, impersonal, abstract code of behavior, and that we obeyed it only because it threatened punishment if we did not. We viewed it as detached from the personal heart of God, and thus our obedience was not from our own heart.

But now we serve, literally, "in newness of spirit." The word "newness" is the same as in 6:4, "newness of life" (NASB) (❋I:429). In my judgment "spirit" in this context is best understood as referring to our own spirit or soul or inner man, rather than the Holy Spirit. A major emphasis of this whole section of Romans is the fact that our conversion includes the regeneration and renewing of the spirit. Thus our "newness of life" (6:4) is a newness of our spirits, which have been made alive toward God and filled with a positive attitude toward his law. This results in a major change in our motivation for obedience: from "have to" to "want to," from "got to" to "get to." (See Deut 15:16-17.)

These last two verses are a general description of before-and-after as experienced by every believer. Paul is not talking here about the difference between the Old and New Covenants, the Law of Moses versus the "law of the gospel" (contra DeWelt, 100; and Moo, 421). The change he describes took place to a degree in the hearts of OT believers; it certainly takes place in the conversion experience of every Christian, with or without reference to the Law of Moses.

C. Does Grace Mean That Law Is Bad? NO! (7:7-13)

This final objection to grace based on a fear of antinomianism focuses on the nature of the law as such. Is there something wrong with law? Is it inherently bad or harmful? Are its consequences purely negative?

Thus far Paul has presented law in a less than favorable light (❋I:430). Thus it is no wonder that he now sees fit to defend the *integrity* of God's law. Despite all the seemingly negative things said about it, the problem is not with law but with sin. Sin, again personified as an opposing tyrant, uses its sinister power to abuse and exploit God's good law for its own negative purposes. Like the serpent in Gen 3:1-6, it distorts the law in a way that leads to sin and death; but this does not mean that the law itself is a bad thing. Indeed, Paul specifically declares that it is "holy, righteous and good" (7:12).

The major exegetical problems in this section stem from Paul's use of the first person singular. Who is the "I" whose experiences are being described here? I believe that Paul is speaking autobiographically, i.e., he is giving intimate details of his own personal spiritual history. This is the common-sense way of interpreting first person singular (❋I:430).

The next question is whether the spiritual events described here are true only of Paul, or whether they are true of Paul as the representative of a larger group. I along with most modern interpreters take the latter view.

But this leads to another question: what is this larger group of which Paul's experiences are representative? Some say Paul is describing his life as a Jew under the Law of Moses, and thus as a representative of all Jews under the Law.

Others say his experiences are those of all people when confronted by the law of God in any of its forms, be it the Mosaic Law or the moral law in general. I accept the latter view, which is in keeping with the fact that Paul has been using the term *law* in this general sense at key points throughout the letter thus far.

A final question remains: what particular stage in his life is Paul describing? I believe he is referring to his "coming of age" as symbolized in the *bar mitzvah* ceremony, when every thirteen-year-old Jewish boy formally became a "son of the commandment" and accepted personal responsibility for his own behavior. This "coming of age," which no doubt preceded the *bar mitzvah* ceremony, refers to the time when he became accountably aware of God as Lawgiver and Judge, of the Law of Moses as the law of *God*, and of his own identity as a sinner condemned by that law. This would correspond to the time when every person reaches the age of accountability (❷ I:431-432).

7:7 Some might object, then, that the law is responsible for sin. This objection is introduced with the same formula as the previous two: first the opening question, **What shall we say then?**; then the specific objection: **Is the law sin?**; finally the emphatic negative, **Certainly not!** The objection has to do with the very nature of law as contained in all law codes. Given the seemingly negative things said about it thus far, is the law somehow included within the sphere of sin or things sinful? Is it in league with sin, on the side of sin? Is it bad or sinful? *By no means*, says Paul. There is absolutely no sense in which this is true.

Indeed I would not have known what sin was except through the law. The word translated "indeed" (ἀλλά, *alla*) is used here to introduce a qualification: "yet" (NRSV). Paul means that the law is definitely not sinful in any way, but still it *does* have an important connection with sin: it gives us a *knowledge* of sin.

Is this knowledge purely cognitive or also experiential? God's law certainly gives us a cognitive (purely intellectual) knowledge of sin (❷ I:433). But the knowledge of which Paul speaks is more than this, as the rest of this section shows. Except through the law, he is saying, I would not have *experienced* the presence of sin in my own life. I may have been doing wrong things, but I would not have *known* them to be wrong without the testimony of the law. When I read in God's law that certain behavior is wrong, and when I see that very behavior in my life, I have a personal consciousness of the fact that I am a sinner; I have a sense of personal sinfulness before God (❷ I:433).

For I would not have known what coveting really was if the law had not said, "Do not covet." Paul's first knowledge of this last of the Ten Commandments no doubt came through the Law of Moses, but it is amply repeated in the New Covenant Scriptures (13:9; Gal 5:16; 1 Pet 2:11). Also, even pagans know that such behavior is wrong (1:24, 32); it is part of the law written on the heart (2:15).

The word for covetousness (ἐπιθυμία, *epithymia*) means "strong desire" (see 1:24). It is used for sexual lust but can also include illicit desires of all kinds, such as are enumerated in Exod 20:17 (cf. 7:8, "every kind of covetous desire"). It is the "desire for something forbidden" (Dunn, I:379). Since desire as such is natural, without the law to tell us which desires are wrong, such desires could be present in our hearts without our knowing them as sinful.

Why does Paul choose this particular example? For one thing, the sin of *epithymia* is appropriate because it is the root of all sin, says James 1:14-15. Also, it was no doubt the particular commandment that first awakened Paul to the reality of sin in his own life.

Thus the law makes us conscious of what sin is and conscious of being a sinner. Does this make the law bad? In no way! This is, among other things, exactly what the law is supposed to do. Unpleasant though it may be, it is a necessary and holy function of God's law.

7:8 But this is not the whole picture of the relation between law and sin. Surely no one can object to the propriety of law as the source of our knowledge of sin (7:7), but now in 7:8-11 Paul describes a relation between law, sin, and death that is much more subtle and which at first glance appears to make the law responsible for the sinner's death. The point Paul makes, though, is that the real culprit is not the law but *sin itself*, which is here personified as a powerful tyrant who seeks our ruin.

But sin, seizing the opportunity afforded by the commandment, produced in me every kind of covetous desire. This is not just a restatement or an explanation of v. 7. Here the law is pictured not simply as revealing and defining sin, but as in some sense *provoking* the very sinful behavior that it condemns. However, this is neither the law's purpose nor its proper function. It does so only indirectly, as an instrument wielded deceitfully by the tyrant sin itself.

The subject of the sentence is *sin* (ἁμαρτία, *hamartia*) as a personified, purposeful power, which some see as standing for Satan himself (Lard, 230; DeWelt, 104). The word for "opportunity" (ἀφορμή, *aphormē*) has a military connotation; it means a base or bridgehead for a military operation, a springboard or starting point for an expedition or attack — and thus in a general way, an occasion or opportunity. Thus sin is pictured as an enemy who is using the law itself, specifically the command against covetousness, to launch an attack upon us.

The prepositional phrase "by [διά, *dia*] the commandment" is taken by the NIV and others as modifying "seizing the opportunity." Others take it as modifying "produced" ("accomplished, worked, brought about"), i.e., sin produced every sort of lust in me through the commandment itself. The latter seems to be the intended meaning, and is more in harmony with vv. 5,11, and 13. Either way the perversity of sin is emphasized: it seizes upon the very commandment that forbids covetousness as an instrument for producing it.

How can the commandment be an opportunity for sin? In what sense can sin produce disobedience in a person through the very means that is designed to prevent it? The most obvious answer is that of Prov 9:17, "Stolen water is sweet." I.e., prohibitions awaken the desire to break them (see Morris, 280; Stott, 203). This is not the fault of the commandment, but is a possibility inherent in the freedom of the will. The commandment (*any* commandment) is misinterpreted as taking away freedom and preventing self-realization, and therefore becomes an occasion for resentment against the Lawgiver. This arouses a spirit of rebellion, which then uses the commandment as an opportunity to express itself. See 7:5 above (JC, I:435).

For apart from law, sin is dead. "Apart from law" means "in the absence of law; where no law exists." The "law" here is not just the Law of Moses, but *any* law of God. This is similar to 4:15, "Where there is no law there is no transgression." The point in 7:8 is somewhat stronger, however. 4:15 says that nothing counts as sin without a law to identify it as such. Here the point is that sin *as sin* lies dormant and ineffective, lacking in power and in this sense "dead," without the law as a weapon to use against the sinner. In such a case there is no commandment to be exploited as a temptation to further sin.

7:9 As stated in the introduction above, this verse is best understood as referring to Paul's "coming of age," or reaching the age of accountability. Also, he presents his experience not as something unique, but as representative of human beings in general. The main point is the role of law in this event.

Once I was alive apart from law . . . . This refers to "the days of innocent childhood" for Paul and for each individual (DeWelt, 106). This is the period when a child is living under the original grace of Jesus (5:12-19), before he comes to understand the significance of living in a world subject to the law of the Creator.

This is the meaning of "apart from law." It does not mean "apart from the existence of law," since there has never been such a time in human history. Nor does it mean "apart from a knowledge of the law"; children can learn the ten commandments at a very young age, and can know that it is wrong to break them. "Apart from law" refers rather to that age of innocence before a child understands the law to be the law *of God*, and before he realizes that breaking God's law has *eternal consequences*.

"Alive" refers to the spiritual state of the individual (the child) before he reaches accountability. His inner man (the soul or spirit) has not yet become dead in his transgressions and sins (Eph 2:1), and he is not yet under the penalty of eternal condemnation. The child in this state does not need conversion; he does not need baptism. If he dies in this state, he dies "alive" and thus is saved.

. . . but when the commandment came . . . . This refers to the coming of the commandment into the consciousness of the child, the time when he first understands its full significance as a commandment *of God* with eternal condemnation for disobedience. In Paul's case the command "Do not covet" awakened within him this full consciousness of sin (❧ I:437).

. . . sin sprang to life . . . . The word here is ἀναζάω (*anazaō*). The prefix *ana-* can give it the meaning "come to life *again*" (as in Luke 15:24), or "revive" (NRSV). But the word can also mean just "come to life" or "become alive" (NASB). The NIV correctly follows the latter sense. That sin "springs to life" in a child coming to the age of accountability does not mean that it was already present in the sense of a state of original sin derived from Adam. It means rather that the *potential* for sin is present in the heart of every free-will creature, just waiting to take on a life of its own.

. . . and I died. (Some texts and versions place this statement at the beginning of v. 10.) Here and in the first part of the verse ("I was alive"), Paul uses the pronoun ἐγώ (*egō*), "I." We should not make too much of this. The main point is the comparison of the self with the personified power of sin: Once *sin* was dead (v. 8) and "*I* was alive; but when *sin* came to life, *I* died" (see vv. 17,20).

This is not the redemptive death *to* sin of 6:2, but the event of becoming dead *in* sin (Eph 2:1,5; Col 2:13). This includes being placed under the sentence of death as a penalty for sin (Lard, 231, 233; DeWelt, 104-105); it also includes entering a state of spiritual death or separation from God, a state of helplessness before the law's demands and sin's lures. In short, it means the infliction of sin's "double trouble."

7:10 The problem that Paul is addressing here is not the fact of this death as such, but the fact that *the law* somehow seems responsible for it. He has declared that the law is not bad or sinful (7:7a). Indeed, it performs the good and necessary function of defining sin and exposing its reality in our lives (7:7b). But the law also in a real sense provokes us to sin and brings about our spiritual death (7:8-9). This leads to an ironic paradox: **I found that the very commandment that was intended to bring life actually brought death.**

"The very commandment" refers to "Do not covet" (7:7), but it stands for the law of God in general. God's law is "intended to bring life" in the sense that obedience to it was meant to be the way of maintaining a right relationship with God and continuing in the blessings of life in his presence. The law can actually accomplish this purpose only when obeyed perfectly, however. Once sin has entered and brought about spiritual death, the law is impotent to restore the sinner to a state of spiritual life. Only grace can do this.

7:11 For sin, seizing the opportunity afforded by the commandment, deceived me, and through the commandment put me to death. This verse basically condenses the ideas already presented in vv. 8-9, and thus reaffirms the conclusion of v. 10, that there is a sense in which the law brings death. (On "seizing the opportunity," see 7:8.) But Paul makes one thing very clear: the real culprit is sin, not the law. Sin is personified as a formidable and powerful enemy who attacks us and kills us. The law is only the instrument used by sin to accomplish this awful deed. Thus sin, not the law, is the true source of death.

The new element here is the idea that sin "deceived me," and that it deceived me "by the commandment." How does sin deceive through the commandment? The reference to deceit draws attention to Gen 3:1-6 (see 2 Cor 11:3; 1 Tim 2:14). There Satan used the commandment of God (Gen 2:16-17) to raise questions about God's motives in making certain things "off limits." In this way the prohibition was used not only to stimulate a curious desire to experience what was forbidden (7:8), but also to arouse in Eve a resentment toward God for denying her something seemingly so desirable and beneficial. In the same way sin continues to use the law to deceive us, clouding our eyes to its life-giving purposes and provoking us to disobey it in resentment toward the Lawgiver and in a futile quest for self-fulfillment. The result is only death.

7:12 So then, the law is holy, and the commandment is holy, righteous and good. Here Paul refers to both "the law" and "the commandment." The former refers to the entire law, or the will of God in general (not just the Mosaic law); the latter refers to each individual commandment of the law, including "Do not covet." With regard to its character, what is true of the whole law is true of all its parts, and what is true of each part is true of the whole.

This verse along with v. 13 is the definitive answer to the question in v. 7. "Is the law sin?" Absolutely not! Rather, it is *holy*, *just*, and *good*. These attributes apply to the law because they are the attributes of God, who is its author and source.

To say that God is *holy* (in the moral sense) means that his nature is totally separate from sin, the very opposite from sin (*GRe*, 251-254). Thus the same must be true of his holy law, which is derived from and based upon his own nature. It too is the very opposite of sin; it stands "as far away from sin as possible" (Morris, 283), contrary to the antinomian accusation of v. 7.

The law in all its commandments is also *just*. To say that God is just means that his actions always are in perfect conformity with his nature (*GRe*, 211-215). The law reflects God's justice in that those who follow its commandments will also be conforming their actions to the perfect norm of God's nature. Thus because of its just nature it produces not sin but righteousness.

The law and its commandments are also *good*. God's goodness is his benevolence, kindness and good will toward his creatures; he desires only what is best for us (*GRe*, 322-323; *GRu*, 289-291). To say that his law is good means that it is intended in every way for man's benefit, not his ruin. When we "uphold the law" (3:31) and allow it to fulfill its proper functions, it will only bless us.

7:13 But does this not contradict one of Paul's main points in this section, namely, that the commandment has produced death in us? The death of which he speaks is certainly not a beneficial death. Thus how can that which produced it be called "good" in any sense?

But is it really the case that the commandment is the source of my spiritual death? **Did that which is good, then, become death to me? By no means!** Paul has already stated in vv. 8,11 that the real culprit, the true source of death, is sin, not the law. Sin deceitfully and perversely *uses* the law as a means of provoking disobedience, which leads to death; but this is not the law's own true purpose. The blame lies with sin, not with the law.

To make this point perfectly clear, Paul now reiterates this idea, as stated earlier in vv. 8,11: **But in order that sin might be recognized as sin, it produced death in me through what was good . . . .** The "good" thing is the law of God; the "death" produced in me or to me is the inner spiritual death of a depraved spirit as well as the penalty of eternal death in hell. The instrument "through" which it is produced is the good commandment. But sin itself is the true and ultimate source of this death.

Why does God allow his law to be used in this perverted way? Is any divine purpose accomplished thereby? This verse actually contains two purpose clauses. The first is stated here: "in order that sin might be recognized as sin." I.e., by its perverse use of the law its true character *as sin* is completely exposed; it is shown to be the evil that it truly is.

This is allowed to happen **so that through the commandment sin might become utterly sinful.** This is the other purpose clause. Again this takes place "through the commandment." I.e., by using the commandment to provoke sin and produce death, sin not only simply exposes itself as sin, but magnifies beyond measure the depths of its perversity and ungodliness.

Thus Paul ends his defense of the law. Even though sin uses the law for its own murderous ends, the law itself remains pure and holy and good. A person could take a hypodermic needle and inject poison into someone's body, but this does not make the needle bad.

II. 7:14–8:13 – GRACE GIVES VICTORY OVER SIN

In this section the subject is still the connection between grace and sin, but with a different focus. Rather than taking a defensive stance against possible objections to grace, Paul goes on the offensive and shows that, rather than encouraging sin, grace provides the means of victory over it. He acknowledges that sin is still present in the life of the Christian and is the source of serious tension and struggle (7:14-25), but he affirms that God's grace gives us victory over sin through the power of the indwelling Holy Spirit (8:1-13).

A. The Christian Continues to Struggle against Sin (7:14-25)

Many see no break between vv. 13 and 14, and include all of 7:7-25 under a single heading. I see a significant break occurring at this point, however, with a new section beginning at v. 14. The change is subtle but real. In vv. 7-13 the main subject is God's law, and personal spiritual history is secondary. In vv. 14-25 this is reversed. The law is still in the picture, but the main point is our struggle to obey it and to conquer sin.

Paul continues to use the first person singular. As in vv. 7-13, he is recounting his own spiritual experience as representative or typical of us all. However, a new element appears in vv. 14-25: the use of the present tense. This raises the much-debated question as to what period of his life and others' lives is in view. Is the present tense to be taken at face value, indicating that Paul is describing his present Christian experience? Or is it just a dramatic way of portraying some past stage of his life? The question is usually couched this way: do these verses apply to an unregenerate sinner, or do they apply to the regenerate Christian? This is one of the major issues in the interpretation of Romans, and there are three main approaches to it. One, some say Paul is describing his and others' past history as an unregenerate person. Two, others say Paul is describing an episode from early in his life as a saved person (❂ I:442-443). Three, many say that Paul is talking about his *present* experience as a regenerated, mature believer, and by extension the experience of all believers. I believe this third view is the correct one, and will now summarize the reasons for it.

First, the major theme of the main section in which this passage occurs (chs 6-8) has to do with the Christian life.

Second, the use of the present tense should be taken at face value. The sudden shift from past to present between vv. 13 and 14 indicates a change in perspective. If Paul were continuing to talk about some past stage of his life, he would only be confusing the issue by using present tense.

Third, the things Paul says about the law of God and about his own inner life are completely incompatible with the heart and life of an unregenerate man as described elsewhere in the Bible. He upholds the goodness of the law and affirms his joyful desire to obey it. He declares his hatred of sin and his desire not to do it. All of this is contrary to the mind of the unregenerate (1:18–3:20; 8:5-8). At the same time Paul sorrowfully confesses his weaknesses and failures in his attempts to obey, and describes himself in the most humble and self-effacing terms. This corresponds to his other humble descriptions of himself as a Christian (1 Cor 15:9; Eph 3:8; 1 Tim 1:15), and contrasts with his pre-Christian attitude of self-righteousness (Phil 3:6; Gal 1:13-14).

Fourth, the intense spiritual struggle pictured here exists only within the heart and life of a regenerate person who has the Holy Spirit (see Rom 8:13; 1 Cor 9:27; Gal 5:16-18). As noted, Paul describes his pre-Christian life as self-complacent and self-assured.

Fifth, the longing for deliverance expressed in v. 24 suggests the tender heart of the Christian.

Sixth, the assurance of triumph in v. 25a is something that only the Christian has (see 8:23).

Seventh, the order of the sentences in v. 25 is incompatible with the experience of the unregenerate. I.e., even after resting his soul upon the salvation provided by Christ, Paul once more describes his inner state as one of conflict with sin.

Eighth, as Smith observes, the experience of spiritual struggle described by Paul is consistent with the experience of countless sincere Christians, if not all of them (I:103).

But what about all the seriously negative self-descriptions: "sold as a slave to sin" (7:14), "nothing good lives in me" (7:18), "evil is right there with me" (7:21), "prisoner of the law of sin" (7:23), "wretched man" (7:24)? Surely these confessions are no worse than Paul's declaration that "I am" (εἰμὶ ἐγώ, *eimi egō*, present tense) "the worst" of sinners (1 Tim 1:15). Only a Christian would be aware of such conflict and admit it with such sorrow. We should remember that it is necessary for regenerate Christians to be exhorted and warned about sin (6:1-2,12-13,19; 8:12-13).

But how can we account for such an intense conflict within the life of the believer? How can a person who experiences such hatred for sin still be a slave to it? How can a person who so strongly desires to do good and who takes such joy in the law say that "nothing good lives in me"? The answer lies in the fact that our nature is twofold, i.e., in the distinction between the flesh (outer man, body) and the spirit (inner man, soul). As we have already seen, we are redeemed in two stages. First, at conversion the sinful soul is crucified with Christ and raised up into a state of spiritual life (6:1-6). Then, at the second coming the sin-infested body will be redeemed through resurrection (8:23) or transformation (1 Cor 15:51-54). But in between these two events, while we are still living on this earth, we exist as an awkward combination of redeemed soul and as-yet-unredeemed body. This is the source of the conflict of which this passage speaks.

1. The Nature of the Struggle (7:14-20)

7:14 We know that the law is spiritual . . . . "The law is spiritual" means primarily that it originates in the mind of God and in its written form comes to us through the inspiration of the Holy Spirit (2 Tim 3:16; cf. Matt 15:4 and Mark 7:10). It probably also means that the law addresses and has a natural affinity with the human spirit (❂ I:445).

Despite my spiritual affinity with the law, a serious problem exists. Though I am in tune with the law in my spirit, my as-yet-unredeemed body is still a source of serious resistance. **. . . but I am unspiritual, sold as a slave to sin.** "Unspiritual" is an unforgivably poor attempt to translate σάρκινος (*sarkinos*). This word is from σάρξ (*sarx*), "flesh," and means "of flesh" (NASB) or "of the flesh" (NRSV). This is not the same idea as "in the flesh" (7:5, NASB; see 8:5,8), which means *controlled* by the flesh. Here it means *made* of flesh and thus refers to the physical part of the self. "I," the *ego*, am (in part) *sarkinos*. I am not only spirit; I am also body.

But this is not just a bare metaphysical statement ("I am physical"); it is also a moral statement. It includes the implication that I am still under the influence of my sin-afflicted physical part. Despite the desires of my spirit, I am still hounded by the lusts of my unredeemed body. This moral implication of *sarkinos* is confirmed by the modifier, "sold as a slave to sin." The Greek says literally, "sold under sin" (KJV), and Paul likely means to say he is sold to sin as a slave-owner and thus is under the power of sin.

But if this is a description of the Christian life, how can it be reconciled with 6:6,15-23, which says that we "used to be slaves to sin" (6:17), but have been "set free from sin and have become slaves to righteousness" (6:18)? The answer is that ch. 6 refers to the liberation of the spirit or inner man from slavery to sin, while ch. 7 affirms that the body has not yet been so redeemed (7:25). It is the body, the fleshly part, that is still "sold as a slave to sin."

This is not an excuse for sin, however. Because our spirits have been renewed and set free, we are now able to take control of our bodies even though they still incline toward sin, and are able to use them in the service of God (6:6,12-13). We can do this not just because our spirits have been renewed, but because we are empowered to do so by the indwelling Holy Spirit (8:13).

Thus this statement ("I am of flesh, sold under sin") neither excuses sin nor consigns us to hopelessness. But it does explain *why* and *how* we, even as Christians, continue to be plagued by sin and are subject to constant struggle and occasional defeat.

7:15 I do not understand what I do. Paul is talking about the fact that he still sins, even though he does not want to. "Understand" is not the best translation of γινώσκω (*ginōskō*) here, since throughout this passage Paul shows that he does in fact understand why this happens (see 7:14). A better translation is "approve," in the sense of "condone, acknowledge the validity of" (see Cranfield, I:358-359; Moo, 457). I.e., "Sin has usurped power over me; I do not accept the legitimacy of its rule over my life."

My true, inner self is very different, in fact. **For what I want to do I do not do, but what I hate I do.** The key words here are "want" and "hate." They represent the basic inner attitudes of the regenerate spirit. "Want" is θέλω (*thelō*), which basically means "to wish or desire something," but also has the stronger connotation of "to will or purpose to do something." In vv. 18-19 Paul indicates that the object of his desire and purpose is "the good," and in v. 16 goodness is identified with the law. Thus the basic desire and purpose of the regenerate heart is to obey God's good and perfect law (12:2).

"Hate" is μισέω (*miseō*), which means to dislike or abhor something; to have a loathing or an aversion toward it; to be filled with hostility and opposition toward it; to be repelled by it and want to avoid it. The object of such hatred is evil (v. 19) or disobedience to God's law. Just as the regenerate heart desires and purposes to do the good, so does it hate every form of sin and evil. Such hatred of sin is an essential aspect of repentance. Both attitudes are characteristic of the believing, regenerate Christian and are the opposite of the way an unbeliever thinks. This is a main reason for applying this passage to the regenerate rather than the unregenerate man.

The tragic irony, though, is that our actual practice is often the very opposite of these inner spiritual attitudes. What we *want* to do goes undone, and we wind up doing the very things we despise. This conflict between willing and doing is the Christian's basic inner tension.

7:16 And if I do what I do not want to do, I agree that the law is good. Some take this as an indication that Paul's main subject is still the law (e.g., Dunn, I:390). But I take it only as a parenthesis in which Paul is reaffirming the point already made in 7:7-13. When a Christian sins, that does not mean he is casting aspersions upon the law and calling it bad. On the contrary, when a Christian sins, he is doing the very opposite of what his heart wants to do. What he truly thinks of the law is shown not by his unlawful deeds, which are the product of his sin-enslaved flesh, but rather by his inward desire to obey it (7:22,25).

7:17 As it is, it is no longer I myself who do it, but it is sin living in me. This further explains why "I do, not what I want, but what I hate." In 7:7-13 Paul made an important distinction between sin (personified as an enemy) and the law. His point was that sin deceitfully uses the law to stimulate our disobedience to it. But the law itself does not cause disobedience; it is simply an instrument in the hands of sin itself. Now in this verse the key distinction is between sin and the *ego* or self (see 7:8-9). When I do the things I hate, says Paul, it is no longer I (ἐγώ, *egō*) who am doing them, but sin itself.

I take the words νυνί (*nyni*, "now") and οὐκέτι (*ouketi*, "no longer") to have a temporal meaning. The allusion is to the regeneration of the inner man described in ch. 6. Now that my spirit has been changed and reborn, I am not doing these hateful things with my whole being. My inner self repudiates them even as I do them. They stem from the sin that still dwells in me. This is not an excuse that relieves me of personal responsibility for my sin; it is only an explanation of why it occurs.

Paul speaks of sin as "living in" or "indwelling in" himself. This may seem strange for a Christian to say, but in the next few verses (esp. 18,23) he makes it clear that sin indwells not his spirit but his body. The power and residue of sin are still present there.

7:18 Verses 18-20 are a restatement of vv. 14-17, with the emphasis still upon the conflict between willing and doing in the Christian life. **I know that nothing good lives in me, that is, in my sinful nature.** This is a negative version of v. 17b and also serves as a qualifier thereof. "In my sinful nature" is literally "in my flesh" and should be so translated. Again "flesh" refers not to the whole of human nature as fallen, but only to the body (vv. 23,25). Paul is not saying that the body is inherently evil, or that it lacks inherent goodness, a false view that is common enough (e.g., Gnosticism). He is speaking rather of the body as it has been commandeered by sin, and which in its unredeemed state is still under the power of sin even for Christians. Thus the statement "nothing good lives in me" is qualified by being limited to the body.

"Nothing good lives in me" is an unduly exaggerated translation. A better rendering is "Good does not live in me" (Newman and Nida, 139). In this context "good" is identified with the law (vv. 12-13,16). Thus "good does not live in me" means that, from the standpoint of my physical nature, I am not inclined to obey God's law.

For I have the desire to do what is good, but I cannot carry it out. I.e., in my heart I want to conform myself to the law, but my body is a continuing source of resistance. Thus in his quest for holiness, the Christian is hindered by the weakness of the flesh. This would be a source of unbearable agony to us (7:24) were it not for Christ's gift to us of the indwelling Holy Spirit (8:4-13). By the power of God the Holy Spirit working in us, we are able not only to will but also to do what God's good law requires (Phil 2:13).

7:19 For what I do is not the good I want to do; no, the evil I do not want to do—this I keep on doing. This is the same lament as 7:15b. "The good" is behavior enjoined by the law, and "the evil" is behavior forbidden by the law. This is not meant in an absolute sense, as if Paul were saying that he *never* does anything good, and that he *always* commits *every* evil deed that he abhors. The comparative frequency of such paradoxical behavior is not the point. For the sensitive Christian even one such incident is too much.

7:20 Now if I do what I do not want to do, it is no longer I who do it, but it is sin living in me that does it. This is the same as 7:16a,17.

2. The Source of the Struggle (7:21-25)

In this section Paul reflects on the source of the tension between willing and doing described in 7:14-20. It lies in the conflict between the redeemed spirit and the as-yet-unredeemed body. He has already indicated as much in 7:14 ("I am of flesh") and 7:18 ("in my flesh"), but here he goes into unambiguous detail.

7:21 So I find this law at work . . . . "I find" means "When I analyze what is going on within myself, this is what I discover." What does he discover? A "law" working within him. Here "law" (νόμος, *nomos*) must mean "the controlling rule of life, the governing principle, the regulating pattern." This meaning of *nomos* appears also in 3:27 and 8:2.

What is this rule or pattern? **When I want to do good, evil is right there with me.** When I intend to keep my temper and speak only kind words, as soon as I open my mouth the angry words fly out. Though I resolve never again to commit that sin, as soon as the opportunity arises, I fall.

7:22-23a Paul now reveals the source of this constant conflict in unmistakable language: **For in my inner being I delight in God's law; but I see another law at work in the members of my body . . . .** Here the two parts of human nature are distinctly contrasted. One is the "inner being" or literally the "inner man" (see 6:6; 2 Cor 4:16; Eph 3:16). This is the soul or spirit or personal center of every human self. In v. 23 it is called "the mind." In the Christian this inner man has undergone the transformation of regeneration and has become the "new man"; the soul of the unregenerate is still the "old man" (6:6; Eph 4:24; Col 3:9-10). The other aspect of human nature is the physical or fleshly body, here simply referred to as "my members," i.e., the members of my body (see 6:13).

Another contrast in this passage is between two kinds of law. One is "God's law," which is the same as "the law of my mind" in v. 23b. It includes whatever code of divine commandments applies to any given person, whether it be written on the heart, on stone, or on paper. Over against this is "another law," which is the same as "the law of sin" in v. 23b. It is called the "law" of sin for the sake of symmetry with the "law" of God. It is a law in the sense of a power or compulsion that exercises control over us.

Spiritual conflict is present in the Christian's life because one part of our being follows the law of God, while the other part follows the law of sin. On the one hand, the regenerated inner man (mind) is fully committed to God's law, and delights in it. We "joyfully concur" in it (NASB). It is the good thing our hearts want to do. (See Ps 119:14,16,24,35,47,97.) It should go without saying that only the regenerate man willingly embraces the law of God with such enthusiasm and joy.

On the other hand, the law of sin is "in my members," i.e., in the members of my body (cf. "in my flesh," v. 18). This law or power of sin still "lives in" the body (vv. 17,20), still permeates it and exploits its appetites and weaknesses.

7:23b This other law is **waging war against the law of my mind and making me a prisoner of the law of sin at work within my members.** This description of the Christian's inner conflict is couched in military metaphors. The law of sin ensconced in my body "wages war" against the law of God which I have embraced with my inner being. My every inclination to do right comes under attack, not just from outside enemies such as ungodly cultural forces and Satan's devices, but from within my very own self.

Not only am I attacked, but sometimes I am defeated. This is the implication of "making me a prisoner," another military metaphor used of taking prisoners of war in battle. This is not a constant state of incarceration, but an occasional defeat. To be sure, the fact that the body is still a captive of sin is a more-or-less constant condition and will be so until its death and resurrection. My soul, however, has been rescued from the enemy and set free. But until the final victory is achieved, I face the danger that my soul may be temporarily recaptured with respect to individual sins.

7:24 This thought is the "last straw" for Paul. He has been describing his struggle against sin in very dark and bleak terms, but this confession that his better inclinations are sometimes overwhelmed by the sin that remains in his body evokes from him a highly emotional outburst: **What a wretched man I am! Who will rescue me from this body of death?**

Here he once more identifies the source of the struggle: "this body of death." "Body" must refer to the physical body, in view of the references to bodily members in v. 23. The Greek is best read as "this body of death." This means first of all that it is still under the curse of physical death as the result of our union with Adam in his sin (5:12-19). But in this context the body's *spiritual* death is in view also. To be a slave to sin (7:14); to be indwelt by sin (7:17-18); to be used as an instrument of warfare against one's own soul (6:13), putting it in danger of eternal death — what is this but a state of spiritual death? Thus even though our inner man has already been raised up from its own spiritual death, the body is still so much in the grip of sin's power that it can be called a "body of death" in a spiritual sense of the word.

No wonder Paul cries out, "What a wretched man I am!" Is this a cry of despair? Many prefer not to use this word, since it implies hopelessness. But surely it is a cry of distress, anguish, and frustration, all of which Paul experiences as he reels under the power of the sin that still resides in his flesh. Though in his heart he deeply desires to obey God's law, he finds himself still assaulted by an opposing power that is still a part of himself.

Paul's distress is expressed in the form of a question: "Who will rescue me from this body of death?" This is not an indication of ignorance, but a humble confession that he *needs* deliverance, that he is unable to win the battle alone, even though his inner man has already been renewed. He cries out for rescue not from bodily existence as such, but from this corrupted body from which sin still wages war against his spirit. He yearns to be free from the constraining power exerted upon him by the lusts of the body (6:12; 7:5).

7:25 In the next chapter Paul shows that deliverance from "this body of death" is possible now through the indwelling of the Holy Spirit (8:13), and is guaranteed ultimately (eschatologically) through the redemption of the body (8:23). But here he pauses, in response to his own question, in order to answer it on the deepest level: **Thanks be to God—through Jesus Christ our Lord!** Here Jesus is presented not as the mediator of this prayer of thanksgiving but as the source of the rescue sought in v. 24b. Both the indwelling Spirit and our new resurrection bodies are gifts from the resurrected and exalted Christ.

After his somewhat premature outburst of anguish and praise, Paul now introduces a summary of the struggle described in vv. 14-23: **So then, I myself in my mind am a slave to God's law, but in the sinful nature a slave to the law of sin.** "I myself" is emphatic αὐτὸς ἐγώ (*autos egō*). This does not mean "I by myself, apart from Christ." The point rather is the unity of his person or self. Even though there is a basic division within him, he is still one person, one *ego*, the man Paul. Though his inner man and outer man are now in a state of conflict, each is an authentic part of his essential self.

On the one hand, says Paul, he is a slave to the law of God with his mind. Here the mind represents the entire inner man, the spirit or soul. In his spirit the Christian has already been delivered from slavery to *sin* (6:6), and from *unwilling* slavery to the law (7:6). Nevertheless he still submits himself as a slave to God's law; but he does so freely, from his heart (6:17), because he delights in the law in his inner being (7:22). This kind of slavery is surely the mark of a Christian.

On the other hand, Paul says he is still a slave to the law of sin with his σάρξ (*sarx*), his flesh (*not* his "sinful nature," contra the NIV). His as-yet-unredeemed body is still under sin's sway and thus is at cross-purposes with his mind. Before conversion we willingly served sin, in both body and spirit; but now our spirits have switched allegiance to God and his law. Even though it is now our responsibility and desire to control our bodies and offer up their members as slaves to God (6:19), the body itself resists and clings to the law of sin. Is there a sure way to victory? This is the subject of the next section.

B. Victory over Sin Comes through the Holy Spirit (8:1-13)

For many people Romans 8 is the high point of the Bible, especially because of its emphasis on the Christian's assurance of victory over all opposing forces (● I:454). It is truly the logical climax of the gospel of grace.

The main theme of vv. 1-13 is the sanctifying work of the Spirit; thus these verses present a conclusion ("therefore") drawn from the preceding context. Then the emphasis shifts in v. 14 to the general subject of glorification, or the Christian's assurance of eternal glory. Thus I see vv. 14-39 as a separate unit (● I:455).

1. God Frees Us from Sin's Penalty and Power (8:1-4)

Paul's heart-cry in 7:24, "Who will rescue me from this body of death?" was immediately answered in brief: "Thanks be to God [because he has rescued me] through Jesus Christ our Lord" (7:25a). While the main concern of this question and its answer is freedom from the *power* of indwelling sin, we need to be reminded again of the main point already established in 3:21-5:21, that the *penalty* for our sin has been paid in full by Jesus. In the midst of our intense spiritual struggle against sin, in which we are sometimes on the losing end, we need not fear that our forgiveness is in jeopardy. Christ has already secured this for us on the cross (● I:455).

8:1 Therefore, there is now no condemnation for those who are in Christ Jesus . . . . "Therefore" shows that a conclusion is being drawn, most likely from the reference to the saving work of Christ in 7:25a. On the judicial or forensic term "condemnation," see the comments on 5:16,18. The word for "no" (οὐδέν, *ouden*) is emphatic and means "not a single one" of any kind (Lenski, 494). "In Christ Jesus" identifies those to whom this wonderful blessing applies, namely, those who have entered into the saving union with Christ described in 6:1-11.

The point of the verse is this: even though sin still lives in our bodies, causing us at times to do sinful things that we hate, we can be assured that these sins will not condemn us because Christ has already died for them and we belong to Christ. Though we may still sin, we are "justified by his blood" (5:9); there is "no penalty" for us (see Dunn, I:435), none of any kind. No disaster or tribulation suffered in this life should now be interpreted as a punishment sent by God. No damnation to eternal hell awaits us after death, and even the sting of physical death has been blunted by the promise of resurrection from the dead (1 Cor 15:53-57) (❧I:456).

8:2 because through Christ Jesus the law of the Spirit of life set me free from the law of sin and death. "Because" (γάρ, *gar*) implies that this verse gives the *reason* for the statement in v. 1: "There is no condemnation *because* we have been freed from it by the law of the Spirit of life" (❧I:457). Verse 2 itself is not limited to the sanctifying work of the Spirit. It speaks rather of freedom from "the law of sin and death" in every respect, including death as the *penalty* for sin.

Through Christ Jesus we are set free from the law of sin and death. This in itself points to the comprehensive nature of this liberation. By applying to us the full scope of the redeeming work of Jesus Christ, the Spirit of life sets us free from every aspect of sin and death, including its penalty.

It is difficult to decide exactly what the two uses of "law" (νόμος, *nomos*) mean here (❧I:457). In this verse they cannot mean "commandments"; thus I conclude that here *nomos* has the general sense of "order, rule, pattern, system," as applied on a cosmic scale. The two "laws" named here are the two competing world orders, the two rival life paradigms. The first is the life system in which the Spirit of life operates and dominates; the second is the life system controlled by sin and death. They are related to the contrasting spheres of flesh and Spirit as discussed in vv. 4b-13 (❧I:457-458).

Paul's point in this section is that, through Jesus Christ, the governing principle and the controlling power of sin and death have been driven out of our lives by and replaced by the governing principle and the controlling power of the Spirit of life. In 8:1-4 the main point is that the regulating principle that sin always brings death has been shattered by Christ's propitiatory atonement, allowing for the justification of the wicked (4:5). In 8:5-13 the point is that the dominating power of the Spirit overcomes the dominating power of the flesh (the body of sin and death — 6:6; 7:24) in the lives of Christians.

How does v. 2 relate, then, to v. 1? Why is there no condemnation for those who are in Christ Jesus? Because, through Christ and the world order that he has made possible, my life is no longer governed by the rules of sin and death. Yes, my sin deserves the penalty of death, but Christ's death has paid that penalty for me, and the Spirit has applied that redemptive act to my life. *This breaks the connection between sin and death!* It has set me free from the principle that sin always brings death, and has restored me — a sinner — to the role of a child of God and heir of eternal life (8:15-17). Thus the liberation of 8:2 is the basis for the justification of 8:1.

But it is also the basis for the sanctification of which 8:5-13 speaks. The indwelling Spirit has broken the power of the indwelling sin which seeks to drag me back down into the pits of spiritual death. When Christ gave me his Spirit, the principle and power of life took over, thus ending the illegitimate reign of those usurping tyrants, sin and death.

We should note that the verb "set free" is aorist (past) tense. The act of liberation that set us free from sin's penalty and power (the "double cure") is a past event for any Christian. Specifically, it happened in our Christian baptism, in which we received not only forgiveness of sins (justification) through Christ's blood, but also the indwelling presence of the Spirit of life (Acts 2:38). In that event the course of our lives as well as our ultimate destiny were totally recast or reprogrammed; the sin-brings-death system was replaced by the Spirit-gives-life paradigm (❂ I:459).

8:3 For what the law was powerless to do in that it was weakened by the sinful nature, God did . . . . The Greek speaks literally of "the impossible thing of the law." What is this "impossible thing"? The answer is in v. 2: the law (God's commandments as such) cannot set a sinner free from the tyranny of sin and death. The law was "intended to bring life" (7:10), and it can do so when followed completely. But once a person has sinned, the law cannot set him free from sin's penalty and power; it cannot restore him to the sphere of life.

That the law cannot give life to sinners is not due to some inherent flaw or failure in the law itself, since it was not designed for this purpose. This weakness is due rather to "the sinful nature"; literally, "it was weak through the flesh." This may refer to the flesh as incapacitated by sin (cf. the NIV), or it could refer to the inherent limitations of human beings simply as finite creatures. I.e., in the hands of mere men, the law can never deliver us from the consequences of our sins.

But what the law cannot do, God can; and he can do it without violating the integrity of his law. As we have seen (1:17), God cannot disregard his own righteousness in his dealings with men; he must always be true to himself and to the requirements of his law. But once sinners have broken the law's *commandments*, the only way God can be righteous is to satisfy his law's requirement for *punishment*. And this is exactly what Jesus came to do — in our place.

The substitutionary atonement of Jesus is the point of vv. 3-4a. Though sin still lives in our bodies, we are not condemned thereby (8:1), because we have been set free from the "sin brings death" principle (8:2). How is this possible? Because God sent his divine Son to suffer the penalty of death in our place

(8:3), thereby satisfying the law's requirement (for penalty) and maintaining his own righteousness (8:4a).

God did this **by sending his own Son in the likeness of sinful man to be a sin offering**. This simple statement contains deep Christological concepts. To say that God "sent" his Son does not in itself imply the Son's pre-existence with the Father in heaven, since the OT often speaks of God's "sending" the prophets. But as Godet suggests (298), when this is combined with the description of Jesus as God's "own Son" (see 8:32), it indicates not only the pre-existence of Christ but his divine nature as well.

On the other hand, "in the likeness of sinful man" refers to the incarnation and human nature of Jesus. "Sinful man" is literally "sinful flesh" or "the flesh of sin." Paul is alluding to his consistent teaching in this context that the human body, though not inherently sinful, has come under the power of sin and remains so to some extent even for Christians. It is "sinful flesh" because it harbors sin.

But what does it mean to say that Jesus came in the "likeness" of sinful flesh (likeness implying "similar but different")? He came in real flesh, but only in the "likeness" of *sinful* flesh. His body was fully human in the truest sense. It had everything a human body is supposed to have, but it did not have the corruption caused by sin (❊ I:460, n. 58). It was not necessary for him to assume a sinful human nature in order to be able to redeem us; he only had to have a genuine and complete human nature, which he did.

The purpose of the incarnation is then stated: "to be a sin offering." In the Greek this is a simple prepositional phrase, "concerning sin." Many give it a very general sense, i.e., Jesus came "to deal with sin" (NRSV). The reason for the NIV translation is that the Septuagint regularly uses this very phrase to translate Hebrew terms meaning "as a sin offering" (see Dunn, I:422; Moo, 480). The following context suggests it is reasonable to think this is how Paul is using it here.

And so he condemned sin in sinful man, or more accurately, "in the flesh." "Condemned" (κατακρίνω, *katakrinō*) is the verb form of the word "condemnation" in 8:1 and in 5:16,18. It refers to God's judicial sentence and pronouncement of penalty against sin.

What does the phrase "in the flesh" modify (JC, I:461)? The context favors the view that "in the flesh" modifies the verb, and that it refers to the flesh (human nature) of Jesus Christ. I.e., the very thing the law could not do because of "the flesh" of sinners (v. 3a), God himself has done in "the flesh" of Jesus. The only way we human beings can gain eternal life through the law is to obey its commandments completely, but in our weakness we have all sinned. But Jesus came to earth in our very same flesh, though untainted by sin; and in his flesh he restored us to the sphere of life by allowing sin to be condemned in himself instead of us.

The nuance of the last sentence is significant. It does not say that God condemned Jesus Christ himself, as if he were a sinner. Nor does it say that God condemned us in Jesus Christ. Rather, it says simply that God "condemned sin in the flesh," i.e., he condemned *our* sin in the flesh of *Jesus*. This is how God has set us free from the law of sin and death (8:2) in reference to its penalty, namely, through the substitutionary (vicarious) atonement of Jesus.

8:4 This substitutionary atonement was necessary **in order that the righteous requirements of the law might be fully met in us . . . .** The word ἵνα (*hina*), "in order that," shows that this is the intended result or purpose of God's condemning sin in the flesh. The main question is whether this intended result is our *justification* (8:1) or our *sanctification* (holy living).

The key to this question is the meaning of δικαίωμα (*dikaiōma*), translated "righteous requirements" by the NIV. It means "an ordinance, a decree, a requirement that expresses or upholds righteousness" (❷ I:462). The *dikaiōma* of the law is not its various commandments, but its decree that sin must be punished. This is how it is used in 1:32 ("righteous decree"). And as we have already seen (1:17), the very essence of the "righteousness of God" which is the content of the gospel is that Jesus came to satisfy the law's requirement for penalty in our place. Here the words "in us" do not mean "by us personally," but as accomplished by Jesus Christ and *imputed* to us, as the basis for our justification (❷ I:463).

At the end of v. 4 Paul makes a transition to the main subject of this section on victory (8:1-13), namely, the sanctifying power of the Holy Spirit. "The law of the Spirit of life" not only sets us free from sin's *penalty of death*; it also delivers us from the *condition* of death as it exists in our souls and bodies (❷ I:463). God intervenes in our battle against sin and rescues us from "this body of death" (7:24) through the power of the Holy Spirit.

The words at the end of v. 4 are not intended to present a *condition* for justification; rather, they simply *identify* those to whom the vicarious suffering of Jesus applies. It does not apply to everyone, but only to those **who do not live according to the sinful nature [*sarx*] but according to the Spirit.**

The word for "live" is "walk," a term often used in Scripture for conduct or behavior regarded from a moral point of view. There are only two kinds of people: those whose lifestyle is based on the *sarx*, and those whose lifestyle is based on the Spirit.

Most people walk according to the *sarx*. Here *sarx* refers not to some nebulous "sinful nature" (contra the NIV), but to the flesh or material body which in its fallen state is indwelt by and enslaved to sin, and thus is the source of sinful lusts and inclinations. Those who are "in Christ Jesus," however, walk according to the Spirit. Though some take *pneuma* here to mean the human spirit, it much more likely means the Holy Spirit (as in 8:2). What it means to walk according to the flesh or Spirit is explained in the introduction to the following section.

2. Sin and Death Are Defeated in Us through the Holy Spirit (8:5-13)

Fighting against sin is an intense struggle (7:7-25), but Jesus has provided us with the means for victory through his gift of the indwelling Spirit. Our deliverance comes through Jesus Christ (7:24-25a) because through his redeeming work the energizing power of the Spirit of life enables us to overcome the insidious power of sin and death that remains in our bodies (8:2). This is what Paul now explains in detail.

Two translation notes are in order. First, where the NIV has "sinful nature" (also "sinful men" and "sinful mind"), the Greek word is σάρξ (*sarx*) and should be translated "flesh." Also, the Greek uses several expressions to describe the two ways of life as lived within the two world orders: walking according to flesh/Spirit, v. 4; existing according to flesh/Spirit, v. 5; existing in flesh/Spirit, vv. 8-9; and living according to flesh/(Spirit), vv. 12-13. The NIV translates vv. 4,5,12-13 the same, i.e., as "live." This may be misleading, especially in v. 5, since there seems to be a difference between being/existing in (according to) flesh or Spirit, and walking/living according to the flesh or Spirit. See v. 12.

Existing in (according to) the flesh or the Spirit refers not to certain specific acts as such, but to a person's life orientation or state of being. On the one hand, a person existing in or according to the flesh is someone whose life is determined by all the things that relate to bodily life in this world. It is someone whose whole being, both body and soul, is basically controlled by the sinful lusts and inclinations of the flesh, e.g., for food, comfort, sex, and pleasure in general. On the other hand, a person existing in or according to the Spirit is someone whose life is oriented around and determined by "the law of the Spirit of life." It is someone who is committed to Spirit-inspired Scripture as his authoritative moral and spiritual compass, and who is committed to using the Spirit's power to live the holy lifestyle prescribed therein.

Walking or living by the flesh or Spirit is different in that it refers to the way a person actually lives. It refers to the lifestyle or conduct that a person chooses to actualize (v. 12). While a person who exists according to the flesh cannot live according to the Spirit (vv. 7-8), a person who exists according to the Spirit *can* choose to continue to live according to the flesh, to his eternal peril (vv. 12-13).

8:5 Those who live according to the sinful nature have their minds set on what that nature desires; but those who live in accordance with the Spirit have their minds set on what the Spirit desires. The literal NASB translation is better: "For those who are according to the flesh set their minds on the things of the flesh, but those who are according to the Spirit, the things of the Spirit." "To set the mind on" (φρονέω, *phroneō*) means "to focus the mind or attention upon, to be preoccupied with."

Thus a major difference between those existing under the two world orders is the content of their minds. This includes one's daydreams, conscious goals, interests, desires, attitudes, and points of view. One whose life orientation is the flesh is constantly preoccupied with the things of the flesh, i.e., things having to do with one's bodily nature as it exists in this physical world. The one whose life orientation is the Holy Spirit, on the other hand, is preoccupied with the things of the Spirit. His desires, goals, and points of view are determined by the truth revealed in Scripture by the Spirit of God.

8:6 The mind of sinful man is death, but the mind controlled by the Spirit is life and peace . . . . Literally, "For the mind of the flesh is death, but the mind of the Spirit is life and peace." "Mind" means the content of the mind in terms of one's worldview, mindset, and thought patterns.

This verse names a second major characteristic of those who are of the flesh or of the Spirit. On the one hand, the mind of the flesh is *death*. This refers both to one's present state and to his eternal destiny. The person controlled by his flesh is in a state of spiritual death; he exists according to "the law [world order] of sin and death" (8:2). This is the state of spiritual depravity (not *total* depravity), which is the second half of the sinner's "double trouble." It is death in the most serious sense, i.e., separation from God (Isa 59:2). Also, to be controlled by the flesh means that one's final destiny is eternal death in the lake of fire (6:23; 7:5; Rev 20:14-15), where separation from God is eternal.

On the other hand, the mind of the Spirit is *life* and *peace*. This also refers first to one's present state. At conversion we were raised from spiritual death to spiritual life (6:4,11; 8:10; John 5:24), and we began to exist in a state of objective peace with God and internal peace of mind (5:1-2). We should note that it is a state of peace with *God*, not peace with *sin*. Thus such peace is consistent with the state of battle against sin described in 7:14-25.

Secondly "life and peace" refer to one's eternal destiny, the final blessings of eternal life and of eternal peace in heaven. To have the mind of the Spirit is to exist according to "the law [world order] of the Spirit of life," and the Spirit's final gift of life is a new body designed for glory (8:11,23).

8:7 the sinful mind is hostile to God. "Sinful mind" is literally "the mind of the flesh," exactly as in v. 6. This statement is preceded in the Greek by διότι (*dioti*), "because" (untranslated by the NIV). This connects with the first part of v. 6. I.e., the mind of the flesh is death, *because* it is hostile toward God. "Hostile" is a noun, ἔχθρα (*echthra*), that means "hostility, hatred, enmity." It is the state that exists between enemies, in contrast with the state of peace in v. 6.

The mind devoted to the flesh is enmity against God because it is committed to everything that God is against. The "carnal mind" (KJV) may not consciously sense itself as being an enemy of God, and may deny that it is so. But the fact remains that "friendship with the world is hatred [*echthra*] toward God" (Jas 4:4). As the maxim says, "The friend of my enemy is my enemy."

The nature of this enmity is explained in the rest of the verse: **It does not submit to God's law, nor can it do so.** This is connected to v. 7a by *gar*, "for, because" (untranslated in the NIV). This shows a causal relation between 7a and 7b. The mind focused on the flesh is an enemy of God *because* it does not and cannot submit to God's law.

"Law" in this context is the general law of God in any and all of its applicable forms. That peace with God and enmity against God are measured by one's attitude toward his law is significant. It shows that God and his law cannot be separated. To reject God's law is to reject God himself.

The choice between the mind of the flesh and the mind of the Spirit is the choice between the attitude of lawlessness, which is the essence of sin (1 John 3:4), and the attitude of submission to God's law (see 7:22). "Submit" is ὑποτάσσω (*hypotassō*), which in the passive voice means to surrender oneself to the authority of someone or something. To submit to the law of God means to acknowledge its authority and to make a conscious effort to obey it. This is precisely what the mind of the flesh does not do. More significantly, it *cannot* do so. This theme of inability is continued in the next verse.

8:8 Those controlled by the sinful nature cannot please God. Literally, "And those who are in the flesh cannot please God." On the phrase "in the flesh," see 7:5. The translation "controlled by" gives the proper sense of it.

This verse is simply reinforcing the point of v. 7b. "Cannot please God" is directly related to "cannot submit to God's law." This shows that what pleases God is inner submission to and external obedience to his law.

Paul says that the one whose mind is set on the flesh cannot submit to God's law (v. 7) and cannot please God. What is the nature of this inability? Calvinists see in this text the concept of *total* inability, which is the idea that sinners are so totally depraved that they cannot respond to the gospel without God's selective, irresistible grace. However, Paul's point here has nothing to do with whether a person controlled by his flesh can respond to the *gospel*. Rather, his inability is related to the *law*. Such a person is unable to obey any command of the law as God wants it done and as the law requires. He may obey it outwardly; but as long as he exists according to the flesh, he cannot submit to God's law in his heart (Gal 5:6; Heb 11:6). One simply cannot do both at the same time: he cannot set his mind on the flesh *and* submit to God's law simultaneously (Morris, 306). Thus as long as he is in the flesh, he cannot please God with respect to his law.

The key words are "as long as." A person cannot be pleasing to God in obedience to his law *as long as* his mind remains set on the flesh. But there is no indication whatsoever in this text that a sinner is unable to respond to the gospel, or unable through the power of the gospel to redirect the set of his mind from flesh to Spirit. The context shows that "cannot please God" refers only to an inability to be subject to the law, and does not imply an inability to respond to the gospel. The failure to make this distinction is the main error of Calvinists' interpretation of these verses. In other passages it is clear that sinners are able and expected to respond to the gospel in faith and repentance (John 3:16; Rom 1:17; Rev 22:17; see Matt 23:37).

8:9 Paul now begins to apply these truths thus: despite the law of sin and death that continues to work in and through your as-yet-unredeemed bodies, and despite the reality of your continuing struggle against its enslaving power, you need not despair, for God has given you a gift of grace second only to the gift of justification through Christ's blood. This second gift of grace is the indwelling Holy Spirit himself. His very presence within you gives you all the resources you need for victory over your flesh now, and for ultimate victory over death in every sense.

You, however, are controlled not by the sinful nature but by the Spirit, if the Spirit of God lives in you. Literally, "you are not in the flesh but in the Spirit." The "you" is emphatic and draws the Christian reader personally into the sphere of the truth enunciated in the text. Paul flatly states that you (Christians) are not "in the flesh," or "controlled by the flesh." Your life is not oriented to this world; your mind is not set upon the things of this earth. Rather, you are "in the Spirit." Some take this to mean the human spirit. I.e., you are not governed by the desires of your bodies but by the higher inclinations of your spirits. As in the preceding verses, however, it is best to take this as referring to the Holy Spirit. That is, your life now falls within the sphere of the Spirit's influence and power.

This is true, of course, only *if* the Spirit of God indeed dwells in you. The word "if" is εἴπερ (*eiper*). "If" or "if indeed" is probably the intended meaning as in 8:17 (see 1 Cor 15:15). It simply states the condition for being in the Spirit. The point is not to create uncertainty as to one's status, but rather to eliminate other conditions, especially those having to do with human achievement. The fact that we are "in the Spirit" depends not upon what we have accomplished in ourselves, but upon what God has accomplished in us through his Spirit.

The word for "lives" is οἰκέω (*oikeō*), and is related to the word for "house, dwelling place." The word implies not a temporary, transient visit, but a permanent settling down. When the Holy Spirit is given to us in baptism (Acts 2:38), he takes up permanent residence and makes himself at home within us. He comes to dwell in our very bodies (1 Cor 6:19), which continue also to be indwelt by sin (7:17,23). Thus he is in position to do battle for us in the very place where we need him most.

And if anyone does not have the Spirit of Christ, he does not belong to Christ. This makes the same point in a negative way. Those who do *not* have the Spirit are outside the sphere of the redeemed. That the Spirit is called both the Spirit of *God* and the Spirit of *Christ* suggests that Christ as God the Son is on the same level as God the Father; it implies his deity.

How can we know whether or not the Holy Spirit is dwelling in us? First we must ask whether we have done that which God has specified as the condition for receiving the Spirit: Acts 2:38; 5:32; 19:1-7. Then we must look for the signs of his continuing presence. These signs do not necessarily include the possession of miraculous powers, since these can be present even where Christ and his Spirit are absent (see Matt 7:21-23). The best sign is the presence of the fruit of the Spirit in our character and conduct (Gal 5:22-26), though even this is not an infallible indicator. What we can say is this, that where such fruit is absent, the Spirit is also absent.

This verse clearly ties our relationship to the Spirit with our relationship to Christ. When the Spirit lives in us and we thus "live in the Spirit," we belong to Christ. (This is the implication from the negative statement that one who does *not* have the Spirit does *not* belong to Christ.) This same connection is made in 1 Cor 6:19-20.

8:10 But if Christ is in you . . . . Here Paul returns to second person, indicating his confidence that this condition is indeed the condition that applies to his Roman readers. Verse 9 says the Holy Spirit dwells in us; now Paul describes our saved state by saying that *Christ* dwells in us. This does not equate Christ with the Spirit, but shows the intimate interrelation between them. It also indicates how difficult it is to give an exact or literal description of the Christian's own intimate relation with both Christ and the Spirit. The Spirit is in us; we are in the Spirit. Christ is in us; we are in Christ. Some say the Holy Spirit dwells in us personally and directly, while Christ dwells in us only indirectly *through* the Spirit (Lard, 258). This is not necessarily the case, however. Both may certainly dwell in us, each for his own purpose.

If Christ is in you, here is where you now stand. First, **your body is dead because of sin . . . .** The body here no doubt is the physical body, as in v. 11. In what sense does Paul say that "the body is dead" (present tense)? The primary and most obvious reference is to physical death (see v. 11), the idea being that the body is subject to death and doomed to die. "Because of sin" must then refer to the sin of Adam (5:12-17), since even sinless infants and young children sometimes die.

But it is also true that the Christian's body is even now still permeated with the spiritual effects of his own sin and thus with a kind of *spiritual* death (see 7:24). I.e., the physical body is spiritually dead because of the sin that indwells it (7:17-18,23). Because the Christian's body has not yet been delivered from the power of this spiritual death, it is thus the source of constant struggle.

That we still have "this body of death" is the bad news, but there is also some very good news: **yet your spirit is alive because of righteousness.** Some say that "spirit" (*pneuma*) here refers to the Holy Spirit; others say it is the redeemed human spirit. I believe a better case can be made for the latter, the strongest argument being the apparent parallel between "body" and "spirit." The NIV translation is appropriate: "your spirit is alive." Either way the phrasing is a bit awkward (❂ I:472).

The spirit is alive "because of righteousness." Many take this to mean the imputed righteousness that is the basis for justification. This would mean that in some sense our regeneration is grounded in our justification through the blood of Christ. This is not at all unlikely since "the law of the Spirit of life" is able to operate only "through Jesus Christ" (8:2) (❂ I:472).

8:11 The Christian is a combination of "a dying body and a living spirit," as Stott says (226). But this is not the whole story. Just as our spirits have already been raised from the dead, so also will our bodies one day be rescued from the grip of sin and death and restored to a state of pure life. **And if the Spirit of him who raised Jesus from the dead is living in you....** Paul has already established that the Spirit of God dwells in all who exist according to the Spirit (v. 9). The word "if" (εἰ, *ei*) does not suggest uncertainty but is simply establishing the basis for our hope regarding the resurrection of our bodies. Some would translate it "since."

We may note that this clause reflects the Trinitarian nature of God. "Him who raised Jesus" is God the Father; "the Spirit" of the Father is God the Holy Spirit; Jesus is God the Son.

... he who raised Christ from the dead will also give life to your mortal bodies .... If God raised Jesus from the dead, he can also raise up our bodies as well (see 1 Cor 6:14; 2 Cor 4:14). The resurrection of Jesus is thus a basis for our assurance that we too will be raised up in the day when Christ returns. "Mortal bodies" refers to the physical body; it is mortal in the sense that it is subject to death and pervaded by death both physically and spiritually (6:12; 8:10). But no matter how strong a grip death has on our bodies, its power will be completely broken **through his Spirit, who lives in you.** The present indwelling of the Spirit is a further assurance of our future resurrection. See 2 Cor 1:22; Eph 1:13-14.

8:12 In vv. 5-11 Paul has told us "what's so" about the flesh and the Spirit. Now he tells us the "so what." The facts that we have been regenerated and that we have received the gift of the indwelling Holy Spirit do not in themselves guarantee holy living. They make holy living possible, but they do not make it automatic and inevitable. As free-will beings we must actualize the possibility created by grace.

Therefore, brothers, we have an obligation .... This is directed specifically and personally to Christians (brothers). It is not a formal exhortation, but it has the force of one. Literally it says "we are debtors" (see 1:14). We *owe* it to God to live a holy life. It is an absolute obligation based on the fact that he is our Creator, and it is a debt of gratitude based on the fact that he is our Redeemer.

... but it is not to the sinful nature, to live according to it. Literally, we are debtors "not to the flesh, to live according to the flesh." We owe nothing to the flesh, to our as-yet-unredeemed bodies. We do *not* "owe it to ourselves" to experience as much physical and earthly pleasure as possible (Phil 3:19).

Actually Paul does not finish his sentence. He tells us we are *not* debtors to the flesh, but he stops before stating the obvious, namely, that we *are* debtors to the Spirit, to live according to the Spirit. Without hesitation we can assume that this is his point, in view of the contrast between flesh and Spirit pervading this context. I.e., we owe it to God to take full advantage of the power and the potential existing within us through the Spirit — the power to overcome the sinful cravings of the flesh and the potential to obey God's commandments to the fullest (❡ I:474).

8:13 The reason Paul breaks off his sentence is so that he can pursue the theme of living according to the flesh. He issues a solemn warning, stressing the danger of continuing to live the lifestyle of the flesh now that we are in the Spirit. **For if you live according to the sinful nature** [literally, "flesh"], **you will die . . . .** "Die" cannot mean die physically, for that will happen regardless. Thus it means die spiritually by reverting to an unsaved condition; or die eternally in hell. Actually these cannot be separated; those who are spiritually dead will die the eternal death. This is the "law of sin and death" (8:2).

This verse is a strong affirmation of the real possibility that a Christian can fall from grace and lose his salvation. Those who cling to the dogma of "once saved, always saved" deny this, of course, sometimes claiming that Paul's warning does not apply to genuine believers (see Moo, 494-495; MacArthur, I:422). But such a position is incredible in view of the fact that Paul here directs this warning specifically to his "brothers" (v. 12). He is not speaking of an anonymous "anyone" (v. 9) who is not a true Christian, but is speaking directly to these brothers in second person plural: "If *you* live according to the flesh, *you* will die." If living according to the flesh is impossible for Christians, then this "warning" is *meaningless* to the very ones to whom it is addressed, and it can be totally ignored (❡ I:474).

The warning is serious and relevant: if believers continue to live according to the flesh, they will die. But the warning is balanced by a glorious promise: **. . . but if by the Spirit you put to death the misdeeds of the body, you will live . . . .** This is the Christian's other possibility. He can continue to live the fleshly lifestyle, yes (and die!); or he can put to death the sins of the body (and live!). "Misdeeds" in this context means "evil deeds." The misdeeds "of the body" are the sinful deeds that result from the law of sin that resides in the flesh, i.e., the as-yet-unredeemed body (6:6; 7:18,23-25).

These and any other sins are to be "put to death," mortified (KJV), killed. This is the opposite of *living* according to the flesh. We can either let these sins continue to live in us and kill us, or we can kill them (see Col 3:5). The latter must be our choice. The sins of the body must be attacked at their very root, where they are imbedded in our flesh on the level of our inclinations and desires. Like Paul, we must beat or buffet our bodies and make them our slaves (1 Cor 9:27), gaining control of our passions. We must train ourselves not only on the level of acting but also on the level of willing or desiring (Phil 2:13).

The point of this is not to punish the body as such, as an end in itself, but to do what is necessary to squelch the *sins* of the body. This requires spiritual discipline, not necessarily asceticism.

We must note here again the Christian's personal responsibility for this discipline: "if . . . *you* put to death." Again, this is not automatic and inevitable; we must personally will it and do it.

But this is not the whole story; it is not even the main point of the story. Yes, we have been renewed in our spirits, but we still find ourselves locked in a discouraging struggle with our indwelling sin (7:14-25). So what is the key to victory in this struggle? Whence comes our rescue from this body of death (7:24)? The key to victory lies in these three words: "*by the Spirit*"! The Spirit's power alone ensures victory in our battle against sin; this is why he lives within us. He gives us the power to put sin to death.

The promise to those who succeed, by the Spirit, is eternal life: "You will live." This can be nothing less than the glory of heaven. This promise is a fitting conclusion to the section on our struggle with and victory over sin (7:14-8:13); and it is also a fitting transition to the next section, which emphasizes our assurance of ultimate victory in the end (8:14-39) (❖ I:477).

III. 8:14-39 — THE ASSURANCE OF FINAL AND TOTAL VICTORY OVER THE FALLEN WORLD

In sections I and II of Part Three, it has become clear that sanctification cannot be completed until our *bodies* have been brought within the scope of Christ's redemptive work (❖ I:477-478). This leads to the subject of glorification, which is the final step of sanctification and the climax of the entire salvation process. When Jesus returns in the last day, the state of glory begins. It will include first of all and primarily the resurrection of believers' bodies into a glorified state (8:23), but will also include the renovation of the universe to be an appropriate home adapted to the eternal needs of glorified human beings (8:20-21; Rev 21:1-7). This is the unifying theme of this present section, in which a key concept is our promised *inheritance* (❖ I:478).

A. The Holy Spirit Marks Us as Sons and Heirs (8:14-17)

The inheritance of glory will be ours because we are sons or children of God. If we have the Spirit of God, we are his children; and if we are his children, we are his heirs. That is the point of this paragraph in a nutshell.

The Spirit plays a key role in this picture, but it is important to define this role carefully. In general, the Spirit provides God's people with two kinds of benefits: those relating to *knowledge* (e.g., the inspiration of Scripture), and those relating to *power* (e.g., sanctification). Most interpreters approach vv. 14-17 in terms of knowledge. They think this passage teaches that the Holy Spirit affects us cognitively, directly implanting knowledge in our minds concerning our status as children of God. I believe Paul's main point is quite different, namely, that the Spirit gives us the power to live the kind of life indicative of a child of God, and the power to confidently claim our filial relationship with the Father.

Thus the point is not that the Spirit *makes* us children of God as such, nor that he makes us *aware* that we are children of God through some mysterious inner revelation. The idea rather is that the Spirit *marks* us as God's children indirectly through what he enables us to do. By objectively observing his mark upon our lives, we ourselves as well as others can have assurance that we belong to God's family and are heirs of his glory.

8:14 because those who are led by the Spirit of God are sons of God. This section expands on the promise at the end of v. 13, "You will live" in eternal glory. You will live, that is, *if* by the Spirit you put to death the sins of the body. But how does putting sin to death lead to eternal glory? Because those who do this "are sons of God," which makes them heirs of eternal life.

The key is to see that putting sins to death by the Spirit in v. 13 is the same general idea as being led by the Spirit in v. 14 (Cranfield, I:395, 401). Those who ignore this connection tend to give "led by the Spirit" a cognitive meaning; i.e., the Spirit leads us by enlightening our minds or "guiding" us in some subjective and mystical way.

But this is not the point. The Spirit leads us not by subjective enlightenment of our minds, but by inward empowerment of our wills. He leads not by overriding our wills and driving or dragging us along. Rather, his leading is an inward prodding of the conscience, an influence upon the heart, an empowerment of the will to do what we already know is right based on the teaching of Scripture. Our problem after all is not ignorance as such but moral weakness.

Being led by the Spirit is another term for walking or living according to the Spirit (8:4,12-13) and includes producing the fruit of the Spirit (Gal 5:18,22-25). It refers to one's lifestyle.

The main point of the verse is this: those led by the Spirit are "sons of God," and *that* is why they can be sure they will live in eternal glory. The Spirit-led lifestyle is a sign of sonship, and in this way the Spirit's influence upon our lives marks us as God's sons. By enabling us to live the distinctive lifestyle of the redeemed, the Spirit becomes our seal (Eph 1:13-14), our distinguishing mark, our "family crest." Being led by the Spirit is not what *makes* us children of God; we "are all sons of God through faith in Christ Jesus" (Gal 3:26). But by allowing the Spirit to lead us, we *show* ourselves to be sons of God; we demonstrate that it is so (see Morris, 313; Moo, 499). We demonstrate it not just to others but to ourselves, and thus we become strengthened in our confidence and assurance of our acceptance with God.

8:15 For you did not receive a spirit that makes you a slave again to fear, but you received the Spirit of sonship [literally, "Spirit of adoption"]. (See 1 Cor 2:12; Gal 4:6; 2 Tim 1:7.) The first question here is whether πνεῦμα, (*pneuma*, "spirit") refers to the Holy Spirit or to a disposition or attitude of the human heart. The NASB says, "a spirit of slavery" and "a spirit of adoption," meaning the attitudes of a slave and of a son respectively. Most expositors reject this interpretation and rightly see this word as a reference to the Holy Spirit. The verb "received" is aorist (past) tense, indicating a single past event when the Spirit was received, namely, baptism (Acts 2:38). See Cranfield, I:396; Lard, 264.

The idea is this: the Holy Spirit, whom we received in our baptism, is *not* a spirit who marks us as slaves and thus engenders a slave's servile and cringing approach to God: obedience motivated by fear of punishment. Rather, the Holy Spirit is one who enables us to see ourselves as true sons of God, whose obedience is motivated by loving gratitude and a genuine desire to please him. Just as the Spirit empowers us to put sin to death and obey God's law, so also does he enable us to change our deepest desires and motives and dispositions, and to adjust them from those of a slave to those of a son. As Phil 2:13 says, God (the Holy Spirit) works in us to empower not just our doing but our very willing itself.

The word "again" refers to our pre-Christian lives, where our basic identity was indeed that of a *slave* to sin and lawlessness (6:17-20) and to the law (7:6). Though the sense of enslavement to sin is still present in us to some degree because of the influence exerted upon us by the sin that still indwells our bodies (7:14-25), we have been set free from sin's inevitability (6:17-22; 8:2), and our basic identity now is that of a *son*. The Spirit does not rescue us from one kind of slavery just to entangle us in another. True, our present relationship to God is that of slave to master (6:22; Eph 6:6). This imagery is still appropriate as a reminder of our absolute *obligation* to obey God's will. But regarding our *motivation*, we now have the freedom of sons. We no longer obey because we feel the yoke on our necks and the whip on our backs. We no longer fear death (Heb 2:14-15); we have no fear of judgment and condemnation. God's fatherly love for us, and our reciprocal love toward him, combine to cast out such fear (1 John 4:18).

The reference to *adoption* distinguishes our sonship from the unique Sonship of Jesus Christ, the only-begotten Son of God (John 3:16), but it does not suggest that ours is a mere pseudosonship. In the Greek and Roman cultures of Paul's day, those adopted into a family became sons in every sense of the word, and possessed the same rights as natural sons (see Dunn, I:460; Moo, 501), especially with regard to inheritance. In fact, one of the main reasons for adopting a son was to appoint an heir for an otherwise sonless father. Now of course, God is not Sonless, and he does not need more heirs in the normal sense of that word (since he is not going to die!), but he *wants* to add as many as possible to his family so that he can share his unlimited "estate" with them, as an earthly father bestows his goods on his children through his will (❂ I:481).

And by him — by the Spirit — **we cry, "Abba, Father."** "Cry" is κράζω (*krazō*), a term used often in the LXX for sincere and urgent prayer, and for heartfelt praise to God (e.g., Isa 6:4). Here likewise it indicates a deeply felt and emotional acknowledgement of our sonship, poured forth from the heart as a positive counterpart to the mournful outcry of 7:24.

The word *abba* is Aramaic, which was the Hebrew-like language spoken by Jews in NT times. *Abba* was the intimate term used by a child to address his male parent (❂ I:482). Use of this term in addressing God has several implications. First, it is "a family word, expressive of family familiarity and intimacy" (Dunn, I:461). When we use it, we are acknowledging that God is our Father and we are his children. Second, it indicates that our relationship to our Father is one of closeness, tenderness, and childlike confidence. It shows that even the transcendent God is not distant and alien from his children (see 1:8). Third, it expresses our family solidarity with Christ, since *our* "Abba" is *his* "Abba." He is "the firstborn among many brothers" (8:29). In a real (though not complete) sense we have a shared sonship and joint heirship with Christ (8:17) (JC, I:482).

To be able to address God as "Abba! Father!" is an indication of our assurance that we are truly his children. By doing so we bear witness to both God and man that we are sons and daughters of God. That we do so *by the Spirit* reflects the Spirit's role in empowering us to live the kind of life expected of a member of God's family and in enabling us to do so in the spirit of sons and not slaves. Again, the Spirit's role is not to add content to our knowledge, but strength to our wills by empowering us to embrace the reality and privileges of our sonship.

8:16 The Spirit himself testifies with our spirit that we are God's children. Most agree that this verse speaks of the Holy Spirit bearing witness in relation to our personal spirit (the soul or inner man). But exactly what does this mean? Does this mean the Spirit "bears witness *with*" our spirit, or "bears witness *to*" our spirit? Most agree that the former is the literal meaning of the word, but they treat it as if it means the latter.

The basic question here is this: *to whom* is the Spirit's witness addressed? Most view it as a subjective, experiential testimony of the Spirit directly to our spirit, giving us assurance that we are indeed children of God. I believe this is a false idea. Paul has already shown us in 3:21–5:21 that our assurance of salvation is based on an *objective* understanding of justification by faith. Also, Paul here says that the Spirit bears witness *along with* our spirit, not *to* our spirit. This cannot be ignored (❂ I:483).

In what way, then, does the Spirit testify *along with* our spirit, that we are children of God? And *to whom* does he testify? The natural understanding of the word is that his testimony is directed toward the same audience as our own, namely, to the Father. When we cry "Abba! Father!" we bear witness to him that we are his children. Then the Spirit adds his own testimony to ours, likewise bearing witness to the Father that we are his children.

We have assurance that someone besides ourselves is confirming our testimony to the Father. The fact that Paul is here *telling* us that the Spirit likewise testifies to the Father that we are his true sons and daughters makes our assurance even more firm. This is similar to the Spirit's intercession between us and the Father in 8:26-27. This is not necessary for the Father's sake, but knowing that it happens gives *us* a sense of calmness and assurance.

8:17 Now if we are children, then we are heirs—heirs of God and co-heirs with Christ . . . . Here we come to the main point of this paragraph, that we are God's *heirs*. The argument is very simple: if we are led by God's Spirit, then we are God's children; and if we are God's children, then we are his heirs (❂ I:484-485).

We are heirs of God and co-heirs with Christ **if indeed we share in his sufferings in order that we may also share in his glory.** As in 8:9, εἴπερ (*eiper*) means "if, if indeed." This specifies a particular condition for heirship, namely, the same one that applied to Jesus: first suffering, then glory. Jesus necessarily followed this path (Luke 24:26; Phil 2:6-11; Heb 2:10; 12:2). If we want to be co-heirs with him, we must be willing to accept this same sequence, since "participation in Christ's glory can come only through participation in his sufferings" (Moo, 506).

What kind of sufferings are indicated here? The text says simply "if we suffer with, in order that we may also be glorified with." What is the implied object of these verbs? It is no doubt Christ: "if we suffer with Christ." The concepts of suffering for righteousness' sake and suffering for Christ's sake are found in many passages. The main point, though, is not that being a Christian guarantees suffering. It is rather this, that faithful suffering with Christ guarantees that we will share in his glory (2:3-4; 2 Cor 4:17).

B. The Redeemed Cosmos Is Our Inheritance (8:18-25)

8:18 I consider that our present sufferings are not worth comparing with the glory that will be revealed in us. This paragraph focuses on our promised inheritance, especially the promise of redeemed bodies (❂ I:485-486). The point in v. 18 is the contrast between our present suffering and our future glory. The former includes everything we suffer specifically as Christians, and all the other suffering that we must endure just because we live in a fallen world. The latter includes such things as natural disasters, disease, frustration, and death (see Moo, 511; Morris, 319). The bad news is that such sufferings exist; the good news is that they are temporary.

Just as this age is marked by suffering, so (for believers) the coming age is the age of glory (see v. 17). This glory will be "revealed in us," or more accurately, "revealed *to* us." In this context the reference is mainly to our new bodies and the new universe. These exist now only in the mind and plan of God (Murray, I:301), and will be unveiled to us upon completion at the time of the second coming. Even though we are already sons and heirs, we do not yet have our full inheritance. There is still plenty to hope for (8:24-25).

The Greek describes this glory as "coming" or "about to come" (μέλλω, *mellō*, not translated in the NIV). Some take this as an indication that Paul expected this eschatological revelation to happen very soon ("about to be" revealed, NRSV). Others take it as emphasizing the certainty of this future revelation, but not necessarily its imminence. The latter view is probably correct (see v. 13), and the translation should read "the glory that will surely be revealed to us" in the age to come.

The main point is the contrast between the present suffering and the coming glory. While the former may seem serious and odious while we are in the midst of it, we should try to "step back" and view it from the perspective of eternal glory. In terms of weight, the sufferings hardly show up on the scale at all, while the coming glory presses it all the way down. See 2 Cor 4:17.

8:19 The creation waits in eager expectation for the sons of God to be revealed. The focus here seems to shift abruptly to "the creation." Though some have included more, the most common and most likely view is that this refers to the physical or natural world, or all of creation except human beings and angels.

This verse depicts the physical universe as earnestly, breathlessly expecting something. The noun translated "eager expectation" is usually identified as a compound word that means "to stretch out the head, to crane the neck forward" in an attempt to see something. Phillips translates, "Creation is on tiptoe." The word conveys a very strong sense of expectation.

What is striking here is that the impersonal creation is pictured as having a personal sense of deep longing and earnest expectation. It is also described as being filled with frustration (v. 20) and groaning (v. 22). In each case nature is being *personified*, or treated as a personal entity for rhetorical purposes.

Exactly what is the object of the creation's "earnest expectation"? Literally, it is "the revelation of the sons of God" (❂ I:487). In one sense we are already sons; but until we get our new bodies, our sonship is not complete. Not even we know all the glory that our sonship entails (1 John 3:1-2). Thus not only we, but the whole of creation is eagerly awaiting the unveiling of the "new model" of the human body.

8:20 For the creation was subjected to frustration . . . . This carries the connection between mankind and the creation back to the Fall. The reason the creation's ultimate deliverance is linked to that of mankind is because its fallenness was caused by man's sin. When God placed the human race in charge of the rest of the material creation (Gen 1:26-28), from that point on the fate of the latter was tied to that of the former. When Adam sinned, God declared, "Cursed is the ground because of you" (Gen 3:17). Instead of man's servant, the earth became his antagonist. Instead of perpetuating man's life indefinitely, it is forced to engorge man's dead body into its dusty maw (Gen 3:18-19).

Through this curse the creation was subjected to frustration. "Subjected" is ὑποτάσσω (*hypotassō*), "to place under the power or authority of." Figuratively, the creation was placed under the power of "frustration." This is the word ματαιότης (*mataiotēs*), which is used 37 times in the LXX version of Ecclesiastes ("Vanity of vanities; all is vanity," 1:2, KJV). It conveys the idea of futility, emptiness, purposelessness, and meaninglessness.

The main idea is that the physical universe was originally created to play the role of servant under the lordship of man (Gen 1:26-28). Under this benevolent dictatorship it was intended to serve man's needs and in so doing to glorify God. Man's first sin, however, included an attempt to manipulate the creation and to misuse it for vainglorious purposes. As a result of this sin and its subsequent curse, man became the creation's slave instead of its master. Thus the creation itself was wrested from its original role in the intended order of things and can no longer fulfill its intended function or purpose (❖I:488-489).

Exactly *who* subjected the creation to this state of futility? Paul says it occurred **not by its own choice, but by the will of the one who subjected it, in hope** . . . . Its state of meaninglessness is not its own fault; it did not choose to rebel against its Maker and abandon its intended role. Its present state is the result of someone else's choice. Indirectly it came from Adam and Eve's decision to sin. Thus some say "the one who subjected it" is Adam. Others rightly see this as referring to God, however. "Subjected" (*hypotassō*) is an authoritative action, a judicial decision, and thus something only God could rightfully have done (Cranfield, I:414). Man committed the sin, but God pronounced the curse and brought it about. Also, attaching the element of hope to the curse is something only God could have done (Murray, I:303) (❖I:489).

The NIV says the creation was subjected "by the will of the one who subjected it." The Greek says it was subjected "because of" or "for the sake of" the one who subjected it. In what sense was God's action of subjecting the creation to meaninglessness and frustration *for his own sake*? It was necessary in order to uphold the integrity of his holiness in the face of sin; he did it to glorify his holy character (see Lard, 272).

8:21 What is the content of this hope that causes the creation to eagerly await the revelation of God's sons? It is the hope **that the creation itself will be liberated from its bondage to decay and brought into the glorious freedom of the children of God.**

The universe is not only "subjected to frustration"; it is also in a state of "bondage to decay." "Decay" (φθορά, *phthora*) here refers to breakdown and decay in the physical world (2 Pet 2:12). Some decay is natural and was no doubt a part of the good creation from the beginning. For example, the growth and seasonal cycles of plants and trees, and their production of edible fruit, vegetables, seeds, and leaves, will necessarily leave a residue that is reabsorbed by the earth through the process of decay.

The cosmic Fall, however, resulted in a *bondage* to decay. This means that death and decay overran their intended boundaries and engulfed what was never meant to die and dissolve — especially the bodies of human beings (Gen 3:19b; 1 Cor 15:42). It also means that the entire universe is undergoing an inexorable process of cosmic decay, which is sometimes called the law of entropy (❋ I:490). This is an unnatural process, being the result of God's curse.

The bad news is that the entire cosmos has fallen with Adam; the good news is that the whole thing "will be liberated" from the consequences brought upon it by sin. The final glory that will be revealed to God's children will include not just new and glorified bodies, but also a completely renewed universe to serve as our eternal home. Thus the second coming of Christ will be the time of "the renewal of all things" (Matt 19:28), or the "restoration of all things" (Acts 3:21, NASB). Out of the cleansing cosmic fire will come new heavens and a new earth, completely purged of sin's effects and fully indwelt by righteousness (2 Pet 3:10-13; see Isa 65:17; 66:22; Rev 21:1). In that day the meek will inherit the new earth, in which there will no longer be any curse (Matt 5:5; Rev 22:3).

No wonder the entire universe is eagerly waiting "for the sons of God to be revealed" (v. 19). That will be the day of its own redemption, a *cosmic redemption* through which it participates in "the glorious freedom of the children of God." The latter phrase is better translated literally, "the freedom of the glory of the children of God," where *glory* stands in stark and utter contrast with *decay*. The glorified universe will be the inheritance of every believer. It is in a sense God's gift to Christ and his new bride (Rev 21:1-2), the ultimate wedding gift of a new universe!

8:22 We know that the whole creation has been groaning as in the pains of childbirth right up to the present time. This verse adds one more description of the (personified) universe's present fallen state. The frustration resulting from being in bondage to decay is depicted as expressing itself in groaning and suffering as if in pain. Two parallel verbs describe this idea: "to groan with" and "to suffer agony with." The prefix "with" (σύν, *syn*), attached to both verbs, signifies that all parts of the creation are jointly participating in the pain of purposelessness.

Without its prefix the first verb means to sigh or groan or even complain because of undesirable circumstances from which one longs to be free (see v. 23). The second verb means especially to be in travail or to suffer the pains of childbirth. This is appropriate in view of the fact that pain in childbirth is

Romans Part Three

part of the very curse which is the source of the creation's pain (Gen 3:16). The main point in referring to "the pains of childbirth" is to emphasize the seriousness of the curse under which the creation groans. "Right up to the present time" indicates that the pain of the curse was constant from Eden up to the very moment of Paul's writing. As the context shows, it will continue without relief until the day of our resurrection.

8:23 Not only so, but we ourselves, who have the firstfruits of the Spirit, groan inwardly as we wait eagerly for our adoption as sons, the redemption of our bodies. Not only does the whole creation groan out of frustration at not being able to fulfill its intended purpose, but so do we also ourselves. "We also ourselves" (the literal Greek wording) is stated twice in this verse for emphasis. We Christians — yes, even *we Christians* — groan inwardly. That is, we also have an inward sense of pain and frustration growing out of our own inability to conform to God's will for us. Having the firstfruits of the Spirit gives us the desire and the ability to live holy lives, but we are still locked in mortal combat with the law of sin that dwells in our unredeemed bodies. To use Stott's term (242-243), as yet we are only "half-saved." Thus we groan because of our own fallenness and sin, and we groan especially out of longing for the completion of our redemption, the gift of a new body (see 2 Cor 5:2,4).

What we already have is called "the firstfruits of the Spirit." The idea of firstfruits was common in Bible times. As the choice part of the harvest, it constituted an appropriate sacrifice or offering to God (Exod 23:19; Lev 23:10-11; Deut 18:4; 26:1-4). The first converts to Christ in a particular area were called "firstfruits" (16:5; 1 Cor 16:15). Christ himself is the firstfruits in reference to the resurrection (1 Cor 15:20,23).

To say that we have the firstfruits of the Spirit means that even though we do not yet have our complete inheritance as God's children, we have already received a significant portion of it in terms of the gift of the indwelling Holy Spirit, along with all he has already accomplished for us in the way of regeneration and sanctification. This is the sense in which the Spirit is the "*earnest* of our inheritance" (Eph 1:13), i.e., the down payment, the first installment, the deposit, the pledge of the fullness of glory (see 2 Cor 1:22; 5:5). In this sense the "firstfruits" are not simply the beginning of the harvest, but are also the guarantee that much more will follow. And as this context shows, the complete inheritance includes the redemption of our bodies and a liberated, glorified universe.

On the other side of this picture, what does Paul say we do not yet have but are eagerly expecting? Our "adoption as sons." But if we already *are* sons and children of God, how can we be "waiting eagerly" for this adoption? Some say our sonship is real but not yet manifested; all we are waiting for is a public announcement of it (e.g., Bruce, 171; Cranfield, I:419). This does not do justice to the intensity of the expectation described in this paragraph, however. The idea is rather that we already have the *status* of adopted sons, but we do not yet have the full *inheritance* that goes with our adoption (Moo, 501, 521). See 8:29. Even though our spirits have already been redeemed by the regenerating power of the Spirit, we will not be fully redeemed until we are clothed with our new bodies. Until then we are only half-saved.

The phrase "redemption of our bodies" has two important implications. First, physical bodies are a natural and necessary part of human existence. We are not complete human beings without them; our spirits are naked without their bodies (2 Cor 5:1-5). Contrary to most religions, we are not redeemed *from* our bodies; our bodies themselves are redeemed. Second, what will happen to our bodies in that event called "the resurrection" will truly be an act of *redemption*. This means that (just as in the physical universe as a whole) all the effects of sin will be gone; all defects and imperfections will be corrected: the blind will see, the deaf will hear, the lame will run, the mentally handicapped will understand, and amputees will be made whole.

But the redemption of the body means much more than this. In the context of Rom 6-8, the true glory of the resurrection body is that it will be totally cleansed not just from the *effects* of sin but from *sin itself*, i.e., from its evil desires (6:12), its sinful passions (7:5), its indwelling sin (7:17-18), and the law of sin (7:23). It will no longer be a "body of sin" (6:6), a "body of death" (7:24), and "sinful flesh" (8:3). Thus the resurrection of the body is not just the issuing of a new and updated model to replace one that is old and worn out. It is a true act of *redemption*, an act of deliverance from sin itself. No wonder Paul depicts us and the entire universe as eagerly awaiting this final inheritance. It will be God's final answer to the question of 7:24.

8:24 For in this hope we were saved. "Were saved" is aorist (past) tense; it refers to the conversion event when we entered the sphere of grace. (For similar language see Eph 2:5,8; 2 Tim 1:9; Titus 3:5.) At that time we were saved, but not completely so. That is why Paul says that we were saved "in hope." The point is that at first our salvation was only partial, but even then we knew that one day it would be made complete. Thus the element of hope has been present in our minds and hearts from the beginning, and we groan and hope at the same time. We groan because part of our salvation is still lacking, but we have the confident expectation that the missing part will one day be ours. (The distinctive element in hope is not uncertainty but *futurity*.)

But hope that is seen is no hope at all. Who hopes for what he already has? Here "hope" refers to the *object* of our hope. If we already see it, or have it in our possession, it can no longer be the object of hope. That would be a contradiction of terms. We only *hope* for things that are still in the future, things we know we will have one day but do not have yet.

The main point of this explanation of the futurity of hope is to remind us that a major aspect of our salvation is still in the future. This is meant to give us encouragement in the midst of our present sufferings (v. 18) and our present struggles against sin. Yes, we have been saved, but not completely so; so do not expect perfection and paradise yet. It will come, but in the meantime do not be discouraged and do not give up.

8:25 But if we hope for what we do not yet have, we wait for it patiently. The latter part of the verse literally reads, "Through patient endurance (ὑπομονή, *hypomonē*) we are eagerly expecting." (The latter word is the same one translated "wait eagerly" in v. 23.) These two aspects of our present attitude correspond to the two elements of hope.

First, since hope involves *futurity*, it is always for something we do not yet have. Thus hope requires patient endurance. On the meaning of *hypomonē* see 5:3-4; it can also be translated "steadfastness" or "perseverance" (❖ I:495).

Also, since hope involves *certainty*, it is always a matter of eager expectation. We can endure the delay, and we can endure the interim struggles and pressures, because we are sure the day of final glory is coming! To have redeemed bodies, to live forever in God's presence in the redeemed universe — what joyous expectations!

C. God Promises to Bring His Family through Earthly Trials (8:26-30)

Overall this main section (8:14-39) assures us of ultimate victory over the fallen world, the key to such assurance being our membership in the family of God. But what about the present, with all its sufferings (8:17-18)? If we are truly God's family — his sons and daughters, why does he let us endure them? And how do we know that they will not overwhelm us and rob us of our victory over sin and the fallen world in general (❖ I:495-496)?

8:26 In the same way, the Spirit helps us in our weakness. We do not know what we ought to pray for, but the Spirit himself intercedes for us with groans that words cannot express. "In the same way" indicates a comparison with something just preceding. Most likely the comparison is between the way *hope* sustains us in the midst of present sufferings (vv. 18-25), and the way *the Spirit* sustains us by personally aiding us in our weakness. The idea is that we have more than enough resources to keep us going in the midst of earthly trials.

What is the nature of "our weakness"? The word refers to our natural finiteness, and to our spiritual weakness or sin-sickness. The latter includes weaknesses related to living in a not-yet-redeemed body and in a sin-corrupted world.

While acknowledging that such weakness exists, Paul's main point is that the Holy Spirit comes to our aid and gives us inward spiritual power at exactly those points where this weakness puts us in danger of doubt and sin. He shoulders the burdens of our suffering and fills in the breaches in our defenses against our spiritual enemies. This is his ongoing work of sanctification, and the very reason for his indwelling. See 8:13; Eph 3:16; Phil 2:13.

One weakness is that we are not even aware of all our weaknesses. Thus we do not always know exactly what to pray for in the prayer aspect of our spiritual warfare (Eph 6:18) (❥ I:496-497). We may know in general what to pray for, but in this and other things we may not know *exactly* what to pray, or how to word our prayers. In such matters there is a proper kind of petition, one that is within God's will ("what we ought"), but we simply may not know what it is or may not be able to articulate it.

Here is one of the ways the Spirit comes to our aid. In our feeble attempts at heartfelt prayer, he intercedes for us, standing between us and the Father. "Intercede" means to make an appeal to someone on another person's behalf. The same combination of words is used in v. 27, "the Spirit intercedes for the saints"; and in v. 34, "Christ Jesus . . . is also interceding for us." Thus we have two divine intercessors between us and the Father: Jesus intercedes for us in heaven at God's right hand (v. 34), and the Spirit intercedes for us from within our hearts.

This does not negate Christ's role as a unique intercessor or mediator (1 Tim 2:5-6), because he is the only one who stands between us and the Father's wrath, the only one who secures for us the decree of justification. The Spirit's intercession is in the realm of our sanctification and is specifically related to our prayer life. By his divine power he looks upon the deepest levels of our hearts and gives content to our unspoken and uncertain prayers, then he lays these prayers before the Father's throne. Knowing that this happens alleviates the frustration and despair that might otherwise arise out of our uncertainty concerning God's will and our inability to know what to pray for.

The Spirit's intercession takes the form of "groans that words cannot express." "Groans" is the noun form of the verb used in vv. 22-23. It refers to the nonverbal vocalizing of deep inward feelings, as in a sigh or groan. Some think these are our own groanings, as stirred up and enabled by the Spirit, but this does not fit the concept of intercession. Others rightly see them as the Spirit's own groanings, as he extracts the deepest unformed prayers from our hearts and presents them to the Father in a kind of intradivine communication that does not need words. This communication is described as "groans" because it conveys to the Father not only our thoughts but also the deep feelings associated with them.

Exegetes debate whether ἀλάλητος (*alalētos*; "that words cannot express") means "unutterable, inexpressible, unable to be spoken"; or simply "unspoken, unexpressed, wordless." In the final analysis this does not matter, since the reference is to the Spirit's communication and not ours. We assume that whatever is in our hearts *could* be expressed in words if we knew exactly what to pray for. What the Spirit carries to the Father may or may not be adaptable to human speech; the point is that this communication is not on that level in the first place.

8:27 And he who searches our hearts knows the mind of the Spirit, because the Spirit intercedes for the saints in accordance with God's will. This continues the thought of the Spirit's intercession for us in our prayers. Just as the Spirit reads our hearts and translates our uncertain petitions into meaningful prayer (v. 26), so does the Father know the mind of the Spirit and thus receives these prayers into his own bosom (v. 27).

"He who searches our hearts" refers to an aspect of God's omniscience or universal knowledge, namely, the fact that he knows the contents of the hearts of all human beings. The "heart" is equivalent to the soul or spirit or inner man, which includes the mind. The Bible often states that God knows what is in our hearts. The argument here is from the greater to the lesser, or from the less likely to the more likely. If God knows what is in the minds of created beings who are qualitatively different from him and relatively independent of him, then surely he knows what is in the mind of the Spirit himself, who is qualitatively equal with God and one in nature with him. What he sees in the mind of the Spirit are the nonverbal groans that convey the contents of the saints' uncertain and unspoken prayers.

If God the Father can directly search our hearts, why is it necessary for the Spirit to intercede for us? It is not a matter of necessity but of choice. In relation to our redemption the triune God has chosen to divide the various aspects of his redemptive activity among the various persons of the Trinity (see *GRe*, 159-161). Since the Spirit is specifically responsible for our sanctification, and since this weakness in our prayer life is a matter of sanctification, this intercession is part of his distinctive work; i.e., it is "in accordance with God's will" that the Holy Spirit should intercede for the saints. (On "saints," see 1:7.)

8:28 And we know that in all things God works for the good of those who love him, who have been called according to his purpose. The verb here is συνεργέω (*synergeō*), "work together"; but how to translate the verse is complicated by a significant textual variation regarding its subject. Some manuscripts include ὁ θεός (*ho theos*), "God," as the obvious subject of the verb; this accounts for the NIV and NASB translations. But many believe that *ho theos* was not in Paul's original text (❖ I:499-500). Still, I believe that the subject of the verb *synergeō* is "he," i.e., God, carried over from the phrase "to the ones who love God," which precedes the verb in the original. *Panta*, "all things," would then be the object of the verb, and the meaning would be exactly the same as the NIV. The main objection to this view is that this verb is usually intransitive; it does not take an object. Despite the objection this seems to be the best choice.

How much is included in "all things"? This must be determined by the context, which specifically deals with the ills and adversities of our present earthly life, "our present sufferings" (v. 18; see vv. 33-39). This includes trials and miseries suffered as the consequence of others' sins, but not necessarily our own (Godet, 322).

The promise is that God will bring good consequences out of all adverse circumstances, including persecution and death itself. This is important: Paul does not say that God *causes* all these circumstances, but that he causes good to *come out of* them (*GRu*, 407-409). This is a function of his special providential control of all things. Also, this promise does not guarantee that each individual adversity will have an "immediate good result" (Smith, II:10). All things *working together* will *ultimately* produce good, but not necessarily for us personally or even in our own lifetimes.

What is the "good" toward which God directs all things? It is surely not the shallow materialism of the "health and wealth" gospel, as Moo rightly points out (529-530). On the other hand, we should not limit it only to the ultimate good of "our completed salvation" (contra Stott, 247). It certainly includes this, and some adversities may produce their benefits only at this final stage. But we should include also a whole host of present or intermediate goods (Moo, 529), spiritual in nature, that contribute toward our sanctification and our ability to serve God and others more effectively (see 5:3-4; 2 Cor 1:3-6; Jas 1:2-4). See *GRu*, 143-153.

This wonderful promise is not made to all human beings, but only to "the saints" (v. 27), i.e., the adopted children of God (vv. 14-16). Here they are described as "those who love God." This is not intended to make a distinction among Christians, as if some love God and some do not. Rather, it is simply a way of distinguishing Christians from unbelievers. Christians are "those who love God," while non-Christians are those who do not.

The persons to whom this promise applies are also described as those "who have been called according to his purpose." On the concept of calling, see 1:6 (❂I:501). God calls men through the gospel itself; his call is universal (John 12:32) and resistible (Matt 23:37).

But why are Christians distinctively described as "the called ones," if others have also received the same call but have just refused to accept it? The answer is that it reminds us of who actually took the initiative in our salvation. Even though we believe the gospel and love God, God loved us first (1 John 4:19) and *called* us unto himself while we were still in our sins. We did not go looking for God and persuade him to love and accept us. He came looking for us, calling us into his family and inviting us to come to him for salvation (10:13).

Paul declares that we have been called "according to purpose." Many early church fathers took this as a reference to human purpose, i.e., to man's free choice to answer God's call. Today it is almost universally, and rightly, understood as referring to *God's* purpose, and most versions insert "his."

What does it mean to be called "according to (God's) purpose"? The purpose includes both the ultimate end or goal God has in mind in issuing his call,

Romans Part Three

and the means he has devised for achieving this end. These are explained in vv. 29-30. The goal (v. 29) is that some will "be conformed to the likeness of his Son, that he might be the firstborn among many brothers." In other words, God has purposed to gather together a family of believers who will love him as their heavenly Father and glorify him forever, and whom he can love and bless as his own children. This is not just God's eternal purpose of *redemption*, but was originally his eternal purpose of *creation* itself. But because mankind has fallen into sin, this purpose can now be accomplished only through Jesus Christ as the firstborn of this family, and only through the process of redemption as summed up in the fivefold process of foreknowledge, predestination, calling, justification, and glorification (vv. 29-30). See 2 Tim 1:9 (❷ I:502).

8:29 For those God foreknew he also predestined to be conformed to the likeness of his Son, that he might be the firstborn among many brothers. Here Paul gives more detail about God's purpose. He states exactly what this purpose is (v. 29b), and sums up the *means* by which God will accomplish it: the act of foreknowledge and the decree of predestination. The relation between this act and this decree may well be the most controversial as well as the most crucial exegetical question in the book of Romans (see *GRu*, ch. 9).

The word for "predestined" combines ὁρίζω (*horizō*), "to determine" (see 1:4), and πρό (*pro*), "before," yielding προορίζω (*proorizō*). This means "to determine beforehand, to predetermine, to foreordain." The translation "to predestine" suggests the nuance "to predetermine the destiny of." When used of persons with reference to salvation it is closely related to the concept of election (v. 33). The prefix *pro* indicates that the determination in view took place before the world was created (see Eph 1:4; Rev 17:8).

In this verse the predetermination of an individual's destiny is the point. God predetermined that those whom he foreknew would one day "be conformed to the likeness of his Son." This is often taken as referring to our spiritual re-creation in the moral image of God as perfectly embodied in Jesus Christ. As such it would include our present and continuing sanctification. But this is not the point. In this context the emphasis is on our final inheritance, the eschatological glory of the redeemed body (vv. 11,23). "The likeness of his Son" refers to the fact that our resurrection bodies will be like that of Christ. It is the same thought and language as Phil 3:21, which says (literally) that our body "will be conformed to the body of his glory." See also 1 Cor 15:49; 2 Cor 3:18.

This interpretation is confirmed by the reference to Christ as "the firstborn among many brethren." In Col 1:15 "firstborn" signifies the unique preeminence of Christ, but the point here is that he is "the firstborn from among the dead" (Col 1:18; see Rev 1:5), i.e., the first to be raised from the dead in a glorified body. (See Acts 13:34; 26:23; Rom 6:9; 1 Cor 15:20.) As such he is the first "among many brethren," i.e., among many others who will also be raised in glorified bodies to constitute God's eternal family.

This is what is predestined: our final salvation, our conformity to Christ's resurrection body, our inheritance of glory. In other words, even before the world was created, God had already predestined that some individuals would go to heaven, and that the rest would go to hell. It is important to see that such predestination applies to specific individuals and not just to an impersonal plan or group. (See *GRu*, 338-343.) Thus far we can agree with Calvinism.

But now comes the crucial question: *on what basis* did God so predestine us (❖I:503-504)? Calvinists say God's predestination of certain individuals to salvation is an *unconditional election*. Prior to creation God unconditionally determined that he would save some sinners and condemn the rest. The key word is *unconditional*. I.e., God did not base his predestination of certain individuals on his foreknowledge of whether these would meet certain conditions, such as faith and repentance. Those whom God has chosen will unconditionally receive not just salvation, but also the prerequisite faith and repentance. God predestines not only the end but also the means.

This is where Calvinism goes wrong. It is biblical to say that God predestines certain individuals to salvation's end result, heaven; but it is contrary to Scripture to say that these individuals will meet the conditions for going to heaven only because God has predestined them to do so. God predestines the end, but not the means. He predestines all believers to heaven, but he does not predestine anyone to become a believer. Salvation is conditional (see 1:16), and individuals must meet these conditions by their own free-will choice. Therefore predestination itself is conditional; God predestined to heaven those whom he foreknew would meet the required conditions. (See *GRu*, 343-345.)

Here we come to the crucial point in this verse, i.e., the relation between foreknowledge and predestination. "Those God foreknew he also predestined." We should note that v. 29 says only that God foreknew certain *persons*; it does not say specifically what he foreknew about them. In view of the Bible's teaching about salvation in general, many assume that God foreknew "that they would comply with the conditions of justification" (Lard, 282).

This answer is not at all unreasonable, but I suggest that v. 28 has already revealed the object of God's foreknowledge, i.e., God foreknew those who would love him. He foreknew that at some point in their lives they would come to love him and would continue to love him unto the end. See the parallel in 1 Cor 8:3, "But if anyone loves God, he is known by him" (NASB). This is exactly the same idea as Rom 8:29a, the former referring to knowledge and the latter to foreknowledge (❖I:504).

Calvinists reject this simple explanation, of course. At issue, they say, is the meaning of the word "foreknow" (προγινώσκω, *proginōskō*). Since *ginōskō* means "to know," and *pro* means "before," it would seem obvious that *proginōskō* means "to know beforehand" in the sense of prior cognitive or mental awareness. God certainly has such precognition. Because of his unique relation to time, his knowledge is not limited to the now; he knows the past and the future as well as he knows the present (*GC*, 255-259, 279-289). The verb "foreknow" is used here and in four other places in the NT: Acts 26:5; Rom 11:2; 1 Pet 1:20; 2 Pet 3:17. (The noun is used twice: Acts 2:23; 1 Pet 1:2.)

Everyone agrees that in Acts 26:5 and 2 Pet 3:17, where it refers to human foreknowledge, it has this simple meaning of precognition or prescience (◐ I:505-506). But Calvinists argue that in all the other passages, and here in 8:29, the words mean *distinguishing love*. "Whom he foreknew" therefore means "whom he foreloved."

The key word is "distinguishing." For Calvinists the foreknowledge of 8:29 is an act by which God (unconditionally) distinguishes or chooses some people out of the mass of future mankind to be the sole recipients of his saving grace. This says "foreknowledge" is the same as "election." On what do Calvinists base this peculiar definition of foreknowledge? Mainly they base it upon a few selected biblical uses of the verbs for "to know," in which they find the connotations of "choose" and/or "love" (◐ I:506). Since "know" in these passages allegedly means much more than simple cognition, they conclude that "*fore*know" in 8:29 and elsewhere also means much more, namely, "distinguishing love bestowed beforehand."

How may we respond to this? By a thorough study of the way the Bible uses the words for "know" and "foreknow." Such a project is outside the scope of this commentary, but we may offer a summary analysis of the NT texts where the words for "know" have persons as their objects (◐ I:507). In order of increasing specificity, the three basic connotations of "know a person" are as follows. (1) *Recognition*. In this case "to know" means to recognize someone, to know who he is, to know his identity or his true identity, to be able to identify him for who he is, to be acquainted with him, to be familiar with him, to understand him, to know his true nature. This is by far the most common connotation (at least 80 times). It is a purely cognitive act. It does not impose an identity upon someone, but perceives that identity. This includes the idea of recognizing someone as belonging to a particular group, as distinct from those who do not. This is the sense in which Jesus "knows" his sheep (John 10:14,27), even as his sheep know him (John 10:14; see 2 Tim 2:19). This is the connotation of "know" that applies to "foreknow" in 8:29.

(2) *Acknowledgment*. Here "to know" means not only to have a cognitive knowledge of someone's identity, but also to admit or acknowledge that identity. As such it is an act of will, though it presupposes an act of cognition. The most important thing is that this acknowledging does not impose a particular identity upon anyone, but simply confesses it.

(3) *Experience*. The third and most intense connotation of "to know" when a person or persons are its object is to know experientially, to experience a relationship with someone. Again, it presupposes cognition but goes beyond it.

Most significantly, such knowing is not an act that initiates a relationship but simply experiences it. This connotation is found especially in 1 John. Matt 7:23; 1 Cor 8:3; and Heb 8:11 could be either (1) or (3).

In each case the act of knowing does not create a person's identity or his distinction from other people. It rather presupposes an already-existing identity or distinction; the act of knowing perceives and in some cases acknowledges that identity or distinction. These connotations for knowing fit the term "foreknowledge" very well as it is used in 8:29 and elsewhere. Those whom God from the beginning recognized and acknowledged as his own, he predestined to be members of his glorified family in heaven. (The connotation of experiencing a relationship does not transfer well to the concept of *fore*knowledge, since foreknowledge as such precedes the existence of its object, precluding an experienced relationship.)

In any case, an analysis of *all* the uses of "know" with persons as the object undermines the notion that it means "choose," and thus does not support the Calvinist idea that foreknowledge is the same as election or choosing beforehand. Also, the other NT uses of "foreknow" and "foreknowledge" do not comfortably bear the connotations of "forelove" and "choose beforehand." Only preconceived dogma will see such meanings in 8:29. (See ❖I:509-510 for a discussion of each of these texts.)

In conclusion, the preponderance of evidence shows that "foreknowledge" is not equivalent to election or choosing, and that in 8:29 it refers to nothing more than the cognitive act by which God knew or identified the members of his family (as distinct from all others) even before the foundation of the world. He identified them by the fact that they were (would be) the ones who loved (would love) him, and who met (would meet) the required conditions for salvation. Knowing through his divine omniscience who these individuals would be, even at that point he predestined them to be part of his glorified heavenly family through resurrection from the dead after the pattern established by the firstborn brother, Jesus Christ.

8:30 And those he predestined, he also called; those he called, he also justified; those he justified, he also glorified. We must resist the temptation to bind these aspects of the redemptive process into too neat a package. Nothing of man's part is mentioned, and some of God's redemptive acts are not named (e.g., regeneration and sanctification). Two of the latter (predestination and glorification) are carried over from v. 29, and two other representative divine acts are added (❖I:511).

"Predestination" has already been explained. "Glorified" refers to the final stage of salvation, eternal life in heaven. This has been a prominent theme in this whole context, and is the point of v. 29b. "Conformed to the likeness of his son" refers to our resurrection in a glorified body.

Why "glorified" is in past tense is a matter of debate, since it has not happened yet. Some say it actually has been accomplished, in the person of Jesus as our representative (see Cranfield, I:433; Godet, 327). But most agree that the past tense refers to the fact that God has already *predestined* it; therefore it is as certain as if it had already occurred (e.g., Bruce, 178; Moo, 536).

This verse adds two steps between predestination and glorification, probably to show us that God's predestining believers to glory does not make a mockery of the intervening process. Some have wondered why, in the Calvinist view, the intervening steps are necessary. But when the biblical concept of free will is retained, we see that what comes between the beginning and the end is what makes it possible for God to predestine some to glory in the first place.

The two divine acts given as links between predestination and glorification are *calling* and *justifying*. We have already examined the meaning of these concepts; the question now is, why specifically are they inserted here? One reason is to show that intermediate steps *such as* calling and justifying are necessary. Another reason, possibly, is to indicate that human decisions are not totally absent from this process but are implicitly present as the objects of the divine foreknowledge in v. 29. As we have already seen, the connection with v. 28 shows that the most likely object of God's foreknowledge is believers' love for God. Now, in v. 30, calling and justification are mentioned. Both of these divine acts are necessarily linked to human decisions: God's call must be answered, and justification is given only to faith. These human decisions may thus implicitly be included here as other objects of the divine foreknowledge by which God predestines us to glory.

The primary reference, of course, is to calling and justification as acts of God himself. Calling (see 1:6; 8:28) is the act by which God initiates personal contact with those whom he foreknew and predestined before even the earth existed. Those whom God foreknew and predestined are those who not only hear the call but also accept it (❥I:512-514).

D. God's Gracious Love Gives Us Unshakable Assurance (8:31-39)

This paragraph is considered by many to be the most blessed and glorious in the entire Bible. In a way that is both spiritually satisfying and poetically pleasing, it sets forth the believer's unshakable assurance and its unassailable foundation in the love of God (❥I:514).

Not surprisingly, we find many commentators attempting to use this passage as a basis for the "once saved, always saved" doctrine. Since the theme here is that *nothing* can separate us from the love of God in Christ, this supposedly means that not even anything we ourselves can do will cause us to lose our salvation (see v. 39 below).

However, this view ignores the element of personal responsibility implicit in the very theme of justification *by faith*. God's love gives us justification through the blood of Christ, and keeps us justified in the same way, but not apart from our continuing active trust in his blood. In 5:1-11 the role of faith was explicit (5:1-2); here it is implicitly assumed that those whom nothing can separate from the love of God are *believers* who *want* to stay within the family of God.

Whether a believer can or cannot lose his faith is not the point in this section. The point is simply this: not even the worst earthly disaster, and not even the strongest spiritual enemy can place us into a circumstance that is so negative that it nullifies and overwhelms the reality of God's love for us as infallibly demonstrated in the propitiatory sacrifice of Christ Jesus our Lord. Not even the worst suffering can outweigh the intrinsic power of the cross to assure us that God loves us and is for us and wants us in his eternal family.

8:31 What, then, shall we say in response to this [literally, "to these things"]? What are "these things"? They include the argument of the entire epistle thus far (Cranfield, I:434-435), but I think they refer especially to the subjects of sonship, heirship, and predestination in 8:14-30. In view of the facts about these things, what conclusion can we draw?

If God is for us, who can be against us? "If" does not imply some sort of uncertainty, but is stating an unassailable argument: "If A, then B." And, based on everything we have just said, we know A is a fact; therefore B is also a fact.

"God is for us" is an excellent way to draw together everything Paul has been teaching about the plan of redemption, all the way from God's precreation purpose to our final glorification. It summarizes perfectly God's attitude toward us, his work on our behalf, and our relationship to him.

Basically this brief statement means that *God is on our side*. He is not only "with us," in the sense that he is present alongside us (Ps 23:4; see Isa 7:14, "Immanuel"); he is also "for us" in the sense that he wants "our side" to win. In our conflict with all the personal and personified enemies who desire to drive us back into unbelief, God is on our side and will protect us and defend us from these enemies (Ps 56:9). In the following verses this conflict is presented in the image of a courtroom where we are on trial. That "God is for us" means that he is our Defender, or more specifically he is the Judge who has already decided the case in our favor (8:1).

"Who can be against us" does not mean that we will never have any opposition in our Christian life. It means only that none of our adversaries stands a chance against the one who is our Champion, the one who is defending us. Certainly, we do have enemies, but they are nothing compared with God. Therefore it really does not matter who is against us, since none can prevail against God.

8:32 He who did not spare his own Son, but gave him up for us all . . . . This recounts the lengths to which God was willing to go to ensure our ultimate victory and our presence in heaven with him, and thereby it establishes the infinite depths of his love for us (John 3:16). Even though his Son, prostrate, cried out for some alternative to the mission that was about to lead him through the very agonies of hell itself (Matt 26:39), God did not spare *him*. As a result he *can* spare *us*!

God "gave him up for us all" (see 4:25) describes the substitutionary atonement of Christ, his propitiatory sacrifice on Calvary (see 3:24-26). Paul's purpose for bringing this up is to highlight the divine love embodied therein (1 John 4:9-10), so that we might be assured that God is indeed on our side.

"His own Son" means God's *unique* Son (see 8:3; John 5:18), as distinct from his adopted sons (8:14-16). "Us all" in this context refers to the believers who will constitute the completed family of God. By using first person plural Paul applies this truth especially to the readers of his epistle (❂I:516).

. . . how will he not also, along with him, graciously give us all things? The argument here is from the greater to the lesser (see 5:9-10). God has already given us the greatest possible gift when he gave up his Son for us. Why should we think he will now for some reason withhold the rest of our inheritance — our glorified body, the redeemed universe — or allow anything to prevent us from receiving it?

8:33a Who will bring any charge against those whom God has chosen? In vv. 33-34 Paul uses explicit courtroom imagery to undergird our assurance of final victory. He continues to press the contrast of v. 31b, "If God is for us, who can be against us?" Christians are pictured as defendants in a judgment scene, with the possibility that witnesses may appear who will bring charges against us and accuse us of being unworthy of salvation. "Bring a charge against" (ἐγκαλέω, *enkaleō*) is a technical legal term referring to such a scenario (see Acts 18:38; 23:29). The primary reference is probably to the final judgment, but in a figurative sense we may think of ourselves as being in this circumstance throughout our Christian life.

Who will dare to bring a charge against God's elect? Actually there are any number of accusers who are eager to rise up against us and magnify our sins and destroy our assurance. Chief among them is Satan, whose name means "adversary," and who is also called "the devil," he who will "bring charges with hostile intent" (BAGD, 181). Thus "the devil" is the slanderer, the accuser, especially "the accuser of our brothers, who accuses them before our God day and night" (Rev 12:10; see Job 1-2; Zech 3:1-2; Luke 22:31). Others eager to accuse us include unbelievers in general (1 Pet 2:12), and certainly anyone we may have harmed at any time during our lives. We may fear that the law of God itself will rise up to accuse us on Judgment Day. And by no means least, our own conscience accuses us with reference to our sinful deeds (2:15).

So what is the point of Paul's question? Not that accusations will never come, but that they will never hold up under the scrutiny of the Judge who will decide our case. None of the charges brought against us will be valid; we need not fear them. Why not? Because we are God's elect, his chosen ones, the ones whom he foreknew and has already predestined to glory (8:29).

"The elect" or "the chosen ones" is a common way of describing believers in the NT. What was said about predestination in 8:29 applies to this concept as well.

8:33b-34a It is God who justifies. Who is he that condemns? (See Isa 50:8-9.) Here the courtroom analogy is most intense. The subject of justification comes to the forefront again. See our comments regarding justification as a legal or forensic term on 3:24 (❖ I:518).

One disturbing thing about the various accusations brought against us by Satan, by unbelievers, even by our own consciences, is that they are so often true! We *have* sinned; we *have* done terrible things. But what the accusers do not take into account is that God has already justified us in relation to our sins, i.e., he has taken away their guilt; he has taken their penalty upon himself; he has broken the connection between our sin and its deserved condemnation; he as Judge has already declared, "No penalty for you!"

Thus the accusers can accuse, but they cannot *condemn*! This is our "blessed assurance."

On the forensic connotation of "condemn" (κατακρίνω, *katakrinō*), see 8:3. The fact that "justify" is used here as the opposite of "condemn" shows that it too is a forensic or legal concept. See 3:24.

8:34b Christ Jesus, who died—more than that, who was raised to life—is at the right hand of God and is also interceding for us. This lays out once more the only basis for our justification, namely, the work of Jesus. Four specific phases of his work are mentioned: his death, his resurrection, his enthronement, and his intercession for us.

The first two are past events that are fundamental to our justification and therefore to our assurance (see 3:24; 4:25). The last two are interrelated and together describe Christ's present and ongoing role in our justification, a role that began with his ascension.

That Christ is seated at the right hand of God the Father is primarily indicative of his exalted status and honor. The "right hand" of God is a symbol of his almighty power; that Christ is seated at God's right hand means he shares in this power (Ps 110; Matt 28:18).

In this context, though, the emphasis is not on the *right* hand or *power* as such, but simply on the close proximity of the crucified and risen Christ to the Father, for the purpose of intercession. This is not the same as the intercession of the Spirit in our prayer life (vv. 26-27). Christ intercedes for us in the sense that he interposes his blood between us and the Father's wrath. As our high priest he presents himself as the sacrifice that has borne this deserved wrath in our place, thus making it possible for us to come to God, to be accepted by him, and to be a part of his intimate family. See Isa 53:12; Luke 23:34; 1 Tim 2:5-6; Heb 4:14-16; 7:25; 1 John 2:1.

8:35 Who shall separate us from the love of Christ? This rhetorical question begins Paul's final celebration of assurance, a crescendo of certainty that finally erupts in a triumphant confession of the all-sufficiency of God's infinite and faithful love. The question is framed in terms of separation: who will separate us from the love of Christ? The rest of the paragraph develops this emphatic answer: NO ONE!

The "love of Christ" is not our love for him but his love for us (v. 37). This is not different from "the love of God that is in Christ Jesus our Lord" (v. 39). This love is not only the subjective love for us within the heart of Jesus, but also all the objective benefits of that love as already bestowed upon us and as promised to us in eternity. Nothing is able to separate us from any of this.

Many persons and many things will try to separate us from his love, i.e., to shake our confidence in his love and tempt us to doubt it and forsake it. Paul has already mentioned sufferings in general (vv. 17-18); here he mentions several specific forms of suffering. None of them, he says, is stronger than Christ's love for us. None of them succeeds as an argument for the proposition that Christ does not really love us after all.

Who shall separate us? **Shall trouble or hardship or persecution or famine or nakedness or danger or sword?** This is not an exhaustive list; it is only intended to be representative.

"Trouble and hardship" are the same two Greek words used in 2:9 for eschatological penalties. Here they refer to general categories of earthly suffering. "Trouble" (θλίψις, *thlipsis*) refers to pressure, or being pressed and pressured by circumstances. "Hardship" (στενοχωρία, *stenochōria*) is not much different. It refers to narrowness, or feeling confined and restricted and hemmed in by circumstances. It is probable that the former refers to the external situations that produce suffering, while the latter is the inner mental state of distress resulting from them.

"Persecution" is a more specific form of trouble and hardship. Probably it refers to persecution suffered because of one's belief (Matt 5:10-12; 1 Cor 4:12; 2 Cor 4:9; 2 Thess 1:4). "Famine" can also mean hunger experienced for any reason, especially because of persecution (1 Cor 4:11; 2 Cor 11:27). The same applies to "nakedness," which can mean destitution in general, being "reduced to rags" (1 Cor 4:11; 2 Cor 11:27). "Danger" refers to being in peril or at risk in general, either from natural or personal threats (2 Cor 11:26). "Sword" is symbolic of violence, especially violent death as in war or judicial penalty (BAGD, 496). To Christians it represents martyrdom (Acts 12:2; see Heb 11:34-37).

8:36 As it is written: "For your sake we face death all day long; we are considered as sheep to be slaughtered." This quote from Ps 44:22 is naturally called to mind from the list of sufferings detailed in v. 35, all of which could result in death. This, along with Matt 5:12 and Heb 11:34-37, shows that such suffering is nothing new in the Christian era but has always been the lot of God's people. The death in view is not so-called "natural" death, but the death of martyrdom.

The NIV translation, "face death," is too weak. The word means "being put to death, being killed." This is happening "all day long." Somewhere, every day, at all times of the day, Christians are being killed because of their belief. We are like sheep for slaughter. This is not a reference to the use of sheep as sacrifices, but to the killing of sheep for food. This is how unbelievers often view believers: we are assigned no real value in society and are fit only for slaughter.

All of these things (vv. 35-36) certainly do not happen to all Christians all the time, but they are always a potential danger. If and when they do happen, certain questions will naturally press themselves upon our consciousness: Where is God? Why is he letting this happen to me? Has he abandoned me? Is he real? Does he really love me? Paul's point is that none of these circumstances and no thoughts such as these are able to eclipse or extinguish the glorious light of God's love that shines forth from the cross.

8:37 No, in all these things we are more than conquerors through him who loved us. Here is Paul's answer to the question in v. 35. Shall any of these things separate us from Christ's love? No! The word is *alla*, the strong adversative often translated "but." Here it means "rather." I.e., rather than these things separating us from Christ's love, we overcome them all. Literally, "in all these things we are more than conquerors!" In the midst of them all and in spite of them all, we emerge victorious.

The word for "to be more than conquerors" means we not only defeat every enemy and conquer in every adverse circumstance; we *over*conquer! We do not just survive; we do not just endure. Rather, we win a glorious, overwhelming victory; we prevail completely. This megavictory happens because the Holy Spirit empowers us to overcome all spiritual foes (8:13), because God's providence brings good out of all adversities (8:28), and because the knowledge of God's grace through the cross of Christ inspires in us a passion for faithfulness that simply will not be denied.

We overconquer "through him who loved us." This is Jesus (v. 35), and the reference is to his cross. This is shown by the fact that "loved" is an aorist participle, referring to a specific act of love. If in our hearts and minds we keep a firm grip on the meaning and reality of this event, *nothing* can shake us in our faith, assurance, and hope.

8:38-39 For I am convinced that neither death nor life, neither angels nor demons, neither the present nor the future, nor any powers, neither height nor depth, nor anything else in all creation, will be able to separate us from the love of God that is in Christ Jesus our Lord. In these verses Paul completes his answer to the question in v. 35a. He declares that *nothing* will be able to separate us from Christ's love. He switches from first person plural to first person singular, indicating that this testimony is not only truth inspired by the Holy Spirit but also his own unshakable personal conviction arising from the depths of his heart. "I am convinced!" he says.

To make his answer more concrete, Paul reels off a list of ten representative things that cannot separate us from the love of Christ. Eight of these are combined into four pairs. Not every item mentioned is necessarily hostile to Christians, though most have the potential for harm. The main point of the listing is to be as comprehensive and inclusive as possible, to cover the whole range of potential sources of "trouble and hardship." This is accomplished especially by the general pairs, life/death, present/future, and height/depth.

Listed first as not having the power to separate us from Christ's love is the related pair, "neither death nor life." It is natural that death should be listed first, since it has just been in the forefront of concern (vv. 35-36). Death, the "Great Separator," scares us because it can come in so many fearsome forms. It is especially threatening in the context of martyrdom.

It may seem strange that "life" is also mentioned as something that cannot separate us from Christ's love. The point seems to be to make these potential threats as comprehensive as possible. Thus "life" includes every possible circumstance that might come upon us before we die, including the things mentioned in v. 35.

The next two items also seem to be a pair, "neither angels nor demons." The second term is not actually "demons," but "rulers" (ἀρχή, *archē*). It could refer to earthly rulers (Luke 12:11; Titus 3:1), but it is also one of Paul's favorite words for angelic beings. As such the KJV usually translates it "principalities." It does not necessarily refer to fallen angels (Col 1:16), but sometimes it does (Eph 6:12; Col 2:15). Though we cannot be sure, that seems to be the connotation here; this is why the NIV translates it "demons."

Though the term "angels" is sometimes used of fallen angels or demons (Matt 25:41; 2 Cor 12:7; 2 Pet 2:4; see 1 Cor 6:3; 11:10), most often it refers to good angels. Thus the NIV translation "angels and demons" seems proper, since pairing these terms in this listing seems intended to cover the whole range of spiritual beings, good and bad.

How good angels can be considered a possible means of separation from Christ's love is somewhat of a puzzle. Men sometimes worship angels (Col 2:18), but good angels always refuse such attempts (Rev 19:10; 22:8-9). Paul poses an hypothetical situation in which "an angel from heaven" preaches a false gospel (Gal 1:8), but if that should happen the angel would no longer be good. We conclude that good angels are included here just to provide a complete spectrum.

The more obvious danger is from demons, who are very active even today in their efforts to thwart God's purposes and to cause believers to stumble

(Matt 24:24; Eph 6:10-18; 2 Thess 2:9-10). But Paul's point is that *no* angel, good or bad, has the power to move us away from the love of Christ. Not even Satan himself, and not even Satan's "best shot," can break the grip of the cross upon our hearts.

The next pair, "neither the present nor the future," does not seem to refer to anything in particular but is included to add to the theme of comprehensiveness. Just as with "death and life," so also "present and future" are all-inclusive with respect to those things that might try to separate us from Christ's love. We are tempted to worry about the future because we do not know what it will bring. But this is irrelevant, since we know that it can bring nothing that is able to nullify the power of Christ's love for us.

The next item, "nor any powers," is not in a pair. Since the word can be used for angelic beings (Eph 1:21; 1 Pet 3:22), some think that is its meaning here. But that raises the question as to why it should be listed separately from "angels and demons." A more likely possibility is that here the term is used in its common meaning of "miracles." The NT has several references to demonic, false miracles (Matt 7:22; 2 Thess 2:9; see Matt 24:24; Rev 13:13; 16:14; 19:20). The point then seems to be that no matter how great a miracle someone might perform, if it is related to a false gospel (Gal 1:8), its power is immediately diminished and negated by the greater power of the cross.

Some see "neither height nor depth" as references to pagan concepts of spiritual beings that rule the regions above the heavens and beneath the earth (or below the horizon), but this is unlikely (see Cranfield, I:443). Probably Paul just adds all-inclusive spatial references here, to go with his all-inclusive temporal references to the present and future. "Neither the highest height nor the deepest depth" can separate us from Christ's love (Cranfield, I:443).

The final item is a catch-all category that includes any other possibility that anyone can imagine: "nor anything else in all creation." The love of God as embodied in the cross of Christ looms so infinitely large that no finite, creaturely contingency can hope to overthrow it.

We should note Paul's language very carefully. He says that none of these things in themselves will ever *be able* to separate us from the love of God. None will have the power to do so. This is God's promise to us, and it is the basis for our confidence and hope and assurance of final victory. But Paul does not guarantee us that none of these things will ever become the occasion for our *separating ourselves* from God's love. As is the case with salvation in general, and justification and predestination in particular, so also is our assurance of salvation conditional. It is conditioned upon our own continued trust in the promises of God, which is something that lies within the power of our own free choice.

Some try to avoid this conclusion by pointing out that Paul says *no created thing* can separate us from Christ's love. Since we ourselves are creatures, that must mean that not even we can do anything to separate ourselves from God's saving love (e.g., Moo, 546-547). However, the believer's abilities and decisions are not at issue here. It is assumed that we *want* to stay within the love of Christ, and that we are going to make every effort to do so. The point and the comfort of this passage is that no third party, no outside circumstance can destroy the saving relationship between us and God, or separate us from his love. That relationship is between us and God alone. Our ultimate salvation is God's loving will and purpose for us, and it will surely come to pass as long as our faith continues to cling to its one and only hope, the cross of Christ.

It is important to see that the love that is the basis for our unshakable assurance is "the love of God that is in Christ Jesus our Lord." God's love is expressed toward human beings in many different ways, especially in his gifts of creation and providence (Matt 5:43-48). But in the experience of many, these expressions of love are often overshadowed by such things as disease, poverty, and natural disasters. But the love of God embodied in the cross of Christ (John 3:16; 1 John 4:10) is different. It is not affected by contrary circumstances. It alone endures as the solid rock upon which our hope and assurance can safely rest (❖I:525).

9:1–11:36 – PART FOUR
THE FAITHFULNESS OF GOD IN HIS DEALINGS WITH THE JEWS

We now begin our consideration of one of the most difficult sections of the Bible, Romans 9–11 (❖ II:23).

A. THE PRINCIPAL THEME OF THIS SECTION

As we read through these three chapters, a number of prominent themes leap to our attention.

a) *The Nation of Israel*. From beginning to end this section is dominated by references to ethnic or physical Israel: their role in God's plan, their historical destiny, and their salvation.

b) *God's Faithfulness*. Another subject introduced near the beginning of this section is the faithfulness of God, specifically, whether God has been just and faithful to his word and his promises concerning his people Israel (9:6a).

c) *The Remnant*. Another key subject is the distinction between Israel as a whole and remnant Israel (9:6b). Membership in the former is determined by physical birth, but the latter is defined in spiritual terms as determined by God. See 9:27; 11:5.

d) *God's Sovereignty in Election*. "God's purpose in election" is another important theme (9:11), especially his sovereignty in making the choices that he does. "For who resists his will?" (9:19).

e) *The Gentiles*. Paul also raises the question of the relation between the Jews and the Gentiles, especially in ch. 11. God's elect, he says, are drawn "not only from the Jews but also from the Gentiles" (9:24).

f) *Law and Grace*. We are not surprised that the main subject in chs. 1–8, law and grace, comes to the surface again in 9:30-31 as the key to the question of why God saves some and rejects others.

g) *The Church*. A final theme, discussed in 11:17-24, is the church. The specific issue in this section is the relation between the church and Israel (❖ II:23-24).

Having named the various topics that arise in this section, we may now ask which of them is the *main point* of 9–11. What overall point is Paul trying to establish?

1. Inadequate Answers

Several inadequate possibilities have been suggested as the main theme of these chapters, including the following three.

God's Sovereignty in Election

A common idea is that Paul's main point here is the sovereignty of God in his election of individuals to salvation. Some see 9-11 as the *locus classicus* (main proof text) for the Calvinist doctrine of predestination (⬥ II:25).

This view must be rejected, however; neither election (predestination) as such nor God's sovereignty in election is the main point of 9-11. This conclusion has nothing to do with one's particular view of predestination since scholars on both sides of this issue generally agree on this. While the subject of God's sovereignty in election is present in these chapters, it is not the main point (⬥ II:25).

Justification by Faith

Another view is that in 9-11 Paul is just continuing the theme of 1-8, that justification before God is by faith in the work of Jesus Christ, with a special emphasis on how this relates to Israel (⬥ II:26).

Certainly the themes of law and grace are prominent in this section, especially in 9:30-10:21. Nevertheless we must conclude that justification by faith is not the main point of 9-11. To be sure, the way the law-grace theme is presented in 1-8 indirectly leads to the question being dealt with here, as we shall presently see. But the main point is something else (⬥ II:26).

The Role of Israel in God's Plan

One other inadequate view is that Paul's purpose in writing 9-11 was to explain the role of the nation of Israel in God's redemptive plan. Many interpreters think this section is mainly concerned with the question of Israel's salvation. Others believe that Paul's main point is to explain the relation between Israel and the Gentiles (⬥ II:26-27).

These chapters are obviously quite heavily focused on the nation of Israel. The Jews are involved in Paul's argument throughout the whole section. However, I disagree that Israel is the *main point* here, whether it be Israel and salvation, Israel and the Gentiles, Israel and the church, or national Israel and remnant Israel.

2. The Faithfulness of God

The real focus of these chapters is not upon predestination as such, justification as such, or Israel as such. The focus is rather upon God himself (see Wright, *Climax*, 235). Specifically, the theme is *the faithfulness of God*. True, Israel figures heavily in this discussion. In fact, it is God's dealings with Israel that give rise to the question of his faithfulness. Has God kept his promises to them (9:6a)? Has he been fair to them (⬥ II:28)?

What, specifically, has raised this issue? Two things: The Jews' rejection of the gospel, and God's consequent rejection of the Jews. First, it was a simple historical fact that most of the nation of Israel did not accept Jesus as the expected Messiah; they rejected the gospel of grace. Second, it was also a fact that God rejected his people (9:3), the nation of Israel as a whole, when they rejected him. That is, he rejected them with respect to salvation. This fact in particular raised the issue of God's faithfulness. How can a righteous God *reject* those whom he has *elected* (Godet, 337)? (❀ II:28-29)

Paul's intent in these chapters is to show that, in spite of the nation's unbelief and God's subsequent rejection of them, God has nevertheless been completely faithful to the Jews and has kept all his promises to them (9:6a) (❀ II:29-30).

B. PAUL'S ANSWER TO THE QUESTION OF GOD'S FAITHFULNESS

How then does Paul answer the question about God's faithfulness? The key to his answer is the distinction between service and salvation, with a corresponding distinction between utilitarian promises and redemptive promises. Being chosen for service is not the same as being chosen for salvation, and promises concerning the former do not necessarily entail promises concerning the latter. Thus it was concerning Israel: when God chose the Jewish nation to play a part in his great drama of redemption, he did not thereby guarantee the salvation of every individual Jew.

1. Chosen for Service

God did indeed choose Israel for a special role of unmatched service, which Paul spells out in detail in 9:4-5 (see 3:1-2). Their mission was filled with wonder and glory, leading up to the grand climax of bringing into the world the Messiah, the Savior of mankind. One cannot imagine a greater privilege.

The fact is, despite all her shortcomings, Israel did indeed accomplish this mission. Nursed along by God's patient and chastising hand, Israel at last yielded the Messiah. This is something in which every individual Jew can take pride. This, along with all the preparatory glories mentioned in 9:4-5, are privileges that will always belong to Israel and to Israel alone. These unique blessings have not been taken away from the elect nation, nor are they shared with anyone else, not even the church.

Israel rendered to God and to the rest of the world the greatest possible service. But it was *service* nonetheless, and service is the *only* thing for which the Jews as a nation were elected or chosen. That God chose them to serve in even this exalted way did not include and was not even directly related to their salvation. Personal salvation — justification by faith — was never intended for nor guaranteed to any individual Jew just because he was a Jew (see Piper, *Justification*, 218). Thus Schreiner misses Paul's whole point when he declares that 9:6a "*refers to God's promises to save his people Israel*" ("Election," 91). Paul's point is just the opposite: the nonsalvation of individual Jews does not negate

God's promises to the Israelite nation, because those promises did not have to do with individual salvation in the first place.

Thus Israel's rejection of salvation in no way implies that God's plan for the Jews *as a nation* was a failure. The problem or challenge concerning God's faithfulness arises only when one misunderstands God's intended role for the Jews in the first place. This was in fact a major mistake that the Jews themselves had made. They assumed that their election for service automatically involved salvation; but this was never the point, as Paul has already shown in 2:1–3:8 (❂ II:32).

Paul's discussion in ch. 9 (vv. 1-29) presupposes that God has the perfect right to make this distinction between service and salvation. One might think (as did the Jews) that God surely cannot deny salvation to the people whom he loved and whom he chose and whom he used in such a marvelous way. Somehow this would just not seem fair! But that is the very point: it *is* fair; it *is* righteous for God to do this. He has the perfect right to make such a distinction and to keep his choice for service completely separate from his choice for salvation. The fact that God used Pharaoh for his redemptive purposes did not require the latter to be saved (9:17-18). The same is true of Israel. If God wants to use the Jews in his service yet deny them salvation because of their unbelief, that is perfectly consistent with his nature and his promises. God is completely within his rights when he does this (9:19-21).

2. Chosen for Salvation

But what about the salvation of the Jews? If they are not necessarily saved, are they then necessarily condemned? Are they totally cut off from Jesus and from his saving grace? No, they are neither automatically included, nor are they automatically excluded from grace. The point is simply that the salvation of any individual Jew — and salvation is open to them all — is an issue that is separate from the nation's election to service. God in his sovereignty has set up a way of salvation according to his own choosing, and he has sovereignly established the conditions under which anyone may receive this salvation, whether Jew or Gentile. Any individual Jew is free to meet these conditions and to accept this salvation.

This way of salvation, of course, is the same that Paul has expounded throughout 1–8: grace, not law; and the means by which any Jew may receive it is just as Paul has explained in these earlier chapters: faith in God's promises concerning the death and resurrection of Christ. See 9:30–10:21.

It is true that most Jews are not saved (9:1-3), but the reason is that they are trying to be saved by a way of their own choosing rather than the way of God's choosing, i.e., by law and not by grace (9:30–10:3) (❂ II:33).

Have any Jews actually believed and been saved? Of course they have! These are the "remnant" (9:27; 11:5) and the "descendants" (9:29, lit., "seed") of which Isaiah spoke. They are the seven thousand who did not bow to Baal (11:4). Though they be relatively few compared with the total number of ethnic

Jews, they were the true Israel (9:6b) in OT times; and they along with believing Gentiles are in NT times the new Israel, the church (9:23-29). This way of salvation is still open to any and all Jews (11:17-24). The way of salvation for individual Jews is the same as for anyone else: grace, not law (❂ II:33). In this way it is possible for all Jews to be saved.

C. THE RELATION BETWEEN 1-8 AND 9-11

Another introductory issue is the relation between 9-11 and the first eight chapters of Romans. How is this section related to Paul's overall argument thus far? What is the flow of his thought here? Is there a logical connection between 9-11 and 1-8?

1. Avoiding Extremes

In answering this question two extremes must be avoided. One is the view that there is no inherent connection, i.e., that chs. 9-11 are a kind of digression or parenthesis, or an appendix only loosely related to what has gone before (❂ II:34).

At the other extreme is the view that 9-11 is not just inherently related to 1-8 but is the logical climax to the argument being developed there. Viewed this way, 9-11 is then regarded as the heart and essence of the entire letter (❂ II:34-35).

Neither of these extremes is acceptable. On the one hand, chs. 1-8 do form a logically complete unit, to which 8:31-39 is a natural climax. These chapters deal with the question of personal salvation, affirming it to be by grace and not by law. But on the other hand, looking at it this way does not require us to regard 9-11 as a mere "aside or appendix, dealing with a different problem." A more moderate view will now be explained.

2. The Nature of the Connection

What has happened in the writing of Romans is this. Throughout Paul's explanation of how we are saved by grace and not by law (1-8), a question comes repeatedly to the surface but is not dealt with in detail lest the flow of the argument be too greatly interrupted. But once the main argument has been completed, it becomes possible, even necessary, to return to this question and to address it more specifically and completely, which is what Paul does in 9-11. Thus 9-11 definitely has a thematic connection with 1-8, though it is not a part of the logical flow of the latter. It *is* a separate unit. The point of 1-8 would stand without 9-11, and we could understand the main point of 9-11 without 1-8. But we would not know *why* Paul wrote these three chapters without referring back to 1-8.

To be specific, the very point of the first eight chapters — that salvation is by grace and not by law — seems in itself to render the Jews irrelevant, to render God's 2,000 years of dealing with them futile and pointless, and definitely to raise the question of God's faithfulness to them.

The argument of 1-8 is that one is saved not by his response to any law code, including the Law of Moses, but only by the grace of God made available to all through the saving work of Jesus Christ (see 3:28; 6:14). But since the Jews are so closely identified with law (in the form of the Law of Moses) and since the way of grace appears to some to disparage or even dismiss the law, the gospel thus appears to be dismissing the Jews from God's plan as well. What then has become of God's promises to the Jews and of God's faithfulness to his promises?

This problem is compounded by the many positive references to the Jews and to the OT in 1-8 (❂II:36). But all of these positive things about the Jews and about law seem to be overshadowed and negated by statements of another kind and by the general contrast with grace. This is especially true in the thematic statements, that we are justified by faith not by works of law (3:28), and that we are not under law but under grace (6:14). See also 2:9-12,25-29; 3:9,20-21; 4:9-16; 7:4-6 (❂II:36).

The fact that the Jews and the law seem to be cast in such a negative light is what raises the question with which 9-11 deals. The message of grace in effect seems to make the 2,000 years of Jewish history superfluous. Why did God focus his loving attention upon the Jews and shower so many privileges upon them, if in the final analysis we are saved by grace, not by law. Has God changed his mind? Has he gone back on his promises to the Jews? (❂II:36-37)

Especially troublesome is the simple fact that most Jews rejected the grace of God and even their Messiah when he came. But if the gospel is so rooted in the OT, why did the Jews refuse it (❂II:37)?

These are the sorts of questions that are left hanging in 1-8, and which Paul's discussion of God's faithfulness to the Jews in 9-11 is intended to answer (❂II:37).

3. The Immediate Contextual Connection: 8:31-39

There is another reason why it is appropriate if not necessary for Paul to defend God's faithfulness at this point in his letter to the Romans. He has just concluded his explanation of the gospel of grace with one of the greatest hymns of hope in the human language, 8:31-39. In this paragraph the Apostle sets forth the precious promises that are the essence of God's new covenant through Jesus Christ.

After reading these promises, however, some may be tempted to ask whether they are as wonderful as they seem to be at first glance. The promises themselves are great, of course. But as some may see it, the problem is whether or not we can truly count on God to keep all these promises! In other words, will he be *faithful*?

Why should anyone raise such a question? Why should anyone dare to challenge the faithfulness of God? Here is where the question of Israel may possibly be raised. Someone may well ask, Did not God make equally great promises to the Jews under the Old Covenant? But where are the Jews now? God seems to have abandoned them. So why should we count on him to keep all these high-sounding promises to us under the New Covenant? If his word has failed for the Jews, will it also fail for us Christians? (See ◐ II:38-39.)

D. THE QUESTION OF GOD'S SOVEREIGN ELECTION

A final issue that must be briefly discussed in this introduction is the question of God's sovereign election as it relates to human responsibility and free will. Though predestination is not the main point of this section of Romans, the subject does figure prominently here, especially in ch. 9. Thus some preliminary remarks are in order before we turn to a detailed examination of the text.

The fact is that there are several key affirmations of God's sovereignty in this section. See especially 9:7,11-13,15,16,17,18,19-21,22-23,24; 11:5,7-8,28,29. These affirmations of God's sovereign election seem to be overwhelming, but at the same time there is considerable emphasis on human freedom and man's responsibility for his own fate. See for example 9:30-33; 10:3,4,9-10,12-13,17,21; 11:14,20,22,23 (◐ II:39-40).

How are we to assess these data? How may we harmonize the references to divine sovereignty on the one hand, with the references to human beings' responsibility for their own fate on the other hand? Some see the answer in the distinction between the election of groups and the election of individuals. It is often argued (by Calvinists and non-Calvinists alike) that the main point in ch. 9 is corporate election, especially the election of Israel as a nation. On the other hand, many deny that the main point is corporate election and argue instead that it is individual election Paul has in mind (◐ II:40-41).

What should we say about this? Surely, in our exegesis of 9–11 it is important to ask whether Paul is dealing with groups or with individuals. But actually this is not the key issue, and to approach this passage as if it were may cause us to miss its whole point. The key issue is the distinction between election for *salvation* and election for *service* (*GRu*, 332-335). Also significant is the distinction between physical or ethnic Jews — the *nation* of Israel, and those who are Jews spiritually — those described as the *remnant* (9:27; 11:5). Paul's main point, though, is the difference between service and salvation, and whether these refer to individuals or groups in the final analysis will not affect the main point.

One point on which almost everyone agrees is that, somewhere in Rom 9, Paul deals at least in part with God's election of Israel as a nation for a role of service, or what Moo calls "this general (and nonsalvific) corporate election of Israel" (559, n. 24). But the problem, the point at issue, is this: exactly *with what* is this corporate election for service being compared or contrasted? Some say the contrast is with election of individuals to salvation, and that this is really the main point of Rom 9. Others say the contrast is with salvific corporate election, with the election of a *group*, not individuals, to salvation (❂ II:41).

Which of these approaches is correct? In my judgment, neither of them. Does this mean that Paul is not concerned here with election to salvation at all? On the contrary, he is very much concerned with it *as a fact*, but especially in ch. 9 he is *not* concerned with any *details* relating to it. Again, the main point is the simple distinction between salvation and service. This is a distinction which the Jews themselves failed to make, and this very failure was the basis for questioning the faithfulness of God. "If God has chosen us, why is he now rejecting us and not saving us?" Because, says Paul, he did not choose you for salvation, but for service.

Election to service applies to the entire nation of Israel, and to every individual within it. Election to salvation applies only to the "Israel within Israel" — the remnant — and to every individual within it. Whether it be nations (groups) or individuals is not the point. This is contrary to the common Calvinist view, which tries to find individual election to salvation in this passage; it is also contrary to the view that salvific election is of groups, not individuals. The simple fact is that in Rom 9 it is not Paul's purpose to explain election to salvation at all.

Paul's discussion of Israel in Rom 9 in fact shows that God has the sovereign right to distinguish between salvation and service. The emphasis is on God's sovereign authority to choose unconditionally any group or any individual to fill any given role in the working out of his purposes, without being bound at the same time to guarantee their salvation. In this way God selected Israel from all the nations of the earth to perform the greatest act of service possible for an earthly agent.

At the same time God is sovereignly free to choose individuals for salvation in a way that is completely different from the way he chooses anyone for service. The fact is that he chooses to bestow salvation on the basis of grace and upon the primary condition of faith. This conditional election to salvation is established in 9:30-10:21. Certainly those unconditionally chosen for service can also be saved, but 9:30-10:21 shows that salvation is given only to those who through faith choose to relate to God in terms of grace instead of law. Those who put their trust in God's way of grace form another group within and distinct from ethnic Israel, namely, spiritual Israel, the remnant of believers.

This resolves the seeming paradox of divine sovereignty and human responsibility in 9-11. Many interpreters, especially Calvinists, are content to regard the presence of these two themes as a paradox, but this is totally unnecessary. God's sovereignty is exercised in his unconditional election of individuals and groups, Israel in particular, to roles of service in the working out of his redemptive plan. His sovereignty is also seen in the way he chooses to distinguish service from salvation, which allows him to choose and use Israel without guaranteeing the salvation of all individual Jews as part of the same package. Another expression of his sovereignty is his right to establish the system of salvation according to a way of his own choosing, in a way independent of works, namely, by grace. Those who accept this way to salvation become part of "the elect."

But it is made very clear from 9:30 onward that becoming a part of this grace category is the result of one's responsible choice to believe God's promises. In other words, salvation is *conditional*. This in no way contradicts the sovereignty of God, but rather upholds it, since it is perfectly consistent with the way God made human beings and configured his way of salvation in the first place.

E. AN OVERVIEW OF CHAPTERS 9-11

Romans 9-11 is divided into three main sections. After a prologue (9:1-5) that sets up the problem to be discussed, the first main section (9:1-29) discusses the fact that God has made a *distinction* within the nation of Israel so that there are in fact two Israels: (1) physical, ethnic, or national Israel, i.e., Israel according to flesh; and (2) remnant or spiritual Israel, i.e., Israel according to faith. The former was chosen for service, the latter for salvation. The second main section (9:30-10:21) explains the *criterion* for distinguishing between the two Israels, i.e., the choice between law and grace. The third section (11:1-32) shows that there is still *hope* for the salvation of all ethnic Jews. The passage closes with a doxology of praise to God (11:33-36).

I. THE PROBLEM OF ISRAEL: THE AGONY AND THE ECSTASY OF THE JEWISH NATION (9:1-5)

The transition from ch. 8 to ch. 9 is quite abrupt. No connecting word (e.g., "therefore," "however") links 9:1 closely with 8:39. There is an obvious shift in subject matter. Also, the tone changes dramatically. The spirit of joy and confidence characterizing the end of ch. 8 is replaced by a spirit of tension and sorrow.

The reason for this new direction in Paul's thought is the problem of his own kinsmen, the Jewish people. In view of the Jews' privileged role in God's plan, the logical expectation would be that they above all others should have been rejoicing in the hope Paul describes in 8:31-39. The shocking and tragic fact, though, was that most Israelites were rejecting the Messiah whose coming was their very reason for being. As a result, rather than celebrating their salvation, they were under God's curse.

Paul's reaction to the plight of the Jews took two forms. On a subjective, personal level his heart was filled with grief because of their lost state. On a more objective, theological level he was concerned that some might take Israel's rejection as an indication that God's word had failed. Though his personal grief was genuine, his greater concern was to show that the tragedy of the Jews in no way violated God's original promises and plans for them as a nation.

The main point of this section (9:1-5) is to set forth the contrast between the plight of Israel (1-3) and her privileges (4-5). How can these be reconciled? Has God's word somehow failed to come true? By raising these questions Paul thus prepares the way for his defense of the faithfulness of God in his dealings with his people.

A. ISRAEL'S AGONY: THEY ARE ACCURSED (9:1-3)

9:1 I speak the truth in Christ—I am not lying, my conscience confirms it in the Holy Spirit— With these introductory words Paul affirms in several ways the truthfulness of what he is about to say in vv. 2-3. In the Greek text of his positive statement, the word "truth" stands first, in the place of emphasis: "*Truth* I speak in Christ!" This point is reemphasized by saying the same thing negatively, "I am not lying."

To further confirm the veracity of his words, Paul invokes three distinct witnesses. One is his own conscience (see 2:15), which, he says, testifies or bears witness along with him. ("Testifies along with me" or "bears witness along with me" is a literal translation and is to be preferred over the NIV's "confirms it.") In other words Paul has no inward reservations at all about what he is saying.

The other two witnesses are Christ and the Holy Spirit. Paul says he speaks the truth "in Christ." This could mean simply that he speaks as one who is conscious of being in union with Jesus Christ, and who thus as a Christian is always bound to speak the truth (see Moo, 555; Cranfield, 2:452). I believe, though, in view of the parallel idea in 1 Tim 2:7, that he is referring to his appointment by Christ to be an apostle; and thus "in Christ" is an invocation of his apostolic authority (see Dunn, 2:523).

Similarly "in the Holy Spirit" could be referring to the indwelling Holy Spirit, through whose moral power every Christian can resist the temptation to lie (see 8:13). More likely, though, Paul is here referring to his consciousness of the fact that he is writing under the inspiration of the Spirit and is thus divinely prevented from speaking falsehood (see 1 Cor 7:40).

Seldom does Paul go to such lengths to reinforce the truthfulness of his assertions. Of course this does not mean that on other occasions he is not telling the truth. This is simply his way of underscoring the seriousness of what he is saying (❧ II:45-46).

9:2 Exactly what is the momentous truth solemnly introduced in v. 1? Strictly speaking, it is the fact that Paul is personally filled with tremendous grief and anguish: **I have great sorrow and unceasing anguish in my heart.** The cause of his grief is not actually stated in this verse, but is made clear in v. 3. It is the fact that his own natural kinsmen, the Jewish people, were under God's curse because of their unbelief.

The words "sorrow" and "anguish" refer to the emotional state of his heart, and their intensity is magnified by the adjectives "great" and "unceasing." Would Paul's spirit be filled with such deep suffering if he thought for a moment that the Jews as such were saved?

Why did Paul think it was so important to state this fact in such an emphatic way? Primarily to make it clear that he is not indifferent to Israel's plight. This establishes his authenticity; it shows that his negative judgment against his countrymen is not just the result of some personal spite against them, but is the true word of God, a word that afflicted him so deeply that he would give anything if it were not true.

9:3 Just how deep are Paul's feelings for his fellow Jews? Just how far would he go to save them? This verse tells us: **For I could wish that I myself were cursed and cut off from Christ for the sake of my brothers, those of my own race, . . .**

Exactly what was Paul willing to endure on behalf of his brethren? To be "cursed and cut off from Christ." The word "cursed" translates ἀνάθεμα (*anathema*), used in other places for eternal condemnation (1 Cor 16:22; Gal 1:8-9) (❈ II:47). There is no word for "cut off" in the Greek text. Literally it reads "accursed from Christ" (see 2 Thess 1:7-10). Most agree that this is a strong and clear reference to condemnation in hell (Lard, 294; MP, 377; Moo, 557).

The verb translated "I could wish" is difficult, not in itself but in view of what Paul was wishing. This word (εὔχομαι, *euchomai*) can mean either "to pray" or "to wish"; either meaning conveys the notion of a sincere desire. The content of Paul's desire is that he himself might be sent to hell in the place of his fellow Jews.

The straightforward meaning of the verb is "I was praying (wishing)," or "I used to pray (wish)"; but a past tense does not fit the context. Thus most agree that it should be treated as a "potential imperfect" (Nash, "Critique," 31). In other words, "I *would* pray or wish this *if* it could be done, but I know it cannot."

But why is such a thing impossible? The Calvinist answer is that this would contradict the doctrine of the perseverance of the saints, or "once saved, always saved" (e.g., Murray, 2:3; Hendriksen, 2:310; MacArthur, 2:11). The more obvious answer, though, is that Paul knew that he as a sinful human being could not be an adequate substitute for even one other sinner, much less for the whole nation of Israel. Paul's words, "for the sake of my brothers," are the language of substitution (compare 6:6,8; see Moo, 559). But only the divine and sinless Messiah could be and was such a substitute (Gal 3:13).

Two things are unequivocally demonstrated by this statement. First is the reality of Paul's concern for his people, and the depth of his grief at their lost condition. "Paul felt such love that he was willing to relinquish his own salvation and spend eternity in hell if somehow that could bring his fellow Jews to faith in Christ!" (MacArthur, 2:11). Second is that Israel as a nation, i.e., the majority of the Jews, were in fact lost. The language "accursed from Christ" certainly refers to eternal lostness, and Paul's willingness to endure this state in Israel's place without a doubt implies that Israel herself was under such a curse (see Moo, 557-558; Piper, *Justification*, 45). The whole discussion in 9-11 is predicated upon this fact.

There is no question that Paul's concern is directed toward the nation of Israel. He calls them "my brothers, those of my own race." Contrary to some interpretations, Paul does not imply that they are saved when he speaks of them as "brothers." In order to make it clear that he is talking here only about physical kinship, Paul adds "those of my own race," literally, "my kinsmen (relatives) according to the flesh." No salvation is implied. In fact, one of Paul's main points in this very chapter is that membership in physical Israel is not equivalent to membership in the true spiritual people of God (9:6; see ch. 2) (❧ II:48-49).

B. ISRAEL'S ECSTASY: THEY ARE RECIPIENTS OF UNSPEAKABLY GLORIOUS PRIVILEGES (9:4-5)

Paul now turns to the other side of the paradox called Israel. The same nation which is the object of God's curse is the one that God chose to receive some of the greatest blessings imaginable. These next two verses give a list of these privileges, a project begun in 3:1-2 and now continued in detail (❧ II:49).

One very important question regarding these privileges is whether they were related only to pre-Christian Israel, or whether they continue to apply to Jews in the Christian era and beyond. Many take the latter approach (❧ II:49-50), but I strongly disagree. It is true that everything in this list of blessings pointed beyond the OT era to this age and beyond, as did Israel's very existence. The single purpose of Israel's election, and of all the preliminary privileges listed in 3:2 and 9:4-5a, is the climactic privilege named in 9:5b, i.e., the first coming of Christ. By serving God's purpose of bringing the Christ into the world, all of these prerogatives have played a preparatory role in the eternal salvation of all believers, both Jews and Gentiles. And every ethnic Jew who ever lived and will live, whether saved or not, has a right to look at this list and take humble and grateful pride in the fact that God chose *his* nation to be the recipients of these blessings and thereby to prepare for the Christ and his saving work.

However, it is one thing to receive the intended *result* of these privileges, as does every saved person; it is quite another to receive the privileges themselves, which was true *only* of the nation of Israel (including every individual within it) up to the time of Christ's first coming. Here Paul is talking only about the latter circumstance. He is referring only to the privileges God bestowed upon the Jewish nation in the OT era, privileges that applied in that day to every Jew whether he was part of the saved remnant or not. But they no longer apply in any direct sense to *anyone*: not to Jews as Jews, whether individually or collectively; not to Gentiles as such; and not to Christians, whether Jews or Gentiles.

Herein lies the nature of the tragic irony of Israel's existence. They were so absorbed with the privileges themselves (and continued to be, in Paul's day), that they neglected and even rejected the intended result of these privileges, God's gracious salvation through Christ. They glorified the means, and ignored the end. The very people who were, by God's gracious choice, responsible for bringing the Redeemer into the world were themselves the object of his wrath.

9:4 At the beginning of v. 4 Paul refers to his brothers and kinsmen (v. 3) as **the people of Israel**. This may be in apposition to "brothers" and "kinsmen," bringing the thought of v. 3 to an end (as in the NIV). Or it may be the first item in the list of the privileges themselves, as the verse division suggests. I prefer the latter view, though this is not a serious issue.

Taking these words as the first blessing, we find a total of nine privileges bestowed upon the chosen people (❋II:51). Schematically the list looks like this:

. . . my brothers and kinsmen —
>— who are Israelites (a better translation than the NIV);
>— of whom [are] adoption, glory, covenants, law, worship, and promises;
>— of whom [are] the fathers; and
>— from whom [is] the Christ.

The first privilege of the Jews, says Paul, is that they are *Israelites*. This seems to point back to the time of Israel's calling, to the period of their very formation as a people from the loins of Jacob, whom God renamed "Israel" (Gen 32:28). It is in itself a title of honor that embodies the totality of their God-given privileges (❋II:52).

Theirs is the adoption as sons . . . . Literally it says, "of whom is the adoption" (❋II:51). Contrary to some interpretations, Paul is not talking primarily about individual Jews but about the nation as a whole. The term refers to God's sovereign choice of Israel collectively to be his son (See Exod 4:22; Jer 31:9; Hos 11:1). In a derivative sense each individual born as a Jew enjoyed this status of adoptive sonship (see Deut 14:1; 32:19; Isa 1:2; 43:6).

This concept of Israel's adoption emphasizes God's initiative and deliberate choice in establishing this relationship with Israel. Also, it indicates that God's relation with his people was one of fatherly affection (Deut 1:31; 8:5; Isa 46:3-4; Jer 3:19).

Though this adoption was extremely significant, its limitations must still be recognized. For one thing, it did not in itself entail the salvation (spiritual sonship) of any individual Jew. (See Lard, 294-295; Moo, 562; MacArthur, 2:13.) Also, this father-son relation with Israel as a nation ended with the beginning of the New Covenant, under which adoption is now a saving relationship with all willing individuals, including both Jews and Gentiles (Gal 3:26-4:7).

[T]heirs is **the divine glory** . . . (literally, "and the glory"). "The glory" has no reference to any alleged future national Jewish participation in eschatological glory. It refers to the fact that God manifested himself to OT Israel and even dwelt among them in a glorious visible form, i.e., the theophany of cloud by day and fire by night (Exod 13:21-22; 40:36-38). Later Judaism began to use the Hebrew term *shekinah* to refer to this glorious manifestation of God's presence. *Shekinah* means "dwelling" or "presence" (Cranfield, 2:462) and was thus a kind of shorthand for "the presence of God's glory." No wonder Paul included this in the list of Israel's privileges (❂ II:53)!

Today God is present in a special way within his church (1 Cor 3:16; Eph 2:22) and within individual Christians (1 Cor 6:19). Though this presence is not one of visible glory, it is even greater than the *shekinah* because it is part of our salvation.

The next privilege is **the covenants**. A major question is, why is this plural? There are several possibilities. One is that Paul is speaking of the several *ratifications* of the Mosaic covenant. Another is that he is talking about all biblical covenants, including the New Covenant. To include the New Covenant, however, violates the intent of this list, which is to name those privileges which are exclusive to Israel. The third and most likely possibility is that "covenants" refers to all OT covenants specifically involving Israel. This would include the covenant with Abraham and the other patriarchs; the covenant at Sinai, as ratified at Moab and at Gerizim-Ebal; and the covenant with David (❂ II:54).

The main point is that Israel is the only nation on earth with whom God chose to enter a special covenant relationship. This is just one more indication of their status of exalted privilege.

The next blessing named by Paul is **the receiving of the law.** This refers to the Law of Moses, and to the fact that being chosen to be the recipients of this law was an honor granted only to Israel. (See Ps 147:20; Rom 3:1-2.)

Israel was also granted the privilege of **the temple worship**. The NIV is probably correct to take it in the narrow sense of the temple services. This would include "the entire ceremonial system" of the Law of Moses (MacArthur, 2:15), and especially the system of sacrifices that dealt with sin and foreshadowed the Messiah's atoning work (❂ II:55).

The last privilege listed in v. 4 is **the promises.** This refers to all the promises included in God's covenants, as well as all the other promises made to Israel. This includes the promises given to the Jewish people generally, and the promises given to individuals (❂ II:55). See Rom 15:8.

All such promises ultimately pointed toward a single goal, the coming of the Messiah. Their fulfilment was the means to this one end. They are like individual notes that lead into the great symphony of messianic promises and prophecies themselves. What is important to see is that all these promises made to Israel were fulfilled when Jesus came the first time; see Acts 13:32-34. Romans 9:5b is the goal and climax of them all. The promises made to Abraham and to the rest were fulfilled *through* Israel, *in* Christ, *to* us. These promises no longer apply to Israel today nor to Christians as such. We are not under these promises, but rather under their fulfilment. The promises of the New Covenant are different, and better (Heb 8:6).

9:5 Theirs are the patriarchs, . . . (literally, "the fathers"; see 11:28; 15:8). This refers especially to the "founding fathers" of the Jewish people: Abraham, Isaac, and Jacob (see 9:6-13; Exod 3:15). From the perspective of the Jews, the fact that God chose these men to be the foundation of his chosen people made them not only national heroes but also the greatest figures in the history of the world (Deut 7:6-8). It was certainly a great privilege to be able to claim them as ancestors.

This leads to the climactic and most wonderful privilege of all: **and from them** [the Jews] **is traced the human ancestry of Christ . . . .** This is the blessing for which all the others were only means to an end, the one purpose for which the others existed in the first place, namely, to bring the Messiah, the Christ, into the world.

The emphasis here is on the human nature of Christ. The Greek text may be translated literally thus: "from whom is the Christ according to the flesh." Christ's saving work required that he have not only a divine nature but also a true and complete human nature. It was Israel's incomparable privilege to provide the latter (see 1:3).

The blessings mentioned earlier in the list are described as belonging to Israel: "theirs" (vv. 4a,5a), literally, "*of* whom." Here the expression changes to "*from* them." This shows that the relation between the Messiah and national Israel was one of origin or ancestry only. Jesus did not "belong" to Israel; he was not their Messiah in the sense of their personal Savior since most Jews remained unbelievers. The very people granted the prerogative of bringing the Christ into the world rejected him when he came. Their greatest privilege was the very obstacle over which they stumbled (❂ II:56-57).

This simple fact that *from Israel came the Christ* was the ultimate fulfilment of all God's promises to and covenants with the Jews as a nation. God's word thus did not fail, and his purpose for physical Israel was thus achieved.

The next clause, **. . . who is God over all, forever praised! Amen**, has been interpreted in two main ways. The basic question is whether the word "God" refers to Christ or not. If it does, this verse is one of the strongest NT affirmations of the divine nature of Jesus (❂ II:57, n. 22).

Those who deny that *theos* (God) refers to Christ insert a period somewhere in the middle of the verse, usually after the word "Christ." Verse 5b then becomes a statement of praise to God that is separate from the statement about

Christ. The RSV is a good example: From the Jews "according to the flesh, is the Christ. God who is over all be blessed for ever" (❷ II:57).

The other main possibility is to take the entire verse (after "the patriarchs") as a single statement about the Christ, which thus would be affirming that he is *theos*, or God. The NIV is an example of this view (❷ II:57).

There are several arguments that favor the latter interpretation. Grammatically, the wording in v. 5b points in this direction. Paul's pattern of usage elsewhere in doxologies and blessings is also a strong indicator (❷ II:58). Based on the grammar and word usage of Paul, if v. 5b were referring to God the Father and not to Jesus Christ, one would expect the wording to have been similar to the following: "Blessed be God, who is over all forever."

Other arguments have to do with the context. For one thing, the reference to Christ's human nature in v. 5a calls for a complementary reference to his divine nature. Also, taking the latter part of the verse as a doxology seems out of place in a paragraph "otherwise expressing sorrow and regret" (Fitzmyer, 549). Finally, taking v. 5b as affirming Christ's deity is compatible with the climactic nature of this last and highest privilege bestowed upon Israel (❷ II:58).

Over against these arguments from wording and context it is argued that Paul nowhere else refers to Christ as *theos* ("God"). It is true that Paul's usual title for Jesus is κύριος (*kyrios*, "Lord"), and that *theos* is usually reserved for God the Father (e.g., 1 Cor 8:6; 12:3-6; Eph 4:5-6; Phil 2:11). But Paul certainly attributes deity to Christ elsewhere (see Gal 1:1; Phil 2:6; Col 2:9), and a strong case can be made that he calls Jesus *theos* in Titus 2:13 and 2 Thess 1:12 (see Murray, 2:247-248). In addition, the title *kyrios* is itself a title of deity (see 1:4; 10:9-13).

Moo is therefore correct in concluding that Paul is calling Jesus *theos* in this verse. This view, he says, is "exegetically preferable, theologically unobjectionable, and contextually appropriate" (568).

The other descriptions of Christ in v. 5b are also indicative of his divine nature. He is the one who is "over all," an expression of his universal Lordship (Acts 10:36), which belongs only to God. He is the "blessed" one (NIV, "praised"), a term which elsewhere in the NT refers only to God (Mark 14:61; Luke 1:68; Rom 1:25; 2 Cor 1:3; 11:31; Eph 1:3; 1 Pet 1:3). He is blessed "forever," indicating his eternality.

In these verses Israel's "ecstasy" (4-5) stands in sharp contrast with her "agony" (1-3). This raises the question, how can Israel's accursedness be reconciled with her blessedness? This is the issue Paul begins to address in 9:6.

II. THE DISTINCTION BETWEEN ETHNIC AND SPIRITUAL ISRAEL (9:6-29)

The main theme of 9–11 is God's faithfulness in his dealings with Israel. The issue is summarized in 9:1-5 thus: in view of the privileges for which Israel was chosen (vv. 4-5), how is it possible for a faithful God to reject them and curse them (vv. 1-3)? Does this mean that God's purpose for Israel has in fact failed? "Have not God's promises to Israel ended in nothing as far as the Jews are concerned?" (Fitzmyer, 558).

Paul's answer, of course, is that God's purposes and promises have not failed (9:6a; see 3:4). The apparent paradox of 9:1-5 is easily resolved by seeing that there is not just one Israel, but two (9:6b), and by discerning the proper nature and purpose of each. National, ethnic, physical Israel was chosen by God to play a primary role in his plan of redemption. This entitled them to all the blessings of 9:4-5, but these blessings did not include the guarantee of personal salvation. Every covenant promise God made to Israel as a nation was completely fulfilled, irrespective of the salvation status of any individual Jew. God has the sovereign right to choose and use any individual or group in this manner. This is the point of 9:6-18.

Is it true, then, that every individual Israelite is actually lost? In 9:3 Paul implies that physical Israel, his "kinsmen according to the flesh," are indeed "accursed" (NASB). But he does not say this applies to every Jew without exception. Yes, some (most) Jews are lost, but some are saved! Those who are saved are still part of national Israel and participate in all the covenant blessings bestowed upon the nation as a whole, but they constitute an "Israel" of a different sort, an "Israel within Israel," one that is defined not just in terms of physical descent from Jacob but also in terms of a saving relationship with God. This is the point of Paul's key statement in 9:6b, "For not all who are descended from Israel are Israel." God's sovereign right to make this distinction within the larger body of ethnic Israel is the point of 9:19-29. He can use the entire nation for his redemptive purposes, while limiting salvation only to spiritual Israel, the remnant. "It is the remnant that will be saved" (9:27b, NASB).

It is extremely important to understand how the issue of salvation figures into the discussion in 9:6-29. Some points are accepted by almost everyone. It is agreed that *election* (choosing, making distinctions) is a key theme in this section. It is agreed that Paul is stressing God's sovereign *freedom* to make distinctions and choices in whatever way he pleases. It is also agreed that belonging to physical Israel was not in itself a guarantee of personal salvation.

But there is sharp disagreement, usually (but not always) along Calvinist vs. non-Calvinist lines, as to which parts of vv. 6-29 refer to God's election to *service*, and which refer to his election to *salvation*. This disagreement occurs in view of the fact that Calvinism generally teaches unconditional election to salvation, and because (especially) vv. 7-23 seem to be affirming unconditional election. Thus it is quite common to see Calvinists use this passage as a proof text for the doctrine of the unconditional election of individuals to salvation (and usually, the unconditional reprobation of all others to hell).

Non-Calvinists of course disagree, and usually take one of two approaches to this passage. Some say the election described therein does have to do with individual salvation, but it is conditional rather than unconditional. Even though the conditions (such as faith) are not specifically named in the text itself, they are taken to be implicit in view of other biblical teaching. A common form of this view is that God made his choices, e.g., of Jacob over Esau, based on divine foreknowledge of the lives and character of each (❧ II:61).

Since the text itself does not mention foreknowledge and seems to exclude human conditions as such, others have taken the approach that Paul is here talking about unconditional election to *service*, not salvation. In my judgment this is the correct view (❧ II:61-62). The following is a summary of the argument in 9:1-29.

First, Paul expresses his grief over the fact that most Jews are accursed — the very Jews who were chosen to receive the greatest of privileges (9:1-5). But how is this possible? Is this some kind of contradiction? Has God's word failed? No! God's purposes and promises have *not* failed (9:6a), basically because there are *two different kinds* of "Israel" (9:6b). One is national Israel, which was unconditionally chosen by God to be a party to the covenant made with the fathers, and thus to receive the blessings of 9:4-5. This was an election and a call to service only, and it was a matter of God's sovereign and unconditional choice with no requirement for saving faith on the part of any individual Israelite. Israel's founders were chosen apart from any decisions, qualifications, faith, or works on their part; and God kept his promises to the nation and carried out his purposes for them not because of their belief but in spite of their frequent unbelief (9:7-13).

The other Israel is composed of those individuals within the ethnic body which do in fact have a saving faith in the God of Abraham, Isaac, and Jacob. Salvation is promised and given not to the nation as a whole, but only to this *spiritual* Israel, which is in a sense the "true" Israel (see 2:28-29), the redeemed remnant. The fact that God has withheld salvation from the majority of Jews is not a violation of his covenant with them, for that covenant as such did not include a promise of automatic salvation based on ethnic heritage alone.

Paul's key point in v. 6b is in effect that God has *made a distinction* within the nation of Israel, using all Jews to serve his saving purpose but giving salvation only to some. This is his solution to the problem raised in vv. 1-5. But his following discussion shows that he anticipates that this solution to the original problem will itself be seen as a problem, namely, its fairness will be questioned (see v. 14). Does God have the *right* to make this kind of distinction within his chosen people, a distinction resulting in two kinds of Israel?

In defense of his statement in 9:6b and in anticipation of such an objection, in 9:7-13 Paul makes a point that no Jew can deny, namely, that in the very events that gave rise to the nation of Israel, God had already made some unconditional distinctions within the progeny of Abraham. These verses are not talking about the distinction within Israel as affirmed in v. 6b, which is a distinction between service and salvation. Rather they describe divine choices whereby some were chosen for service and others were passed by, choices by which Israel as a nation was created in the first place.

This has two applications. The first refers to the distinction specified in v. 6b. To those who might suggest that such a distinction is unfair, Paul is simply pointing out that making such distinctions is nothing new for God; he did this sort of thing in the very beginning when he brought Israel into existence. Granted, that was a matter of selecting certain individuals and a certain people for service rather than for salvation, but it set a precedent showing that God was not acting out of character or contrary to established patterns when he made the distinction between the two Israels as such.

The second application of 9:7-13 relates directly to the problem of Israel's lostness raised in vv. 1-5. The point is that this lostness does not negate God's promises because his original choice of the founders of Israel had nothing to do with their works, character, merits, faith, or salvation status in general. It was simply his sovereign will to use these individuals (Isaac and Jacob) rather than the alternatives (Ishmael and Esau), and the purpose for which he chose them was such that they did not have to be personally saved to carry it out. God could and did choose to use them just as they were. The same is true for the entire nation of Israel that sprang from their loins. God intended to use them for his service whether or not they believed and were saved. Thus there is no conflict between vv. 1-3 and vv. 4-5.

In 9:14-18 Paul specifically raises the problem of fairness that some are bound to see in such divine distinguishing. Doesn't it seem unjust for God to choose people for service in this way? Shouldn't individuals have the right to volunteer, or at least consent to being thus used? And if they are going to be conscripted into service, as it were, shouldn't they at least be rewarded with salvation?

In response Paul simply *declares* that God has the right to choose whomever he wills to use for his purposes, whether they be saved or not. The subject is election for service, not salvation. The mercy and compassion of which Moses spoke is not saving grace, but God's selection and appointment of a person (or a nation) to have the privilege of serving him (see below). That such a person does not have to be saved to serve God's redemptive purposes is perfectly illustrated by Pharaoh, upon whom God had mercy by choosing him for a vital role in his plan, but who at the same time was hardened in order that he might fulfill that role. In like manner God chose the nation of Israel for his grand redemptive purpose, and he used them for it even though most individual Jews (like Pharaoh) were hardened.

In 9:19-29 Paul turns specifically to the original distinction set forth in 9:6b, the distinction between national Israel as a whole (used for service) and the spiritual Israel existing within it (blessed with salvation). Does God have a right to make this distinction? The objection is put into the mouths of those Israelites who are lost, as they try to blame God for their lost state (9:19). They say, if God is orchestrating this whole thing, how can he hold us responsible and condemn us for our unbelief? Hasn't God made us the way we are?

Paul's primary answer at this point is that the lost person (specifically, the unbelieving Jew) has no right to complain to God at all, since God is indeed the sovereign Lord who has by decree created this single "lump of clay" known as Israel (9:21). It is *his* plan and *his* clay, and he (like a potter) can do with it what he wills. Since it is his to begin with by right of creation (9:7-13), it is also his right to divide it as he chooses and to make different kinds of vessels from it. Some are vessels of wrath and are under the curse of v. 3; others are vessels of mercy and will be saved. These vessels of mercy are the remnant of which the prophets spoke, i.e., the true believers, or spiritual Israel, to which in this church age are added all true believers from among the Gentiles.

This main section comes to a close with this point, but in itself it does not resolve the issue of divine faithfulness raised in 9:1-5. It simply establishes the *fact* that God has made a distinction between the two Israels, only one of which is saved. It shows clearly that ethnic Israel's role of service had no essential connection with personal salvation. It also asserts God's sovereign right to make this distinction between the serving and the saved (9:19-29), but it does not go into detail as to the *nature* of such a distinction. In particular, this section does not raise the question as to the basis, or conditions, upon which God distinguishes the remnant from the larger group of Israelites according to the flesh.

Those of a Calvinist bent will insist that this is an improper question to begin with, since they are convinced that election to salvation is unconditional. But this conclusion is invalid in view of the fact that the language of unconditionality in 9:7-18 applies only to election to service. Election to salvation is a completely different issue. The divine distinguishing that separates the saved from the lost is conditioned upon the free human choice either to accept or to reject the saving promises of God. This is the point of the next main section, 9:30–10:21. Only when this point has been made is the issue of divine faithfulness regarding Israel completely resolved.

A. ISRAEL'S SITUATION AND GOD'S FAITHFULNESS (9:6-13)

It is clear that these verses deal with divine election, but election *to what* (❦ II:65)? The relevant choices are election to *service* and election to *salvation*. This distinction relates to the two Israels named in 9:6b: ethnic Israel, chosen for service; and spiritual Israel, chosen for salvation. But which of these two is the main subject of 9:6-13?

Many simply assume that spiritual Israel is the main subject, and that God's choice of Isaac and his choice of Jacob are prime examples of how God distinguishes the true spiritual Israel (the saved) from ethnic Israel as a whole. They argue that the terminology used in these verses can only be salvation language: seed or children of Abraham, children of God, children of promise, God's purpose, God's call as opposed to human works, God's love.

A brief reflection upon the individuals and incidents being discussed in these verses will show, however, that Paul is *not* talking about how God makes distinctions *within* Israel (between the ethnic and the spiritual, as in v. 6b), but how he established ethnic Israel in the first place. Ishmael and Isaac as a pair were not the original "ethnic Israel" from which God elected only Isaac to be the first member of "spiritual Israel." Ishmael was never a part of Israel in either sense; he was chosen neither for service nor for salvation (as far as we know). The same is true of the twins Esau and Jacob.

The point of these verses is that Isaac and Jacob were chosen to be the first representatives of *ethnic* Israel (after Abraham himself). Whether they were saved or not, i.e., whether they were also part of spiritual Israel, is not relevant. In fact, the nonrelevance of their salvation status is the key to Paul's argument: Isaac and Jacob, like ethnic Israel as a whole, could be chosen and used for God's service whether they were saved or not. This is the key to v. 6a, "It is not as though God's word had failed." God's promises to physical Israel have not failed, even though most Jews are unbelievers, because these promises did not include salvation as such.

But what about the language used in this section? Is it not the language of salvation? This depends solely upon the context. In other NT contexts the terminology does refer to salvation and the saved, but it is not inherently limited to this. It is covenant language, to be sure, but covenant language is not always salvation language. A common error in modern theology is to erase the proper distinction between the Abrahamic covenant and the New Covenant, and to project the salvation content of the latter back into the former. This is common among Calvinists, and it is why someone such as Murray or Piper cannot separate the covenant realities of 9:4-5 from salvation, and why they cannot see anything but salvation in the language of 9:7-13.

The point of the Abrahamic covenant, though, was not the salvation of its recipients. Its point was rather that *through* Abraham and his (physical) seed the means by which all peoples could be saved would be brought into the world. This was a covenant of service; and the recipients of this covenant, i.e., ethnic Israel, were chosen to render this service and to experience its accompanying temporal privileges and rewards (vv. 4-5).

The language of 9:7-13 is perfectly consistent with the role played by ethnic Israel in God's plan. God had a definite purpose for choosing this nation (9:11), which he did by choosing its forefathers, Isaac and Jacob. He called them into his service without regard for any meritorious qualifications on their part and without even asking for their own conscious participation in the choice (9:11-

12). It was all a matter of God's choice and promise, i.e., his covenant promise to bless and to use these individuals and their physical descendants for the purpose of bringing the Savior into the world. In this context "children of Abraham," "children of God," and "children of promise" (9:7-8) are perfectly consistent with God's purpose for ethnic Israel, and perfectly applicable to Isaac and Jacob and their natural descendants in contrast with Ishmael and Esau and their descendants. Isaac and Jacob were the progenitors not just of spiritual Israel, but of ethnic Israel as a whole.

Thus I agree with Lenski (597-598), that Isaac and Jacob are not types of election to salvation: "Paul's two illustrations have nothing to do with an eternal election or predestination of Isaac and of Jacob to salvation and with a reprobation of Ishmael and of Esau to damnation."

Shall we say, then, that 9:6-13 has no bearing at all upon the election of individuals to eternal salvation? Not necessarily. The error is to take the references to Isaac and Jacob as *examples* of election to salvation and therefore as *exact models* for the way God saves any individual. In other words, according to this erroneous view, just as God unconditionally chose Jacob and rejected Esau, so he unconditionally predestines some to heaven and some to hell. But this is not Paul's point. At the most, we may possibly say that God's choosing Isaac and Jacob for service is *analogous at some points* with his electing of individuals to salvation. For one thing, members of spiritual Israel are "children of promise" and not "children of the flesh," even though the promises that apply in this case are not the same promises that set ethnic Israel apart from the rest of the world. Members of spiritual Israel are also chosen and called, though not in the same way that God chose and called ethnic Israel. "Not by works" (9:12) is likewise a key ingredient in being chosen for membership in spiritual Israel, though such membership does require the precondition of faith, as Paul goes on to show in 9:30–10:21 and 11:20-23.

In other words, there are some similarities between election to service and election to salvation, but they are not the same in every detail. To assume that they are would defeat Paul's whole purpose in this section (9:6-13), which is to answer the charge that God is somehow being untrue to his word unless all ethnic Israel is saved. The very essence of his answer is that being chosen for service is *different* from being chosen for salvation. The two Israels are constituted differently, or are established on different bases. The process by which God established ethnic Israel, i.e., through the unconditional choosing of Isaac and Jacob, did not in itself involve their personal salvation, which requires a specific decision of faith (❧ II:68).

1. God's Word Concerning Israel Has Not Failed (9:6a)

9:6 It is not as though God's word had failed. If it is true that much of Israel is "cursed and cut off from Christ" (v. 3), has something thus gone wrong with God's plan for Israel? Has he failed to keep his word to his people? Paul immediately rejects any such suggestion. His response begins with a strong negative expression, "But it is not as if."

The word "failed" is ἐκπίπτω (*ekpiptō*) (see Acts 12:7; Jas 1:11; 1 Pet 1:24). Here it has the general meaning of "fail, come to nothing, be annulled."

Paul declares that "God's word" (ὁ λόγος τοῦ θεοῦ, *ho logos tou theou*) does not fall away or fail. What is meant by "God's word"? In this context "God's word" refers specifically to his words of *promise*, i.e., the promises he made to and about OT Israel (Dunn, 2:539) (❍ II:69). These promises have not failed.

2. The Key to the Puzzle: The Existence of Two Israels (9:6b)

But in view of Israel's lostness and the apparent inconsistency between vv. 1-3 and vv. 4-5, how can it be said that God's promises to Israel have never failed? The answer, says Paul, lies in the fact that there is not just one Israel, but two. **For not all who are descended from Israel are Israel.** This statement clearly affirms the existence of two groups, both called "Israel" but in two different senses: ethnic Israel and spiritual Israel. The former includes all those who bear Abraham's genes through physical descent from Isaac and Jacob, i.e., the Jews; the latter is composed only of those Jews who also share Abraham's faith in the God of salvation.

The first group is called "the ones of [or from] Israel." This expression may mean simply "the ones who belong to the *nation* of Israel," or it may mean (as the NIV suggests) "the ones who can trace their physical lineage back to the *man* Israel," i.e., to Jacob whom God renamed Israel. The second group is simply called "Israel," but it is usually (and rightly) referred to as *spiritual* Israel or even as the *true* Israel, to distinguish it from the former.

These two Israels are not two totally distinct groups, with some Jews belonging to one and some to the other. In fact, *all* Jews belong to the first group, and only *some* to the second. I.e., those in the latter group actually belong to both. The relationship between the two Israels may be depicted not by two side-by-side circles, but by two concentric circles, thus:

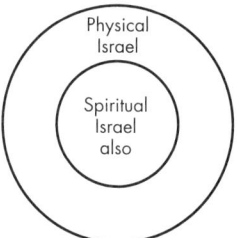

We should note that this passage has in view Jewish people only, and thus the "spiritual Israel" in this verse includes only Jewish believers (as the concentric circles indicate). Other NT teaching warrants the conclusion that in this dispensation the church as a whole, including believing Jews and believing Gentiles, may be called the true Israel or spiritual Israel. (See Rom 9:23-30; 11:17-24; Gal 6:16.) This may be depicted thus:

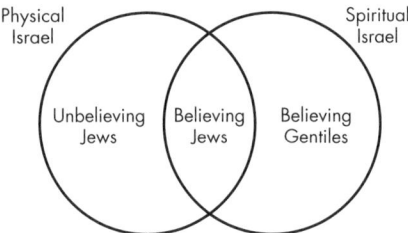

This is not the point of 9:6b, however. See Moo, 573-574.

A key word in this second sentence in 9:6b is γάρ (*gar*), "for" or "because." This word indicates that 6a is explained by 6b, i.e., the latter is the *reason why* the former is true. God's promises concerning Israel have not failed, *because* there are really *two* Israels.

Everyone seems to agree that this is how the two parts of the verse are meant to be connected. There is a serious disagreement, though, as to the *nature* and *recipients* of the promises included in the phrase "God's word." Some take God's word (of promise) to be referring specifically to his promises of *salvation*, or "all his promises relative to the salvation of Israel" (Lard, 298). How can one say, then, that this promise of salvation has not failed, in view of the *lostness* of most Jews (v. 3)? Here is how the point about the two Israels enters in, according to this view: the promises of salvation were made not to ethnic Israel as a whole, but only to spiritual Israel, the remnant (Lard, 298).

In my judgment this misses Paul's point completely. "God's word" does indeed refer to "the promises made to Israel and its patriarchs" (Fitzmyer, 559), but the main reference is to the promises made to ethnic Israel as a whole, especially the covenant promises. made to the patriarchs regarding God's messianic purpose for the nation collectively and including the accompanying privileges that served as a means to this end. In other words, God's promises to ethnic Israel included everything named in vv. 4-5, and every one of these promises was kept.

But did not God's OT promises include forgiveness and eternal life? Certainly, but here is where the distinction between the two Israels is crucial. Personal salvation was not among the unconditionally guaranteed promises enjoyed by the entire nation of Israel. This blessing was promised only to *spiritual* Israel, the believing remnant. The existence of the two Israels thus resolves the dilemma of vv. 1-5. "All who are descended from Israel" experience the covenant blessings of vv. 4-5, but only the true Israel escapes the curse of eternal damnation. The promises of salvation applied only to the latter. This had always been God's plan; this is the way it happened; thus his word did not fail.

3. Ethnic Israel Exists by God's Sovereign Choice (9:7-13)

The subject of these next seven verses — this is very important — is not spiritual Israel but ethnic Israel. See my introductory summary of 9:6-29 above. The import of v. 6 is that God is free to use the nation of Israel for service without giving them salvation. This paragraph (7-13) responds to expected resistance to this idea (❖ II:72-73).

Thus we must not interpret vv. 7-13 as further elaboration upon the distinction between the two Israels in v. 6, as if these verses are describing *how* or *why* God made that distinction. Nor are these verses somehow meant to *justify* this distinction, contrary to Moo's view (570-571). They are in fact making a point that is separate from 9:6b. The progression of thought from 6b to 7a is thus: Not all members of physical Israel are also members of spiritual Israel; *neither* are they called the children of Abraham just because they are physically descended from Abraham. Thus v. 7 begins a separate thought. The paragraph through v. 13 focuses on the origin and role of ethnic Israel as such, explaining the manner in which God called them into his service. The main point is that this is *different* from the way he calls individuals to salvation. Only when the two are confused do questions about God's faithfulness to Israel arise.

The Choice of Isaac (9:7-9)

9:7 Nor because they are his descendants are they all Abraham's children. This verse begins Paul's response to the erroneous assumption of the Jews that just because they were descendants of Abraham, God was obligated to treat them in a certain way. Paul's point is that this is not true even with regard to Israel's role of service in God's historical plan of redemption, much less their participation in eternal life (❖ II:73-74).

The most common error here is the assumption that v. 7 is parallel to v. 6b, which it is not. Spiritual Israel is not in view in v. 7, thus neither term ("seed," "children") applies to it in this context. The distinction rather is between *all* the physical descendants of Abraham, including those born to Hagar (Gen 16:15) and Keturah (Gen 25:1-5) as well as to Sarah, and *only* those physical descendants of Abraham born through Sarah and Isaac (Gen 21:1-3). Only the latter may be called Abraham's true seed or children. Just being physically descended from Abraham did not establish someone as the "seed of Abraham" named in the Abrahamic covenant (Gen 15:5,18; 17:6-8; 22:17-18). Something more than physical descent is required, as v. 8 specifies.

On the contrary, "It is through Isaac that your offspring will be reckoned." God made this promise to Abraham as he was explaining to him why the patriarch should not hesitate to sever his connections with his son Ishmael (Gen 21:8-21). The sense of it is, "Through Isaac *alone*, not through Ishmael or any other possible progeny, will come the seed specified in my covenant with you."

The word translated "reckoned" literally means "called." Here it does not have the theological connotation of "called unto salvation." At most it may refer to God's call to *service*, i.e., only children born to Isaac will be called upon to continue the covenant responsibilities and receive the covenant blessings given to Abraham. Only those connected with Isaac will be called (named, counted as, recognized as, acknowledged as, reckoned to be) Abraham's true covenant seed. The only thing to remember is that this covenant did not include the promise of salvation as such (❖ II:75).

9:8 In other words, it is not the natural children who are God's children, but it is the children of the promise who are regarded as Abraham's offspring. "In other words" ("this is to say," "this means") introduces the basis upon which God chose Isaac. Though this may well be a general principle that God applies in the context of salvation, that is not how the statement functions here. In this case it relates to the choice of Isaac and thus to the manner in which Israel came into existence.

"The natural children" is literally "the children of the flesh," or children born by purely natural means. It is similar to the expression in 1:3 and 4:1 (κατὰ σάρκα, *kata sarka*, "according to the flesh"), where "flesh" is used in a morally neutral sense. "The children of the promise" refers to God's promise to Abraham and Sarah concerning the birth of Isaac, as v. 9 shows. They are "children of promise" because they are "born as a result of a promise" (Morris, 354). These children of the promise are identified as "God's children" and as "Abraham's offspring." The latter expression is a loose but accurate paraphrase for one word, "seed" (*sperma*). "Regarded" is λογίζομαι (*logizomai*), the same word used for the concept of imputation almost a dozen times in Rom 4. Here it simply means "considered to be, counted as, looked upon as." It is equivalent to "reckoned" ("called") in v. 7.

It is easy to see why many take this verse to refer to the distinction between physical Israel and spiritual Israel, and thus take it as referring to the way God elects some to salvation while rejecting others. "God's children" and "children of the promise," as well as the verb *logizomai*, all have salvation connotations in other contexts. (See Moo, 577.) Indeed, we may agree that there is a significant analogy between the way God chose Isaac for service and the way he chooses individuals for salvation. The concept of *promise* is the main similarity. See Gal 3:14,16-22,29; 4:23.

We must remember, though, that such terminology does not always connote the eternal salvation of individuals. The covenant made with Abraham (and Isaac and Jacob) was primarily a series of promises, culminating in the promised coming of the Messiah (Acts 13:23,32; 26:6; Rom 15:8; Heb 8:6; 11:9). Thus it is appropriate to think of Israel as a whole as "children of the promise." The expression "children of God" is surprisingly rare in Scripture. Sometimes it refers to those in a saving relationship with God (Rom 8:16,21; Phil 2:15); at least once it refers to the Jews as a nation (John 11:52; see also Deut 14:1 and Ps 82:6, "sons" of God). It is not inappropriate to see the latter sense here.

We conclude, then, in accord with the present context, that it is ethnic Israel that is here identified as "God's children" and "children of the promise," and that these terms describe Israel's role as the special family through whom God brought the Messiah into the world. This is consistent with 9:4, which says that the Israelites received "the adoption as sons" and "the promises."

What is Paul's point? He is simply reminding Israel that their status as God's children and Abraham's seed was not something they possessed by an accident of nature, by inherent right, or by meritorious acquisition. It was theirs only by God's gracious choice and promise. God alone controls the selection process and the terms of selection. In this case God demonstrated his sovereign control by specifying that Abraham's covenant family would come into existence through one whose own existence was dependent upon nothing except the promise and power of God.

9:9 For this was how the promise was stated: "At the appointed time I will return, and Sarah will have a son." Paul's statement of the promise concerning Isaac is a combination of thoughts from Gen 18:10 and 18:14. God spoke these words during a glorious visitation (a theophany) to Abraham and Sarah (Gen 18:1-15). "At the appointed time" is usually taken to mean "about this time next year." "I will return" is literally "I will come." This does not necessarily mean that God was promising another visible manifestation of himself to Abraham and Sarah a year later; no such theophany is recorded in Genesis. It means only that God would come upon Abraham and Sarah in his providential power, opening Sarah's barren and "dead" womb (Gen 11:30; 18:11; Rom 4:19; Heb 11:11-12) and causing her to conceive contrary to all natural means.

This verse is important because it shows us that Paul's main concern here is not the general promise of salvation made to all who will believe in God's mercy, but rather the specific event of the choice of Isaac rather than Ishmael as the one who would carry on the covenant line of his father Abraham — which was a call to service, not to salvation. In fact, v. 8 says that the Israelites were "the children of *the* promise," meaning the specific promise identified in v. 9.

The first part of this verse specifically reads, "For the word [λόγος, *logos*] of promise is this." The term *logos* ties this in with 9:6a, where Paul says, "It is not as though God's word [*logos*] has failed." This shows that he is mainly concerned here with the charge that somehow God's words of promise to the *nation* of Israel had failed. The promises are those which establish Israel as the covenant nation, and as words of *promise* they establish God as the one who is in complete control of Israel's tenure as the covenant people.

Thus there is no reason for anyone to think that God has lost control of the situation with respect to Israel. Though most individual Israelites are accursed, God has still kept every promise he ever made to them as a people, as is evidenced by the way he kept one of the very first promises that brought them into existence in the first place.

The Choice of Jacob (9:10-13)

These next four verses show how God chose a particular son of Isaac to be the one who would carry on his covenant purposes. The debate continues, of course, as to whether this incident is intended to describe the way God chooses individuals for salvation. Does God's choice of Jacob demonstrate the way he distinguishes true spiritual Israel from ethnic Israel as a whole, or does it tell us how he chooses those who will serve him in the carrying out of his redemptive purposes? In my judgment *only the latter point is being made here*. The focus is exactly the same as in vv. 7-9, namely, the sovereignty of God in establishing the nation of Israel.

9:10 Not only that, but Rebekah's children had one and the same father, our father Isaac. This truth does more than simply repeat the lesson from Isaac and Ishmael; it strengthens it and clarifies it. Regarding the earlier example, someone might try to argue that the natural circumstances surrounding the births of Abraham's (first) two sons were so different that the choice of Isaac was no surprise. After all, the boys had different mothers, and Ishmael's mother was not even Abraham's true wife. But this cannot be said of Jacob and Esau. As twins, they were the product not only of the same mother, but of the same pregnancy. In addition, Esau was the first-born twin. Thus according to every natural expectation, Esau should have been selected as the covenant seed. The fact that God chose Jacob for this role shows unequivocally that his election of those who will serve his purposes need not be conditioned upon any human circumstance or qualification.

The grammar and syntax of this section are notoriously difficult, but the NIV generally sorts it out quite well (❖ II:78). It is worth noting that based upon the underlying Greek some give the words "from one" a dual force: not only were Jacob and Esau conceived from *one father*, namely, "our father Isaac," but also from just *one act of intercourse*. The point is to minimize any natural distinctions between Esau and Jacob.

9:11 Yet, before the twins were born or had done anything good or bad.... See the NRSV: "Even before they had been born" (❖ II:79). The point is that God had already made his decision as to his choice between Jacob and Esau, and had already announced it to Rebekah (v. 12) before anything had happened from the human side that might have any possible bearing upon that choice. "Before the twins were born" indicates that the birth order would be irrelevant. Before they "had done anything good or bad" shows that their future conduct was not a factor in the selection.

To introduce divine foreknowledge into the picture here, as some non-Calvinists do, misses the point. Certainly the omniscient God had a complete foreknowledge of the entire lives of both the twins, including which would be born first (v. 12b). But that is not only irrelevant; it tends also to obscure the very point Paul is making, namely, that the choice had nothing to do with either the works or the faith of either twin, whether foreknown or not. God wanted Jacob and not Esau, and that's that.

But someone will say that this sounds a lot like unconditional election, which is a main doctrine of Calvinism, and that we need the concept of foreknowledge here in order to avoid it. I will reply that the choice of Jacob over Esau *was* a case of unconditional election. But this is not a concession to Calvinism, because Paul is not talking about election to *salvation*, but to *service*.

Calvinists themselves usually fail to understand this point. They assume that God's choice of Jacob and his rejection of Esau had to do with the twins' eternal destinies, thus seeing this passage as biblical proof of the Calvinist doctrine of unconditional election (❧II:79-80).

Such statements are true as they apply to God's selection of Jacob for covenant service, and they may be true of election to service in general; but the context does not warrant applying them to election to salvation as some do.

—in order that God's purpose in election might stand. This is the first part of a parenthetical comment (vv. 11b-12a), in which Paul is explaining why God's choice of Jacob (and thus of the nation of Israel) was unconditional (v. 11a), namely, so that his purpose according to election might not fail. What was God's purpose for choosing one or the other of these twins? It was the same purpose he had for choosing Abraham in the first place, then Isaac. It was the purpose expressed when God first made his covenant with Abraham: "All peoples on earth will be blessed through you" (Gen 12:3). This purpose was fulfilled with the birth of the Messiah (9:5b; Acts 13:32-33).

This redemptive purpose was too important to be allowed to depend on the vicissitudes of human behavior. Thus God made it clear from the very beginning that he was going to accomplish his purpose through this particular family regardless of their individual decisions and the direction of their personal piety. He showed this by the very way in which he chose Jacob over Esau, i.e., unconditionally. This means that even if he had chosen Esau over Jacob, he would still have accomplished his purpose.

How this applies to the issue under discussion should be clear. At stake is God's faithfulness in his dealings with the Jews. How could he shower them with the covenant blessings of 9:4-5 and allow them to be lost at the same time? The answer is that the covenant did not include a promise of individual salvation for all Jews; it was limited to God's special use of the nation of Israel as the conduit for bringing Christ into the world. From the beginning God determined that he was going to do this, regardless of whether any individual Jews were saved. Just as "God's purpose in election" did not depend upon the spiritual status of the twin he chose from Rebekah's womb, so it did not depend upon the salvation status of the Jews in Paul's day (❧II:79).

9:12 . . . not by works but by him who calls. "Not by works" simply explains or restates "before the twins . . . had done anything good or bad" (9:11) (❁ II:81), and (as we have seen) this refers to Jacob's unconditional election for service, not salvation. God's choice of Jacob had nothing to do with any superior qualifications he might have possessed, and it was in spite of any of his potential weaknesses or character flaws. It was simply God's sovereign decision to choose him and use him, and this was a paradigm representing his choice of the nation of Israel as such.

This entire phrase modifies 9:11b; it tells us why it is that God's purpose in election will stand, namely, *not* by virtue of the accomplishments, faith, or faithfulness of the ones called to fulfill that purpose, but solely by the invincible power of the God who called them.

Contrary to some interpretations, the *calling* Paul mentions here has nothing to do with salvation. "It is election to privilege that is in mind, not eternal salvation," as Morris says (356). The terminology of calling is not used exclusively for calling to salvation in the NT, but on several occasions refers to calling to service. See Heb 5:4; 11:8; Matt 4:21; Rom 1:1; 1 Cor 1:1; Gal 1:15. Jesus himself says, "For many are called, but few are chosen" (Matt 22:14, NASB). The "many" who are called are probably the nation of Israel as a whole, which was called into God's service; and the "few" who are chosen are probably the spiritual Israel of Rom 9:6b. This verse from Matthew, especially in its context of the parable of the wedding feast, definitely helps us to understand the nature of the calling to which Paul refers here in 9:12 (❁ II:81-82).

—she was told, "The older will serve the younger." This picks up the thought from v. 11a: before the twins were even born or had done anything good or wrong, God had already told Rebekah which one he was choosing for his covenant purposes. The quote is directly from Gen 25:23 (LXX). The "older" is Esau, who was born first; "the younger" is Jacob.

Commentators argue over whether this divine decree refers to Jacob and Esau as individuals or to the two nations established by each. From Jacob, of course, came Israel; and from Esau came the Edomites. God's full statement to Rebekah, recorded in Gen 25:23, shows that he originally had the two nations in mind: "Two nations are in your womb, and two peoples from within you will be separated; one people will be stronger than the other, and the older will serve the younger." That is probably the main point here. The OT does not record any instance where Esau personally assumed the role of a servant to Jacob, but it does refer to times when the Edomites were in a kind of servitude to Israel or Judah (see Num 24:18-19; 2 Sam 8:14; 1 Kgs 11:15-16; 2 Kgs 14:7).

This is not a serious issue except for those who want to read election of individuals to salvation into this context; they may be inclined to limit Paul's reference to Jacob and Esau to these men as individuals. Even if this is the case, though, election to service (not salvation) is Paul's point. The language of servanthood is simply a way of indicating which of the twins would be favored by God and chosen to be the covenant son, and which would not.

9:13 Just as it is written: "Jacob I loved, but Esau I hated." This quotation, from Mal 1:2, continues the thought already elaborated in vv. 10-12 and carries it a step further. By introducing it with the formulaic "it is written," Paul presents it as a proof text for the point he is making. The main idea is that God's choice of Jacob and his rejection of Esau were based not on something within these men but upon something within God himself, i.e., his own love and hate.

Two main issues arise here. One is the common question of whether God's love and hate relate to Jacob's and Esau's temporal fortunes or to their eternal destinies. Consistent with their approach to the passage as a whole, many see God's love as the basis for his unconditional election of Jacob to salvation, and God's hatred as the basis for his unconditional reprobation of Esau to hell. This is then generalized into the Calvinist doctrine of unconditional election as such (see Moo, 585-586).

As we have already seen, however, the subject here is not individual salvation but election to service. This election is unconditional to be sure, but it is election to *service* nonetheless. In reference to this verse we can see this is the case by examining the context of the quotation as it appears originally in Malachi. There it is clear that the main point is not God's attitude toward and treatment of the two brothers themselves, but of the two nations springing from them. Even more significantly, the consequences of these contrasting attitudes are not eternal destinies but different earthly fortunes.

The other main issue is the meaning of "Esau I hated." In what sense did God "hate" Esau? Some say Paul is merely employing a semitic hyperbole, in which the strong term "hate," when used in comparative conjunction with "love," sometimes simply means "to love less." Others agree this is a valid meaning of "hate," but say that it does not apply here. They equate love with election, and see "hatred" as God's nonemotional decision to reject Esau (decline to choose him) and just set him aside. Still others believe, and I agree, that neither of these explanations is strong enough. Murray correctly observes that the treatment of Esau (Edom) in Mal 1:1-5 can hardly be called just a less intense love or even nonselection. It is "a positive judgment, not merely the absence of blessing." It is "disfavour, disapprobation, displeasure," a true "holy hate" (2:22-23).

It is difficult to think of this "holy hate," even in the form of temporal destruction as described in Mal 1:1-5, as unconditional and in no sense related to Edom's conduct. Here is where I believe the thought of 9:13 goes a step beyond the basic point of 9:10-12. The main point throughout is God's sovereignty in his selection of those who will carry out his purposes. His initial choice of Jacob over Esau stresses this sovereignty, even to the point of unconditionality. This quotation seems to show, though, that God's subsequent historical treatment of their respective nations *was* conditioned to some extent upon their conduct.

In OT references to Edom it is made clear that God's wrath is divine vengeance against Edom because of its wicked treatment of Israel (❂ II:84). Thus even if God's original choice of Jacob and rejection of Esau were totally unconditional, his subsequent treatment of them did have respect to their conduct. This does not contradict Paul's basic premise regarding the manner of God's original choice of Jacob (and the people of Israel); it simply adds another dimension to his continuing historical relationship with this nation.

The overall main point of this section (7-13) is still the sovereign freedom of God to set up his plan of redemption as he chooses. He can choose whomever he pleases, whether individuals or nations, to carry out his redemptive purposes, apart from their own choice or cooperation if necessary. His chosen servants do not have to be a part of "spiritual Israel" to be of service to him, and he is not obligated to reward them with eternal life just because they have played their intended part in the messianic drama. There is no inherent connection between service and salvation (❂ II:84-85).

B. GOD'S RIGHT TO CHOOSE AND USE PEOPLE WITHOUT SAVING THEM (9:14-18)

As we have said earlier, Paul's main purpose in Rom 9 is to affirm God's sovereign right to choose any individual or group for *service* without at the same time choosing them for *salvation*. The emphasis is not simply upon God's right to choose some while rejecting others; it is also upon the *manner* in which God makes his choices (❂ II:85). God is free to choose people for service in whatever way he wishes.

This present paragraph lies at the heart of this argument. In the previous paragraph Paul demonstrates that this is the way God works by citing the concrete examples of Isaac and Jacob. Now in vv. 14-18 he affirms the general principle of divine sovereignty that underlies all such specific examples: "I will have mercy on whom I have mercy, and I will have compassion on whom I have compassion" (v. 15).

This is not an argument in the sense that Paul is attempting to justify God's actions before the bar of reason. He is not trying to defend God by appealing to some cosmic code of conduct that is independent of God and to which God himself is bound. Rather, by citing the general principle as stated in OT Scripture, Paul is simply showing that God's choices of Isaac and Jacob — and therefore of the nation of Israel — were consistent with his own nature and with his own plainly stated principles of action. This is the only sense in which this paragraph may be called a theodicy.

Throughout this study of Rom 9 we must keep in mind that the main issue is *the status of physical Israel*. I.e., if they have been chosen for covenant service, why are they not saved? Thus in 9:14 the question ("Is God unjust?") is not about those whom God has *not* chosen (such as Ishmael and Esau), but about those whom he *has* chosen, i.e., Isaac and Jacob — as forerunners of the nation of Israel. Like Isaac and Jacob, physical Israel did not receive its role in God's plan through personal achievement but solely through God's unconditional choice (vv. 15-16). Therefore it does not have any claim on God's saving grace, and can be chosen *and hardened* at the same time, like Pharaoh (vv. 17-18).

Again we must insist that the issue here is not how God chooses individuals for salvation, contrary to the common Calvinist effort to use this text as a proof for unconditional election (❂ II:86).

1. God's Righteousness Is Challenged (9:14)

9:14 What then shall we say? Is God unjust? Not at all! Paul dialogues thus with himself when he knows he has just said something that is likely to be misunderstood or to raise objections or false conclusions in the minds of his hearers. "What then shall we say?" is parallel to 3:5; 6:1,15; 7:7. "Not at all!" is μὴ γένοιτο (*mē genoito*), the very strong negative expression frequently used by Paul; see 3:4 above. The question itself, "Is God unjust?" is stated in such a way in the Greek (using the negative particle *mē*) that a negative answer is implied and expected. Also, "unjust" is actually a noun, ἀδικία (*adikia*). The NASB has a literal translation: "There is no injustice with God, is there?"

The term *adikia* has been used several times already, always for human unrighteousness or wickedness (1:18,29; 2:8; 3:5; 6:13). Righteousness as such means conformity to the proper norm or standard. That God is righteous does not mean that he conforms to some norm outside himself, since such a norm does not exist. God's essence is itself the highest and ultimate norm, even for his own actions. To say, then, that God is righteous means that his actions always conform to his own essence. He never goes against himself and never acts in a way that is inconsistent with or contradictory to his own nature. He is always faithful to himself.

Thus to say that God is unrighteous or unjust is to accuse him of doing something that violates his very nature — which is impossible. Since it is his nature to be true (3:4) and never to lie (Titus 1:2), his righteousness thus requires that he always be faithful and true to his word. In the context of Rom 9, to suggest that God may be unrighteous or unjust is simply to raise the question again as to whether or not God's word of promise to Israel has failed (9:6a). "The question is — Is God *righteous*? — i.e., has he been true to his covenanted word?"

We must remember that the issue here is the status of national Israel. Thus the objection stated in 9:14 is one that would most likely be raised by the Jews regarding God's treatment of them as a nation. It is a mistake to see this question as something that relates only to the immediately preceding section, and especially to limit it to the rejection of Ishmael and Esau. It relates rather to everything Paul has said in vv. 1-13. "What then shall we say — about the way God chose and has been using Israel? Has his treatment of the nation been unjust? Has his word failed as some seem to think? No! Absolutely not!" Paul's answer has the intensity and the content of Abraham's conviction in Gen 18:25, "Will not the Judge of all the earth do right?"

Why is God's treatment of Israel not unjust? Because, as 9:6b says, there really are *two* Israels, and God is not obliged to treat them in the same way. Specifically, he is free to use the nation as a whole for his covenant purposes, while limiting salvation only to those who trust his saving promises. Ultimately, the question raised in v. 14 is a statement of the implied objection that underlies this whole chapter, and the answer given in vv. 15-18 is really no different from what Paul has already discussed (❧ II:88).

2. God's Sovereignty in Election for Service (9:15-16)

9:15 For he says to Moses, "I will have mercy on whom I have mercy, and I will have compassion on whom I have compassion." Here the connecting word "for" (*gar*) introduces the cause or reason for the preceding statement. I.e., "No, God is *not* unjust, *because*"—look what he says to Moses! But how does God's statement to Moses show that God is not unjust? The best answer is that Paul believes that the *quoting of OT Scripture* is sufficient to establish his point. (See also v. 17.) Since the main source of the objection in v. 14 would be the Jews, refuting it from their own Scripture would be especially effective.

How then does the Jews' own Scripture answer the question in v. 14? No, God has not acted unjustly in his choice of Isaac, in his choice of Jacob, and especially in his choice of the nation of Israel, because Scripture itself records his sovereign right to choose anyone he pleases according to his own terms. He has simply acted in accord with his established word.

The divine statement cited by Paul was spoken "to Moses." It was part of God's reply when Moses requested to see the very essence of God: "Then Moses said, 'Now show me your glory'" (Exod 33:18).

Paul's citation of this statement by God raises several questions. First, does it apply to the eternal salvation of individuals or to temporal election for service? Second, how does it relate to the overall argument of ch. 9? Third, why is the statement only *positive*, with no corresponding negative reference to exclusion from God's mercy?

The most crucial (and by now, most familiar) issue, of course, is whether the statement applies to God's choice for salvation or for service (❧ II:89). In answering the question every interpreter must show how his view fits into the overall context. But since this statement in 9:15 is a quotation from the OT (Exod 33:19b), this raises the question as to which context should be used to determine whether Paul is referring to salvation or service: Exod 33 or Rom 9?

Actually, both contexts are important, and in the end they yield the same result regarding the issue of salvation or service.

Why did God make this statement to Moses in its original context? What was its intended application? I.e., *to whom* was the statement originally intended to apply: to Moses himself, or to the nation of Israel? Many have concluded the former, i.e., that God was telling Moses that he would be the recipient of God's blessing, specifically, that God would grant his request. This would happen not because of any meritorious accomplishment on Moses' part, however, but solely because of God's sovereign choice (❂ II:90).

In my judgment this view is correct, being true to the context and to the terminology used (as will be explained shortly). But I have concluded that this is not the whole picture, and that the statement in 33:19b must be taken also in the broader context of the immediate crisis concerning Israel, and thus also applies to the nation as a whole. Only then is it relevant to Paul's argument in Rom 9.

Israel's episode with the golden calf, as an act of great sin and even apostasy, certainly raised the question of the salvation of those who were involved (Exod 32:25-35). But it also raised the question of Israel's preservation as the people chosen to serve God's covenant purposes. Moses was very concerned with the latter, especially when God told the people that from that point on he would not be personally present among them on their journey (33:3-5). The visible presence of God had up to that time been a crucial factor in their lives (33:7-11), and Moses argued before God that without his continuing visible presence among them they would not really know if they were still God's unique people, nor would anyone else know (33:12-16).

At this point in the narrative the issue is not the eternal salvation of individual Jews, but Israel's preservation as a nation and her continuing role in God's plan. In reference to God's threat to withdraw his presence, Moses reminds him, "Remember that this nation is your people" (33:13).

In the face of Moses' intercessory prayer God relents and tells Moses that he will indeed once more bestow his personal presence upon them (33:15,17). This is the point at which Moses makes his bold request, "Now show me your glory" (33:18), i.e., as an assurance that he and Israel had been restored to God's favor. What follows is the marvelous event of God's unique revelation to Moses, both visibly and audibly (33:19–34:7). Moses' response is a final and humble plea for the nation's reinstatement as God's "inheritance" (34:8-9), though they obviously did not deserve it. God concludes the matter by reestablishing his covenant with Moses and with Israel (34:10-28).

The point is that the critical statement in 33:19b refers not only to God's sovereignty in his choice of which prayers to answer (according to which he granted Moses' request), but also to his sovereignty in his choice of those who will serve him in the accomplishment of his plan of redemption. That God answered

Moses' prayer and showed himself to Moses in a unique way was symbolic of his intention to relent and once more to grace the nation with his presence.

In this light we can see why Paul chose to quote Exod 33:19b in support of his own argument that God's word toward Israel has not failed and therefore that he cannot be accused of injustice in his treatment of them. The issue in Exod 33 and Rom 9 is very much the same: not the salvation of individuals, but the role of the nation in God's plan. The point is that God is free to choose whomever he will, according to whatever conditions he pleases.

One main problem that many will have with this interpetation is the meaning of the terms "have mercy" and "have compassion." Do not these terms refer to eternal salvation? Not necessarily. These terms and their Hebrew counterparts have a variety of uses, depending upon context.

The verb for "have compassion": (רחם, *raham*) in Exod 33:19b and οἰκτείρω (*oikteirō*) and its cognates refer to the attitude of compassion, mercy, or pity upon someone in any kind of need. It *can* refer to salvation, but it can also refer to compassion expressed only in temporal blessings without any reference to spiritual salvation. For the latter see, e.g., Isa 14:1; Jer 13:14; 21:7; 33:26; 42:12; Ezek 39:25; Zech 10:6.

The word for "have mercy" is used much more often in both testaments. In Hebrew the word refers to saving grace in some contexts; but that is actually one of its lesser meanings. Basically it means to show favor, to be merciful and kind, or to bestow a blessing. Thus in the Exodus account God could very well be simply saying to Moses, "All right, Moses; I will answer your prayer this time; but remember that it is my sovereign prerogative to determine which prayers I will answer and which I will deny." In light of its OT usage it is completely consistent with the meaning of "have mercy" to interpret Exod 33:19b as referring to God's sovereign choice to answer Moses' prayer and to spare the people of Israel and to continue to use them as his servant nation (❃ II:93).

In Rom 9:15 the Greek word translated "have mercy" also has a range of meanings other than saving mercy. A few times it does refer to salvation. More often, though, it refers to showing compassion to the poor, sick, or needy (see Matt 9:27; 15:22; Rom 12:8; Phil 2:27). Most significantly, it is sometimes used to refer to God's choosing or calling someone for service, specifically, Paul's call to apostleship: 1 Cor 7:25; 2 Cor 4:1. This last meaning is the one Paul intends in 9:15, I believe; and it has special reference to God's choice of the nation of Israel to play a crucial role in his covenant purposes. In other words, when God chooses anyone for service, it is the bestowal of a great favor upon that person (or nation), whether that person (or nation) is saved or not.

The next question is how Paul's citation of Exod 33:19b relates to his overall argument in Rom 9. The answer should be obvious. At stake is the righteousness or faithfulness of God in relation to Israel. Does not his choosing of Israel for covenant service imply that all Jewish people should be saved? No, says Paul; as in his choice of Isaac and Jacob, God chooses as it pleases him. He is free to choose *whomever* he likes. He can choose and use people, including the whole nation of Israel, whether they are saved or not. Salvation is neither a prerequisite for nor a necessary result of such a choice. The quote from Exod 33:19b states this as a general principle; the example of Pharaoh in 9:17-18 is a specific example.

The last question about v. 15 is, why does the statement refer only to a positive choice, i.e., one grounded in mercy and compassion? Why is there no reference to God's sovereign rejection of others? This question is meaningful only when one concludes that the passage is talking about the eternal salvation of individuals rather than election to service. For those who hold the former view, the issue is whether or not there is such a thing as double predestination, i.e., both election to salvation and reprobation to damnation (❂ II:94-95). If this passage is indeed discussing election to salvation, there can be no doubt that the double-predestination folks are correct. To say that God is free to show saving mercy unconditionally on whomever he chooses definitely implies that he is free to withhold saving mercy unconditionally from whomever he chooses, and his decision to do the former necessarily entails his decision to do the latter. Such a decision to withhold mercy is in effect a decision to send these nonrecipients to hell, with all the resulting negative implications for the nature of God.

This is why it is so important to see that the issue is not a kind of sovereignty by which God chooses some for salvation and condemns others to hell. Rather, the issue in vv. 7-13 is his sovereignty in choosing one (Isaac, Jacob) *rather than* another (Ishmael, Esau) for a role of service, and the issue in the chapter as a whole is his sovereignty in choosing and using the nation of Israel apart from the promise of individual salvation. Such choosing of Isaac, Jacob, and national Israel was a matter of (temporal) mercy and favor, but the nonchoosing of Ishmael and Esau was not *ipso facto* an act of eternal condemnation. Those who were not so chosen are just no longer relevant to the discussion. Thus to have added "I will condemn whomever I will condemn" would have been irrelevant and beside the point, not to mention untrue. Even the references to Pharaoh and hardening in 9:17-18 are not about condemnation as such.

9:16 It does not, therefore, depend on man's desire or effort, but on God's mercy. The issue here is not the eternal salvation of individuals (❂ II:95). Rather, the main point is that God's final decision to select someone for his covenant service is based not upon anything in the person himself, but entirely and only upon the divine purpose. If it is God's purpose to choose someone, he will do so, whether that person is willing or unwilling, or whether he is prepared or not. Of course, God would rather use a willing person who will devote his entire strength to God's cause. Also, for those tasks that require someone who is especially gifted and trained, God will prepare such a person through his providential control of life circumstances. Examples are Moses and Paul.

But for other tasks he can use those who are unwilling and even hostile toward him. Examples are Balaam (Num 22-24) and, of course, Pharaoh (9:17-18). Many in Israel were in this last category.

The thought of this verse is not different from that of v. 15 and is set forth as a logical conclusion ("therefore") from it. The subject of v. 16 ("it") is not stated but must be supplied from the context (❂ II:96). Whatever the subject is, it *depends* "on God's mercy;" Therefore, contrary to some, the subject cannot be mercy itself. In keeping with our overall interpretation, I believe the subject is simply "being chosen for God's service."

Being thus chosen does not depend upon human desire or willing. Jacob is a perfect example; he was chosen before he was born and contrary to the will of his father Isaac (Gen 27). Nor does it depend on human effort. "Effort" is literally "the running one" or "the one who runs." This refers to "moral attainment" (Piper, *Justification*, 153) or vigorous, purposeful striving as in the running of a race. This applies, of course, to election to service in general, and specifically to God's purpose for Israel (❂ II:96).

Such election for service is a matter of "the one who shows mercy, namely, God," as the text literally says, and as v. 15 says.

3. God's Purposes Can Be Served by the Unsaved (9:17-18)

9:17 For the Scripture says to Pharaoh: "I raised you up for this very purpose, that I might display my power in you and that my name might be proclaimed in all the earth." Paul takes this quote directly from Exod 9:16. Obviously "the Scripture" did not say this to Pharaoh. God himself, through Moses, spoke these words to him (❂ II:97).

Once again the sentence begins with "for" (*gar*). This *gar* does not give a reason for what is stated in v. 16. Rather, it is parallel to the *gar* in v. 15, with each relating equally to v. 14. Thus vv. 15-16 and vv. 17-18 are two distinct points, each confirming that God's treatment of the Jews is not unjust (v. 14) by citing data from the OT (❂ II:97).

The point of this entire section is that God is free to choose whomever he pleases, including the Jews, for roles of service (❂ II:97-98). But the specific question here is if God is going to use the Jews for service, is he not thereby obligated to save them? This is the point addressed in vv. 17-18. Here Paul shows from the OT that God's sovereignty in election for service includes the prerogative of choosing and using someone without saving them. His premiere example is Pharaoh. Not only was he chosen ("shown mercy"), but he was also hardened (confirmed in his unbelief).

A very common approach to this text is to take Pharaoh as an example of *reprobation* (condemnation to hell), in contrast with Moses, who is an example of election to *salvation*. Verses 15-18 are taken as parallel to the two parts of v. 13. "Jacob I loved" is equivalent to the positive example of Moses in vv. 15-

16, while "Esau I hated" corresponds to the negative example of Pharaoh in vv. 17-18 (Moo, 593; Morris, 360). According to Pendleton (MP, 398), Moses and Pharaoh are a pair between whom God chooses, just as he chose between Isaac and Ishmael, and between Jacob and Esau. And in this "third case he granted favor to Moses, and *meted out punishment* to Pharaoh."

I believe this approach is a very serious error, not only because the context is not dealing with the question of eternal destinies, but also because it is not warranted by what the text specifically says about Pharaoh and the others. For one thing, Moses is not introduced here as the object of election, whether for service or for salvation. He is simply the one to whom God spoke the statement in 9:15 and is not being used as an example of anything. Thus it is not proper to speak of a "contrast between Moses and Pharaoh." For another thing, there is no parallel between Esau and Pharaoh. Esau was not chosen for anything; but Pharaoh *was* chosen for a significant role, a fact that is crucial for Paul's point.

God's rejection and punishment of Pharaoh are indeed significant, but *not* as a parallel with Ishmael and Esau, and not even as a contrast with Isaac, Jacob, or Moses. They are significant only insofar as they make Pharaoh an exact parallel of the nation of Israel itself. God chose both Israel and Pharaoh for a role of service, and he used both of them not only *despite* their hardness of heart, but even *because* of it. Pharaoh is not an example of God's freedom to *reject* whom he will, contrary to Godet (352-353). Rather, he is an example of God's freedom to elect some for service while at the same time withholding salvation from them. See also King Cyrus (Isa 44:28-45:7) (❂II:99).

In the affirmation "I raised you up," God is saying that he exercised his sovereign prerogative to choose Pharaoh for a very specific role in his redemptive plan. "For this very purpose" stresses the fact that Pharaoh was being used by God, even when it seemed that he was most emphatically opposing God. He was carrying out the divine purpose in and through his hardened heart.

God's purpose for Pharaoh was twofold: to be an instrument for displaying God's power and for proclaiming God's name in all the earth. The power to which God refers is not the power to save individuals from their sins (1:16), but the power to overthrow opposing earthly rulers and their so-called deities, and thereby the power to deliver his people from Egyptian slavery and oppression. How did God display this power "in" or "through" Pharaoh? By hardening his heart so that he continued to refuse to let the people go, thereby giving God the opportunity to add plague upon plague all the way to the climactic death of the Egyptian firstborn. What God needed from Pharaoh was not his immediate acquiescence but his continuing resistance. This he achieved by his providential power to harden the Egyptian's heart (*GRu*, 203), thus providing the occasion for the public and overwhelming display of his might.

The second part of God's purpose for Pharaoh (a direct consequence of the first) was the proclamation of the name of the true God in all the inhabited earth. "My name" does not have to refer to any one particular name, such as Exod 3:14, or Exod 33:19 or 34:6-7. The point is simply that God intended his utter defeat of Pharaoh's gods (via the plagues) and Pharaoh's forces (in the Red Sea) to be trumpeted abroad, so that everyone would know that Israel's God was the one true God, and that all other so-called "gods" are nothings.

In fact, thanks to the way God used Pharaoh through the whole episode of the Exodus, God's name and power *were* magnified in all the nations. The display of power in Egypt shook the surrounding nations and was a continuing testimony to God's omnipotence for the Israelites themselves. Indeed, it continued to be celebrated throughout their history (❖II:100).

That God is free to use as his instruments even hardened unbelievers such as Pharaoh was something any Jew would have granted. Paul simply wanted the Jews to see that the same principle applied to them as a nation. They could serve God's purposes, whether they were believers or not. Such is not contrary to his justice.

9:18 Therefore God has mercy on whom he wants to have mercy, and he hardens whom he wants to harden. "Therefore" indicates this is the logical conclusion or summarized result, not just from vv. 15-17, but from the whole discussion in vv. 6-17.

Two errors must be avoided from the outset. One is the mistaken notion that this chapter and this verse refer to eternal destinies; the other is the assumption that the objects of the two verbs ("have mercy on" and "harden") cannot refer to the same individual or group. If these two errors are accepted one cannot easily avoid the conclusion of double unconditional predestination. This whole approach, however, is negated by the understanding that the sovereign choices to which Paul refers in 9:18 are for historical roles of service, not eternal destinies (❖II:100-101).

God's divine sovereignty is the main emphasis here: "on whom he wants." This verb is θέλω (*thelō*), "to wish, to will." God's choice of the one to receive mercy and the one to harden is purely a matter of his own will. He does not have to justify his choices; his sovereignty is grounded in the very fact that he is, after all, *God*. Just because he is God, he "is free to choose whom he will for what he will" (MP, 400).

The common approach to this verse, whether seen as dealing with salvation or service, is that 18a refers to Moses and 18b to Pharaoh. Murray's statement is typical: "As Moses, in this context, exemplifies mercy, so Pharaoh hardening" (2:28) (❖II:102).

In my judgment, though, this is not the point of v. 18. The mercy and the hardening are not exclusive, but may be bestowed upon the *same person* (or group). We have already seen that "mercy" in this context is not a salvation word. "God has mercy on whom he wants to have mercy" refers thus to God's sovereign choosing of whomever he pleases to serve his purposes. This means that the second half of v. 18 does not have to refer to individuals or a group of individuals that are separate and distinct from those in 18a. It refers rather to certain individuals *within* the first, inclusive category. God has mercy on whom he wants to have mercy, i.e., he calls into his service whom he wants to call into his service; *but* some of these can serve his purposes only by being hardened. Thus it was with Pharaoh. God bestowed favor upon him by selecting him for a key role, but he could fill that role only by being hardened (❂ II:102).

The obvious and intended application of this whole section, 9:14-18, is to the nation of Israel, with v. 18 being the climax. Just as both statements in v. 18 refer to Pharaoh, so do they both refer to Israel. God bestowed a temporal mercy upon the latter when he chose to use them in his redemptive plan, but he also hardened at least some of them (11:7,25) in reference to the role he wanted them to play. There is no divine inconsistency or contradiction here, either with Pharaoh or with Israel, because there is no inherent connection between service and salvation (❂ II:102-103).

What is the nature of the *hardening* of which Paul speaks? This is obviously a reference to the OT teaching about Pharaoh, and to the fact that God used him in his service specifically by hardening his heart. The Greek word is σκληρύνω (*sklērynō*), which means "to make firm, to harden." It can refer to something physical but is more often used figuratively for a hardened attitude or state of mind. In Scripture it usually refers to a hardened attitude toward God, an attitude of resistance and rebellion toward God's will. Also, in Scripture it is something that a person does to himself; hence the warnings in Hebrews to "not harden your hearts" (Heb 3:8,15; 4:7, quoting Ps 95:8).

The Exodus narrative refers to the hardening of Pharaoh's heart in various ways: (a) his heart "became hard" or "was hardened" (7:13,14,22; 8:19; 9:35; 13:15); (b) he hardened his own heart (8:15,32; 9:34); (c) God promises to harden his heart (4:21; 7:3; 14:4); (d) God did harden his heart (9:12; 10:1,20,27; 11:10; 14:8). God also hardened the hearts of other Egyptian officials and soldiers (9:34; 10:1; 14:17).

Much is made of these different ways of speaking. It is assumed from them that the occasions when Pharaoh hardened his own heart are somehow distinct from those occasions when God hardened it. Then it is usually declared that Pharaoh's self-hardening preceded God's action (❂ II:103-104).

I believe this analysis is unnecessary and misleading. Throughout the series of encounters between Moses and Pharaoh, from beginning to end, God was working providentially to harden Pharaoh's heart. On every occasion where his heart was hardened, the hardening was accomplished by *both* God *and* Pharaoh. On each occasion it was Pharaoh who made the conscious and deliberate decision to not let the people go. But prior to this moment I suggest that God was working within Pharaoh's mental processes, causing such thoughts to enter his consciousness that he could not bear to grant or follow through with permission to let the people go (❂ II:104). How did God harden Pharaoh's heart?

Perhaps by flooding his mind with thoughts such as what a great loss of free labor it will be to lose these Israelites! or what a laughingstock the king of Egypt will be when other nations hear how a bunch of slaves had their way with him! Such thoughts would have great validity in the mind of Pharaoh, and God could have pressed them upon his consciousness at just the right time, i.e., when he was weakening and about to let the people go (*GRu*, 203).

While it is true that Pharaoh's heart was already self-hardened toward God in a general way before God hardened his heart, this was not in fact the *reason* why God worked this specific hardness upon him. Many emphasize such a cause/effect connection, though, because they think God's hardening of Pharaoh's heart had something to do with his *salvation*. But the two are not causally related. Like any pagan unbeliever, Pharaoh had a heart that was self-hardened toward the true God (1:18-32), and God may already have confirmed him in that unbelief according to the principle implied in 1:24,26,28. But the divine hardening of Pharaoh in 9:18 is of a different kind. It is not about salvation as such; it is about how someone whose heart is already self-hardened by sin can in fact be fitted into God's cast of characters for working out his redemptive plan.

Thus we do not have to think of God's hardening of Pharaoh's heart as some kind of *punishment* for his sins (❋ II:105). This sort of thinking, while popular, is a serious misunderstanding of Paul's concept of hardening. It confuses the general self-hardening of rebellious unbelief with God's providential hardening in order to accomplish a specific temporal purpose. The hardening of Pharaoh, both in Exod 4:14 and here in 9:18, is of the latter type, not the former. It in fact had only one specific goal: to cause Pharaoh to oppose God's demand that he set the Israelites free. God expressed his purpose clearly: "I will harden his heart so that he will not let the people go" (Exod 4:21).

This particular hardening was not a natural consequence of Pharaoh's already rebellious heart, nor an act of divine retribution against him because of this rebellion. It did not cause him to be lost, nor did it somehow intensify his lostness. It simply brought him to a state of mind that resulted in his decision to forbid the Israelites to leave. This occurred over and over, which in turn allowed God to send plague after plague, which in turn accomplished the purposes stated by Paul: "that I might display my power in you and that my name might be proclaimed in all the earth" (9:17).

What this shows, in reference to Paul's overall point in Rom 9, is that God can call into his service someone who is lost (by his own choice), and can use him in a significant way even if that person's heart must be divinely hardened in some special manner. The ultimate application of this truth is to the nation of Israel. It demonstrates how God could take Israel, a nation comprised mostly of self-hardened sinners, and use them in their lost state to carry out his purposes. Paul's point is not to explain *why* such people are lost, but simply to affirm that God can use them even though they *are* lost (❋ II:106).

C. GOD USED ETHNIC ISRAEL TO PRODUCE SPIRITUAL ISRAEL (9:19-29)

We must remember two things: First, the main point in Rom 9-11 is the issue of God's faithfulness in his dealings with the nation of Israel. Though blessed with covenant privileges (9:4-5), the nation as a whole was "cursed and cut off from Christ" (9:3). Second, the reason why first-century Jews saw this as a problem was that they assumed that God's calling them into his covenant service guaranteed their final salvation. Paul is in the process of pointing out that this is a false assumption (❧II:106).

But is not God the God of *salvation*? And is not salvation the inherent and ultimate purpose of the covenant with Israel? So how can God be true to his word and at the same time cut Israel off from this very salvation? The basic answer is that there are *two Israels* (9:6b). Israel the *physical* nation was God's main historical instrument or means for making salvation a reality (9:5); the Israel whose origin and essence is *spiritual* is the actual recipient of the salvation.

Paul develops this thought in two stages. First, in 9:7-18 the subject is physical Israel, i.e., the unconditional election of Israel the nation to covenant service despite their unbelief (❧II:107). Now in the second stage of this explanation, of which 9:19-29 is a part, the focus of attention is *spiritual* Israel, the group which is the recipient of God's saving mercy. A major point of this section is the fact that the calling and saving of spiritual Israel was all along a part of the very purpose for the existence of ethnic Israel. In other words, it has always been God's sovereign purpose to distinguish between the two Israels, as the remnant prophecies show (9:27-29). The *means* by which God distinguishes between them is explained in 9:30-10:21.

In summary, just as 9:7-18 explains how God separated physical Israel from the rest of the world, so does 9:19-10:21 explain how God separates spiritual Israel from physical Israel.

Here is how the present section (9:19-29) unfolds. First, by way of transition, Paul words an objection he anticipates from his Jewish readers (v. 19). His immediate response (vv. 20-21) is to issue a stern generic warning about how presumptuous it is for the creature (the clay) to challenge the ways of the Creator (the potter).

Applying the potter-clay analogy to the particular issue at hand, Paul then begins his specific reply to the objection in v. 19 by succinctly summing up God's purpose and intention for the two Israels (vv. 22-24). Like a potter, God has the right to take one lump of clay (the original nation of Israel) and make two completely different kinds of vases from it. One consists of those individuals who are Israelites by physical birth only. Like Pharaoh, they are unbelievers and will ultimately suffer the wrath of God. This is actually the bulk of Israel. So why does God put up with these "vessels of wrath"? Because only through

Romans Part Four

them can he bring into existence the "vessels of mercy," i.e., spiritual Israel, which is the *church* — a group composed not only of believing Jews but of believing Gentiles as well.

In these three verses (22-24) is summed up one whole major aspect of the history and purpose of Israel. It is a supplement, as it were, to vv. 4-5.

To show that this is not some new and alien concept that he has hatched out of his own brain, Paul then cites prophecies from Hosea and Isaiah. These biblical texts show that this has been God's intention for Israel — and the Gentiles — all along (vv. 25-29), i.e., God's final purpose was never physical Israel as such.

This does not end Paul's reply to the objection in v. 19, "Why does God still blame us?" Actually it only prepares the way for the main response to this question, which is given in 9:30-10:21. The curse upon physical Israel (9:3), and upon the individual Jews of which it is composed, is *not unconditional,* as if God were arbitrarily assigning some to eternal wrath. Nor are the individuals within spiritual Israel unconditionally elected to salvation. As 9:30-10:21 shows, the difference between the two Israels is *justification by faith*. Physical Israel, the vessels of wrath, are those who seek to be justified by their own righteousness, while spiritual Israel, the vessels of mercy, accept Christ's salvation through faith. This connection between 9:19 and 9:30-10:21 must not be missed.

This point *is* missed, of course, by those who think ch. 9 is a fundamental proof text for unconditional election. They find this doctrine especially in vv. 19-23, which they see as simply repeating the point of vv. 7-18. However, this approach hopelessly confuses two entirely distinct acts of God: one, his dealing with physical Israel in terms of unconditional election to service; and two, his way of distinguishing between physical Israel and spiritual Israel by the condition of faith.

It is important to see that in this present section (9:19-29), unlike in vv. 7-18, eternal destinies are now an important part of the picture, since the distinction between the two Israels has eternal consequences. But we must be careful not to apply the affirmations of God's sovereign, unconditional choice of the nation as such (vv. 7-18) to the respective eternal destinies of the individuals within the two groups.

In this paragraph, for the first time in this major section (chs. 9-11), Paul introduces the issue of the Gentiles. For some, the incorporation of the Gentiles into spiritual Israel is the key point of the paragraph (❂ II:109). Now, it is true that believing Gentiles are here identified as being included within the new Israel. Nevertheless, in my opinion, this is not a major point of the paragraph. The main emphasis here is still God's faithfulness in his dealings with physical Israel. I.e., his use of them has been in every way consistent with his stated purposes.

1. The Objection (9:19)

9:19 One of you will say to me: "Then why does God still blame us? For who resists his will?" The context here indicates that this objection is placed in the mouth of a typical first-century Jew (❂ II:109-110). The issue is the status of the Jewish nation as such. In 9:3 Paul clearly implies that the bulk of his physical brethren were under eternal condemnation, "cursed and cut off from Christ." He recognizes that the intervening references to God's unconditional decisions regarding mercy and hardening may cause some Jews to conclude that this explains why they were lost, even though this is not his point. This in turn generates their objection, which "runs thus: But, Paul, if God shows mercy to whom he will, and if he hardens whom he will, then it is he who has hardened us Jews in unbelief against the gospel. Why, then, does he still find fault with us, since he himself, according to your argument, has excluded us from blessedness, and made us unfit for mercy?" (MP, 402). How can God hold us responsible for our unbelief and therefore condemn us to hell (v. 3) if our hardening and therefore our unbelief are his own doing? Does this not all the more suggest that he is unjust (v. 14)?

In his second question — literally, "For who has resisted his will?" — the objector seeks to justify his first question by appealing to what seems to be an unassailable theological axiom: no one can resist the will of the sovereign God. Has not Paul himself appealed to this very axiom in vv. 15 and 18 (❂ II:111)?

But is it not possible for a free-will creature to resist or oppose God's will? Is this not the very essence of sin? Yes, if by "will" we mean God's *preceptive* will, i.e., his laws, his commandments, and even his desires. God's preceptive will can be rejected and thwarted by human beings. (See *GRu*, 310-313.) But if we are talking about God's *purposive* will, i.e., his deliberate purposes and determinative decisions, then the answer is no, it is *not* possible for any human being to oppose, violate, or resist his will in this sense (Ps 33:11; Prov 19:21; Isa 14:27; John 6:40; Acts 2:23; 4:28; Eph 1:11; *GRu*, 304-310).

In 9:19 the objector's questions seem to have the latter aspect of God's will in mind, and so the objection does involve a valid theological truth, i.e., no one has ever truly resisted God's purposive will. But if this is the case, then why is God blaming *us* for our sin and rebellion against him? If "he hardens whom he wants to harden" (9:18), then our sin and rebellion are actually *his* will, are they not? So why is he punishing us as if we were *resisting* his will, when in reality we are not — since no one can? (See Cranfield, 2:489; Piper, *Justification*, 186.)

A crucial issue at this point is whether or not the objection is valid in the sense that it correctly and accurately represents the meaning of Paul's teaching in the previous verses. Is this a legitimate conclusion to draw from vv. 15-18? Many say that it is (❂ II:112). However, I conclude that this approach is incorrect. The objection raised here by the Jew misrepresents Paul's teahing.

Wherein lies the error? First, we should emphasize that it does not lie in the objector's second question, "For who has resisted [resists, can resist] his will?" As noted above, there is such a thing as God's *purposive* will, his eternal purpose which is irresistible and immutable, and which therefore cannot be opposed by mere creatures.

Wherein, then, is the error? The objector's misunderstanding was in assuming that this purposive will of God applied to Israel's salvation status (9:3) as well as to the nation's historical role in accomplishing God's redemptive plan. To say it another way, the objector took Paul's statements in vv. 15-18 as explaining why most Israelites were hardened to the point of rejecting their Messiah and thus being cursed. However, as we have seen, this is not Paul's point. In these verses he is affirming God's right to sovereignly choose and use anyone, even sinners, to serve his covenant purposes, and even to harden them with regard to certain decisions if this is necessary (❂ II:112-113).

One reason why interpreters assume that the objector must have understood Paul correctly is that they conclude that the Apostle does not try to refute the objection; he simply rebukes the objector for his presumptuous attitude. But this is simply not true, as I have explained in the introduction to this section. Paul does rebuke the questioner (20-21), and he does reaffirm and explain God's inviolable purposive will for Israel the nation (22-29). But then (9:30–10:21) he sets forth a lengthy reply to the objector's first question, "Then why does God still blame us?" The reply, in effect, is simply this: "Because you refused to believe in your own Messiah." The attempt to excuse such unbelief by illegitimately applying God's purposive will to this circumstance is thereby repudiated.

2. Paul's Initial Rebuke of the Objector's Attitude (9:20-21)

These two verses are not a specific response to the objection worded in v. 19, nor are they meant to preclude such a response. They are only a preface to the more detailed response which follows. As a rebuke, they are directed more toward the tone of the objection than its content. The rebuke is actually generic and may be applied to many a presumptuous and misguided complaint against God's purposes and providence.

9:20 But who are you, O man, to talk back to God? In the NIV, "but" translates a much stronger Greek expression better rendered "on the contrary," as in the NASB. This indicates that Paul is about to correct the erroneous thinking by which the objector seeks to justify himself: "Hey, it's not *my* fault! God made me do it. So why should I be blamed?" "On the contrary," says Paul; "you have missed the whole point. Let me explain it to you" (❂ II:114). Unfortunately, many overlook the fact that Paul spends the rest of ch. 9 and all of ch. 10 correcting the objector!

The first part of Paul's correction (vv. 20-21) is directed toward the objector's presumptuous attitude; the Apostle rebukes him for arguing with God.

We must realize that the objector is not portrayed as simply raising a sincere question concerning God's ways. Rather, the man is described as arrogantly taking a debater's stance against God; he is "talking back" to God, says Paul.

The objector is addressed as "O man." This seems to be a way of emphasizing his mere creaturehood, in contrast with the all-powerful and all-knowing Creator. "Who are you, a mere *human being*, a 'feeble morsel of sinful dust' (MP, 403), to argue against *God*?"

"Shall what is formed say to him who formed it, 'Why did you make me like this?'" The NIV puts this question in quotation marks because it represents the thought of Isa 29:16 and Isa 45:9, where the clay and the vessel made from it are likewise depicted as sitting in judgment on the potter. As Paul uses the metaphor in v. 20b, the complaint comes not from the clay as such but from the piece of pottery formed from it. The scene is almost comical: a finished pot is lifted from the potter's wheel and, personified, looks upon itself with disappointment. It then glares accusingly at the potter and reprimands him thus: "Why did you make me to look like this? I'm a mess! Is this the best you could do? Haven't you made some sort of mistake?"

The potter-clay analogy can be used to teach many lessons, and we are rightly warned to stick to the point Paul is making here and not to try to apply all the details indiscriminately (Cranfield, 2:491). What is Paul's point? Just this: in a potter-clay relationship it is obviously the potter who decides how the clay will be used. Once his decision is made and the vessel has been formed, it is the height of absurdity and arrogance for the vessel to criticize the potter.

Why does Paul use this metaphor here? To what or whom does it specifically apply? Not to the original creation event; not just to individuals such as Pharaoh; and especially not to the destinies of individual men. Its specific application is to the nation of Israel. This is how the analogy is used in Jeremiah: "Then the word of the LORD came to me: 'O house of Israel, can I not do with you as this potter does?' declares the Lord. 'Like clay in the hand of the potter, so are you in my hand, O house of Israel'" (Jer 18:5-6) (❧ II:115).

Thus Paul is rebuking the objector of v. 19 not in the latter's role as a creature nor as a condemned sinner as such, but in his role as a representative of Israel who is complaining that God's treatment of the nation is basically unfair. To such an objection Paul simply says, "Whoa! Let's not forget who we are, shall we? Remember: God is the potter; you (Israel) are just clay in his hands. Who do you think you are, to challenge the one who formed you in the first place?"

9:21 Does not the potter have the right to make out of the same lump of clay some pottery for noble purposes and some for common use? While Paul's reference to the potter and the clay in v. 20 was somewhat general, here he gets more specific. He refers to the potter's right and authority to do with the clay (Israel) whatever he chooses, particularly to his right to make from the same lump the two Israels of 9:6b (❧ II:116).

It is obvious that the potter here represents God, but to whom does the "same lump" refer? Many think this "lump" is the human race in general, a view that usually leads to Calvinist conclusions. In my judgment this is a serious error. In keeping with the overall context, the "same lump" here refers not to the mass of human individuals as such but to the totality of Israel, from which God makes the two derivative groups, physical Israel and spiritual Israel (❖II:116-117).

From the same lump of clay, says Paul, the potter has the right to make pieces of pottery that are very different in their nature and disposition. On the one hand he can make from it a vessel εἰς τιμήν (*eis timēn*), "unto honor"; on the other hand he can make from it a vessel εἰς ἀτιμίαν (*eis atimian*), "unto dishonor."

This statement raises some key issues. First, how are these terms — honor and dishonor — related to each other? One approach is to take them in a comparative sense: one vessel is given more honor, the other less honor. This is the point of the NIV: some "for noble purposes and some for common use." However, a better approach is to take the terms in their more natural sense as *opposites* rather than as comparatives. If the vessels unto honor and unto dishonor in v. 21 are equivalent to the vessels of mercy and vessels of wrath in vv. 22-23, then they must be taken in an opposite and not just a comparative sense (❖II:117). This also seems to better fit the actual meaning of the terms used. As a result, the NIV rendering is misleading.

This leads to the second and more overriding issue: do these terms refer to God's creation of all individuals for the specific purpose of saving some ("for noble purposes") and sending the rest to hell ("for common use")? Or do they refer to God's preparation of some individuals and even some nations for specific uses in the accomplishment of his historical plan of salvation? Those taking the former view naturally see the terms *timē* and *atimia* as opposites; advocates of the latter view see them as comparative.

Calvinists argue for the former view; others, especially non-Calvinists, argue for the latter view (❖II:118). I cannot accept either of these two views. I do agree that the main reference here is to the nation of Israel, and not to the human race as such. But at the same time I believe Paul is referring not to how God used this nation in his historical plan, but to the eternal destinies of individuals within it.

It is unlikely that the point here is simply God's right to prepare and use individuals and nations — especially Israel — for his covenant purposes, because Paul has already made this point in vv. 7-18. An even more convincing reason, though, is the use of the word *atimia*, or "dishonor." The source and nature of the objection worded in v. 19 indicates that Paul is addressing here in vv. 20-21 the status of the Jews; thus the terms "honor" and "dishonor" must apply in some way to this group. Most who take the latter view outlined above would see unfaithful Israel as an example of a "vessel of dishonor" (e.g., Morris, 366).

My contention, though, is this: if this verse applies only to the way God *uses* nations, especially Israel, for his historical redemptive plan, there is *no way* that the role of Israel — believing or unbelieving — can be described as dishonorable or even menial. The term *atimia*, however interpreted, simply does not fit the use God made of the nation of Israel. Theirs was indeed the most exalted and honorable role imaginable, apart from that of the Messiah himself (9:4-5). Thus this interpretation of v. 21 cannot stand.

What, then, is the alternative? I believe Calvinists are right to see "honor" and "dishonor" as referring to eternal destinies, heaven and hell. But I believe they are wrong on two counts. First, they are wrong to assume that the "clay" refers to the human race in general. The clay is not the mass of humanity, but the nation of Israel only. Second, Calvinists are wrong to think that God made two separate vessels from this clay for the express purpose of sending one to heaven and the other to hell. "Unto honor" and "unto dishonor" do indeed refer to the eternal destinies of individuals within Israel, but these respective destinies are not determined by God himself. The next main section, 9:30–10:21, shows that individuals determine their own eternal destinies according to whether or not they put their trust in God's saving promises.

This distinction applies even to the people of Israel. God used the nation in its totality to accomplish his exalted redemptive purposes, and this honor belongs to believing and unbelieving Jews alike. But with regard to eternal destinies, God has exercised his sovereign right, like a potter, to make an internal separation among the individuals of whom this nation is composed. He makes from the one lump a vessel of honor, *spiritual Israel*, whose distinguishing characteristic is faith in God's gracious promises. Also from this same lump he makes a vessel of dishonor, the majority of the original nation, whose distinguishing characteristic is that, even though they are Jews physically, they have never given their hearts to God (❖II:120).

A key point here is that this distinction between the vessel of honor and the vessel of dishonor, though decreed by God, is ultimately the responsibility of the individuals placed within each group. This view is supported by Jer 18:1-12, where God compares his relationship with Israel as that of potter to clay. "'Like clay in the hand of the potter, so are you in my hand, O house of Israel'" (18:6b). But God makes it clear that this potter-clay relationship does not mean that he arbitrarily determines the destiny of the nation. He declares that he tailors his final decision regarding any nation or kingdom to the way it responds to his warnings (18:7-12; see Smith, 2:20). In his role as a potter, God's method of dealing with nations must surely also apply to his dealing with individuals.

We should remember that the main point of vv. 20-21 is to rebuke the objector in v. 19 for his presumptuousness in talking back to God. The metaphor of the potter and his clay is a generic warning applicable to anyone who presumes to do the same in any sort of circumstance. We know that Paul intends that it

Romans Part Four

be applied to Israel in the way explained above because of the way he himself continues the metaphor in vv. 22-24.

3. Beyond Ethnic Israel to Spiritual Israel (9:22-24)

In these next three verses Paul begins his specific response to the objection in v. 19. Basically he grants the objector's second point, that no one truly resists God's purposive will. This is surely true regarding Israel. Undeterred by massive unbelief, yea, even enduring it, God used this nation to accomplish his intended purpose for them.

That purpose first and foremost was to bring the Messiah himself into the world (9:5). But that is not the whole story. In these three verses Paul reveals another purpose for which God was using the nation of Israel: through them he brought into existence the other Israel, the true Israel, spiritual Israel, the remnant (9:6b). And here he mentions for the first time in this chapter the fact that believing *Gentiles* are also included within this spiritual Israel, the entity for which it was the glorious purpose of physical Israel to prepare.

In its fullness, then, spiritual Israel is no less than the church of Jesus Christ, which is composed of believing Jews and believing Gentiles, i.e., of anyone who accepts Jesus as Savior and Lord. It was God's *purposive* will to use ethnic Israel as an instrument for bringing forth the church. In this respect the objector is correct: no one could have resisted God's purpose to do this.

But the objector erred in thinking that this same principle ("Who resists his will?") was the explanation for Israel's state of accursedness (9:3). As Paul will explain in the next section (9:30-10:21), the reason for their condemnation was their resistance to God's *preceptive* will, i.e., that believing submission to Jesus Christ is a requirement for salvation.

The tragic irony of this, of course, is that most Israelites were lost because they refused to become a part of the very group whose origin was a major reason for their own existence (❖ II:121).

This section is difficult to understand and translate because, even though the syntax is quite extended and complicated, it does not form a complete sentence. Verse 22 begins with the word "if," but as is sometimes the case in Greek literature, the expected second part of such a sentence, the "then" part, never appears (❖ II:122).

There is a fairly general agreement that the NIV captures the intended sense very well. Paul asks, "What if God endured the vessels of wrath, in order that he might bring forth vessels of mercy?" (❖ II:122).

How does this relate to the objection in v. 19? The thought seems to be this: "What if it is so, in accordance with his role as a potter, that God sovereignly forms the nation of Israel and bears with their unfaithfulness in order to accomplish his purpose for them? So what if it is true, as you say, that no one can resist his will in this matter? Does this explain and excuse your sin? Does this shift responsibility for your condemnation to God? No!"

9:22-23 What if God, choosing to show his wrath and make his power known, bore with great patience the objects of his wrath—prepared for destruction? What if he did this to make the riches of his glory known to the objects of his mercy, whom he prepared in advance for glory . . . ? (See ❖II:122.)

These verses form a single unit of thought, a thought which can be discerned only by working through a series of very difficult exegetical questions: Who are the "objects of his wrath"? How are they "prepared for destruction"? In what sense does God *choose* to show his wrath? Who are the "objects of mercy"? How are they "prepared in advance for glory"? As we have often seen, the Calvinist and the non-Calvinist give very different answers to such questions.

The Calvinist View

The Calvinist interpretation is as follows. As to the scope of Paul's remarks, it is assumed that he is dealing here with the human race in general. The "objects of wrath" are the reprobate, the total number of lost human beings (Calvin, 367; Hendriksen, 2:328). The reprobate are lost because they were from the beginning "prepared for destruction" by God himself (❖II:123).

God determines to create a certain amount of human beings as objects of wrath simply as a decision of his secret, purposive will (which is the implication of the word "choosing" in the NIV). Calvinists usually speak of two types or levels of God's will: his revealed, expressed will and his secret, ultimate will. Things do not always happen according to the former, but the latter is all-inclusive and all-determinative (see *GRu*, 301-310) (❖II:124).

On the one hand this determinative counsel by which God determines the fate of the lost is said to be "secret" and "incomprehensible," says Calvin (367). But on the other hand it seems that it is not hidden very well, because Calvin and others believe that in v. 22 Paul is telling us the reason why God prepares some for destruction, i.e., "to show his wrath and make his power known." Because he wants to display his wrath and power in punishing the wicked, God assigns some to eternal condemnation in hell. In fact, according to Calvinism the very reason God is patient is to magnify his wrath. As Stott says, "His forebearance in delaying the hour of judgment" is designed to "make the ultimate outpouring of his wrath the more dreadful" (272) (❖II:124).

But this is not the whole story. Verse 23 adds another reason why God "bore with great patience the objects of his wrath." He did it in order "to make the riches of his glory known" to the elect, which are chosen unconditionally for salvation. As Calvin interprets it, this means that God delays punishing the reprobate, thus increasing their punishment, because the greater the punishment poured out upon the reprobate, the greater will appear the mercy bestowed upon the elect (❖II:125).

Seeing Paul through Non-Calvinist Eyes

Since Calvinists tend to see this entire chapter in terms of the unconditional predestination of individuals to their eternal destinies, it is not unexpected that they interpret these two verses as outlined above. But as we have seen, unconditional individual election and reprobation are not the point of this chapter. It deals rather with God's faithfulness in all his dealings with the nation of Israel. That is the subject of these two verses as well.

One point that Paul has stressed throughout this chapter is that God has the sovereign right to choose and use both individuals and nations in whatever ways he pleases for the accomplishment of his covenant purposes. No one "resists his will" in such matters (v. 19). These verses are simply reaffirming God's right, like a potter, to manipulate his clay in any way he chooses.

The "objects of his wrath" in v. 22 are not the total mass of lost human beings, but rather the nation of Israel, specifically the ethnic Jews who rejected God's promises of grace and were thus accursed (9:3). These unbelieving Israelites, viewed collectively as a nation, in spite of their indispensable role in God's plan, are nevertheless indeed the objects of his wrath (❡ II:126).

What is the "destruction" for which Israel has been prepared? It is possible that Paul is thinking about temporal destruction, such as the destruction of Jerusalem in A.D. 70 (Godet, 360). But it is also likely that Paul is referring to the final, eternal destruction of sinners in hell, since its counterpart of "glory" in v. 23 also likely includes eternal life (❡ II:126).

Who, then, is the agent by which these vessels of wrath, these unbelieving Jews, are "prepared" for such destruction, whether temporal or eternal? The difference between the term used here in v. 22 and the comparable term in v. 23 ("he prepared in advance") makes it very likely (contrary to Calvinism) that *they prepared themselves* for such destruction (Godet, 361; MP, 406). The verb in v. 23 is active and has the prefix *pro-*, and clearly means that God himself prepared in advance the vessels of mercy for glory. But in v. 22 the verb seems to be deliberately different. It is either passive voice: "they were prepared," or (more likely) middle voice: "they prepared themselves" (AG, 419). I.e., they are responsible for their own destruction; by their sin and unbelief and refusal to repent, they sealed their own doom. Even if the agent of preparation were God himself, the lack of the prefix *pro-* ("in advance, beforehand"), unlike the verb in v. 23, would suggest that God prepared them for destruction only after they manifested their adamant unbelief. The more likely meaning, though, is that they prepared themselves.

The "objects [vessels] of his wrath," then, are ethnic Israel, viewed in terms of its unbelief. Like a potter God made the nation as such for his glorious purposes, which they did indeed fulfill. But in reference to their individual eternal destiny, the Jews' personal unbelief makes them the objects of divine wrath. Thus they ultimately become vessels of dishonor and shame (v. 21).

Exactly what is Paul saying about these vessels of wrath prepared for ultimate destruction? He says that God "bore" or "endured" them "with great patience." This refers to God's relationship with his chosen people throughout OT history, especially to the fact that he refrained from completely destroying them despite their blatant and repeated idolatry (❀ II:127).

This next point is crucial to our understanding of this whole section. The question is, what is meant by the expression, "choosing to show his wrath and make his power known"? As we have seen, Calvinists usually take this as referring to God's infallible, purposive will: because God has determined (chosen) to display his wrath and power upon the objects of wrath whom he has prepared for destruction, he patiently withholds this wrath until the time comes when it can be exhibited in its most spectacular intensity. I.e., he exercises patience in the interests of greater wrath. In my judgment this interpretation is atrociously inaccurate and is an insult to the mercy and grace of God. What does the expression mean, then?

First of all, "choosing" is an unacceptable translation for the verb θέλω (*thelō*), used here by Paul. Basically it means "to be willing, to want, to desire, to wish" (❀ II:127). At this point Paul is simply saying that God *was willing* or *wanted* to show his wrath and power against Israel, not that he purposed or determined to do so.

A second point is that the form of *thelō* is a present participle, indicating that this "wanting" is simultaneous with the action of the main verb, "bore." But the very nature of a participle requires that we determine from the context just how it relates to the main verb. Here it appears that the participle has either a *causal* or a *concessive* relationship with "bore." I.e., it means either, (1) "*Because* he was willing to show his wrath and make his power known, *therefore* he bore with great patience the objects of his wrath"; or, (2) "*Although* he wanted to show his wrath and make his power known, *nevertheless* he bore with great patience the objects of his wrath." For the latter, see the NASB.

In general, Calvinists accept the causal view. I.e., *because* God wants to display his wrath as impressively as possible, he patiently withholds it until he can do this. Likewise in general, non-Calvinists accept the concessive view. I.e., *even though* God actually wanted to go ahead and abolish the nation of Israel and send unbelieving Israelites to hell, still he bore with them in order to achieve his ultimate saving purposes.

Is it possible to tell from Scripture itself which of these two views is correct? Yes. The key to the right understanding here is the reference to "patience." Paul says that God bore (endured, put up with) the vessels of wrath — not with just a little patience, but with *great* patience. Why? According to the causal interpretation of *thelō*, accepted by Calvinists, God exercises his patience toward the vessels of wrath for the express purpose of being able to heap even greater wrath upon them. Such a view, however, violates the very essence of divine patience. Is "patience" for the purpose of increasing wrath *patience* at all? Not according to Scripture. Romans 2:4 expressly says that God's kindness and patience are designed to lead to repentance. Second Peter 3:9 says that God is patient because he does not want anyone to perish but for everyone to come to repentance. The Calvinist view of 9:22 makes a travesty of such texts.

I would suggest that the *cause* of God's great patience cannot be found in v. 22. This verse simply asserts the reality of this patience: *even though* God many times wanted to pour out his wrath upon idolatrous and unbelieving Israel, and bring upon them the destruction they deserved, he bore with them with great patience. *Why* he did so is stated only in v. 23 (❂ II:129).

What is this purpose? "To make the riches of his glory known to the objects [vessels] of his mercy." In continuity with everything we have seen in ch. 9 thus far, we take these vessels of mercy to be the spiritual Israel alluded to in 9:6b; and in view of the reference to the Gentiles in v. 24, we take this specifically to refer to the NT church. For hundreds of years God endured with great patience the unbelieving multitudes of ethnic Israel because it was his purpose to produce through them, in the fullness of time, the true Israel.

It was certainly the case that any of these unbelieving Israelites along the way could have "circumcised their hearts" (Jer 4:4) and turned in penitent faith toward the gracious God; and many did so. But strictly speaking God did not exercise his great patience toward OT Israel just for the purpose of allowing time for individual Jews to repent. The fact is, according to v. 22, he actually *wanted* to wipe them all out. What prevented him from doing so, and what caused him to be patient, was his determination to accomplish his final historical purpose for them as a nation: the establishment of the church of Jesus the Messiah consisting of both Jews and Gentiles who accept the gospel (❂ II:130). Collectively they form the church, which is the new and true Israel, or the Israel which is identified by spiritual rather than physical criteria.

How shall we understand "the riches of his glory" which he makes known to these vessels of mercy? Some take this to mean that God's purpose is to display *his own* glory by bestowing salvation upon the elect (Murray, 2:35). The NIV might be taken in this sense in that it refers to making the riches of God's glory "*known to* the objects of his mercy." I believe it is better, though, to interpret "the riches of his glory" to mean the riches of salvation as bestowed "*upon* vessels of mercy" (NASB, emphasis added). The preposition *epi* is better translated "upon" than "to." Thus it is God's purpose to manifest the glorious riches of his salvation by lavishly bestowing them upon the new Israel.

Does this "glory" refer to eschatological glorification, the final blessings of heaven itself? It certainly must include this, since "glory" most often has this specific reference (e.g., 2:7,10; 5:2; 8:18,21,30; Col 1:27). But it must not be limited to the glory of the end times; from the very beginning of the Christian life God pours "the riches of his glory" into the vessels of his mercy. This exact phrase is used in Eph 3:16 to refer to the sanctifying work of the Holy Spirit within us. See also 2 Cor 3:18; Eph 3:13; Phil 4:19; Col 1:11; 1 Thess 2:12.

In what sense are the vessels of mercy "prepared in advance for glory"? Here the verb "prepared in advance" (προετοιμάζω, *proetoimazō*) is different from the verb translated "prepared" (καταρτίζω, *katartizō*) in v. 22. Because the latter is middle or passive voice, we may conclude that the vessels of wrath prepared themselves for destruction. But in v. 23 the word is active voice and no doubt means that God is the one who has prepared the vessels of mercy for glory. Also, unlike v. 22, the verb in v. 23 has the prefix *pro-*, which means that God prepared them "in advance" or "beforehand."

If "prepared in advance for glory" refers to the final glory of heaven, then this statement is no different from 8:28-30. I.e., whom he foreknew would respond favorably to his gracious promises, he predestined to be in heaven (see ❖I:502-514).

But it is possible that "prepared in advance" refers to the plan that God had begun to work out from the time he called Abraham and Isaac and Jacob, the plan whereby he would use the ethnic people of Israel to lay the groundwork for the establishment of the church. That he prepared them "for glory" would then mean that he had already determined that he would pour out the riches of salvation upon all who accepted the Messiah, whether Jew or Gentile. See Eph 2:10; 1 Pet 1:2 (❖II:131).

In other words, the church is the ultimate objective of God's advance preparation; its members are the vessels of mercy God "prepared in advance for glory." Every time a sinner is converted, God "make[s] the riches of his glory known" by pouring them out upon the convert.

We must not lose sight of Paul's main point, which is to declare God's faithfulness in his dealings with the Jews. As he has insisted all along, the members of ethnic Israel did not have to be personal believers as a prerequisite for being used to carry out the divine plan. Even as vessels of wrath, they were used collectively as an instrument for bringing the church into existence. This was God's purpose, and as the objector in v. 19 rightly observes, no one can resist his purposive will.

It is important to see that the ultimate purpose of God is not wrath, but mercy. He used vessels of wrath (unbelieving Israel) to accomplish this purpose, but the purpose itself is to make known the riches of his glory on vessels of mercy. And here is the most glorious truth of all: no unbelieving Jew — no individual vessel of wrath — needs to remain as such. Though the nation in general remains under God's curse because of unbelief, any individual Jew can respond to the gospel of Jesus Christ and *become* a vessel of mercy! After all, the gospel is "first for the Jew" (1:16).

9:24 . . . even us, whom he also called, not only from the Jews but also from the Gentiles? The main point of this verse has already been set forth in the above discussion, namely, that the vessels of mercy for which God had long been preparing would include not only Jews but Gentiles as well.

Once the advance preparation through ethnic Israel was completed, God "called" (καλέω, *kaleō*) from the larger masses of Jews and Gentiles those who would receive his mercy. This is not the Calvinist "effectual call," which is identical with the doctrine of irresistible grace; it is rather the call that is extended to all sinners through the preaching of the gospel, though it is accepted by only a few (see ❂I:83-84, 500-501, 512-513).

The word "from" is ἐκ (*ek*), which can be more forcefully translated "out of." Thus Paul is here identifying the vessels of mercy as "called-out ones," which is etymologically related to the NT word for "church," which is ἐκκλησία (*ekklēsia*). This comes from the same two words used here in v. 24, *ek* and *kaleō*. This is completely consistent with what was said above, that Paul's whole point in this chapter is the way God used ethnic Israel to produce spiritual Israel, the church (❂II:132-133).

4. Prophetic Confirmation of God's Purpose (9:25-29)

This section does not add any new content to Paul's argument. It is a series of quotations from Hosea and Isaiah, cited to provide prophetic confirmation of God's purpose for Israel as it culminates in the birth of the NT church. These quotations, especially those from Isaiah, show that the present state of Israel's unbelief and accursedness was no surprise to God, and that his original purpose had not failed (❂II:133). The nation itself was always intended to be a means to an end; the end itself is spiritual Israel, which consists of both the believing remnant from old Israel and all believers from among the Gentiles. This end, and therefore God's purpose for Israel, have been accomplished, in fulfillment of these prophecies.

9:25-26 As he says in Hosea: "I will call them 'my people' who are not my people; and I will call her 'my loved one' who is not my loved one," and, "It will happen that in the very place where it was said to them, 'You are not my people,' they will be called 'sons of the living God.'" A major question is whether or not Paul really intends to apply these quotes from Hosea to the calling of the Gentiles. This is problematic because Hosea's prophecy was originally addressed to Jews, specifically to the ten tribes of the northern kingdom. Still most interpreters believe that Paul is applying the Hosea texts to the evangelization of the Gentiles (❂II:134).

But how could Paul justify applying the Hosea prophecies to the Gentiles? The consensus seems to be that the ten "lost" tribes' permanent exile has so intermingled them with the Gentiles that the evangelization of the one group will necessarily involve the evangelization of the other (Godet, 365). These Jews had become "not loved" and "not my people" through the judgment of the exile; the Gentiles were "not loved" and "not my people" by nature, so to speak.

Thus in the NT age, when the church goes into all the world, the gospel appeal reaches Jew and Gentile alike, and the words of Hosea take on a new and expanded meaning (❂II:135). Thus it seems proper to apply the Hosea prophecies to both Jews and Gentiles.

In v. 25 Paul introduces what is actually a paraphrase of Hosea 2:23 thus: "As he says in Hosea." The "he" is God. For God to punish Israelites by stripping them of their status as "my people" was a severe blow; being the people of God was their greatest treasure. Thus the messianic promise that God would one day bestow this title upon them again would have special meaning for Jews. Gentiles who have never had this status to begin with may not at first realize what a great promise this is. To be "God's people" means to come into a special family relationship with him (see 8:14-17) (❂II:135-136).

The word "call" in both v. 25 and v. 26 does not refer to the gospel call but to the giving of a new name or title. Verse 26 is a citation of Hosea 1:10; its main point is the same as v. 25 and Hos 2:23 (❂II:136).

Paul says, citing Hosea, that this calling (naming) will happen "in the very place where it was said to them, 'You are not my people.'" This probably refers to the Gentile world. As applied to exiled and scattered Jews it means that they do not have to return to their "homeland" in order to become God's sons once again. Through the preaching of the gospel adoption into God's family takes place in whatever nation one is found, whether one be Jew or Gentile.

9:27-28 Isaiah cries out concerning Israel: "Though the number of the Israelites be like the sand by the sea, only the remnant will be saved. For the Lord will carry out his sentence on earth with speed and finality." Paul takes this quote from Isa 10:22-23 and specifically applies it to Israel. He says that Isaiah "cries out" this prophecy, indicating that the words were spoken with fervent emotion.

Though his message surely applies to the whole of Israel, Isaiah's ministry, unlike that of Hosea, was to the southern kingdom. The prophet is assuring Israel that even though they must suffer conquest and captivity, at least a remnant will survive and return to the Lord. But at the same time, the fact that only a remnant will be saved means that the rest will be destroyed.

Isaiah 10:21 says, "A remnant will return, a remnant of Jacob will return to the Mighty God." Isaiah speaks here of a *spiritual* return — a returning to the Lord. This is the way Paul understands it; thus in v. 27b he words the promise, "The remnant *will be saved*." He sees Isaiah's prophecy as being fulfilled through the preaching of the gospel and the entry of many Jews into spiritual Israel, the church, through their conversion to Christ (❂II:137).

That the prophet Isaiah himself declares that only a remnant would thus be saved is a primary vindication of Paul's main point, "that the covenant promise did not contemplate or guarantee the salvation of all ethnic Israel" (Murray, 2:39). Everything that God promised to Israel as a nation *was* fulfilled. But the remnant prophecy shows that this great nation was chosen only for service, not for salvation; and the fact that only a small proportion were saved was in no way contrary to God's promises and God's faithfulness (❂II:137).

The remnant doctrine is both a promise and a judgment. As a promise, it is an assurance that *at least* a remnant of Israel will be saved. There will always be an Israel, at least a spiritual Israel. But as a judgment, it is a solemn recognition that *only* a remnant will be saved. Emphasizing this judgment, v. 28 "explains how it will come about that only a remnant of Israel will be saved" (Cranfield, 2:502). It will be the result of God's λόγος (*logos*), translated "sentence" in the NIV. This probably refers to the decree of destruction of which Isaiah speaks (❂II:138).

The Lord himself will carry out this decree of judgment upon the nation "with speed and finality." These last words are an attempt to translate two participles. The first word (*synteleō*) looks to the past and means that in carrying out this sentence God is accomplishing an existing purpose, bringing it to completion, and fulfilling it completely. The other word (*syntemnō*) looks to the future and means that in carrying out this sentence God is cutting something off and bringing it to an end; it will not continue to exist in the future. In my opinion this means that the establishment of the remnant (spiritual Israel) marks the end of God's dealing with Israel as a nation; his purpose for ethnic Israel is now completed, and they are cut off as his special people. From this point on his focus is upon spiritual Israel.

The words translated "on earth" probably should be translated "upon the land," i.e., the land of Israel, with "land" actually standing for ethnic Israel or physical Israelites as such (❂II:139).

9:29 It is just as Isaiah said previously: "Unless the Lord Almighty had left us descendants, we would have become like Sodom, we would have been like Gomorrah." This last quotation, from Isaiah 1:9, reemphasizes both the seriousness of God's judgment upon unbelieving Israel and the divine provision for preserving at least a remnant of his people. In Scripture the destruction of Sodom and Gomorrah is a type of final and decisive judgment. Thus without the remnant, Israel would have become like these two cities: extinct. By preserving only the remnant, God brought a judgment just short of this upon Israel.

"The Lord Almighty" preserved this remnant. Both Isaiah and Paul actually say "the Lord of Hosts," contrary to the NIV. "Hosts" refers to all the heavenly or angelic hosts (❂II:139).

The word "descendants" would be better translated "seed." The word connotes not a relationship to what is past (i.e., to one's ancestors), but a preparation for the future. The purpose for leaving behind a few survivors is to reseed and replant for the future. The "new growth" that springs forth from this seed is the new spiritual Israel, the church (❂II:140).

The Lord "left us" this remnant. The verb used here means "to allow to remain." Though the Lord carried out his sentence of destruction upon the nation in general, he allowed this seed-remnant to remain.

In what sense did *the Lord* leave this remnant? He left it in the sense that he "bore with great patience the objects of his wrath" (v. 22) until the time that he was ready for the spiritual Israel to come into existence (❂II:140).

This brings the first main section of Rom 9–11 to a conclusion. Paul has shown that God has not been unfaithful to Israel nor treated them unfairly. He has kept every promise he made to them, and fulfilled every purpose he had for them as a nation.

The one question raised in this section that has yet to be addressed is the lost state of the great majority of the Jews, or more specifically, who is responsible for their lostness? The objector raised the question in v. 19a, "Then why does God still blame us?" The implication is that somehow God is responsible for the Jews' rejection of their Messiah; therefore they should not be blamed and punished. This is the issue that Paul will address in the next section.

III. ISRAEL'S CHOICE OF LAW RATHER THAN GRACE (9:30–10:21)

There is considerable agreement that 9:30–10:21 forms the next major section of 9–11, but how it relates to the previous section is a matter of dispute. A common view is that ch. 9 explains Israel's lostness in terms of God's sovereign decision, while ch. 10 explains it as the result of Israel's own unbelief. For Calvinists especially, ch. 9 presents the picture of a sovereign God who unilaterally and unconditionally chooses which individuals he will save and which he will send to hell, while ch. 10 presents him as giving human beings the choice of whether to believe or not to believe, with salvation being conditioned on this choice. This seeming contradiction between divine sovereignty and human responsibility is a paradox with no ready explanation (❂II:141).

In my judgment the point of these two sections is something quite different. Paul's main purpose in 9–11, as discussed earlier, is to vindicate God's faithfulness in view of (a) his promises to Israel and (b) Israel's lostness. Chs. 9 and 10 present two separate but related reasons why this situation does not violate God's faithfulness. First (ch. 9), his faithfulness is not violated because his promises to the nation as a whole involved only their role of service and not their salvation. The second reason (ch. 10) why God's faithfulness is not violated by this situation is because Israel's lostness (their exclusion from spiritual Israel) is the result of their own free choice of law rather than grace as the way of salvation. Paul makes it clear that any and all Jews could have been saved if they had accepted God's gift of righteousness on his gracious terms instead of trying to attain salvation through their own works or personal righteousness. Such saving grace had always been available to individual Jews based on God's

Romans Part Four

loving offer of forgiveness of sins; but the offer was usually spurned, as the gospel of Christ itself came to be. In other words, it is the Jews themselves, not God, who have been unfaithful (◉ II:142-143).

A. PERSONAL RIGHTEOUSNESS VERSUS THE RIGHTEOUSNESS OF GOD (9:30–10:3)

This paragraph presents the essence of this section in terms of the concept of righteousness, i.e., the righteousness on the basis of which one is accepted by God. The Jews were lost, says Paul, because they sought acceptance by God through their own personal righteousness or law-keeping, which can never be good enough. They rejected the gift of God's righteousness, which is the only hope for salvation.

"God's righteousness" (10:3) in this context is the same as the "righteousness from God" that is revealed in the gospel (1:17). It is not the attribute of God by which he is personally righteous, but rather a gift of righteousness that God offers to sinners, thus allowing him to accept them as righteous even though in reality they are not. Specifically, it is Jesus Christ's payment of the penalty of the law in our place (see ◉ I:116-120).

Though the Jews are the main focus of this section, the Gentiles are mentioned here by way of contrast. The very thing the Jews were seeking but failed to attain, the Gentiles attained even though they were not seeking it (9:30-31) (◉ II:143).

1. The Reason for the Gentiles' Acceptance (9:30)

9:30 What then shall we say? Sometimes when Paul asks this question, he does so to introduce a false inference or idea, which he then proceeds to refute (e.g., 6:1; 7:7; 9:14). But here it serves simply to introduce the new section. What follows is not an objector's question but Paul's own teaching (as in 8:31; 11:7).

"What then shall we say?" — about what? What has triggered this question? No doubt it is the whole of the previous section that is in view. I.e., what shall we say about the lostness of most Jews (9:3,22,28), especially in view of the fact that even some Gentiles (!) are being saved (9:25-26)?

This is Paul's answer, **That the Gentiles, who did not pursue righteousness, have obtained it,** . . . This refers not to all Gentiles, but only to those who accept the gospel. What is the righteousness they have obtained? Most agree that Paul is not speaking of moral righteousness or righteous character, but rather a "righteous status in God's sight" (Cranfield, 2:506), or a right standing with God (e.g., Hendriksen, 2:333; Morris, 374). It is not the same as justification (contra Lard, 317; DeWelt, 159), but is rather the result of it. On the basis of his gracious act of justifying (declaring or counting righteous), believing Gentiles obtain their right standing before God.

Whether righteousness be taken as right moral character or as a right standing before God, it was characteristic of the Gentiles that they sought for neither. Regarding the former, there were no doubt some exceptions, but in general the pagan world was noted for its wickedness (1:18-32; Acts 14:16; 17:30; Eph 4:17-19). But this very fact shows that the Gentiles were not striving for the latter, either. This is true because without special revelation the only known means of being right with God is earnest moral striving; but as just noted, this was not typical of the Gentile world.

But even though they were not pursuing a right standing before God, they obtained it anyway! The words "pursue" and "obtain" go together. Literally they can refer to pursuing a quarry and catching it, or running after a prize in a race and winning it. Figuratively they refer to seeking after or pursuing a goal, and attaining it. What is so unusual is that the Gentiles attained this goal or prize without even seeking it. This refers to the fact that under the New Covenant God is actively seeking Gentiles to be his people through the worldwide preaching of the gospel. By accepting the gospel when it is presented to them, Gentiles obtain this right standing before God.

Specifically, Paul says, the Gentiles obtained **a righteousness that is by faith** . . . . That is, they obtained a right standing with God based on the free gift of God's own righteousness, a gift which they received by putting their trust in Christ's saving work (1:17; 3:21-22; Phil 3:9). "Righteousness by faith" is a shorthand expression for the grace system as a whole and is similar to "justified by faith" in 3:28 (see ❂I:267-268).

2. The Reason for the Jews' Lostness (9:31-33)

9:31 [B]ut Israel, who pursued a law of righteousness, has not attained it. Here is the tragic irony. The Gentiles did not pursue righteousness but obtained it anyway; Israel pursued it but did not attain it. "Israel" refers to the physical nation in general. "Pursued" is a present participle (literally, "pursuing"), to which both the NASB and the NIV give a purely descriptive meaning. Another possibility, which I favor, is that the participle is concessive: "*although* they pursued." Although Israel, unlike the Gentiles, vigorously pursued a law of righteousness, they did not attain it.

The difficult part of this verse is the expression, "a law of righteousness" (νόμον δικαιοσύνης, *nomon dikaiosynēs*). Why didn't Paul just say "righteousness," making the language parallel with v. 30? Why did he say "*law* of righteousness"? (❂II:146.)

First, the best understanding is that "law" here refers to the Law of Moses, which the Jews obviously pursued and after which they hastened with the greatest of zeal (2:17-20; 10:2) (❂II:146-147). But in what sense is the Law of Moses a law of *righteousness*? We should remember that righteousness as such means "conformity to the proper and relevant standard or norm." Thus any form of God's law for mankind (heart-engraved [2:15], Mosaic, New Covenant) is a law of righteousness in the sense that it is the norm or standard to which all human beings in their respective contexts are obligated to conform. The Law of Moses was the norm by which the righteousness of the Jews was to be measured. As such it was meant to be meticulously and sincerely obeyed, which was the professed goal of every Israelite (see Ps 119).

Paul's lament is that, although the Jews pursued their law of righteousness, they did not attain it. Contrary to the Gentiles, who did obtain righteousness, the Jews did not arrive at their goal (❂ II:147).

Exactly what did the Jews hope to gain by pursuing the law of righteousness, i.e., by conforming their lives and conduct to the Law of Moses? Not just righteousness in the sense of perfect moral character, but righteousness in the sense of right standing before God — the very thing the Gentiles attained without seeking it. But why did the Jews not attain it?

9:32 Why not? Because they pursued it not by faith but as if it were by works. Here is a point that must not be overlooked: it was possible for the Jews to obtain a right standing with God by pursuing the Law of Moses, their "law of righteousness," as long as they pursued it in the right manner. Of course, if anyone had obeyed it perfectly, he would have been justified before God for that very reason; but Paul has already shown that no Jew ever accomplished this (2:1-3:20), and he is not just repeating that point here. Rather, Paul says the reason the Jews did not succeed was that they did not pursue their law "by faith." This implies that they *could* have pursued it by faith; and if they had done so, they *would* have obtained the same righteous standing with God that the Gentiles did. In fact, we must assume that a large number of Jews throughout OT history *did* in fact follow after the law by faith and attain righteousness thereby (11:4), though most did not.

But how is it possible for the Jews to follow after the Law of Moses *by faith*? The most obvious way is that the Jews living in the Christian era can put their trust in the very one to whom their law points, namely, Jesus. But what of those who lived in pre-Christian generations? How could they pursue the *law* of righteousness *by faith*? Doesn't this sound like a contradiction?

It is not a contradiction. The Law of Moses as a law code was unique, in that it contained not just moral and legal precepts to be obeyed, but also religious provisions that embodied the very essence of grace (i.e., forgiveness of sins). Pre-Christian Jews did not know Jesus as such, but they knew that they were sinners and law-breakers as measured by all the moral and legal requirements of their law, and they knew from the laws of sacrifice the principle of atonement via substitution. Thus they knew that their sin and idolatry could be forgiven when God's promises of mercy displayed in the sacrifices were embraced by faith (see 3:21). Those Jews who trusted in the gospel aspects of the Law of Moses rather than its legal aspects are the ones who obtained a righteous status before God. In this sense the Jews' law was not an enemy of faith, but was in fact designed to engender faith (❂ II:148-149).

A biblical example of one who pursued the law by faith is the publican or tax collector in Jesus' parable in Luke 18:9-14. In the temple as he prayed for acceptance by God, he was overwhelmed by his unworthiness and cried simply, "God, have mercy on me, a sinner." Jesus declared that this man went home "justified before God." Though this story may have been fictional, it shows how any Jew at any time in OT history was able to attain by faith a righteous standing with God, as guided by the law.

Many were thus driven, but most were not. Indeed, most were like the Pharisee in the same parable. Instead of pursuing the law of righteousness by faith, Israel as a whole pursued it "by works." Instead of simply trusting the law's manifested grace as the source of their righteous standing before God, they trusted that their own ability to obey its precepts would make them worthy of acceptance by God. Instead of depending on God's forgiving grace, they trusted that they had achieved a satisfactory degree of personal righteousness, "as if the accumulation of works-righteousness were God's way of salvation" (Stott, 276).

What Israel did, in effect, was to transform their law *code* into a law *system*. As a law code, the Law of Moses was a simple set of commands to which the Israelites were obligated to conform their lives and conduct. To use it as such was to use it properly (3:31). But the moment they began to regard such obedience as the means or basis for gaining acceptance by God, their law code became the centerpiece in the law system as a way of salvation. But this is exactly why Israel was lost: the law system cannot save sinners (1:18–3:20).

They stumbled over the "stumbling stone." This is a reference to Yahweh's warning to Israel in Isa 8:13-15. "The LORD Almighty," he said, "is the one you are to fear, he is the one you are to dread." Though he will be a sanctuary or place of safety, at the same time "for both houses of Israel he will be a stone that causes men to stumble and a rock that makes them fall." Many of the Jews "will stumble; they will fall and be broken."

Though 9:33 as well as other NT references show that the "stumbling stone" ultimately applies to Jesus Christ, originally the stone was Yahweh as such. To Jews in Old Covenant times, God presented himself as a sanctuary, i.e., as the holy place where one could find refuge from all his enemies (see 1 Kgs 1:50-51; 2:28-29). As such he placed himself squarely in the path of his people (Isa 65:1-2). Thus if they refused to take shelter in his grace, they ran headlong into him and crashed against him and fell. Thus it was with all Jews throughout OT history who pursued the law of righteousness by works instead of by faith.

Thus it is no surprise that when Yahweh came in the flesh, the Jews of that generation stumbled against him as well. They were conditioned to do so by the chronic misuse of the law by their ancestors (❂ II:151).

9:33 As it is written: "See, I lay in Zion a stone that causes men to stumble and a rock that makes them fall, and the one who trusts in him will never be put to shame." This verse expands the "stumbling stone" concept and implicitly applies it to Christ. I say "implicitly" because Christ is not specifically mentioned in the verse, yet these same OT quotes are applied to him elsewhere in the NT. In fact, the second part of this verse, a quote from Isa 28:16b, is explicitly applied to Christ in 10:11 (❖ II:151).

"As it is written" is a common NT way of introducing material from the OT, which in this case is a composite of two passages from Isaiah. "See, I lay in Zion a stone" is from Isa 28:16; "a stone that causes men to stumble and a rock that makes them fall" is from Isa 8:14; and the rest of the verse is from Isa 28:16 again. The way Paul combines them is an ingenious blending of the two texts. Isaiah 8:14 presents Yahweh as both a refuge (sanctuary) and a stone of judgment, with the emphasis being on the latter. Isaiah 28:16 concentrates on the stone as a place of refuge and safety. Paul simply combines the two and presents the one stone as the source of both judgment and promise.

One reason for saying v. 33 refers to Jesus is that, while in Isa 8:14 Yahweh himself is the stone, in Isa 28:16 Yahweh is the one who lays the stone. That the latter is a messianic prophecy is indicated by the fact that Matt 16:16-18 is clearly based on Isa 28:14-19. Christ's person and work as summed up in Peter's confession are the foundation stone on which the church is built, and all the forces of Hades (=Sheol in Isa 28:15,18) cannot overpower it. Thus most scholars agree that the stone of stumbling in 9:32-33 is Jesus, especially in his role as the crucified Messiah (see 1 Cor 1:23).

But how can Paul apply both Isaiah texts to Jesus? In Isaiah 28:16, to be sure, the stone does appear to be the Messiah, but in 8:14 the stone is Yahweh himself. So how can they both refer to Jesus? The answer is simple: "Christ is God!" (Hendriksen, 2:335). The Messiah-Stone "is therefore Jehovah in His final manifestation" (Godet, 369; see Rom 10:9,13). This does not mean that God the Father and Jesus Christ are one and the same person; it means only that Yahweh in the OT revelation is the entire Trinity: Father, Son, and Holy Spirit.

Jesus is "a stone that causes men to stumble and a rock that makes them fall." This does not mean that God *wants* anyone to stumble over him or that he *intended* the Jews to fall because of him (Lard, 319). The stumbling is a *result*, not a purpose (❖ II:152).

In what sense does anyone stumble or fall over Jesus? The verb for "stumble" (v. 32) is προσκόπτω (*proskoptō*); it means literally "to strike or bump against, to stumble against or over"; figuratively it means "to give offense, to take offense at, to reject." The noun, πρόσκομμα (*proskomma*), is used in this verse to refer to the act of stumbling. The word for "fall" is the noun σκάνδαλον (*skandalon*) (❖ II:152-153). A *skandalon* is something which one opposes or to which one takes offense only to his ruin and destruction. In this light it is easy to see how Jesus is a stumbling stone. Those who oppose him or who take offense at the gospel of the cross fall into eternal ruin and death. This is what happened to the Jews (1 Cor 1:23), and it can happen to anyone else.

But this is not the whole story. God lays in Zion a stone; some fall over him, but "the one who trusts in him will never be put to shame." This part of v. 33 is based on Isa 28:16b, where the Hebrew verb in the latter clause seems to be "will not be in haste," or "will not be in a hurry" (NASB margin). The passive verb used by Paul means "to be disgraced, to be put to shame," and speaks more of the reason for such panic or hasty flight than the fleeing itself. The idea is that those who take refuge upon the Rock by trusting in him will never have to slink away in shame for having made a humiliating decision.

In these three verses (31-33), then, Paul vindicates the faithfulness of God by declaring that Israel as a whole is responsible for its own lost condition. The essence of their failure was that they trusted in themselves rather than in God's promises and in their own Messiah; they pursued acceptance with God by works rather than by faith; they chose law rather than grace.

Such a path to perdition is not limited to the Jews, of course. Anyone living in the New Covenant era can respond to the New Covenant revelation in exactly the same way, i.e., by zealously pursuing its commands in an effort to win God's approval on the basis of such works. The fate of those who do so will be the same as Israel's.

3. The Jews' Rejection of God's Righteousness (10:1-3)

These three verses expand further the reason for the Jews' lostness, namely, they rejected the gift of God's own righteousness, preferring to stake their claim to heaven on the worthiness of their own works.

10:1 Brothers, my heart's desire and prayer to God for the Israelites is that they may be saved. Paul addresses his "brothers" (ἀδελφοί, *adelphoi*), which are his fellow Christians (not just Jewish Christians, contra MP, 418). In general Greek usage *adelphoi* was often inclusive of men and women and thus could be translated "brothers and sisters" (BAGD, 16).

Paul's sentiment here is directed toward his fellow Jews: his prayer is "for the Israelites." It reminds us of 9:1-3 where the Apostle expressed his grief over Israel's lostness and declared his willingness to take their place if only they could be saved. Here he echoes that desire for their salvation.

"Desire" is εὐδοκία (*eudokia*), which is basically a feeling of good will toward others out of which a desire for their well-being naturally arises. Paul's reference to his "heart" (the spirit, the inner man) expresses the depth and sincerity of his desire.

"Prayer" is δέησις (*deēsis*), which is a petitionary prayer, an entreaty, a supplication, a request (see Phil 4:6). He lays his request before God on behalf of Israel "unto [εἰς, *eis*] salvation," i.e., for the purpose of their salvation.

Here is the situation: the Jews as a whole were lost, and Paul yet says he prays for them to be saved. How can such a prayer be meaningful? In the following way: Paul has already declared on the basis of divine prophecy that only a remnant will be saved (9:27-29), he does not know the exact number of this remnant. Thus he can pray for all Israel in the hope that as many as possible will be included in that number. (See ❖ II:155-156.)

10:2 For I can testify about them that they are zealous for God, but their zeal is not based on knowledge. This is a partial explanation of why Paul earnestly desires and prays for Israel's salvation, i.e., because they did seem to be genuinely sincere in their efforts to honor God. Literally Paul says "I bear witness" or "I do solemnly testify" that they have such zeal. How did Paul know this? Because this was his own state of mind prior to his conversion. He was truly zealous for God even while he was opposing Christ and his church in ignorant unbelief (Acts 22:3; Gal 1:13-14; 1 Tim 1:13). The problem is that one can be zealous, sincere, and enthusiastic and at the same time be deadly wrong. This was true of the Jews, whose zeal, says Paul, "is not based on knowledge" (see Prov 19:2). Unfortunately, where zeal serves the cause of error and ignorance, it is not a virtue but a vice (❖ II:156).

Paul's testimony concerning the Jews' uninformed zeal is a good corrective for those who think that sincerity is the deciding factor in one's relationship with God. If that were true, then the Jews would surely have been saved. But Paul makes it crystal clear that they are lost in spite of their sincerity. They are lost not because of their lack of knowledge as such, but because they refused to accept the knowledge that was available to them (see 10:16-21; see 1:18-25, about the Gentiles). One is not held responsible for knowledge that is actually unaccessible to him (4:15), but willful ignorance is inexcusable.

The Jews' zeal was blameworthy not because of its ultimate object, which was God, but because of the *way* they sought to honor him. This is explained in the next verse.

10:3 Since they did not know the righteousness that comes from God and sought to establish their own, they did not submit to God's righteousness. As we saw in our discussion of 1:17 (see ❖ I:115-121), "the righteousness that comes from God" is the very heart of the gospel of grace. It is the same as "the righteousness that is by faith" in 9:30. In this context it is not his righteous nature as such, but the gift of a right standing before him which he offers to bestow on believing, penitent sinners. See 1:17; 3:21-22; 4:6; 2 Cor 5:21; Phil 3:9.

This is the righteousness by which God has always saved sinners, even before its basis was not specifically known. The actual basis for it is the propitiatory sacrifice of Jesus Christ; the righteousness of God is literally Christ's satisfaction of the penalty of the law (eternal punishment in hell) in our place (see ❖ I:119). This is the gift of righteousness which God offered to all of Israel throughout OT history, through their humble acceptance of the gospel provisions of the law. This is also the gift he offered to them in the very person of their Messiah, Jesus.

But, says Paul, the Jews *did not know* this righteousness. They did not know it when it was initially offered to them in God's promises in OT history, and especially they did not know it when it was offered to them in Jesus himself. This is the climax of their not-knowing: the rejection of Jesus of Nazareth as their Messiah and Savior (DeWelt, 164).

To say that the Jews did not *know* this righteousness of God does not mean that they had never been exposed to it and were somehow ignorant of the very existence of the promises of God and the reality of the gospel facts. Rather, it means that they did not *acknowledge* the good news of God's righteousness; they did not accept it and welcome it and submit to it (Hendriksen, 2:342).

Instead, they continued to seek acceptance with God on the basis of their own righteousness, i.e., "as if it were by works" (9:32). They sought to use their law code as if it were a law system; they sought to achieve a level of personal obedience that would make them deserving of heaven. Rejecting the gift of the "robe of righteousness" (Isa 61:10), they relied on their own "filthy rags" (Isa 64:6).

"Their own" righteousness means the personal self-righteousness achieved by each individual, not the national or corporate righteousness of the Jewish nation as compared with other nations. Only if we take this in the former sense does it have universal application. I.e., every one of us, not just Jews living under the Mosaic Law, must fight the temptation to plead our case before God based upon our own moral and spiritual accomplishments rather than upon the blood of Christ (❥II:158).

The word for "submit" (ὑποτάσσω, *hypotassō*) is often used for submission to authority. In what sense is a rejection of grace a refusal to submit to authority? It is so in the sense that grace is the way of salvation established by God himself and declared by him to be the only possible and acceptable way; thus to reject God's way by refusing his gift of righteousness is an act of rebellion against God. It is so also in the sense that accepting the gift of God's righteousness requires a humble and submissive attitude along with a repudiation of personal worthiness, to which human pride stubbornly clings.

How, then, does one submit to the righteousness of God? By accepting *God's* way as the only way, thereby abandoning all claims to salvation based on self-righteousness. The only way to do this in the Christian era is to accept Jesus as the only Messiah and Savior, and to do so by fulfilling the gracious conditions for receiving God's righteousness as spelled out in the Word of God (see ❥I:108-115, 268-271). Chief among these conditions is faith (9:32a,33b; 10:4-17), the very essence of which is in part the act of submitting or surrendering oneself into the hands of God (see ❥I:108).

B. CHRIST ALONE IS THE SOURCE OF SAVING RIGHTEOUSNESS (10:4-13)

Israel's lostness does not violate God's faithfulness for two reasons. First, God's promises had to do with the nation's service, not salvation (9:1-29).

Romans Part Four

Second, their lostness is the result of their own free-will rejection of God's offer of grace, not the result of some secret, unconditional choice on God's part (9:30–10:21). Thus ch. 9 shows that ethnic Israel was unconditionally elected to service, and ch. 10 shows that spiritual Israel is conditionally elected to salvation.

The point Paul is making in this section presupposes the law/grace distinction spelled out in 1–8, especially the nature and role of the righteousness of God in justification (see ❋I:115-120; 250-265). Here Paul is simply applying what he has already taught on the subject to the question at hand, i.e., the question of God's faithfulness in view of the Jews' lostness. The bottom line is that the law/grace distinction, and more specifically the distinction between God's righteousness and personal righteousness, is the key to why God saves some (even Gentiles) and rejects others (even Jews).

In 9:30–10:3 Paul has shown that the Jews are lost because they deliberately chose to trust their own personal righteousness rather than God's righteousness (10:3). Many Gentiles, on the other hand, have chosen to accept the gift of God's righteousness through faith (9:30), and thus are saved.

Now in 10:4-13 Paul goes into more detail about the distinction between the two kinds of righteousness. Speaking especially about the present era, he gets specific about "the righteousness that comes from God." How can it be said that the Jews have rejected God's righteousness? Have they not cherished God's law and been zealous in their attempts to obey it? Yes, but the point is that righteousness according to law is *not* God's righteousness, the righteousness that saves. God's saving righteousness is to be found in Jesus Christ alone. So when the Jews rejected Jesus of Nazareth as their Messiah, they were rejecting the only source and basis for saving righteousness.

The content of this section unfolds thus. First Paul simply states the choice that anyone must make regarding his salvation: either law-righteousness, or faith in Jesus (10:4). The typical Jew chose the former, using his relationship with the Law of Moses as the basis for his claim to salvation. But Moses himself said that the only way to be saved by law is to obey it completely, which is a futile pursuit (10:5).

But the grace of Jesus Christ can set anyone free from the futility of this universal tendency to pursue righteousness via law-keeping. The gospel of grace is readily available to all. The key to receiving it is to trust in the mighty works of Jesus Christ, not in our own works (10:6-10). Saving faith understands that Christ's works alone are the basis for salvation.

This way of trust is open to all, to Jews and Gentiles alike. When it comes to salvation, God makes no distinction between these groups. Whoever calls on the name of the Lord will be saved (10:11-13).

1. An Either-Or Choice: Works-Righteousness or Faith in Christ (10:4)

10:4 Christ is the end of the law so that there may be righteousness for everyone who believes. Contrary to many, I believe that v. 4 begins a new paragraph. How then does this verse relate to the preceding paragraph? Verses 2,3,4, and 5 all begin with the particle *gar*, a word that usually introduces an explanation, a confirmation, or a reason for what precedes. (The NIV translates it only in v. 2). Thus the point is that something in the previous verse or context is true, because v. 4 is true. The key is the reference to the Jews' ignorance of true righteousness in v. 3 ("not based on knowledge") and v. 4 ("they did not know"). Their pursuit of righteousness via law was zealous, but it was ignorant and futile *because* (*gar*) Christ has shown once for all that law-keeping cannot make one acceptable before God.

The distinction between law and grace as contrasting ways of salvation is central to this paragraph (Moo, 644). This distinction has existed from the very moment sin entered the world, but it has now come into sharpest focus with the coming of Jesus the Christ. It is clear beyond the shadow of a doubt that the choice between works-righteousness and faith in Christ is an either-or choice. Jesus is the definitive end to all attempts to use the law as a way of being accepted by God.

This verse is without question "one of the fundamental theses of Pauline theology as a whole," as Cranfield says (2:515), and thus its interpretation is crucial (❂II:161-162). Two principal interpretations emerge. The first can be summarized thus: "Christ is the goal and fulfillment (and thus the termination) of the Law of Moses, so that now, in the NT era, there is righteousness for all who believe." The second is this: "Christ is the termination of the law-system as a way of righteousness for each individual who puts his trust in God's gracious promises." Here I will defend the latter view.

The first issue to be settled is what it means to say that Christ is the "end" of the law. The Greek word *telos* has many meanings, but only two or three are relevant here. One possibility is that it means "goal" or "fulfillment." The other relevant meaning is "termination." Christ is the end of the law in the sense that he terminated it or brought it to an end (❂II:162). In my judgment "termination" is the correct view, as the following discussion will show.

The second issue, closely intertwined with the above, is the meaning of "law." Christ is the *telos* of the law — but which law? One main view is that this means the Law of Moses. Another is that Christ is the end of all forms of law or law in general, as a way of attaining righteousness before God. This would apply certainly to the Law of Moses, but also to the law written on the heart as well as to the law-commandments of the NT. In other words, Christ is the end not just of this or that or all law *codes*; he is the end of any form of law as a *system* of salvation (❂II:163). If this is the meaning of "law," then *telos* must mean "termination," since it does not make sense to say that Christ is the aim or purpose or fulfillment of all law.

I accept this latter view of "law" in this verse, and thus take Paul as saying that Christ is the termination of any form of law as a way of righteousness or acceptance with God. It is certainly true that Christ is the *telos* of the Law of Moses. He both fulfills it, and brings it to an end; thus what Paul says is surely intended to apply to the Jews and to their law. But his point is not restricted to this. Indeed, Paul says Christ is the end of law for righteousness to *every* person who believes. This reference to "every person" (παντί, *panti*) shows that Paul is thinking not only of those to whom the Law of Moses applied but to those who have other forms of law as well (see SH, 284). The following conclusion concerning *eis* also confirms this view.

The third issue in exegeting 10:4 is the connection between "the end of the law" and "righteousness." In the Greek text the connecting word is the preposition *eis*, a preposition which the NIV translates as "so that there may be," as if the last part of the verse states the *purpose* for the first part. In my judgment the NIV translation is wrong here. *Eis* should be connected only with the word "law," introducing a simple prepositional phrase (εἰς δικαιοσύνην, *eis dikaiosynēn*) that modifies that word alone. Thus the verse is saying that Christ is the end of "law for righteousness" or law "as a means toward righteousness" (Dunn, 2:596). This is how the NASB translates it: "For Christ is the end of the law for righteousness to everyone who believes." This view is acceptable grammatically and is theologically consistent with the theme of Romans in general and with Paul's point in this context (9:30–10:21) (❂II:164-165).

A final question is this: what sort of event is this τέλος νόμου (*telos nomou*, "end of law")? Is it a one-time event accomplished by Christ in the process of salvation history? Or is it an ever-recurring event that takes place in each individual's experience when he comes to trust in God's saving grace? Those who take "law" as referring to the Law of Moses say the former. I totally disagree with this view. Paul's point is that Jesus Christ is the termination of the law-system as a way of righteousness, as a way of acquiring God's favor, for everyone who comes to believe in him. Even before Christ came, and not just in this new era, his planned and foreknown atonement was the basis for God's offer of righteousness to those who accepted his loving promises (❂II:165-166).

It is important to see that ever since sin entered the world there has never been a time when law was an actual way of righteousness before God. Thus to say that Christ is the end of law for righteousness means that he is the end of all false and futile attempts to base righteousness on law-keeping. When we understand the work of Jesus Christ as the embodiment and source of grace, we understand that our righteousness is in him alone (2 Cor 5:21).

2. The Futility of Law-Righteousness (10:5)

10:5 Moses describes in this way the righteousness that is by the law: "The man who does these things will live by them." This and the next five verses set forth in more detail the contrast between law-righteousness and God's righteousness, explaining why Christ has ended the former and established the latter. Verse 5 explains the way law-righteousness works, with the implied conclusion that it is futile for anyone to attempt to actually achieve a right status before God by this method. This is in essence the same message as 1:18–3:20.

To make his point Paul paraphrases a statement by Moses from Lev 18:5: "The man who does [the righteousness of the law] will live by it." See also Luke 10:28 and Gal 3:12 (☯ II:166-167).

Paul, guided by the inspiration of the Holy Spirit, sees in these words of Moses a reference not just to the Mosaic Law but to law in general, and to the necessity of absolute obedience as a condition for eternal life. Thus the statement by Moses is presented as a terse summary of law as a way of salvation. When one chooses the law-system as his way of gaining acceptance by God, the only way to gain such acceptance is to obey the requirements of the law without exception. Thus Paul takes the statement from Moses to read, "*Only* the man who does these things *perfectly* will live *eternally* by them" (see *GRe*, 202-209).

In the background, however, lies the fact that "all have sinned" (3:23; see 1:18–3:20). Thus law as a way of righteousness is tragically futile; this is why it is so important to see that Christ has brought an end to all attempts to establish righteousness by law (v. 4).

3. Saving Righteousness Comes through Trusting Christ's Works, Not Our Own (10:6-10)

10:6a But the righteousness that is by faith says . . . . The next five verses set forth a contrast between law-righteousness and faith-righteousness, a contrast indicated by the word "but" (δέ, *de*). The main point seems to be that whereas law-righteousness depends on human works and accomplishments (which can never be adequate), faith-righteousness depends on the all-sufficient works of Christ. What is left for us to do is to humbly acknowledge these works and rest our hope of heaven on them.

Much of the content of vv. 6-8 consists of statements drawn from the words of Moses in Deut 30:12-14 (☯ II:168-169). Here Paul is simply taking the *form* of Moses' statements about the law, including some of the same wording, and applying it to grace instead. He is not attempting to quote Moses or interpret Moses. He simply wants to say the same thing about grace that Moses said about the law: we do not have to do something heroic to know about it and receive it; it has already been made available to us, namely, through Jesus Christ (☯ II:169).

It is important to note that Paul personifies faith-righteousness here. That faith-righteousness *says* these things means simply that it is *characterized* by them.

The first words of the personified faith-righteousness are in the form of an exhortation, **"'Do not say in your heart . . . .'"** "Heart" refers to the entire spiritual side of man's nature, including the intellect and the will as well as the emotions. According to Lenski, "'To say in the heart' is a Hebraism for 'to think

Romans Part Four

secretly' and is used especially regarding some unworthy thought which one fears to utter aloud" (650) (❂ II:169).

10:6b-7 What does Paul warn us not to say? Do not say **". . . 'Who will ascend into heaven?'" (that is, to bring Christ down) "or 'Who will descend into the deep?'" (that is, to bring Christ up from the dead).** This is certainly an allusion to Deut 30:12-13, where Moses says this concerning God's law: "It is not up in heaven, so that you have to ask, 'Who will ascend into heaven to get it and proclaim it to us so we may obey it?' Nor is it beyond the sea, so that you have to ask, 'Who will cross the sea to get it and proclaim it to us so we may obey it?'"

Moses' emphasis is clearly on the accessibility and understandability of God's law. It is not an esoteric message hidden in some secret place or located at some far corner of the universe. Possession of it is not dependent on some act of Herculean proportions, such as ascending into the heavens or crossing the sea. As Moses explains in v. 11, "What I am commanding you today is not too difficult for you or beyond your reach." You already have it; all you have to do is obey it.

By wording his questions in much the same way as Moses, Paul makes the same point about grace that Moses does about law, except he refers not just to the *knowledge* of saving righteousness, but to the actual *possession* of it. How can one be accepted as righteous before God? Not by personal obedience or "doing" ("the man who does these things," v. 5), but only by the works of Jesus Christ! So do not ask yourself, what great work must I do to be justified before God? Do not ask, "Must I ascend into heaven?" — as if you could! and as if Christ has not already been there and has not already come down to us, bringing salvation with him. Do not ask, "Must I invade the empire of death and Satan himself?" — as if you could! and as if Christ has not already done that and returned from the dead in triumph. Do you think you can match what Christ has done, or somehow participate in his work or improve upon it?

Paul's reference to ascending into heaven is the same idea and has the same force as Deut 30:12. As Moo points out, in the OT this act was "almost proverbial for a task impossible for human beings to perform" (654). The reference to descending into the deep makes the same point, using the figure of extreme depth rather than extreme height. In the second question Paul does not follow Deut 30:13; Moses speaks of crossing the sea while Paul speaks of descending into "the deep" (ἄβυσσος, *abyssos*, "the abyss"). In the Greek OT this word was often used for the depths of the sea, and the concept is sometimes paired with the heavens (Ps 107:26; see Ps 139:8, which has *hades* instead of *abyssos*). In either case, crossing the sea or descending to its depths, along with ascending to the heavens, to the Jews represented the most extreme effort imaginable.

Paul's reference to the abyss, though, probably has significance beyond the fact that it is simply the opposite vertical extreme compared with the heavens.

In the OT the abyss is sometimes comparable to *sheol* (*hades*), the abode of the dead (Ps 71:20), and in the NT it is elsewhere depicted exclusively as the proper abode of Satan and his demonic angels (e.g., Luke 8:31; Rev 9:1,2,11). Thus descending into the abyss means coming face to face with man's greatest enemies, death and Satan.

What is the significance of Paul's christological comments appended to these questions? They are not meant to be a commentary on or an interpretation of Moses' questions in Deut 30:12-13. They are meant rather to point out that the only one who is capable of performing mighty works of salvation is Jesus Christ, and he in fact has already done them. There is no need to ask, "Who will ascend into heaven?" as if such an act on man's part would merit his salvation. In the first place, no human being can do this by his own effort. In the second place, even if he could, the only purpose for doing so would be to come before God and beg for a Savior. But this is unnecessary, because the Savior has already by his own initiative come down out of heaven for us, in the incarnation.

At the same time there is no need to ask, "Who will descend into the deep (the abyss)?" as if by this act we could in some way forge our own deliverance from sin. In the first place it would be futile, since the lords of the abyss, death and Satan, are both stronger than we are. In the second place, the Christ who came down from heaven has already through his death invaded the abyss, and he has defeated its inhabitants and been victoriously raised from the dead. He has done this by his own glorious power; he needs no help from us.

These questions are not meant to represent an attitude of denial and disbelief with respect to Christ's incarnation and resurrection. Rather, they represent either an attitude of self-righteousness, as if a man could actually do works great enough to save himself — in which case the references to Christ are a rebuke; or (more likely) they are a cry of despair at the impossibility of saving ourselves — in which case the references to Christ are a comfort and a relief.

10:8 But what does it say? The subject of the verb "say" is the same as in v. 6, "the righteousness that is by faith." What does faith-righteousness say to us? **"The word is near you; it is in your mouth and in your heart"**. . . . This statement closely follows part of Deut 30:14, "No, the word is very near you; it is in your mouth and in your heart so you may obey it." This completes the thought begun in Deut 30:11, where Moses tells his people that God's commands are not beyond their grasp, as if they could find them only by ascending to heaven or crossing the sea (30:12-13). On the contrary, his word is as close to you as your own mouth and heart. You already have God's law; all that remains is for you to obey it.

Though Paul in 10:8 is obviously echoing key elements of this verse in Deuteronomy, he is not just repeating it but is adapting it to his own purposes. When Moses said, "The word is very near you," he meant the word of command. Deuteronomy 30:11 speaks literally of "[this command which] I am commanding you today"; v. 14 says this word (of command) must be *obeyed*. But to show that he is not speaking of the same word, Paul adds this specific qualification: **. . . that is, the word of faith we are proclaiming . . . .** Moses spoke a word that must be obeyed; Paul proclaimed a word that must be believed.

The term for "word" is ῥῆμα (*rhēma*), not *logos*, probably because the LXX uses *rhēma* in Deut 30:14. It refers to the message Paul proclaimed or preached, the message of the gospel of Jesus Christ.

Why is it called "the word of faith"? One reason is that the proper and natural response to the word (message) of the gospel is to *believe* it (as contrasted with the proper and natural response to the word of law, which is to *obey* it). Another reason is that this word is what stimulates and evokes faith (10:17). Finally and primarily, as is often the case for Paul, the term "faith" stands in contrast with "works" (9:32) and with the "doing" required by law (10:5). Thus "the word of faith" is another shorthand expression for the entire way of grace.

The main point is that the word of faith is *near* you. This simply reinforces what was said in vv. 6-7, that the source of our salvation is not works that we do but the saving work of Jesus, which is made known to us through the word of the gospel.

Just how near is this "word of faith"? It is so close that it is "in your mouth" and "in your heart." Deuteronomy 30:14 says the same thing about the word of law. The Israelites had heard the word of the law spoken by Moses; thus they were fully able to repeat it with their own mouths and understand it in their hearts. Likewise, through the proclamation of the word of faith, the saving righteousness of God is immediately present to the hearing sinner, so near and familiar to him that he can talk about it and mull it over in his mind.

10:9 It may be that in the original reference (Deut 30:14) the mouth and heart were mentioned simply because they are the epitome of nearness. I.e., what could be closer to the center of a person's being than something in his mouth or in the deep recesses of his heart? But Paul is not content to let these figures stand as simple symbols for nearness. In the next two verses he gives them a spiritual or theological application, showing that the mouth and the heart are both involved in receiving for oneself what the close-at-hand "word of faith" promises.

Moses declared that the word of command was very near to the Israelites, but it still had to be obeyed: "The word is very near you; it is in your mouth and in your heart *so you may obey it*." Paul likewise tells us that the word of faith demands a response. The gospel may be in someone's mouth in the sense that he can repeat it, and it may be in his heart in the sense that he knows about it and understands it. But such a person is not actually saved unless he believes the gospel message to be true and both internally and externally surrenders himself to the Lordship of Jesus Christ.

Paul sums up this response in v. 9: **That if you confess with your mouth,**

"Jesus is Lord," and believe in your heart that God raised him from the dead, you will be saved. This verse begins with the Greek word ὅτι (*hoti*), which the NIV and others translate as "that." Taken thus, v. 9 would be the content of the word of faith that Paul proclaimed. Others take *hoti* as meaning "because" (e.g., Moo, 657; NRSV). I.e., the word of faith is as near as your mouth and heart, because the simple hearing of the word puts one in the position of immediately being able to use his mouth and heart to receive salvation.

The Greek for "confess" is ὁμολογέω (*homologeō*), which literally means "to say the same thing, to agree," and thus to acknowledge the truth of something. Of course such a confession could be hypocritical, but the very sense of the word implies sincerity, and in this context Paul ties it to sincere heart-belief.

Paul says that this confession is "with your mouth," which shows that he is referring to an oral, public confession of one's faith. In 1 Tim 6:12-13 Paul reminds Timothy that he confessed the "good confession in the presence of many witnesses," and notes that even Jesus "made the good confession" before Pontius Pilate (see John 18:37).

The essential content of our confession is specified: "Jesus is Lord." The Greek is κύριον Ἰησοῦν (*kyrion Iēsoun*), literally "Lord Jesus." The KJV speaks of confessing "the Lord Jesus." It is generally accepted, though, that this double object of the verb "confess" has the sense of confessing "Jesus [to be] Lord." The NASB puts it "Jesus *as* Lord." The NIV gives the correct sense of the statement. (See 1 Cor 12:3, where the same formula, *kyrios Iēsous*, obviously means "Jesus is Lord.")

The confession of Jesus as Lord early became the standard way of acknowledging oneself to be a Christian. See John 20:28; Acts 2:36; 10:36; 1 Cor 12:3; 2 Cor 4:5; Phil 2:11.

What does it mean to confess Jesus as *Lord*? It ascribes to him two things: ownership and deity (see Cranfield, 2:529). The basic connotation of the word is that of the owner or master of something (cf. the English "landlord"). To confess Jesus to be our Lord is thus to confess that he is our owner and we are his slaves. It is the external expression of an internal spirit of complete submission to every aspect of his word and will.

In accord with the religious significance attached to the title *kyrios* in biblical times, it is clear also that confessing Jesus as Lord is to confess that he is deity, that he is fully divine, that he is God the Son, equal with God the Father and God the Holy Spirit in essence and power and honor. "Lord" is the name above every name (Phil 2:9-11); it is Paul's trinitarian title for Jesus (1 Cor 8:6; 12:4-6; Eph 4:4-6). It is also the Greek word used by Greek-speaking people to represent the holy name of God — Yahweh — in the OT, orally at first and then ultimately in copies of the Septuagint (see Moo, 660, n. 77; see *GRe*, 121).

There is still no greater and no more significant confession than "Jesus is Lord." To confess him as "the Christ" and "the Son of the Living God" (Matt

16:16) is accurate and appropriate, but to omit the central confession of his Lordship is to ignore the fundamental pattern of NT Christianity. MacArthur points out (2:74), "In the book of Acts, Jesus is twice referred to as Savior but ninety-two times as Lord. In the entire New Testament, He is referred to some ten times as Savior and some seven hundred times as Lord. When the two titles are mentioned together, *Lord* always precedes *Savior*."

The other necessary response to the word of faith mentioned by Paul in this verse is to "believe in your heart that God raised him from the dead." To "believe that" (πιστεύω ὅτι, *pisteuō hoti*) is to acknowledge or assent to the truth of some statement. This is a necessary aspect of saving faith, but must be accompanied also by "believing in/on" Jesus, which is the element of trust. (See ❥ 1:107-108.) Here the element of trust is not specifically mentioned but is implied in the confession of Lordship, by the phrase "in your heart," and by association with "trusts in" (πιστεύω ἐπί, *pisteuō epi*) in v. 11.

To "believe in the heart" means not only to accept the bare facts about something but also to accept its full meaning and significance and to be committed to applying its implications to one's own life. It is comparable to being "obedient from the heart" (6:17, NASB).

It is significant that believing and confessing are linked together; it shows that in the Christian life they cannot be separated. Confession without faith is of no value for salvation (Matt 7:21-23), and faith without confession is simply unthinkable.

It may seem strange that Paul mentions confession before faith, since the logical order would seem to be the reverse. The order in v. 9 is dictated, however, by the order of "mouth" and "heart" in Deut 30:14 as reflected in v. 8. In v. 10 Paul recapitulates v. 9, using the reverse (expected) order.

Exactly *what* must be believed in the heart about Jesus as a means to salvation? We must believe "that God raised him from the dead." In view of the centrality of the atonement in God's provision for our justification (see ❥I:118-120), it may seem strange that Paul should here omit any reference to the cross and mention only the resurrection. The resurrection is not unrelated to our justification, however (see 4:24-25). Also, we should not jump to the conclusion that Paul's list here in 10:9 is meant to be exhaustive (see below). Also, he focuses specifically on faith in the resurrection because in the NT the resurrection of Christ is directly related to his Lordship (see below).

That Jesus actually died and came back from the dead are two of the most firmly attested facts in the NT, and are completely indispensable to the gospel (1 Cor 15:1-4). Faith in the resurrection is the keystone (the top wedge of an arch) that gives legitimacy to all the other elements of our belief about Jesus. We cannot believe in his incarnation, virgin birth, deity, propitiatory sacrifice, and Second Coming if we deny his resurrection.

We must believe not just that he came back from the dead, but more specifically that *God raised him* from the dead. As such we acknowledge that his resurrection is not just some isolated and unexplained accident of nature, nor a part of some sinister hoax by an unidentified but malevolent power. No, his resurrection was an act of *God*, the God of the Bible, the God of the Jews, the God of our Lord Jesus Christ himself. Thus the resurrection establishes the entire biblical worldview, especially its claim that our justification before God is not by our own righteousness but by his righteousness alone.

Belief in Christ's resurrection is naturally linked with confession of his Lordship, since in the NT his resurrection and Lordship are inseparable. As the final and victorious stage in his battle against death and Satan, the resurrection is the supreme and conclusive expression and validation of the Lordship of God the Son in his incarnate form as Jesus of Nazareth. Because of the resurrection there can be no doubt that this man is, in Thomas's words, "my Lord and my God" (John 20:28). There are many others for whom deity and lordship are claimed (1 Cor 8:5), but the claims of Christ and Christ alone are vindicated once for all by his resurrection. See Matt 28:18; Acts 2:36; Rom 1:4; Eph 1:20-22; Phil 2:9-11; Rev 1:17-18.

This brings us to Paul's main point. Grace as a way of salvation is simple and relatively easy (compared with law), because the message has already been proclaimed to you, and the reality of which it speaks can be appropriated without delay by the activity of your own mouth and heart. You must respond as instructed, to be sure; but if you do respond, you can be assured that "you will be saved." This salvation includes the present down-payment of the "double cure" for sin (see ❧I:248), followed by the full inheritance of eternal life (8:17-25).

This verse clearly states that salvation is conditional: "*If* you do these things, you will be saved." This is in keeping with Paul's main point in this chapter, namely, that the Jews' lostness is not the result of some action (or lack of action) by an unfaithful God, but is the result of their own refusal to meet the gracious conditions for receiving salvation.

Regarding the specific conditions named here, v. 9 presents a dilemma for those committed to a faith-only view of salvation. On the one hand, the verse omits any reference to baptism, and thus seems to refute the claim that baptism is somehow a condition for salvation. On the other hand, it does speak of deliberate oral confession as a condition for salvation, and thus seems to go against the common view of justification by faith alone.

At the same time, this verse presents a problem for those who do believe that baptism is a condition for salvation. Paul seems to be saying that the *only* conditions for salvation are faith and confession; he makes no specific mention of baptism.

Regarding the former dilemma, some faith-only advocates simply ignore the implications of this verse for their view; others openly deny the parallel significance given by Paul to confession and faith. See, e.g., Moo, 657; Murray, 2:55-56; Lenski, 657 (◉II:178).

Such attempts to discount the significance of confession in order to preserve a concept of "faith only" that has been around only since Zwingli (16th century) are unfair to Paul's teaching, however. The references to confession and faith are grammatically parallel; the two verbs are identical in form and are related to "if" in exactly the same way, i.e., as equal conditions for salvation. If faith is a condition for salvation, then so must confession be. This is not to say that these two acts are related to salvation in the same way. I.e., both are conditions for salvation, but they do not play the same role in bringing the sinner to that point.

This verse shows the folly of taking any passage regarding the way of salvation in isolation from others that address the same subject. It especially shows the fallacy of drawing faith-only conclusions from texts such as John 3:16; Acts 16:31; and Rom 3:28. I have commented several times that when Paul uses expressions such as "righteousness by faith" (9:30; 10:6) and "word of faith" (10:8), these are shorthand expressions that stand for the entire grace system as contrasted with the law system. (See ◉I:266-271, on 3:27-28.) Just as works are the central element in the law system, so is faith the central element in the grace system. The frequent reference only to faith is due to this centrality, and the absence of a reference to other acts (such as repentance and baptism) cannot be taken as ruling them out as conditions, as this verse shows.

Lard notes that Hodge says, "The two requisites for salvation mentioned in this verse, are confession and faith." Lard then comments, "But the reader may ask, Do you regard this condition [confession] as indispensable? I will answer the reader by asking, Are you ready to assume the responsibility of dispensing with it? I at least am not" (330).

The bottom line is that Paul's teaching about faith and confession is inconsistent with the prevalent Protestant understanding of salvation by faith alone. (See v. 14 below for a further problem with this view.)

But what about the absence of any reference to baptism here? Even if we grant that faith is not the only condition for salvation, the only other one mentioned here is confession, not baptism. How can we explain this?

The same cautions explained above apply to this concern as well. We cannot assume that any one NT passage includes the entire list of conditions for salvation — not even this one. In fact, this very verse contains something that shows us that it was not intended to include all the conditions necessary for salvation, namely, the limited nature of the content of the faith specified here. Paul says if you believe "that God raised him from the dead," you will be saved. But virtually all Christians agree that the content of faith must include more than this; it must especially include "faith in his blood" (3:25). Thus the abbreviated content of the faith described here shows this verse is not intended to be a comprehensive, exclusive list of conditions.

Compiling such a list requires looking at all that Scripture has to say about the way of salvation. (See ❧ 1:112-115.) In Romans, Paul has already explained the saving significance of baptism (6:3-4); he need not repeat it here. Many other texts do the same. (See Cottrell, *Baptism*.)

One thing about this verse suggests that baptism may not have been absent from Paul's thinking after all, even though it is not specifically mentioned. That is the fact that the verbs "confess" and "believe" are aorist tense, which suggests that Paul had in mind a specific past act that was associated with the sinner's initial and decisive confession of faith. In early Christian practice, this act was baptism. Bruce says, "If we are to think of one outstanding occasion for such a confession to be made, we should more probably think of that first confession — 'the answer of a good conscience' (I Pet. iii.21) — made in Christian baptism" (205). Also, Cranfield (2:527) notes that the confessional formula "Jesus is Lord" was probably "used in connexion with baptism (the present verse — perhaps also the fact that baptism was in, or into, the name of Jesus — would seem to point in that direction)." This confession, says Dunn, was "a public confession of a solemn nature," and "would no doubt be used at baptism" (2:607). The confession of Jesus as Lord is also referred to as "calling on the name of the Lord" in 10:13; and this is something associated with Christian baptism as a saving event (Acts 22:16; see Joel 2:32; Acts 2:21).

10:10 For it is with your heart that you believe and are justified, and it is with your mouth that you confess and are saved. Literally this reads, "For with the heart one believes unto [εἰς, *eis*] righteousness, and with the mouth one confesses unto [*eis*] salvation." The NIV equates "unto righteousness" with being justified, which is probably accurate.

Do "justified" and "saved" refer to two different things in v. 10? I do not believe so. As Dunn says, here the words "could be reversed without loss of meaning" (2:609) (❧ II:181).

The two parts of the verse are strictly parallel in form. In each case Paul is talking about how a sinner initially receives the gift of God's righteousness, which is the same as entering into the state of salvation. Thus this verse does not add anything to v. 9, in which being saved (the only term used there) is conditioned on both confession and faith.

One problem with the NIV is that it obscures the precise relation shown in the Greek text between believing and righteousness, and between confession and salvation. Paul says the sinner believes "unto (*eis*) righteousness" and confesses "unto (*eis*) salvation." *Eis* expresses purpose (and therefore result). I.e., the sinner believes for the purpose of receiving the gift of righteousness, and that is indeed the result of his faith. The sinner likewise confesses for the purpose of receiving the gift of salvation, and that is indeed the result of his confession.

When we understand that the two parts of this verse are parallel in form and that "righteousness" and "salvation" here have the same connotation, we can see why the faith-only approach to salvation cannot be true. This view assumes that righteousness or justification *by* faith means that one is justified *as soon as* he has faith, in the instant he has faith. Such simultaneity, however, is not inherent in the preposition "by" in the phrase "justified by faith," and this verse is evidence of it. The fact that another, separate act besides faith (i.e., confession) is also a condition for receiving salvation shows that one does not receive it *as soon as* the faith is present. This same logic also shows that justification by faith does not exclude from the salvation package the act of baptism, which in other texts is shown to be the precise *time* when the salvation is received (e.g., Col 2:12, "in baptism").

4. God's Righteousness Is Available Equally to Jews and Gentiles (10:11-13)

Why are so many Jews lost, while so many Gentiles are being saved? It all comes back to the question of righteousness, and *how* a person seeks to be accepted as righteous by God. The question has always been, "In whose righteousness do you trust?" Anyone who trusts in his own righteousness will come short of the glory of God and be put to shame on Judgment Day; but anyone who humbly, by faith, accepts the gift of God's own righteousness will be saved. This applies to Jews, covenant service notwithstanding; it also applies equally to Gentiles. In this New Covenant age, the focus of this trust must be Jesus Christ, whose saving work is the very source and essence of this gift of righteousness.

This brief section speaks of the universality of God's righteousness, and how it is intended for and available to every human being.

10:11 As the Scripture says, "Anyone who trusts in him will never be put to shame." Unlike v. 6, this is specifically identified as a quote from Scripture, namely, Isa 28:16b. This was quoted earlier in 9:33; see the comments there for its basic meaning.

"Will never be put to shame" means that those who meet God on the day of judgment wearing the free gift of the robe of Christ's righteousness (Isa 61:10; 2 Cor 5:21) will not be ashamed; those who refuse the gift (i.e., refuse to put their trust in Christ) will show up for the judgment wearing only their own filthy rags (Isa 64:6) and will be eternally ashamed. See Phil 3:9.

The "him" who is the object of trust is without question Jesus. In 9:33 this was implicit, but the context of 10:11 makes it explicit. He is the *Lord* of whom this whole passage speaks (vv. 9,12,13).

Paul cites Isaiah to once again provide OT confirmation for his teaching. His main point is righteousness by faith, and in vv. 8-10 Jesus Christ is the specific object of this faith. This is what Isa 28:16b means, he says.

Isaiah is quoted exactly the same in 9:33 and 10:11, except for the addition of one word in the latter. In each case the subject is a participle, "the one who believes/trusts" (ὁ πιστεύων, *ho pisteuōn*). Universality is implicit here, but in 10:11 Paul makes it explicit by adding the word πᾶς (*pas*), "all, everyone, anyone." Thus he emphatically affirms that God's offer of righteousness by faith is open to everyone. It is open to all Jews; those who refuse to accept it do so by their own choice. It is also open to all Gentiles, many of whom have accepted it (9:30). Those who exercise their freedom to trust in him constitute the true Israel, spiritual Israel, the remnant.

10:12 For there is no difference between Jew and Gentile . . . where the true Israel is concerned. Paul has already declared, in 3:22b, that "there is no difference" between these groups. In that verse his point was that there is no difference between them with regard to *sin*, "for all have sinned and fall short of the glory of God" (3:23); "Jews and Gentiles alike are all under sin" (3:9). In this verse, though, the statement sounds the joyful note that there is no difference between Jews and Gentiles with regard to *salvation*. The promise in v. 11 applies equally to all. As Peter learned through his encounter with Cornelius, "God does not show favoritism" when it comes to salvation (Acts 10:34). The Old Covenant distinction between Jews and Gentiles was a matter of the formers' election to service; faith-righteousness as the only way of salvation is offered to all. See 1 Cor 12:13; Gal 3:28; Col 3:11.

The all-inclusiveness of the gospel is grounded in the universality of the Lordship of the one Lord, Jesus Christ: **. . . the same Lord is Lord of all and richly blesses all who will call on him . . . .** In 3:29-30 Paul affirmed the unity of Jews and Gentiles by declaring that there is only one God who is the *God* of them both. The idea here is the same, with attention focusing specifically on Jesus as the one *Lord* who is over all. That "Lord" here refers to Jesus is clear from v. 9 (see 1 Cor 12:5; Eph 4:5; Phil 2:9-11). He is elsewhere declared to be "Lord of all" (Acts 10:36; see Rom 9:5; Eph 1:22).

"All" refers specifically to all *people*, Jews and Gentiles; but the reference to riches means he is also Lord over all *things*, especially the spiritual bounty of salvation. God is "rich in mercy" (Eph 2:4) and supplies all our needs "according to his glorious riches in Christ Jesus" (Phil 4:19) (❧ II:184).

Paul says that God richly blesses "all who call on him." We might have expected him to say, "all who believe in him," since his main emphasis thus far has been on faith (10:11). Why does he now change to "call on him"? Probably for two reasons. First, "calling upon the Lord" is a way of confessing him with our mouths; thus by using this language Paul reinforces the essentiality of confession as explained in 10:9-10. "Calling upon him" unites faith with the act of confessing. Second, Paul uses this word here to set up the quotation from Joel 2:32 in the next verse. To "call upon" (ἐπικαλέω, *epikaleō*) was a word widely used in biblical times in both secular and religious senses. In the middle voice (as here) it meant "to appeal to someone" for a favor or a blessing. It is the word

Paul used when he "appealed" to Caesar (Acts 25:11-12,21,25; 26:32; 28:19). When used in reference to God, it often had the sense of petitionary prayer (1 Kgs 18:24; Acts 7:59). To call upon the *name* of God was the same as calling upon God, as vv. 12 and 13 show.

Calling upon (the name of) the Lord — confessing his Lordship — has always been a distinguishing characteristic of God's people. Calling on the name of Yahweh set Israel apart from all the nations: "Pour out your wrath on the nations that do not acknowledge you, on the kingdoms that do not call on your name" (Ps 79:6; see v. 4). In the NT Christians are identified as the ones who call on the name of the Lord (Acts 9:14,21; 1 Cor 1:2; 2 Tim 2:22). To call upon the Lord is in essence a humble confession of his absolute, universal Lordship.

10:13 Most important, calling upon the Lord is specifically related to salvation: **for, "everyone who calls on the name of the Lord will be saved."** In some contexts this may refer to praying for deliverance from temporal troubles, as in Ps 116:4, "Then I called on the name of the LORD: 'O LORD, save me!'" In other contexts, as here, it is an appeal to God for salvation from sin.

This verse (except for "for") is an exact quotation of Joel 2:32 (LXX, 3:5). In Acts 2:21 the Apostle Peter cites this as part of a Messianic prophecy that refers to calling on the name of the Lord Jesus Christ for salvation (Acts 2:36-38; see 4:12; 8:12). Here we see again how "calling on the name of the Lord" is equivalent to "confessing with your mouth that Jesus is Lord" (10:9), and how confessing with the mouth results in salvation (10:10).

The relation between calling on the Lord and salvation from sin also helps us to understand how baptism is related to the initial reception of salvation. In Acts 22:16, God's messenger Ananias tells the penitent but as-yet-unsaved Saul to do what Joel 2:32 says and call on the name of the Lord, i.e., for salvation. Do this, he says, while you are being baptized and washing away your sins. The very act of baptism is both a humble acknowledgment (confession) of the Lordship of Christ, and a prayer for him to save by washing away sins through his blood. The baptismal act should also be accompanied by a verbal prayer that "calls on his name," i.e., calls upon the Lord to keep his promises and wash away all sins. This is the sense of 1 Pet 3:21, which says that baptism saves us because it is "an appeal to God for a good conscience" (NASB; the NIV's "pledge" is incorrect). (See Cottrell, *Baptism*, chs. 6 and 13.)

One last point about 10:13 is that it is a clear affirmation of the deity of Jesus. There can be no question that "the Lord" here refers to Jesus, especially in view of the content of our saving confession in v. 9. Also, there can be no question that Paul is here quoting Joel 2:32 and applying it to Jesus. But in the original Hebrew of Joel 2:32, "Lord" is actually the tetragram, the name *Yahweh*. Thus Paul is identifying Jesus of Nazareth with Yahweh, the God of the OT. (This is not to say that Yahweh and Jesus are identical. Yahweh as known in the

OT is actually all three persons of the trinity — Father, Son, and Holy Spirit — as known in the NT. See *GRe*, 127-128.)

The main point of this paragraph (10:4-13) is that Jesus Christ alone is the source of saving righteousness. The emphasis throughout has been upon him. Now, by climactically applying Joel's prophecy to Jesus, Paul shows why we can have such utter confidence in him: he is no less than God himself.

C. THE JEWS HAVE NOT BELIEVED IN CHRIST, AND THEIR UNBELIEF IS INEXCUSABLE (10:14-21)

The Jews in general are responsible for their own lost condition, having chosen law over grace (9:30–10:21). They have rested their hope of salvation on their own righteousness, not on the righteousness of God (9:30–10:3). But salvation comes only through God's righteousness, the only basis for which is the work of Jesus Christ; and the only way to receive it is by faith in Christ (10:4-13).

This leads to the specific question now being discussed in this paragraph (10:14-21): it is true that the great majority of Jews have not believed in Jesus, but is their unbelief really their fault? Maybe they have not believed simply because they have never had the opportunity!

In response to such an idea, Paul makes it clear that the Jews have had every opportunity to believe but have simply refused to do so. Thus they are without excuse and are personally responsible for their own lost state (❧II:187).

The flow of Paul's thought here is as follows. He has just asserted that everyone who calls on the name of the Lord will be saved (v. 13). But Israel has not called on his name (v. 16). Why not? Maybe it has something to do with the chain of contingencies that must precede the act of calling on the Lord's name, i.e., calling-on is contingent upon faith, which is contingent upon hearing, which is contingent upon preaching, which is contingent upon being sent (vv. 14-15a).

So maybe Israel's unbelief can be traced to one of these other contingencies, one over which they have no control. Faith can come only from hearing the message, which can come only through the word of Christ. So maybe the message has never been brought to them — which would not be *their* fault (v. 17).

In response to this idea Paul specifically affirms (in vv. 18-21) that the Jews have both heard and understood the gospel. In fact, their own Scriptures — including both the Law and the Prophets — should have prepared them for it. Therefore they have no excuse; their problem is not ignorance but stubborn, willful unbelief. (See Smith, 2:27.)

1. The Necessary Prerequisites to Saving Faith (10:14-15)

Even though their immediate application was to Paul's Jewish contemporaries, these two verses (along with v. 17) are general doctrinal principles with many other applications. For example, they have long been regarded — and rightly so — as crucial for such theological issues as the salvation status of the unevangelized, the necessity of missions, and the nature of conversion as such.

10:14-15a The four main verbs in this passage are third person plural with no subject specified; thus the general translation, "they." Though its scope is ultimately universal (see vv. 12-13), "they" refers specifically to the Jews. Though they are not expressly mentioned until v. 19, they are the implicit subject all along.

These four rhetorical questions are similar in form, beginning with "how" (πῶς, *pōs*) and a subjunctive verb. The sense is "How is it possible . . . ?" and the expected answer is, "It is impossible!"

The issue is, why have the Jews not called on the name of their Lord and Messiah, and thus received salvation? The question being explored is whether they may possibly have some excuse for not doing so. After all, a number of prerequisites must be in place before one can call on the Lord's name and be saved. These are listed here, in a kind of reverse order, as a chain of effects and causes. If any one of the links in the chain is missing, then it would be impossible for one to call on the Lord's name and be saved.

How, then, can they call on the one they have not believed in? A genuine appeal for help presupposes a belief that the one to whom the appeal is made is able to comply. It is also a confession of need and dependence. As in vv. 9-10, mouth and heart are inseparably linked.

"Believed" is aorist and probably refers to the initial birth of faith in the heart. Believed "*in*" is εἰς (*eis*), which is equivalent to ἐπί (*epi*) in v. 11. These expressions refer primarily to that element of faith usually called trust, which is a heartfelt surrender and commitment of the self to Christ. This involves a sense of dependence upon him, and a total confidence in his ability and willingness to keep his promises and to meet our needs.

In the discussion of 10:9 above, it was pointed out that the listing of both faith and confession as conditions for salvation disproves the common faith-only doctrine of salvation, which alleges that a person is saved the instant he believes. The question Paul asks here in v. 14a has the same effect. Paul's point is that these three things occur in a cause-effect sequence: believing, calling on the Lord's name, and being saved. One cannot contend that these events are only logically sequential while being in fact temporally simultaneous. The act of calling upon the Lord, as a public confession of one's faith, will almost never occur at the instant faith begins. The fact that Paul lists it here as an intermediary link between faith and salvation shows that salvation is not given at the moment one begins to believe. Faith is a prerequisite for calling upon the Lord, and calling upon him is a prerequisite for salvation.

And how can they believe in the one of whom they have not heard? This is not a literal translation, because the Greek says neither "believe *in*" nor "*of* whom." It says literally, "How can they believe whom they have not heard?" As the next questions show, the one who is heard is actually the preacher of the gospel of Jesus Christ. But the previous question (indeed, the entire context) implies that the object of faith is Jesus himself. This has led many exegetes to suggest that "Christ is present in the preachers; to hear them is to hear him" (Morris, 389-390). This may well be true in the sense that the inspired message is the words of Jesus (John 16:12-15; see Luke 10:16), but the main point is surely as the NIV translates it.

Just as calling-on and faith are necessarily linked, so are faith and hearing. Hearing does not always produce faith; indeed, the main point of this paragraph is that the Jews have heard (v. 18), but have not believed. But on the other hand, there can be no faith without hearing (see v. 17). In other words, hearing is a *necessary* condition for faith, but not a *sufficient* one.

The hearing of which Paul speaks is more than mere sense perception; it is also an act of the mind. It involves at least a minimal level of understanding of the message heard, i.e., enough understanding to create culpability for failure to believe (see v. 19).

We must not underestimate the importance of hearing in the salvation process. On several occasions Jesus gave this exhortation: "He who has ears, let him hear" (Matt 11:15. See Matt 13:9,43; Mark 4:23; Luke 14:35; Rev 2:7,11,17,29; 3:6,13,22). This hearing is the responsibility not just of the messenger, but even more so of the listener, who is the one addressed in the exhortation. I.e., the listener is responsible for paying attention to the message, and for studying it and searching out its proper meaning.

And how can they hear without someone preaching to them? A proper hearing of the message of Jesus Christ presupposes and requires the work of a third party. God of course could speak his message directly to each individual, but instead he has chosen to use intermediaries to act as his messengers and ambassadors; and without their faithful preaching there will be no hearing.

"Someone preaching" is a form of the verb κηρύσσω (*kēryssō*), which means "to announce, to proclaim aloud, to preach, to herald abroad." Its noun form is κήρυξ (*kēryx*), a "*herald*, whose duty it is to make public proclamations" (BAGD, 431). We should remember that Paul wrote this long before the invention of the printing press and electronic media, in a time when the role of the herald was indispensable for spreading news. For our time we may properly assume that this "preaching" can be done via such media as printed material, television, and the internet.

This question shows how important is the whole enterprise of evangelism, and specifically the office of evangelist (Eph 4:11) and the work of preaching the gospel. Murray says this verse refers to "the institution which is the ordinary and most effectual means of propagating the gospel, namely, the official preaching of the Word by those appointed to this task" (2:58-59). This includes local evangelists and ministers, as well as missionaries engaged in worldwide evangelism.

Paul's point is not just that this heralding work is *important*; it is actually *necessary*. It is a prerequisite to the hearing that must precede faith. "Hence arises the necessity of proclaiming the gospel world-wide" (Bruce, 205). Some think that general revelation alone provides enough knowledge of God to enable pagans to believe and call upon God and be saved, but this text shows otherwise. The hearing that leads to salvation comes only through a personal, human messenger.

Since the hearing involves not just receiving but also understanding the message (as noted above), the heralding must include not just a bare speaking of the message but an earnest attempt to explain it as well. Hence the importance of sound exegetical and doctrinal training for those who proclaim the gospel.

And how can they preach unless they are sent? With this question Paul has traced the chain of prerequisites back to its beginning point: the *sending* of the heralds or preachers. At first glance this may seem to be out of place in a list of such obviously significant and interconnected events as preaching, hearing, believing, calling-on, and being saved. It may not appear to be on the same level with these other factors. Nevertheless, Paul through the Spirit has included it here. Therefore we must not weaken the connection between preaching and being sent; sending is just as necessary as the other elements in the chain.

The obvious question is, sent by whom? The first answer is, sent by *God*. This certainly applies to Paul himself, and to the other apostles, all of whom were commissioned and sent directly by Christ, who is God the Son. After his resurrection Jesus said to the Eleven, "As the Father has sent me, I am sending you" (John 20:21). Paul's commission came directly through Jesus and God the Father (Gal 1:1,15-16). In fact, the very word "apostle" is from ἀποστέλλω (*apostellō*), "to send," and means "one who is sent."

But God has sent more than these who are the "official" apostles. Jesus, God the Son, gave us his "great commission" (Matt 28:18-20), which most take to apply to all Christians. Even though it was spoken directly only to the apostles (28:16), Jesus told them to teach the rest of us to obey everything he commanded *them* to do (28:20). In the early church all Christians who were scattered abroad via persecution "preached the word wherever they went" (Acts 8:4). By the very fact that we possess the message, the word of the gospel, we have been inducted into the army of heralds who have been commissioned to take that word to the world. God himself has sent us.

The second answer to this question (sent by whom?) is, sent by *the church*, through the act of ordination. By ordaining an individual Christian to a specific ministry, the leadership of a local church acknowledges that servant's spiritual gift, puts an unofficial "stamp of approval" upon him (e.g., on his doctrinal soundness and his readiness for ministry), recommends him to the brotherhood at large, and establishes a relationship of encouragement and accountability. Various NT men and women were "apostles" — "ones who were sent" — in this generic sense, e.g., as missionaries (see Acts 13:1-3; Rom 16:7; 2 Cor 8:23). When we apply this verse to the sending of missionaries, we should think more in terms of ordination than financial support (❷ II:192).

10:15b As it is written, "How beautiful are the feet of those who bring good news!" This quote is from Isa 52:7, which was first of all a prophecy relating to the end of Israel's Babylonian captivity c. 536 B.C. It speaks of the herald "who brings good news as he runs on mountain ridges and announces to Jews left in ruined Jerusalem that deliverance from Babylonian captivity has come" (Fitzmyer, 597). But since that great event was itself an historical type of the Messiah's work of delivering his people from captivity to sin, Paul appropriately applies the prophecy to the work of preaching the gospel of Jesus Christ.

Why are the feet singled out? The implication is that the original messenger traveled from Babylon to Jerusalem on foot to bring his message of deliverance. His feet were responsible for bringing him and his beautiful message to those set free from Babylon's oppression; therefore his feet were looked upon as sharing in the beauty of the message. Also, after such a long, hot, dusty journey, the messenger's feet would be the least attractive part of his appearance. But the messenger's news was *so good* that even his *feet* looked beautiful to those receiving his word!

Why exactly does Paul quote this text from Isaiah at this point? Some answer that it shows "the need for heralds"; it is "Paul's case for evangelism" (Stott, 286; see Moo, 664). This is at best a secondary point, however. The main reason for quoting Isa 52:7 is to affirm through OT testimony "that the 'gospel' has indeed been preached to Israel" (Fitzmyer, 597). Thus "the last condition for salvation listed by Paul in vv. 14-15a has been met: God has sent preachers" (Moo, 664). Paul knew this was true, because he himself was such a preacher.

2. Most Jews Have Not Believed the Gospel Message (10:16)

10:16 This verse states the obvious: **But not all the Israelites accepted the good news.** Literally this reads, "But not all obeyed the gospel." The context shows that the "Israelites" are indeed the subject, but this word is not in the original. "Not all" is rhetorical understatement, and simply highlights the fact that "only a few" Jews — a remnant — obeyed the gospel (9:6b,27b).

"Accepted" is too mild a translation of ὑπακούω (*hypakouō*). It has the connotation "to heed, to submit, to be subject to, to obey." It means "to submit and yield to what is heard" (Lenski, 665).

To "obey the gospel" is a significant NT concept (2 Thess 1:8; 1 Pet 4:17), similar to "obeying the faith" (Acts 6:7; see ❷ I:81, on 1:5). It means submitting to God's instructions (meeting the conditions) for receiving the saving grace promised in the gospel. The primary (and representative) condition for salvation is faith, as v. 16b shows; that other conditions are also required has already been made clear in vv. 9-10 (confession) and vv. 13-14 (calling on his name).

To show that the Jews' rejection of the gospel was just part of a longstanding pattern of chronic unbelief, Paul quotes Isa 53:1 from the LXX: **For Isaiah says, "Lord, who has believed our message?"** This was true in Isaiah's own day, when apostate Jews rejected God's words spoken through his prophets (see Acts 7:51-52). It was true of the Jews whom Jesus confronted during his earthly ministry. See John 12:37-38, where John quotes this same passage and declares that Israel's unbelief is the fulfilment of Isaiah's prophecy. And alas, much to Paul's dismay (9:1-3; 10:1-3), the prophecy was still being fulfilled in his own time.

That most Jews have not obeyed the gospel is just a restatement of v. 3b, which says "they did not submit to God's righteousness." In terms of the prerequisites for salvation listed in vv. 14-15a, they have not believed and have not called upon the Lord's name. The issue at hand is how to account for this, which is addressed in the next few verses.

3. The Jews' Problem Is Not Ignorance but Stubbornness of Will (10:17-21)

10:17 Consequently, faith comes from hearing the message, and the message is heard through the word of Christ. How this verse fits into the logical progression of Paul's argument is a bit puzzling (❂ II:194-195). The logic is something like this: "Most Jews have not believed, even as Isaiah says. Consequently, in view of the chain of prerequisites listed earlier, some will say that Israel's unbelief must have something to do with that chain. There must be a breakdown in it somewhere. I.e., one of the necessary prerequisites for faith must be missing. Did we not say that faith comes from hearing, and hearing comes through the preaching of the gospel? Thus there must not have been any preaching or hearing, since if there had been, surely the Jews would have believed." The NASB is literal and to the point: "So faith comes from hearing, and hearing by the word of Christ" (❂ II:195).

"The word of Christ" could mean either "the word Christ speaks" or "the word spoken about Christ." The latter is probably Paul's intent, since it is no doubt the same as "the word of faith" that he proclaimed (v. 8), i.e., the message about Christ's saving work.

The verse restates the important principle given in v. 14b, "And how can they believe in the one of whom they have not heard?" It also restates and expands v. 14c — "And how can they hear without someone preaching to them?" — i.e., preaching the word of Christ. It is exceedingly important that we acknowledge these necessary cause-and-effect connections. Faith must be preceded by hearing the word of Christ; it cannot arise under any other circumstances. The role of the word is indispensable. Also, this "word" must be the word or message about *Jesus Christ*. Saving faith cannot arise in a context of general revelation only, which tells us nothing about Jesus.

We must not conclude, however, that wherever the word of Christ is present, faith will automatically follow. As said earlier, the word is a *necessary* condition for faith, but not a *sufficient* condition (❧ II:196). The Jews have indeed heard the gospel, and have understood it. But hearing it is not the same as believing it, and does not automatically lead to saving faith. Such faith is a decision the individual must make, and a stubborn will may refuse to believe even in the face of clearly attested facts. Herein lies the real cause of the Jews' unbelief: they are simply "a disobedient and obstinate people" (v. 21).

Paul now discusses this point in detail.

10:18 So why has Israel not believed? Is it possible that they never really heard the word of Christ? Here is Paul's question, and his answer: **But I ask**, on behalf of all who may want to raise this question: **Did they not hear?** And I answer: **Of course they did.** It is true that no one can believe in someone of whom they have never heard (v. 14), but the Jews cannot use this excuse. In fact, the words of David in Ps 19:4 apply here: **"Their voice has gone out into all the earth, their words to the ends of the world."** (This is a verbatim quote from the LXX.)

Paul is not implying that these words from the Psalms are an actual prophecy of first-century evangelism. Thus he is not citing this passage to *prove* that the Jews have heard the gospel; the authority of his own words as an apostle is sufficient for this purpose.

In its original context this quote refers to the universal availability of general revelation (see also 1:18-20). The personified natural world is pictured as declaring the glory of its Creator to all people on earth. Paul's citation of the verse is by way of analogy: "The dissemination of the gospel is becoming as world-wide as the light of the heavenly bodies" (Bruce, 209) (❧ II:197).

When Paul said that the gospel had gone out into "all the earth" and "to the ends of the world," did he mean that this had already happened (❧ II:197)? When we remember that Paul is speaking here specifically of the Jews, we need not press his words beyond the scope of their scattered colonies. The main point is that "the Jews had, indeed, gotten to hear!" (Lenski, 671). Thus ignorance cannot be cited as an explanation for their unbelief.

10:19 Paul now deals with one last attempt to excuse the Jews for their failure to obey the gospel: maybe they *heard* the message, but just did not *understand* it. He says, **Again I ask: Did Israel not understand?** As we saw above (v. 14), the concept of "hearing" in itself includes a basic understanding of the message received. Thus to distinguish here between hearing (v. 18) and understanding (v. 19) is grasping at straws, and Paul does not even consider the objection worthy of a direct answer.

The way Paul deals with this question shows that the Jews' "not knowing" in 10:3 was a *willful* ignorance (Stott, 289). As was the case with the Gentiles and general revelation in 1:18-25, knowledge of the gospel was there for the Jews but was willfully ignored or suppressed, the result being that there was no excuse.

Paul makes his point by quoting three passages from the Jews' own Scriptures (the OT). He implies that they should have understood from these texts that the Gentiles were ultimately going to be included within God's people, and the Jews excluded. But they also should have understood that in the final analysis God did not do the excluding; the Jews excluded themselves (v. 21).

Paul quotes first from Moses and then from Isaiah. **First, Moses says, "I will make you envious by those who are not a nation; I will make you angry by a nation that has no understanding."** This comes from Deut 32:21 (❂ II:198). As quoted by Paul, "those who are not a nation" and "a nation that has no understanding" refer to the Gentiles in general. They are "not a nation" because God did not call them into a special covenant relationship with himself, the way he called Israel. Also, in contrast with Israel, they had "no understanding" (ἀσύνετος, *asynetos*) of God's redemptive purposes and plans. Paul uses this same word to describe the Gentiles in 1:21 ("foolish") and 1:31 ("senseless").

There may be a sense in which this prophecy was fulfilled in OT history in the various occasions when God used heathen nations to punish Israel (e.g., the Babylonian captivity), but its ultimate fulfillment lies in the NT era, in the continuing influx of Gentiles into the church in the face of Jewish unbelief.

The irony and the tragedy of these words in relation to Israel is this, that the nation that took such great pride in being God's chosen people and in being entrusted with God's special revelation would some day be humiliated by a "no-people" with "no understanding"! That is, the messianic blessings that were intended first of all for the Jews (1:16b) are being lavished upon the Gentiles, who are turning to Jesus the Messiah, calling upon his name, and being saved (10:11-13).

What are the implications of this for the Jews? First, Paul seems to be suggesting that Israel should have understood from this text that Gentile evangelism and conversion were part of God's plan. Second, the Deuteronomy text says that the conversion of the Gentiles would have the effect of arousing envy and anger in the hearts of the Jews (❂ II:199). Certainly God did not embrace the Gentiles just to make Israel jealous. He wanted to save the Gentiles for their own sake; Israel's jealous anger would be an indirect result of this (Lard, 341-342). Paul's earnest hope was that this jealous anger would then lead to Israel's own conversion (see 11:11-14).

10:20 And Isaiah boldly says, "I was found by those who did not seek me; I revealed myself to those who did not ask for me." After quoting from the Law, Paul now quotes from the prophets to make the same basic point. This verse is from Isa 65:1a, with the clauses being transposed. As in v. 19, the words of the prophecy are actually spoken by God. Isaiah, like Moses, is the prophet through whom he speaks (❧ II:200).

It seems likely that when Isaiah wrote 65:1, he had the Jews in mind. Paul sees in Isaiah's words "a principle which in the situation of his day is applicable to Gentiles" (Bruce, 211). "As he did with Hos. 1:10 and 2:23 in 9:25-26, Paul takes OT texts that speak of Israel and applies them, on the principle of analogy, to the Gentiles" (Moo, 669). See 10:18b.

Thus Paul takes Isa 65:1 as having the same general impact as Deut 32:21. Even if this were not Isaiah's original point, in view of the reality of widespread Gentile conversions, Israel should have been struck by the way these words precisely described what was happening among them. Thus, "as used by [Paul], the quotation from Isa 65:1 is parallel to the quotation in v. 19, and serves to confirm that Israel must have known, since God has actually been found by Gentiles who were not seeking Him" (Cranfield, 2:540-541). It is an argument from the lesser to the greater: if the Gentiles (who had no prior understanding based on special revelation) could understand the gospel and accept the Messiah through apostolic preaching, surely the Jews (with their long history of divine preparation) should be able to understand and obey the same gospel.

It is easy to see how these words apply to Gentiles. Paul's description of them in 1:18-32 shows emphatically that they do not seek God and do not ask for him. Nevertheless God "revealed" himself or "became manifest" to them through the word of Christ. This is the very nature of evangelism. In preaching the gospel we do not passively wait for people to come to us, but actively seek them where they are.

10:21 But concerning Israel he says, "All day long I have held out my hands to a disobedient and obstinate people." There is neither doubt nor disagreement that these words from Isa 65:2 apply to Israel; Paul expressly says so. His point goes back to 10:19: "Did Israel not understand?" He implies that the Jews of his day should have seen and understood how Isa 65:2 applied to their situation. They should have understood that the inclusion of the Gentiles in the messianic kingdom was not meant to exclude them. They should have learned from this text that they too were being invited into the kingdom, and that the only reason they were not included in it was their own stubborn refusal to believe in their Messiah, Jesus.

This image of God as one who constantly stands with welcoming arms outstretched toward rebellious sinners is one of the Bible's most graphic pictures of God as a God of grace. "All day long" indicates God's persistence and patience in his desire to save sinners. Stretched-out hands are a gesture of invitation, as God pleads with sinners and implores them to return to him.

Just as important is the verse's description of Israel as "a disobedient and obstinate people." Paul has already emphasized the Jews' refusal to obey the gospel (v. 16), and here he suggests the reason for it. Their failure to believe cannot be blamed on ignorance, as if no one had ever been sent to preach the gospel to them. No, their unbelief is due to their own obstinate will.

Cranfield (2:541) recalls vv. 9-10 and takes "disobedience" as the very opposite of believing, and "obstinate" as the very opposite of confession. "Obstinate" is a form of the verb ἀντιλέγω (*antilegō*), which means "to speak against, to contradict, to oppose, to refuse" (BAGD, 74). Instead of using their mouths to confess Jesus as Lord and to call upon his name, the Jews chose to speak against him, to oppose him, to deny him.

This is how this main section ends. Is Israel's lost state a reflection on God, evidence of his unfaithfulness, an indication that his word has failed (9:6)? No, God has faithfully kept his word to Israel in every way. He kept every promise he made to the nation relating to their covenant purposes and privileges (9:1-29). He has sent the Messiah and given them every opportunity to trust in him for personal salvation (9:30–10:21). Their refusal to accept him is their own fault. In summary, "The Apostle demonstrates the inexcusableness of Israel and does so by appeal to their own Scriptures" (Murray, 2:64) (● II:202).

Chapter 10 thus ends on a negative, pessimistic note. Where does this leave the question of the Jews and their salvation? Is v. 21 God's final word on the subject? No! There is much more to be said — in ch. 11.

IV. THE SALVATION OF GOD'S TRUE ISRAEL (11:1-32)

Thus far in chs. 9–10 Paul has painted a very dark picture of Israel and an encouraging picture of the Gentiles (● II:203). Such teaching naturally raises the question, "Did God reject his people?" (11:1). Has he simply given up on Israel, and turned his attention solely to the Gentiles? Romans 11 addresses this question and answers it with an emphatic No! God's desire and intention are still to save as many Jews as possible, even to the point when ultimately "all Israel will be saved" (11:26).

This chapter discusses not just the *fact* of Israel's salvation, but also the *means* by which God is accomplishing it. This involves intricate interrelationships between the Jews and the Gentiles, which God uses for the salvation of both. Even as Paul writes about this, he is overwhelmed with awe and amazement at the wisdom and mercy of God, and most appropriately closes out the chapter and the entire section with a hymn of praise to the Creator and Redeemer (11:33-36).

It is important to see that the question addressed here is different from that in ch. 9, which focuses on God's covenant faithfulness to ethnic Israel, i.e., how he kept his promises to them and how they fulfilled their purpose in God's plan. In ch. 11 the focus is not on the Old Covenant purpose for Israel as fulfilled in Jesus Christ (9:4-5), but on God's intended place for Jews as individuals under the *New* Covenant, in terms of salvation and eternal destiny.

Throughout this chapter, the issue is *salvation*. What is God's plan for Israel with regard to salvation in this New Covenant age?

In this connection a major issue of interpretation is the place of Israel *as a nation* in this NT era. One main view is that God is still under obligation to save, restore, and preserve national Israel because of the covenant promises he made to the patriarchs (❈II:204). Another main view is the one defended here, i.e., that only the Old Covenant was made with Israel as a nation, that the essence of this covenant for Israel was service and not salvation, and finally that all God's covenant obligations to national Israel were fulfilled when Christ came into the world the first time. Under the New Covenant God is dealing with the Jews as individuals, not as a nation. He is now gathering together the remnant, the new Israel, the true spiritual Israel, from among both Gentiles and Jews. Those who believe the gospel and accept Jesus as their Messiah are added to this remnant. See Lard, 345; McGuiggan, 319-320.

The following exposition will show that Paul's teaching in Rom 11 is more consistent with the latter view.

A. GOD'S TRUE ISRAEL IS THE REMNANT CHOSEN BY GRACE (11:1-6)

Has God rejected Israel? The answer to this question is already obvious in chs. 9–10. In the first place, God has not rejected them; *they* have rejected *him*. "All day long I have held out my hands" to invite them to myself, God says (10:21), but "they did not submit" (10:3). See Matt 23:37.

In the second place, even if there is a sense in which God has "rejected" Israel, he has not rejected them all. Some Jews are still among "the objects of his mercy, whom he prepared in advance for glory" (9:23-24). These are "the remnant" of whom Isaiah spoke (9:27-29); they are the Jews who accepted God's righteousness on God's terms (10:1-17). They are still "his people," Israelites in the truest sense of the word.

Near the beginning of this main section (9:6b) Paul declares that "not all who are descended from Israel are Israel." This means in effect that there are two Israels. One is the physical nation descended from Jacob (renamed Israel, Gen 32:28), which was called as a group into covenant relationship with God to serve his redemptive purposes. The other is the remnant, the relatively small part of the nation who as individuals put their heartfelt trust in God's promises as the basis of their personal salvation. This remnant is "his people" in a double sense, both ethnically and spiritually.

The remnant is the subject of this paragraph. Paul's point is that God can never be accused of rejecting "his people," because there has always been a remnant from among the Jews who have accepted his way of grace and are thus in personal fellowship with him. Thus no matter what happens to the nation as a whole, "Israel" will never perish, because "the *real* Israel has always been less than the nation" (McGuiggan, 317).

1. God Has Not Rejected His People (11:1-2a)

11:1 I ask then: Did God reject his people? By no means! The word "then" (οὖν, *oun*, "therefore") indicates that this question might naturally arise from the preceding chapters. Paul simply anticipates it and responds to it. The word for "reject" is ἀπωθέω (*apōtheō* — here in the middle voice). It means "to push away, cast away, or thrust away (from oneself); to repel; to spurn; to reject; to disown; to repudiate."

To be rejected or cast away by God is a terrible prospect for anyone, but for the Jews it was an absolutely unthinkable idea, given the facts that God had chosen them through Abraham (Gen 12:1-3), had established his covenant only with them at Sinai (Exod 19:5-6; see Deut 14:2), and thus had regarded them as his unique people for some 2,000 years. God described them as "my people, my chosen, the people I formed for myself" (Isa 43:20b-21a). "I will be your God and you will be my people," he promised them (Jer 7:23; see Lev 26:12).

But in view of 9:6b, we may ask, to which Israel does "his people" refer? Some think it refers only to the remnant, since "from Abraham onward only believing Israelites were 'his people'" (Lenski, 680). Others say it refers to "the *nation* as a whole" (Godet, 391; see MacArthur, 2:99). Strictly speaking neither view is correct. Contra Lenski, at this point "his people" is not spiritual but physical, as Paul's self-identification in v. 1b shows. But neither is it a reference to physical Israel as a whole, as if such a question ("Has God rejected the nation of Israel as such?") could be answered yes or no. Rather, Paul *is* thinking of ethnic Jews, but he is thinking of them *as individuals*. Has God rejected all of them?

The answer depends upon what is meant by "rejected." Does this "rejection" relate to Israel's role of service in God's redemptive plan, or does it relate to their personal, individual, eternal salvation? It cannot refer to the former, because such a question is irrelevant and meaningless. There is no sense in which God has ever rejected or will ever reject his nation Israel, either as a whole or as individuals, in reference to their role as the covenant people who prepared for the Messiah's coming into the world. God cannot *reject* them in reference to this role, because every purpose for which he thus chose them has already been fulfilled (9:4-5). Because of this it is true, to be sure, that there is no longer any rationale for Israel's continuing existence as a nation, or as Jews as distinct from Gentiles. Their existence as God's special, unique physical nation has thus come to an end (10:12; Gal 3:28; Col 3:11). But this is not the same as being "rejected." We may say, rather, that in full accordance with God's plan Israel as a nation has been honorably retired from service.

"Rejected" in this context must then refer to the question of personal salvation. Has God excluded his own people, the Jews, from salvation? Has he shut them out of heaven? Is the gospel invitation closed to Jews? Such a question does not (indeed, cannot) apply to Israel as a nation, but it does apply to all Israelites as individuals.

"Did God reject his people?" The question itself contains a Greek particle (μή, *mē*) which shows that a negative answer is intended. The question could thus be worded, "God has not rejected his people, has he?" Paul's answer is an emphatic and resounding NO! (μὴ γένοιτο, *mē genoito*; see 3:4; ❧I:228). The very idea is unthinkable, and the evidence shows that it is not in fact the case.

The first bit of evidence that God has not rejected his people, the Jews, is Paul himself: **I am an Israelite myself, a descendant of Abraham, from the tribe of Benjamin.** Here Paul emphasizes his physical Jewishness. He is an "Israelite," which at the very least is equivalent to "Jew" (see 9:4). He is also "of the seed of Abraham" in the literal, physical sense (see 2 Cor 11:22), specifically of "the tribe of Benjamin," which along with Judah was one of the only two original tribes to be restored to their homeland following captivity and to remain intact into NT times. Thus "Paul shows that he is as firmly located within Judaism as anyone can be" (Dunn, 2:635).

Why does Paul make a big deal of his Jewish credentials? Some think he does so in order to make it clear that he is expressing "an authentically Jewish viewpoint" (Dunn, 2:635; see Fitzmyer, 603) (❧II:207). This answer is possible, but more likely Paul thoroughly identifies himself as a Jew in order to give "living evidence" that God has not rejected "his people" (Moo, 673). "How do I know that God has not excluded Jews from salvation? Because *I, Paul* am the most Jewish of Jews, and *I* am saved!" Thus Paul himself is "proof that God had not abandoned Israel" (Bruce, 211), proof that a remnant does exist.

11:2a God did not reject his people, whom he foreknew. Again Paul emphatically denies that God has rejected his people. The wording here (as in 11:1a) seems to be taken from 1 Sam 12:22 and Ps 94:14, which use the future tense to assert God's promise: "The LORD will not reject his people." Paul changes it to past tense and thus states it as a fact; God has kept his promise!

Why does Paul add the qualifier, "whom he foreknew"? This again raises the crucial question as to the essential meaning of προγινώσκω (*proginōskō*; see 8:29; ❧I:505-511). Many, especially Calvinists, declare that it refers to an act of distinguishing, choosing love, and is thus the same as election or predestination. In this context it thus becomes a reason why God has not rejected his elect remnant, spiritual Israel. How could he reject the very ones he has "foreknown," i.e., chosen from eternity for salvation? (❧II:208).

Many of those who equate foreknowledge with predestination do not think it refers to the eternal salvation of the elect in this verse, however. This is because they take "his people" as referring to the Jewish *nation* as such. I.e., God cannot reject the nation of Israel, because he unconditionally chose it and set it apart with his electing love (i.e., his "foreknowledge"). "Israel is the only *nation* God has foreknown and predetermined to be his people," says MacArthur. Thus "he can never totally reject them" (2:100) (◉II:208).

The problem with each of the above views is its erroneous understanding of foreknowledge as such. As I have shown earlier (see ◉I:505-511), foreknowledge means just that: knowing beforehand, in the sense of prior cognitive or mental awareness. "Foreknew" here could then mean the same as in 8:29, i.e., God did not reject those from among his people whom he foreknew would accept his grace through faith. The effect then would be to narrow the meaning of "his people" from the nation in general to the remnant. I.e., has God rejected his people? No, he has not rejected *all* of them. To be more specific, he has not rejected the ones foreknown to become believers, who by their very faith are the only ones who are truly "his people."

I do not think this is the point, however. I take "his people" in v. 2a to be the same as in v. 1a, i.e., it refers to all ethnic Israelites and thus to the nation of Israel; but it refers to them as individuals and not as a national unit. To say that God "foreknew" his people Israel means that even before he singled them out for a central role in his redemptive plan, he knew in advance the kind of people they would be all along the historical path to the Messiah and beyond. Nothing about them — their weaknesses, their failures, their unbelief, their idolatries — took him by surprise. He foreknew all these things and chose them anyway, because he also foreknew that there would always be a faithful remnant who would turn to him with believing hearts, who would keep the messianic hope alive, and who would turn to the Messiah when he came.

Thus God's foreknowledge of his people included a foreknowledge of their persistent rebellion (see ◉I:509), as well as a foreknowledge of a continuing, faithful remnant. The latter is the main point, as vv. 2b-5 show. Because he foreknew there would always be an abiding remnant who is the true *spiritual* Israel, he did not abandon his ethnic people, even though he foreknew that most of them would never respond to his gracious invitation (10:21).

2. God Had a Remnant of Believers in the OT (11:2b-4)

11:2b-3 Don't you know what the Scripture says in the passage about Elijah—how he appealed to God against Israel: "Lord, they have killed your prophets and torn down your altars; I am the only one left, and they are trying to kill me"? In v. 1 Paul cited himself as evidence that God has not rejected his people; now he refers to a familiar incident from the OT as a further, more general proof (Godet, 392; Hendriksen, 2:361). In so doing he explicitly affirms the remnant concept introduced in 9:27-29.

"Don't you know" implies a positive answer: "You surely know, don't you?" "In the passage about Elijah" refers to 1 Kgs 17:1 through 2 Kgs 2:11. Students of Scripture in Paul's day would have known where to find this, even though they did not have chapter-and-verse divisions as we do today.

Paul refers to the specific place in the Elijah section where "he appealed to God against Israel," i.e., 1 Kgs 19:10,14 (❖II:210). Elijah's words sum up his perception of the religious crisis facing Israel at that time. God's prophets were certainly being killed on Jezebel's orders (1 Kgs 18:4), and the altars were being demolished (1 Kgs 18:30-32). Elijah's lament that he was "the only one left," even if it refers to prophets and not just true believers in general, is surely an exaggeration reflecting more his mood of despair than the facts as he knew them (see 1 Kgs 18:13,22).

The term translated "left" ("I am the only one left") is important because it ties in with several other words that represent the remnant concept. The word is the passive form of ὑπολείπω (*hypoleipō* – used only here in the NT), and means "to be left behind." Two other one-time words from this same family used in this context are λεῖμμα (*leimma*, 11:5) and ὑπόλειμμα (*hypoleimma*, 9:27). Both mean "the ones left behind," i.e., the remnant. In v. 4 a more common word meaning "to leave" καταλείπω (*kataleipō*) is used. Thus when Elijah complained, "I am the only one *left*," he was to the point of thinking he alone constituted the remnant of true believers (or at least true prophets).

11:4 And what was God's answer to him? "I have reserved for myself seven thousand who have not bowed the knee to Baal." In order to shake Elijah out of his black mood, God gave him a demonstration of his solemn majesty (1 Kgs 19:11-13) and some concrete instructions (1 Kgs 19:15-17). He added the firm yet gentle reminder that Elijah was not alone; there were seven thousand other true worshipers of Yahweh in Israel (1 Kgs 19:18).

Many think the number "seven thousand" is not meant to be literal, but (since it involves the perfect number 7) is symbolic for the complete and perfect number of believers among Israel (see Cranfield, 2:547; Dunn, 2:638). Paul follows the LXX and adds the word ἀνήρ (*anēr*, "male") after "seven thousand," i.e., "seven thousand *men*." For a parallel see Acts 4:4. (The NIV translates *anēr* ["men"] in Acts 4:4, but leaves it out here.) If the number itself is symbolic and not literal, this is irrelevant. If not, then the total number of believers in Elijah's day were even greater than seven thousand, including women and youth (see Matt 14:21).

God's statement, "I have reserved for myself," uses the verb καταλείπω (*kataleipō*), another "remnant" term (see v. 3). Its usual meaning is "to leave." Those with Calvinist leanings see an oblique reference to unconditional predestination in this word (❖II:212).

But this is not the point. Certainly this is an act of God regarding these men, but God's act is conditioned on the fact that they "have not bowed the knee to Baal." God is telling Elijah, "There are more than just you who have remained faithful. Indeed, I have identified and singled out from the great majority of Israelites a group of seven thousand true worshipers. I have separated them from the rest; in my sight they are a different group, a remnant. These are the ones I have kept in my saving grace and in close fellowship with myself."

They are the ones, God says, "I have reserved *for myself*." They are "his people" in a special, spiritual sense. In this spiritual sense only these seven thousand belonged to God; the rest were Baal's. This remnant alone was the true Israel of 9:6b (McGuiggan, 319). Thus God did not reject his people Israel. Though most rejected him, he still counted as his own those who sought him in faith. Though most abandoned him, these are still enough — a remnant to be sure — to constitute "his people."

3. Those under Grace Are God's New Covenant Israel (11:5-6)

11:5 Paul's reference to the Elijah incident is a good example of the remnant reality in OT times, but his main point is that this is an analogy of the Jewish situation in his own day. **So too, at the present time there is a remnant chosen by grace.** Paul uses three words to connect this verse with the preceding one: "so therefore also." He does not want us to miss the parallel, i.e., there is no difference between Elijah's day and "the present time."

What is the nature of the parallel? The main point is the very *existence* of a remnant from among the people of Israel. God is no more rejecting his people in this gospel era than he was in Elijah's day. In the earlier time of national apostasy at least seven thousand remained true to God, "and so in Paul's day there was a faithful minority who had not rejected the gospel" (Bruce, 211). The existence of this remnant is sufficient to prove that God has not rejected his people, and thus that he is still faithful to his word and to his promises (❂ II:213).

The second part of the parallel has to do with the *means* by which the remnant of Israel is distinguished from the nation as a whole, i.e., the remnant is "chosen by grace." Literally Paul says that in this present time a remnant "has come into existence according to an election [or choice] of grace." Even though this was not stressed in the OT itself, by virtue of the parallel being drawn here we must conclude that the Old Covenant remnant, such as the seven thousand in Elijah's day, were also established according to an election or choice of grace.

Paul says that the New Covenant remnant has "come into existence" or has "come to be" (NASB). The word is γίνομαι (*ginomai* — a word the NIV completely ignores), which basically means "come to be, become, originate" (BAGD, 158). The perfect tense of the verb may be referring to a single past historical event that brought the New Covenant remnant into existence, i.e., the establishment of the NT church (Acts 2).

Paul's statement that the remnant has come into existence "according to a choice of grace" is often interpreted as an affirmation of Calvinist unconditional election, and is thus equated with the Calvinist understanding of 9:7-18 (❂ II:214).

I reject this meaning for Paul's statement. For one thing, this election is *not* the same as that in ch. 9. The subject here is election to salvation; in ch. 9 it was election to service. Also, we have already seen in our discussion of 8:29 that election to salvation is based upon divine foreknowledge (precognition) of human choices. The remnant *is* a group chosen by God, but chosen according to his foreknowledge.

What does it mean to say that the remnant has come into existence according to a choice of grace? We must keep in mind that Paul is here explaining how the remnant is different from the nation as a whole, and I believe that he does intend for us to understand this by comparing it with the election in 9:7-13. In that passage Paul emphasizes that being chosen as an instrument for God's use in carrying out his redemptive purpose was not a matter of natural right based on natural birth, but was a matter of God's sovereign choice. It was "God's purpose in election" (9:11) that led him to select Isaac over Ishmael and Jacob over Esau. None of these sons had an inherent claim to the privilege.

Likewise, being part of the saved remnant (spiritual Israel) is not a matter of physical birth as a Jew; no ethnic Israelite has an inherent claim to salvation. Being a part of the remnant is a matter of God's choice, and he has the sovereign right to establish the basis or criterion by which he chooses some Israelites rather than others. Thus the remnant is according to choice, not birth. Here the election of 9:11 and that of 11:5 are similar.

But there is an important difference between these two elections. Since 9:11 was not election to salvation, it was not described as an "election of grace." But in 11:5 the issue is salvation. The remnant consists of those within the nation of Israel who are saved, and the only way for sinners to be saved is by receiving God's gift of his own righteousness through faith (9:30–10:13) — in other words, by grace. This speaks to another main difference between the mass of ethnic Israel and the remnant. The former sought salvation by works or by their own righteousness (9:32; 10:3), while the latter sought it by faith in the righteousness of God. Thus to say that the remnant has come into existence according to an election of grace means that God chooses to save those Jews (and Gentiles, 9:30) who themselves choose his way of grace rather than the futile way of law.

We must not lose sight of Paul's purpose for even mentioning the remnant here. His point is to show that God has not rejected his people; the existence of the remnant is evidence that he has not. The fact that he is willing to constitute this remnant according to the terms of grace rather than law shows how faithful he is, and just how determined he is to preserve "his people" in spite of their sin.

11:6 And if by grace, then it is no longer by works; if it were, grace would no longer be grace. This verse sums up some of the main conclusions concerning law and grace as ways of salvation that were discussed in chs. 1–5 (see also 9:30–10:4). It also reinforces the point made under 11:5 above, that the main difference between ethnic Israel and remnant Israel is the latter's choice of grace instead of law as the only way to a saving relationship with God.

The first part of v. 6 has no stated subject in the Greek; translators usually supply "it." We may conclude from v. 5 that "being included in the remnant" is the understood subject.

The term "no longer" is used here in a logical sense, not temporal. I.e., Paul is not saying that in earlier times remnant membership was by works, but is so no longer. Rather, he is saying that once one sees that remnant membership is by grace, then he can no longer consider it to be by works.

Dunn notes that this is the first time Paul "brings 'works' and 'grace' into direct antithesis" (2:647). This is true of the terms themselves, but not of the concepts. The whole point of chs. 1–5 was the antithesis between law (works) and grace (faith) as ways of salvation. Since faith is a key element in the grace system, sometimes "faith" or "by faith" is simply shorthand for the system as a whole. Likewise, since works are a key element in the law system, sometimes "by works" or "from works" is just shorthand for the law system as a whole – which is the case here. In 10:5-6 Paul contrasts "righteousness by law" and "righteousness by faith"; this is exactly the same contrast as that between "by grace" and "by works" in 11:6.

It is crucial that we correctly understand the meaning of "works," which is the same as "works of law" in 3:28. As explained there (see ❂I:268-271), "works" includes any response to the laws or commandments of the Creator given to human beings as creatures, without restriction as to dispensation (Old Covenant or New Covenant), form (written or innate), and motives (good or bad). Thus it is wrong to limit "works" to obedience to the Law of Moses. It is also wrong to expand the term to include "anything that human beings do" (contra Moo, 678; see 250), since it does not refer to the Redeemer's instructions on how to be saved, i.e., the conditions for receiving salvation. These are not a part of the Creator's law, and are not works in the Pauline sense. (See ❂I:270; MP, 449.)

Those who wrongly expand the concept of works to include "anything a person does" usually then proceed to use v. 6 to support their Calvinist interpretation of v. 5. If "works" means *anything* a person does, this must include not only repentance, confession, and baptism, but even faith itself, insofar as it is a decision of man's will. Thus to Calvinists, even faith, regarded as something a person does as a result of his own choice, is a grace-canceling work. As Murray says, "If grace is conditioned in any way by human performance or by the will of man impelling to action, then grace ceases to be grace" (2:70) (❂II:217).

This whole approach to grace is a serious error, since it includes more in the category of works than Paul intends (as discussed above). Also, it is a false concept of the freedom that is inherently involved in grace. That grace is conditioned on certain human acts is not a violation of God's freedom in the bestowal of grace, since he himself is the one who freely chose to do it this way and the one who freely chose what the conditions shall be. Besides, the conditions he has chosen are completely consistent with the essence of grace. (See *GRu*, 184-185, 226-227; *GRe*, 383-399.)

Also, election according to foreknowledge does not contradict grace because the crucial object of God's foreknowledge is not the presence or absence of human works but the acceptance or rejection of God's free offer of grace in accord with the gracious conditions which he himself has laid down.

Paul's point in this verse is simply to sum up the main message of Romans, that the only way for a sinner to be saved is by grace through faith, not by the system of law. The two systems are mutually exclusive; one must choose either God's righteousness (grace) or personal righteousness (works) as the basis for his salvation. One must rely either upon himself or upon Jesus Christ; he cannot do both. Any trust in the worthiness of one's own achievements or the merit of one's own accomplishments is simply incompatible with grace. Trying to get to heaven by being "good enough" nullifies the way of grace.

As applied to remnant Jews, this means that they belong to the remnant not because they are essentially better than the rest, i.e., less sinful or more law-abiding, but because they have submitted to God's way of righteousness (10:3), which is grace. If everyone were to be accepted or rejected on the basis of his works, there would be no remnant. By its very nature the remnant is a grace entity. Though Paul is making this point specifically regarding the remnant of the Jews, it applies equally to the Gentiles, and thus to the church as a whole.

B. UNBELIEVING ISRAEL HAS BEEN HARDENED (11:7-10)

If only a remnant of Israel is saved, what has happened to the rest? Are they totally abandoned and forgotten by God? Having served their covenant purposes as a means of bringing Christ into the world, and paradoxically having refused to accept him as their Messiah, are they now to be completely ignored? Paul's answer is No, but exactly how they continue to be the object of God's attention is somewhat surprising. This is Paul's subject in this paragraph.

11:7 What then? What Israel sought so earnestly it did not obtain, but the elect did. The others were hardened, . . . The first part of this verse is a transitional statement that sums up the preceding thoughts in terms of a contrast between "the elect" on the one hand, and "Israel" ("the others") on the other hand.

Paul does not use the usual word for "the elect" (ἐκλεκτός, *eklektos*; see 8:33), but carries over the noun used in 11:5 (ἐκλογή, *eklogē*, "choice, election"). In this context it is synonymous with "the remnant." The term "Israel" here refers to the physical nation in general, or "Israel as a corporate whole," as Moo says (679). But strictly speaking, Paul is referring not to the totality of physical Israel, but only to unbelieving Jews, "the others" in contrast to the elect.

What was Israel "so earnestly" seeking? The answer can be found in 9:30–

10:3; they were pursuing *righteousness*, a right standing before God (Denney, 677; Morris, 402; Moo, 680). In 9:30-31 Paul says the Gentiles found such righteousness though they were not seeking it, while Israel was pursuing it but did not find it. The reason they did not find it, he says (9:32; 10:3), was that they were seeking it in their own works and not in God's gift.

The NIV translates the verb as past tense ("sought"), which is consistent with the past tense of the verbs in 9:31-32; 10:3. But here the Greek is present tense ("that which Israel is seeking for," NASB), which implies that the Israelites in general were still seeking for this righteous standing before God.

The emphasis, though, is not on the action of seeking, but on the result of the search. The good news is that the elect remnant did obtain the sought-for righteousness. The bad news is that the vast majority, Israel as a whole, did not (see 9:30). These are simply called "the others," or "the rest" (NASB), i.e., the rest of the Jews (not the rest of mankind in general, contra Morris, 403).

At this point Paul introduces a new and surprising thought: "the others," the unbelieving Jews, *were hardened*. This theme is a prominent part of the argument in the rest of this chapter, either implicitly or explicitly. Thus it is crucial that we understand it aright. The following facts concerning this hardening will emerge in the course of Paul's argument, but may profitably be summed up before we go any further. (1) Whatever the nature of this hardening, it is not the cause of anyone's unbelief. The only ones hardened are those who have already rejected God's righteousness in Christ. (2) Whatever the nature of the hardening, it is not irrevocable and final. Those hardened are still able to come to faith, as the next point indicates. (3) God's purpose for this hardening is to use it as a means of converting many Gentiles, which in turn will be a means of converting many of the hardened Jews themselves. Thus paradoxically the ultimate goal and result of the hardening is the salvation of those who are hardened! The sequence of events is as follows: the bulk of the Jews reject the gospel; they are hardened; as a consequence Gentiles are saved; as a consequence of this, many of the hardened Jews are made jealous and are saved; and as a consequence of this, even more Gentiles are saved!

The word for "hardened" is πωρόω (*pōroō*), the noun form of which (πώρωσις, *pōrōsis*) is used in 11:25. (The meaning is the same as the verb used in 9:18, σκληρύνω [*sklērynō*].) The verb *pōroō* "is a medical term used in Hippocrates and elsewhere of a bone or hard substance growing when bones are fractured, or of a stone forming in the bladder" (SH, 314). Hence it means "to harden, to petrify"; in the NT it is used in the figurative sense: "to make dull, obdurate, insensitive." It refers to "the heart becoming hardened or callous," i.e., to a state in which "a covering has grown over the heart, making men incapable of receiving any new teaching however good, and making them oblivious of the wrong they are doing" (SH, 314).

In this verse the verb is passive, and the agent of the hardening is not identified. Some declare that the Jews hardened themselves. The hardening came about "through their own rejection, choosing rather to obey Satan . . . than the grace of God" (DeWelt, 176). Such self-hardening is certainly a biblically attested reality (Exod 8:15,32; Heb 3:8,15; 4:7). Some identify Satan as the agent of the hardening, by God's permission (Lard, 351; MP, 451; Godet, 398). Others say the agent of the hardening is "intentionally left vague" and indefinite (Denney, 677; Morris, 403).

There is some truth in each of these views, but the context requires us to identify God himself as the main agent in the hardening of the Jews (see 9:18; 11:8; see Murray, 2:72; Moo, 680; Stott, 293). How he did so is not explained. It is very possible that he hardened them by allowing Satan a free hand to blind their eyes. Citing 1 Kgs 22:19-23, the book of Job, and 2 Cor 4:4, Godet says that "God proves or punishes by leaving Satan to act" (398). It is also possible that God hardened the Jews simply by diminishing or withdrawing his own positive influences toward them, as he did with the Gentiles when he "gave them over" to the destructiveness of their own sinful desires (1:24,26,28; see ❂I:149-150).

In any case there is general agreement that the Jews had already hardened themselves into a state of unbelief before God performed this act of hardening upon them. Thus the divine hardening is not the cause of their rejection of the gospel, but a punishment for it. They were hardened because they deserved it; it was retribution (v. 9) for their sin. It was "a judicial penalty for refusal to heed the Word of God" (Bruce, 215; see Lenski, 686) (❂II:221).

What is the result of this hardening? Some interpret it as a final sealing of these Jews in a state of unbelief, and equate it with the eternal decree of reprobation that (in Calvinist thinking) predestines some to hell, just as the eternal decree of election unconditionally predestines others to heaven (Calvin, 417; Murray, 2:72).

This view is a serious error, however, and must be vigorously rejected. Not even all Calvinists agree with it. Hendriksen (2:365) says, "To include Rom. 11:7 . . . in a list of passages proving reprobation is an error," because "even for the hardened ones there is hope," as the following context shows. So whatever result this hardening has, it is something done only to unbelievers, and it does not ultimately prevent them from becoming believers. It is neither absolute nor irreversible. Hence it does not contradict the principle that God does not violate any individual's free will to choose his own eternal destiny.

The result of the hardening is Paul's subject in vv. 8-10. It certainly involves an insensitivity toward God's word, blinding one's spiritual eyes and deafening one's spiritual ears toward God's truth. In the act of hardening God takes away "from the heart the faculty of being touched by what is good or divine," and he takes away "from the understanding, the faculty of discerning between the true and the false, the good and the bad" (Godet, 395). In so doing God is simply confirming what is already present in the unbeliever's heart.

Why has God so hardened the Jews? As noted above, it is in the first place a judicial act, a recompense for unbelief. But there is an even deeper reason, a positive one that flows from the deepest and wisest recesses of God's loving heart. God has used many people, including the Jews as a nation, to carry out his redemptive purposes. Sometimes this can be done only by a limited and temporary hardening, as in the case of Pharaoh (9:18). So it is here, that by hardening "the rest" of the Jews, he can use them "as an instrument of his good pleasure" in bringing many people to salvation (see McGuiggan, 322). As Paul goes on to explain in 11:11ff., the hardening of the Jews is intended as a means by which the Gentiles may be saved, which in turn is a means by which the hardened Jews themselves may be brought to faith in their Messiah.

11:8 [A]s it is written: "God gave them a spirit of stupor, eyes so that they could not see and ears so that they could not hear, to this very day." In this and the next two verses Paul draws from three OT passages to reinforce his assertion about the hardening of Israel. These texts are not treated as prophecies but as precedents. In v. 8 two passages are used. "God gave them a spirit of stupor" is from Isa 29:10a, "For the LORD has poured over you a spirit of deep sleep" (NASB). The last part of v. 8 is from Deut 29:4.

The words from Isa 29:10 make it clear that God is the one who is responsible for the hardening in 11:7. The word for "stupor" suggests not so much a deep sleep as a state of numbness, of being bewildered and stunned. Sometimes a person who has been struck on the head may seem to be fully conscious but is mentally confused and unaware of his surroundings. Just so, says Paul (as did Isaiah before him), God has enveloped Israel in a state of spiritual numbness, in "an attitude of deadness towards spiritual things" (Morris, 403), in a "mental and moral dulness [sic] or apathy" (Hendriksen, 2:364).

The word "spirit" probably means an attitude or a state of mind, but it is possible that it refers to a demonic spirit whom God permits to inflict Israel with this spiritual blindness. See 1 Sam 18:10 and 1 Kgs 22:20-23 for precedents. Whether this be the case or not, the result is God's intention: a "punitive hardening which follows after self-hardening has fully set in" (Lenski, 687). "The eyes of their souls are shut; they see nothing rightly" (Lard, 351).

So that there may be no mistake, the "spirit of stupor" is explained with the reference to Deut 29:4, "eyes so that they could not see and ears so that they could not hear." Again, Paul says *God gave* to Israel these nonseeing eyes and nonhearing ears. The mass of Israel seemed to be spiritually conscious and God-fearing; indeed they had "a zeal for God," but it was "not in accordance with knowledge" (10:2, NASB). God reinforced their own willful ignorance by covering their spiritual eyes and stopping up their spiritual ears.

"To this very day" is part of the quotation from Deut 29:4. Moses' point was that after forty years of wilderness wandering the Israelites still had not come to understand and appreciate what God had done for them in delivering them from Egypt and giving them their own land, even on the very eve of their possession of that land. Paul seems to be saying that the Jews of his day were still laboring under the same spiritual blindness that caused them to crucify their Messiah (1 Thess 2:14-15), and that this blindness had not yet been lifted or counteracted as 11:11-32 suggests will some day happen.

11:9-10 And David says, "May their table become a snare and a trap, a stumbling block and a retribution for them. May their eyes be darkened so they cannot see, and their backs be bent forever." These two verses are taken from Ps 69:22-23. This is appropriate because Ps 69 is widely recognized as Messianic and is cited or alluded to frequently in the NT. As David wrote the Psalm, it was his prayer for God to deliver him from his enemies and to give those enemies the punishment they deserved. As Paul applies it to his time, he suggests that "what David prayed would happen to his persecutors, . . . God has brought upon those Jews who have resisted the gospel" (Moo, 683).

Paul's main point in citing these imprecations seems to be to reinforce the idea that the hardening affirmed in v. 7 is actually deserved by the unbelieving Jews. David's prayer was for three curses to come upon his enemies. The first is that "their table become a snare and a trap, a stumbling block." Here "table" may be an allusion to the OT law in general, and especially to its sacrificial system, which involved an altar and a table for eating the sacrificial meal (Denney, 678; Dunn, 2:642-643, 650). Or it may simply be a household table representing the food and fellowship of ordinary mealtime and earthly prosperity in general (Lenski, 689; Murray, 2:74). In either case the prayer is "a wish that even the good things which these enemies enjoy may prove to be a cause of disaster to them" (Cranfield, 2:551).

The second curse is that "their eyes be darkened so they cannot see." This clearly ties in with the "spirit of stupor" in v. 8 and the hardening in v. 7, and indicates that Israel as a whole was blinded toward the truth of the gospel.

The third curse is that "their backs be bent forever." It is difficult to tell exactly what calamity this is supposed to represent. It may be a figure for the hard labor of slavery, the heaviness of a burden, a state of weakness, or the overwhelming effects of grief or fear. Any of these could apply to first-century Judaism (❂ II:225).

The main point, though, is expressed in v. 9b, where the wish is that their table may become "a retribution for them." The sense of this term is that of being repaid or paid back in kind. The implication is that all these curses are a recompense or retribution, a deserved penalty upon the Jews "rightly demanded by their wickedness" (Lenski, 690).

C. THE HARDENING OF UNBELIEVING ISRAEL BECOMES A BLESSING FOR BOTH THE GENTILES AND THE JEWS (11:11-16)

In this paragraph Paul is still developing his answer to the question in 11:1,

"Did God reject his people?" He has supported his emphatic negative answer by pointing to the existence of the "remnant chosen by grace" (vv. 1-6). But what about the mass of unbelieving Jews not included in the remnant? They "were hardened" (11:7-10).

This leads to the question of the ultimate fate of hardened Israel. Are they simply and finally lost? Is there no place for them in the kingdom? Are they totally excluded from God's mercy and God's plan? "What about the sinning majority? Are they lost forever?" (Morris, 405).

Paul's answer is another emphatic No! It is true that this majority rejected their Messiah, and that God hardened them. But this is not the final word; it is not the whole story. In this section the Apostle shows how even hardened Israel is part of the larger picture of God's mercy, or "how Israel's failure fits into the salvific plan of God" (Fitzmyer, 608). God can use this unbelieving nation for his own redemptive purpose, and even his hardening of them furthers this purpose.

In essence, Paul explains that God's hardening of Israel (especially the withdrawing of direct evangelistic efforts to win them) is intended to start a chain reaction that leads back to the conversion of Jews by indirect means. In summary, the hardening of unbelieving Israel "is the occasion for the coming in of the Gentiles, which, in its turn, is to have the effect of awakening the unbelieving Jews to a realization of what they are missing and so to lead to their repentance" (Cranfield, 2:553). Thus "even the hardening of Israel serves the purposes of mercy" (Achtemeier, 181).

Nearly everyone agrees that this section shows that Israel's fall and hardening are not meant to be final. Just as vv. 1-10 show that her rejection is only partial, these verses show that it is intended to be only temporary. "God's punitive action against the majority" is "not his last word concerning Israel" (Dunn, 2:666). The Jews *can* be saved.

Unfortunately, many interpreters take Paul's basic message of hope for Israel and expand it into a veritable philosophy of history. They see in this paragraph the seeds of a complicated eschatology involving a renewed special role for the Jews as a nation. I.e., they take Paul's statements about Israel's salvation as referring to a large-scale future conversion of the Jews *en masse*, and a restoration of the nation as such to their original status as the people of God. Many regard this as the key precursor to the end of this age and the final resurrection (v. 15). This theory will receive some attention in the following discussion.

11:11 Again I ask: Did they stumble so as to fall beyond recovery? Not at all! Of whom is Paul speaking? Not Israel as a whole, as a corporate nation (contra Moo, 686), but only the individual Jews who rejected their Messiah and were subsequently hardened, i.e., "the others" of v. 7 (Cranfield, 2:554; Denney, 678).

The first verb, "stumble" (πταίω, *ptaiō*, "to stumble, to trip") is used in a figurative or moral sense, "to make a mistake, go astray, sin" (BAGD, 727; see Jas 2:10; 3:2; 2 Pet 1:10). The second verb, πίπτω (*piptō*), has a straightforward meaning: "to fall, to fall down, to collapse." In a moral sense it means "to fall into sin, to go astray," and may have an even stronger sense: to "fall from a state of grace, be completely ruined, perish" (BAGD, 659-660).

There is no question that hardened Israel stumbled (9:32-33), but did they *fall*? Despite Paul's emphatic No! (μὴ γένοιτο, *mē genoito*; see 3:4), the answer to this question is not as simple as it seems. The main reason is that v. 22 refers to these same Jews as "those who fell," and uses the same word as in v. 11 (*piptō*).

So what does Paul mean in v. 11? The most common approach is to give *piptō* an exceptionally strong meaning here, as in the NIV: "to fall beyond recovery." It means to be "finally lost" in the sense of "a complete and irrevocable fall," say Sanday and Headlam (320-321). Paul does imply that falling is more serious than merely stumbling, so this interpretation seems to fit (❂ II:227-228).

Is this interpretation acceptable? Yes. It surely fits the context, since one of Paul's main points is that fallen Israel can indeed be saved. A serious problem, though, is that it does not seem consistent with v. 22.

Thus out of concern for v. 22, some have suggested another understanding of v. 11. The point of the question, they say, is this: did Israel stumble "merely for the purpose that they might fall" (Murray, 2:76)? Paul's No! is not intended to deny that they have fallen; it simply means that there is more to the story than this. They have not stumbled just for the purpose of falling, or with the simple result that they are now fallen and that's that. No, Paul's whole point is that God has incorporated Israel's stumbling and falling into a much larger and more glorious plan.

Is this interpretation acceptable? Yes, and in my opinion it is preferable. If anything, it fits the immediate context even better than the more common view, and it takes full account of v. 22. The main problem is that the concept of "merely" must be read into the question.

Another issue is the meaning of the word ἵνα (*hina*), which connects the two verbs ("so as," NIV). This word can imply either purpose or result. If Paul intends the former, he is asking whether hardened Israel stumbled "in order that they might fall" or "for the purpose of falling." If we read it in this sense, then Paul would be implying that God *caused* Israel to stumble (to reject their Messiah), and that he had a *purpose* for causing them to stumble. This of course assumes a Calvinist view of sovereignty and free will (❂ II:228).

Most interpreters, however (even among Calvinists), take *hina* as stating result rather than purpose. That is, has hardened Israel stumbled "with the result that" they have *fallen*? This meaning "makes excellent sense," says Dunn (2:653); and this is so however one understands the concept of "falling."

The bottom line is that most Jews have indeed stumbled, i.e., have rejected Jesus and his grace, and consequently have fallen into a state of lostness and spiritual ruin. But that is not the whole picture; that is not the end of the story. The drama of Israel does not end on such a negative note. **Rather, because of their transgression, salvation has come to the Gentiles to make Israel envious.**

Paul refers here to "their transgression" (singular). Is this different from the stumbling and falling in v. 11a? It may be useful to bring together and analyze the variety of terms Paul uses to describe Israel's downfall. It seems that he distinguishes three steps in the process, the first two of which are attributable to the sinner's will and the last of which is an act of God. The first step is the sin of rejecting God's way of grace, most significantly the initial sin of rejecting Jesus as the only Savior. The second step is falling out of a saving relationship with God and into a state of lostness. The third step is God's placing those who have so fallen under his wrath and curse.

The first of these steps is what Paul means by "their transgression." It is the word παράπτωμα (*paraptōma*), which is "frequently used by Paul to denote 'trespass,' 'sin' (in the sense of a particular sinful deed)," as Cranfield says (2:555). It is the same as the stumbling in v. 11a, i.e., their stumbling over Christ (9:32-33), their rejection of Christ as the Messiah. It is called "unbelief" in vv. 20,23, and "disobedience" in v. 30.

The second step is the Jews' "fall" in v. 11a (see v. 22), also called their "loss" in v. 12. This is not so much an *act* of the sinner as the natural result of the first step (the unbelief).

The third step is God's act of hardening (vv. 7,25), which is his punitive response to the first two steps. This is also called his "rejection" of the Jews (v. 15), and his act of breaking off or cutting off the unbelieving branches (vv. 17,19-20,22).

In reference to the Jews' downfall, these three steps always go together; even when only one is mentioned, the other two are assumed to be a part of the total picture. Thus here when Paul says "because of their transgression," he does not mean the transgression alone, as distinct from the fall and the hardening. Rather, because of the transgression along with the consequent fall and the divine hardening, salvation has come to the Gentiles.

Herein lies the first element in God's plan that evokes Paul's extreme sense of awe and wonder at his wisdom (11:33-36), namely, that God has determined to use the Jews' unbelief and fall (along with his own act of hardening) as a means of bringing salvation to the Gentiles! Out of sin, salvation comes! Out of wrath, mercy comes!

This could refer to the fact that by delivering Jesus over to the Romans for crucifixion, the Jews were inadvertently helping to bring about the one great act of redemption that is the source of salvation for all. More likely, though, it refers to the ordinary process of evangelism reflected in the book of Acts. I.e., once Gentile evangelism finally began (Acts 10), the missionary strategy was still to preach to the Jews first. But when the Jews typically rejected the gospel message, attention was turned to the Gentiles (◉ II:230).

But even this is not the whole story. If it were, hardened Israel would still be abandoned in their lostness. But this is not God's plan. The other element in the divine strategy that evokes Paul's reverent amazement is that God intends the conversion of the Gentiles to arouse the hardened Jews to jealousy (or envy) and thereby cause them to turn at last to their Messiah (see v. 14). I.e., "the salvation of the Gentiles was intended in the divine providence to arouse in Israel a passionate desire for the same good gift" (Morris, 407). "Thus that hardening of which v. 7 spoke has for its ultimate purpose the salvation of those who are hardened" (Cranfield, 2:556).

Paul has already introduced this theme of "provoking to envy" in 10:19, where he cites Deut 32:21. Some may be concerned that God can speak of envy or jealousy as a motivation for accepting the gospel. Because they think of jealousy as always being sinful, it sounds to them like an "end justifies means" scheme (❂ II:231).

In the Bible jealousy is always the point of this word, but it is not always an evil attitude. God himself is often described as a "jealous God" (see *GC*, 409-416). Stott well says that "not all envy is tainted with selfishness, because it is not always a grudging discontent or a sinful covetousness." The essence of envy, he says, is the desire to have for oneself what is possessed by another. It is good envy or evil envy depending on the nature of what is desired and on whether one has a right to it (297). Surely in this case the salvation possessed by the Gentiles is something good and something God wants the Jews to have anyway, and the Jews' desire to have it will in no way diminish the Gentiles' possession of it. Thus it is not at all an unworthy motive for accepting the gospel.

In this verse three things are linked in a cause-and-effect chain: the Jews' transgression (their initial negative response to the gospel), Gentile salvation, and Jewish envy. It is significant that in the latter part of the verse there are no verbs, and thus no tenses (past, present, future). We know the first step has already occurred; we assume the second has at least begun ("salvation *has come*," NIV, NASB). Many assume the last step (Jewish envy) is still in the future, but our conclusion on this point must be based on the following verses.

11:12 But if their transgression means riches for the world, and their loss means riches for the Gentiles, how much greater riches will their fullness bring! Most of the content of this verse, rightly understood, has already been either affirmed or implied in v. 11 (Lard, 356; MP, 456-457). I.e., if the Jews' *transgression* (stumbling, unbelief) results in riches (salvation) for the world (the Gentiles), and if their *loss* (fall) similarly results in riches (salvation) for the Gentiles, then how much more likely it is that the *fullness* (salvation) of the Jews will result in spiritual riches for all.

We should note that in the Greek there are no verbs (and thus no tenses) in this entire verse; thus we should be cautious about assigning to any one of these three clauses an entirely past or entirely future enactment.

The first two clauses seem to be restating the link between the Jews' downfall and the Gentiles' salvation taught in v. 11. "Their transgression" is the same word used in v. 11 and has the same meaning, i.e., their stumbling over and rejecting their Messiah in unbelief. "Their loss" is equivalent to the "fall" in v. 11 (❂ II:232).

The basic meaning of "loss" (ἥττημα, *hēttēma*) seems to be "defeat" (Isa 31:8, LXX; 1 Cor 6:7), but the emphasis here seems to be more on the loss (e.g., of possessions, of freedom) that results from an actual defeat. "Loss" is thus a good translation. As a result of their rejection of their Messiah, the Jews suffered the loss of their relationship with God and of the spiritual riches of Christ's kingdom.

The point is that the Jews' trespass, along with their consequent loss, is a means of bringing spiritual riches upon the Gentiles, as pointed out in v. 11. "Riches" refers to the spiritual riches of salvation and is equivalent to "salvation" in v. 11. See Eph 1:18, which refers to "the riches of his glorious inheritance in the saints" (See also 2:4; 9:23; 11:33; Eph 1:7; 2:7; 3:6,8; Phil 4:19).

The last clause in this verse is extremely difficult. Literally it is very succinct: "by how much more their fullness" (no verb). How does this fit into the overall structure of the verse? The phrase "by how much more" (πόσῳ μᾶλλον, *posō mallon*) shows that some kind of comparison is being made between the first two clauses and this final clause. The common assumption is that "riches" is being compared with "more riches," i.e., if the Jews' transgression and loss bring *riches* to the Gentiles, their fullness will bring even *greater riches*.

I believe this misses the point, however. In six of its eight NT occurrences, the phrase *posō mallon* means "how much more likely it is that," and is usually part of an argument from the lesser to the greater. This meaning fits very well here. Thus the clause is not an argument from riches to more riches, but this: "If the Jews' *transgression* and *loss* mean riches for the Gentiles, *how much more likely it is that* the Jews' *fullness* [means riches for the Gentiles]."

This conclusion will affect not only how we interpret v. 12, but also v. 15, where "life from the dead" is often identified with the alleged "greater riches" in v. 12 (e.g., see Moo, 689; DeWelt, 182). Speculation then abounds. I.e., if the *riches* brought to the Gentiles by the Jews' sin is (rightly) understood as their *salvation* (v. 11), then the *greater riches* ("life from the dead") must be something even more significant than personal salvation; indeed, it must be something spectacular, such as a great future universal revival or the final general resurrection at the end-time.

But when we see that *posō mallon* is not really talking about "greater riches," the basis for such speculation is gone; and when we realize also that there is no verb (and thus no future tense) in this clause, the assumption that this word refers to some great eschatological event is also weakened.

This brings us to the difficult question, what is the nature of the Jews' "fullness" (πλήρωμα, *plērōma*)? There are two basic views. One is that this is a *quantitative* fullness, and refers to the ultimate conversion of the "full number" of

Jews; the other is that the fullness is *qualitative* and refers to the Jews' participation in the fullness of salvation.

The former view, that *plērōma* means "full and completed number," is, as Cranfield notes, "widely accepted." The TEV translates it "complete number." This is often paralleled with a numeric interpretation of *hēttēma* in the previous clause; see the NEB: "If their falling-off [*hēttēma*] means the enrichment of the Gentiles, how much more their coming to full strength!"

To what, then, would this refer? The most common idea is that it refers to a future large-scale conversion of Jews, in contrast with the present "remnant" situation. Some expand this idea to include the restoration of the Jews to their original status as God's chosen people (❂II:234). This is often linked with the establishment of a millennial kingdom in the premillennial sense (e.g., MacArthur, 2:110-111).

Others agree that "fullness" means "full number," but interpret this (in a Calvinist sense) to mean the full number of elect Jews as they are gradually converted over the full course of Christian history (❂II:234). The meaning of v. 12 would then be, in Cranfield's words, as follows: "If the present unbelief of the majority of Israel actually means the enrichment of the Gentiles, how much more wonderfully enriching must the situation resulting from the provoking to jealousy of this majority of Israel be!" (2:557-558).

The second view, and in my opinion the correct one, is that the *plērōma* of the Jews is meant in a qualitative sense and refers to spiritual fullness, or being filled with all the abundance of salvation. The word itself as used elsewhere in the NT does not refer to "full number" but to "completeness, abundance." See, e.g., John 1:16; Rom 15:29; Eph 1:23; 3:19; 4:13 (❂II:235).

This meaning also fits the context. In v. 12 itself, "fullness" is in contrast with both "transgression" and "loss," words that sum up the lost state as opposed to salvation. This is an especially appropriate contrast with "loss," which as we have seen does not have a numerical connotation; the point is simply the lost state as compared with the saved state.

Also regarding context, this meaning is better in view of the connection between v. 11 and v. 12. Verse 11 describes a cause-and-effect chain: the Jews' transgression leads to Gentile salvation which leads to Jewish envy. The reference to Jewish envy implies Jewish salvation, since this is its intended result (see v. 14). As noted above, v. 12 is giving further reflection on the relations among these three items, especially the idea that the Jews' transgression results in riches (salvation) for the Gentiles. The one thought added in v. 12 is that the Jewish envy (and thus salvation) produced by the Gentiles' conversion would in turn lead to even more Gentiles being saved. Thus it is natural to take "fullness" in v. 12 as referring to the Jews' salvation, which in context corresponds to (since in fact it grows out of) their envy in v. 11.

As another contextual note, we shall see later that this meaning best corresponds to the meaning of *plērōma* in v. 25.

Thus I agree with McGuiggan when he says that the Jews' fullness is the "rich blessedness" they receive when they abandon their unbelief and accept their Messiah's salvation. "Israel by unbelief lost blessings, Israel by faith would be fully blessed." McGuiggan rightly says, "There is no ground in the text whatever for supposing that 'fulness' is somewhat equivalent to a conversion of Jews 'on a national scale' or 'on a scale commensurate with their rejection' (numerically speaking)." In fact, in v. 12 "there is no allusion to the number of Jews lost and (therefore, in the antithesis) there is no mention of the number of Jews (to be) saved. . . . 'Fullness' speaks of a rich state of blessedness as opposed to 'loss'" (324). See Lenski, 695.

We must also emphasize that the text does not project this conversion of the Jews to some distant future date; it does not preclude that it could already be happening at that very time. (Remember: the verse has no verbs and no tenses.) In fact, in vv. 13-14 Paul implies that his own ministry is already producing this result.

We must remember that the main point of v. 12 is not about the Jews but about the Gentiles, i.e., what will happen to the Gentiles as a result of the Jews' unbelief as well as their belief. If some Gentiles are saved as the result of the Jews' *rejection* of the gospel, then we have even more reason to expect Gentiles to be saved as the result of the Jews' envy-induced *acceptance* of the gospel.

11:13-14 I am talking to you Gentiles. Inasmuch as I am the apostle to the Gentiles, I make much of my ministry in the hope that I may somehow arouse my own people to envy and save some of them. Many think v. 13a shows that the Gentiles were in the majority in the church at Rome (e.g., Dunn, 2:655, 669; Moo, 691, n. 39), but Cranfield is right that such a conclusion cannot be drawn from this verse (2:559). Paul is simply saying that he wants the Gentiles among his readers to pay special attention to what he is saying, not just in what follows but in the preceding verses as well.

This is true for two reasons. One, in this whole main section, Israel has been the focus of attention; the Gentiles have entered the discussion only marginally. Thus the latter group "may well have been reasoning that all this about the Jews had little to do with them. They may have wondered why the apostle to the Gentiles should be spending so much time worrying about the Jews" (Morris, 408). Thus Paul stops to reassure the Gentiles that he has not forgotten the main focus of his ministry. What he is showing them is that the welfare of the Jews and the Gentiles is intertwined.

Paul's other reason for addressing the Gentiles specifically is the possibility that what he teaches about Gentile salvation in vv. 11-12 may lead some to develop an attitude of arrogance toward the Jews (see v. 20), as if the latter were merely a means to the end of Gentile salvation. Paul assures them of his own genuine concern for the Jews' salvation, and in the next section he shows them how much they owe to the Jews (vv. 17-24) (❂ II:237).

Paul says, "I make much of my ministry." It is possible that διακονία (*diakonia*, "ministry") here means "office" (KJV) in a special technical sense (see, e.g., Acts 1:25; 2 Cor 4:1; Col 4:17). More likely it means simply "ministry" or "area of service" or "mission," i.e., his specific assignment to be the apostle to the Gentiles. "Make much of" is δοξάζω (*doxazō*), which means "to honor, to praise, to glorify." It is usually used of giving glory to God, and is rarely used of men or anything human (see 8:30; 1 Cor 12:26; negatively, see Matt 6:2). Paul does not say that he honors or glorifies himself, but he glorifies his *ministry* as a task given to him by God. Thus he honors it not because of its fulfillment in himself but because of its origin in God.

Paul's point is that he has the highest respect for his calling, and approaches it with the utmost seriousness and diligence.

To what end does Paul honor his ministry? It is taken for granted that he does so in order to win converts from among the Gentiles, but in view of the divine plan spelled out in v. 11, he knows that his ministry is also an indirect means of bringing his own kinsmen to faith in Christ. "My own people" is literally "my flesh" (see 9:3), i.e., the Jews, "Israel according to the flesh" (1 Cor 10:18, lit.). The relation between their envy and their salvation has already been implied in vv. 11-12 (see the explanation of "fullness" in v. 12 above). Thus he glorifies his ministry, because "the more Gentiles Paul converts, the more of this jealousy he creates, . . . which results in conversions of the Jews" (Lenski, 697).

Paul understands that this process will not be automatic and will not convert every Jew. He pursues his apostleship to the Gentiles "in the hope that" some Jews may be saved thereby. "In the hope that I may somehow" translates εἴ πως (*ei pōs*) plus the subjunctive case of the verb. This is "an expression of expectation," says Dunn (2:656), but as Moo says, it is a "hesitant expectation" (692, n. 46).

Why does Paul say "some of them"? Some interpreters think he says this because he knows that the number of Jews who will be saved through his own ministry will be few in comparison with the great ingathering and restoration of the Jewish people in the future. I believe this misses the point, especially since the whole idea of a future large-scale conversion of Jews is far from certain. We must look elsewhere for the reasons why Paul says "some of them." First, he refers here only to the results of his own ministry, and he knew that Jews were being won to Christ by other evangelists and would continue to be won by others in later generations. Second, Paul knew from experience that the salvation of every individual Jew was too much to hope for. He knew that the unbelieving Jews of his own generation were hardened and strongly resistant to the gospel. But at the same time he knew that they still had the free will to believe, and that arousing them to envy was a means to this end. Thus by fulfilling his ministry to the Gentiles, he expected "some" of his ethnic brothers to be saved, but not all.

11:15 For if their rejection is the reconciliation of the world, what will

their acceptance be but life from the dead? (See ❂ II:235.) I think it is best to see v. 15 as reaching back into both v. 12 and vv. 13-14. I.e., it repeats v. 12 in more specific terms, and explains why Paul is so enthusiastic about his ministry to the Gentiles (13-14). The key thought linking the end of v. 12 and the end of v. 14 with v. 15 is the salvation (fullness, acceptance) of some of the hardened Jews. In v. 15 Paul is stating why he wants to see as many as possible from this group come to salvation, because that is nothing less than "life from the dead."

We cannot ignore the fact that the form of this verse is very close to that of v. 12: if A leads to B, then surely C leads to D. "Their transgression" and "their loss" in v. 12 correspond to "their rejection" in v. 15. In both cases "their" refers to the unbelieving, hardened Jews. In v. 12 their transgression and loss refer to their unbelief and subsequent lost state. But what is the meaning of "rejection" in v. 15?

The word translated "rejection" is ἀποβολή (*apobolē*), which comes from the verb ἀποβάλλω (*apoballō*), which means "to throw away, to reject, to remove, to lose." Dunn is correct (2:657) that the contrast with "acceptance" in v. 15b means that *apobolē* refers to the deliberate act of throwing away or rejecting something, rather than the passive act of losing something. But the question is, who is rejecting whom?

Some say it is the Jews' rejection of Christ and the gospel of his grace. Thus it would be equivalent to "transgression" in vv. 11-12. However, in spite of v. 1, most take v. 15 to mean God's rejection of the Jews, "their temporary casting away by God" (Cranfield, 2:562; see Moo, 692-693). This is equivalent to God's hardening of Israel (v. 7), and his breaking off of some of the branches (vv. 17-20).

But in v. 1 did not Paul emphatically deny that God has rejected his people? How then can he say here that they have been rejected? The Greek words are different, but the concepts seem to be the same. Is there a contradiction, then? The answer is No, and the reason for this is very important. In v. 1 the issue is whether God has rejected the Jews as such, just because they are Jews. I.e., has he rejected *every one* of "his people"? The answer is obviously No, because there is a remnant of true believers who have not been rejected. But in v. 15 Paul is talking only about the nonremnant Jews, the unbelieving Jews who rejected the gospel and whom God hardened. After their initial refusal to accept their Messiah, God rejected them (hardened them, broke them off the tree).

It is important to understand this so that we do not interpret v. 15 as referring to Israel *as a nation*. This verse says nothing about God's relationship with the nation as a whole (❂ II:240). When we try to interpret v. 15 as referring to the Jews in general, or to the Jews as a corporate group, then we place it in conflict with v. 1.

God's rejection of the unbelieving Jews leads to the "reconciliation of the world." Here "world" must be taken in light of v. 12, where it refers especially to the Gentiles (Murray, 2:81; Lenski, 699-700). Thus the point is exactly the same as in the first two clauses of v. 12. "Riches for the world" (v. 12) and "the reconciliation of the world" (v. 15) both refer to the salvation of the Gentiles, with "reconciliation" being a specific aspect of that salvation (see 5:10; ❈ I:326-327). Reconciliation basically means the removal of hostility and the restoration of peace and friendship between two estranged parties. Some think this possibly refers to "the reconciliation of Jew and Gentile in one new people of God" (Barrett, 215; see Stott, 298). Others think it refers to the objective reconciliation of the whole world to God through Christ's propitiatory sacrifice, even if it is not accepted by all and applied to all (see 5:10-11; 2 Cor 5:19). This is Cranfield's view (2:562). Most probably, though, it refers to the actual subjective reconciliation of the believer to God, which is one aspect of individual salvation and the conversion process (see Lenski, 699; Moo, 693, n. 58). This reinforces the point made in the last paragraph, that Paul is thinking here of individuals rather than groups.

We now turn our attention to the second part of the verse, which is similar to the last clause in v. 12, both in its meaning and in its relation to the rest of the verse. I.e., if the assertion in the first part of the verse is true, then that gives us all the more reason to believe the second part.

"What will their acceptance be" is literally "what the acceptance." There is no verb, and no possessive pronoun ("their"). The latter should probably be understood, in view of the similarity to v. 12; but the insertion of the future tense ("will be") is based as much (if not more) on doctrinal presuppositions as on exegetical considerations. The word for "acceptance" is used only here in the NT, but the uses of its verb form support the translation "acceptance." Other possibilities are "reception," "taking to oneself," "acquisition" (Dunn, 2:657), and "the act of welcoming" (Godet, 403).

As with v. 15a we must ask the question, who is accepting whom? Some take it as referring to the Jews' "acceptance or welcoming of the gospel" (Fitzmyer, 612), but most take it to mean God's acceptance of repentant Jews back into a saving relationship with himself (Moo, 693). God has rejected them because of their unbelief (15a), but he is just as eager to receive them back to himself if they will but turn to him.

What is this acceptance? Since it is the grammatical equivalent of "fullness" in v. 12, and since many interpret that fullness to mean a dramatic, large-scale, end-time conversion of the Jewish people, this is a common interpretation of "acceptance" as well (❈ II:241).

There is no reason other than a dogmatic one to interpret the acceptance thus, however. We have seen that "fullness" in v. 12 need not have this meaning and more likely refers to the salvation of individual Jews, something that was already occurring even as Paul wrote. Also, the "rejection" in v. 15a refers to the unbelieving Jews as individuals, not to the Jews as a nation; the same must be true of their "acceptance." We must also remember that there is no future-tense verb in the original text. Thus it is altogether appropriate to interpret this acceptance of the Jews as referring to the ongoing conversion of individual Jews, something that was already happening in Paul's day (Lenski, 700).

What happens when hardened Jews are converted? Well, says Paul, if God's casting away of the Jews results in the reconciliation of Gentiles to God, what can we expect as a result of their return and reception except "life from the dead"? This leads to our discussion of one of the most controversial expressions in this chapter, "life from the dead." Only v. 26 has "sparked more disagreement," says Moo (694).

What does it mean? Stott has identified three main answers: the literal, figurative, and spiritual views (298). Now, giving life to the dead in any sense is a marvelous event (see 4:17), but defenders of the first two of these views believe that in this case it must refer to some future, worldwide, awesome resurrection of unprecedented magnitude. This approach is based on their perception of Paul's lesser-to-greater arguments in both v. 12 and v. 15.

The common assumption is that in v. 12, the lesser element of the argument includes "riches," so the corresponding greater element must be "greater riches." Likewise it is assumed that in v. 15 the lesser includes "reconciliation," so the corresponding greater must be "life from the dead." In both verses what is perceived as the lesser element is identified with the individual's present experience of salvation. Therefore the "greater riches" and "life from the dead" must be something greater than present salvation. Therefore since regeneration is part of this present salvation, then "life from the dead" cannot be regeneration but must refer to something of much greater magnitude (❂II:242-243).

What, then, is this greater "life from the dead"? The *literal* view says it refers to the final bodily resurrection of all the dead at the Second Coming of Christ, as preceded and signaled by the mass conversion of the Jews (❂II:243).

The second view identified by Stott agrees that "life from the dead" must refer to some sort of sensational, unparalleled event, but interprets it in a *figurative* sense. It says that the Jews' fullness and reception will trigger some sort of "world-wide blessing which will so far surpass anything before experienced that it can only be likened to new life out of death" (Stott, 298). This will be "a great spiritual movement" (Morris, 411), "an unprecedented, semi-miraculous revival" (MP, 458). Since this is something triggered by the mass conversion of Jews, it must be a mass conversion of the Gentiles (Godet, 404) (❂II:243).

The final view, the *spiritual* view, is that "life from the dead" refers to an element of the individual's present salvation experience, namely, regeneration (see 6:4,11; 8:10; Eph 2:1-5; Col 12:12-13). Thus it is part of the "salvation" and the "riches" mentioned in vv. 11-12, and is in the same category as the "reconciliation" named in v. 15a. This, I believe, is the correct view.

But what about the common assumption that "life from the dead" must be something much different from and greater than this, in view of the fact that Paul is arguing from the lesser to the greater? In my judgment this is a major error based on a faulty understanding of the lesser-to-greater argument as Paul uses it here. As explained above in v. 12, the whole concept of "greater riches" misses Paul's point. There he is not arguing that if a lesser cause produces a significant effect ("riches"), then a greater cause will produce an even more significant effect ("greater riches"). Rather, he argues that if the lesser cause produces a significant effect, we have even *greater reason* to expect a greater cause to produce a similar effect. No greater effect is mentioned in the verse. The point is that the first two views above are based mainly on the assumption of an equivalence with the argument in v. 12, which itself is misinterpreted.

But what about v. 15? Indeed, there is a lesser-to-greater argument here, but the language is different from v. 12 and the logical force is weaker (Lenski, 701). But it is equivalent to v. 12 in the sense that the lesser-to-greater element in v. 15 (as in v. 12) lies only in the comparative *causes* in the two clauses, not in the effects. I.e., if the lesser cause (rejection of the Jews) produces a significant effect, then surely a greater cause (acceptance of the Jews) can be expected to produce a similarly significant effect. Thus the argument that "the logic of the verse" rules out the spiritual view is without foundation in fact.

Other considerations should be kept in mind. For example, we must remember that there are no verbs in this verse, and therefore no grammatical reason to think that "life from the dead" refers to some event that is only future. Also, the argument that the terminology "from the dead" refers only to the future bodily resurrection is offset by other linguistic data spelled out in detail by Murray (2:82-83). Also, apart from unfounded speculation regarding the meaning of "fullness" (vv. 12,25) the whole theme of eschatology simply does not appear in this context. The subject of personal salvation is dominant.

Thus we must see "life from the dead" as referring to the spiritual experience of regeneration, of passing over from the state of spiritual death to the state of spiritual life (John 5:24; Col 2:12-13). Paul may be including the Gentiles within the scope of this statement, but its main application is to the Jews themselves. I.e., if the Jews' rejection results in reconciliation for the Gentiles, then the Jews' reception results in their own resurrection to new life in Christ (◉II:245).

When we understand it this way, we see that v. 15 is just summing up what Paul has said thus far in this paragraph. Verse 15a focuses on the spiritual riches enjoyed by the Gentiles, brought about by the Jews' unbelief and rejection (vv. 11-12); and v. 15b focuses on the salvation of the Jews themselves, brought about by their own envy of the Gentiles (vv. 13-14).

11:16 If the part of the dough offered as firstfruits is holy, then the whole batch is holy; if the root is holy, so are the branches. Though many take this verse as starting the next paragraph, I agree with the NIV that it concludes the thought begun at v. 11. The general subject is still that there is hope for the salvation of the hardened portion of Israel. The main point is that God still has a special place in his heart for "his people," even those who have rejected their Messiah. This does not mean that they receive special treatment with reference to salvation (see 2:1-3:20), but it does mean that God still loves them and will make every possible effort to save them.

This verse uses two metaphors. The first is based on the fact of the divine ownership of all things. To reinforce this fact in the minds of the Jews, God required that the first portion of any product be set apart (made holy) to him in a special way. Paul is here alluding to one example of this general practice, i.e., presenting as an offering to God a portion of bread made from the meal ground from the first-harvested grain (Num 15:17-21). Though Num 15 does not specifically state this, based on the general practice it is assumed that the offering of the firstfruits "thereby consecrated to the Lord the entire grain harvest" (Hendriksen, 2:369), or all the flour and dough made from it.

The second metaphor is the relation of a tree's root to its branches. Since the root is the beginning of the pipeline through which the rest of a tree is watered and nourished, the condition of the root naturally affects the status of the branches as well. I.e., "if the root is holy, so are the branches."

The question is, what do these metaphors represent? In answering this question, two cautions must be observed. First, we should not assume that they are identical in meaning. Second, we should not assume that the point of the root-branches metaphor in v. 16 is the same as the point of the extended root-branches metaphor in vv. 17-24.

Some do take the metaphors to be parallel. For example, some have understood the firstfruits and the root to refer to Jesus Christ. In view of the context, though, it is more probable that they refer somehow to the Jews. The most common view is that the firstfruits and root refer to the patriarchs, especially Abraham, while the "whole batch" or entire "lump" (KJV, NASB), as well as the branches, refer to all the Jews who have descended from them. According to most who hold this view, the Jews as a nation will always be treated in a special way because of their relation to "the patriarchs" (v. 28).

What, then, would be the nature of this shared holiness? In a generic sense, to be holy means to be separated or set apart from all the rest; in a religious generic sense it means to be set apart for God or consecrated to God in a way that is special but does not necessarily involve salvation. Some interpret v. 16 thus, as God's promise that the nation of Israel will always be a distinct and special people, just as the patriarchs were set apart in the beginning. Many tie this in with the idea that God will one day restore the Jewish nation to its "original pre-eminence as leaders in the worship of Jehovah" (MP, 464). This does not assert "the salvation of every Israelite but the continuing 'special' identity of the people of Israel in the eyes of the Lord" (Moo, 701) (◐ II:247).

Some do interpret "holiness" in a salvific sense, however, and see this verse as a promise that all Israel will one day be saved (see v. 26). To some this means spiritual Israel only, i.e., "all the spiritual descendants" of the patriarchs (Lenski, 703). To others it is a promise that one day all (or a great majority of) ethnic Jews will be saved (❧ II:247).

I disagree with all of the above views. A key point is that the two metaphors are not parallel in their meaning, as if the firstfruits and the root refer to the same thing, and the lump and the branches refer to the same thing. What do they mean, then? In other texts Paul uses the term "firstfruits" (ἀπαρχή, *aparchē*) to refer to the first converts in a particular context (16:5; 1 Cor 16:15). That is the point of the first metaphor here. The firstfruits are the early Jewish converts, the Jewish Christian remnant; the "batch" is the Jews as a whole, especially the unbelieving and hardened ones.

Also, "holy" here does have the connotation of salvation. This does not imply, though, that just as the first converts *have been* saved, so ultimately all Jews *will be* saved. It means this, rather: if *some* Jews can be saved, then *all* Jews can be saved. It is the same hope that Paul holds out in this paragraph when he refers to the "fullness" and "acceptance" of the Jews (vv. 12,15).

The second metaphor is slightly different. The root includes the patriarchs but not them alone; it refers to the entire OT Israelite nation considered as a whole. The branches are all ethnic Jews living in the NT era, considered as individuals. Here the primary connotation of "holy" is the generic concept of "set apart" or "consecrated" to God, but its ultimate reference is still to salvation. The point is this: under the Old Covenant God chose the nation of Israel to be the instrument by which he worked his redemptive purpose in the world (9:6-29). Even though he no longer has a special purpose for Israel as a nation, nevertheless the love and concern he had for "his people" in OT times carries forward into the gospel era. Every branch, i.e., every individual Jew, is just as personally precious and special to him today as was the root, the nation of old. Thus the door of salvation is still open even to the hardened, unbelieving Jews. God is waiting to add them to the remnant.

The point of the verse, then, is not to promise that Israel as a nation will be restored to its OT prominence, nor to guarantee that all Jews actually *will* be saved. Rather, it is to stress the fact that any and all Jews *can* be saved (v. 16a), and that God *wants* them to be saved (v. 16b). Following up on this, the point of the next paragraph is to show exactly *how* they can be saved.

D. THE OLIVE TREE: A METAPHOR OF JUDGMENT AND HOPE (11:17-24)

Introduction

In this paragraph Paul stays with the metaphor of the olive tree, but he expands it considerably and uses it for different purposes. In brief, he uses it to show how the NT church is related to OT Israel, and how Jews and Gentiles are related to the church. The main point of vv. 17-22 is a double warning to Gentile Christians. They are warned not to have an attitude of self-righteous superiority toward unbelieving Jews, and not to presume that they are any more immune to falling away than the Jews who fell. The main point of vv. 23-24, on the other hand, is an explanation of how the fallen and hardened Jews can be saved.

Why has Paul used the olive tree as a basis for making these points? For one thing, the OT compares God's people with an olive tree (Jer 11:16; Hos 14:6). Also, it was something his initial readers would have been very familiar with. Also, the common practice of grafting branches from one olive tree to another was a perfect illustration of the points he wanted to make.

Since Paul has just used the root-branches metaphor in v. 16, we would expect these two elements to have the same basic meaning in this new paragraph; and most agree that this is so. E.g., those who identified the root with the patriarchs in v. 16 do the same here. I agree that this is the best approach. Thus, as in v. 16, I identify the root with OT Israel as a national unit, and I identify the branches as (in part) including (some) individual Jews who live in this NT era.

In vv. 17-24, however, Paul has expanded the metaphor in at least three ways. First, the concept of the tree as a whole is important here. Whereas v. 16 was about the relationship between generic roots and branches, here a particular tree is in view. How the roots and branches of this tree are related is still important, but it is also important that we understand the character of the tree as a whole. Second, the branches are not limited to individual Jews, but refer also to individual Gentiles. Finally, the grafting of branches is a central element of the metaphor in this paragraph.

The rest of this introduction will explain, first, the concept of the olive tree as a whole, and second, the imagery of the pruning and grafting of the branches.

The Meaning of the Olive Tree as a Whole

Exactly what does this olive tree stand for? It represents the people of God in a general sense, including both OT Israel and the NT church, the latter including both Jews and Gentiles (see Moo, 698). This tree cannot be limited to ethnic Israel alone, as some think (see Fitzmyer, 610, for examples).

In one sense the nation of Israel as it existed in the OT era was a kind of prototree, and was a precursor of Paul's olive tree. This is suggested by the references to the breaking off of some of the Jewish branches (vv. 17-21). If they were broken off, then they were already attached to something. Also, Paul calls his tree the Jews' "own olive tree" (v. 24). In this sense pre-Christian Israel was itself a tree, but this is not Paul's main point. Also, it is important to remember that the OT tree had no implications regarding the salvation of the individual Jews attached thereto as branches. The tree as a whole was an instrument by which God was working out his salvation purposes; some of the individual branches were saved and some were not.

Whatever the nature of this prototree which led to the existence of Paul's olive tree, we must recognize that it underwent a radical transformation in character and purpose with the coming of the NT era. In Paul's metaphor OT Israel is not identified with the tree as a whole, but only with its root. His focus is on the individual branches as they relate to this root. These branches themselves constitute an entirely new group: the NT people of God, the church. Most importantly, unlike the OT prototree, Paul's olive tree is a soteric metaphor. Its branches as a whole are the aggregate of all saved individuals in this new era.

We may now look more closely at the composition of the olive tree. As in v. 16, the root stands for OT Israel as a whole. Thus it includes but is not limited to the patriarchs. It represents the entire nation throughout its entire history from the patriarchs forward, not as the aggregate of saved individuals (the remnant), but as God's covenant servant. It represents Israel in its role of fulfilling God's redemptive purposes, culminating in the coming of the Messiah. Thus the root includes all blessings enumerated in 9:4-5: the patriarchs, the covenants, the promises, and in a sense even the Messiah himself.

The branches of the tree, which are the focal point of the metaphor, are the saved individuals of the NT era. As such they are the new Israel. The olive tree as a whole represents the two Israels to which v. 9:6b alludes, "For not all who are descended from Israel are Israel." The root is OT ethnic Israel; the branches are NT spiritual Israel. When the Messiah came and the OT prototree was transformed into the olive tree, this transformation was a moment of crisis for all Jews. Prior to this time all individual Jews – unbelievers as well as believers – were part of the prototree as an instrument of service to God. But with the coming of Christ and the transformation of the tree, all unbelieving Jews as individual branches of the old tree were broken off. There are no unbelievers on the olive tree; its branches consist of believers only.

The olive tree metaphor teaches us that there is a definite *discontinuity* between OT Israel and the NT church. Paul's tree is not the same as the OT prototree. The latter was transformed at Pentecost (see MP, 464-465) into something different. What once was an entire tree is now just the root of a new tree. The church is as different from Israel as a tree's branches are different from its root.

But this fact in itself implies a *continuity* between OT Israel and the NT church. The old tree was not simply cut down and replaced with a completely new one. The church by itself is not the entire tree, but only the branches that are growing from a root that is part of that same tree. The two parts of this one tree have never existed simultaneously but are sequential in time. I.e., the root and the branches represent two interconnected stages in salvation history. Though the root itself no longer exists, its prior existence was an essential preparation for the present reality of the branches. Herein lies the basis for one of Paul's main points in this section: the relationship of dependence between the two Israels. I.e., the church as the new Israel is dependent upon what was accomplished by old Israel. The NT branches would have no existence apart from their OT root, and they constantly reap the rich benefits of what God has done through the latter (vv. 17-18). This is one reason why Paul warns the Gentile Christians not to boast over the fallen Jews (v. 18a).

The Imagery of the Pruning and Grafting of the Branches

While the meaning of the olive tree as a whole tells us something about the relation between OT Israel and the NT church, the imagery of the pruning and grafting of individual branches tells us something about the salvation of Jews and Gentiles in the NT era. Unlike the root-branches illustration in v. 16, which dealt exclusively with Jews, the branches in the extended metaphor include both Jews and Gentiles. While Jewish Christians are described as belonging naturally to the "cultivated" olive tree, Gentile Christians are pictured as belonging by nature to a "wild" olive tree and being grafted into the cultivated one (v. 24).

Paul's discussion of Jews and Gentiles in this paragraph is in terms of God's pruning some branches from the tree and grafting others into it. A crucial point is that, when the OT prototree was transformed into the present olive tree, some of the original branches (Jews) that were attached to the former were broken off, which is an indication of their lost state. Before the transformation some of these attached branches were already lost, since the prototree did not have a soteric significance. But when Christ came and the tree was changed, *all* Jews who refused to accept him as their Savior were removed from the tree. We have every reason to assume that this included some Jews who were previously in a saved state because of their faith in Yahweh as he was known through OT revelation, but who rejected Jesus as the promised Messiah. On the other hand, all Jews who did believe in Jesus remained as branches on the new tree.

At the same time, all Gentiles who accepted Jesus as their Savior were taken from the wild olive tree (the pagan world) and were grafted into the cultivated and transformed olive tree, alongside the believing Jews, in the community of salvation.

Some have raised questions about the accuracy of Paul's knowledge of the olive industry. It seems that the usual procedure for grafting olive branches is to take a shoot from a cultivated but depleted tree and graft it into a wild but vigorous tree, but here it is just the opposite. Some have concluded that Paul as a naïve city boy was just showing his ignorance. Others point to a few ancient sources which show that wild-to-tame grafts were sometimes made, just as Paul describes. Still others say that Paul knew wild-to-tame grafts were not a natural procedure, but he reversed the process in order to show that grace deliberately contravenes nature (v. 24). Either of the last two explanations is acceptable. The details of grafting as an agricultural practice are not crucial to Paul's point. He simply incorporates the general concept into his metaphor and adapts it for his own purposes; one does not have to be an olive tree expert to understand what he is saying.

Paul uses the practice of grafting to make two main points. One is that the Gentile Christians, as wild olive branches grafted into a cultivated tree, have absolutely no room for boasting or considering themselves superior to the Jewish branches that were broken off the tree (vv. 17-22). One reason is that they are dependent upon the Jewish root of the tree for their very salvation and sustenance (v. 18b). The other reason is that their being grafted into the tree is due to their faith in what Christ has done, not to some boastworthy achievement accomplished by their own hands. If they ever reach a point where they no longer believe in Jesus, they too will be broken off just as the unbelieving Jews were (vv. 20-21).

Paul's other point is a continuation of his theme in vv. 11-16, that the lopped-off Jews are not irrevocably lost but can still be saved, even though they are now in an unbelieving and hardened state. Here he is not just declaring that they *can* be saved, but showing *how* they can be saved, namely, by being grafted again into their own (transformed) olive tree, the church (vv. 23-24). This regrafting is done branch by branch, as individual Jews come to believe in their Messiah. It has absolutely nothing to do with a supposed "future restoration" of the Jewish nation (contra Godet, 404), or a time when "the natural descendants of Abraham will . . . once again be the Lord's chosen people of blessing" (contra MacArthur, 2:118). It is a possibility that is open to all Jews, any time, anywhere. The stated requirement is simply that they "not persist in unbelief" (v. 23). If they do not, then they will become branches on the tree, i.e., members of the church of Jesus Christ. This is the one hope of Gentiles and Jews alike; this is how "all Israel will be saved" (v. 26).

We should note Paul's emphasis on faith or the lack of it as the key to whether one is part of the olive tree or not. This is consistent with the main theme of Romans, that sinners are saved by grace through faith, and not by works of law (3:28), and consistent with his emphasis on faith in the previous main section (9:30–10:21).

1. Words of Warning to Gentile Christians (11:17-22)

The first part of this paragraph is a specific warning to Gentile Christians not to think of themselves as somehow superior to the Jewish branches that were broken off the tree. This may reflect some tension within the Roman church between Gentile Christians and Jewish Christians, and it may reflect a general cultural anti-Semitism carried over into the church by converted Gentiles. But these are matters of speculation and need not concern us, since the arrogant attitude of which Paul speaks could have been readily aroused just by unsound reflection upon Israel's history and the early decades of church history.

11:17-18a If some of the branches have been broken off, and you, though a wild olive shoot, have been grafted in among the others and now share in

the nourishing sap from the olive root, do not boast over those branches. This is an "if-then" sentence in which the if-clause (the protasis, v. 17) is assumed to be true, with the then-clause (the apodosis, v. 18a) naturally following.

Paul keeps the root-branches metaphor introduced in v. 16 and begins to apply it to the way individual Jews and Gentiles are saved. He refers first to the Jews, who are compared with branches on a tree, some of which have been "broken off." This refers to the Jews who refused to accept Christ as their Messiah, and to God's punitive act of hardening and rejecting them (vv. 7,15). That Paul says only "some" branches were broken off is a deliberate understatement reminiscent of 3:3. Actually the majority of Jews were in this category.

Next Paul refers to the Gentile Christians, whom he is addressing (v. 13). He uses the singular "you" to put his admonitions on a more personal level. This "you" is the typical Gentile Christian representing the whole group (Dunn, 2:673). Paul addressed the Jews in a similar way in 2:1ff.

The Gentile Christian is here described as "a wild olive shoot" (a branch cut from a wild or uncultivated olive tree) that has been grafted into the cultivated olive tree "among the others." The branches of this cultivated tree represent the NT church, and "the others" are the Jews who were the first converts to Christ and thus the first branches on the tree. That the wild branches were grafted in "among" them (beginning in Acts 10) means that they were placed alongside the Jewish Christians who had already been there from Acts 2 and following.

The last part of the protasis also speaks of Gentile Christians. It describes the result of their being grafted into the olive tree alongside the believing Jews. When this happened, says Paul, the Gentile Christians immediately became "fellow partakers" or "sharers together" (i.e., along with the Jewish Christians) of "the nourishing sap from the olive root." This root is OT Israel as it fulfilled its covenant purpose of bringing the Messiah into the world. As such OT Israel is the indispensable source of all the "nourishing sap" or spiritual benefits that are absorbed by the branches, i.e., by each individual member of the church. When a Gentile becomes a Christian, he immediately begins to draw upon all the spiritual blessings made possible by two millennia of Jewish history—blessings which are a natural inheritance for Jews who accept their Messiah (❧ II:255-256).

In v. 18a Paul draws his conclusion from v. 17: "Do not boast over those branches." This is in the form of an exhortation, but its logical force is "you have no reason" to boast over them. Paul still addresses Gentile Christians (in the person of their typical representative); "those branches" are the Jews. Do these Jewish branches include both Jewish Christians ("the others") and the broken-off branches, or do they include only the branches that were broken off? I agree with Murray (2:86) that the latter is probably the case, in view of v. 19.

Thus in this exhortation Paul warns Gentile Christians not to brag or boast over against the Jews who were broken off the tree, as if becoming a Christian were the result of some kind of competition between the two groups, with the

Gentiles being the winners. You have no reason to boast, he says, as if being grafted into the tree were a sign of your superiority over those rejected Jews.

11:18b If you do, consider this: You do not support the root, but the root supports you. This is not an implicit permission to go ahead and boast. Rather, Paul is saying, "If you are still inclined to boast, or if you still have a boastful spirit, please remember this . . . ."

What Paul asks them to remember is very close in meaning to v. 17c, but here he is more forceful: "*You* [emphatic] do not support the root, *but* [emphatic] the root supports you." It is important to see that the root is not just the patriarchs, as many believe, and especially not just "the covenant of salvation that God made with Abraham" (contra MacArthur, 2:115), but the entire scope of the Jews' covenant service from Abraham to Christ. Paul is thus asking the Gentile Christians, "What, historically, do the Jews owe to you? Which of their glorious blessings (9:4-5) came through you? Obviously, none; so your boasting is vain. The relationship of dependence is actually the other way around" (❧II:257).

11:19 Wanting to drive this point home further, Paul puts a question in the mouth of the proud Gentile Christian: **You will say then, "Branches were broken off so that I could be grafted in."** The way Paul words the question highlights the egotism that he wants to turn aside: "Branches were broken off so that *I, even I*, could be grafted in!" The implication is that this person thinks God excluded some Jews from the church just to make a place for Gentile believers.

11:20a Granted. But they were broken off because of unbelief, and you stand by faith. Paul's opening word, "Granted" (καλῶς, *kalōs*), can be taken as "qualified agreement" (Moo, 705); it is "a form of partial and often ironical assent" (MP, 467). In other words, "There is some truth in what you are saying." Here Paul is probably referring to the point made in vv. 11-16, that "because of their transgression, salvation has come to the Gentiles" (v. 11), and "their rejection is the reconciliation of the world" (v. 15).

Paul's next statement can be paraphrased thus: "But this is not the whole story, and it is not even the most important part of the story. It's true that many Jews were broken off, and it's true that you, a Gentile, were grafted in. But this is not a neat, self-contained cause-and-effect sequence, as if there were some sort of intrinsic connection between these two events. No, the important fact is this: the Jews were broken off *because of their unbelief*! They refused to believe in Jesus! Those who believed in him were not broken off; would that this had been true for all of them! And you: why have you been grafted into the tree? Not because the Jews were broken off, but only because you have put your faith in Jesus. Even if every Jew had believed, you would still have been grafted into the tree by virtue of your faith."

The implied conclusion, again, is that the circumstances of the Jews' rejection and the Gentiles' acceptance gave the latter absolutely no room for boasting against the former. This warning is reinforced by the reminder that the

Romans Part Four

Gentiles stand, i.e., are saved, only by faith — a way of salvation that insistently excludes any reason for boasting (3:27; Eph 2:8-9).

11:20b-21 Do not be arrogant, but be afraid. For if God did not spare the natural branches, he will not spare you either. Here Paul tells the Gentile Christians the proper attitude to develop in place of arrogance: the fear of God. "Do not be arrogant" is literally "do not have high-minded thoughts" (see 12:16; 1 Tim 6:17), i.e., do not think so highly of yourselves. Instead, you should "fear" (NASB), or "be afraid" (NIV).

Either of these translations may be a proper rendering of the Greek φοβέω (*phobeō*), but they do not necessarily have the same connotation. The fear of God takes two different forms. One is the healthy, reverential awe of the creature before his Creator. The other is the terror and dread of the sinner in the presence of the holy Lawgiver and Judge.

To which of these kinds of fear is Paul referring? Certainly to the first, which is always a main element of holy living. Also, there is no better antidote to arrogance, nothing more conducive to humility, than to come to a full realization of our creatureliness before God Almighty. But what about the second, being afraid of the Judgment? Certainly when it is truly felt, this kind of fear likewise cancels out arrogance as fire consumes tissue paper. As a rule, such fear is inappropriate for Christians, since we are free from condemnation thanks to justification by faith in the blood of Christ. But there is one context in which the fear of terror is still necessary even for Christians, namely, when we stand on the brink of apostasy or falling away. In such a situation, how can we not call to mind that "it is a dreadful thing to fall into the hands of the living God" (Heb 10:31)? In view of Paul's warning to the Gentile Christians in v. 21, I think he probably also has this kind of fear in mind in v. 20b, i.e., terror at the prospect of being cut off.

We should make no mistake: in v. 21 Paul holds before us all the real possibility of falling from grace and losing our salvation. This is another reason why Gentile Christians, and Jewish Christians as well, should realize the folly of arrogance regarding their salvation status. Here Paul uses an argument from the greater to the lesser. The "natural branches" are the Jews, who in view of their natal association with the root are inherently suitable for being attached as branches to the tree. But even so, when some refused to believe in Jesus, God did not spare them. I.e., he rejected them and broke them off the tree. This was true even if they were in a saved state before being confronted with the gospel. If they refused to convert their faith in Yahweh to a Trinitarian faith, they were broken off, and given no place in the transformed olive tree. And if God did not spare even these, he will certainly not spare the wild olive branches — Gentile Christians — that have no natural connection with the tree, if they return to their unbelief.

11:22 Consider therefore the kindness and sternness of God: . . . This refers to what are rightly called "the two sides of the Divine character" (SH, 329).

"Kindness" (χρηστότης, *chrēstotēs*; see 2:4) is an attitude of goodwill and generosity toward others, a goodness of heart or "kindly disposition" (SH, 55) that desires the happiness of others and especially their salvation. "Sternness" (ἀποτομία, *apotomia*; "severity," NASB) is an attitude of relentless and vigorous commitment to justice, including retributive justice; a strict upholding of the requirements of the law; an "inflexible hardness and severity" in judging (see Köster, "τέμνω," 107-108). Obviously, then, "the kindness and sternness of God" are "a fascinating contrast of attitudes, held simultaneously," as Morris says (416).

These two attributes are generally equivalent to God's love and God's holiness, which I believe are the two most basic and equally ultimate moral attributes of God. God's love is his basic goodwill toward other moral beings. Other attributes within the sphere of his love are mercy, patience, grace, and kindness. God's holiness, on the other hand, is his perfect moral character, which is the basis of his work as Lawgiver and Judge. It embraces other attributes such as wrath and vengeance. See *GRe*, 238-239, 255-257.

Because these two sides of God's nature are equally ultimate, it is a serious misconception to think that they are just two different ways of expressing the same divine attribute. There is probably no more widespread false doctrine in Christendom than this, and few with more serious consequences. (See *GRe*, 303-314.)

At the same time I will agree with Dunn's contention that these two aspects of God's nature are not of "equal weight," since in Scripture the "stronger emphasis is on grace and mercy" (2:665). This makes his holiness and wrath no less real, no less distinct, and no less ultimate, however. (See *GRe*, 372-375.)

Why does Paul admonish the representative Gentile Christian (and us) to "consider" or "observe" the kindness and sternness of God? Because these are the two basic attributes that God expresses toward sinners, depending on their response to the grace of his Son, Jesus Christ. In this context they are the attributes that lie behind the breaking off of the unbelieving Jewish branches and the grafting in of the believing Gentile branches: **sternness to those who fell,** i.e., the Jews who rejected Christ (v. 11), **but kindness to you** as a Gentile who has accepted Christ.

In v. 20 Paul stressed that the reason the Gentile Christians were grafted into the tree was their faith in the Messiah, not some merit on their part. Here he shows that God's willingness to accept someone on the simple basis of faith in Christ is a matter of his gracious kindness. There is no merit in faith itself.

Paul says all these things to set up his final warning to Gentile Christians, which also applies to all branches on the olive tree (all members of his church) in all times and places. I.e., the very fact that you are on the tree (and by implication saved) means that you have received the kindness of God. But be warned: you will remain on the tree as a recipient of God's kindness **provided that you continue in his kindness. Otherwise, you also will be cut off.**

"Provided that you continue" is ἐάν (*ean*) with the subjunctive, a form that expresses a contingency that may or may not be the case in the future. (For the same form see 13:4; 14:8.) God will continue to bestow his kindness upon you, *if and only if* you "continue in his kindness." To "continue in" God's kindness means to continue to *trust* his kindness and grace as embodied in the saving work of Jesus. What will happen if you *do not* continue to trust God's grace? Paul's answer is very clear: "you also," like the Jews who refused to believe, "will be cut off." You will lose your salvation.

This verse brings into sharp focus the issue of whether or not salvation is conditional, which includes the issue of "once saved, always saved." In general Calvinists believe that God's grace is sovereignly bestowed and maintained in an unconditional way, and non-Calvinists believe that it is conditional. But even some non-Calvinists hold that once a person believes by his own free choice, he will unconditionally continue to believe from that point on. This is the essence of the "once saved, always saved" doctrine.

In my judgment this verse unequivocally supports the view that salvation is conditional. Just as *becoming* saved is conditioned upon faith, *staying* saved is conditioned upon continuing to believe. You will remain as a branch on the olive tree "if you continue" (NASB) in God's kindness. (See Col 1:23 for the very same point.) More specifically this verse shows that falling from a saved state and thus losing one's salvation is possible. Dunn rightly says, "The possibility of believers 'falling away' . . . apostatizing, is one which Paul certainly did not exclude." He adds, "Perseverance is a Christian responsibility rather than an unconditional promise" (2:664-665).

How do Calvinists handle this text? One may be surprised to see the strong Calvinist William Hendriksen conclude from this verse that God's kindness is "not unconditional. It requires genuine faith on man's part" (2:375). At the same time this verse does not imply "that those who truly belong to him will ever be rejected," as Stott explains (301).

But how could anyone believe that salvation is truly conditional, and at the same time deny the possibility of falling away? The answer, for the Calvinist, is as follows. First, God does require sinners to have faith in Jesus as a condition for being saved. Therefore, technically, salvation is conditional. But at the same time God sovereignly determines who will have faith and who will not. To those whom God has unconditionally chosen for eternal life, he unconditionally gives the gift of faith. Once the faith has been given, of course, it is the person who believes, and not God. Thus the person is fulfilling the condition for salvation. Hendriksen (2:375) says of 11:22 that it

> must not be understood in the sense that God will supply the kindness, man the faith. Salvation is ever God's gift. It is never a 50-50 affair. From start to finish it is the work of God. But this does not remove human responsibility.

God does not exercise faith for man or in his place. It is and remains man who reposes his trust in God, but it is God who both imparts this faith to him and enables him to use it.

This, says Hendriksen, is the "sound, biblical sense . . . in which we can speak about salvation as being *conditional*."

I sincerely believe that this and other such explanations are nothing but theological double-talk. To say that this is a "sound, biblical sense" in which salvation is conditional, and that such a system "does not remove human responsibility," is a sham. It is not enough just to say that God sets conditions for salvation. The Calvinist may begin with this premise, but then he declares that God unconditionally decides *who* will meet the conditions, and then unilaterally *causes* them to meet these conditions. In such a scenario there are no conditionality and human responsibility in any normal sense of these terms.

If persevering faith is a sovereign gift of God, what is the purpose of warnings in the Bible, such as the one in 11:22? Moule (197) grants that such passages imply "*contingency*" in man's continuance in the mercy of God," but they are nevertheless in harmony with "sovereign and prevailing Divine grace." This is true because God both gives and preserves faith in the elect. The chosen will without fail persevere in faith, because God will infallibly enable them to do so. As Moule says, "Grace imparts *perseverance* by imparting and maintaining faith." And how does grace maintain faith? Among other things, "faith is properly animated and energized" through these warnings themselves.

In my opinion all such attempts to harmonize the "if" in 11:22 (or elsewhere) with Calvinism, or with any "once saved, always saved" belief, amount to more double-talk and reduce Paul's warning to a travesty. Unless there is a genuine possibility that this warning may be disregarded by a genuine believer, then it is not a warning at all, and its very presence in the Bible is deceptive.

Moo's attempt (707, n. 57) to reconcile 11:22 with a denial of the possibility of falling away is a little different but just as untenable. His view is that not every branch on the tree is a true believer in the first place. This must be true, he says, because the unbelieving Jews who were cut off the tree in reality were never part of the tree at all. It is only for the sake of his metaphor that "Paul presents them as if they had been. In the same way, then, those Gentiles within the church . . . who appear to be part of God's people, yet do not continue in faith, may never have been part of that tree at all."

This explanation fails for three reasons. One, it is an unwarranted assumption that *all* the Jews who were originally cut off from the tree were never truly saved to begin with. As I have already stated, it is quite likely that many Jews who had a faith adequate to save them in light of the limitations of the OT revelation refused to elevate their faith to the NT level when first confronted with the gospel. (Paul himself may have been in this category.) These would be among the branches that were broken off.

Second, Moo's explanation does not take account of the difference between the OT prototree and the olive tree as it has existed under the New Covenant dispensation. All Jews were branches on the former, but this had no soteric implications. The latter is occupied solely by those who are saved, Jews and Gentiles. Is this not the point of the breaking off of the unbelieving Jewish branches in the first place?

Third, the speculation that the Gentiles who do not continue in the faith may never have been part of the tree at all goes against everything Paul says in this paragraph. "You stand by faith," he says to the Gentile representative in v. 20. If the addressee is not saved — not truly part of the tree, then everything about this statement is false. God's kindness has been given to you, Paul says in v. 22, in contrast with the fallen Jews who received God's sternness. There is no way to reconcile this affirmation with a mere appearance of salvation.

The focus in vv. 23-24 will shift to the fallen Jews, but at this point we may note that the conditional promise about Jewish unbelievers in v. 23a is parallel in every way to the conditional warning about Gentile believers in v. 22b. If we cannot take the warning seriously, why should we take the promise seriously? If we say that v. 22 does not imply that an *actual* falling away can take place, must we not assume that v. 23 does not mean that any fallen Jews will *actually* be saved? But no one would ever consider the latter. Here is a statement by Stott (301): "After this warning to Gentile believers against pride and presumption, Paul is ready with his promise to Jewish unbelievers. His argument is that if those grafted in could be cut off, then those cut off could be grafted in again." Just so! But the "once saved, always saved" doctrine completely destroys the symmetry between the two conditions and leaves the latter open to doubt. Indeed, Stott himself says of the warning in v. 22, "Not that those who truly belong to him will ever be rejected . . ."! However, I have yet to see him or anyone else say of v. 23, "Not that those Jews who truly rejected him will ever be accepted . . . ."

2. Words of Hope for Hardened Jews (11:23-24)

In these last two verses about the olive tree, Paul returns to the main theme of the chapter, that God has not completely rejected the Jews. It is true that only a remnant accepted the Messiah in the beginning, and that the rest were hardened, rejected, and broken off the tree. But since v. 11 Paul has held forth the possibility and the hope that individuals in this latter group may still return to God. Here he reaffirms that hope as he shows how the rejected Jews may be saved.

11:23 And if they do not persist in unbelief, they will be grafted in, . . . The parallelism between v. 22b and v. 23a is obvious when we slightly reword 22b while keeping the same thought:

> If you [believing Gentiles] do not continue in God's kindness, you will be cut off the tree.
>
> If you [unbelieving Jews] do not continue in unbelief, you will be grafted back into the tree.

The subject here is obviously "those who fell" (v. 22), the Jewish unbelievers. Literally Paul says, "And those also," or, "Yes, and they too" (SH, 330). The verb translated "persist" is the same one translated "continue" in v. 22; and the conditional form is the same, *ean* with the subjunctive. The then-clause is just the simple future tense of ἐγκεντρίζω (*enkentrizō*, used in vv. 17,19), "they will be grafted in." To be grafted into the tree is the equivalent of "life from the dead" in v. 15.

This is a clear indication that God has not abandoned the Jewish people but is ready and willing to receive them back to himself at any time.

It is also clear in this verse that the Jews' return to and acceptance by God is *conditional*. It is conditioned upon their change of heart concerning Jesus. They will be grafted into the tree *if* they do not continue in unbelief, but turn to Jesus in full faith and surrender. The promise that they will be grafted in is a promise that they will be saved (❂ II:265, n. 174).

In spite of the clear and obvious conditional nature of this promise, some interpreters completely ignore the stated condition and take Paul's statement as an absolute promise that the Jews — all of them — will one day be saved (❂ II:266).

What is happening here? Just as in reference to v. 22b, we are witnessing an inability — or an unwillingness — to take seriously the significance of Paul's "if." In v. 22, in the interest of preserving the "once saved, always saved" doctrine, some declare that the if-clause is something that *will not* happen, period. Here in v. 23, in the interest of supporting a particular view of the end-times, some declare that the if-clause is something that *will* happen, period. Paul might just as well have omitted the "if" in both cases.

We must take Paul at his word. He does not say "when"; he says "if." Hendriksen rightly reminds us that "the apostle does not say or imply that one day all unbelieving Jews are going to be grafted back into their own olive tree" (2:376). As McGuiggan says (331), the tone of the verse suggests that he was *not* predicting "a national scale conversion of the Jews" (❂ II:266).

We cannot say, of course, that this will never happen. But whether few or many Jews do come to faith in Christ, this verse shows *how* they will be saved and restored to God, namely, by being grafted into the olive tree, which is the church. There is absolutely nothing here about a restoration of the nation of Israel to its role as a separate and special people of God. The only thing Paul promises the Jews here, conditioned upon faith in Christ, is that they will be grafted into the olive tree. But this is not the same tree from which they were broken off in the first place. This is a transformed tree, only the root of which is OT national Israel. The branches are the new Israel, the church, and they consist of both believing Jews and believing Gentiles. To be joined to the tree is to be united with the Gentiles, not set apart from them again. To expect a national restoration to an OT-like special role is to go against the very essence of the olive-tree metaphor.

We must not allow such false hopes to blind us to the very real possibility Paul sets forth here. The Jews *can* become a part of the tree, **for God is able to graft them in again.** The promise does not depend on what was possible with regard to literal grafting practices; it depends on the supernatural power of God: "God is able." Denney says, "Even in the most hardened rejector of the Gospel we are not to limit either the resources of God's power or the possibilities of change in a self-conscious, self-determining creature" (681).

We should note that God's grafting the Jews into the tree is not the same as causing them to believe. The first part of this verse makes it clear that there is a difference between the believing and the grafting-in. God can and will graft them in, i.e., will add them to his church, but they must first meet the stated condition of not persisting in unbelief.

11:24 After all, if you were cut out of an olive tree that is wild by nature, and contrary to nature were grafted into a cultivated olive tree, how much more readily will these, the natural branches, be grafted into their own olive tree! This verse does not add anything new; it simply reinforces the last statement in v. 23, that *God is able* to graft the fallen Jewish branches back into the tree. It is an argument from the greater to the lesser. Paul says it is a lot easier to graft a broken-off branch back into its own olive tree than to graft wild and alien branches into that tree. Since God has already done the latter (in saving the Gentiles), we can be sure that the former (saving the Jews) will be no problem for him.

Using the singular, Paul still addresses the typical representative of all Gentile Christians. The first part of the verse sums up the Gentiles' situation in terms of the olive tree. The phrase "by nature" probably does not modify the wild olive tree itself (contra the NIV), but rather the branch that was cut out of it (see Cranfield, 2:571; Moo, 708, n. 63). I.e., it should read, "If you, who by nature belong to a wild olive tree, were cut off from that tree and contrary to nature were grafted into a cultivated olive tree . . . ."

This means that the Gentiles by nature belonged to the pagan world. This is where they were born and reared; this is where they learned and lived by the antibiblical worldview. This is where they were "at home," i.e., on the wild olive tree. But when they came to Christ they were cut off from this tree and grafted into the "cultivated olive tree," which is described as "cultivated" because of its Jewish root. The cultivation process includes all of God's dealings with the Jews from Abraham up to the first coming of Christ. Because of this background the earliest Jewish Christians — the first branches of the transformed olive tree — in a sense grew naturally out of this root. But when Gentiles were pried loose from their paganism and united with this OT root (Lenski, 712), this was definitely "contrary to nature," i.e., against everything they had thus far stood for.

On the other hand, v. 24b says that when unbelieving Jews ("these") are converted, this is like grafting broken-off branches back "into their own olive tree." Because of its Jewish root, even unbelieving, broken-off Jews have a natural affinity with the olive tree. Indeed, it is called "their own tree" for this very reason. OT ethnic Israel is not the tree as such, but it is the *root* of the tree. Thus when a Jew is converted to Christ he is being attached to his true roots; he is taking his natural place among the branches (the church) that were the divinely intended goal of the Israelite nation all along. What could be more natural than this? (II:265.)

The main point is to show that from God's side, there is absolutely no obstacle to the Jews' salvation. Their hardening (v. 7) and their rejection (v. 15) need not be the final word concerning their eternal destiny. God is ready and willing to receive them back, if they will believe in their Redeemer. He has already added repentant, believing Gentiles to the church; and if he has done this, *how much more likely is it* that believing Jews will also be added? (II:265.)

Two implications from this olive tree metaphor must be emphasized. First, there is in this New Covenant age only one olive tree, only one chosen people, only one way of salvation. Any Jews who are saved will be saved by being grafted into this one tree. The Jewish branches and the Gentile branches are joined together into one aggregate of saved persons (the church) where the Jew-Gentile distinction is irrelevant (II:269).

A second implication is that, contrary to a common misconception, *it is possible* for someone who has fallen from grace to be restored to full fellowship with God. Hebrews 6:4-6 is often misinterpreted as teaching the opposite, that it is impossible for a once-saved but now-fallen person to be brought back to a saved state. Some translations perpetuate this error by the way they translate Heb 6:6 (e.g., the word "because" in the NIV, and "since" in the NASB).

The olive-tree metaphor, however, shows that this interpretation of Heb 6 is false. This is true because we must assume that *some* of the Jews who were broken off the tree (v. 17) were believers in Yahweh as they knew him from the OT revelation and were thus in a saved state *until* they heard the gospel of Jesus and initially refused to accept it. E.g., Acts 2:41 says about 3,000 persons were baptized and added to the church on the day of Pentecost, when the church began. Unless this number includes the entire Pentecost audience, or unless it constitutes one hundred per cent of the pre-Christian Jewish believers who were present, then we must assume that some believing Jews who were present at Pentecost "fell away" by not accepting Christ on that day. Since both of these possibilities are highly unlikely, we can assume that some of the "natural branches" being grafted back into the tree are fallen-away believers who are being restored to salvation. This means the alternative translation of Heb 6:6 given in the NIV and NASB margins ("while," i.e., "as long as") is the correct one.

In other words, Paul's teaching about the olive tree refutes both the "once saved, always saved" error, *and* the "once fallen, always fallen" error. Both are equally unbiblical.

E. GOD'S PLAN FOR ISRAEL'S SALVATION (11:25-32)

In this paragraph all eyes are usually focused on v. 26a, "And so all Israel will be saved." This is "the center of this paragraph," says Moo (712); the NIV makes this statement the heading for the entire section. What it means, though, is notoriously difficult, and is the subject of endless discussion. Every part of it is controversial. How extensive is the word "all"? Does "Israel" refer to ethnic or spiritual Israel? To what status is Israel "saved"?

One of the more common conclusions based on this text is that at some time in the future, at or near the end of this age, most living Jews will turn to Christ and be restored as a nation to a place of preeminence in God's kingdom. As Moule says, in this text Paul "now, in plain terms, reveals and predicts a great future Restoration" (197).

I cannot accept this interpretation, for reasons that will be made clear in the following exposition. At this point I will simply say that in v. 26a, emphasis is usually placed on the wrong word, namely, "all," with the verse being read thus: "And so *all* Israel will be saved." In my judgment the emphasis should be on the word "so," taken in the sense of "thus, in this manner." Thus we should read it: "And *in this way* all Israel will be saved." I.e., regarding Israel's salvation Paul's point is "How?" and not "How many?"

This does not mean that there is a question whether Israel's salvation will be by some means other than faith in Jesus. That issue has already been settled, especially in ch. 10. Rather, the question has to do with the interrelationship between Israel and the Gentiles, continuing the discussion begun in v. 11. Paul has already emphasized that Israel's sin and rejection have been used by God as a means to save the Gentiles (❂ II:271). Now he is focusing on the climactic second step of God's plan, namely, that God will use the salvation of the Gentiles as a means of bringing salvation to the Jews. This is the way in which "all Israel will be saved." In v. 26a the word *all* is meant to be contrasted with the *remnant* saved "at the present time" (v. 5). I.e., in v. 5 Paul affirms that a saved remnant existed at the time of his writing. But what about "the others" — the mass of unsaved Jews, both present and future? They can be saved, too; and the burden of vv. 11-32 (vv. 25-32 in particular) is to show how this is done. I.e., *all* Israel, not just the presently existing remnant, will be saved. But *how* will they be saved? In this way: by the *fullness of the Gentiles* (v. 25), *if* they put their *faith in Jesus Christ*. (v. 23).

These two main aspects of God's complex plan for showing mercy upon all are summed up in vv. 30-31: because of the Jews' disobedience the Gentiles have received mercy (v. 30; see vv. 11-16); and likewise because the Gentiles have received mercy, Israel will also receive mercy (v. 31; see vv. 25-32)!

The purpose of this paragraph is not to present new data about Israel's future, but simply to sum up the main points of ch. 11, especially emphasizing the way God uses the salvation of the Gentiles to bring mercy upon Israel. This serves as a fitting climax to chs. 9–11 as a whole, in that God is shown to be not just fair and faithful in his relationship with the Jews, but much more than fair in that he offers them his undeserved grace and mercy.

1. The Mystery of Israel's Salvation (11:25-27)

First of all Paul declares the mystery of Israel's salvation: its reality, its means, and its nature. He begins with a word not translated in the NIV: γάρ (*gar*, "for, because"). This word links vv. 25ff. with the olive tree illustration. Especially, the imagery of grafting the broken-off natural branches back into the tree helps us to understand how Israel will be saved.

11:25 I do not want you to be ignorant of this mystery, brothers, so that you may not be conceited: . . . . "I do not want you to be ignorant" is a formula Paul sometimes uses to call attention to an important point (see on 1:13; ❥I:96-97). "Brothers" is part of the formula. It indicates he is addressing the entire church, but the context shows he has Gentiles mainly in mind (see 11:13). In 11:17 he began using second person singular, addressing a typical representative Gentile Christian; but here he switches to second person plural. In this paragraph "you" and "they" still refer to Gentiles and Jews respectively.

Specifically, Paul does not want the Gentile Christians to be ignorant of "this mystery." The word "mystery" does not mean something that is and forever will be mysterious and incomprehensible. In the biblical context it refers to a truth once hidden in the mind of God and undiscoverable by human reason, but now made known by divine revelation and fully open to human understanding. Thus Paul is claiming that what he is teaching here is a revelation from God (❥II:273).

The reason Paul wants Gentile Christians to understand the mystery is "so that you may not be conceited," or "lest you be wise in your own estimation," as the NASB literally translates it. In vv. 18-20 Paul has already warned Gentile Christians against arrogant boasting in view of the fact that they were being gathered into the church while only relatively few Jews were being saved. Here he warns them again (❥II:273).

Exactly what is the content of the mystery that will nullify the Gentiles' pride? In the NT the word μυστήριον (*mystērion*) is often used in a general way for revelation concerning Christ and his church (❃ II:273, n. 176). A mystery that was of special importance to Paul, though, was the revelation that God had always intended to include Jews and Gentiles together in the church of Jesus Christ (Eph 3:3,4,9; see 2:11–3:11). In Eph 3 the emphasis is on the fact that God is bringing the Gentiles into the church; here in 11:25 the emphasis is on the fact that unbelieving Jews may still be brought into the church.

More specifically, in 11:25 the mystery focuses on "interdependence between the salvation of the Gentiles and that of Jews" (Hendriksen, 2:378). I.e., not only are the Jews and Gentiles united together in the one church, but in accordance with God's plan each group in part owes its inclusion to the other. This is spelled out in the rest of this verse and the beginning of v. 26 in three clauses: (1) "Israel has experienced a hardening in part"; (2) "until the full number of the Gentiles has come in"; (3) "and so all Israel will be saved." This is the mystery, once hidden and now revealed, with special emphasis on the *way* Israel will be saved, as explained in vv. 11-24 (❃ II:274).

The first element of the mystery is that **Israel has experienced a hardening in part . . . .** Paul has already referred to this hardening in v. 7. As we saw there, it is God's response to Israel's initial rejection of Jesus as their Messiah. But Israel's hardening was only "in part" (ἀπὸ μέρους, *apo merous*). Most seem to understand this phrase in a numerical sense, i.e., only a part of Israel were hardened (❃ II:274).

In my judgment, though, this is not what Paul means. The sentence says literally that "hardness from a part has happened to Israel," not "hardness has happened to part of Israel." It means that even though Israel was hardened, the hardening was only partial; the unbelieving Jews were not completely hardened so as to preclude the possibility of repentance. The NIV ("a hardening in part") reflects this view, as does the NASB ("a partial hardening").

Is this a new point, not made known until v. 25? Not really. That the hardening is only partial is clearly implied in the earlier references to Israel's salvation (vv. 12,14-15,23-24). Thus it would seem that there is nothing new in this statement in v. 25 about Israel's hardening. This part of the "mystery" has already been set forth.

The heart of the mystery is in the next clause, i.e., that the hardening will last **until the full number of the Gentiles has come in.** Combined with the preceding clause, and read in the light of vv. 11-12,15,18, this implies that the hardening of Israel has something to do with the coming of the full number or fullness of the Gentiles. At the same time, taken with the following clause (26a), and read in the light of vv. 11,13-14, it implies that the fullness of the Gentiles has something to do with the salvation of "all Israel." As said earlier, the "mystery" thus is how salvation of Jews and Gentiles is interrelated. It is important for the Gentile Christians to see this, in order to avoid thinking too highly of themselves.

The key question is the meaning of the expression "the full number of the Gentiles." The word translated "full number" (πλήρωμα, *plērōma*) is the same word the NIV translates as "fullness" in v. 12, where it refers to the fullness of the Jews. It seems that most interpreters favor the numerical connotation of the word, both here and in v. 12 (❂ II:275).

As was the case in v. 12, I cannot accept a numerical connotation for *plērōma*. Hence (contra the NIV) I do not see this as referring to the "full number" of Gentiles, but rather to the fullness of salvation as it was proclaimed to and accepted by the Gentiles, beginning in Acts 10. (See on v. 12 above.) The NT nowhere else uses *plērōma* in a numerical sense, but does use it for the fullness of salvation. Thus Paul is not saying anything basically different from v. 11: "Because of [the Jews'] transgression, salvation has come to the Gentiles"; or from v. 12: "Their loss means riches for the Gentiles"; or from v. 15: "Their rejection is the reconciliation of the world" (❂ II:276).

In what sense does this full salvation of the Gentiles "come in"? This is εἰσέρχομαι (*eiserchomai*), the common word for "go in, enter." In the NT it is occasionally used for people entering the kingdom (e.g., Matt 5:20; 7:21; John 3:5) or entering eternal life (Mark 9:43,45). Thus many take it in v. 25 as referring to the full number of Gentiles entering the kingdom or the church. But on some occasions the word means simply to come or to appear (see Luke 1:28; Acts 10:3; 19:30). I take it in a similar sense here, i.e., "until the salvation of the Gentiles has appeared or arrived or come into the picture." Compare 5:12, where Paul uses this word to declare that *sin* entered or came into the world. Here he uses it to affirm that *salvation* came into the Gentile world.

The point is that the hardening of the Jews was the occasion for the commencement of the preaching of the gospel to the Gentiles. Thus the Gentile Christians should not gloat over the Jews' lost state; in one sense they owe their very salvation to it.

The other side of this coin is that the partial hardening of Israel has happened (and by implication will persist) *until* the fullness of the Gentiles has come in. This places a limit on the hardening of Israel. Once the Gentiles' participation in the blessings of salvation has become fully established, the period of Israel's hardening will be over.

Those who interpret "fullness" as referring to a final ingathering of Gentiles at or near the second coming must naturally see this hardening as still present and as continuing up to or near the end. However, if we see the "fullness" as referring to the initial ingathering of Gentiles into the church, then the time of Israel's hardening was relatively brief and perhaps was coming to an end in Paul's own day. This is why he can say in v. 31 that the Jews "may *now* receive mercy as a result of God's mercy to you [Gentiles]."

Paul implies that the Gentiles' experience of the fullness of salvation in some way leads to the cessation of Israel's hardness (see the references to arousing the

Jews' envy in vv. 11,13-14). The further implication is that Gentile Christians, rather than feeling conceited because they are saved and most Jews are not, should instead be actively preaching the gospel to the Jewish community.

We may note again that what Paul affirms here in v. 25 has already been either stated or implied in vv. 11-24; hence this verse is not revealing anything new but is summarizing the "mystery" already set forth.

11:26a The last element in the mystery is this: **And so all Israel will be saved,** . . . This is the conclusion drawn from the first two parts of the mystery, and in fact from 11:1-25 as a whole. Has God rejected his people? It is true that most of them were hardened. But in God's plan this hardening is instrumental in bringing the fullness of salvation to the Gentiles. Once the Gentiles have experienced this fullness, the Jews will be moved to envy and will be ready to receive God's mercy. Thus the hardening will last only until the fullness of the Gentiles has come in. After this they may be grafted back into the olive tree, if they accept the mercy offered to them through the gospel. And in this way, all Israel will be saved. So how can anyone say that God has rejected his people?

As we discuss this verse, three questions must be kept in mind at the same time. First, what does "Israel" mean? Also, how extensive is the "all"? Finally, what kind of salvation is Paul talking about? The key issue, of course is this: does this verse predict and thus guarantee the salvation of a large mass of Jews at some point in the future, or does Paul have something else in mind?

Before we examine the phrase "all Israel," it is important to have a proper understanding of the first two words in the verse, "and so." The word "and" clearly ties this sentence to the last two clauses, but the word "so" (οὕτως, *houtōs*) does so in an even clearer and more crucial way. Some take this word as indicating a temporal sequence between v. 25b and v. 26a: Israel has experienced a partial hardening until the fullness of the Gentiles has come in, and "when this is done" all Israel will be saved. Such a temporal meaning for *houtōs* seems to be lacking elsewhere in Greek writings (Fitzmyer, 622; Moo, 719-720). Thus it is best to reject this meaning for the word.

Rather, *houtōs* here should be given its common meaning of "in this manner, thus, so" (BAGD, 597). The point is not *when* all Israel will be saved, but *how*. Cranfield says the word is emphatic: "It will be in this way, and only in this way," that all Israel will be saved (2:576). And what is this way? Here the term points us not to what follows but to what precedes. I.e., Israel will be saved by the coming of salvation to the Gentiles (v. 26b), which will arouse jealousy in the Jews themselves (vv. 11,13-14).

But exactly what is meant by "all Israel"? There are three major views: (1) "all Israel" means *ethnic Israel as a whole*; (2) it means *the whole of spiritual Israel*, including both believing Jews and believing Gentiles; and (3) it means *the remnant portion of ethnic Israel*. In my judgement this last view is correct. (See ◐ II:279-283 for an explanation and analysis of the first two views.)

This third (correct) approach says that "all Israel" means all believing Jews in all generations. Thus in v. 26 the term "Israel" is taken in a slightly different sense as compared with v. 25 and elsewhere. I.e., it may be true that the mass of Israel has been hardened (v. 25), but all of true spiritual Israel will be saved (v. 26). They will be saved not in a single mass conversion but in the normal process of evangelism, being brought to faith in Christ and added to his church over the whole course of church history.

What reasons can we give in support of this interpretation of "all Israel"? The first argument is that (contrary to the claims of some) it is consistent with the way Paul uses the term "Israel" in 9–11. To say that Paul uses this term elsewhere in this section only for ethnic Jews may be true; but that does not affect our view, which agrees that v. 26a refers to ethnic Jews. The only issue is whether Paul uses the term only in the sense of the nation *as a whole*, and 9:6 shows that he does not. In 9:6 Paul uses the term "Israel" twice, first referring to the nation as a whole and then referring only to spiritual Israel, the remnant. In the Greek text of 9:6 these two uses are almost consecutive, being separated by only one Greek word. Thus 9:6 is more than enough justification for regarding "Israel" in 11:26a as referring to spiritual Israel, even though the same term in 11:25 refers to Israel as a whole.

The second argument for this position is that it is totally consistent with the context in general. Some say that v. 26a must be talking about the nation as a whole, because the status of the nation as a whole is exactly what 9–11 is all about: How can we reconcile Israel's lostness with God's faithfulness? But this is not the whole picture. It is true that in 9–11 the unbelief of Israel in general is the *problem*, but it is also true that the existence of a remnant who believe is part of the *answer* to the problem. Hence the remnant concept is a prominent theme in the context as a whole. See especially 9:6,23-29; 11:1-7a.

Third, this view is also consistent with the line of thought Paul is developing in ch. 11 specifically. Has God rejected his people? No. Though most are hardened, he has a remnant. But is there any hope for those who are hardened? Yes. Especially now that salvation has come to the Gentiles, all hardened Jews may believe in Jesus and *become a part of the remnant*. Paul has just declared that God can and will graft the broken-off branches back into the olive tree, conditioned upon their abandoning their unbelief (v. 23). In v. 24 Paul assures us that God *will* graft these natural branches back into the tree, but the condition of faith is obviously meant to be carried over from v. 23. The same is undoubtedly true in v. 26. When Paul says "All Israel will be saved," in view of v. 23 we must understand it as "all Israelites who believe in Jesus Christ — i.e., the remnant — will be saved." This shows the importance of translating *houtōs* as "thus, in this way." When Paul says "in this way" all Israel will be saved, he is referring not just to the summary statement in v. 25, but to the more complete explanation in vv. 11-24, including the emphasis on conditionality in vv. 23-24.

A fourth argument for our position is that it does justice to the word "all" in "all Israel." One of the most serious flaws of other interpretations is that they really do not take the word "all" seriously. Often it is said that the only Jews who are saved are those who happen to be living at and possibly after a point of time still in the future, and for many it is only that final generation of Jews who are saved. Most individual Jews in the scores of generations before that time are actually *not* saved (❖II:285). How can this be evidence of the faithfulness of God toward "all Israel," if only the last generation of Jews will actually be saved? But if "all Israel" means "the entire remnant of Jews," then this refers to *every* believing Israelite in *every* generation. *All* who meet the condition of v. 23 will be saved.

A fifth argument for our understanding is that it is consistent with Paul's teaching in the following verses that "all Israel" is being saved *now*. As we shall soon see, the OT texts cited as confirmation of v. 26a refer to the *first* coming of Jesus and to the present salvation from sin by God's grace. They do not refer to the Second Coming and to some future national restoration (Hendriksen, 2:380). Especially, in v. 31 Paul says it is God's plan that the Jews "may *now* receive mercy as a result of God's mercy to you [Gentiles]" (❖II:285).

A final question in reference to "all Israel will be saved" is the meaning of "saved." At stake is whether this salvation includes something special for the Jews, or whether Paul is referring simply to the ordinary salvation from sin enjoyed by Gentile believers as well. Those who hold to the eschatological salvation of the then-existing ethnic Jews usually take the former approach, saying that this salvation includes the restoration of Israel as a political entity to its original Palestinian homeland as a preparation for the millennium (see MacArthur, 2:128-129; Cranfield, 2:577-578). Almost everyone else, though, in view of vv. 26b-27, understands "saved" to mean the ordinary way of salvation which Paul has been expounding throughout Romans. As Stott says, it is "salvation from sin through faith in Christ. It is not a national salvation, for nothing is said about either a political entity or a return to the land" (304). Moo agrees that there is no evidence in Rom 11 that salvation includes restoration to the land (724, n. 59).

If this is the case, how does the salvation of all remnant Israel depend on the fullness of the Gentiles? The main thing is that the latter is an occasion for envy on the part of the Jews (11:12,13-14), but DeWelt reminds us also that it must involve "nothing short of the faithful preaching of the gospel by the Gentiles to the Jews" (188).

11:26b-27 . . . as it is written, "The deliverer will come from Zion; he will turn godlessness away from Jacob. And this is my covenant with them when I take away their sins." This is a brief OT confirmation that God is now saving "all Israel" through the gospel of Jesus Christ. These lines are taken from the LXX version of Isaiah. Verse 26b is basically the same as Isa 59:20; v. 27a is from Isa 59:21a; v. 27b is from Isa 27:9 (❖II:286).

The word for "deliverer" can also be translated "redeemer" (see *GRe*, 15-20). This originally would have been applied to Yahweh, but Paul's use of it here shows it is definitely a messianic prophecy. The "deliverer" is Jesus Christ. See 1 Thess 1:10.

"Jacob" of course was the original name of Isaac's favored son before it was changed to Israel. OT poetic and prophetic literature often used it as a synonym for Israel when referring to the Jewish people. That is its meaning here. It simply means "Israel" or "the Jews."

"Zion" was one of the hills on which Jerusalem was built. In the OT sometimes the nuance was Zion (Jerusalem) as the location of the temple and thus the dwelling place of God (e.g., Ps 76:2; 132:13; Isa 8:18; 18:7; 24:23; Jer 2:19; Joel 3:17,21). In this way "Zion" came to represent heaven itself as God's dwelling place (e.g., Ps 9:11; 14:7; 20:2; 50:2; 53:6; 110:2; 134:3).

In the New Covenant era "Zion" represents the new temple, the new people of God, the church. Messianic prophecies about Zion, such as Ps 2:6 and Isa 28:16 (see also Isa 2:3 and Micah 4:2) could be referring to the fact that the church was established in the earthly city of Jerusalem (Acts 2), from which the gospel then was taken into all the earth. But these texts could also be referring to the church itself, which seems more likely in view of Rom 9:33; Heb 12:22-23; and 1 Pet 2:6. See also Gal 4:26.

How does Paul intend for us to understand "from Zion" in this quote from Isa 59:20? Possibly it just means "Israel," i.e., Christ came forth from the people of Israel. Or it may mean "Jerusalem" in the sense that this is where the church and the preaching of the gospel originated. Most likely, though, it means Zion as God's heavenly dwelling place, i.e., God the Redeemer will come forth from heaven itself.

It makes a considerable difference whether this refers to the Messiah's first coming or his second coming. If it is the latter, Paul would be saying that all Israel will be saved when the Messiah returns from heaven. The better understanding, though, is that this refers to the first coming of Christ. It is in future tense ("will come") from Isaiah's standpoint, not Paul's. Christ's first coming was just as much from the heavenly Zion as the second will be. The strongest reason for taking it to be the first coming is the specific stated *purpose* for which the Redeemer comes from Zion. The redemptive acts mentioned by Isaiah and recited by Paul refer not to a political restoration of the Jewish nation but to the personal salvation of individuals. This is why Jesus came the first time: to die for the sins of his people, and thereby to establish a new covenant with them, a covenant to take away their sins.

Specifically the deliverer has come to "turn godlessness away from Jacob" (v. 26b) and to "take away their sins" (v. 27b). This is the saving grace of forgiveness (justification), regeneration, and sanctification. It is a *spiritual* restoration, not a political one (Godet, 413; Denney, 684). This is the very thing Peter preached to the Jews in his second sermon in Acts: "When God raised up his servant, he sent him first to you to bless you by turning each of you from your wicked ways" (3:26). This taking away of sins, says Isaiah, is the purpose and result of God's "covenant with them."

Of which covenant is Isaiah speaking? Some assume it is the covenant God made with Abraham and his physical seed, the Jewish nation (e.g., Moo, 728-729). From this they conclude that God has promised salvation to the Jews as a nation (e.g., Fitzmyer, 625) and that for this covenant to be fulfilled God must ultimately bring about "the future restoration of Israel" (Murray, 2:100; see Moo, 729). This is completely off the mark, however. The covenant with Abraham *was* with the *nation* of Israel as a whole, but its promises were principally temporal blessings relating to Israel's role of bringing the Messiah into the world (9:4-5), not the spiritual blessings of salvation as such. I.e., the Abrahamic covenant did not guarantee salvation to every Jew living under it. Also, the Abrahamic covenant was fulfilled with the first coming of Christ.

The covenant to which Isaiah's messianic prophecy refers is thus not the Abrahamic covenant, but the New Covenant prophesied in Jer 31:31-34, and established through the death and shed blood of Christ (Luke 22:20; Heb 8:7-12; 10:15-17). The central promise of the New Covenant, as stated in Jer 31:34, is this: "For I will forgive their wickedness and will remember their sins no more." This is exactly what Paul is emphasizing in his quote from Isaiah: God covenants to take away the sins of "all Israel" through the blood of Christ if they will but trust in him. This covenant is conditional (11:23), and God gathers Jews into it one by one over the whole course of church history. This is how all true Israel will be saved.

2. God's Continuing Love for Israel (11:28-29)

11:28 Speaking of the Jews, Paul continues to address the Gentiles, explaining the reason why God's salvation is offered to "all Israel." **As far as the gospel is concerned, they are enemies on your account; but as far as election is concerned, they are loved on account of the patriarchs, . . .** This verse reflects the tension within God's nature that sums up God's relation to all sin and all sinners, i.e., the tension between his holiness and his love. This is seen in a special way in his attitude toward the Jews; they are at the same time his enemies and his beloved, the objects of both his hatred and his love (see on 11:22).

The word ἐχθρός (*echthros*) is usually translated "enemy" in the NT; it speaks of an attitude of enmity and hostility and hatred. The main point here is not the sinner's hatred of God, but God's hatred of the sinner (see *GRe*, 286-287), in contrast with his love for the sinner in v. 28b (Morris, 422). To be hated by God is to be under his wrath, rejected by him, and shut off from him (SH, 337; Cranfield, 2:580). This divine hostility is not directed toward all Jews, but only toward those who have rejected the gospel. They are God's enemies "as far as the gospel is concerned," i.e., because they have refused to accept the gospel and to believe in Jesus as their Messiah (9:30–10:21).

Paul never ceases to remind the Gentile Christians, however, that God's enmity toward the Jews has been the occasion for bringing the gospel to them. The Jews are enemies, yes; but they are enemies "on your account," for your sake, "in order to open His kingdom wide to you" (Moule, 201). See vv. 11,12,15.

But this is only part of the picture, and the lesser part at that. Even though the hardened Jews have chosen to become God's enemies by rejecting the gospel, *God still loves them* because of the original relationship he established with them through the patriarchs (Abraham, Isaac, and Jacob). Thus he cannot forget them; he cannot pretend that this relationship never existed. Even if they no longer have a special role in God's ongoing plan, they still occupy a special place in his heart.

"As far as election is concerned" has been taken two ways. In vv. 5,7 Paul uses this same term (ἐκλογή, *eklogē*, "election, choice") for the elect remnant; some interpret it this way here, saying that v. 28b refers only to the remnant within Israel, and thus limiting God's love to the elect alone. Others (correctly) interpret "election" here as referring to God's original choice of Abraham and through him of the entire nation of Israel. This is not an election of individuals to salvation, but the election of the Jews as a corporate body to covenant service, as in 9:11.

Thus, whereas v. 28a reflects the reality of ch. 10 above, v. 28b reflects the reality of ch. 9. God chose Israel as a nation to serve his special redemptive purposes, and poured out upon them his special covenant blessings. Even though this relationship did not automatically guarantee salvation to every individual Jew, God cannot help but regard every natural descendent of Abraham with a special affection. Thus for the Jews perhaps more than others, God is "not wishing for any to perish but for all to come to repentance" (2 Pet 3:9, NASB). That is why he wants to include them in his new covenant, the covenant of salvation (v. 27). God's enmity to the hardened Jews is real (v. 28a), but it does not cancel out his love for them.

That all Israel is loved by God "on account of the fathers" does not mean that the patriarchs did anything to merit or deserve this continuing love for their descendants. (See Cranfield, 2:580-581.) Nor does it mean that God still has unfulfilled covenant obligations toward the fathers. This latter view is quite common, especially among those who believe there is just one covenant of salvation, beginning with Abraham and continuing through the NT era. According to this view, this is why God still loves the Jews and *must* save them (❥II:291).

This view errs in thinking that the covenant with the patriarchs is the same as the covenant of salvation Jesus established on the cross. Thus it errs in thinking that the patriarchal covenant promised salvation to Jews as Jews in perpetuity. The truth is that every promise to Israel as a nation through the patriarchs was completely fulfilled when Jesus came into the world the first time (9:4-5; Acts 13:32-34).

11:29 This is not contradicted by what Paul says in the next verse: **for God's gifts and his call are irrevocable.** This refers still to God's original general election of the nation of Israel. The "gifts" are not the gifts of salvation (contra Moule, 201; Hendriksen, 2:384; MacArthur, 2:131). They are the benefits described in 9:4-5, which, though glorious in every respect, are still temporal and nonsalvific in themselves. The "call" likewise is not the salvific call to which only the elect respond, as in 8:30 (contra Denney, 684; Hendriksen, 2:384; MacArthur, 2:132; Lenski, 734). It refers to the original call to Abraham and thus the call to Israel as a nation "to be His special people, to stand in a special relation to Himself, and to fulfil a special function in history" (Cranfield, 2:581).

These gifts and this call are "irrevocable," Paul says. This is the first word in the verse in the Greek text and therefore is in a place of emphasis. What does it mean? It comes from μεταμέλομαι (*metamelomai*), which means "to regret, to repent, to change one's mind." Here, with the negating alpha, the word is ἀμεταμέλητος (*ametamelētos*, "not to be regretted, not to be repented of." (See 2 Cor 7:10.) "Irrevocable" is not the best translation. The point is not that God must save the Jews because he has made an irrevocable promise to Abraham *et al.* to do so. Rather, it is that God does not regret his choice of Israel as the nation through whom he brought the Christ into the world. Despite the centuries of their heartbreaking unfaithfulness and idolatry in OT times, and despite their current rejection of the gospel, God does not regret all he did for them and through them to carry out his purposes.

This is why they are still beloved to him. Paul begins this thought with γάρ (*gar*), "for, because." The Jews are still beloved because of the patriarchs (v. 28b), because God has never regretted this Old Covenant relationship he established with them in the first place. As Lard says, "Their fathers were chosen and loved, and on their account their rejected descendants are still loved" (373).

3. God's Ultimate Purpose Is Mercy (11:30-32)

In describing God's dealings with the Jews and Gentiles, this chapter has strongly emphasized both sides of God's nature: his sternness and his kindness (v. 22), his enmity and his love (v. 28). It has not attempted to soften or disguise the wrath of God against the unbelieving Jews (vv. 7-10,19-22,28a). But this is not the main point of the chapter. The main point is that, in spite of the unbelief and disobedience of Gentiles and Jews alike, God wants the gracious side of his nature to prevail. His ultimate goal and purpose are *mercy*, not wrath. And the most marvelous thing of all is that God can use the universal disobedience of mankind as a part of his plan to show mercy unto all. By explaining how this is so, this paragraph is a striking example of 8:28.

11:30-31 Just as you who were at one time disobedient to God have now received mercy as a result of their disobedience, so they too have now become disobedient in order that they too may now receive mercy as a result of God's mercy to you. The parts of these two verses are so carefully composed and so deliberately parallel that both must be printed together here. Dunn says this sentence is "the most contrived or carefully constructed formulation which Paul ever produced in such tight epigrammatic form, with so many balancing elements" (2:687). It may be diagrammed thus:

> For just as YOU GENTILES
> *then* were disobedient to God, but
> *now* have received mercy
> by the JEWS' disobedience;
>
> So also THESE JEWS
> *now* have become disobedient, so that
> *now* they also may receive mercy
> by the mercy shown to you GENTILES.

In a real sense this sentence sums up everything Paul has said in this chapter. As Godet puts it, "Ver. 30 describes the rebellion of the Gentiles, then their salvation determined by the rebellion of the Jews; and ver. 31, the rebellion of the Jews, then their salvation arising from the salvation of the Gentiles" (414).

The word ποτε (*pote*, "then, at one time") in v. 30a refers to the pre-Christian era when the Gentiles were limited to general revelation and were given over to the sinful excesses of their rebellion against God (1:18-32). The word νῦν (*nyn*, "now") in v. 30b refers to the New Covenant era when Christ has commanded that the gospel be taken to all nations. Morris (424-425) points out that the contrast is not between disobedience and obedience, as if one could make up for his sins by beginning to obey the commandments of the law. As in 3:21–5:21, the only remedy for disobedience is the mercy and grace of God.

To say that the Gentiles have received mercy "as a result of their [the Jews'] disobedience" is simply to repeat vv. 11,12,15. God takes the Jews' rebellion against the gospel of Christ as an occasion for sending that gospel to the Gentiles.

These verses continue to undermine Gentile smugness in relation to the Jews. Paul reminds the Gentiles (1) that they too were once in a state of disobedience; (2) that in one sense they owe their present state of grace to the Jews' disobedience; and (3) that God's plan is for the Jews to ultimately receive the same mercy now enjoyed by the Gentiles, even though they will arrive at it by a slightly different route.

To say that the Jews "have now become disobedient" refers to their initial rejection of the gospel at the beginning of the New Covenant era.

The word translated "in order that" is ἵνα (*hina*). It usually denotes purpose, as the NIV chooses to translate it here. But if that is what it means here, this would suggest that somehow God *caused* the Jews to be disobedient, *so that* he might accomplish the stated purpose. Thus it is important to know two things about *hina*. First, it can denote simple result rather than purpose (BAGD, 378). Also, "contrary to regular usage" *hina* sometimes "is placed elsewhere than at the beginning of its clause, in order to emphasize the words that come before it" (BAGD, 378). I believe both of these points are in evidence here in v. 31b. We should especially note that, for emphasis, "by your [the Gentiles'] mercy" is placed at the very beginning of this clause, even before the word *hina*. Taken thus it reads quite naturally as follows: "The Jews have now become disobedient, with the result that, *by means of the mercy shown to you Gentiles*, they too may now obtain mercy."

This shows that God's ultimate goal, even for the hardened Jews, is that they may receive his mercy and be saved. It also emphasizes again that the salvation of the Gentiles is the means of bringing this about (❋ II:294-295).

The inclusion of the word "now" in v. 31b is very significant. It shows that the statement, "And so all Israel will be saved" in v. 26a does not refer to a mass conversion of ethnic Jews at some far distant point in the future (relative to the time of Paul's writing), but that it refers to the ongoing conversion of remnant Jews beginning even "now," in the first century (Hendriksen, 2:385). Those who take the former view give "now" some other meaning, such as "at any time" (Moo, 735), or "the eschatological now" (Cranfield, 2:586), i.e., sometime during this final messianic age, even if it is toward the end of it (Morris, 425). But the parallel with the "now" in v. 30b shows that Paul is thinking of the "now" in which he was living. Thus as Wright says, it indicates "a steady flow of Jews into the church, by grace through faith," from that very time (*Climax*, 249).

11:32 For God has bound all men over to disobedience so that he may have mercy on them all. In this final verse of the present section Paul emphasizes once again that God's goal and purpose are to bring mercy to all. The "all" in both clauses probably is not intended to refer to every individual as such, but to all in the sense of both *groups*, i.e., both Gentiles and Jews (❋ II:295).

As a matter of fact, though, all individuals in both groups *are* bound over to sin (3:23). Also, there is a sense in which God has mercy on all individuals, in that his mercy is intended for all and is offered to all. It is not the case, though, that all will in fact accept it.

The word translated "bound over" literally means "to enclose, to confine, to shut up, to imprison." How did God imprison the Gentiles in disobedience? This does not mean that he caused them to sin, or made it impossible for them not to sin. It refers to 1:18-32, and to God's decision to "give them over" to the sinful desires of their hearts (vv. 24,26,28). How did he imprison the Jews in disobedience? Again this does not mean he caused them to sin. It refers rather to 2:1-29, and to the conclusion that the law, in which the Jews trusted, has but one verdict for sinners: condemnation. It refers also to 11:7 and the hardening of Jewish unbelievers.

From another standpoint, to say that God shuts up all men in their sin refers to the divine pronouncement that all have in fact sinned (3:23) and have become trapped in the consequences of their sin with no hope of escaping through any deeds or schemes of their own. "By the works of the Law no flesh will be justified in His sight" (3:20, NASB) (❧II:296).

But this is not the last word, because God has provided a way of escape from this dungeon, this prison of sin. It is the way of mercy, the way of grace (3:21–5:21); and it is the *only* way. This is the whole point of Romans: "a man is justified by faith apart from works of the Law" (3:28, NASB). "We are not under law but under grace" (6:15). This is the point to which all of ch. 11 has been leading: that God can and will provide this mercy to all, Jews and Gentiles alike. "As they have been together in the prison of their disobedience, so they will be together in the freedom of God's mercy" (Stott, 307).

V. DOXOLOGY: GOD'S WAY IS RIGHT (11:33-36)

Godet rightly remarks regarding this paragraph, "Like a traveller who has reached the summit of an Alpine ascent, the apostle turns and contemplates. . . . The plan of God in the government of mankind spreads out before him," and his heart is filled with admiration and gratitude (416). His response to God's work is nothing less than a doxology (see 1:25, ❧I:154), a hymn of highest praise.

How does this doxology tie in with what precedes it? In a sense we may see it as "the conclusion to the whole of the doctrinal section of Romans (1:16–11:36)," as Fitzmyer says (633). It is more appropriate, though, to take it as the capstone for chapters 9–11, where the overall subject is God's faithfulness in his dealings with Israel. The question has been, Does the combination of God's original covenant with the patriarchs and Israel's present lostness mean that God has been unfaithful and untrue to his word? In answer to this question, under divine inspiration, Paul has set forth a theodicy: God's way is right, especially his way with Israel. He has shown that the first covenant dealt with Israel's *service* as a *nation*, and that God has faithfully kept every promise he made to them under this covenant (ch. 9). He has also shown that the reason for Israel's lostness is not unfaithfulness on God's part but Israel's own unbelief (ch. 10). Finally he has shown that under the New Covenant God's redemptive plan incorporates Israel's unbelief in a way that leads ultimately back to her salvation (ch. 11).

These are the mysteries that fill Paul with wonder. Paul no doubt has ch. 11 especially in mind, and particularly the summary statement in vv. 30-32, which emphasizes the mercy of God. Thus he marvels that God has vindicated his faithfulness in the face of Israel's unbelief in a way that glorifies both his holiness and his mercy (❂ II:297-298).

11:33 Oh the depth of the riches of the wisdom and knowledge of God! There is disagreement over how this exclamation was intended to be structured. Some take "the depth of the riches" as a single idea, with "wisdom and knowledge" being its double object. See the NIV and NASB. According to this interpretation, the main emphasis of the whole section would be on God's wisdom and knowledge.

Others take the three nouns, "riches and wisdom and knowledge," as three parallel objects of "depth." In my judgment this view is preferable (contra the NIV), since "the depth of the riches" as a single idea is redundant. According to this view, then, the doxology is emphasizing not just God's wisdom and knowledge, but his *riches* as well. (The phrase "of God" goes with all three nouns.)

The word "depth" is "a common Greek expression for inexhaustible fullness or superabundance" (MP, 479). The idea is that God is a bottomless, infinite resource of riches, wisdom, and knowledge.

Paul marvels first at the depth of God's *riches*. This word can mean material wealth (Matt 13:22; 1 Tim 6:17), but usually Paul uses it for spiritual riches, the riches of salvation (e.g., Eph 1:7,18; 3:8; Phil 4:19) (❂ II:299).

Paul refers next to the depth of God's *wisdom*, which is a common OT theme (see Dunn, 2:699). Generally speaking, wisdom "is the ability to choose the best possible end, and to choose the best possible means of achieving that end. It is not the same as knowledge, but is rather the ability to put one's knowledge to practical use" (*GRu*, 285; see 285-289). Here Paul is thinking specifically of the wisdom of God in working out the salvation of sinners, especially the interplay between Jews and Gentiles as explained in ch. 11 (❂ II:299).

Finally Paul extols the depth of God's *knowledge* (*GC*, 273-292). God's knowledge is his constant, comprehensive, immediate consciousness or awareness of all facts — past, present, and future. This certainly refers to his omniscience, or his general knowledge of all things; and this includes his foreknowledge of man's free choices, of which he takes account and which he incorporates into his own plan of salvation. Few truths about God are more awe-inspiring than his foreknowledge of man's future free-will choices. It does not behoove us to reject the reality of such foreknowledge just because we do not understand how it is possible.

How unsearchable his judgments, and his paths beyond tracing out! This basically says the same thing as v. 33a in different words. "Unsearchable" and "beyond tracing out" correspond to "depth," and are similar in meaning and implication. They convey the idea of "unfathomable, inscrutable, incomprehensible." I.e., the thoughts and ways of God are beyond our unaided ability to seek out and discover (❂ II:300).

This applies to both God's judgments and his paths. Stott rightly says that

God's judgments are "what he thinks and decides," and his paths are "what he does and where he goes" (310). The word for "judgments" is κρίμα (*krima*), which often refers to a judicial decision to punish wrongdoers (e.g., 2:2-3; 3:8; 5:16). Here it probably is inclusive of all God's decisions as to how he will deal with mankind, and especially "his 'executive' decisions about the direction of salvation history" (Moo, 742; see Lard, 376). The word for "paths" is ὁδός (*hodos*), the common word for "road, way." A better translation here would be "ways" (NASB). The ways of God are simply his works or deeds, "the paths along which God moves in executing his plans and purposes" (Lard, 376). See Ps 95:10; Isa 55:8-9.

These two statements are a confession that the wisdom and the ways of God that work out our salvation surpass our knowledge and are beyond anything we can ask or imagine (Eph 3:19-20). Once they are explained to us, we may understand *what* God has done, but *how* he can do it and *why* he should even want to do it we will never fully comprehend. As finite creatures and sinners saved by grace, we can only do what Paul did and utter heartfelt expressions of praise.

11:34-35 "Who has known the mind of the Lord? Or who has been his counselor? Who has ever given to God, that God should repay him?" These three questions are based on texts from the OT (thus the NIV quotation marks). The first two (v. 34) are adapted from Isa 40:13, "Who has understood the [Spirit] of the LORD, or instructed him as his counselor?" The last (v. 35) is based on the Hebrew text of Job 41:11 (see 1 Chr 29:14; Job 35:7). The fact that Paul does not say "It is written" or "Isaiah says" indicates that he, under inspiration, is adapting these texts for his own purposes.

It is very likely that the three questions correspond, in reverse order, to the three elements in v. 33a. "Who has known the mind of the Lord?" refers to the depths of God's *knowledge*. God alone has access to the content of his own mind, but he graciously chooses to reveal some of this content to us through his inspired prophets and apostles (1 Cor 2:9-16). "Or who has been his counselor?" refers to the depths of God's *wisdom*. A counselor is one who gives advice on how to live and how to act, i.e., how to discern the best ends and the best means to achieve them. God needs no such advice; he does not need to ask anyone for help in devising his plan of salvation and in carrying it out.

The third question, "Who has ever given to God, that God should repay him?" corresponds to the depths of God's *riches*. The point is that we give nothing to God prior to his bestowing his riches upon us; therefore God's gifts to us are truly gifts and not just a repayment of something he owes to us. It is impossible for us to perform a service for God that puts him in our debt.

This applies of course to the specific subject of God's dealings with the Jews. God placed himself under obligation to them when he entered into the covenant with their father Abraham. But the covenant itself was a gift and not an obligation; his promises both as made and as fulfilled were his free gift to them. And

Romans Part Four

since those promises have now been fulfilled (9:4-5), the Jews can lay no claim upon God whatsoever, not even one based on the truth of his own word.

This also applies to the whole subject of salvation as a matter of grace rather than works. Only when salvation is by grace can it be a gift and not wages due (see 4:4). This is how God saves any sinner, Gentile or Jew. As far as salvation is concerned, "God is debtor to none, his favour is never compensation, merit places no constraints upon his mercy" (Murray, 2:107) (❊ II:302).

11:36 This verse first tells us why God is free from any obligation under which someone might try to place him: **For from him and through him and to him are all things**. In three succinct prepositional phrases the sovereign freedom and glorious supremacy of God are declared. He is related to all things as their *source*, originator, or Creator: "from him." He is related to all things as the *means* by which they came into existence and remain in existence: "through him." He is related to all things as the *goal* or purpose for which they exist: "to him," i.e., unto his glory and for his good pleasure. See Eph 4:6; Heb 2:10.

One should not take these three phrases as referring respectively to the three persons of the Trinity, as some ancient writers did. The Bible makes similar statements concerning Jesus Christ, God the Son (1 Cor 8:6; Col 1:16), but that is not the point here. Each phrase applies to all three persons of the Trinity.

To say that all things are "from God" does not mean that he makes them out of his own essence, a concept that would be equivalent to the false worldview called pantheism. This phrase refers rather to the act of creation *ex nihilo*, by which God in the beginning brought all things into existence out of nothing. (See on 4:17, ❊ I:300-301; see *GC*, 97-117.)

The expression "all things" should not be limited. The statement is a general truth that applies to the whole of creation, even if the immediate application is to the establishment of the new creation through the work of redemption. We should not be surprised to find such a reference to God as Creator in this final verse of the theological portion of Romans, in view of 1:18-25.

A final word of doxology closes this part of Romans: **To him be the glory forever! Amen.** The glory of God is his infinite and total greatness as it is manifested and as it shines forth for all to see (see *GC*, 446-452); it is "the reflection of all His perfections in all that exists" (Godet, 419). To ascribe glory to God ("to him be the glory") is not to give him anything or add anything to his nature, but simply to acknowledge and confess that he *is* glorious, and to call upon others to acknowledge this glory as well. Adding the word "forever" (lit., "unto the ages") intensifies the praise even further. On this and on "Amen," see 1:25 (❊ I:154).

This brings us to the end of what may properly be called the theological section of Romans, namely, chs. 1-11. It is only fitting that it should end on a worshipful note, since, as Stott says (311-312), theology and worship should never be separated.

12:1-15:13 – PART FIVE
LIVING THE SANCTIFIED LIFE

Up to now Romans has taught us *theological* doctrine (what is true and false); this section is devoted mainly to *ethical* doctrine (what is right and wrong). All ethical teaching is ultimately grounded in some theological truth such as the nature of God, the nature of man, or the nature of salvation (❂ II:305). Here in Romans, the specific theological foundation for ethical living is the doctrine of salvation: "In view of all that God has accomplished for His people in Christ, how should His people live?" (Bruce, 225). Specifically, Romans is intended to expound the fact that salvation is by *grace* rather than by works of law (❂ I:52-54). In this exposition Paul makes it clear that grace is not simply justification by faith in the blood of Christ, but also regeneration and sanctification by the power of the Holy Spirit. I.e., grace is a double cure (❂ I:248, 370). In chs. 6-8 the second part of this double cure (regeneration and sanctification) is set forth in a forceful way. The material here in Part Five is directly related to that.

The exact nature of this relationship seems to be something like this. In chs. 6-8 Paul sets forth the reality of the new life in Christ (ch. 6) and the indwelling power of the Holy Spirit (ch. 8) in general theological terms. I.e., he tells us what God did for us when he saved us by grace. But now in chs. 12-15 he describes the character of this sanctified life in specific terms. He has already said (1:5) that the goal of his preaching is to bring about the "obedience that comes from faith"; now he tells us exactly what that obedience should be. In 6:4 he tells us that in our baptism we were raised up from spiritual death so that we "may live a new life"; now he tells us in precise terms what the content of this new life should be.

The material in this section is divided into two main parts. The first (12:1-13:14) is a catalogue of virtues that does not seem to be in any particular order. The important point is that these virtues have the character of law. They are rules for Christian living, laws to live by. They are nonnegotiable absolutes, not matters of opinion. This corrects any possible misunderstanding of 6:14-15, that we are "not under law but under grace." In that passage Paul means that we are not under law as a way of *salvation*, but he does not mean that law no longer applies to Christians in any sense. We are still under law – the moral law – as a way of life (❂ I:409-410). We may think of this present section as a good (but not necessarily complete) synopsis of God's moral law, the law that applies equally to all people in all times.

The second main part is 14:1–15:13, the presupposition for which is that not everything in our Christian lives is regulated by law. In this section Paul teaches us how to deal with such "matters of opinion" (❂II:307).

I. A CATALOGUE OF VIRTUES (12:1–13:14)

As stated above, the instructions in this section have the essence of *law*. This should never be confused with legalism, however. As Morris points out, legalism says, "Do these things and live." Grace, on the other hand, says, "Live, and you will do these things" (431).

A. GRACE DEMANDS A TRANSFORMED LIFE (12:1-2)

This transitional passage asserts in a general way that the theology and the experience of grace as set forth in chs. 1–11 must necessarily bring about profound changes in every aspect of a believer's life. The very contemplation of the mercies of God, says Paul, compels us to offer up our bodies as living sacrifices to God (v. 1). How is this accomplished? By refusing to conform our lives to the prevailing anti-Christian cultures of this age, and allowing ourselves to be transformed instead according to the standard of God's preceptive will (v. 2a). And how can this be done? Only by the renewing of the mind through initial regeneration by the Holy Spirit and continuing instruction from the written Word of God. As a result of this renewing we can discern which moral choices are in conformity with the will of God, i.e., the way of life that is truly good, truly pleasing to God, and truly fulfilling.

Three underlying themes are presupposed by the language of this brief passage. First, the language of worship, especially OT ritual worship, is prominent. This is seen especially in the expressions "offer," "sacrifices," and "act of worship," and to a lesser extent in the descriptions of the sacrifices in v. 1. Second, the theme of anthropological dualism is seen in the references to "bodies" (v. 1) and "mind" (v. 2), and to an extent in "spiritual" in v. 1. Paul's teaching in chs. 6–8 is definitely in the background here (❂I:372-374).

Third, contrary to the concept of sovereign or monergistic grace (as in Calvinism), the language of this passage reflects a synergistic concept of salvation, i.e., the basic and efficacious grace-works of God are joined with the human acts of submission and surrender in order to bring about the transformed life. The reality of human responsibility is in the foreground (❂II:308).

12:1 Therefore, I urge you, brothers, in view of God's mercy, to offer your bodies as living sacrifices, holy and pleasing to God—this is your spiritual act of worship. The word "therefore" links what follows not just to the immediately preceding verses, but to the entire message of the epistle thus far, which is summarized as "God's mercy." The word translated "mercy" (lit., "mercies") is οἰκτιρμός (*oiktirmos*, "pity, mercy, compassion") (❁II:309).

The word translated "urge" has a number of meanings. The main question is whether Paul is using it in the sense of an authoritative command or a personal plea. It is certainly a plea on a personal level (they are "brothers"), one that is explicitly grounded in the mercies of God. On the other hand, "I urge you" is surely an authoritative exhortation (❁II:309). So is it a command or a plea? Actually it is both. The key is to distinguish obligation (why we *ought* to do something) from motivation (why we actually *do* something). As an inspired apostle, Paul always speaks with apostolic authority unless he specifically suspends it (Phlm 8-10). Thus the authority of the writer imparts authority to what is written, and we who read are under obligation to obey. The main emphasis, though, is on motivation. By appealing to the mercies of God, Paul wants to ensure that we offer our bodies as living sacrifices not just because he says we should, but because we are inwardly convicted that this is the only "appropriate and expected response to God's mercy as we have experienced it" (Moo, 749).

Exactly what does Paul exhort us to do? Literally, "to offer your bodies as a sacrifice." The language here would have immediately reminded Paul's first readers of the common practice of offering up animals as sacrifices or burnt offerings to God in acts of worship. The word "offer" (παρίστημι, *paristēmi*) is found also in 6:13,16,19, but it is not used there in the sense of offering up a sacrifice to God. It does have this technical sense here, however (Cranfield, 2:598; Dunn, 2:709; Moo, 751). The word "sacrifice" (θυσία, *thysia*) is the common word for the animal or thing being offered up in such a ritual.

As Christians, says Paul, we must offer up our *bodies* (σώματα, *sōmata*) as sacrifices to God. At issue here is whether he really means bodies, or whether this is just shorthand for the entire self. Many take the latter approach, especially those who deny the reality of anthropological dualism (❁II:310).

While it is true that we should offer our entire selves to God, this is not the point here. Paul knows how to say "offer yourselves" and to distinguish this from "offer your bodies." This is the very language he uses in 6:13. After he says "offer yourselves" (παραστήσατε ἑαυτούς, *parastēsate heautous*), in a separate exhortation he urges us to offer the members of our *bodies* to God (❁I:402-404). Here in 12:1 he means exactly what he says: offer your *bodies*.

This exhortation shows the importance of the body in itself as an authentic part of our human nature, and shows how important it is to use the body to the glory of God. It also recalls especially the teaching of chs. 6–8, that in this present stage of our redemption only our souls/spirits have been renewed; the redemption of the body awaits the day of resurrection. In the meantime, our unredeemed bodies remain the seat of sin and the source of many temptations; thus they must be constantly and consciously offered up to God as part of the process of sanctification. This is how we fulfill the commands of 6:12-13.

The nature of this bodily sacrifice is described with a string of three adjectives: "living," "holy," and "pleasing to God." In what sense is our sacrifice a "living" one? Some think this refers to the *new* life received in regeneration (6:4). But if "bodies" literally means *bodies*, this cannot be, because the body as yet does not participate in this new life (8:10-11). It is better to take "living" as a deliberate contrast with OT sacrifices, in which the animals were killed in a one-time act. Under the New Covenant we no longer offer such sacrifices, but instead offer up our bodies with all their vital energies in continuing, day-after-day worship (MP, 487; Moo, 751).

We offer our bodies also as *holy* sacrifices. "Holy" basically means "set apart in consecration to God." In this sense every true sacrifice is holy (Moo, 751), and so must we set our bodies apart from the world in daily service to God. Such separation from the world is not so much physical as it is ethical, i.e., refusing to use our bodies for participation in the defilements of sin (Murray, 2:112). This is the ethical equivalent of the OT requirement that sacrifices be without physical defects (e.g., Lev 1:3; 3:1,6).

Finally, the sacrifice of our bodies is described as "pleasing to God." It is pleasing to him just because it is living and holy. Such a sacrifice is a delight to God's heart. This is equivalent to the way the OT sacrifices provided "an aroma pleasing to the Lord" (e.g., Lev 1:9,13,17; 2:2,9,12; see Gen 8:21).

The offering of our bodies as living, holy, and God-pleasing sacrifices is a "spiritual act of worship." The interpretation of the key words in this phrase — λογικός (*logikos*) and λατρεία (*latreia*) — is disputed. The issue regarding *latreia* is whether it means "service" to God of a general nature, as distinct from acts of worship as such, or whether it actually means "worship."

Whether or not this distinction between service and worship is valid, we cannot limit this word to the former concept only. *Latreia* and its cognate verb, λατρεύω (*latreuō*), often are used for ritual worship, as in 9:4. The imagery of ritual sacrifice in 12:1 leads us to interpret *latreia* here in that sense also; the NIV's "worship" is correct. The point is that all Christian living is worship offered up to God. Public, corporate worship is special and must not be neglected, but that is not the only part of the Christian life that may be called "worship." Christians must do *everything* "for the glory of God" (1 Cor 10:31), and whatever is done for his glory is an act of worship.

The other key word in this phrase, the adjective *logikos*, can be interpreted several ways. The NIV and the NASB render it "spiritual," which seems to be its meaning in its only other NT use, 1 Pet 2:2 (❂ II:312). If Paul is using *logikos* in the sense of "spiritual," his point is that even the way we use our physical bodies is a spiritual matter.

A second possibility is that *logikos* should be interpreted as "rational" in the sense of involving the mind, the reason, the intellect. The Greeks used this word to distinguish human beings from animals, and to distinguish reason-based worship from superstition (Dunn, 2:711-712; Moo, 752). Some see such a connotation here. I.e., offering our bodies as living, holy, and God-pleasing sacrifices is worship that is "worthy of thinking beings" (Jerusalem Bible).

A third interpretation is that *logikos* means "reasonable" in the sense that offering our bodies as sacrifices to God is the only reasonable, logical thing to do once we understand the depths of his mercies toward us in the work of Christ (Cranfield, 2:604-605; Lard, 380; MP, 485, 488; see the KJV, "reasonable service").

Any one of these views is possible in view of other biblical teaching, and is appropriate to the present context. I favor the first two views combined, because together they emphasize the internal nature of true worship, even when externals (e.g., the body) are involved. As the NEB puts it, this is "the worship offered by mind and heart." Jesus spoke of it as "worship in spirit and in truth" (John 4:24), i.e., worship that comes from the heart ("spiritual") and is consistent with reason ("rational").

12:2 Do not conform any longer to the pattern of this world, but be transformed . . . . How shall we go about offering our bodies as living sacrifices? This is explained in the two general exhortations in v. 2 (which in the best texts are present passive imperatives). We offer our bodies by refusing to be conformed to this world, and instead allowing ourselves to be transformed by the renewing of our minds.

The two verbs in this part of the verse are derived from two basic Greek nouns, namely, σχῆμα (*schēma*), from which comes "conform," and μορφή (*morphē*), from which comes "transform" (❧II:313-314). Some see a significant difference between these two words, but the "large consensus" (Dunn, 2:712) is that these are more or less synonyms, and that we should not read any significant distinction into the two verbs here in 12:2a (Cranfield, 2:605-607; Stott, 323; Moo, 756). The true contrast in this verse is not between two *kinds* of change, but between two totally different *models* according to which one may shape his life. These two competing models are "the pattern of this world" and "God's will" (12:2b). Paul emphatically commands us *not* to shape our lives according to the anti-Christian cultures of this world, but instead to continue allowing ourselves to be recreated according to God's will, a process which began in the act of regeneration (6:1-11) and which continues through the truth of his Word and the power of his Spirit.

The form of these verbs is as important as their meaning. They are *present* tense, which means that these are not one-time acts but are part of the ongoing process of progressive sanctification (see "living sacrifices," 12:1). They are also *passive* in form, which means that the change in view is not something we do or can do for ourselves; it is something that is done to us. Thus the transformation (and the renewing) can be accomplished by God alone. Finally, the verbs are *imperative*, which means that we have the responsibility of desiring the change and consenting to it and yielding ourselves up to the power of the Holy Spirit within us. Cranfield brings out all these nuances with the translation, "Continue to let yourselves be transformed" (2:607).

The negative command is literally, "Do not let yourselves be conformed to this age." (The NIV phrase "any longer" is not in the original text.) The term translated "world" in the NIV is αἰών (*aiōn*), which is better translated "age." Such an "age" is not just a bare historical era, but a period of history as marked by a certain ethical or spiritual character. "This age," the age to which we must not be conformed, is the world as fallen, the world as it has existed under the power of Satan, sin, and death since the Fall and as it will continue to exist until the Second Coming. Paul calls it "this present evil age" (Gal 1:4) since it is controlled by Satan, "the god of this age" (2 Cor 4:4; see 1 Cor 2:8). The new age or the "age to come" in one sense has already begun, being inaugurated through the death and resurrection of Christ; it will come in its fullness when Christ returns. (See Matt 12:32; Mark 10:30; Luke 18:30; 20:34-35; Eph 1:21; Heb 6:5.)

We are thus commanded not to be influenced by the false, anti-Christian religions and worldviews that are always springing up and embodying the spirit of "this age." We are admonished not to buy into the relativistic and sin-justifying value systems that exert constant pressure upon us. "Don't let the world around you squeeze you into its own mould" (Phillips translation). This means that we must consciously avoid, for example, "the use of dirty or offensive language, the singing of scurrilous songs, the reading of filthy books, the wearing of tempting attire, engaging in questionable pastimes, associating, on intimate terms, with worldly companions" (Hendriksen, 2:404).

The positive command, "Let yourselves be transformed," thus means by implication to shape your lives according to the biblical worldview, to orient your lives around the age to come, and to "set your hearts on things above, where Christ is seated at the right hand of God. Set your minds on things above, not on earthly things" (Col 3:1-2). "Live as those whose lives are governed by the principles and hopes of a holy eternity in prospect" (Moule, 206).

The means for accomplishing this ongoing transformation is **by the renewing of your mind.** This renewing has its beginning in the Spirit's work of regeneration that takes place in the moment of Christian baptism (6:3-5; Titus 3:5); and it continues as the ongoing process of sanctification, which is described in Col 3:10 as the renewing of the image of God in which we were originally created.

This is specifically a renewing of the *mind*. The "mind" is "the faculty by which the soul perceives and discerns the good and the true" (Godet, 427); it is "the seat of intellectual and moral judgment" (Fitzmyer, 641), the powers of our moral consciousness. Thus the renewing of the mind is the renewing of our ability to think correctly, especially about spiritual and moral matters.

But the mind is not just our formal intellectual and logical powers. It includes the inclinations and contents of our thought-life as well. It is our "inner disposition" (Hendriksen, 2:406); it includes our "inner thoughts, drives, and desires" (McGuiggan, 358). It involves the adoption of the Bible's comprehensive worldview, which usually requires a complete paradigm shift or reprogramming for most converts. It means to exchange the mind of the flesh for the mind of the Spirit (8:5-8).

Such a radical renewing is not something we can do by our natural powers; it can be accomplished only by the instrumentality of the Word of God and the Holy Spirit (Stott, 324). The Spirit renews our *ability* to think straight; this is part of his regenerating and sanctifying work (see chs. 7, 8). Then the Word of God, the Bible, renews the *content* of our minds (see Col 3:10,16) (❂ II:316).

What is the result of this renewing of the mind? **Then you will be able to test and approve what God's will is—his good, pleasing and perfect will.** "Test and approve" translates one Greek word, δοκιμάζω (*dokimazō*). It has several connotations: "put to the test, examine"; "prove by testing"; "accept as proved, approve" (BAGD, 202). The object of the verb is "God's will." The circumstance Paul is describing seems to be this. Like everyone else, Christians are confronted with a myriad of conflicting choices with regard to how to act and to live. But because they have been transformed by the renewing of their minds, they are able to subject all the options to the test of God's Word and are able to discern and distinguish the will of God from the false and demonic choices. The best translation is actually "discern," i.e., "so you can discern what conforms to God's will" (Achtemeier, 195).

Moule says this renewing of the mind instills within us a "holy instinct" by which we "can discern, in conflicting cases, the will of God from the will of self or of the world" (207). This does not make the Word of God superfluous, of course (❂ II:317). A mind that has been truly renewed can discern God's will in making moral decisions *just because* it has been saturated with the teachings of his Word. Moo is probably right, that Paul is talking about "Christians whose minds are so thoroughly renewed that we know from within, almost instinctively, what we are to do to please God in any given situation" (758). But such an instinct is thoroughly dependent upon the written Word. Paul himself shows that this is the case in the very next section of Romans, in which he gives us several chapters of moral instruction telling us in detail what the will of God is (12:3–15:13).

The will of God of which Paul speaks is his *preceptive* will, his commandments, as distinct from his purposive and permissive wills (see *GRu*, ch. 8). This preceptive will of God is declared to be equivalent to three things. First, the will of God is the same as what is called "the good." This means primarily "good" in the sense of morally right (Cranfield, 2:610) since God himself is absolute goodness and since God's will is the verbalization of his good nature. Second, the will of God is defined as that which is acceptable or pleasing, i.e., pleasing *to God*. The phrase "to God" does not appear here, but it is used in v. 1 with this same word and is no doubt to be understood here. Third, the will of God is identified with "the perfect," i.e., with what is "ethically adequate and complete" (Denney, 688). It is all that we need to lead a life that is holy and fulfilled. The same word (τέλειον, *teleion*) is used in Matt 5:48.

The last part of v. 2, whether it expresses purpose or result, shows that a transformation that renews the mind is a necessary prerequisite for being able to discern God's will. An unsaved person cannot trust his "moral instinct." Romans 2:15 is true in principle, but only the transformed Christian can even begin to use this inward inscription of the law as a trustworthy moral guide.

B. USING THE GIFTS OF GRACE FOR UNSELFISH SERVICE (12:3-8)

Paul now begins to instruct us as to the specific nature of the transformed life. He tells us first of all that it is characterized by humble, unselfish service to our fellow believers. As in 1 Cor 12, he makes this point by using the metaphor of the human body.

Also as in 1 Cor 12, Paul teaches here that the functions performed by the various parts of the body are in accord with the different gifts or abilities bestowed upon us by God. Based on 1 Cor 12:1-11, we usually refer to these as spiritual gifts or gifts of the Spirit. In Rom 12 Paul calls them gifts of grace rather than gifts of the Spirit, but the point is the same. Other listings of such gifts are found in 1 Cor 12:8-10,28-30; Eph 4:11; and 1 Pet 4:10-11. Some gifts appear in more than one list; others appear in only one. No list is exhaustive in itself, and probably all taken together are not exhaustive.

In these verses Paul exhorts us to *evaluate* our gifts honestly and humbly (v. 3), to *dedicate* them to the good of the body as a whole (vv. 4-5), and to *activate* and use them conscientiously (vv. 6-8).

12:3 For by the grace given me I say to every one of you: . . . Here the word "grace" refers not to salvation from sin but to the gift of Paul's apostleship and thus to his apostolic authority (see 1:5; ❷ I:77-78). Thus the meaning is "I say to you in my capacity as an Apostle."

The exhortation is directed to the entire church, "to every one of you." The implication for the subject of spiritual gifts is that every Christian has a gift or a special ability of some kind that can be used to build up the body as a whole. See 1 Pet 4:10.

Identifying one's gift calls for honest and impartial self-examination: **Do not think of yourself more highly than you ought, but rather think of yourself with sober judgment, . . .** In v. 2 Paul has just indicated that the Christian's life is transformed by the renewing of his *mind*; here he gives one example of how the renewed mind must think. The key word is "think" (φρονέω, *phroneō*); it appears four times in this short statement, twice as such and twice in compound forms. It means "to set one's mind on, to have a specific opinion about or attitude toward" something (see 8:5).

The first (negative) side of this command is an exhortation to humility, an exhortation not to have too exalted an opinion of oneself, "not to over-think." The context shows that this applies especially to the subject of spiritual gifts. The Christian "is not to overvalue his abilities, his gifts, or his worth but make an accurate estimate of himself" (MacArthur, 2:158).

The second (positive) part of the command is an exhortation to be sober-minded and to think clearly (σωφρονέω, *sōphroneō*), i.e., to examine oneself as honestly and objectively as possible with a view to assessing the gift with which one has been endowed by God. Such "sober judgment" not only excludes an exaggerated opinion of oneself, but also warns us not to *under*estimate the abilities God has given us. Sometimes a false modesty may be just as detrimental to the church as pride.

One's judgment is accurate when it is **in accordance with the measure of faith God has given you.** The NIV is not very precise here. Instead of "given," Paul actually says "divided, distributed, apportioned, allotted" (μερίζω, *merizō*). Instead of allotted to "you," he says "allotted to each." The NASB is better: "as God has allotted to each a measure of faith." The main point is that a person's sober estimate of himself must correspond with the "measure of faith" distributed to him by God.

The expression "measure of faith" is notoriously difficult. The word for "measure" (μέτρον, *metron*) can mean either an instrument or a *standard* by which something is measured, or it can mean the amount or *quantity* measured out in a particular situation. "Faith" could refer to the subjective faith by which a person is initially saved (Moule, 208; Cranfield, 2:615; Moo, 761) or the subjective faith by which a person lives the Christian life (Murray, 2:119; MacArthur, 2:161-162). Or "faith" could refer to objective faith, the doctrine or object in which we believe, especially Jesus Christ (Fitzmyer, 646). Or "faith" may be the special miracle-working faith which is one of the gifts of the Spirit (1 Cor 12:9; 13:2; Lard, 382-383; MP, 492).

Other views have been suggested (❂ II:320-321), but in my opinion, the specific gift God has distributed to each Christian is not the faith as such, but rather the "measure" itself. In this case *metron* does not have the sense of the standard by which we measure ourselves, but the sense of "quantity" or "limited amount." I.e., *God has given to each Christian a measured ability that is appropriate to or that corresponds to his own faith.* This, I believe, is the meaning of this difficult clause. As Murray points out (2:119), faith is involved not only in becoming a Christian but also in the day-by-day living of the Christian life (see 14:23; Phil 4:13). "In the church there is distribution of gift [*sic*] and each member possesses his own measure for which there is the corresponding faith by

Romans Part Five

which and within the limits of which the gift is to be exercised" (Murray, 2:119, see also MacArthur, 2:161-162).

The main points of this verse are 1) *each* Christian has a gift; 2) these gifts are not all the same; 3) each one's gift has been given to him by God (1 Cor 4:7); and 4) one's gift is therefore no basis for feelings of superiority over others.

12:4-5 Just as each of us has one body with many members, and these members do not all have the same function, so in Christ we who are many form one body, and each member belongs to all the others. The analogy between the church and the body is also found in 1 Cor 10:17; 12:12-31; Eph 1:23; 4:4,11-16; 5:23-30; Col 1:18,24; 2:19; 3:15. Sometimes the point is the relation between the body as such and its head, Jesus Christ; sometimes it is the interrelations among the various members of the body. The latter is the point here. Like the human body, the one church has many members with different yet interdependent functions. I.e., there is *variety* in *unity*.

The unity of the "one body" is "in Christ." No matter how many members a local congregation may have, whether 50 or 5,000, and no matter how many Christians exist worldwide in the invisible church, we are all one body because we have the same Savior and Lord, Jesus Christ.

At the same time we are not an army of identical clones. Like the members of the human body, the members of the church do not all have the same "function" (πράξις, *praxis*, "activity, task, function").

Rather than separating us from one another, though, the variety of gifts only brings us closer together when we see how much we depend on one another. "Each member belongs to all the others," says Paul (v. 5). No matter how humble my gift may be (1 Cor 12:22-24), every other member of the body depends on it; and no matter how honorable my gift may be, I am dependent upon and blessed by even the humblest contribution of every other member.

12:6 The terseness of the material in vv. 6-8 makes interpretation difficult. Verse 6 begins with a participle ("having"), which begins a new sentence and is dependent on the implied imperative verbs in the clauses that follow. What makes this difficult is that in the Greek the seven units comprising vv. 6b-8 are not really clauses and contain no verbs at all. These must be supplied, with the imperative mode being assumed.

The NASB supplies a whole imperative clause in the middle of v. 6, "let each exercise them accordingly," and intends for this to govern the seven units that follow, which it translates quite literally, e.g., "if service, in his serving" (v. 7a). In terms of the NASB's supplied imperative the thought would then be, "If your gift is serving, then involve yourself in the work of serving."

The NIV takes a different approach, but the result is the same. Each of the seven units in vv. 6b-8 is converted into an exhortation. The imperative "let him" is added in each case, and the prepositional phrase that ends each unit is converted into a verb. Thus "if serving — in the serving" becomes "If it is serving, let him serve." Both the NASB and the NIV are acceptable; both convey the "underlying hortatory sense" of these verses (Moo, 764; see Murray, 2:121; Cranfield, 2:618).

The beginning of v. 6 emphasizes the *variety* of spiritual gifts: **We have different gifts, according to the grace given us.** On the word for gifts (χαρίσματα, *charismata*; singular, χάρισμα, *charisma*), see 1:11 (❂:93-94). This does not refer to the gift of salvation as such, but to the gifts that endow the recipient with the right and the ability to render special service to the church. Likewise "grace" (χάρις, *charis*) here does not refer to saving grace, but is used in the more general sense of "a gift that brings joy or gladness" (see Rom 1:5; 1 Pet 4:10).

What follows is a series of (implied) exhortations urging conscientiousness in the exercise of the gifts discerned through the "sober judgment" mentioned in v. 3. In effect Paul is telling us: "Whatever your gift, be satisfied with it and use it diligently." The seven gifts which are named should be considered as a representative list, not an exhaustive one.

The first gift is prophecy: **If a man's gift is prophesying, let him use it in proportion to his faith.** The gift of prophecy was very important in the early church, being regarded as second only to the apostleship itself (1 Cor 12:28; Eph 2:20; 3:5). Paul stresses its preeminence in relation to other gifts, especially tongues (1 Cor 14:1,39).

Some equate prophecy in the NT with the ordinary proclamation of the Word. This view is quite unacceptable, however, in view of the lofty place given to this gift as noted above. The NT prophets performed the same function as the OT prophets, namely, they received revelation from God and spoke their revealed messages to God's people under divine inspiration.

Thus the gift of prophecy was a *miraculous* spiritual gift in the same category as speaking in tongues, and thus has no place in the church today (1 Cor 13:8-13). What a prophet proclaimed was "inspired speech, words given as from 'without' (by the Spirit) and not consciously formulated by the mind" (Dunn, 2:727). An apostle's personal authority was more general and abiding than that of a prophet, but the inspired words of a prophet were just as true and authoritative as the inspired words of an apostle. It is true that a prophet's words had to be weighed and tested (1 Cor 14:29; 1 Thess 5:20-21; see Stott, 327), but even an apostle's authority had to be substantiated by miraculous signs (2 Cor 12:12).

The implied exhortation is that if one does have the gift of prophecy (as was true in the early church), he must "use it in proportion to his faith." The Greek text does not say "*his* faith," but simply "the faith," with the definite article. This leads some to conclude that Paul is not talking about subjective faith (contra the NIV), but objective faith, i.e., "the faith" in the sense of the content of established biblical and gospel truth (see Jude 3).

This view is possible, but the very nature of prophecy makes it unlikely. I.e., if prophecy is the proclamation of revealed and inspired truth — which it is —

then a prophetic message may in fact be adding completely new material to the existing canon and thus will not be measurable by that canon. I conclude, then, that Paul is referring to a prophet's subjective faith, in the sense explained above in v. 3b. I.e., one who has the gift of prophecy should allow himself to be used by God to the full extent of his faith in the power of God working through him. Thus Paul's exhortation has to do not with the content of the prophecy (over which the prophet has no control anyway), but with the spirit of complete submission with which a prophet must exercise his gift.

12:7 If it is serving, let him serve . . . . I.e., if your spiritual gift is serving, then apply yourself to the task of serving to the full extent of your faith in the power of God which is working through you. The word for "serving" is διακονία (*diakonia*), which is the term for general service or ministry, as in 1 Cor 12:5; and it is similar to the term from which we get our word "deacon," as in 1 Tim 3:8. Some take it in the general sense here (Moule, 209; Morris, 441); see 1 Pet 4:10-11, where the verb form of the word is used inclusively. Many others take it in the more narrow sense of "deacon," not necessarily as the formal name of an office but as representing a specific function. The latter is more likely, since here it is part of a longer list of specific gifts.

What specific function is in view? Some speculate that it refers to the ministry of the Word (Acts 6:4), a ministry of *spiritual* service, since it is listed between prophecy and teaching (Lenski, 762-763; see Murray, 2:123-124). Others, rightly concluding that the order of the list is not decisive, see it as referring to the ministry of benevolence, or meeting the *material* needs of the less fortunate in the congregation (Acts 6:1). I agree with the latter view. *Diakonia* here is probably similar to the "helps" listed in 1 Cor 12:28 ("those able to help others," NIV). In some ways it may be similar to the office of deacon as this is understood by many today.

[I]f it is teaching, let him teach . . . . I.e., if you have been given the ability to teach, then apply yourself fully to the task of teaching (see 1 Cor 12:28-29; Eph 4:11).

"Teaching" is best understood by comparing it with the gifts of prophecy and encouragement or exhortation (v. 8). Whereas prophecy is the gift of speaking messages directly inspired by God, teaching is the insightful exposition of the meaning and application of such inspired material, including OT Scripture and New Covenant revelation. As such the work of a teacher is directed toward the mind or the understanding, as compared with the work of an encourager (exhorter), which is directed mainly toward the feelings, the conscience, and the will (Murray, 2:125).

12:8 This leads us directly to the next gift: **if it is encouraging, let him encourage . . . .** The word is παρακαλέω (*parakaleō*), translated "I urge" in v. 1, and better translated here as "exhorting" (see the NASB). Literally it reads, "If one who exhorts – in the exhortation." I.e., if you have been given the ability to exhort, then apply yourself fully to that task.

The main work of an exhorter is to encourage and persuade Christians to act upon the knowledge received through prophecy and teaching. One with the gift of exhorting knows how to touch the heart; he is able to deliver "a stirring appeal to men to do their duty" (Lard, 386).

[I]f it is contributing to the needs of others, let him give generously . . . . When this terse exhortation is fleshed out in view of carry-over elements from vv. 6-7, it has this sense: "If you have been given the gift of sharing, then apply yourself fully to this task to the full extent of your faith in the power of God at work within you; and do so with simplicity of motive" (❧II:326-327).

The NIV interprets the single word, "sharing," to mean "contributing to the needs of others." This is no doubt Paul's point, probably in the sense of private benevolence, or meeting others' needs from one's own funds. The essence of the gift includes the ability to earn significant amounts of money (or the simple possession of wealth), plus a "God-given inclination to give" (Cranfield, 2:625) (❧II:327).

The noun in this final phrase is ἁπλότης (*haplotēs*), the basic meaning of which is "simplicity [KJV], singleness, single-mindedness." When applied to actions it connotes pure motivation and thus sincerity (Eph 6:5; Col 3:22). But this noun also came to mean "generosity" or "liberality" in reference to giving. Either connotation is appropriate here (❧II:327).

[I]f it is leadership, let him govern diligently . . . . The verb can mean "to stand before people for the purpose of protecting, aiding, or helping them," or "to stand before people for the purpose of leading, governing, or presiding over them" (❧II:328). The NIV correctly gives it the connotation of leadership and governing (so also the NASB and NRSV). Some see this as referring to leaders of all kinds (SH, 358), or "anyone who is placed at the head of others" (Lenski, 765). Indeed, the term may be used for one who manages his household (1 Tim 3:4,5,12), but here it probably refers to those who are leaders in the church (as in 1 Thess 5:12 and 1 Tim 5:17), specifically the elders. It is probably the same as "gifts of administration" in 1 Cor 12:28.

The elders are exhorted to "govern diligently," i.e., with eagerness, earnestness, zeal, and devotion. That is to say, elders must not approach their work with idleness and indifference (DeWelt, 200), because the very salvation of those under their care is at stake (Acts 20:28; Heb 13:17).

This brings us to the final gift: **if it is showing mercy, let him do it cheerfully.** Paul has already named the gift of serving (general church benevolence) and the gift of sharing (private benevolence). But there are many acts of mercy that do not involve the giving of money or material goods, and these are probably what Paul refers to here. These include such things as visiting the sick at home or in hospitals, visiting and helping shut-ins, comforting the dying and

Romans Part Five

the bereaved, visiting and corresponding with prisoners, and sending cards to or telephoning any of these. To show mercy "cheerfully" means to do so not from a sense of begrudging duty but from the desire of a joyful heart (◕ II:329).

C. MISCELLANEOUS MORAL TEACHING (12:9-16)

In this paragraph Paul continues to instruct us about the content of the sanctified life, with a slight change of direction. Whereas in the previous paragraph the exhortations about spiritual gifts apply individually only to those who have the particular gift in view, here the exhortations are general and apply equally to all Christians. This is not an exhaustive handbook on ethics, though, but rather a list of some of the more basic characteristics of the transformed life.

Though this teaching has a decidedly Christian flavor, for the most part it is not something newly revealed to and through Paul. Included are "maxims of traditional Jewish wisdom" rooted in the OT, and echoes of the teaching of Jesus as it was already being circulated among the churches (Dunn, 2:738, 745). Especially reflected here are the exceptionally high moral standards established by Jesus, representing a pattern of behavior regarded as foolish by the carnal mind and attainable only by the regeneration and renewing of the Holy Spirit (◕ II:330).

There does not appear to be any logical order to this series of admonitions. They are a miscellany of mandates, a potpourri of prescriptions summing up the essence of the sanctified life.

An introductory question is whether the first declaration, "Love must be sincere" (v. 9a), is intended to be a heading over the entire section, or whether it is just the first exhortation in the list. Many interpreters take it as a heading, and see what follows as an elaboration of what it means to love one another.

There is an important truth here, since every command is always in a sense just a facet of the general commandments to love God and one's neighbor (Matt 22:36-40; Rom 13:8-10). I question the idea that the love command is the intended general heading for this paragraph, however. Actually it is not a command, and not even a full statement. It is a phrase which reads literally, "Love sincere." If it were meant to be a heading, we would expect the words to be reversed: "[This is] sincere love: . . . ." As it stands, it has the force of a commandment about the *character* of love, i.e., "[Let your] love [be] sincere" (◕ II:331).

12:9 Love must be sincere. It is appropriate for this injunction to appear first, given the supreme importance of the virtue of love. Jesus singled it out as the essence of God's law (Matt 22:36-40) and as the central demand of the New Covenant (John 13:34-35).

This applies primarily, of course, to the kind of love called ἀγάπη (*agapē*), which is the subject here. The Greeks knew several kinds of love, including a form of *agapē* (see Lewis, *Loves*; *GRe*, 327-328, 336-345); but the noun *agapē* was first used with "theological density" by the LXX (Spicq, *Lexicon*, 1:18), and was taken over and given a uniquely Christian meaning by Jesus and the NT writers (Dunn, 2:739; Moo, 775). This Christian meaning is drawn from the nature of God himself as displayed in his work of salvation through Jesus Christ, i.e., his selfless and sacrificial concern for the happiness and well-being of others (8:39; John 3:16; 1 John 4:10).

This is the essence of the *agapē* enjoined upon us as Christians. It differs from the other forms of love in that it does not depend upon some uncontrollable inner emotion or desire or need for fulfillment within the one who loves, but rather is a deliberately willed attitude of concern and good will based on the needs of the one who is loved.

The point of Paul's injunction is not that Christians should love one another, since this commandment should be something engrained on every Christian's mind from the beginning of his renewed life. Rather, the point is that the love we profess must be *sincere*; it must be from the heart and not be an external mask only.

The word for "sincere" is ἀνυπόκριτος (*anypokritos*), which means "without a mask, unhypocritical, genuine, not counterfeit, without pretense or sham." Metaphorically and morally, a *hypokritēs* (a hypocrite) is anyone who pretends to be something he is not. Christians are commanded to be without hypocrisy not only in love (see also 2 Cor 6:6; 1 Pet 1:22) but also in faith (1 Tim 1:5; 2 Tim 1:5) and wisdom (Jas 3:17).

Hate what is evil; cling to what is good. (See Amos 5:15, "Hate evil, love good.") Here good and evil are general terms, representing everything that is morally wicked and ungodly, and everything that is morally good and holy.

The verbs are very forceful. The word for hate "expresses a strong feeling of horror" (SH, 360), and implies loathing, abhorrence, and disgust. It means that Christians cannot just passively ignore evil, but must actively and aggressively oppose it and speak out against it (DeWelt, 200-201) and flee from it (1 Tim 6:11; 2 Tim 2:22). The hatred of sin, especially one's own, is the starting point for repentance.

The verb for "cling to" is likewise strong. In the active voice it means to join or glue two things together. Here in the middle voice it means "attach yourself closely" to everything that is good.

The message here is clear: there can be no neutrality in the moral realm. We cannot hide behind some alleged moral or cultural relativism. Good and evil objectively exist in God's own nature and in God's law. Christians must take a clear and unequivocal stand against the evil and for the good.

12:10 Be devoted to one another in brotherly love. Here Paul moves from the general love (*agapē*) Christians must have for all people, to the more intimate love we must also have toward one another. He uses words compounded from two other Greek words for love, φιλία (*philia*) and στοργή (*storgē*). The former is used for the affectionate love between friends; the latter, the tender affection among family members.

"Be devoted" (φιλόστοργος, *philostorgos*) is a combination of both these terms, but has the nuance of *storgē*. It is a kind of instinctive affection, like that which parents and children feel toward one another. It implies that the relationships among Christians should involve intimacy, understanding, and acceptance.

The other word is φιλαδελφία (*philadelphia*). It is a combination of φιλία (*philia*) and ἀδελφός (*adelphos*, "brother") and literally means "brotherly love." As members of God's family and spiritual siblings of Jesus Christ (1:13; 8:12-17; 2 Cor 6:18), Christians truly have a sibling relationship with one another. Thus we are exhorted to develop the close and affectionate relationship that should exist among brothers and sisters (❀ II:333).

Honor one another above yourselves. "Honor one another" is straightforward; it means to treat one another with genuine respect. This includes the general respect due to all Christians as members of the King's own household, and the specific respect and appreciation due to those who have made special contributions to the work of the kingdom.

"Above yourselves" is not so easy. This is a rendering of the verb προηγέομαι (*proēgeomai*), which literally means "to go before, to lead the way." Some thus take it to mean "set an example," or "show the way to one another," i.e., in this matter of giving honor to others. Others take it to mean "to surpass, to outdo, to take the lead." I.e., "when it comes to bestowing honor, we are to take the lead" (McGuiggan, 368); we should try to "outdo one another in showing honor" (RSV).

A third interpretation, reflected in the NIV, is that this verb can be translated "to prefer, to put first." This is the choice of the NASB also: "Give preference to one another in honor." I.e., give honor to your fellow believers "by putting them first" (MacArthur, 2:189). The main problem with this view is that this verb is not known to be used in this sense anywhere else (it appears only here in the NT). Many give it this meaning anyway, seeing a parallel between this verse and Phil 2:3b, "in humility consider others better than yourselves" (see Cranfield, 2:632-633; Hendriksen, 2:415).

Any one of these views is possible. Whichever we adopt, the main point is that we must exhibit toward one another the spirit of courtesy, unselfishness, and humility. (See Murray, 2:130.)

12:11 This verse expresses three basic Christian states of mind (❀ II:334). The first appears in the NIV thus: **Never be lacking in zeal, . . .** The word for "zeal" (σπουδή, *spoudē*) means "fervor, zeal, eagerness, ardor, passion, enthusiasm." "Never be lacking" is literally "not slow, not slothful, not lagging behind (NASB), not hesitant, not lazy, not complacent." "Lacking" describes a loafer or a sluggard who is slow to get started, or who puts off fulfilling his Christian duties (❀ II:335).

[B]ut keep your spiritual fervor . . . . "Fervor" is used of water boiling or of metal glowing with heat. In the context of Christian service (as here), it means "to be full of energy, to be on fire with zeal and enthusiasm." It is a warning against settling into comfortable, shallow ruts in our spiritual lives.

Paul says literally that we must be glowing or burning "in the Spirit" (◐ II:335). The meaning would be that "the Christian is to allow himself to be set on fire . . . by the Holy Spirit" (Cranfield, 2:634). Rather than depending on external stimulation (such as innovative worship programming), we must look to the Spirit within us to energize us and fire us up for Christian service.

. . . serving the Lord. "The Lord" is specifically Jesus Christ. "Lord" (κύριος, *kyrios*) has the connotation of owner or master; "serving" (δουλεύω, *douleuō*) has the connotation of serving as a slave, a δοῦλος (*doulos*). This exhortation to serve the Lord as a slave refers not just to external obedience but also to the inner spiritual attitude of submission to the Lord's authority over us.

12:12 Here is another triad of exhortations that are loosely related to each other. The first appears in the NIV as **Be joyful in hope, . . .** Over and over the NT exhorts us to "Rejoice!" (e.g., Matt 5:12; Phil 3:1; 4:4; Rev 19:7). The word is χαίρω (*chairō*), which is related to the word for grace (χάρις, *charis*).

Paul indicates that one specific source of our joy as Christians is our *hope*, which of course is based on the grace bestowed upon us in Christ Jesus. Christian hope is not just a fond wish, but is an earnest and confident expectation of the full salvation awaiting us at the *eschaton* (see ◐ I:301, 315; ◐ II:336).

The next admonition is to be **patient in affliction, . . .** This follows naturally from the former; our hope-inspired joy gives us the courage to hold up under the afflictions of this age. Afflictions include the various sufferings to which all men are susceptible because of the fallenness of this present world; they also include the opposition and persecution Christians can expect just because we are Christians (John 16:23; Acts 14:22; Rev 7:14).

"Be patient" is ὑπομένω (*hypomenō*). Cranfield says this translation is too weak; he suggests "hold out steadfastly" (2:637). The word has the nuance of "bearing up with courage" and "enduring what is hard to bear" (◐ II:337).

The next exhortation is related to this sort of situation but cannot be limited to it: be **faithful in prayer.** It is natural and proper to fall back on prayer in the midst of affliction or persecution, but we must not wait for trouble to befall us before we are moved to pray. The word translated "be faithful" is used with reference to prayer also in Acts 1:14; 2:42; 6:4; Col 4:2. It means "to continue steadfastly in, to persevere in, to persist in" prayer (◐ II:337).

12:13 The two exhortations in this verse fall under the general heading of benevolence. They direct us to cultivate the spirit of giving, which befits those who are saved by grace. First, **Share with God's people who are in need.** Literally this refers to "the needs of the saints," with physical needs such as food and clothing being specifically in view. "To share with" is κοινωνέω (*koinōneō*), which is related to κοινωνία (*koinōnia*, "fellowship, sharing, participation (in).") These words are used elsewhere for the sharing of one's money or material goods (❂ II:338).

Some Christians are especially gifted to meet the needs of the saints, whether in a leadership capacity (12:7) or individually (12:8); but here Paul tells us that every Christian has a responsibility to participate in the church's ministry of benevolence to some degree. See Gal 6:10.

The Apostle zeroes in on a very specific kind of need when he says, **Practice hospitality.** "Hospitality" (φιλοξενία, *philoxenia*) is literally "love of strangers," or treating a stranger (ξένος, *xenos*) as a friend (φίλος, *philos*). It refers to the practice of hosting travelers. In NT times it was not nearly as easy for travelers to find safe and reasonable accommodations as it is today, so this would have been an important service. In most ancient cultures hospitality was a prized virtue, and it is identified as an important Christian virtue as well (see Matt 25:35; 1 Tim 3:2; Titus 1:8; Heb 13:2; 1 Pet 4:9; 3 John 5-8). It was especially necessary to care for itinerate preachers and Christians fleeing persecution.

"Practice" is an inadequate translation for the strong verb διώκω (*diōkō*; see v. 14). It means "to run after, to chase, to pursue, to strive for, to earnestly aspire to or seek after." In other words, we should take the initiative in this matter of hospitality (❂ II:339). Some Christians have been known to build extra rooms on their houses in order to provide for traveling evangelists and missionaries on furlough.

12:14 Bless those who persecute you; bless and do not curse. This admonition may have been suggested to Paul by the fact that the word *diōkō* can mean both "pursue" (as in v. 13) and also "persecute" (as here). That Christians may expect to be persecuted, i.e., forced to suffer hurt and hatred and unjust treatment, is a common theme in the NT (Matt 5:10-11; John 15:20; 2 Tim 3:12).

Exactly what is God here requiring of us? Not just to endure persecution, not just to refrain from striking back at our persecutors, and not even just to refrain from wishing them harm. Rather, he is requiring us to pray a prayer of *blessing* for our persecutors. To "bless" in this sense is to ask God to bestow his favor upon someone. To "curse" would be the opposite, i.e., to call upon God to bring harm upon someone (Dunn, 2:744).

But how is this possible? To *bless* those who persecute us seems to be the very opposite of the so-called "natural" response. This is what makes this admonition so striking and, on the face of it, so impossible to obey (❂ II:339).

But this is the whole point of the renewing of the mind and the transformed life (v. 2): the regeneration of the Holy Spirit enables us to do what may seem impossible in the eyes of those still held captive by the powers of sin. God may require the "impossible," but he empowers us to achieve it! Jesus himself has shown us how to do this even in the most extreme circumstances (Luke 23:34), and the martyr Stephen has demonstrated that even an ordinary human being can follow Jesus' example (Acts 7:60) (❂ II:340).

12:15 Rejoice with those who rejoice; mourn with those who mourn. Here Paul calls for *empathy*, which is the ability to identify with and actually experience the feelings and inner dispositions of others (see 1 Cor 12:26). To "rejoice with those who rejoice," to "share in one another's triumphs, joys, and successes," is probably the harder of the two commandments, as Fitzmyer observes (655). To see others succeed (especially where we may have failed) leads easily to negative feelings of envy, jealousy, and resentment; but through the power of the indwelling Spirit we must overcome such tendencies and be genuinely happy when others have cause to rejoice.

To feel compassion toward others who are suffering may seem easier, but often it too requires deliberate, Spirit-assisted effort. It is easy to be indifferent toward the troubles and sorrows of others, especially when we ourselves are caught up in troubles of our own. Even worse, more often than we like to admit, we have a tendency to be glad when misfortune overtakes certain people. We must guard against such urges (❂ II:340).

12:16 Live in harmony with one another. "Live in harmony" is a very loose translation of "think the same thing." The idea is that we should all have the same attitude toward one another.

Some take this to mean that all Christians should have harmony and agreement in our doctrinal thinking, at least on the basics (see Cranfield, 2:643; Dunn, 2:746). Such doctrinal harmony is required of the church, to be sure (15:5-6; 1 Cor 1:10; Eph 4:13-15), but this is probably not Paul's point here. He does not just say, "Have the same mind," period. Nor does he say, "Think the same thoughts *along with* one another." Rather, he specifically says, "Think the same thing *toward* [εἰς, *eis*] one another." The NEB (first edition) captures this idea: "Have equal regard for one another." The TEV says, "Have the same concern for everyone." Exactly what is the content of this common mindset? He has just been telling us: sincere love (v. 9a), family affection (v. 10a), mutual honor and respect (v. 10b), a spirit of sharing (v. 13), and empathetic joy and sorrow (v. 15) (❂ II:341).

What is the greatest hindrance to such harmonious attitudes? Putting oneself and one's own happiness ahead of that of others; having too high an opinion of oneself; in a word, pride. Thus in the interest of removing this barrier to harmony, Paul enjoins us thus: **Do not be proud, but be willing to associate with people of low position.** Literally he says, "Do not think high things," about yourself. This is basically the same as the admonitions in 11:20 and 12:3. The word for "associate with" (in the passive voice) literally means "to be led along or carried away with" something or someone. The thought here is this: do not place yourself above others, but be willing to associate comfortably with "the lowly."

A major question is whether "the lowly" (ταπεινός, *tapeinos*) here is masculine ("humble people") or neuter ("humble things") (❂ II:342). Since *tapeinos* is used elsewhere in the NT only for people, and since the main point of the verse seems to be interrelationships among Christian people, most take this as a reference to humble *people*.

This approach (as in the NIV) is to be preferred: Associate with people who are *tapeinos*. In the Greek world such a person was not "humble" in the sense of showing humility, but in the sense of having a position in life regarded as inferior because of his origin or occupation. The *tapeinos* person was "base, ignoble, of low birth . . . , servile . . . , working at a humble occupation . . . , held in low esteem" (Spicq, *Lexicon*, 3:370).

Paul's point is that, insofar as we are able, we must ignore the caste distinctions and social classes imposed by our various cultures, and look upon all people, especially our Christian brothers and sisters, in the same way. The Apostle does not tell us to associate *only* with "people of low position" and to ignore others. It would be appropriate, though, to pay special attention to those regarded as lowly in one's particular culture, since these are the ones more likely to be shunned by the world in general.

The final admonition in this paragraph is, **Do not be conceited**, or "Do not become wise in your own eyes" (see discussion on 11:25). "Wise" is φρόνιμος (*phronimos*), which is a positive attribute in itself ("sensible, thoughtful, wise"). The idea here, though, is not to consider yourself to be the ultimate measure of wisdom. As McGuiggan words it, "Don't take yourself too seriously. Others really *can* teach you something" (373).

D. PERSONAL VENGEANCE IS FORBIDDEN (12:17-21)

Paul is still explaining the essence of the sanctified life, but this is a new paragraph for two reasons. First, regarding form, the previous section (vv. 9-16) was basically a series of one-liners: short, terse exhortations in no particular order, handed to us like beads on a string. This section, though, seems to be a substantial development of a single theme. Second, for the most part, insofar as personal relationships are in view, vv. 9-16 tell us how Christians should relate to one another. In the present paragraph the emphasis is mainly on our relations with unbelievers, in particular those who in some way have caused us harm or injury.

Exactly what is the topic being discussed here? Our heading identifies it as personal vengeance. This is stated at the beginning in v. 17, "Do not repay anyone evil for evil," and is repeated in v. 19, "Do not take revenge." Sometimes these exhortations are equated with v. 14, "Bless those who persecute you"; but they are not exactly the same. Persecution is a specific kind of injury; it is injury inflicted upon a Christian just because he is a Christian ("because of me," Matt 5:11). Verses 17-21 are more general and speak of evil done to someone for *any* reason, including persecution but not limited to it.

What should a Christian do when harmed by another person, i.e., when he is cheated, insulted, assaulted, cursed, robbed, or treated unjustly in any way? The almost-universal tendency is to personally strike back, to retaliate, to try to get even, to make the evildoer pay for the harm he has done, i.e., to seek personal revenge. Paul's point is that this tendency must be resisted. It is wrong for anyone to take it upon himself, personally, to exact vengeance upon someone who has harmed him.

This is not to say that vengeance as such, or seeing that the evildoer pays for his wrongdoing, is wrong. This is nothing more and nothing less than retributive justice, which as an ethical principle is just as eternally valid as mercy itself. The point is that there is an important limitation on who is permitted to be the instrument of retributive justice: vengeance is *God's* prerogative, not that of the person whose rights have been violated as verse 19 states clearly.

A crucial question, though, is *how and when* God pours out his vengeance upon evildoers. The answer is twofold. On the one hand, God's vengeance in the form of eternal wrath will be poured out upon all unbelieving evildoers at the final judgment (Heb 10:30). But on the other hand — and this is *extremely important* — God's vengeance in the form of temporal punishment is poured out *now* through his appointed servants, those who work in civil government.

The break between Rom 12 and Rom 13 is quite unfortunate, since it tends to obscure the deliberate connection between 12:17-21 and 13:1-7, which are two sides of one coin. Individuals (not just Christians, but *all* individuals) should not take their own revenge (12:17-21), because God has assigned the responsibility for exacting vengeance in his name here on earth to human government (13:1-7).

The proximity of these two passages, one forbidding personal revenge and the other affirming government's responsibility for retributive justice, shows the continuity between the Old Covenant ethic and the New Covenant ethic on this matter. Very often, Christian pacifists and others interpret Christ's teaching in Matt 5:38-48 as a repudiation of the OT ethic and a prohibition of vengeance in any form. Paul's teaching shows this is not the case. The key to understanding Christ's teaching is the distinction between personal vengeance, which is forbidden, and God's own vengeance rendered through civil government, which is necessary and right. Jesus was speaking only of the former, not the latter.

The Law of Moses included both teachings. On the one hand, it absolutely forbade personal vengeance: "Do not seek revenge or bear a grudge against one of your people, but love your neighbor as yourself" (Lev 19:18). Thus neither Jesus nor Paul was the first to teach this. On the other hand, Moses' Law required civil judges to measure out punishment to evildoers that fit the crime, no more and no less. This was the point of the *lex talionis*, the "eye-for-an-eye" principle. This principle is stated three times in the Mosaic Law: Exod 21:23-25; Lev 24:19-

20; and Deut 19:21. In each case it is set forth as a rule to be applied only in a judicial context, not by individuals or by the injured parties themselves.

In Rom 12:17–13:7 Paul teaches the same two moral rules: no personal vengeance, and retributive justice only in the context of a court of law. The latter is the same as the "eye-for-an-eye" principle, which has *not* been repealed. Jesus does not repeal it in Matt 5:38-48. In that part of the Sermon on the Mount our Lord corrects rabbinic misinterpretations and misapplications of OT Law. One such misapplication was the wrongful use of the "eye-for-an-eye" principle as justification for personal revenge. This is what Jesus is repudiating. He is not contradicting the OT Law, nor is he setting this principle aside. He is simply saying, like Moses and Paul, that individuals do not have the right to take their own *personal* revenge. The *lex talionis* as it stood in the Law of Moses was never meant to apply to personal revenge; it was meant to be applied only by civil government. This is Paul's point in Romans. Jesus himself makes no reference to the role of civil government; he is concerned only with the way *individuals* should respond to those who have wronged them. But Jesus does not contradict anything said by Paul. The following chart summarizes this:

	Law of Moses	Jesus	Paul
No personal revenge:	Lev 19:18	Matt 5:38-48	Rom 12:17-21
Governmental retribution:	Exod 21:23-25; Lev 24:19-20; Deut 19:21	[silence]	Rom 13:1-7

Clearly there are continuity and harmony among the Law of Moses, Jesus, and Paul on this subject. The prohibition of personal revenge and the approval of governmental retribution are not contradictory but complementary. Thus it is not wrong for governments to punish criminals, nor is it wrong for Christians to punish criminals when they are serving in an official capacity as representatives of civil government, e.g., as jurors, judges, or correctional workers. What is wrong is for *anyone*, Christians and unbelievers alike, to take justice into their own hands.

12:17 Do not repay anyone evil for evil. By "evil" Paul means any injury or injustice, any situation in which someone "does you wrong." Our first inclination when we have been thus wronged is to strike back and "get even." This spirit of revenge, retaliation, and vindictiveness is what Paul is forbidding here.

As explained in the introduction above, this is not a condemnation of vengeance as such, but *personal* vengeance only, i.e., making oneself the instrument by which the wrongdoer is made to suffer. Vengeance is God's prerogative, and he has his own ways of working it out (❷II:346).

Be careful to do what is right in the eyes of everybody. "Be careful" is προνοέω (*pronoeō*). It means to give serious thought to something. "What is right" is καλά (*kala*; neuter plural of καλός [*kalos*]), "good things." In this context it refers to what is morally good or right; this is in direct contrast with "evil" (κακός, *kakos*) in v. 17a. As Wuest explains it, *kalos* refers "to exterior goodness, or goodness that is seen on the exterior of a person, the outward expression of an inward goodness" (218). Such exterior goodness is necessary because what we do as Christians is observed by those around us, and it is important that our conduct, which is open to "the eyes of everybody," brings honor to our God (⊙II:347).

"In the eyes of everybody" is literally "before or in the sight of all men." Jesus taught that we should let our light shine before men, "that they may see your good deeds and praise your Father in heaven" (Matt 5:16; see 2 Cor 8:21; 1 Pet 2:12). This is a general principle and applies to all areas of our lives. The point is that we should always be sensitive to how our conduct is viewed by others, so as not to cause anyone to stumble or reject the gospel, and so as not to be an occasion for anyone to mock the God we profess to serve (1 Cor 10:32; 2 Cor 4:2; 1 Tim 3:7; 5:14; 1 Pet 2:15).

We must be careful not to misunderstand Paul here. He is not saying that we should do only what other people consider to be right, as if we are conforming to the world's norms after all, contrary to the command in v. 2. Rather, since the conduct of the law is written on the hearts of everyone (2:15), Paul assumes that there is a common core of decency acknowledged by all, or what Hendriksen calls a "public conscience" (2:420). Even if the world itself does not live up to such a standard, it is aware of it and is also keenly aware that Christians have openly subscribed to it. Thus the world is quick to notice when Christians' lives do not conform to this standard, and in such cases is even quicker to mock our faith and our Lord. (See Dunn, 2:748; Fitzmyer, 656; Moo, 785.)

12:18 If it is possible, as far as it depends on you, live at peace with everyone. As in v. 17, the admonition is about our relationships not just with other Christians but with everyone in general. Our goal should be to live in such a way that we would never antagonize anyone or give anyone an occasion for doing evil against us. We should never take the initiative in disturbing the peace (Morris, 452). In fact, we should go out of our way, doing all that is *possible*, to establish and maintain peaceable relations with others (see Matt 5:23-24). As Jesus says, we should *make peace happen* (Matt 5:9).

If it depended *only* on us, we could, through the power of the Holy Spirit working in us, be at peace with all men. But it does not depend just on us. Unfortunately, even after we have done everything in our power to live peaceably with others, sometimes they themselves simply will not allow it. Despite our best efforts they continue to perpetuate a spirit of hostility from their side.

In fact, if we live consistent, faithful lives, and if we take a firm stand for the truth of God's Word and for the uniqueness of Jesus Christ as the only Savior, we can expect to arouse enmity and be openly opposed and hated by those who hate Jesus (Matt 10:22,34-36; John 16:33). The only way to avoid all such enmity is to compromise our commitment to Jesus, and this we cannot do (⊙II:348).

12:19 Do not take revenge, my friends, but leave room for God's wrath, . . . "Do not take revenge" is literally "not avenging yourselves," or "Never take your own revenge" (NASB). The issue is *personal* revenge, as explained in the introduction to this section. Some see this verse as different from "Do not repay anyone evil for evil" in v. 17. If there is a difference, it is minimal. The verb here is ἐκδοκέω (*ekdokeō*), which means to avenge or punish. "Do not avenge yourself" means "Do not take it upon yourself to punish someone for some wrong he has done to you."

The alternative to personal vengeance is not *no* vengeance, but *God's* vengeance. Paul says, "Leave room for God's wrath." The expression "leave room" means the same thing as in Eph 4:27, i.e., "make room for, give place to." Here Paul means, "Get out of the way and allow God to handle the matter in his own way" (see Lenski, 780). Step aside, back off, and leave it up to the wrath of God (❥II:349). Thus whenever we suffer harm or injustice, we must allow God to be our avenger. Wrath is his prerogative, and we must not attempt to usurp it.

[F]or it is written: "It is mine to avenge; I will repay," says the Lord. Here Paul lets us know immediately that he is referring to the wrath of God, by quoting an OT text in which God (the Lord, Yahweh) specifically says, "Vengeance is mine." This is a paraphrase of Deut 32:35, where the Hebrew text says, "To me belongs vengeance and recompense." This is also cited in Heb 10:30, where it refers to the final judgment. The word order is emphatic: "*To me* belongs vengeance; *I* will repay." This shows that vengeance *per se* is not wrong. The moral issue is simply, who has the *right* to exact vengeance on evildoers; the answer is, God does.

We must ask, though, exactly when and how God inflicts his wrath upon these evildoers. As explained in the introduction, he does this in two ways. The ultimate expression of divine wrath, of course, is the eschatological wrath of *eternal punishment* in hell (Heb 10:30). Some think Paul is referring to this here (Fitzmyer, 657), or at least mainly to this (Morris, 454). I believe this is an error, though, because God has another means of inflicting his wrath on evildoers, and he is already in the process of doing so even now in this world. The means by which he is doing so is *civil government*, as Paul goes on to explain in this very context, in 13:1-4, especially v. 4. Thus it is a mistake to separate the wrath of government from the wrath of God; ideally they are the same thing. I believe God's wrath as expressed through civil government is Paul's primary reference here.

We may identify two reasons why God has not left vengeance in the hands of those who have been wronged, but has appointed civil rulers to take care of it instead. First, it is almost always impossible for the wronged party to be objective and even-handed in deciding on a proper punishment for the evildoer; the tendency will always be to go beyond what is warranted. Civil government as a third party (theoretically) can evaluate and decide on such matters objectively and fairly.

Second, some people who are wronged will not on their own have the power or the resources to see that justice is done and the evildoer punished. Thus it is necessary to have a civil government that is strong enough to take vengeance on even the most powerful wrongdoers.

12:20 On the contrary: "If your enemy is hungry, feed him; if he is thirsty, give him something to drink." The strong contrast between the world's tendency to seek personal revenge for wrongs suffered, and the response God demands and expects from those leading a transformed life, is seen in the opening phrase, "on the contrary" (ἀλλά, *alla*). Except for this phrase, this verse is a direct quote from Prov 25:21-22a (LXX).

In a circumstance crying out for revenge, it is not enough for us as individuals to passively refrain from retaliating while allowing God's vengeance to prevail. Invoking the passage from Proverbs, Paul shows that the wronged party must also have a positive, loving attitude toward the wrongdoer and must actively take steps to meet needs that he might have (❧ II:351).

The rest of the quotation from Proverbs reads thus: **"In doing this, you will heap burning coals on his head."** This is a very difficult clause because we simply are not sure of the significance of heaping burning coals on someone's head. Two major approaches have been pursued (❧ II:351).

The first view had adherents in the early centuries of the church, and has an occasional defender in modern times. In this view the burning coals represent the *wrath of God* (see Ps 11:6; 140:10). The idea is that the acts of kindness bestowed by a victim upon his enemy will in the final judgment only increase his guilt and thus intensify his eternal punishment, if he has not repented by then. Such action could thus be regarded as "a more noble type of revenge," as Fitzmyer puts it (658).

The biggest problem with this view is that it seems to suggest a motive for such acts of kindness that is the exact opposite of everything Paul is teaching about the transformed life. Deeds of kindness done for the express purpose of increasing an enemy's eternal punishment would not be more noble than tit-for-tat retaliation, but less noble. This is why most who have taken this view say that the increased punishment is just the *result* of showing kindness to an enemy, and should never be one's *purpose* or motive (Cranfield, 2:649; Moo, 788). But such a distinction, while clear in theory, would be difficult to maintain in practice, and would only create unnecessary ambiguities for the person who only wants to do the most loving thing for his enemy. Besides, the teaching from Proverbs as quoted by Paul seems to suggest that heaping coals on an enemy's head is the *very reason why* (*gar*) one should do such acts of kindness, and not just the result. Thus the context seems to be against this view.

The second view, rightly accepted by most modern scholars, is that the burning coals are meant to symbolize an *attitude* that may develop within the enemy's heart as a result of his victim's acts of kindness. This attitude is usually identified as the "burning pangs of shame and contrition" (Cranfield, 2:649), or "the vehement pangs and pains of conscience, the torments of shame, remorse, and self-reproach" (MP, 505). This is considered to be a positive result of the kind deeds, since burning shame and a tormented conscience may lead to genuine repentance (❋ II:352).

Whatever the origin of the metaphor, this view sees the acts of kindness as nothing but a positive expression of love, performed in order to influence the enemy to repent. Whether such repentance actually occurs is not the point; what matters is that we have done for our enemy what our transformed life requires and makes possible

12:21 Do not be overcome by evil, but overcome evil with good. This could be an unlimited exhortation that applies to our battle against evil in general, but Paul more likely intends it to sum up his teaching about personal revenge in this paragraph.

"Do not be conquered by evil," or "Do not let evil gain the victory over you," means "Do not give in to the temptation to get even with your tormenter. Do not seek personal revenge." To "overcome evil with good" means first to resist the temptation to retaliate in kind against one who has wronged us, and then to respond with acts of kindness instead (❋ II:353).

E. THE RELATION BETWEEN CITIZENS AND GOVERNMENT (13:1-7)

In this section we have what appears to be an abrupt change of subject, as Paul turns his attention to the relationship between citizens and government. The main point, as Stott says, seems to be "conscientious citizenship" (338). The paragraph as a whole is "a coherent and well-organized argument about . . . the need for submission to governing authorities" (Moo, 790). But there is another side to the coin. While stating the citizens' responsibility toward government, Paul gives us very valuable information about the government's responsibility toward its citizens. Indeed, this passage presents the clearest biblical teaching concerning the divine origin and God-intended purpose of human government.

Why does Paul introduce this subject at this particular point? Some have argued that the passage has no logical connection with the context, and may even be an interpolation by someone other than Paul. One reason some regard it thus is that there is nothing christological about the passage (see Cranfield, 2:651) (❋ II:354).

Actually we do not have to go outside the immediate context to see how this paragraph fits into Paul's purposes in this section of his epistle. The subject here is the virtues required of those who are living the transformed life. Submission to authority is simply one aspect of God's will for us — "his good, pleasing and perfect will" (12:2; see Murray, 2:145). God's will for Christians includes not just specifically Christian duties such as the unselfish use of spiritual gifts (12:3-8), but also the laws of the Creator that apply to all human beings as his creatures. This passage falls into the latter category; its application is universal and applies to "everyone" (13:1). This reminds us that Christianity is not just a "religion"; it is a *worldview*.

Without a doubt the most immediate contextual connection is with the preceding paragraph, 12:17-21. The teaching concerning the role of government in 13:3-4 deliberately complements the teaching about personal nonretaliation in 12:19. These doctrines are in a sense just two sides of one coin, despite the unfortunate chapter division after 12:21. Paul wants to make it clear that the prohibition of personal vengeance does not mean that evildoers are free to do all the harm they please without restraint and without fear of any kind of punishment at all. While individuals are not allowed to take their own vengeance against those who do them wrong, God has established civil government to be his earthly agent to see that such vengeance (i.e., justice) is carried out. We should never teach or preach from either of these paragraphs (12:17-21 and 13:1-7) without referring to the other.

Before turning to a detailed exegesis of this passage, I will give a brief systematic summary of its teaching. I must reemphasize that this instruction is not just a temporary expedient to be applied to some local problem only, but is "an important basis for a general theology of the state," contra Dunn (2:768). We are dealing here with "broad general principles" that apply to all times (SH, 369). We should also note that Paul is here describing the role or purpose of government in the *ideal*, as God intends for it to be carried out according to his preceptive will.

Paul's instruction on the one hand sets forth the responsibility of government toward its citizens; on the other hand it describes the responsibility of citizens toward their government. Regarding the former, the purpose of government is to *uphold justice*, which includes both the protection of the rights of all citizens, and the punishment of evildoers. It is important that these functions not be separated as if they were unrelated to one another. Actually they belong together as *means* and *end*.

The ultimate goal or purpose of government is a positive one, i.e., to protect the rights of its citizens. As such it is "the guardian of justice," as Godet puts it (439). This positive task is described in 13:4, "he is God's servant to do you good." It is stated in more detail in 1 Tim 2:2, which says we should pray for governing authorities to the end "that we may live peaceful and quiet lives in all godliness and holiness." The ultimate purpose of government is to make this possible.

The means by which government is meant to accomplish this is the punishment of those who do in fact violate the rights of others. This "punishment of evildoers" (1 Pet 2:14, NASB) is government's negative purpose. In one sense such punishment can be regarded as an end in itself since the wrongdoer deserves it as a matter of retributive justice (wrath and vengeance – 12:19; 13:4). But in another sense punishment of criminals, functioning as a deterrant, is just a means of preserving the general state of peace and tranquility.

Thus ideally, government exists "to make justice reign by checking evil and upholding good" (Godet, 445). This is the reason why God ordained it in the first place. And we should not overlook this point: God is the one who has established human government and decreed its purpose. He has not prescribed any one particular *form* of government; any type that can accomplish his declared purpose is acceptable. But government as such is God's creation and God's servant. It is not inherently evil, and there is no inherent conflict between being a good Christian and being an instrument of the state.

We may now ask, what are the requirements of a good citizen, according to this passage? First and most important is the obligation to acknowledge and submit to the authority of civil rulers and obey the various laws and regulations they impose on us in the interest of justice (13:1). We should remember that Paul's instruction here applies to the ideal situation. He does not go into the many "what if" circumstances that may require civil disobedience (see Cottrell, *Questions*, 2:33-35). Civil government is inherently good, but it can be corrupted just like any other institution. If it becomes perverted to the point that it requires us to do something contrary to God's revealed will, then "we must obey God rather than men" (Acts 5:29). Governmental authority is binding upon all citizens, but it is not absolute (see Stott, 342).

The second requirement of good citizens is that they must have an attitude of respect toward government and its representatives, insofar as the latter are functioning in their governmental roles as God's own servants (13:7b). A final requirement is that citizens must pay taxes to support those who devote themselves to the work of government, and to provide the equipment and programs that are necessary to uphold justice.

13:1 Everyone must submit himself to the governing authorities, ... This exhortation reflects the most fundamental aspect of the relation between government and its citizens. Paul deliberately uses the universal terminology, "everyone" (πᾶσα ψυχή, *pasa psychē*), to show that what he is about to say applies to all people and not just to Christians (contra Cranfield, 2:656). The word *psychē* is the Greek word for "soul"; thus the KJV translation, "every soul." Here it does not mean the inner spiritual nature as distinct from the body (as in Matt 10:28; Rev 6:9), but refers rather to the whole person, body and spirit (see 2:9). This is a common meaning of the term. "Everyone" or "every person" (NASB) is a good translation.

"Authorities" is the plural form of ἐξουσία (*exousia*), the common word for "right, power, authority." The concept of authority includes the right to tell others what to do, and the right to enforce compliance through the exercise of power. In the plural, as here, it refers to the individuals who bear and exercise such authority (❂ II:357).

The word "authorities" is modified by a term (ὑπερέχω, *hyperechō*) that means "to surpass, to rise above, to be in a high position" (see the KJV, "higher" powers). The main point of the modifier is to distinguish *governmental* authorities from other kinds of authorities, as will be explained below. The NIV's "*governing* authorities" makes this point very well.

The basic relation between citizens and government is here summed up in one word: "submit." This is the Greek word ὑποτάσσω (*hypotassō*), which along with its noun form ὑποταγή (*hypotagē*) is used over forty times in the NT. *Hypotassō* means "to place under, to subordinate, to arrange in order of rank" (❂ II:358). In our text it is in the middle voice, which usually means "to subject oneself, to submit, to obey." In the NT the term refers to an order or arrangement set in place by God himself, and the action in the middle voice refers to acquiescence to this divinely willed order.

One question is whether this word means or includes the concept of *obedience*. Some versions translate the word as "obey" (e.g., Phillips; TEV) or "be obedient" (Weymouth), and some exegetes use these terms in their explanation of the verse. Murray is on the right track when he says the term includes but is not limited to obedience. "It implies obedience when ordinances to be obeyed are in view," as is the case with submission to government, but also includes an *attitude* of "willing subservience" to governmental authority (2:148) (❂ II:359).

[F]or there is no authority except that which God has established. The authorities that exist have been established by God. Most if not all commentators take these statements as referring to individual rulers and governments, and thus to God's sovereign choice and appointment of all such authorities. Now, it is true that God is in complete control of all the nations and rulers of this world. He appoints and arranges specific governments by his special providence as his purposes call for it, and his omnipotence and omniscience enable him to control all others within his general providence and permissive will. This is a common OT theme: Prov 8:15-16; Isa 45:1-7; Jer 27:5-6; Dan 2:21,37-38; 4:17,25,32; 5:21. (See my discussion of this in *GRu*, 117-228.)

The fact remains that if we take Paul to be referring here to individual governments and rulers, then we have no choice but to say that God has hand-picked and personally put into office every blood-thirsty tyrant, every genocidal dictator, every anti-Christian regime, every crooked politician and judge, every sadistic sheriff and police officer, and every immoral and bribe-taking public official who now exists, has ever existed, and ever will exist. Most take it exactly this way. For example, Moo says this is "a universally applicable truth about the ultimate origin of rulers"; it refers to "specific governmental officials" (798).

It is easy to see how such an understanding can be used to justify every form of tyranny and to coerce citizens into blind obedience to the most degrading and antibiblical demands. It is no wonder that J.C. O'Neill has said of 13:1-7, "These seven verses have caused more unhappiness and misery in the Christian East and West than any other seven verses in the New Testament" (cited in Morris, 457, n. 1).

In my opinion, this whole approach to 13:1b is wrong. Paul is referring here not to individual governments and rulers at all, but rather to the various *forms* or *spheres* of authority which God has established, including governmental authority along with all the others. In fact, I suggest that vv. 1b-2 are a parenthesis in which Paul is asserting the general truth that *all* forms of authority have been established by God, and that rebellion against *any* of them is rebellion against God himself and deserves his condemnation. In other words, vv. 1b-2 express the general principle, of which v. 1a is a specific application.

The second clause in v. 1 ("For there is no authority except that which God has established") begins with "for" and states a *reason* why everyone must submit to the governing authorities. The reason is that all valid human authority comes from God himself. He is the only one who has absolute, inherent authority. When he delegates authority to others, it is in a real sense still his own authority. Thus, because governing authorities are wielding authority given to them by God, we should be submissive to them.

In this second clause the word "authority," which is singular, should not be taken as referring to civil authority as such, but to authority of whatever type, i.e., "For there is no authority *of any kind* . . . ." The last part of the clause literally says, "except by God," and means, "except that which has been established by God." Thus the entire clause reads thus: "For there is no authority of any kind except that which has been established by God."

The last clause in the verse is simply a positive restatement of the preceding one. "The authorities that exist" refers to all the existing authority relationships, including but not limited to governmental authority. All such authorities have been "established by God." The word for "establish" is *tassō*, which as explained above means "to ordain, to determine, to appoint." Since all authority ultimately comes from God, all existing authority-submission relationships have been ordained and arranged by God himself.

My contention, then, is that the word *exousia*, "authority," as used within the parenthesis (vv. 1b-2) means *authority in general*, authority in all of its forms. This is why *exousia* is modified by *hyperechō* in v. 1a — to specify *which* authority Paul has in mind (❧ II:361).

Thus by qualifying the *exousiais* in v. 1a as *governing* authorities, Paul makes it clear that he is talking about *that* kind of authority in particular, as distinct from the other kinds. The use of the expression οἱ ἄρχοντες (*hoi archontes*, "the rulers") in v. 3 marks Paul's postparenthetical return to his discussion of *governing* authorities in particular.

What other kinds of human authority has God ordained, in addition to governmental authorities? We can easily determine this by examining the way the NT uses *exousia* and other words denoting authority, along with their "natural correlatives" (Dunn, 2:761), i.e., words denoting submission and obedience (◐II:361, n. 51). Having done this we may list without further comment the following authority-submission relationships:

1. Man/woman   1 Cor 11:3,10 (*kephalē, exousia*)
   1 Tim 2:11 (*hypotagē*)
2. Husband/wife   1 Cor 14:34 (*hypotassō*)
   Eph 5:21-24 (*hypotassō, kephalē*)
   Col 3:18 (*hypotassō*)
   Titus 2:5 (*hypotasso*)
   1 Pet 3:1,5,6 (*hypotassō, hypakouō*)
3. Parents/children   Luke 2:51 (*hypotassō*)
   Eph 6:1 (*hypakouō*)
   Col 3:20 (*hypakouō*)
   1 Tim 3:4 (*hypotagē*)
4. Elders/congregation   Heb 13:17 (*peithō, hypeikō*)
   1 Pet 5:5 (*hypotassō*)
5. Master/slave   Eph 6:5 (*hypakouō*)
   Col 3:20 (*hypakouō*)
   Titus 2:9 (*hypotassō*)
   1 Pet 2:18 (*hypotassō*)

13:2 Consequently, he who rebels against the authority is rebelling against what God has instituted, . . . According to the interpretation I am offering here, this continues the parenthesis and thus refers to rebellion against authority (*exousia*) of all kinds, but with special contextual reference to rebellion against civil authority.

The NIV term "rebel" translates two different Greek words. One is ἀντιτάσσω (*antitassō*), which refers to an attitude that is the very opposite of *hypotassō*, "submit," v. 1. The other is ἀνθίστημι (*anthistēmi*), which literally means "to take a stand against." "He who rebels against the authority" refers to anyone who opposes authority as such, or to anyone who resists a particular kind of authority or any individual who exercises that authority.

The opening word, "consequently," indicates that a conclusion is being drawn from the latter part of v. 1. Since all human authority ultimately derives from God, those who rebel against authority are really rebelling against God himself. Paul says they are setting themselves against "what God has instituted," literally, "the ordinance of God" (NASB).

. . . and those who do so will bring judgment on themselves. "Judgment" is κρίμα (*krima*), which usually stands for a negative judgment, i.e., punishment or condemnation (see 2:2-3). The main point is that those who refuse to submit

Romans Part Five

to God's ordained authorities will bring his own divine condemnation upon themselves, to be meted out at the final judgment. Since in this context the main reference is to governmental authority, it is possible that the *krima* also refers to the punishment exacted upon wrongdoers by civil rulers acting as agents of God's wrath (v. 4).

13:3 For rulers hold no terror for those who do right, but for those who do wrong. After the parenthesis concerning authority in general, Paul now returns to the specific subject of *governing* authorities, calling them "rulers" (ἄρχων, *archōn*) to distinguish them from the other kinds of authority. He is answering the question, *why* should everyone submit to the governing authorities (v. 1a)? The parenthesis in vv. 1b-2 gives the most fundamental answer, i.e., because every authority including civil authority is ordained by God himself, and those who oppose authority of any kind must answer to God. Here he begins to give a more pragmatic answer: because (*gar*, "for") those who do not submit will be punished by the civil authorities themselves.

Paul presents this thought in terms of "terror," or fear (φόβος, *phobos*) in the sense of fear of punishment. He states the principle thus (lit.): rulers are not a (cause for) terror to the good work (i.e., good conduct), but to the evil (i.e., bad conduct). Since government exists to uphold justice by protecting the rights of its citizens, the evil deeds which should be forbidden by law and thus punished by rulers are those acts that violate the rights of others (e.g., disturbing the peace, theft of property, bodily harm).

Civil rulers have a divine mandate to punish evildoers; thus (ideally) anyone who contemplates breaking the law should be terrified by the thought of being caught and punished, and thus should decide to refrain from the evil deed. It is clear that fear of punishment is a proper motivation for obeying the laws of the land. This means that our legal systems should operate at least in part according to the principle of deterrence (see Deut 13:11; 17:13; 19:20; 21:21).

The obvious fact is that citizens have but two options in reference to civil laws: we may either obey them (vv. 3b-4a) or disobey them (v. 4b).

First Paul explains the relation between government and law-abiding citizens. **Do you want to be free from fear of the one in authority? Then do what is right and he will commend you.** Switching to second person singular, Paul addresses each of us in a more intimate way. After asking us if we want to live without being afraid of civil authority, he tells us how to do this: "Do what is right," or what is "good." Since in this context "good" and "evil" are defined in terms of respecting the rights of other people, "doing right" is simply living in such a way that your conduct does not interfere with the rights of others.

If we do this, we not only should be free from the fear of punishment, but should also actually be commended or praised by our civil authorities (see 1 Pet 2:14) (❂ II:364).

13:4 For he is God's servant to do you good. Paul is still speaking to "you" as the law-abiding citizen, the one who does what is right, whether Christian or non-Christian. He urges submission to the civil ruler on the basis of the fact that he is a servant or minister (διάκονος, *diakonos*) of God. "Of God" is in a position of emphasis in the Greek, i.e., he is a minister *of God!* The term *diakonos* was frequently used in secular Greek for civil officials and had no specific religious connotation (Dunn, 2:764; cf. "prime minister," "minister of defense"). Paul's point is that such "ministers" are not just servants of the people but are first of all servants *of God*. This is true because governmental authority as such has been established by God (v. 1); therefore anyone who functions as an enforcer of civil authority is serving God's purposes whether he acknowledges it or not (see Isa 45:1).

God's purpose is that the civil ruler exercise his authority "to you for good." I.e., he should do so for the benefit of you who want to live peaceably and abide by the laws of the land. Government exists not for its own sake, but for the sake of its citizens. It seeks their "good," which consists of the "civic well-being" which government provides by protecting us from unjust treatment from others (see 1 Tim 2:2).

Paul now switches gears and describes the relation between government and law*breakers*. He still uses direct address: **But if you do wrong, be afraid, . . .** The appeal is still to the fear of punishment, a simple statement of fact: **for he does not bear the sword for nothing.** In the NT the word "sword" is used quite frequently for a weapon of violence and death (Matt 10:34; 26:52,55; Luke 21:24; Rev 6:4; 13:10,14), including capital punishment (Acts 12:2; Rom 8:35; Heb 11:34,37). The form of the verb translated "bear" implies "repeated or habitual action," and thus can mean "wear" (Dunn, 2:764). In NT times the sword was worn as a symbol of governmental authority. To "wear the sword" meant to possess the right and the power to coerce obedience to law via threat of punishment, and to punish lawbreakers even unto death.

There can be no serious doubt that Paul is here sanctioning capital punishment as a legitimate instrument of the state (see Stott, 344-345). In view of the way the sword is so frequently associated with death by execution, says Murray, to deny that it includes capital punishment in 13:4 "would be so arbitrary as to bear upon its face prejudice contrary to the evidence" (2:152-153). Those who argue that the transformed life replaces wrath with grace miss Paul's point altogether. God's purpose has always been that individuals respond to personal attacks with grace and forgiveness (12:17-21), but at the same time the government's job has always been — and still is — to punish evildoers according to the demands of justice, including the death penalty (Gen 9:6). This is why the evildoer should fear: because the government authorities wield the power of life and death, and they do not wield it "for nothing," in vain, to no avail. It is not — or *should* not be — an empty threat.

He is God's servant, an agent of wrath to bring punishment on the wrong-

doer. Here for the second time the civil ruler is called God's servant, or "a minister of God." In the former instance (v. 4a) he is God's servant for the positive purpose of doing good for law-abiding citizens. Here he is God's servant for the negative purpose of bringing vengeance and wrath upon evildoers. *Both aspects of the government's task are equally valid and equally good.*

The NIV's weak translation "agent of wrath" obscures the force of Paul's language and its deliberate connection with 12:19. The NASB is literally accurate: the civil ruler is "an avenger who brings wrath upon the one who practices evil." The references in both verses to vengeance and wrath make the connection obvious. "Avenger" is ἔκδικος (*ekdikos*), a noun form of ἐκδικέω (*ekdikeō*), "take revenge" (12:19). "Wrath" (ὀργή, *orgē*) is the same in both verses.

The point is clear: punitive wrath and vengeance are forbidden to individuals, but are delegated by God to civil authorities. When Paul in 12:19 commands us as individuals to "leave room for God's wrath" and refers to God's dictum, "It is mine to avenge; I will repay," he is laying the foundation for ascribing these tasks to the government in 13:4. Stott is correct: "It is important to hold Romans 12:19 and 13:4 together" (345). Taken together they show that the government's wrath and vengeance toward evildoers are no less than God's own wrath and vengeance. As a penal force the government is God's agent, God's servant.

13:5 Therefore it is necessary to submit to the authorities, not only because of possible punishment but also because of conscience. "It is necessary" states our *obligation* to "submit" (*hypotassō* — see v. 1). Paul gives two reasons for such submission. One is pragmatic: "because of wrath." I.e., if we want to avoid the government's penalties, then we should obey its laws.

Fear of the government's punishment in itself, however, is not the only reason to avoid civil disobedience. If it were, this would leave us morally free to break the law (e.g., zoning, tax, and speeding regulations) as long as we were reasonably sure we would not get caught or as long as we were willing to pay the penalty if caught. But Paul adds a second reason why it is necessary to submit, i.e., "also because of conscience." This means that our obligation to obey civil laws is absolute and unqualified. We must do it just because God says so, just because it is right. I.e., we must do it not just for our own sake (to avoid punishment) but also "for the Lord's sake" (1 Pet 2:13), "out of a sense of obligation to God" (Murray, 2:154). This requirement is for all citizens as God's creatures, and not just for Christians.

We should remember that Paul is here setting forth the *ideal* relation between citizens and government; it is not his purpose to comment on situations where a particular government has perverted its God-given mandate to uphold justice in accordance with God's moral law. In other places the Bible allows — even requires — civil disobedience where obedience to a human law would require us to break a divine commandment (e.g., Acts 5:29; see Cottrell, *Questions*, 2:33-35).

13:6 This is also why you pay taxes, for the authorities are God's servants, who give their full time to governing. The first clause is not an imperative (contra the KJV); Paul is simply referring to paying taxes as a fact of life. His main point is to explain the *reason* why we pay taxes. What exactly is this reason? Some think he is referring back only to v. 5b, "because of conscience." I.e., you pay taxes in order to have a clear conscience. Others (correctly) think Paul is referring back to the general teaching of vv. 1-4, i.e., you pay taxes in order to support the government's divinely mandated program of protecting law-abiding citizens and punishing evildoers.

The latter view is supported by the second clause in the verse, which alludes to the civil ruler's task as set forth in vv. 1-4. Here the governmental authorities are again called "God's servants," though Paul uses λειτουργός (*leitourgos*) instead of *diakonos* (❂II:368). The religious nature of their service is again connoted by calling them servants *of God*.

Paul says we pay taxes because the authorities are servants of God who (literally) "devote themselves constantly to this very thing." "Give their full time to" (NIV) is a good translation of the verb here. But what is the meaning of "this very thing"? Not just collecting taxes, but the *governing* itself, i.e., the twofold purpose of government as set forth in vv. 1-4. The NIV interpretation ("to governing") is correct.

13:7 Give everyone what you owe him . . . , or "Render to all what is due them" (NASB). This *is* an imperative, and thus makes the payment of taxes (along with other things) a divine command, an obligation we owe not only to the government but also to God himself. The word for "give" is the same as in Mark 12:17, in Jesus' command to "*render* to Caesar the things that are Caesar's" (NASB). The similarity of the language and subject matter make it very likely that Paul is consciously thinking of Christ's teaching on this topic.

Because of the context it is probable that "everyone" here means "every governmental authority." The words for "give" and "owe" both include the connotation of obligation or debt. The idea is that, because of their position as servants of God and their purpose as ordained by God, civil authorities are *owed* certain things by their citizens; and as conscientious citizens we are obligated to give them these things.

"What you owe" is followed by four short phrases listing what citizens owe to their government: taxes, revenue, respect, and honor. Each phrase is governed by "what you owe" and has the same compact form, literally, e.g., "to the one taxes, taxes," i.e., "to the one [to whom you owe] taxes, [give him your] taxes." The NIV renders the phrases thus: **If you owe taxes, pay taxes; if revenue, then revenue; if respect, then respect; if honor, then honor.** Actually the Greek text does not make these obligations conditional ("if"). The sense is more of an imperative: "Pay taxes to the one to whom you owe taxes," etc.

Paul uses two different words to stress our obligation to pay taxes of all sorts, i.e., "taxes," φόρος (*phoros*), and "revenue," τέλος (*telos*) (❧ II:369). These commands to pay taxes clearly show that tax fraud is a sin, that refusing to pay taxes is an act of direct disobedience to God. This is true even of taxes levied by pagan governments such as Rome.

The other two things Paul says citizens owe to civil authorities are respect and honor. The word for "respect" is *phobos*. Most agree that it is used here in the sense of veneration or respect (see Eph 5:33; 1 Pet 2:18). It refers to "the respectful awe which is felt for one who has power in his hands" (SH, 368).

Paul says finally that "honor" should be paid to rulers. This is not greatly different from respect. One possibility is that respectful fear is internal, an attitude of the heart, while honor is the overt expression of respect toward its object. A complementary possibility is that the former is a constant attitude toward those in government simply because of the nature and divine origin of their roles as such while the latter is contingent upon the actual accomplishments of individuals.

F. THE RELATION BETWEEN LOVE AND LAW (13:8-10)

Paul cannot draw his discussion of Christian virtues to a close without returning to the most important virtue of all, namely, love (see 12:9-10). His main point is to show the relation between the love command and all other commands, which he does in two correlative statements: "Love is the fulfillment of the law" (vv. 8b,10b); and, all commandments "are summed up" in the rule of love (v. 9b).

The "law" here is not just the Law of Moses, contrary to the approach of many interpreters, but is the totality of the moral law as such, the sum total of all the commands that apply to those living in the New Testament era. In this context this "law" includes the very instructions Paul has been setting forth since 12:1. Since most of these have to do with interpersonal human relationships, Paul focuses here only on the second greatest commandment, the one enjoining neighbor-love.

After setting forth his definitive teaching that sinners are justified by faith apart from works of law (chs. 1-5), Paul knew that some would erroneously conclude that the principle of faith negates the necessity of obeying God's commands. Thus, beginning in 6:1, he shows that this is definitely not the case. Now, in view of the prominence given by Jesus himself to the command of love (Matt 22:34-40; Mark 12:28-34; Luke 10:25-28; John 13:34-35), Paul knows that some might erroneously conclude that the principle of love makes all law obsolete. Thus in this brief paragraph he shows that this is not the case either.

It is true that the love command is special. As Godet says, "Love is not in the law a commandment *side by side* with all the rest; it is itself the essence of the law" (446). It is the *general* commandment; all the others are just the specific ways in which it is expressed. To truly love one's neighbor is to keep these other commandments.

13:8 Let no debt remain outstanding, except the continuing debt to love one another, . . . The concept of debt or obligation is the bridge between this and the previous paragraph. In v. 7 Paul says, "Give everyone what you owe him"; "what you owe" is the noun *opheilē*. He begins this verse with the verb ὀφείλω (*opheilō*, "to owe, to be indebted, to be obligated"). The result sounds almost like a contradiction. "Pay what you owe," and (lit.) "Owe nothing to anyone" (NASB).

Now, it is obvious that v. 7 is talking not about obligations entered into voluntarily, but about duties inherent in the relation between citizens and government. We have no choice about such "debts." Does v. 8a, then, forbid voluntarily entering into debt? Does it rule out car loans, house mortgages, and credit cards? No, this is not the point. Other Scriptures show that borrowing and lending on reasonable terms (e.g., no interest charged to the poor) are not prohibited; see Exod 22:25; Lev 25:35-37; Ps 37:26; Matt 5:42; Luke 6:35. The point rather is that when you enter into a loan agreement, the payments must be submitted promptly and honestly and in accordance with the terms of the contract. The NIV captures the intent of the command quite well.

The command not to owe anyone anything is actually just a way of leading into the main commandment, "to love one another." By saying we should have no unpaid debts *except* to love one another, Paul says that love itself is a *debt*, in the sense of a moral or spiritual obligation; he is also saying that (unlike other debts) it can never be completely paid off (● II:371).

The love of which Paul speaks is *agapē*; see 12:9 above.

What is the scope of "one another"? Some say this expression in Paul's writings always refers to one's fellow Christians, which must be the primary application here. However, they point out that the rest of the paragraph uses universal language ("his fellowman," 8b; "your neighbor," 9-10), which means that our debt of love ultimately extends to all human beings (Murray, 2:159-160; Moo, 813). It is generally agreed that the scope is unlimited. Even in this context personal enemies (12:14,17-21) and government officials (13:1-7) would seem to be included. See Matt 5:44; Luke 10:25-37; Gal 6:10.

It is necessary to love one another, **for he who loves his fellowman has fulfilled the law.** "His fellowman" is literally just "the other" (● II:372). Loving "the other" is open-ended; Paul does not specify any particular "other." As Morris says, it refers to "any other person whatever" with whom we have anything at all to do (468).

"Law" here is not the Mosaic Law as such, but simply the moral law as it governs interpersonal relationships, in whatever form one may possess it (see Lard, 403; Lenski, 798).

How does neighbor-love fulfill the law? It is absolutely not the case that love fulfills the law by taking its place and making it unnecessary (● II:372). How then does it do this? We can sum it up thus, that love fulfills *the requirements of* the law. The one who loves *will* do the things required by all the other commandments regarding interpersonal relationships because these other commandments are simply the contents of love, or the verbalization of the various expressions of love. This applies even to negative commandments such as those in v. 9a; the one who loves will *not* do such things because they are the very opposite of love.

One can obey the commands outwardly without love, in which case the commands are not fully obeyed (i.e., fulfilled); but one cannot love the other without obeying the commandments and thus fulfilling the law.

13:9 The commandments, "Do not commit adultery," "Do not murder," "Do not steal," "Do not covet," and whatever other commandment there may be, are summed up in this one rule: "Love your neighbor as yourself." This verse is intended to explain v. 8b. The commandments in v. 9a are *examples* of the law Paul has in mind, and are not intended to be an exhaustive list, as v. 9b shows. These are, of course, four of the "ten commandments," nos. 6, 7, 8, and 10. They are listed in the order of the LXX in Deut 5:17-21. Though originally appearing in the Law of Moses, they are not limited to that particular law code. Paul condemned the Gentiles for covetous desires (ἐπιθυμία, *epithymia*, 1:24) and murder (1:29). These commands are all repeated as binding on people today: no adultery (Jas 2:11; 1 Cor 6:9; Heb 13:4), no murder (Jas 2:11; 4:2; Rev 9:21; 21:8; 22:15), no stealing (Eph 4:28; 1 Cor 6:10; Titus 2:10), and no covetousness (Col 3:5; 1 Tim 6:9; Jas 4:2; 1 Pet 2:11; 4:3).

The actions represented in these and other such commands are simply the opposite of love and are prohibited for that very reason. To deride and disparage such commands because they are negative in form ("Thou shalt not . . .") demonstrates a failure to understand the nature of love. True love does demand positive action (1 Cor 13:4a,6b,7), but just as validly rules out nonloving deeds and attitudes (1 Cor 13:4b-6a).

Paul's reference to "whatever other commandment there may be" shows these four to be just a few examples to which many more could be added, from both the Law of Moses and the NT revelation. He seems to have in mind just those commands that cover interpersonal relationships, though. These are all included in the "law" in v. 8b.

All such commands, he says, are summed up in the one rule or command, "Love your neighbor as yourself." This is not an exclusively NT command, being taken directly from Lev 19:18; but Jesus identified it as one of the two greatest of all commands (Matt 22:34-40) and declared mutual love to be the identifying mark of his disciples (John 13:34-35). See Matt 5:43; 19:19; Gal 5:14; Jas 2:8.

All other commands, says Paul, are "summed up" in this one rule. The word for "summed up" is used in the NT only here and in Eph 1:10. Literally it means "to bring together under one head," or (in literary terms) under one heading. I.e., the love commandment is the category heading, and all the other commands are listed under love as part of it or expressions of it. This helps to explain how these other commands ("the law") are fulfilled by love.

In Lev 19:18 "neighbor" probably meant one's fellow Israelite (see "one of your people," v. 18a); but by NT times the Jews themselves had begun to give it a wider meaning (see Dunn, 2:779-780), and Christ's illustrative parable of the Good Samaritan definitely gives it a universal scope (Luke 10:25-37). MacArthur rightly defines one's neighbor as "anyone with whom we have contact, especially if he is in need" (2:251).

Does this command justify self-love ("Love your neighbor *as yourself*")? Yes, there is nothing wrong with self-love as long as it is of the *agapē* type (see Eph 5:28-29). As Murray correctly points out, not all self-love is *selfish* love (2:163). We can and must have the same kind of concern for our basic well-being, including our temporal health and our eternal salvation, as God does. Not to care about ourselves in this sense is to deny God's own purposes for us.

The main point, though, is not self-love, however pure, but a love that embodies an equally deep concern for the well-being of others.

13:10 Love does no harm to its neighbor. Therefore love is the fulfillment of the law. This verse basically recapitulates the point of the paragraph. "Love does no harm" is simply the converse of "Love seeks the neighbor's well-being." It sums up the essence of the negative commands given in v. 9a. Adultery, murder, theft, and covetousness all cause great harm to other people. Thus if we truly love others, we will not do these or any other harmful things.

G. WALKING IN THE LIGHT (13:11-14)

This main section ends as it began, with an appeal to believers to lead the sanctified life. In 12:1-2 the appeal is based upon the mercies of God, which include his saving work *for* us through Jesus Christ, and his saving work *in* us in justification and regeneration, the latter being specifically cited ("by the renewing of your mind," 12:2). In 13:11-14 the appeal is based more on the reality of an already-accomplished, external, cosmic change, i.e., the transition from the old age (old creation) to the eschatological new age (new creation).

This brief paragraph abounds in temporal references to these contrasting ages and our relationship to them: "the present time," "the hour," "salvation is nearer," "the night," "the day," "darkness," "light," "the daytime." The following chart will prepare us for a brief discussion of the significance of these terms:

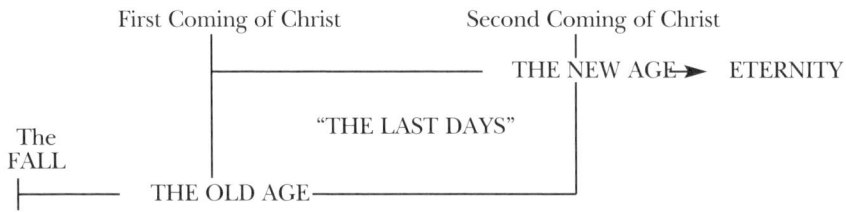

In our text the "old age" is the "night," the time of "darkness." It is the sphere of the old, fallen creation. It is the same as "this world" in 12:2, and "this present evil age" in Gal 1:4. Christ's first coming, in particular his death and resurrection, brought judgment (*krisis*) upon this world (John 12:31). Its end is certain. At the time of the Second Coming it will be burned up and replaced by "new heavens and a new earth" (2 Pet 3:10-13, NASB). Between the first coming and the second coming of Christ, the status of this old age resembles that of a murderer who has been condemned to death. They are both existing between the time of sentencing and the time of execution.

What is called the "new age" on our chart is in our text the "day," the time of "light." It is the sphere of the new, redeemed creation, which is an eschatological reality that has already begun. It was inaugurated by the death and resurrection of Jesus, and now exists in embryo form alongside the old age. Its reality consists mainly in the presence of the Holy Spirit, who is a foretaste and pledge of the future fullness of the new age. This "day" will unfold in its fullness at the Second Coming, which will bring into being our resurrection bodies, the new heavens and new earth, and eternal life.

The "last days" on the chart is the church age, the period when the old age and the new age coexist temporarily side by side. As Stott says, "At present the two ages overlap" (351). The "last days" concept is well established in Scripture; see Acts 2:17; 2 Tim 3:1; Heb 1:2; 1 Pet 1:20; 2 Pet 3:3; 1 John 2:18; Jude 1:18. The phrase has a double meaning. It refers at the same time to the final period of the old age and to the initial period of the new age. With reference to the former meaning, these "last days" are indeed the last stage of the old creation; the very next step in God's plan is the Second Coming itself. This is one sense in which we can say that the Second Coming is "near," regardless of the actual temporal length of the "last days."

"Understanding the present time" (13:11) simply means understanding this scheme and its terminology, and where we are in the scheme. "The hour" in 13:11 refers to the opportune time for the Christian to recognize that he has experienced his own personal transition from the old age to the new age (John 5:24; 2 Cor 5:17). That is, it is time to recognize that we are already, now, living in the *eschaton*, and should thus awaken from our apathetic indifference and begin to live the kind of life that belongs to the light of day.

This section thus is a call for Christians to live the lifestyle that is appropriate to the new age. We are a part of that age (vv. 11-12a); therefore ("so") we should live like it (vv. 12b-14).

Most agree that Paul presents this old-age-to-new-age transition in order to motivate Christians to live a holy life. This is called the "eschatological motivation of Christian obedience," i.e., an "appeal to eschatology as an incentive to moral earnestness" (Cranfield, 2:679-680).

Most interpret Paul as basing this appeal on *future* eschatology. I.e., because

Christ's coming is "near," we must devote ourselves to holy living in order to be prepared for him when he returns (❂II:377). I agree that Paul's appeal is eschatological, but I believe his emphasis is not so much on future eschatology as on *present* eschatology. I.e., his exhortation to holy living is based not on something that is yet to come, but on the eschatological reality of the new age that has *already begun*. He does not say, "Live right, so that you will be ready for Christ's return and so you will be rewarded in heaven." He says rather, "Live right, because this alone is consistent with the new age which was inaugurated by Christ's death and resurrection, and in which you are already participating by virtue of your conversion." The *eschaton* has already begun and we are a part of it; therefore our lifestyle must be consistent with it.

13:11 And do this, understanding the present time. "This" could be just the preceding paragraph about neighbor-love (Murray, 2:165), or more likely the entire section on holy living, chs. 12–13 (Cranfield, 2:680; Moo, 820). The verb "do" is supplied; the Greek simply has the idiomatic "And this." The NIV and a few other translations make it an imperative by adding "do," which probably captures the meaning best (Fitzmyer, 682; Moo, 819).

This simple phrase gathers together "all the Apostle has just been enjoining" (Lard, 407) and introduces the main point of the paragraph, i.e., the immediate motivation for doing all these things. We should do them, he says, because we understand the significance of the time in which we live. "Time" is καιρός (*kairos*), which refers not to clock time or a calendar date, but to an era or epoch of a certain character or significance, e.g., a welcome time, a critical time, an opportune time, the right moment (BAGD, 395). As we saw in the introduction above, the time in which Christians live is "the last days," the epoch immediately preceding our Lord's return. Paul's point is that we should be all the more diligent in living the transformed life in view of the nature of the time in which we live.

The hour has come for you to wake up from your slumber, because our salvation is nearer now than when we first believed. These clauses explain the nature of the *kairos* in more detail. "The hour has come" (literally, "the hour is now," or "it is already the hour") emphasizes the urgency of the situation. You know, says Paul, that the moment for action has arrived. Specifically, it is time to wake up, to get out of bed, and to apply yourselves to the business of holy living as if there were no tomorrow.

The metaphor of sleep is used in the NT to represent a state of inattention and unpreparedness (Matt 25:1-13; Mark 13:35-37; Rev 16:15). It also stands for a state of spiritual apathy, lukewarmness, complacency, and indifference, in short, "a lethargic Christian life" (Morris, 471; see Eph 5:14-16; 1 Thess 5:4-8; Rev 3:2-3). Both of these ideas are present here, especially the latter.

The urgency of the time — the fact that "our salvation is nearer now than when we first believed" — is the reason why we should awake from our slumber. Paul refers again to the eschatological *now*, i.e., the "last days," and to the nearness of the end. Every passing day brings us closer to our salvation. This is true, of course, whether we are thinking of the moment of our death (MP, 519-520) or the Second Coming of Christ (Murray, 2:165; Moo, 822; see Titus 2:11-13). The latter is probably the case, since "our salvation" most likely refers to our full and final salvation (5:9-10; 8:23; 1 Thess 5:8-9; 1 Pet 1:5), our state of glorification. We receive such salvation not at our death, but at the time of the Second Coming (Hendriksen, 2:445) (❂ II:379).

13:12 The night is nearly over; the day is almost here. This contrast between night and day is a key concept. "Night" is a negative image, being associated with indifferent sleep (v. 11), darkness (v. 12b), and evil deeds (v. 13). "Day" is a positive image, representing light (v. 12b) and decent living (v. 13). Here they stand for the two eras of salvation history. "Night" is the *old* age, "this present evil age" (Gal 1:4), the sphere of the old creation as it stands under God's curse and Satan's dominion. "Day" is the *new* age, the sphere of the new creation, the eschatological age, the kingdom age, the era of truth and power and freedom in the Holy Spirit.

As explained in the introduction, these two ages overlap in what are called "the last days." The old age (the "night") still exists and will exist until the Second Coming, but its power is broken and it is "nearly over," "far spent" (KJV), or "almost gone" (NASB). The new age (the "day") will not fully arrive until the Second Coming; but it has already been inaugurated by the saving death and resurrection of Jesus, and its light is already shining over the horizon (1 John 2:8; Rev 22:16).

A serious question arises in reference to Paul's assertion that this "day" is "almost here" (literally, "has drawn near"). If this "day" will begin in its fullness only at the Second Coming of Christ, in what sense can Paul say, just decades after the first coming, that it "has drawn near"? Some have taken this reference to the nearness of the day as an indication that Paul and other early Christians believed Christ would return in their own generation. Since this did not happen, they were obviously wrong — according to this view.

If we believe that Paul's inspired writing cannot be wrong (as I do), then how may we explain the *nearness* of the Second Coming, especially from the perspective of the first century, since almost 2,000 years have passed since then? There are three main points. First, the Second Coming was near, even then, in the sense that its spiritual power had already been unleashed via Christ's death and resurrection, and Christians had already begun to taste of its power and glory (2 Cor 1:22; Eph 1:13-14; Heb 6:4-5), as we still do today. Second, Christ's first coming and the redemptive events associated with it began the final stage of history ("the last days") leading up to the Second Coming, and left nothing more to be accomplished but the Second Coming itself. Thus the latter is near in the sense that it is "the next great epochal event" (Murray, 2:168), whether the actual lapse of time between the two comings is 20, 200, or 2,000 years. Third, God's way of counting time is not necessarily the same as ours. "But do not forget this one thing, dear friends: With the Lord a day is like a thousand years, and a thousand years are like a day. The Lord is not slow in keeping his promise, as some understand slowness" (2 Pet 3:8-9a; see Hendriksen, 2:446-447).

In view of these considerations, we should never say, "Christ *is* coming soon"; but we should always think and say, "Christ *may be* coming soon." The final day is "always imminent — its coming certain, its time incalculable" (Moo, 822). See Matt 24:36; Acts 1:7; 1 Thess 5:1-2.

So let us put aside the deeds of darkness and put on the armor of light. Paul now turns from the eschatological presence of the new age (vv. 11-12a) to the consequent necessity of living the kind of life that is consistent with it. The rest of this paragraph is governed by the word "so" (οὖν, *oun*, "therefore"). I.e., because we have in fact experienced the transition from the age of night to the newly dawning day (Acts 26:18; 1 Pet 2:9b), let us live like it.

The contrast between darkness and light is parallel to that between night and day (v. 12a). "Darkness" relates to the old, evil age; "light" is characteristic of this new age of salvation in Christ.

"Deeds of darkness" are evil, sinful deeds (e.g., v. 13), "the deeds that are done under the cover of night" (Fitzmyer, 683), "the sort of things which were frequently indulged in during the night in a pagan city" (Cranfield, 2:686). The word for "put aside" was often used for taking off garments. It was used figuratively for getting rid of or laying aside sinful deeds (Eph 4:22,25; Col 3:8; Heb 12:1; Jas 1:21; 1 Pet 2:1).

The "armor of light" is equivalent to the "full armor of God" in Eph 6:13-17 (see 1 Thess 5:8). The word for "armor" is ὅπλον (*hoplon*), which can mean either "an instrument" in general (6:13), or "a weapon" in particular. The military connotation seems to be intended here. The implication is that the Christian life is a state of spiritual warfare against the forces of evil; thus we must be dressed for battle so that we may fight off and defeat the lingering enemies of the night.

Our battle gear is called the armor of *light* because it consists largely of truth (Eph 6:14a) and holiness (Eph 6:14b; 1 Thess 5:8), which are the principal forms of light associated with God. Truth and holiness are the main weapons with which we are able to defeat the forces of darkness. The word for "put on" is used for putting on garments; in the NT it is often used in the figurative sense of incorporating works of holiness into one's character and lifestyle (13:14; Eph 4:24; 6:11,14; Col 3:12; 1 Thess 5:8).

The message is clear: we as Christians have passed from the sphere of darkness and death into the sphere of light and life. Therefore we must at once cast away from us everything associated with darkness and evil, and wrap ourselves completely and exclusively in the lifestyle of moral purity and truth (Eph 5:8-9).

13:13 Let us behave decently, as in the daytime, ... This basically says the same thing as v. 12b; it is repeated to set up the examples of "deeds of darkness" in v. 13b. "Behave" is the word περιπατέω (*peripateō*), which literally means "to walk around" but is often used figuratively for daily conduct (e.g., 6:4; 8:4; 14:15). "Decently" refers to conduct that "would generally be regarded as decent, proper, presentable in responsible society" (Dunn, 2:789). "As in the daytime" refers to the fact that in Christ we have already passed from darkness to light and are therefore expected to "walk in the light, as he is in the light" (1 John 1:7).

The rest of this verse gives examples of the dark deeds that must be abandoned if we are serious about walking in the light: **... not in orgies and drunkenness, not in sexual immorality and debauchery, not in dissension and jealousy.** Though six specific sins are mentioned, they clearly are meant to be taken as three related pairs, with each pair referring to things closely associated with each other.

The first works of darkness are "orgies and drunkenness," or drunken revelry. The former term (κῶμος, *kōmos*) (❂ II:382) came to have the negative connotation of excessive, uninhibited revelry, carousing, wild partying, or boisterous brawls and riots. Since such revelry usually was accompanied by excessive drinking, Paul couples with it a word for drunkenness (μέθη, *methē*), as in Gal 5:21.

The second pair is "sexual immorality and debauchery." The former is the word κοίτη (*koitē*), which literally means "bed," but was used as a euphemism for sexual intercourse, either in a good sense (Heb 13:4) or bad (as here). As used here in the plural it refers to sexual promiscuity, sexual excesses, and harlotries. The second word (ἀσέλγεια, *aselgeia*) refers to sensual excesses of all kinds, but especially sexual excess, lewdness, licentiousness, or "uninhibited and unabashed lasciviousness" (MacArthur, 2:267). These words picture a lifestyle of unrestrained sexual promiscuity.

The final pair of words refers to sins of a different kind, but deeds of darkness nevertheless. "Dissension" is ἔρις (*eris*), the same word translated "strife" in 1:29. It refers to a quarrelsome disposition, a spirit of contention and bickering. This sin pairs up well with jealousy (ζῆλος, *zēlos*), since the latter is often the source of the former. *Zēlos* can mean "zeal" in a good or neutral sense (10:2), but is usually used in the negative sense of envy or jealousy, or "the various forms of venomous and hateful feelings leading to discord" (MP, 521) (❂ II:383).

Many other deeds of darkness could be added to these examples. What is striking is that the ones chosen here are certainly some of the ugliest and most detestable sins we can imagine, yet Paul deems it necessary to warn *Christians* not to engage in them! This suggests that even Christians are not completely immune to temptation regarding such behavior.

13:14 Rather, clothe yourselves with the Lord Jesus Christ, and do not think about how to gratify the desires of the sinful nature. Paul closes this section with a positive and a negative exhortation, which together sum up the moral instruction presented in it. "Clothe yourselves" is the same word translated "put on" in v. 12b, where the "clothing" was the "armor of light" or Christian virtues in general. Here the clothing is a person, the Lord Jesus Christ. As Christians we have already been clothed with Christ in one sense (Gal 3:27). When we were immersed into Christ, we received the robe of his own righteousness (Isa 61:10; Phil 3:9), i.e., his blood shed in payment of the penalty for our sins. We have been "wearing" Christ in this sense from the moment of our baptism, and this has been the basis for our continuing justification before God.

But in this verse Paul *exhorts* Christians to "put on Christ," implying a reference to something not yet completed. Thus it is generally agreed that he must be using this metaphor in a sense different from Gal 3:27, i.e., that here he is talking about *sanctification* rather than justification, which is what we would expect in this context. Thus "putting on Christ" is here equivalent to being transformed by the renewing of our minds (12:2). It is the same as putting on "the new self," which is the process of the re-creation of the image of God within us (Eph 4:24; Col 3:10). Thus to clothe ourselves with Christ in this sense means to gird ourselves outwardly and inwardly with the same holy character exhibited by the sinless Christ during his earthly sojourn.

The concluding negative exhortation is parallel in meaning to "put aside the deeds of darkness" (v. 12b), such as those named in v. 13. "Do not think about how to gratify" translates words that literally mean "take no forethought for," or "make no provision for." I.e., we should not try to hold on to certain sins, planning our lives and our daily schedules in such a way that we have time and opportunity to indulge ourselves in them (see Ps 36:1-4).

"Desires" (ἐπιθυμία, *epithymia*) here means sinful desires or "lusts" (NASB), as in 1:24 and 6:12. "The sinful nature" is literally "the flesh" (σάρξ, *sarx*). As explained earlier (❁I:373-377), I believe that faithful exegesis leads us to reject the prevalent understanding of *sarx* as "sinful nature" (contra the NIV), and see it as referring to the unredeemed physical body. Thus, what the NIV calls "the desires of the sinful nature" here are the same as the lusts or "evil desires" of the "mortal body" in 6:12 (❁I:401-402). Lenski is on the right track when he says it is "the body we all have, through which so much sin tries to invade us" (809).

This verse in no way prohibits us from taking care and forethought for the health and well-being of our bodies (see the reference to self-love in 13:9). It is concerned only with those propensities toward sin that still lurk without our unredeemed bodies. All in all, in attending to the needs of the body, we must be careful to distinguish its genuine needs from its sinful lusts. Thus we "must, as it were, go on tiptoe, and be exercised with extreme caution, so as not to waken in us those slumbering dogs of lust which, if aroused, will tear our spiritual life to pieces" (MP, 523).

II. CHRISTIAN LIBERTY IN MATTERS OF OPINION (14:1–15:13)

In this main section (12:1–15:13) the general subject is "living the sanctified life." A Christian's sanctified life is basically divided into two areas, corresponding to the two parts of the slogan, "Where Scripture speaks, we speak; where Scripture is silent, we are silent." The former is the area of the Christian life governed by God's law, i.e., the specific commandments and general principles he has spoken to us through his inspired apostles and prophets in the pages of the Bible. Such are the "good, pleasing and perfect" will of God (12:2), which was the subject of the previous subsection (12:1–13:14). In matters where God has spoken, we are not free to decide what is right and what is wrong; we are free only in the sense of having the free will to choose whether to obey God's law or not.

In this subsection (14:1–15:13), Paul turns his attention to areas of Christian living corresponding to the second part of the slogan, i.e., matters upon which Scripture is silent. These are the issues and aspects of our daily life that are not addressed by any "Thus saith the Lord." That Scripture is silent about these things means that it neither commands (requires) them nor forbids them. They are called the "adiaphora," i.e., "things that make no difference," or matters of indifference. They are also called "matters of opinion," referring to issues for which opposite viewpoints or opinions are equally valid (❖ II:385, n. 75).

Here is where the expression "Christian liberty" applies. In matters of opinion individual Christians are free to choose whichever course of action seems best to them, whether it is a mere preference or a matter of conscience. In this connection it is important to remember that Christians are *not* free from law as such (see chs. 6–8). Paul's point here is not "the problem of law versus freedom" (contra Fitzmyer, 687), as if the Christian must choose between law and freedom. It is not a question of either/or, but both/and. Some aspects of the Christian life are governed by law; some rightly fall under the heading of freedom of opinion. Paul is discussing the latter category here.

Paul's point here is not to give us a complete list of those things which are matters of opinion and therefore of Christian liberty, though he does cite three issues as examples: eating meat (14:2-3,6,14-15,20,23), keeping special days (14:5-6), and drinking wine (14:21). His point is to tell us how to manage our Christian liberty, and to warn us not to sin against each other in these matters. The implication is rather ironic if not paradoxical, i.e., that how we use our *liberty* is a matter of *law*!

Paul indicates that there are two basic approaches to matters of opinion: the way of the *weak* and the way of the *strong* (14:1; 15:1). The weak are those who tend to include too much under the heading of law. Because of their weak understanding of Scripture, they treat issues that are actually matters of opinion as if they were matters of law. This group is especially warned against the sin of condemning those who do not agree with them on such issues (14:3,10). By implication, i.e., by the very fact that they are called "weak," they are encouraged to pursue a more mature approach to these matters.

The strong, on the other hand, are those who better understand how to distinguish matters of opinion from matters of law. This is not a question of having a stronger faith in Christ, nor is it a question of having a better or more sophisticated view of biblical authority. Both the strong and the weak may be in agreement on these points. Rather it is a question of hermeneutics, or how to interpret and apply God's revealed will. The hermeneutical issues that are especially relevant here are the nature of the distinction between the covenants, the implications of biblical silence, how to make proper inferences from general principles, and how to distinguish between eternal principles and cultural expressions thereof. In general, the strong are those who have a better grasp of these points, and therefore are able to distinguish which elements of God's revealed will are binding as law upon Christians throughout the church age, and which are not. Because of this better understanding, the strong are able to do certain things (e.g., eat meat) with a clear, biblically informed conscience, whereas weak Christians doing the same things would be violating their consciences.

Although the strong have a better understanding of matters of opinion than do the weak, the former are not without responsibilities. First, they are commanded to accept the weak without looking down on them for their weakness (14:1-3,10). Second, they must be ready to sacrifice their freedom if it appears that the exercise of it could become a stumbling block to the weak (14:13-15,21).

It is interesting that Paul condemns neither the weak nor the strong as such. Though he clearly considers himself to be one of the strong (15:1), he nevertheless "expresses himself in a very gentle and subdued manner" toward the weak (Hendriksen, 2:455). This indicates that the weak brethren, unlike the Judaizers in Galatia, were not attempting to impose their convictions upon others as conditions for salvation. I.e., the issue between the weak and the strong is not justification by faith as such, but what truly constitutes the sanctified life.

It is generally agreed that the Roman congregation was experiencing a conflict between weak and strong Christians, and that Paul had heard about it and was thus specifically addressing the situation here. There is no general agreement, however, as to the exact nature of the problem and the exact identity of the weak. The most widely accepted view is that the weak brethren were mainly some converted Jews, and perhaps some converted God-fearing Gentiles who had come under Jewish influence, who were unable to let go of certain crucial aspects of OT ceremonial law, especially the rules regarding diet and special days.

Another major approach is simply to say that we cannot be sure who the weak Christians were, and that they probably came from not just one but several backgrounds. Some converted Jews were probably included, but all of

Paul's references to the weak do not neatly apply to this group. Also, the teaching here is similar to 1 Cor 8:1-13; 10:23-33, where the weak were converted pagans who could no longer conscientiously eat meat that had been offered to idols. Though Paul does not specifically mention this problem in Romans, a similar situation probably existed in the Roman church, thus accounting for the vegetarianism mentioned in 14:2. I believe this latter approach helps us to explain more of the data more reasonably.

In any case it is not crucial that we know the exact identity of the weak in Rome. The teaching is clear enough and general enough to be applied to similar problems regarding Christian liberty, whether it be in the first or twenty-first century. In fact, we must not think that Paul's treatment of this subject was solely occasioned by a problem in Rome, and that it has no inherent connection with his overall topic. As we saw at the beginning of this introduction, instruction on how to handle matters of silence follows naturally and logically upon the section dealing with issues governed by God's law.

In this section Paul first speaks to both the strong and the weak and instructs them not to sit in judgment upon one another (14:1-12). He then addresses the strong in particular, admonishing them to respect the conscience of the weak and not to do anything that would cause the latter to go against their own convictions (14:13-23). Finally he urges all Christians to live in unity and peace with one another (15:1-13).

A. DO NOT JUDGE OTHERS IN MATTERS OF OPINION (14:1-12)

As Morris observes, there will always be differences within the church, since "Christians are not clones" (476). When it comes to matters of opinion, however, these differences will not lead to divisions unless we perversely allow them to do so. Paul now tells us how we can have acceptable differences without divisions, namely, by not sitting in judgment upon other Christians who do not agree with us on specific matters of opinion.

Paul begins this paragraph by admonishing us to accept in full fellowship and unity all whom God has accepted (vv. 1-3). He then reminds us that we are all servants of the same Lord, and we all answer to our Lord rather than to each other (vv. 4-9). He concludes by assuring us that a final judgment will occur and that each of us will indeed be judged by God (vv. 10-12).

1. We Should Accept All Whom God Has Accepted (14:1-3)

14:1 Accept him whose faith is weak, without passing judgment on disputable matters. Precisely what Paul means by "faith" in this and the next verse is not easy to determine. It may help to recall that faith has two basic elements, assent and trust (see ❂I:107-108). Saving faith includes "believing that" the facts of the gospel are true, and "believing in" or trusting specifically in Jesus for one's salvation.

Some scholars locate the weakness in the *trust* element of faith. Dunn says that "to be 'weak in faith' is to fail to trust God completely and without qualification." The weak Christians in Rome were not trusting in God alone, but trusting "in God *plus* dietary and festival laws" (2:798). What was at stake, then, was the very principle of justification by faith apart from works of law.

I disagree with this approach, since nowhere in this section does Paul relate this problem to justification by faith as such. The emphasis is not on trusting in Jesus as Savior, but on conscientious submission to him as Lord (vv. 4-9). Also, if this weakness were somehow a challenge to justification by faith, we would expect Paul to vigorously expose and condemn it as such; but he does not do this.

The problem, then, would seem to be related to the *assent* element of faith. Assent is that act by which the mind or intellect acknowledges the truth of a statement. I.e., it means believing the content of the Christian faith, or accepting the truth of "the faith that was once for all entrusted to the saints" (Jude 3). This is how some understand "faith" here. In v. 1 it actually has the article, "*the* faith." Thus Lenski says the "weak in faith" are those who do not understand and thus do not accept (assent to) what the Christian faith teaches. This does not mean they are doubting the saving facts of the gospel, but simply are failing to comprehend "what Christian doctrine involves in regard to food, observance of days, etc." (814). (See MacArthur, 2:275.)

A similar approach says that "weak in faith" means a failure to understand all the implications of believing in Jesus as Savior. According to Moo, Paul is not saying that these weak brethren have a faulty trust in Jesus. "Rather, he is criticizing them for lack of insight into some of the implications of their faith" (836; see Morris, 477). "Weak in faith" means they lack the assurance that their faith permits them to do certain things, as Cranfield puts it (2:700).

This understanding of "weak in faith" is consistent with Paul's similar teaching in 1 Cor 8:7-12; 9:22, where the weakness is located in the conscience and consists in a *lack of knowledge* about the true nature of God and idols (❧ II:390).

Paul does not specifically address this command to "the strong"; this term is not used until 15:1. He just addresses it to the church in general, which suggests that "the weak" were a minority in the congregation. To "accept" the weak brother means not just to formally receive him into church membership, but to warmly welcome him into one's heart in the spirit of affection and true fellowship. For other uses of the same verb see John 14:3; Phlm 17.

The last part of this verse is quite difficult. Its structure tells us that Paul is laying down a qualification as to the *motive* for accepting the weak brother into close fellowship. It begins with the words μὴ εἰς (*mē eis*), literally, "not unto." The preposition "unto" denotes purpose. The NASB rightly translates this as "but not for the purpose of." The next word (the object of the preposition) is διακρίσις (*diakrisis*), which means "decision, judgment, quarrel, dispute." The NIV rendering, "passing judgment," is good.

The last word in the verse is διαλογισμός (*dialogismos*), which basically means "a thought, an opinion," and can mean "a doubt, a dispute." The best translation in this context is simply "opinions," which is after all the subject of the whole section. The NASB says it best: "but not for the purpose of passing judgment on his opinions." I.e., accept the weak brother as one of the group, but not just so you can stand in judgment upon him and pick him apart for his sincere but faulty convictions about practices that are neither required nor forbidden in themselves.

What Paul is trying to eliminate through this qualification, says Dunn, is a situation where a "strong" majority welcomes weak brethren simply as an opportunity to debate the disputed issues and settle them in their own favor (2:798). The implication, he says, is that a congregation "should be able to embrace divergent views and practices without a feeling that they must be resolved or that a common mind must be achieved on every point of disagreement" (2:799). This applies, of course, only to things that are truly matters of opinion.

14:2 One man's faith allows him to eat everything, but another man, whose faith is weak, eats only vegetables. Here Paul introduces an example of an issue where either side is acceptable, i.e., eating "all things" (including meat), or eating only vegetables. This does not mean that both sides are equally correct in their thinking, since the one who practices vegetarianism is described as "weak." I.e., his conviction and practice are based on a faulty understanding of the implications of his faith. He could actually eat meat without sinning, but he does not see it that way. Thus, since it is no sin *not* to eat meat, it is perfectly acceptable for him to restrict his diet to vegetables; and the rest of us should not make a fuss about it.

On the other hand, "we who are strong" (15:1) eat everything, because our "faith allows" it. The implication is not just that we *believe* it to be legitimate to eat, but that we *rightly* believe it. Thus the Christian who eats all things is the one who has correctly sorted out the relation between faith in Jesus and the kinds of food one may eat. See 14:14,20; 1 Tim 4:3-5.

What sort of circumstances in NT times would cause some Christians to practice vegetarianism as a matter of conscience? For one thing, certain pagan beliefs forbade the eating of meat (see Cranfield, 2:693, n. 5; Dunn, 2:799-800; see Col 2:16-23); therefore some Gentile Christians from this background may have found it difficult to change their habits. Also, much of the meat sold in the ancient markets came from animals that had been offered as sacrifices to idols. Some converted pagans still could not in their minds separate this meat as such from the idolatrous use that had been made of it, and thus violated their consciences if they ate it (1 Cor 8:4-13). The uncertain source of meat sold in the market caused them to avoid meat altogether.

This same course of action was followed by many converted Jews. Even though the Mosaic Law did not forbid the eating of all meat, it did distinguish between the clean and the unclean (see 14:14,20) and prescribed that even clean meat be prepared in a certain way (see Lev 7:22-27; 17:10-16). Some Jewish Christians apparently could not bring themselves to eat what God's own law had forbidden for 1,500 years. And since it was next to impossible to verify the "clean" status of meat sold in the markets or served in someone else's home, many of them apparently renounced the eating of meat altogether rather than risk unwittingly eating something unclean (see Dan 1:8-16).

Any one of these would have qualified as an early Christian who "eats only vegetables" because his "faith is weak." Paul was probably not thinking of any one of them in exclusion of the others.

14:3 The Apostle's point is that within the Christian community both strong and weak should be allowed to follow their consciences on this matter without being hassled by the other side. It is, after all, a *matter of opinion*. To enforce this point, Paul has an exhortation for each group, speaking of them in the representative singular. First he instructs the strong, **The man who eats everything must not look down on him who does not, . . .** "Look down on" is ἐξουθενέω (*exoutheneō*), a strong word meaning "despise, disdain, regard with contempt." The more liberated Christian must guard against the temptation to feel superior toward the less enlightened Christian. It is easy for the former to regard the latter as legalistic and nit-picking, and perhaps narrow-minded and a bit dense. All such temptations must be resisted. The strong must have full respect for the integrity and the conscience of the weak.

On the other hand, the weak are not without their own temptations to sit in judgment on the strong, whom they may regard as morally lax or at least inconsistent. Thus Paul exhorts the weak Christian: **. . . and the man who does not eat everything must not condemn the man who does.** "Condemn" is κρίνω (*krinō*), which can mean either "pass judgment on," or the stronger "condemn." It probably has the latter connotation here, and not just "criticize" (contra Lenski, 817). Dunn is right to point out that Paul's command implies that (sometimes at least) the weak Christian looks upon the strong as "not actually to be reckoned as a Christian" (2:813). As Lard says, he "is sure to adjudge the strong a sinner" and is "ready to refuse him fellowship" (415). Not all weak Christians may go this far, but at least they will be tempted to condemn the *conduct* of the strong (e.g., eating meat) as being sinful and unacceptable to God. Because of such a "holier-than-thou," censorious attitude, Morris observes that "not infrequently the weak is the greater tyrant" (479).

In the last part of v. 3 Paul gives the reason why the strong should not despise the weak, nor the weak condemn the strong: **for God has accepted him.** It is possible that "him" here refers only to the one who eats meat (and thus by implication to any strong Christian), as some argue. In my judgment, though, "him" refers to both the strong and the weak. In 15:7 Paul exhorts both groups to "accept one another," using the same verb. In 14:1 he begins this paragraph by urging the strong to "accept" the weak (same verb). Thus it is reasonable to conclude that the acceptance in v. 3c applies not just to the strong eater in v. 3b but to the weak noneater in v. 3a as well (Moule, 224; MacArthur, 2:279). Thus the strong should not despise the weak, *for God has accepted him.* Neither should the weak condemn the strong, *for God has accepted him.*

The bottom line is this: "How dare we reject a person whom God has accepted?" (Stott, 361). Acceptance by God thus becomes the basis for all genuine Christian fellowship. We cannot accept as brothers and sisters in Christ a smaller group than God himself has accepted as his children.

2. We Answer to Our Lord and Not to Each Other (14:4-9)

Another reason why Christians, both weak and strong, should not judge one another in matters of opinion is rooted in the nature of the servant-Lord relationship. Only the owner (lord) of a slave has the right to sit in judgment on the slave's conduct. In the church the only Lord is Jesus Christ (10:9); all Christians are equally his slaves. He alone is our arbiter and judge; we answer only to him. See Matt 7:1; 1 Cor 4:3-5.

14:4 Paul states this as a general principle, with obvious application to the church: **Who are you to judge someone else's servant? To his own master he stands or falls.** "Judge" is *krinō*, the same Greek word translated "condemn" in v. 3; "servant" is οἰκέτης (*oiketēs*) or house-slave, the kind of servant who was usually close to his master.

Since in v. 3 "judging" ("condemning") is the act of the weak toward the strong, some think the question in v. 4a is directed only toward the weak (Cranfield, 2:702). But in v. 13 the same word (*krinō*) is applied to both sides, and it is better to apply it to both here in v. 4a.

Paul's question is a strong rebuke, and it reveals the presumptuousness of any Christian who either ridicules the weak or condemns the strong for following his conscience in the area of opinions. We must not think Paul is ruling out honest and respectful discussions about such issues, however; he is especially not ruling out loving attempts to lead the weak to a better understanding of the implications of Christian belief, and thus into freedom from unnecessary prohibitions (❀II:395).

"Stands or falls" refers to the Master's acceptance or nonacceptance of his slave's conduct. I.e., it is the Lord's place either to approve him and lift him up for his conscientious service, or to condemn him for his wrongdoing. The implication is that in matters of opinion any course of action (e.g., eating meat, or eating vegetables only) offered in good conscience to God is accepted by him (v. 3c), and the conscientious servant stands before his Lord with the latter's full approval and without guilt.

And he will stand, for the Lord is able to make him stand. Even if your fellow Christian's conduct makes it appear to you that he has stumbled and fallen (because he does not agree with you), as long as he is true to his conscience on indifferent matters (14:22-23), he will stand approved by the Lord. "The Lord is able to make him stand" may mean only that the Lord has accepted him; or it may refer to the Lord's gift of the Holy Spirit (Acts 2:33-39), whose sanctifying power enables the Christian to remain true to his conscience.

14:5 One man considers one day more sacred than another; another man considers every day alike. Here Paul introduces a second example of an issue that is a matter of opinion, i.e., whether or not to observe special days. The one who considers some days to be more holy than others is equivalent to the one who makes distinctions among foods; he is therefore presumed to be the weak brother on this issue. The one who considers every day alike is thus equivalent to the strong brother who eats any kind of food.

Interestingly, the word for "considers" is *krinō*, the same word translated "condemn" and "judge" in vv. 3 and 4. Here in v. 5 it obviously has the neutral meaning of "judge between, distinguish, decide" (❂II:396). Literally Paul says the weak Christian judges "a day more than a day," i.e., one day to be more important or more sacred than another day.

What is the issue here? Most likely it is the question of whether Christians must continue to honor the special days set apart under the Old Covenant (❂II:396). In other texts (Gal 4:10; Col 2:16) Paul is very clear that observing such days is no longer a matter of law, and that insisting that all Christians do so is a kind of legalism that destroys Christian liberty. His point here, though, is that a Christian may continue to observe these special days as a matter of personal conviction, as long as he does not condemn those who decide otherwise.

The latter (the strong) are those who judge "every day alike." From the Christian point of view, to consider every day alike does not mean to regard them all as *secular*, but rather to consider "every day as equally to be dedicated to the service of God" (Bruce, 245). The main point is that the one who judges all days alike is no less Christian than the one who feels that some days are special.

Each one should be fully convinced in his own mind. Whichever of these acceptable views one chooses, he should do so only after examining the case for both sides and coming to a conclusion he judges to be reasonable. To "be fully convinced" is to have "a settled conviction . . . that the pattern of conduct followed is in accord with the will of God" (Dunn, 2:806). Our opinions may be personal ("his *own* mind"), but we must believe they are adequately supported by good evidence ("his own *mind*"). This applies to both the strong and the weak. Thus in matters of opinion it is not wrong to believe we are right, even if we are wrong — which is exactly the situation of those who hold the "weak" side in such issues.

Is the teaching of this verse meant to be applied to the observance of the first day of the week (Sunday) as a special day in the church age? Most Christians have traditionally regarded Sunday observance as a matter of law (based on apostolic precedent) rather than a matter of opinion (see Acts 20:7; 1 Cor 16:2). Therefore they see this verse as applying only to the holy days of the Mosaic Law, not to the Christian Sunday. Others take this verse to mean that even the observance of Sunday is a matter of opinion, and therefore they have no problem with Thursday communion and Saturday night worship. I personally am "fully convinced" that a better case can be made for the former position.

14:6 In this verse Paul again shows how the servant-Lord relationship is the reason why it is wrong to judge one another in matters of opinion. He makes his point in reference to both special days and dietary preferences. **He who regards one day as special, does so to the Lord.** By implication the same can be said of the one who treats all days alike. Also, **He who eats meat, eats to the Lord, for he gives thanks to God; and he who abstains, does so to the Lord and gives thanks to God.**

The main point is that whatever convictions a Christian has about these and similar matters, he lives out (or *should* live out) his convictions "to the Lord." In other words, it is a matter between him and his Lord, and he is motivated by a conscientious desire to bring honor and glory to his Lord. This is a warning to both the weak and the strong not to regard those of differing opinions as being impious or selfishly motivated.

Paul notes that both the eat-anything Christian and the vegetarian Christian are equally diligent in giving thanks to God for their food, each regarding his meal as a gift from God. Paul saw himself in the former category (1 Tim 4:4-5), but respected the vegetarian's conscience.

This verse probably refers to "the blessing spoken at meals" (Dunn, 2:807), and thus supports the common practice of "saying grace" before eating. It "indicates that grace before meals was the universal practice of Christians in Paul's day" (MP, 527). See Matt 15:36; John 6:11,23; Acts 27:35; 1 Cor 10:30; 1 Tim 4:4.

14:7 For none of us lives to himself alone and none of us dies to himself alone. To be sure, Christians "are members of one another" (Eph 4:25, NASB). Paul's point here, however, is not our connections with other people, but our continuing relationship with our Lord, as v. 8 shows.

14:8 If we live, we live to the Lord; and if we die, we die to the Lord. I.e., none of us lives and dies to himself alone, *because* we all live and die "to the Lord" (see Phil 1:21-24). This basically reinforces the point of v. 6, that every Christian, no matter what position he takes on matters of opinion, is doing so in his capacity as a servant of Jesus Christ. This is true, because *everything* we do is done "in the name of the Lord Jesus" (Col 3:17) and for his sake. The reference to both living and dying emphasizes the all-inclusiveness of this principle. No part of our life or death, not even our seemingly insignificant opinions about matters of indifference, is outside the boundaries of our responsibility to our Lord.

How does one "die to the Lord"? It may mean that at death our bondservice to Christ does not end; rather, we simply pass into another sphere or form of service to him (Moule, 226; Morris, 482). More likely, though, it refers to the circumstances of one's death. Whatever the mode of our bodily death, as Christ's servants we are determined to fully trust his promises and be fully surrendered to his purposes. Whether it be a peaceful transition while asleep or a martyr's violent death, we will bring glory to our Lord by confidently praying, "Lord Jesus, receive my spirit" (Acts 7:59).

So, whether we live or die, we belong to the Lord. He is our owner; we are his slaves, his possessions. We live (and die) to serve him, not to please ourselves.

14:9 For this very reason, Christ died and returned to life so that he might be the Lord of both the dead and the living. The servant-Lord relationship between Christians and Jesus Christ is the key to harmonious relationships within the church in the area of opinions. But this servant-Lord relationship is not something we should take for granted. Jesus is Lord only because, in his role and nature as the incarnate Christ, he met and defeated his enemies through his glorious death and resurrection. It was unto this end, or "for this very purpose," that he died and returned to life.

The word for "returned to life" is not the usual word for "raised up," but the word ζάω (*zaō*), which means simply "to live." Some may conclude from this word that Paul is referring just to Christ's earthly life ("he lived") and his death ("he died"). But if that were the meaning, the verbs would have been reversed. Paul says Jesus "died and lived." There is no doubt that he means "lived again, came back to life, returned to life," as the NIV has it.

As the result of his death and resurrection, Jesus is "Lord of both the dead and the living." This unusual order — we would expect "the living and the dead" — is probably determined by the reference to Christ's death and resurrection in the first part of the verse. It is not that Christ's death made him Lord of the dead, and his resurrection made him Lord of the living. Rather, his death and resurrection together made him Lord over all people, whether they have already died or are still living (see Cranfield, 2:708).

There is a cause-and-effect relation between Christ's death and resurrection on the one hand, and his Lordship (sovereign ownership and rule) on the other hand. The eternal Logos was by nature the sovereign Lord over all things, but the God-man Jesus Christ earned his right to Lordship by means of his victorious work of death and resurrection. As the risen Redeemer he could rightly lay claim to all glory and power and honor, and exercise his Lordship over all. See Matt 28:18-20; Acts 2:36; Rom 1:3-4; Phil 2:7-11; Col 2:15; Heb 2:14-15; Rev 1:18; 5:9-12.

The point is that this is why *Jesus*, and no one else, is the Lord over all Christians. Unless we can say that *we* have died and come back to life by our own power in direct triumph over sin and death and Satan, we have no right to sit in judgment on our fellow Christians and their conscientious decisions in matters of opinion.

3. Each of Us Will Be Judged by God (14:10-12)

Here is the final reason why Christians should not judge one another in matters of opinion, namely, because each of us will one day *be* judged in the final accounting before God's judgment seat. The emphasis is on the exclusive right of God to judge others, which is a corollary of his sovereign Lordship over all. We who are servants do not have this right. Instead, we will all one day stand alongside one another before the same Lord and Judge.

14:10 You, then, why do you judge your brother? Or why do you look down on your brother? The emphatic "You, then!" gets our attention. Reminding us that we are brothers only magnifies the inconsistency and presumptuousness of sitting in judgment on one another: "These are your *brothers and sisters* in Christ! Why are you so eager to condemn them and belittle them?" Paul returns to the terminology used in v. 3, where "judge" (*krinō*) is the act of the weak toward the strong, and "look down on" (ἐξουθενέω, *exoutheneō*) is the act of the strong toward the weak.

"Why do you judge or look down on your brother?" Paul has already given two reasons why this is wrong (vv. 3-9). Now he adds a third reason: **For we will all stand before God's judgment seat.** Anticipation of our own judgment should cause us to think twice before judging a brother. It should remind us that we too are sinners whose only hope in that day will be God's abundant grace, gratitude for which should even now cause us to regard our fellow Christians with a gracious spirit.

"Judgment seat" is βῆμα (*bēma*), a word used for the platform upon which a judge's chair might rest, and thus for the chair or seat itself (see Matt 27:19; John 19:13; Acts 12:21), and also for the tribunal before which one was judged ("the court" – see Acts 18:12,16,17; 25:6,10,17). *Bēma* is also used in 2 Cor 5:10 for "the judgment seat of Christ." This is not different from the "great white throne" of Rev 20:11.

A main emphasis is on the universality of this event: *all* will stand before God's *bēma*. This is true even of Christians, as 2 Cor 5:10 confirms: "For we must all appear before the judgment seat of Christ, that each one may receive what is due him for the things done while in the body, whether good or bad." See 1 Cor 3:13. Some mistakenly think that Christians will not be brought into the judgment, or that their sins will not be made manifest there; but these ideas are incorrect. God "remembers our sins no more" (Heb 8:12; 10:17) in the sense that they are forgiven and will never condemn us, but the Bible is clear: "The judgment embraces not only all persons but also all deeds" (Murray, 2:184).

14:11 Paul reinforces the universality of the final judgment by citing the OT: **It is written: "'As surely as I live,' says the Lord, 'every knee will bow before me; every tongue will confess to God.'"** Most of this quote is from Isa 45:23, but the introductory words ("'As surely as I live,' says the Lord") are found in a number of texts as a solemn preface to a prophetic word from God (e.g., Isa 49:18; Jer 22:24; 46:18; Ezek 5:11; 14:16; Zeph 2:9).

To bow the knee before God is an act of submission, and to confess God with the tongue is to acknowledge that he and he alone is truly God. The word for "confess" is ἐξομολογέω (*exomologeō*), which in the middle voice means "to acknowledge, to confess, to admit." This does not refer to confessing sins to God (contra Fitzmyer, 692), but rather to confessing or acknowledging his sovereign Lordship, his worthiness to be worshiped, and his right to bring us into judgment. See Phil 2:9-11.

The emphasis again is on the universality of this homage: *every* knee will bow; *every* tongue will confess. Some will do so in terror and grudging resentment, having rebelled against God in their lifetime. Others will do so with the same sincere and willing worship they offered up to him while on the earth. Only the latter will receive the gift of eternal life.

14:12 So then, each of us will give an account of himself to God. This restates the point already made in vv. 10-11. "So then" indicates that this is the logical conclusion from the preceding affirmations. "Each" reaffirms the universality of the judgment. No one, not even Christians, are exempt from it. "Of us" makes this prospect very personal. All of us Christians, including the strong who are tempted to belittle the weak, and the weak who are prone to condemn the strong, will experience our own personal judgment.

We "will give an account" of all our deeds, including our sins (2 Cor 5:10). We will have to answer for how we have despised our weak brethren, or condemned fellow Christians who are stronger than we are, in matters of indifference (❖ II:402).

All of these points together emphasize the folly of judging others, and provide the material basis for the transitional exhortation in v. 13a, "Therefore let us stop passing judgment on one another."

B. THE STEWARDSHIP OF CHRISTIAN LIBERTY (14:13-23)

The previous section (14:1-12) presumes that "the strong" can discern between matters of law and matters of opinion, while "the weak" cannot. The present paragraph is addressed to the strong, i.e., those who understand the nature of Christian liberty and whose conscience allows them to choose as they please in matters of opinion. Paul's message to this group is that such freedom is not absolute, and that one must not insist upon exercising his rights in such matters if this should prove harmful to the weaker brother and to the cause of Christ. Specifically, in the spirit of Christian love the strong must be willing to sacrifice their liberty, if necessary, where there is a danger that the weak may imitate them and thereby sin against their own consciences (❖ II:403).

1. We Must Sacrifice Our Liberty for the Sake of the Weak (14:13-15)

14:13 Therefore let us stop passing judgment on one another. This is addressed to both the strong and the weak, and basically is a transitional statement that sums up vv. 1-12. "Let us stop" implies that such judging was occurring in the church at Rome. See Matt 7:1.

Instead, make up your mind not to put any stumbling block or obstacle in your brother's way. From this point on the paragraph seems to be directed mainly to the strong. "Make up your mind" is *krinō*, the same word translated "condemn" in vv. 3,22; "judge" in vv. 4,10; "pass judgment" in v. 13a; and "consider" in v. 5. Here its meaning is "make a decision about," or "let this be your decision."

The strong Christian is warned not to place a stumbling block (πρόσκομμα, *proskomma*) or an obstacle (σκάνδαλον, *skandalon*) in a brother's path. These words are very similar in meaning and refer to an obstacle which causes someone to stumble and fall. See 9:32-33, where the same words describe Jesus as a stone over which the Jews stumbled, to their destruction. The stumbling in this verse is spiritual, not physical; it refers to stumbling and falling *into sin*.

It is important that we understand that the stumbling to which Paul refers is not just becoming offended or having one's feelings wounded. It refers to real spiritual harm (see 9:33; 11:9), a true "spiritual downfall" (Moo, 851). The cause for such spiritual stumbling would be an act on the part of the strong brother that is not wrong in itself, but which is perceived as wrong by a weak brother. Such an act becomes a stumbling block when the weak brother observes it and is influenced thereby to do the same thing, *even though in his heart he believes it is wrong*, which is sin (v. 23). In this way the strong brother has inadvertently influenced the weak brother to "fall into sin and potential spiritual ruin" (Moo, 852) just by exercising his Christian liberty (see 1 Cor 8:9). The point is that we must be sensitive to how our conduct is affecting others, and we must be willing to forgo perfectly legitimate behavior if it has the potential of causing someone to sin against his conscience. Verses 14 and 23 in particular show how this may happen.

14:14 The main example of such behavior is the eating of certain kinds of food (see 14:2). **As one who is in the Lord Jesus, I am fully convinced that no food is unclean in itself.** The word "food" actually does not appear in this verse; literally Paul says that *"nothing* is unclean in itself." By "nothing" he means "nothing in the created world"; the following context shows that he has food in mind as a primary example of this.

Under the Old Covenant certain foods were declared to be "unclean," but they were not inherently so. For Old Covenant purposes God simply pronounced them ceremonially unclean and forbade the Jews to eat them; but this restriction does not apply under the New Covenant (Mark 7:15; Acts 10:9-16; 1 Tim 4:4-5; Titus 1:15). That Paul at least has in mind this OT distinction between clean and unclean foods is shown by his use of the term "unclean." He may also have in mind meat offered to idols, which is not inherently polluted for those who know the difference between the true Creator-God and vain idols (1 Cor 8:4-6; 10:23-33).

Paul is very emphatic in his conviction that no food is unclean in itself. The source of this conviction is "the Lord Jesus." The Greek phrase (ἐν κυρίῳ Ἰησοῦ, *en kyriō Iēsou*) probably means "by the Lord Jesus," with Paul thus referring to a special revelation given to him in his capacity as an apostle, or perhaps to Christ's public teaching as recorded in Matt 15:10-11,15-20; Mark 7:15-23. The NIV translation reflects another common view, that the phrase indicates that Paul's conviction is based in a general way on "his status as a Christian" and "his association with the risen Christ" (Fitzmyer, 695). I.e., "Everything I know about Jesus tells me that this is true."

That "no food is unclean in itself" is the fundamental principle from which the rest is deduced. Thus "in principle the 'strong' are right" (Morris, 486). Idols are nothing, so idol-meat is not really polluted; and Christ has abolished the clean/unclean distinction of the Mosaic Law.

But what if someone does not fully understand these points? What if, because of his weak understanding, he still regards eating OT foods and idol-meat as wrong? In this case, says Paul, another principle applies: **But if anyone regards something as unclean, then for him it is unclean.** And because he truly thinks of it in his heart as unclean according to God's own law, his conscience tells him that it would be wrong to eat it. And if he does in fact eat it, contrary to what his conscience tells him, he is guilty of sin. In such a case the sin is not in the eating *per se*, but in the violation of the conscience.

This is the principle that applies to the weak. See also 1 Cor 8:7.

Since no object is in itself evil or unclean, sin is always in the heart, mind, and actions of a person. Some acts and mental states are always sinful (e.g., murder, greed), but some are wrong only because a person mistakenly thinks they are (see Lenski, 834). In the former case moral standards are absolute; only in the latter case are they relative, and these have to do only with things that are in reality matters of opinion.

Where a weak conscience thus exists, the ideal approach, as Moule indicates, would be "*correction by better light*" (229); but in the meantime the weak believer must follow his mistaken conscience on such matters or else be guilty of sin.

14:15 If your brother is distressed because of what you eat, you are no longer acting in love. The NASB is more literal here: "For if because of food your brother is hurt . . . ."

It seems best to consider the statement of principles in v. 14 as a parenthesis, with this verse linking up directly with v. 13. In v. 13 Paul urges the strong Christian not to put a stumbling block in the way of the weak; here in v. 15 he gives one *reason* for this, i.e., it is not consistent with love (*agapē*; see 12:9). As Stott says, "Love never disregards weak consciences" (365). To the one who loves, a weak brother's spiritual well-being is always more important than indulging the right to eat whatever one likes.

A crucial question is the meaning of "distressed" ("hurt" in the NASB). The word is λυπέω (*lypeō*), which in the passive means "to be grieved, distressed, hurt" (BAGD, 481). The issue is whether Paul is referring simply to hurt feelings, or to actual spiritual harm. If the former, then he is saying that one must sacrifice his Christian liberty even if its use merely *upsets* or *annoys* the weaker brother or is offensive to his feelings. Since "the weak are always with us," this interpretation would seem to seriously limit if not practically eliminate Christian liberty.

The other view, that *lypeō* here refers to actual spiritual harm, is more in keeping with the context and thus appears to be the right interpretation. The meaning would then be that one is not acting in love if his exercise of liberty influences a weak brother to follow his example and thus fall into sin by violating his own conscience (❧ II:407).

The rest of the verse supports this interpretation: **Do not by your eating destroy your brother for whom Christ died.** The Greek word for "destroy" is ἀπόλλυμι (*apollymi*), a very strong word which means "to ruin, destroy, kill, put to death, cause to perish" (BAGD, 95). There seems to be an increasingly stronger description of the harmful results of the insensitive exercise of Christian liberty: the weak are caused to stumble (v. 13); they are gravely hurt (v. 15a); they are destroyed (v. 15b).

What are the implications of this warning? Just how serious is this destruction? Is Paul referring to loss of salvation and condemnation to hell? Those committed to Calvinism and especially to "once saved, always saved" of course deny that Paul has this in mind. They must rule this out since Paul is talking here about "brothers" (vv. 13b,15a) who have already been saved; and (according to their view) once they have become saved, they can never be lost. Thus the destruction is limited to "loss of spiritual well-being" and "utter devastation" in the area of Christian growth (MacArthur, 2:294). It refers only to serious damage to Christian discipleship, says Stott (366). Though this could potentially lead to "eternal perdition" if not corrected, Paul is not implying that it actually will do so; he uses this dire language only to show the strong brother how serious his offense is (Murray, 2:192; see Moo, 854).

I must conclude, though, that this strong warning does imply that the careless and unloving exercise of Christian liberty can lead to actual loss of salvation for a weak brother. *Apollymi* is frequently used in the sense of eternal destruction in hell (e.g., Matt 10:28; Luke 13:3; John 3:16; Rom 2:12). The reference to the fact that Christ died for these weak brethren supports this meaning here. I.e., the destruction in view would negate the very purpose of Christ's death, which is to save them from eternal condemnation.

Stott is correct to point out that a weak Christian's single sin against his conscience does not in itself bring him under eternal punishment (365-366), but here Paul is not referring to a single act of stumbling. He has in mind the ultimate outcome to which a single act of this kind could potentially lead. By violating his conscience the weak brother is weakened even further and could ultimately give up his faith altogether and return to idolatry (Lard, 425). The weak brother's destruction is thus his "actual and complete ruin" (Lenski, 837), his "final eschatological ruin" (Dunn, 2:821; see Cranfield, 2:715). The verse cannot be reconciled with "once saved, always saved."

We must remember that this passage is addressed to the strong brother. By showing him the potential disastrous consequences of the indiscriminate use of his Christian liberty, Paul attempts to motivate him to a discreet and even sacrificial use of it. Just what is your weak brother's eternal life worth to you? he asks. To Jesus, it was worth his very life. If Jesus was willing to give up his life to save your brothers, surely you can give up meat! "Shall we set a higher value on our meat than Christ did on his divine life?" (MP, 530). Do you love your freedom more than you love your brother or sister for whom Christ died? See 1 Cor 8:11.

2. Do Not Allow What You Consider Good to Be Spoken of as Evil (14:16-18)

In these three verses Paul gives another reason for the strong to be discerning in his use of Christian liberty. I.e., he must never insist upon his "rights" if exercising them creates a situation within the church that gives outsiders a bad impression of Christ, Christianity, or the kingdom of God. I.e., we must be sensitive to how the kingdom of God is perceived by those who are not a part of it.

14:16 Do not allow what you consider good to be spoken of as evil. By using the phrase "your good," Paul seems to be referring to the good conduct of the strong brother, i.e., conduct which in accordance with the principle of Christian liberty (v. 14a) is inherently good. Paul thus exhorts the strong Christian not to use his liberty in such a way that it is "spoken of as evil." This is the word "to blaspheme, to speak against" (see 2:24; ❥I:214). What would cause someone to speak evil of the practice of Christian liberty? When that liberty is used in such a way that others are harmed thereby.

Those who are led to thus blaspheme the conduct of the strong are not the weak (contra SH, 391; Moo, 855), but those outside the church (see 2:24 for a parallel). As Hendriksen observes concerning conflict between the strong and the weak, "Open quarrels between the two groups would certainly result in slanderous talk on the part of outsiders" (2:463). Thus strong Christians are admonished to consider "the impact of [their] insensitive conduct upon any onlooking or visiting unbelievers" (Dunn, 2:831).

14:17 For the kingdom of God is not a matter of eating and drinking, but of righteousness, peace and joy in the Holy Spirit, . . . In most places where Paul speaks of the "kingdom of God," he refers to "the future inheritance of the people of God" (Bruce, 252; see, e.g., 1 Cor 6:9-10; 15:50; Gal 5:21; Eph 5:5), but here (and in 1 Cor 4:20) he speaks of God's kingdom as it presently exists. The most basic meaning of the "kingdom" (βασιλεία, *basileia*) of God is the *reign* or *rule* of God; in a secondary sense it refers to the realm over which God reigns, and specifically to that body of people who acknowledge and submit to his dominion. In the NT era, this is the church.

Paul's point is this: when outsiders observe God's church, what characteristics or phenomena should they immediately see as a demonstration of the true essence of God's reign on earth? What is the primary evidence that God is truly ruling in the hearts of Christians and in the midst of his church?

No wonder people have nothing good to say about Christians when they see the latter fighting over such trivial things as "eating and drinking." Are rules about food and drink the essence of the kingdom of God? Does true Christianity consist of getting one's way with regard to eating and drinking? *No*, says Paul; the kingdom of God is not about such ultimately unimportant matters (see Matt 15:11-20), *but* is rather about "righteousness, peace and joy in the Holy Spirit" (❧II:410).

In this context the main point seems to be how the church appears before the world, so that it is either spoken against (v. 16) or "approved by men" (v. 18). Thus the righteousness, peace, and joy that are the true essence of the observable church are better understood in a horizontal or "social sense" (Godet, 461), i.e., as having to do with how Christians get along with each other. "Righteousness" thus is the daily righteous conduct of Christians, especially in the right use of Christian liberty. "Peace" is the state of loving harmony among all the members of the church (see v. 19), of "the loving, tranquil relationship of believers" (MacArthur, 2:298). "Joy" is the happy and cheerful spirit that always is obvious among people who enjoy being together. Godet calls it "that individual and collective exultation which prevails among believers when brotherly communion makes its sweetness felt" (461).

The phrase "in the Holy Spirit" goes especially with joy (Acts 13:52; 1 Thess 1:6), but the Spirit's presence is rightly the source of all three of these virtues (see Gal 5:22-23).

Paul's point is that the very nature of the kingdom of God is another reason why the strong brother should not make an issue of his liberty to eat meat or to take any other stand on things that are just matters of opinion anyway. For the sake of the kingdom of God and its impact on the world, he will surely be willing to forgo his rights.

14:18 . . . because anyone who serves Christ in this way is pleasing to God and approved by men. The verb in "serves Christ" is δουλεύω (*douleuō*), which means to serve as a slave, a δοῦλος (*doulos*; see 1:1; ❧I:59-60). It is important when thinking of Christian *liberty* to remember that such freedom is not absolute; we are still subject to Christ's will for us.

To what does "in this way" refer? No doubt it means doing those things that bring about righteousness, peace, and joy in the life of the church (Lard, 426;

SH, 392). When we do those things we not only please God, but earn the approval or respect of our fellow men, who expect to see these virtues exhibited in the church. This is the counterpart to living a life of strife and hypocrisy, which elicits the contempt and blasphemy of the world (v. 16).

This section makes it clear that we Christians cannot be indifferent to others' observations and opinions about the church (see Matt 5:16). Everything about matters of opinion is not a matter of opinion. We are free to decide either way in such matters, but *how* we decide concerning them, and how we perceive them in relation to the kingdom of God, are *not* matters of indifference. Rather, these things are a part of serving Christ as his slaves.

3. We Must Do Only Those Things Which Build Others Up (14:19-21)

14:19 Let us therefore make every effort to do what leads to peace and to mutual edification. This exhortation is based especially on the foundational principle in v. 17, and generally upon the entire teaching of vv. 13-18. It is a call to action, urging all Christians, but especially the strong, to deliberately work to maintain peace and harmony among all believers.

This is accomplished when Christians do and say only those things which lead to "mutual edification," or "the building up of one another" (NASB). Here Paul invokes the familiar image of God's saving work as a construction project. The main emphasis is on the building up of individuals, i.e., causing them to grow and be strengthened in Christ (❧ II:412).

This is just another way of describing the limit which love places on our Christian liberty. Love must constrain us to curb our own freedom, and to forgo even good behavior if indulging in it is actually destructive rather than edifying to others.

14:20 Do not destroy the work of God for the sake of food. "The work of God" is the work God is doing, the work he is in the process of accomplishing. Some think this refers specifically to God's building up of the church as a whole. While this cannot be ruled out, the main emphasis again (as in v. 19) seems to be upon the individual Christian viewed as God's "new creation" (2 Cor 5:17) or as "God's workmanship" (Eph 2:10).

This "work of God" is the weak Christian in particular, and Paul is again admonishing the strong not to bring spiritual harm to the weak by insisting on his right to eat any food he pleases, any time he pleases. The thought is exactly parallel to v. 15b: *destroying the work of God* for the sake of food is equivalent to *destroying the brother for whom Christ died* by the same careless act. A moment's sober reflection should show the strong brother how disastrously absurd this would be.

The word for "destroy" is not the same as in v. 15b; here it is καταλύω (*katalyō*), which has the connotation "to tear down, to demolish." It is used in direct contrast with the work of edifying or building up in v. 19. Do what it takes to build a brother up, says Paul; do not do anything that will tear him down. We are in the construction business, not the demolition business.

The word "destroy" in this verse is thus a very strong word, as is the word in v. 15b. Again it includes the possibility that the strong believer can cause the weak believer to stumble in a way that leads to his ultimate loss of salvation.

All food is clean, but it is wrong for a man to eat anything that causes someone else to stumble. "All food is clean" is a positive restatement of the basic principle given negatively in v. 14a. The rest of the sentence is a clear statement of the ethical principle that underlies all the exhortations to the strong in this paragraph. Although all food is clean, there is at least one circumstance where eating even clean food is wrong, i.e., if it causes a brother to stumble.

"It is wrong" (κακός, *kakos*, "evil") is meant to be in contrast with "it is better" (καλός, *kalos*, "good") in v. 21a. To cause the weak to stumble by what one eats is a moral evil on the part of the strong, and at the same time it has evil or injurious consequences for the weak.

The sentence structure in the Greek is quite terse and leaves open the possibility that the "man" in this sentence is the *weak* brother, who by eating in violation of his conscience commits a sin. This would make the sentence equivalent to vv. 14b,23. Most agree with the NIV, though, that the "man" is the strong brother who commits sin by using his freedom in such a way that his eating becomes a stumbling block to the weak. The use of "stumbling block" (πρόσκομμα, *proskomma*) recalls the exhortation to the strong in v. 13b, "not to put any stumbling block" in a brother's way (II:414).

14:21 The next verse does in fact extend the principle beyond the example of eating certain foods: **It is better** [lit., "good"] **not to eat meat or drink wine or to do anything else that will cause your brother to fall.** This is, as Moo (861) says, "the basic practical point" of the whole paragraph. This is the way of unselfish love (v. 15a).

Being free to eat any kind of meat is the main example of Christian liberty in this whole section, though this is the first specific reference to "meat" in the Greek text. It is clearly implied in v. 2, however, which says that the strong eats "everything" while the weak eats "only vegetables."

This verse also uses drinking wine as an example of Christian liberty. The reference to "drinking" in v. 17 alludes to this, but it is not mentioned anywhere else in Paul's discussions of the subject of liberty. In biblical times wine was commonly drunk with meals, though it was usually diluted considerably with water. The fact that Paul uses this practice as an example of Christian freedom shows that we cannot say that drinking wine in and of itself is wrong.

We are not sure what circumstances would have required the strong brother in NT times to abstain from drinking wine. Idol worship sometimes involved the pouring out of wine as a sacrifice to the gods; some converted pagans may have thus associated wine with idol worship as they did meat. Thus their overly sensitive consciences may have prevented them from drinking wine altogether. In such a situation the strong Christian is under obligation not to drink wine, just as he is under obligation not to eat meat, if his eating or drinking carries the risk of causing the weak brother to imitate him and thus sin against his own conscience.

"Or to do anything else" leaves the category of opinions open so that this principle may be applied according to our informed Christian wisdom in all times and cultures (❂II:415).

We should note that the prohibition against meat and wine is not absolute, but must be applied only when such eating or drinking would be a stumbling block for the weak (see Lenski, 849-850; Moo, 861). This means that the strong Christian must conscientiously use his best judgment as to when the exercise of his freedom might lead another into sin. If he cannot be sure, then total abstention would be the loving decision. See 1 Cor 8:13.

4. Each Christian Must Be True to His Own Convictions (14:22-23)

14:22 So whatever you believe about these things keep between yourself and God. "Whatever you believe about these things" is literally "the faith which you have." Since Paul is addressing the strong, the meaning of "faith" here is similar to the faith in v. 2a, in contrast with the faith of the weak in vv. 1,2b. Thus the Apostle is not really talking about "whatever" faith one happens to have; he is rather referring to the correct faith of the strong Christian, who is strong *just because* he has a right understanding of the implications of Christian faith with reference to matters of opinion.

I do not take the word "faith" (πίστις, *pistis*) in itself to mean "conviction," contrary to a common understanding of this verse. As in vv. 1-2, it refers to the content of the Christian faith along with the implications thereof, to which we must give assent and which we must seek to understand. This *understanding* is what is at issue here. The strong have a proper understanding; the weak do not.

Paul's point is that those who have this proper understanding should not flaunt it or wave it in the face of the weak. Rather than make a big issue of it, it is better just to keep it "between yourself and God." Even if you cannot exercise your freedom when you are in the presence of the weak, you can do so when you are alone before God (❂II:416).

Blessed is the man who does not condemn himself by what he approves. To be "blessed" is to have inward happiness. Κρίνω (*krinō*) here is properly rendered "condemn" by the NIV.

This beatitude has been understood in two ways. Some take it thus: Blessed is the strong Christian who does not bring God's condemnation upon himself by flaunting his freedom regarding those things he rightly regards as acceptable, in such a way that a weaker brother is caused to stumble. This meaning is possible, but the second interpretation sets up a better contrast with v. 23, namely:

Blessed is the strong Christian who does not condemn himself or feel guilty about his understanding that there is nothing wrong with eating meat, drinking wine, or doing other things about which the revealed will of God is truly silent. He is blessed because he can do these things with a clear conscience.

14:23 But the man who has doubts is condemned if he eats, . . . On the word "has doubts," see 4:20. Here it means "to be uncertain, to waver between two judgments" (Lenski, 853). This refers to the weak Christian who does not understand the true implications of Christian belief in this area of opinions. It is not a sin to have this inadequate understanding or to have doubts about such things as eating meat offered to idols, though it would certainly be better to come to a right understanding of such things. But it *is* wrong, in the presence of these doubts, to go ahead and eat the meat anyway. The one who does so is "condemned." This word is κατακρίνω (*katakrinō*), an intensified form of *krinō*; it leaves no doubt that eating or doing anything else contrary to one's conscience is condemned by God as a sin.

This verse makes it clear that stumbling or falling on the part of the weak, which the strong are warned not to cause, is not just an inward disapproval of the strong's eating, or an inward distress caused by just witnessing it. It lies rather in being led to actually partake of the disapproved food: "if he eats."

Such an act is wrong for the weak Christian **because his eating is not from faith . . . .** As in vv. 1-2, the "faith" here is not one's inner trust, as if the weak Christian's faith in God and in Jesus Christ for salvation are somehow in question (contra Dunn, 2:835). Rather, it has to do with the weak brother's understanding of the content and implications of Christian faith as such. His understanding is faulty to begin with, but the problem is compounded when he yields to temptation and goes against what he believes his faith requires. His action therefore is not consistent with Christian faith as he understands it; thus he is violating his own conscience, to his own condemnation. Even though the action is not wrong in itself, he *thinks* it is wrong; therefore if he does it anyway, for him it is a sin.

[A]nd everything that does not come from faith is sin. It is tempting to take "faith" here in the specific sense of "trust in Jesus Christ," and to make this a general principle affirming that literally everything an unbeliever does is a sin before God. This may well be true, but most likely this is not Paul's point in this verse. The context limits the "everything" to the debate about matters of opinion.

Thus the point is to extend the statement in v. 23a about *eating* contrary to one's conscience, to cover *all* acts that violate one's convictions about what Christian faith requires. This again is the meaning of "does not come from faith," as in v. 23a. Thus we may paraphrase Paul thus: "Every act that is in fact a matter of opinion but is nevertheless inconsistent with one's (even faulty) understanding of Christian faith is a sin."

C. LIVING IN UNITY AND HOPE (15:1-13)

These verses form the conclusion of the larger section on Christian liberty in matters of opinion (14:1-15:13). The language in both 15:1 and 15:7 shows that Paul still has this subject in mind. The main concern seems to be how the church's handling of such matters affects its internal unity and the integrity of its witness to the watching world. The foundation and the example for such unity, says the Apostle, have been supplied by the redeeming work of Christ.

These verses conclude not only the section on Christian liberty, but also the entire unit on the application of the theological doctrine of the gospel to practical Christian living ("Living the Sanctified Life," 12:1-15:13). It likewise brings to an end the main body of the letter as a whole, and prepares the way for Paul's concluding personal remarks (15:14-16:27).

1. Selfless Service Produces a Unified Witness (15:1-6)

Like much of this section on Christian liberty, these verses are addressed mainly to the strong, which leads Dunn to comment that the primary responsibility for maintaining harmony in the church regarding matters of opinion lies with the strong (2:841). The main hindrance to harmony is the spirit of selfishness, and the key to achieving harmony is to imitate the example of Jesus Christ.

15:1 We who are strong ought to bear with the failings of the weak and not to please ourselves. The contrast is still between the weak and the strong, and these terms are still limited to the one issue of Christian liberty regarding opinions. The "weak" were described with a different term in 14:1-2, but the basic concept is the same. This is the first time Paul has used any specific term for the strong. (By saying "we who are strong," Paul includes himself in this group.)

The "strong" are those who, because of their better understanding of the implications of Christian faith, are *able* to do various things (in the category of opinions) with clear consciences. The "weak" are those who are *unable* to do these same things without violating their consciences.

The word "ought" introduces a moral obligation on the part of the strong, a debt which the strong owe to the weak. Stated positively, the strong "ought to bear with the failings of the weak." The term translated "bear with" (βαστάζω, *bastazō*) can mean "to bear with, to tolerate, to put up with, to endure," as the NIV renders it here. Most of the time in the NT, however, it means "to bear, to carry," as the NIV translates it in Gal 6:2. Most scholars believe it has this latter connotation here, too. Also, the term translated "failings" in the NIV is simply "weaknesses"; the word "failings" has a negative connotation not evident in the Greek.

All in all the NASB translation is better here: the strong "ought to bear the weaknesses of those without strength." This is a specific instance of the general principle in Gal 6:2, "Carry each other's burdens." I.e., the strong should not merely tolerate the weaknesses of the weak, but should help them carry the burden of their scruples. How may we — the strong — do this? By trying to understand the weak, and by putting ourselves in their place.

Why should the strong be the ones required to make this sort of concession? Because, as Lard says, the strong can do so without violating their consciences, but the weak cannot (431).

The negative aspect of the moral obligation of the strong is "not to please ourselves." Here Paul identifies the real key to unity, harmony, and peace within the body of Christ, i.e., *selflessness*, or the willingness to sacrifice one's personal rights and personal happiness in order to meet the needs of others (❡II:420).

15:2 Each of us should please his neighbor for his good, to build him up. "Each of us" could refer to all Christians (Morris, 497-498), but most likely it refers still to strong Christians, the "we" in v. 1 (Moo, 866-867). Thus "each of us should please his neighbor" is simply the same obligation as v. 1b, stated positively. In this case the "neighbor" is the weak Christian.

The rest of this verse — "for his good, to build him up" — identifies and limits the kind of neighbor-pleasing to which Paul is referring. First, this description distinguishes "neighbor-pleasing" from the sinful "man-pleasing" condemned elsewhere by Paul (Gal 1:10; 1 Thess 2:4; see Eph 6:6 and Col 3:22, NASB). In the latter the contrasting choices are pleasing *men* and pleasing *God*; in such circumstances "man-pleasing" means trying to win someone's favor for one's own personal, self-serving purposes. But here in 15:1-2 the contrasting choices are pleasing *ourselves* and pleasing *others*, where "neighbor-pleasing" means that we sacrifice our own desires for the good of the other.

Second, this description — "for his good, to build him up" — limits the extent to which we should go in pleasing our neighbor. Such neighbor-pleasing is not absolute, as if "we are always to defer to the whims and wishes of others" (Murray, 2:197-198). The context shows that Paul is talking about pleasing one's neighbor in areas of opinion where his conscience is threatened by his weak faith. Pleasing the weak "for his good" means "for his spiritual profit or spiritual advantage." It means doing what is necessary to help him maintain a clear conscience in these areas. This includes making an effort to lead the weak out of his unnecessary scruples.

15:3 For even Christ did not please himself . . . . Here Jesus is cited as a model for the virtue of selflessness, one which we should imitate. This is also the main point of Phil 2:5-11, which declares that the selfless attitude of the eternal Logos is exhibited in the incarnation, in his accepting the role of a servant, and especially in his submission to the cross. In every way the Logos put the needs and the interests of the lost human race before his own. It was the Father's will that Jesus undergo an unimaginably agonizing death to save us from our sins, and Jesus surrendered his will to that of his Father. (See Heb 10:7; Matt 20:28 [Mark 10:45]; Matt 26:39 [Luke 22:42]; John 4:24; 5:30; 6:38.) When we as Christians relate to one another in this same spirit of selfless service (Phil 2:5), unity and harmony will surely follow (Phil 2:1-4).

Paul cites just one OT prophecy concerning Jesus to illustrate and confirm his spirit of unselfishness: **. . . but, as it is written: "The insults of those who insult you have fallen on me."** This is taken directly from Ps 69:9b, where David is lamenting that God's enemies are also his enemies and are taking out their hatred of God on him. Paul in effect puts David's words in the mouth of Christ, thus making David's suffering a type of Christ's suffering on the cross. Christ thus declares that, in his submissive life and especially in his substitutionary death, the insults (reproaches, blasphemies) that sinners direct against God are being borne by him. And if Jesus himself made such a selfless choice, we should all the more be willing to do so for the sake of our weak brothers.

15:4 The next verse is a parenthesis in which Paul reminds us of the validity of citing OT texts as a basis for ethical exhortation to Christians: **For everything that was written in the past was written to teach us, . . .** "Everything that was written" refers to OT Scripture, and declares that every part of it has meaning and value for those living under the New Covenant. It was written not just to teach us theological truths, but also to be a source of practical instruction for Christians concerning how to live. Paul was thinking mainly (but not exclusively) of OT Scripture when he said, "All Scripture is God-breathed and is useful for teaching, rebuking, correcting and training in righteousness, so that the man of God may be thoroughly equipped for every good work" (2 Tim 3:16-17). See 1 Cor 9:10; 10:6,11; Rom 4:23-25.

In particular, says Paul, the OT was written **so that through endurance and the encouragement of the Scriptures we might have hope.** "Endurance" (ὑπομονή, *hypomonē*) is the same as "perseverance" in 5:3; it indicates patient endurance, steadfastness, the ability to bear and to bear up under whatever comes along. "Encouragement" (παράκλησις, *paraklēsis*) has the connotation of "exhortation" in 12:8, but here it means "comfort, consolation, encouragement." "Hope" (ἐλπίς, *elpis*) for Christians is the confident and joyful expectation of the future possession of full salvation, as explained under 4:18 and 5:2.

This is a purpose clause, introduced by ἵνα (*hina*, "so that, in order that"). I.e., God intends for us to be taught by the OT Scriptures, to the end that "we might have hope." How does the study of the OT give hope to Christians? Paul says it does so specifically "through endurance and the encouragement of the Scriptures."

In my judgment the context (Paul's explanation for citing the OT) favors the view that "of the Scriptures" is meant to modify both endurance and encouragement (❧II:423). The point is that when we read the OT accounts of and testimony to God's just and faithful dealings with Israel, this reinforces our confidence in God's promises to us through the New Covenant, and thus gives us patience and encouragement in times of personal spiritual doubt and distress. The result of such endurance and encouragement is that our hope — our assurance of salvation — is in turn strengthened. This hope is fortified even further by "reading the OT and seeing its fulfillment in Christ and the church" (Moo, 870). On the relationship between endurance and hope, see 5:3-4; 1 Thess 1:3.

15:5-6 The next two verses are a prayer for God to bless the church with the spirit of unity: **May the God who gives endurance and encouragement give you a spirit of unity among yourselves as you follow Christ Jesus, so that with one heart and mouth you may glorify the God and Father of our Lord Jesus Christ.**

The Greek text speaks literally of "the God of endurance and encouragement"; the NIV rightly takes this to mean that God is the *source* of these blessings in the Christian life. The idea is that God by his words and deeds gives us every reason to have patient endurance and to be encouraged even in the bleakest of circumstances, and he gives us knowledge of and access to these words and deeds through his Spirit-inspired Scriptures (see v. 4).

The heart of Paul's prayer is that God "will give you a spirit of unity among yourselves." Just what is the nature of the unity for which Paul prays (❀ II:424)? Paul's language here shows that this unity is not just a harmonious spirit, but also a unity of faith, i.e., an agreement as to the *content* of what is believed. "A spirit of unity" is literally "to be of the same mind." This phrase does not necessarily refer to intellectual agreement, since it occurs in the same or similar form in 12:16 and Phil 2:2, where it refers to the general unity of love and purpose. But the reference to the "mind" does leave the door open for the concept of intellectual agreement; and the expression "with one mouth" in v. 6 definitely shows that this is part of what Paul is praying for.

"With one mouth" shows that the church's unity must be on a verbal level, which certainly involves a unity in worship (SH, 396; Dunn, 2:841); but this presupposes a unity of *what we believe* about the one whom we worship. Lenski says it involves outward agreement wherein all confess "the one same gospel truth" (863).

This prayer for unity regarding what we believe certainly does not prescribe total agreement regarding matters of opinion, since matters of opinion by definition do not require agreement. In reference to opinions, the most Paul can be praying for is that all Christians have the same understanding of the *nature* of *adiaphora* or opinions, and of how to *handle* them with mature faith. But at the very least this prayer is instructing us to seek basic agreement concerning the fundamental truths about God and the gospel (see Cottrell, *Faith's Fundamentals*) over against the idea that "each man may have . . . the right to his own personal views" about the truths affirmed in God's Word (Lenski, 864).

Paul prays that the church will have such unity "as you follow Christ Jesus," or better, "according to Christ Jesus" (NASB). Some take this to mean "according to Jesus' example" (SH, 396; Murray, 2:201; Dunn, 2:840); others "according to Jesus' will" (Cranfield, 2:737). Paul may have both of these in mind (Lard, 433; Hendriksen, 2:473), but the main point is that Christ Jesus must always be the touchstone of the church's unity. That is, we must never pursue unity just for the sake of unity. God is not interested in unity at all costs, especially at the cost of truth. Those things on which the church is united must correspond to Christ's way, Christ's will, Christ's gospel, and Christ's word as we know it through inspired Scripture.

What is the purpose of seeking this inner harmony and this unity of confessed faith? So that "you may glorify the God and Father of our Lord Jesus Christ." To glorify God is to acknowledge and declare his greatness before others, and to lead them to do the same (see 1:21). A church with internal dissensions and conflicting beliefs brings dishonor to God and to Jesus its Head. A church united in heart and mind brings glory to both. See 1 Cor 1:10; Eph 4:11-15.

Some may raise questions about the description of God as "the God and Father of our Lord Jesus Christ." No one will have a problem with calling God "the *Father* of our Lord Jesus Christ." But since Jesus himself is divine, i.e., God the Son, how can we speak of "the *God* of Jesus Christ"? The KJV translates it "God, even the Father of our Lord Jesus Christ"; Lard agrees (434). But there is no problem with the language as it stands in the NIV. In his incarnate state as Jesus of Nazareth, the human nature of Jesus was in full submission to God the Father as *his God*. In John 20:17, speaking to Mary, Jesus refers to God the Father as "my God and your God." Eph 1:17 uses the very phrase, "the God of our Lord Jesus Christ." See also Matt 27:46 (Mark 15:34) and Heb 1:9. There is no conflict between this concept and the divinity of Christ.

2. Through Christ's Selfless Service, Jews and Gentiles Glorify God Together (15:7-12)

Some see this paragraph as standing alone and serving as a conclusion to the doctrinal body of the letter (Dunn, 2:844). Most, however, see it as belonging to the section on Christian liberty. The main emphasis still seems to be on the unity of the body of Christ, which was being threatened by false approaches to matters of opinion.

The main point is the way the saving work of Jesus has united two groups, the Jews and the Gentiles, into one body and into one voice singing praises to God. This is significant because in the ancient world these two groups would surely have been regarded as the least likely to be reconciled. In the immediate context this serves as another argument from the greater to the lesser. If Christ's selfless service can succeed in unifying such disparate groups as the Jews and the Gentiles, surely we as Christians can do what is necessary to establish accord among strong and weak believers within the church.

Paul's bringing together of Jews and Gentiles in this paragraph serves other purposes, too. It means that Paul has come full circle in his presentation of the gospel, which in the introduction was announced to be God's way of salvation, "first for the Jew, then for the Gentile" (1:16). It calls attention again to the fact that God's faithfulness to the Jews has always involved his intention to save the

Gentiles as well (chs. 9–11). Finally, Paul's citation of OT prophecies concerning the salvation of the Gentiles serves as a transition to his personal remarks about his own mission to the Gentiles (15:14-33).

Some think the reference to Jews and Gentiles at this point supports the view that the weak and the strong in the church at Rome were divided mainly along these lines, with the weak being mainly from the Jews and the strong mainly from the Gentiles (SH, 397; Cranfield, 2:740-741). Others are rightly reluctant to draw this conclusion (Lenski, 866; Murray, 2:204). Even if we think there is a hint in this direction, this discussion of Jews and Gentiles is better explained by the points mentioned above (see Dunn, 2:852).

15:7 Accept one another, then, just as Christ accepted you, in order to bring praise to God. It seems clear that this paragraph is meant to be the conclusion to the section on Christian liberty (Moo, 874). This verse begins with the conjunction διό (*dio*, "wherefore, then"), indicating that the following exhortation is an inference from the preceding discussion (14:1–15:6). The exhortation to "accept" one another also ties this paragraph to this same discussion, since 14:1 uses the same verb to exhort the strong to "accept" the weak. Another link is the stated bases for the two exhortations: accept the weak, "for God has accepted him" (14:3); accept each other "as Christ accepted you" (15:7).

While this exhortation is parallel to 14:1, it also goes beyond it by addressing the entire church and not just the strong. In fact, it has the nature of a general principle that applies to all potential causes of division in the church. The fact that Christ has united Jews and Gentiles together serves as a paradigm for the healing of all divisions. His acceptance of both groups is the reason why we should embrace all believers in full fellowship despite differences that do not affect our common salvation. Paul's point is "that all are to accept those who differ from them" (Morris, 503) (❂ II:427-428).

15:8a For I tell you that Christ has become a servant of the Jews on behalf of God's truth, . . . Here Paul begins to explain how Christ has "accepted you" through the redeeming work performed in his role as the Jewish Messiah. The words "I tell you" introduce "a solemn doctrinal declaration" (Cranfield, 2:740). "Servant" is διάκονος (*diakonos*), which can mean "deacon" or "minister," but is rightly translated here with its basic generic sense, "servant." "Has become" is in the perfect tense, indicating past action (perhaps the incarnation but certainly the atonement and resurrection) with a lasting result; Christ is still "a servant of the Jews" (Morris, 503). "Jews" is literally "circumcision," a term often used for the Jews as a nation (see 3:30; 4:12; Gal 2:8-9). This emphasizes the fact that the Jews were under the covenant God made with Abraham, of which circumcision was the covenant sign (Gen 17:1-14).

That the Logos entered the world in the role of a servant is clear; see v. 3 above, and see Phil 2:7-8, where he is called a "slave" (δοῦλος, *doulos*). Jesus says that he "did not come to be served, but to serve" (Matt 20:28; Mark 10:45; see

Luke 22:27). He was primarily a servant of the Father himself (Isa 52:13), but in that role he served the lost world by giving "his life as a ransom for many" (Matt 20:28).

Most specifically Jesus performed his redeeming work as "a servant of the Jews." This refers to his role as the Jews' Messiah (the Christ). In order to fulfill this role Christ Jesus came into the world *through* the Jews (John 4:22; Rom 9:4-5) and *for* the Jews, i.e., so that the Jews themselves might be the first to receive the gospel of salvation (Matt 15:24; Rom 1:16; 2:10; Gal 4:4-5).

Paul affirms that Jesus became a servant of the Jews "on behalf of God's truth." "Truth" (ἀλήθεια, *alētheia*) here refers to an attribute of God and may better be rendered "truthfulness," "fidelity," or "faithfulness." The specific reference is to God's faithfulness to his covenant promises. Everything Christ did as the Jewish Messiah was in fulfilment of what God has been promising to do for his people (both Jews and Gentiles) from the very beginning of his covenant with Abraham (Gen 12:1-3).

15:8b-9a The rest of this section shows how Christ's Jewish Messiahship has affected not only the Jews but the Gentiles as well. Christ was a servant of the Jews **to confirm the promises made to the patriarchs so that the Gentiles may glorify God for his mercy, . . .** (See ❧ II:429.) The first intended result of Christ's Messiahship was "to confirm the promises made to the patriarchs" (Abraham, Isaac, and Jacob). This reference to the patriarchs (or "fathers"; see 9:5), along with the very phrase "servant of the Jews," shows that Paul is here referring to promises concerning the Jews themselves. See Gen 12:1-3; 13:14-17; 15:1-5; 17:1-8; 18:19; 22:15-18; 26:3-4; 28:13-15.

Paul has already affirmed that God in his faithfulness has fulfilled all his promises to the Jews as a nation (9:4-5) and as a believing remnant (see the entire discussion in chs. 9–11). Here he says that Christ's work as the Jews' servant has *confirmed* these promises. This means that he has proved the promises to be reliable and trustworthy, but it means more than this. Christ has confirmed the promises by fulfilling them, by establishing them, by bringing them to realization. What was in the beginning just a promise is now a reality for the Jews.

The second intended result of Christ's Messiahship, and the one Paul emphasizes, was to enable the Gentiles to "glorify God for his mercy." This purpose is seen in the fact that the covenant promises made to the patriarchs included the blessing of salvation for all peoples and nations on earth (Gen 12:3; 17:3-5; 22:18; 26:4; 28:14; Rom 4:13,16-17). Though Christ's earthly ministry was conducted almost entirely among the Jews, his "great commission" directs that the gospel be preached to all nations (Matt 28:19; Luke 24:47; Acts 1:8). By thus including the Gentiles within the scope of his salvation, Christ causes them to glorify God (see v. 6), specifically for having mercy upon them (see 11:30-32).

15:9b The rest of this section is a series of four quotes from the OT showing that God all along intended to bring the Gentiles within the scope of his mercy, thus uniting Jews and Gentiles together into one harmonious chorus of praise to God.

The first quote is as follows: **. . . as it is written: "Therefore I will praise you among the Gentiles; I will sing hymns to your name."** This is a direct quote from Ps 18:49 (LXX, 17:50) and 2 Sam 22:50, except for the omission of "O LORD." In this Psalm David is praising God for giving him victory over his enemies and for making the nations subject to him. In verse 49 he announces that he will sing hymns of praise to the Lord among these nations (i.e., Gentiles), so that the Gentiles may know the true God and join in the praise.

Paul sees in this Psalm an indication of God's plan to include the Gentiles in the Messiah's people. As Cranfield notes (2:795), it is possible that the Apostle sees David's words as foreshadowing his own mission to the Gentiles, a subject he is just about to expand upon (15:14ff.).

The word for "sing hymns" is simply ψάλλω (*psallō*), which Morris says "referred originally to plucking the strings of a musical instrument; later it appears to have been used of singing with accompaniment and then simply of singing. There is nothing in the Greek to correspond to NIV's *hymns*; the translators have assumed (not unreasonably) that it is hymns that would be sung to God" (505, n. 51).

15:10 Again, it says, "Rejoice, O Gentiles, with his people." This next quotation is the first line of Deut 32:43 (LXX). Deuteronomy 32 is a song of Moses celebrating the righteousness of God that takes vengeance on his enemies and saves his people. In this line Moses invites the nations (Gentiles) to join with God's people (the Jews) in rejoicing over this. The key phrase is "with his people," which contemplates Jews and Gentiles praising God with a single voice. Paul sees this as an expression of God's plan to unite the two groups.

15:11 And again, "Praise the Lord, all you Gentiles, and sing praises to him, all you peoples." This is a close paraphrase of Ps 117:1 (LXX, 116:1). The main point again is the reference to the Gentiles and the fact that they are invited to sing praises to the Lord, the God of Israel. This is another indication that the work of the Messiah was intended to bring Jews and Gentiles together into one body so that "his people" (v. 10) along with "all you peoples" (v. 11) may glorify God together for his mercy.

15:12 And again, Isaiah says, "The Root of Jesse will spring up, one who will arise to rule over the nations; the Gentiles will hope in him." This is taken from Isa 11:10 and is closer to the LXX than to the Hebrew text. It is a specific messianic prophecy, "the Root of Jesse" being a title for Jesus. Jesse was David's father; thus this title is equivalent to "the Root of David" in Rev 5:5; 22:16, which refers to Christ. The word translated "root" can mean either the root itself or a shoot or sprout that comes forth from the root. In this case "Jesse," standing for the family and dynasty of David (see Luke 2:4), is the root itself; Jesus is the shoot or sprout that springs up from that root (Isa 11:1; 53:2).

The main point is that when "the Root of Jesse" rises up, the Gentiles will rally around him and submit to him and find their salvation in him. The Hebrew text of Isa 11:10 says that "the Root of Jesse will stand as a banner for the peoples." The LXX interprets the banner or ensign as a symbol of command and authority; thus when the Gentiles rally around this banner (which is Jesus himself), they are submitting to him and he is ruling over them.

The messianic rule of which Isaiah speaks is not a military conquest of rebellious and unwilling foes, but a benevolent embrace of willing subjects for the purpose of bestowing mercy upon them. As a result, "the Gentiles will hope in him," i.e., they will find their salvation in him. The startling thing about this is that the *Gentiles* will be saved by submitting to the Messiah of the *Jews*! (❧ II:432).

In view of God's majestic and glorious program for uniting all believers into a single ensemble of praise, how can we refuse to obey the simple command to "accept one another" (15:7)?

3. A Prayer That All Believers May Abound in Hope (15:13)

15:13 May the God of hope fill you with all joy and peace as you trust in him, so that you may overflow with hope by the power of the Holy Spirit. This last verse of the main body of the letter expresses Paul's desire that all Christians may experience the fullness of the spiritual benefits that come from knowing, understanding, and receiving the gospel of God's grace. As such it draws together many of the main threads that the Apostle has woven into the carefully designed pattern of his doctrinal essay about this gospel. Specifically mentioned are faith, joy, peace, hope, and power.

The first and primary benefit that comes from knowing the gospel is faith itself (10:17). All the other blessings come only "as you trust in him," or literally, "in connection with believing" (❧ II:433).

Paul prays that we as believers may be filled with joy, peace, and hope, all of which come from knowing that we are justified by faith in the blood of Christ (5:1-2). *Peace* is first of all the objective state of being reconciled to God (5:1,10). It is also an attitude of inward tranquility and freedom from worry about salvation (1:7; 8:6); this is the main point in view here. Finally peace is the corporate harmony that exists among brethren (14:17).

Joy is the inward delight and jubilance that keep us excited about being Christians, about being under the blood of Christ, and about living the sanctified life (5:2-3,11; 12:12,15; 14:17). Joy and peace together are "two of the great human desirables," as Dunn says (2:853), and they are available to mankind only through the gospel of Jesus Christ.

The last of this trio of related blessings is *hope*, which is a key aspect of assurance and in many ways is equivalent to it. Assurance is first of all a peaceful confidence about our *present* relationship with God through Jesus Christ; second, it is a joyful expectation of the *future* fullness of glory to be received when Christ returns. The latter is the essence of hope.

Knowing that we are justified by faith is the key to such hope or assurance (5:1-2). That God is here called "the God of hope," i.e., the source of everything that gives us hope, shows how important hope is in the context of the gospel.

Paul's prayer and wish are not just that believers might *possess* joy, peace, and hope, but that we might be *filled to overflowing* with these blessings. Since they are linked to faith, they will increase as our faith increases (Luke 17:5). Faith consists of *assent* and *trust* (1:16; ❂ I:107-108). Assent increases as we grow in our understanding of what we believe about Jesus and the gospel, and trust increases as we grow in our love for Jesus and in confidence in his promises.

The ultimate means of our being filled to overflowing with joy, peace, and hope is the fifth blessing mentioned in this verse, i.e., *power* — "the power of the Holy Spirit." Paul has made it clear in Romans that all spiritual growth comes from the power of the indwelling Spirit (2:29; 5:5; 8:3-16,26-27; 14:17; see Gal 5:22-23). Here he prays that the Spirit's power may work within our hearts to make us abound in hope. There could hardly be a more appropriate conclusion to the didactic body of the Epistle to the Romans!

15:14-16:27 — PART SIX
PERSONAL MESSAGES FROM PAUL

What remains of the epistle is a kind of epilogue containing many of the same elements found in the conclusions of Paul's other letters and written on a very personal level (❖ II:435).

I. PAUL'S MINISTRY AS THE APOSTLE TO THE GENTILES (15:14-33)

As he begins his conclusion, Paul first of all expresses his confidence in the spiritual maturity of the Christians at Rome, and suggests that the sternness of some of his exhortations is not meant to imply weakness on their part (14-15a). All of his ministry, including the writing of this letter, is carried out in his specific role as the Apostle to the Gentiles, which he regards as a kind of priesthood in which he offers up converted Gentiles as sacrifices pleasing to God (15b-16).

Paul realizes that his work has produced significant results, but he gives God all the glory (17-19a). Up to the time of this writing, he has concentrated his efforts in the geographical area ranging from Jerusalem to Illyricum, using the strategy of starting new churches in unevangelized areas (19b-21). This has kept him so busy that he has been unable to fulfill his dream of visiting Rome (22).

But the situation is different now. He has accomplished his purpose for this eastern area and is now ready to travel west, stopping off to visit the Christians in Rome on his way to evangelize Spain — an endeavor for which he hopes to enlist the aid of the church in Rome (23-24).

But before he can begin to carry out this plan, he has one other very important task to complete. He must journey to Jerusalem and deliver the contributions he has collected from the Gentile churches for the poor saints in the Jerusalem church (25-27; see ❖ I:35-36). Then he will head directly to Rome and on to Spain (28-29).

The side trip to Jerusalem is anything but routine, however. Paul anticipates the possibility of serious problems there, including attacks upon him personally from non-Christian Jews, and a reluctance on the part of the Jewish Christians to accept gifts from Gentile Christians. Therefore he urges the Roman brethren to join him in praying that the Jerusalem trip will go well, so that he may subsequently go on to Rome in a joyful spirit (30-32). He prays for God's peace to be with them (33).

Some see this section as the key to Paul's purpose for writing Romans in the first place, or at least the key to "the content and emphases of the letter" (Moo, 885). Some think Paul's long essay is intended to demonstrate his doctrinal orthodoxy to the Roman Christians, showing them the gospel he would preach in Spain as part of his effort to persuade them to back his mission there. Others think Paul is rehearsing the defense he will give in Jerusalem, in case his orthodoxy is challenged in connection with the delivery of the Gentile Christians' gifts to the Jerusalem church. (See ❋I:40-42; see Dunn, 2:884.)

In my opinion, though, these factors are secondary in Paul's mind as he writes this letter. His main purpose, as explained earlier (❋I:44-45), stems from his eager desire "to preach the gospel also to you who are at Rome" (1:15).

While the themes of this section definitely overlap the contents of the introduction to the epistle (1:1-17; see Moo, 886), there is significant new information here, as the above summary indicates. We may break it down into paragraphs dealing with Paul's past service (14-22), his future plans (23-29), and his request for prayer (30-33).

A. REFLECTIONS ON HIS PAST SERVICE (15:14-22)

This paragraph gives us important insights, first into Paul as a person, and then into his self-understanding of his apostolic ministry. The former is manifest in vv. 14-15, in the way he deals with his concern that the Christians in Rome might misunderstand the occasionally serious tone of his letter. He has uttered some rather stern rebukes and strong exhortations along the way, and now he wants to make sure that the brethren in Rome do not take these to mean that he had a low opinion of their Christian faith and life. Thus he expresses his own confidence in them and compliments them on their personal maturity as Christians (see 1:8; 16:19). At the same time he wants them not to see him as insensitive and presumptuous but to understand that it is his duty as the Apostle to the Gentiles to address them with authority. (See MacArthur, 2:326; Stott, 377; ❋II:437.)

15:14 I myself am convinced, my brothers, that you yourselves are full of goodness, complete in knowledge and competent to instruct one another. We must not forget that the just-completed essay on the doctrine of salvation was not written just for the sake of the church at Rome, but was intended by the Holy Spirit to apply to the entire body of Christ in all ages. At times Paul's admonitions seem rather severe, e.g., 6:1-3,15-16; 11:17-22; 13:12-14; 14:1-4,10-16; and in the church as a whole some Christians will feel their sting more than others will.

This is why Paul wants the Christians in Rome to know that he is not necessarily implying that they are personally lacking in these areas. "I myself" translates an emphatic phrase, as does "you yourselves." "As far as I personally am concerned," Paul says, "I am persuaded that you personally are Christians of solid maturity." He knew their good reputation (1:8; 16:19), and he knew some of them on a personal basis. His praise is neither insincere flattery nor oily diplomacy, nor is he apologizing for anything he has said.

Paul compliments the Roman Christians in three areas. First, he says they are "full of goodness" (ἀγαθοσύνη, *agathosynē*). This basically refers to a morally upright character, a general goodness of the heart that loves righteousness and opposes all that is evil. That the Romans were *full* of goodness is hyperbole since perfection eludes all. It means, says Morris, that they had a "plentiful supply" of goodness and not just an occasional episode of it (509). In any case it is a high compliment (❦II:438).

Paul next praises the church at Rome for being "complete in knowledge," or "filled with all knowledge" (NASB). This again is hyperbole, since omniscience belongs to God alone. Paul is saying that they have a solid and practical understanding of Christian teaching (❦II:438-439).

In his third compliment Paul declares that the Romans are "competent to instruct one another" (❦II:437.) He is basically saying that they do not need for him to admonish them, for they are fully capable of admonishing one another.

15:15 I have written you quite boldly on some points, as if to remind you of them again, because of the grace God gave me . . . . In what sense is this letter somewhat *bold* (audacious, daring)? Paul may be referring to those places mentioned above where his admonitions are rather severe. He may also be referring to his explanation of the fundamental facts of the gospel, the deeper implications of which is here setting forth. He says he is *reminding* them *again* of these things, implying the prior knowledge mentioned in v. 14 (❦II:439-440). In the last part of the verse Paul declares that he has reminded them of these things somewhat boldly on account of "the grace God gave to me." This grace is the gift of apostleship, his commission to be the Apostle to the Gentiles (see 1:5; ❦I:77-78).

15:16 Paul now explains the essence of his apostleship. God gave me this grace, he says, **to be a minister of Christ Jesus to the Gentiles with the priestly duty of proclaiming the gospel of God, so that the Gentiles might become an offering acceptable to God, sanctified by the Holy Spirit.** Three words in this verse show that Paul viewed his ministry as a (metaphorical) *priesthood*. First, he says God's grace has made him a "minister" (λειτουργός, *leitourgos*; see 13:6). This word does not always have a religious connotation, but the present context, especially in light of the other two words discussed below, shows that Paul has this priestly connotation in mind here. He thus identifies himself as a priestly minister serving Jesus Christ "to the Gentiles," or for the sake of the Gentiles.

The second religious or cultic word used here is the verb ἱερουργέω (*hierourgeō*), translated "priestly duty" in the NIV. Most agree that it means "to serve or act as a priest." Thus Paul says that his specific work as a minister of Christ is to perform the work of a priest, and to do so with reference to "the gospel of God." The latter phrase can mean "by proclaiming the gospel," i.e., by using the gospel as an instrument. Or it can mean "for the cause of the gospel," i.e., to bring about the ultimate purpose sought by the gospel: the salvation of sinners (or in Paul's case, *Gentile* sinners).

The third word identifying Paul's ministry as a priesthood is "offering," or προσφορά (*prosphora*), which in this case means the *thing* offered or sacrificed to God (see Acts 21:26; Eph 5:2; Heb 10:5,8). The main work of a priest is to offer sacrifices to God on behalf of sinners in order to restore them to a proper relationship with God. This is why Paul was called to his priestly ministry, i.e., for the purpose of presenting an offering before God.

What offering does Paul the priest present to God? Literally, "the offering of the Gentiles," i.e., the offering that consists of the Gentiles. As the result of Paul's ministry, converted Gentiles are themselves offered up to God as sacrifices that are well-pleasing and acceptable in his sight. This does not mean simply that he leads them to *offer themselves* as living sacrifices (12:1); in his role as priest, Paul is the one who presents them to God (Stott, 379; contra Morris, 511). See Isa 66:19-21.

Paul says that this offering is "acceptable to God" because it is "sanctified by the Holy Spirit." Just as OT temple sacrifices had to be ritually clean and acceptable to God, so must NT sacrifices be acceptable to him. In the eyes of the Jews, the Gentiles were considered to be unclean and therefore unacceptable by nature, just because they were not Jews (Acts 10:9-16,28,34-35; 11:1-18). But God makes the Gentiles acceptable to him by *sanctifying* them through the Holy Spirit. This was done symbolically for all time when God poured out his Spirit on Cornelius and his household (Acts 10:44-47; 11:15-17; 15:8-9); and it is done for every individual Gentile convert when he receives the gift of the indwelling Spirit in Christian baptism (Acts 2:38,39; 1 Cor 12:3). At this point he is initially sanctified or set apart unto God "by the Spirit" (1 Cor 6:11).

Thus the essence of Paul's apostolic ministry is priestly service. The same can be said also of all those who preach the gospel. Paul's priestly offerings were specialized (the Gentiles), but in a real sense "all evangelists are priests because they offer their converts to God" (Stott, 379). Actually, every Christian is a priest and has some sort of sacrifice to offer. The Protestant Reformers rightly spoke of the "priesthood of all believers." The church, says Peter, is "a holy priesthood, offering spiritual sacrifices acceptable to God through Jesus Christ" (1 Pet 2:5; see 2:9; Rev 1:6; 20:6). These "spiritual sacrifices" are the "sacrifice of praise," or *good words* (Heb 13:15), and also the sacrifices of *good works* (Heb 13:16).

15:17 Therefore I glory in Christ Jesus in my service to God. "I glory" is literally "I have a reason for boasting." In terms of both the quantity and the quality of of his service — winning converts, starting churches, writing books of the Bible! — Paul certainly could have put together a very impressive resume. But he was not interested in bringing glory to himself. He knew that his apostleship as such was a gift of grace (v. 15b), that the gospel is the real power that saves (1:16; 10:17), and that he owed his accomplishments to God's power working through him (v. 19a). See Jer 9:24; 1 Cor 1:31; 2 Cor 10:17.

15:18 I will not venture to speak of anything except what Christ has accomplished through me in leading the Gentiles to obey God by what I have said and done. . . . Christ certainly accomplished many things through Paul, resulting in obedience on the part of many Gentiles (see 1:5, ❧I:78-82). But here Paul reiterates and explains the determination expressed in v. 17, not to call attention to himself or to speak of his accomplishments as if they were his own. He will talk about them, but only as things that Christ has done through him, using him as an instrument. "Not I, but Christ" is his theme. See Acts 15:1-2; 21:19.

Verse 18 ends with the short phrase, "by word and deed" (NASB). The NIV interprets this, as do most scholars, as modifying "accomplished," i.e., as referring to *Paul's* words and deeds. In this case it is a brief but comprehensive reference to his total ministry. "By word" refers to his preaching and teaching; "by deed" refers to his journeys, his sufferings, his miracles, and his many labors. See 2 Cor 10:11.

It is also possible to take this phrase as modifying "the obedience of the Gentiles," in which case it would mean that Paul's priestly ministry is intended to lead the Gentiles into a life of total obedience, in word and deed. See Col 3:17; 2 Thess 2:17.

15:19a *How* did Christ accomplish the evangelization of the Gentiles through Paul? He did it **by the power of signs and miracles, through the power of the Spirit.** He did it first of all by "the power of signs and wonders" (NASB). All three of these words are used elsewhere to refer to miracles (Acts 2:22; 2 Cor 12:12; Heb 2:4; see 2 Thess 2:9; see *GRu*, 229-231). "Signs" refers to miracles in terms of their purpose, namely, to function as proof or evidence for the validity of an accompanying truth-claim (see *GRu*, 231-240). They can function thus because they are also "wonders." I.e., because miracles are observable events that are outside the laws of nature (*GRu*, 244-261), they elicit awe and wonder in those who observe or hear of them. Miracles are also called "powers," referring to their source in the mighty power of God. (Here in 15:19a the word "power" is not referring to the miracles as such, but to the divine power from which they come.)

As an Apostle, Paul had the ability to perform miracles, and used it to attest to the truth of the message he proclaimed. These miracles confirmed the authenticity of his apostleship (2 Cor 12:12).

"Through the power of the Holy Spirit" could be saying only that the signs and wonders were done through the Spirit's power, but most (rightly) take it as setting forth a more general reason for the success of Paul's work among the Gentiles. I.e., *everything* Christ did through Paul was accomplished through the power of the Spirit working in him (❧II:444).

15:19b Having reflected on the source of, essence of, and power behind his ministry as the apostle to the Gentiles, Paul now tells us (in vv. 19b-22) something of the *strategy* behind it, and how that strategy has affected and is still affecting his choices of *where* to serve. He says, **So from Jerusalem all the way around to Illyricum, I have fully proclaimed the gospel of Christ.**

Here he sums up where he has preached the gospel thus far, i.e., within the boundaries of an arc-like span around the northeastern portion of the Mediterranean Sea, reaching from Jerusalem in the southeast to Illyricum in the northwest (❂ II:444-445).

What does Paul mean when he says he "fully proclaimed the gospel of Christ" in this area? Literally he says he "fulfilled the gospel" there. This could possibly refer to the *content* of his preaching, indicating that he left nothing out of his message (see Acts 20:20,27); but that does not seem to be his point here. In this context he is focusing on the *places* where he preached.

Is he affirming, then, that he has already preached the gospel in every city, town, and village within the Jerusalem-Illyricum arc? No, this would have been physically impossible. The reasonable consensus is a little different, namely, that he "fully proclaimed the gospel" in the entire area named, but only according to the strategy explained in vv. 20-21. I.e., he preached in all the strategic cities and population centers in these provinces, going where no one had yet carried the gospel, and planting new churches which could then take up the task of spreading the Word to the surrounding regions. Thus in terms of his special mission as a trailblazing, pioneer preacher, he had indeed "fulfilled the gospel" within the described arc.

15:20 It has always been my ambition to preach the gospel where Christ was not known, so that I would not be building on someone else's foundation. This verse begins with Greek words unfortunately not translated by the NIV, οὕτως δέ (*houtōs de*). (See the NASB, "And thus.") *Houtōs* means "thus, in this way." It connects v. 20 with v. 19 by explaining *how* Paul was able to fully proclaim the gospel from Jerusalem to Illyricum. I.e., he was able to complete this task because it was his policy always to be covering new ground in his effort to get the message out.

Paul states his strategy in two ways. First, his goal has been to preach "where Christ was not known," or literally, "not named." That is, he wanted to go into virgin territory where the Gentiles had not yet heard about Jesus and had not had the opportunity to name him as their Savior and Lord (10:9-13; 2 Tim 2:19).

Second, he has made it his practice to concentrate on unevangelized areas "so that [ἵνα, *hina*] I would not be building on someone else's foundation." This was exactly how he had worked in Corinth (1 Cor 3:6,10; ❂ II:446).

While this was his general strategy, it was not an absolute rule and did not prevent him from making certain exceptions under special circumstances. For example, he was planning an immediate trip to Jerusalem to deliver the Gentile

Christians' offering to the poor saints there (15:25-27). Also, he had long desired to visit Rome (1:9-15; 15:23) and was planning to go there as soon as he completed his business in Jerusalem (15:24,28).

While his planned visit to Rome would clearly be an exception to his usual policy, it was at the same time subordinated to it. The main reason he had not visited there earlier, he says (vv. 22-23), is that he was concentrating on the unevangelized regions in the East. Also, his visit to Rome would be part of a larger plan to begin a pioneer gospel mission in the West, specifically, in Spain (vv. 24,28). Finally, the visit to Rome would be just that: a brief visit (vv. 24,28).

15:21 Paul now cites an OT text which he sees as validating his pioneer-preacher policy. **Rather, as it is written: "Those who were not told about him will see, and those who have not heard will understand."** (The quote is from Isa 52:15, LXX.) This text is about the Servant of Yahweh and is undoubtedly messianic; it prepares the way for the great prophecy of Christ's propitiatory death in Isa 53. Paul cites this verse because the first part of it clearly indicates that Isaiah is talking about the Gentiles: "So will he [the Suffering Servant] sprinkle many nations" (i.e., to purify them; see 15:16).

The Gentiles are the ones "who were not told" about the Messiah, and "who have not heard." The point of the prophecy, however, is that they *will* see, and they *will* understand. Paul clearly implies that his own work as the Apostle to the Gentiles is a fulfillment of this prophecy, in that he is the means by which the nations are seeing and understanding.

15:22 This is why I have often been hindered from coming to you. Paul has already indicated in 1:13 that he had planned many times to visit Rome but had been prevented from doing so until now. While other factors were also responsible, the main reason why he had not yet been able to go to Rome was the urgent need to preach the gospel to the unevangelized in the Jerusalem-Illyricum arc.

B. HIS PLANS FOR THE FUTURE (15:23-29)

Paul has now formulated a plan for a totally new phase in his missionary work, one that will definitely allow him to spend a short time in Rome. It is no small undertaking. His ultimate goal is Spain, in the far western regions of southern Europe. But instead of traveling directly there from Corinth (his location when he wrote this letter), he felt the need to personally present the Gentiles' offering to the Jerusalem church. Only then would he go back westward to Spain, stopping at Rome on the way. Stott (384) calculates that this itinerary would require Paul to travel (mostly by boat) about 3,000 miles: c. 800 from Corinth to Jerusalem, c. 1,500 from Jerusalem to Rome, and c. 700 from Rome to Spain. Such a trip would be long, perilous, and uncomfortable.

15:23-24a But now that there is no more place for me to work in these regions, and since I have been longing for many years to see you, I plan to do

so when I go to Spain. Here Paul names two basic factors that have shaped his upcoming travel plans. The first has to do with the completion of his missionary work in the eastern area. "Place" is τόπος (*topos*), which can also mean "opportunity," a meaning that fits well here. "These regions" are the area described in v. 19b. Paul is simply saying that now that he has laid the foundation for the church there, he is ready to move on to a totally new area. In terms of the strategy affirmed in v. 20, there is no more opportunity for him to pursue his calling here.

The second factor shaping his itinerary is his long-standing desire to visit Rome itself, as described in 1:9-15. "Having been longing" is a rather rare noun that suggests a very strong desire.

The NIV (❂ II:448-449) has rightly added a main clause at the beginning of v. 24, "I plan to do so" In order to complete Paul's thought. But this is not in the original; the next clause, "when I go to Spain," is actually how v. 24 begins. (See the NASB for a literal rendering of vv. 23-24a.)

Verse 24a and v. 28 are Paul's only references to his intention to evangelize Spain. We do not know if he was ever able to do this. The Bible says nothing more about it, but this does not rule out the possibility. Two statements from early Christian writings are sometimes interpreted as affirming that Paul did get to Spain, but these cannot be verified (see Murray, 2:217, n. 27). Nonetheless, Spain's growing significance as a cultural and commercial area was no doubt why Paul saw it as a logical next step in his plan to evangelize those who had not yet heard.

15:24b In the rest of v. 24 Paul explains to the Christians at Rome the place of his intended visit there in relation to his overall plan. **I hope to visit you while passing through and to have you assist me on my journey there, after I have enjoyed your company for a while.** First, he says he will just be stopping by "to visit you" as he is "passing through." Both of these terms indicate that his stay in Rome will be "not much more than a stop on his way to his ultimate destination, which is Spain" (Moo, 898). Second, he says he will be able to stay only "for a while," literally, "in part." I.e., it will only be a partial visit compared with what he would prefer.

But even though his visit in Rome will be brief, he hopes to accomplish two things. First, he will attempt to persuade the church in Rome to assist him in his mission to Spain. The word translated "assist me on my journey" likely means "help on one's journey with food, money, by arranging for companions, means of travel, etc." (BAGD, 709). It suggests at least that Paul was expecting the Roman Christians to give him substantial aid for the remainder of his journey to Spain. It may be that he was even hoping they would become a "supporting church" for his mission there, perhaps by providing him with a missionary recruit to help him in his work, as Philippi had sent Epaphroditus (Phil 2:25-30).

The other thing Paul hoped to accomplish by his visit with the Roman

Christians was to "enjoy their company" in Christian fellowship. The word used here literally means "to be filled full"; it is appropriate to interpret it (as does the NIV) to mean something like "filled full with the pleasure of your company."

15:25 Now, however, I am on my way to Jerusalem in the service of the saints there. Here Paul informs his Roman brothers that there is still one more thing he has to do before making his journey to Rome and Spain. He is just now beginning a trip to Jerusalem (Acts 19:21; 20:16), to deliver money collected from the Gentile churches during his third missionary journey, to help the poor Christians in the Jerusalem church. Thus he would be "serving the saints" (NASB).

The word for "serving" is διακονέω (*diakoneō*), the verb form of διακονία (*diakonia*). These words can have the general sense of serving or ministering to others' needs (see 16:1), or they can signify a more specific kind of service. As we have seen, *diakonia* in 12:7 probably refers to benevolent work in the church, just as *diakoneō* refers here to the collection taken for the poor in Jerusalem (as in Acts 11:29; 12:25; Rom 15:31; 2 Cor 8:4,19-20; 9:1,12-13).

"Saints" is a word used for all Christians (see 1:7); here it refers specifically to the poor saints in Jerusalem (v. 26).

Ten or eleven years earlier, Paul (along with Barnabas) had already carried an offering to the Jerusalem church, sent by the church at Antioch (Acts 11:28-30; 12:25). The occasion then was a famine, and the motivation was simply Christian love.

What was the purpose of this present offering? First, there is no doubt that Paul encouraged this offering simply as an act of benevolence, as a way of helping the poor (Gal 2:10) in the spirit of Christian love (2 Cor 8:8,24). There is no indication that there was another widespread famine in the Jerusalem area at this time, but there did seem to be quite a number of poor saints there who needed continuing help.

Second and more significantly, Paul apparently regarded this offering as a concrete symbol of the unity and interdependence of Gentiles and Jews under the banner of the gospel of Christ. He has already written at length about this interdependence in ch. 11, and he will refer to it again in v. 29 (❧ II:451).

15:26 After the initial general reference to his Jerusalem trip in v. 25, Paul now states its purpose explicitly: **For Macedonia and Achaia were pleased to make a contribution for the poor among the saints in Jerusalem.** The churches of these two areas are the ones Paul had been working with most recently, though other areas were also involved (❧ II:451-452). The Christians in these areas, says Paul, were "pleased" or delighted to participate in Paul's collection for the poor in Jerusalem. Though Paul had urged them to give (1 Cor 16:1-4; 2 Cor 8:7,24), he made it clear that it was not a matter of necessity but of free and cheerful choice (2 Cor 8:8; 9:5,7). This free and cheerful spirit in which the gifts were given is indicated in the word "pleased"; Paul thinks this point is important enough to repeat the word in v. 27a. As v. 31b indicates, he hopes the gifts will be received by the Jerusalem church in a similar spirit.

The word translated "contribute" is κοινωνία (*koinōnia*), which literally means "fellowship, participation, sharing in." The same word is used for this collection in 2 Cor 8:4; 9:13, where it is translated "sharing." Since money earned as salary or wages is indeed "coined life," when one gives his money to help meet the needs of others, it is truly an act of fellowship, of sharing one's very life with the recipient of the gift. Thus the very nature of benevolent giving (as an act of fellowship) made Paul's collection an ideal means of drawing the early Jewish and Gentile Christians closer together.

"The poor *among* the saints" rightly indicates that only *some* of the Christians in Jerusalem were poor. This had been true from the beginning, and the other Christians in the church there had always been ready to help them (Acts 4:34-37; 6:1). What is significant here is that so many *Gentile* Christians were willing to do the same.

15:27 This verse indicates *why* the Gentile Christians were so eagerly pleased to help the poor saints in Jerusalem: **They were pleased to do it, and indeed they owe it to them. For if the Gentiles have shared in the Jews' spiritual blessings, they owe it to the Jews to share with them their material blessings.** Here for the first time Paul indicates that the main thing at stake in this collection was the relation between Jews and Gentiles in the church. The Gentile Christians were happy to share with the Jewish Christians (at Jerusalem), because they felt they *owed* it to them. Literally Paul says "they are debtors," using the same word he used of himself in 1:14 (❄I:99-100). This is not a legal debt but a moral obligation, a debt of gratitude. The Gentiles owed this debt to the Jews because of what the latter had done for them.

Paul explains the debt in the rest of the verse. The Gentiles, he says, "have shared in the Jews' spiritual blessings." The "spiritual things" of which Paul speaks are the blessings of salvation, and his point is that the Gentiles must remember that "salvation is from the Jews" (John 4:22; see Rom 11:11,17; 15:8). It was through the Jews that the Savior came into the world (9:5), and in this sense all Christians owe an unpayable debt to the Jews. Also, it was from Jerusalem, through the early Jewish Christians, that the gospel was first proclaimed and from which it spread into all the earth (Acts 1:8; see Isa 2:3-5; Micah 4:2-5).

The word translated "share" is λειτουργέω (*leitourgeō*) (the verb form of *leitourgos* in 15:16), which indicates that the collection was an act of servanthood and an act of worship.

15:28 So after I have completed this task and have made sure that they have received this fruit, I will go to Spain and visit you on the way. Having explained his imminent trip to Jerusalem (vv. 25-27), Paul now returns to the main point he was making in v. 24, about his planned trip to Rome and then to

Spain. He will make the latter trip only after he has finished the business about the collection, i.e., after he has delivered it to the Jerusalem church in person.

At this point Paul adds a participial phrase that most find difficult to understand. It explains what, to Paul, was involved in completing the task of delivering the collection. He describes this act as, literally, "having sealed to them this fruit." "This fruit" is the collection itself, but in what sense is it "fruit"? This may mean that it was the fruit of Paul's own labor, i.e., of the effort he expended in raising these gifts. More likely Paul means it was the fruit produced among the Gentiles as a result of the spiritual blessings sent forth to them by the Jerusalem Christians (Cranfield, 2:775; Murray, 2:219).

The difficult question is, what does Paul mean when he says that he will *seal* this fruit to the Jerusalem church? (On "seal," see ❧I:291.) To place one's seal upon something means to put one's unique identifying mark upon it in order to guarantee its authenticity (❧II:454). The most likely meaning here is that Paul put his seal on the collection in the sense that he attested and certified to the Jewish Christians in Jerusalem that this money was a gift of genuine love from their Gentile brethren. He made this long and arduous trip to Jerusalem just to make sure that the Jewish Christians understood the significance of the gift as an instrument that was meant to join them and their Gentile brothers together in a bond of Christian fellowship.

Once this has been accomplished, Paul says, "I will go on by way of you to Spain" (NASB). The NIV's "visit you on the way" is literally "through you," i.e., through Rome. This is another indication that his visit to Rome was going to be brief and was secondary to his purpose of taking the gospel to Spain (see v. 24).

15:29 I know that when I come to you, I will come in the full measure of the blessing of Christ. Here Paul expresses a measure of confidence that he will finally be able to fulfill his longing to visit Rome, once the Jerusalem task is completed. "I know," he says; "I will come," he says. We know from the book of Acts that he did indeed go to Rome, though not exactly according to his original plan.

In any case, he was sure that when he came, it would be with the full blessing of Christ. That is, he knew that Christ's blessing would be upon him, and he knew that he would be able to bestow the fullness of Christ's blessing upon them (see 1:12).

C. HIS REQUEST FOR PRAYER (15:30-33)

Despite the confidence expressed in v. 29, Paul is still somewhat apprehensive about his trip to Jerusalem, especially about how he and the contribution would be received there. Thus he closes this section of the letter with a request for prayer concerning his announced itinerary.

15:30 I urge you, brothers, by our Lord Jesus Christ and by the love of the Spirit, to join me in my struggle by praying to God for me. This is surely more a personal plea than an authoritative command (see 12:1). It is an urgent plea; the word for "urge" (παρακαλέω, *parakaleō*) often has the connotation of pleading and begging. The language shows that Paul feels a serious need for the intercessory prayer of his brethren.

Paul names two bases for his appeal. First, he pleads for prayer "by [διά, *dia*] our Lord Jesus Christ." This may be a reference to the authority by which he makes his request (Moo, 909), but more likely he is just appealing to the fact that he and his Roman brethren both worship the same Lord ("*our* Lord"): "I urge you, as one Christian to another . . . ."

The other basis for his appeal is "the love of the Spirit." This is no doubt the Holy Spirit, but it is not clear just how the Spirit and the love (ἀγάπη, *agapē*) are related. Grammatically it could mean either the Spirit's love for us or our love for the Spirit (❍ II:456). Most likely, though, it means the love which the Holy Spirit imparts to us as part of his sanctifying work, and which is one aspect of the fruit of the Spirit (Gal 5:22). Paul is saying, "If you really love me — and Spirit-filled Christians should love one another — you will pray for me."

Paul beseeches his brethren not just "to pray," but to strive or struggle along with him in prayer. The word for "struggle" is συναγωνίζομαι (*synagōnizomai*, cf. "agonize") (❍ II:456). To what struggle does Paul refer? Quite possibly he is thinking of the struggle he anticipates in Jerusalem, where he expects to meet with resistance from both his unbelieving Jewish enemies and the Jewish Christians (see v. 31). The NIV suggests this meaning; it pictures Paul beseeching the Christians at Rome to march alongside him in this struggle, not by their physical presence but by their prayers for him (see Dunn, 2:878).

The other possibility, which is more likely, is that the struggle to which Paul refers is the praying itself, in which case he is not talking about ordinary, casual prayer but earnest, forceful, and persistent prayer like that of Jesus in Gethsemane (see Cranfield, 2:777) (❍ II:456-457).

15:31 Now Paul instructs the saints at Rome to pray for two things in particular: **Pray that I may be rescued from the unbelievers in Judea and that my service in Jerusalem may be acceptable to the saints there, . . .** The "unbelievers in Judea" are the unbelieving, unconverted Jews in Jerusalem and the whole surrounding area. Paul was well known to them as a former leader among the Jews (❍ I:27-28) and was considered to be a betrayer of his people and his religion, and the Apostle was well aware of their hostility toward him. They had already tried to kill him, and would do so again. He was not afraid to die, but he wanted to live in order to fulfill his plans to evangelize Spain (❍ II:457).

Paul specifically requests that his brethren pray that he might "be rescued" from the unbelieving Jews. The word for "rescue" (ῥύομαι, *rhyomai*) can mean "to protect or preserve from harm," but often it has the connotation of delivering or rescuing someone from a peril that has already come upon him. At the time Paul wrote this letter he may already have known that he was going to be captured and bound by the Jews in Jerusalem; it was certainly made clear to him shortly after this (Acts 20:22-23; 21:10-14). Thus he may be requesting prayer that God will literally rescue him out of this certain captivity.

As a matter of fact, this *is* the way it happened. If Paul was praying and asking for prayer that he not be captured at all, then his prayer was not answered. If he was praying and asking for prayer that he be delivered from his Jewish enemies after they had captured him, then this prayer was definitely answered — but not necessarily in any way that Paul could have anticipated. He was in fact rescued from his Jewish captors, but only by becoming a prisoner of the Roman government.

Paul's other specific prayer request is that the Jewish Christians in Jerusalem ("the saints," vv. 25,26) would accept the offering he was bringing to them. This is a prayer that the existing tension between Paul and his Gentile converts on the one hand, and the Jewish Christians in Jerusalem on the other hand, would not lead to a rejection of the offering but instead would break down that very tension and unite them all in true brotherhood (❧II:458).

15:32 [S]o that by God's will I may come to you with joy and together with you be refreshed. While Paul's main concerns were his safety and a congenial acceptance of the offering, he did have a secondary concern, one relating to his planned trip to Rome. If the first prayer was not answered, Paul knew that he might not get to Rome at all; and even if that one was answered but the second one was not, his heart would be heavy and his visit to Rome would be tainted with melancholy. Thus he requests fervent prayer for these two things, "so that" (ἵνα, *hina*) he may indeed be able to come to Rome, and to come with joy.

If this does happen, says Paul, it will be "by God's will" (❧II:458). It may refer only or at least partly to the *permissive* will of God (*GRu*, 313-317), by which God in his sovereignty allows historical events to unfold according to human free will choices. Or it may refer to God's *purposive* will (*GRu*, 304-310), according to which God intervenes via his special providence in order to accomplish certain purposes, particularly in answer to prayer (see *GRu*, 376-378).

Paul knew that his itinerary was subject to God's will in these senses (Acts 16:6-10; 18:21; Rom 1:10; 1 Cor 4:19; 16:7). So in this case, he knew God either could allow his adversaries' evil purposes to unfold as they may, or could intervene in the historical process in answer to prayer and cause positive results to occur. Either way, he knew it would be God's will — either permissive or purposive. And either way, he knew it would all work together for good (8:28).

The fact is that Paul did get to go to Rome and visit with the brethren there (Acts 28:15), but not according to his own plan. His plan was to stay there for a short time and "be refreshed" by his visit with the brethren. It did not happen this way, though. Instead, he came to the city as a prisoner of the Roman government, and was under house arrest for two years (Acts 28:16,30) (❧II:459).

15:33 After his request for prayer in his own behalf by the church at Rome,

Romans Part Six

Paul cannot close this section without himself uttering a prayer on their behalf. Thus he says, **The God of peace be with you all. Amen.**

Paul has just recently spoken of God as the God of endurance and encouragement (v. 5), and the God of hope (v. 13). Now he calls him the "God of peace" (see also 16:20; 2 Cor 13:11; Phil 4:9; 1 Thess 5:23; Heb 13:20), i.e., the God who bestows upon believing sinners a state of peace and reconciliation with himself (5:1), a feeling of peace and tranquility within (8:6; 15:13), and a relationship of peace and harmony among brethren (14:17) (◐II:459-460).

II. PAUL AND HIS FELLOW WORKERS (16:1-24)

(See ◐II:460.) This section is almost altogether about specific personalities, many of them Paul's fellow workers. First comes a brief word of commendation for Phoebe (vv. 1-2), followed by a long list of personal greetings to Christians living in Rome (vv. 3-16). These warm and encouraging words to sincere Christian workers are followed by a solemn warning to be on guard against false teachers (vv. 17-20). Finally, some of Paul's coworkers in Corinth send their greetings to the Roman Christians (vv. 21-24).

A. COMMENDATION OF PHOEBE (16:1-2)

Paul is writing this letter from Corinth and is just about to depart for Jerusalem. At this same time a Christian woman from the nearby town of Cenchrea is about to leave on a trip to Rome. Apparently Paul has asked her to carry this letter with her and deliver it to the church at Rome. In these two verses he provides her with a statement of introduction and recommendation, ensuring that she will be well received by the Roman Christians.

16:1 I commend to you our sister Phoebe, a servant of the church in Cenchrea. The word "commend" (συνίστημι, *synistēmi*) was the usual term, a "technical epistolary expression," for introducing and recommending a friend to other acquaintances (Fitzmyer, 728; Cranfield, 2:780) (◐II:458).

Phoebe is not mentioned anywhere else in the NT. Her name (which means "bright, radiant") indicates that she was probably a Gentile by birth, since *Phoibē* was the name of a pagan goddess. Paul calls her "our sister," meaning our sister in Christ, a part of the family of God, one of "our own." Paul also describes her as "a servant of the church in Cenchrea." Cenchrea was the eastern seaport for Corinth, and obviously a church had been established there, perhaps by Paul himself.

What does Paul mean when he calls Phoebe a *servant* of the church in Cenchrea? This is a matter of considerable controversy. Paul uses the Greek word διάκονος (*diakonos*), a word which is masculine in form but was used for both men and women. Its basic connotation is "servant, helper, one who carries out the will or purpose of another, one who ministers to the needs of others." The NT usually uses it in this generic sense for Christian workers (and others). In this case the English word "servant" is most appropriate.

But on at least three occasions (Phil 1:1; 1 Tim 3:8,12) this word seems to be used for a more or less "official" role of service in the church — "official" in the sense that the individual is selected and appointed by the local congregation to be responsible for a specific task within or on behalf of that congregation. In this latter case the English word "deacon" is used.

In what sense does Paul call Phoebe a *diakonos*? (See the discussion of this concept, ❂ II:462-463.) For one thing, there is no warrant whatsoever for referring to her as a "minister" of the church at Cenchrea, in the sense of the modern-day "senior minister" or pulpit minister. But was she a deacon(ess), implying some sort of official leadership status in the church at Cenchrea? Many so affirm. "Deaconess" is the way the word is translated in the RSV, the NAB, and Phillips; the NRSV says "deacon" (❂ II:463).

The strongest argument for this view is the fact that Phoebe is called a *diakonos* of a specific congregation (Spencer, *Curse*, 115; Walters, "Phoebe,'" 181; Moo, 914). Such a phrase appears nowhere else in the NT. But such phrasing does not necessarily imply that Phoebe held the *office* of deacon in the Cenchrean church (contra the NEB, "who holds office in the congregation at Cenchreae"). There is no reason to think that Paul is doing anything more than specifying where Phoebe came from, i.e., where her home church was, for the simple purpose of identifying her to the Roman church.

The most we can say with any confidence is that Phoebe was a *servant* of the church in Cenchrea (see KJV, NASB, NIV), "servant" being the most basic meaning of *diakonos*. I.e., Phoebe had a significant ministry at Cenchrea. She was a *diakonos* like Paul, Timothy, Epaphras, Tychicus, and Archippus, i.e., someone who faithfully carried out a specific task in service to others (❂ II:464).

Two more things need to be said. First, to deny that Phoebe was a deacon(ess) in the church at Cenchrea in no way detracts from her service and influence in the church there, nor from her stature as a role model for Christian women today. Phoebe was a woman whom Paul was able to commend in the highest terms — not because she held some (rather nebulous) "office," but because of the important service she rendered to the church.

Second, even if we grant that Phoebe was a deacon(ess) in the Cenchrean church, this in no way violates the clear teaching of 1 Tim 2:12, that women may not teach men or have authority over men in the church. The "office" of deacon is neither a teaching office nor an office of authority. Thus if anyone feels compelled to speak of Phoebe as a deacon(ess), he should not fear that he is in any sense capitulating to egalitarianism (feminism); nor should egalitarians assume that this would be some sort of victory for their cause (❂ II:464).

16:2 In v. 2 Paul makes two specific requests of the church at Rome: **I ask you to receive her in the Lord in a way worthy of the saints and to give her**

Romans Part Six

any help she may need from you, . . . "Receive her" (the first request) is not the same word used in 14:1 and 15:7, where the issue was potential division over matters of opinion. Here the idea is something like, "Welcome her into your midst with the open arms of fellowship" (see Phil 2:29). To receive her "in the Lord" means to receive her as a fellow-believer in the Lord, as a "sister" in Christ (v. 1). To receive her "in a way worthy of the saints" means to do so in a manner one would expect from a follower of Jesus, i.e., with loving respect, unselfish generosity, and a cheerful heart.

The second request is for the Roman church to assist Phoebe in any way that she might need help. She would be in need of hospitality from trusted people. Also, she was traveling to Rome for some specific purpose, perhaps relating to some business or legal matter (❖II:465). The Roman Christians would be able to advise Phoebe as to "how things worked" in business and legal circles in Rome. On the other hand, Paul may not have had anything specific in mind beyond general hospitality.

At this point Paul says there is a reason to help Phoebe besides the general obligation of Christian love. You should help her in any way you can, he says, **for she has been a great help to many people, including me.** The noun used to describe Phoebe is προστάτις (*prostatis*). It has two possible meanings. It can mean "helper, benefactor, patron, protector," as in the NIV's "a great help." Or it may mean "leader, director, ruler, presider." Some, especially egalitarians, assume the latter meaning and declare that Paul thus calls Phoebe a ruler or elder in the church (e.g., Spencer, *Curse*, 115-116).

It is true that the verb form of this word in the NT most often means "to lead, rule, direct, manage, be over" (see Rom 12:8; 1 Thess 5:12; 1 Tim 3:4,5,12; 5:17), but the word also can mean "to assist, help, protect, care for" (see Reicke, "προΐστημι, 700-701). The key to the meaning of the noun *prostatis* here must be the context; and in every way, the context excludes the concept of ruler and supports the connotation of helper.

Here are three textual considerations. One, if Phoebe had an official position in the church, such as elder, she would be the *prostatis* of *all*, not just of "many." Two, she was a *prostatis* of Paul himself. There is no acceptable sense in which she could have had authority over Paul. Three, the first part of this verse clearly requires the meaning "helper." Note the reason Paul asks the Roman Christians to be of assistance to Phoebe. *You* should help *her*, he says, because *she herself* has been a helper to many, even to me. This is why she deserves your help. As Murray says, "There is exact correspondence between the service to Phoebe enjoined upon the church and the service she herself bestowed upon others. The thought of presidency is alien to this parallel" (2:227, n. 1).

The two words for helping are slightly different, but they convey the same general sense. The verb "give [her any] help" is *paristēmi*, literally, "stand by or beside." The verb form of *prostatis* is *proistēmi*, literally, "to stand before, stand in front of." Thus Paul is saying something like this: "You stand by her, because she has stood up for many."

The concept of a *prostatis* in the sense of a helper, especially a *patron*, was well established in Paul's day. A patron (*prostatis* or *prostatēs*, woman or man) was usually a prominent, well-to-do person who used his or her position, wealth, and influence for the public good. They sometimes helped the whole community, sometimes groups within the community, and sometimes individuals, e.g., by opening their homes to travelers and taking care of their needs.

Phoebe was no doubt "a figure of significance, whose wealth or influence had been put at the disposal of the church at Cenchreae" (Dunn, 2:889). Since the Cenchrean church was in the eastern seaport town for Corinth, it would have the occasion to host many travelers. This was probably Phoebe's special ministry, and the nature of her work as a *diakonos* of that church. In this sense she was a helper to many, including the traveler Paul; and the Roman Christians are asked to reward her in kind.

B. GREETINGS TO INDIVIDUAL ACQUAINTANCES (16:3-16)

Sending greetings to specific individuals in his letters is something Paul seldom did. In Col 4:15 he greets Nympha; in 2 Tim 4:19 he greets Prisca and Aquila. But here at the end of Romans he sends greetings to 24 named individuals, two specific but unnamed individuals (vv. 13,15), and several groups. The groups include two households and (apparently) three house churches.

Who are these individuals whom Paul specifically names? Most of them are completely unknown to us except for what we are told in this list. We know Prisca and Aquila for sure (v. 3). We probably know Rufus (v. 13) from one other NT reference. It is possible that the men whose names are attached to the two households (Aristobulus, v. 10; Narcissus, v. 11) can be identified with prominent individuals known from secular sources, but this is less certain than the identification of Rufus.

The fact is that the other 21 individuals whom Paul greets by name are simply otherwise unknown. In view of this, it is rather amazing that so much space is devoted to discussing them in the commentaries! In most cases the only thing we can do with these brothers and sisters is to analyze what Paul says about them and compare their names with lists of the same names compiled from contemporary inscriptions and other sources from ancient Rome. But even then, there is no sure way to connect any of the individuals here with any individuals mentioned on inscriptions.

We can, however, draw some basic general conclusions about the Christians in this list, including the unknown individuals. First, Paul obviously knows some better than others. He takes pains to say something complimentary about the first 16 persons listed (vv. 3-13), but then greets ten others without elaboration (vv. 14-15). Some in the group of 16 he obviously knew quite well; others he may have known only casually. The last ten were known to him, but perhaps only through communications he had received from friends in Rome, such as Prisca and Aquila.

Concerning the ones Paul knew personally, since he had never been to Rome, he would have met them somewhere during his missionary work in the eastern regions before they migrated to Rome.

Second, we know for sure that several of these individuals are Jewish, some because we know them otherwise (vv. 3,13) and some because Paul calls them his "kinsmen" (vv. 7,11, NASB). The rest, obviously the majority, are most likely Gentiles, since their names were used by Gentiles of that day. This does not necessarily prove that the church as a whole was predominantly Gentile, but it points in that direction (see Moo, 918).

Third, many of the names on the list are otherwise found to be common among slaves and former slaves (freedmen, freedwomen). Many of these names were prominent among slaves in the emperor's household. According to Lampe ("Romans 16," 227-228), only the names Urbanus, Rufus, Prisca, and Aquila "do not indicate any affinity to people born into slavery." Of the rest, ten are most probably slave names; the rest cannot be determined one way or the other. (The households of Narcissus and Aristobulus no doubt would also include slaves.)

Fourth, the prominence of women in the list is noteworthy. Nine of the 26 individuals are women. Of these, Prisca is described as Paul's fellow worker; Junia is praised for her outstanding missionary work; and four others are praised for their labor for the Lord (Mary, Tryphena, Tryphosa, and Persis). Only three men are complimented in these same terms (Aquila, Urbanus, and Andronicus). This shows that faithful Christian women had important roles in the church in the apostolic era, and should have the same today. This, along with the reference to Phoebe in vv. 1-2, shows that women can have high-profile ministries in the church without violating the limitations imposed in 1 Tim 2:12.

Since such a long list of names is unusual in Paul's letters, we may ask why he went into such detail here in Rom 16, even regarding people he probably did not know or know very well. The answer no doubt lies in the fact that Paul had never been to Rome and was not the founder of the church there, but he was on the verge of paying them a visit and seeking aid from them for his mission to Spain (15:23-24). A list like this would impress not only those who are named, but those who are not mentioned as well. This would prepare the way for a positive reception by and fruitful relationship with the whole congregation, once he arrived in Rome (Moo, 918).

16:3 Greet Priscilla and Aquila, my fellow workers in Christ Jesus. That "greet" should be an imperative plural is not unusual in an epistle like this. It was a standard epistolary way of saying "Greetings to . . ." (Dunn, 2:891; Moo, 919).

That Prisca and Aquila should be greeted first is no surprise, given their prominence in the NT in relation to Paul's ministry (❧II:470). This husband-wife team is mentioned three times by Paul (16:3; 1 Cor 16:19; 2 Tim 4:19), who always calls the wife Prisca; and three times by Luke (Acts 18:2,18,26), who always refers to her as Priscilla, the diminutive form of Prisca (❧II:470-471).

There is no doubt, based on the NT information, that Prisca's service in the church was just as significant as that of her husband. They were both involved in evangelism (Acts 18:24-26), and Paul was certainly impressed with the work of both, judging from his other references to them and from what he says about them here (❧II:471). They may well have been his best friends, and were surely his best liaison with the church at Rome.

Thus it is not surprising that Paul has more to say about this couple than anyone else on the list. In what ways does he commend them? First, he calls them his "fellow workers in Christ Jesus." Since Paul's work specifically was missionary in nature, focusing on evangelism and church planting, we can assume that all the fellow workers he refers to were associated with him in some way in this kind of ministry. Since new converts must be gathered together into local congregations, one thing associated with missionary work is organizing and providing for these newly established congregations. By hosting "house churches" (v. 5; 1 Cor 16:19) Prisca and Aquila were very much involved in this aspect of missions.

Paul calls them his fellow workers "in Christ Jesus." He is not talking about their common secular trade of tentmaking (Acts 18:3), but about "gospel work" (Lenski, 903). They and Paul served a common Savior and Lord.

16:4 Paul's second commendation of Prisca and Aquila is this: **They risked their lives for me. Not only I but all the churches of the Gentiles are grateful to them.** "Risked their lives" is literally "risked their neck." At some point in their laboring together, these two friends of Paul put their lives on the line for his sake. Paul suffered many perils in his many years of service (2 Cor 11:23-29), but we do not know the specific event he has in mind here (❧II:472).

Because of this especially, and no doubt for countless other reasons, Paul says he gives thanks to God for Prisca and Aquila. In fact, he says, all the Gentile churches thank God for this great servant couple. Why? Probably, because if they had not saved his life, his mission to the Gentiles would have been cut short, and many of these Gentile churches may never have existed (Lard, 454; MP, 546).

16:5a Paul adds one more item to his greeting to Prisca and Aquila: **Greet also the church that meets at their house**. In the apostolic era, in some times and places, it may have been possible for the whole church in an area to meet together (1 Cor 11:18; 14:23), but church buildings as such did not exist, and often the Christians just met together in smaller groups in the houses of indi-

Romans Part Six

vidual Christians (Acts 12:12; Col 4:15; Phlm 2). Prisca and Aquila hosted house churches both in Ephesus (1 Cor 16:19) and in Rome (indicated here).

16:5b Paul now turns his attention to other saints in Rome. **Greet my dear friend Epenetus, who was the first convert to Christ in the province of Asia.** Otherwise unknown to us, Epenetus must have been well known to Paul, who refers to him literally as "my beloved." This probably means that he was Paul's "dear friend" (NIV), though this is an interpretation and not a translation. Paul says Epenetus was literally the "firstfruit" of Asia for Christ, a term that was used for the first converts in a particular context (see 8:23; 11:16; 1 Cor 16:15) (❂II:472-473).

16:6 Greet Mary, who worked very hard for you. There is no reason to equate this Mary with any other Mary in Scripture. It was a common name in Rome and was used among both Jews and Gentiles, more commonly among the latter (Lampe, "Romans 16," 225). Whoever this Mary was, Paul gives her a high compliment when he says she "worked very hard for you."

The verb for "worked hard" is κοπιάω (*kopiaō*), "to toil, labor, struggle, strive, work hard." In a note of praise such as this (❂II:473), the verb indicates that Mary and others (v. 12) have probably devoted themselves to some "voluntary, laborious activity on behalf of the gospel" (Fitzmyer, 737). The language may be used of those in leadership roles (1 Thess 5:12; 1 Tim 5:17), but is not limited to this. Laudably laboring for the Lord is something that can be done by both men and women. In this list of greetings Paul uses the term only for four women and no men.

16:7a Greet Andronicus and Junias, my relatives who have been in prison with me. These individuals, along with Herodion (v. 11), Lucius, Jason, and Sosipater (v. 21), are called Paul's "relatives." This is a misleading translation, because Paul almost certainly means not "close relatives," but "fellow Jews," "those of my own race" (9:3, same word).

These two disciples are also called "my fellow prisoners." Paul uses this term also for Aristarchus (Col 4:10) and Epaphras (Phlm 23), who were with him during his Roman imprisonment. We do not know when Andronicus and Junia(s) were fellow prisoners with Paul. The Apostle says he was "frequently" in prison (2 Cor 11:23), but the only such episode recorded in Acts prior to this writing is Acts 16:24. Whether Andronicus and Junia(s) were in the same prison at the same time as Paul, or whether they had simply suffered the same kind of imprisonment for Christ as Paul did, we cannot tell.

A major question is whether the individual called "Junias" was a man or a woman. In the Greek text *Junian* is the accusative case either for a man named Junias or a woman named Junia. Interpreters have been divided on this issue (❂II:474).

The main reason some have argued that the name must be masculine is that v. 7b describes these two workers as "outstanding among the apostles," and gender-role considerations rule out the possibility that a woman could be an apostle. But since egalitarianism has changed many people's thinking about gender roles, it is fairly easy for modern interpreters to accept the fact that Junia was a *woman*, indeed, a woman *apostle*.

Apart from preconceptions about gender roles, what evidence can be adduced one way or the other on this issue? The deciding factor seems to be the existence or nonexistence of these two names in contemporary Roman inscriptions. The facts are that the feminine name Junia has been found about 250 times in such inscriptions, while the masculine form Junias has thus far been found *nowhere* (Lampe, "Romans 16," 223, 226). The reasonable conclusion, then, is that Junia was a woman, and that Andronicus and Junia were husband and wife.

16:7b With this conclusion, the rest of the verse now presents a major problem. It says of Andronicus and Junia, **They are outstanding among the apostles, and they were in Christ before I was.** The latter statement is not difficult. That they were "in Christ" before Paul just means they were converted to Christ before Paul was, which must have been within the first few years after Pentecost. Thus they had been laboring for Christ for over 20 years, and possibly for as long as 25 years.

The problem lies in Paul's statement that Andronicus and Junia are "outstanding among the apostles." If this means what it appears to mean, then Paul is affirming not only that Junia, a woman, was an apostle, but that she was one of the *very best* apostles. One way to avoid this conclusion is to interpret this statement to mean that Andronicus and Junia were outstanding *in the eyes of* the apostles. This is grammatically possible, and has some support among scholars (see MP, 547; Moule, 248; Lenski, 906-907; Murray, 2:230). I believe it is a reasonable interpretation.

Most conclude, however, that the much less awkward and more natural interpretation is that Andronicus and Junia were outstanding members in the group known as apostles. If this is the case, how does the fact that Junia is called an outstanding apostle affect our view of gender roles in the church?

The answer depends on what is meant by "apostle." If we think that the word always refers to someone on or near the level of the original twelve apostles, the ones (like Paul) upon whom (along with the prophets) the church is built (Eph 2:20; see ●I:62-63), then Paul is saying that a woman, Junia, held the highest authoritative office in the NT church, thus obliterating all gender-role distinctions and vindicating egalitarianism. This view has many defenders (●II:475-476).

This is by no means the only possible, nor even the more likely, understanding of "apostle" in this verse, however. As we saw earlier (1:1; ●I:62), the word ἀπόστολος (*apostolos*) comes from the common verb ἀποστέλλω (*apostellō*), "to send (on a mission)." Thus the noun *apostolos* is sometimes used in the NT in the general (generic) sense of "someone sent on a mission," i.e., an ambassador, a messenger, or (in the context of Christian work) a missionary. When it is used in this sense it has no connotation of "an authoritative leadership position" (Moo, 923).

This is the sense in which Jesus himself is called an apostle, i.e., he was someone sent on a mission (Heb 3:1). The word is applied to Saul and Barnabas in this sense in Acts 14:4,14, because they were sent out as missionaries by the church at Antioch (Acts 13:1-3). In Phil 2:25 Epaphroditus is called the *apostolos* (NIV, "messenger") of the church at Philippi, because they had sent him to help Paul in his work. In 2 Cor 8:23 Paul speaks of several unnamed brethren who are "*apostoloi* of the churches," i.e., messengers (NASB) or representatives (NIV) sent out by the churches. In modern terms, they were *missionaries*.

There are good reasons for the word "apostles" here in v. 7 to be taken in this latter, generic sense. One is that this is consistent with a proper understanding of 1 Tim 2:12 (❀ II:476, n. 46). Another is that if Andronicus and Junia were "outstanding among the apostles" in the sense of authoritative leaders in the church (equivalent to Paul himself), it is very strange that we have no other references to them anywhere in the NT.

The best understanding of Paul's laudatory statement about this couple is that they were "outstanding missionaries" (Stott, 396), "commissioned itinerant evangelists" (Fitzmyer, 739), a "married missionary couple" (Lampe, "Romans 16," 224). While women missionaries would be most effective in witnessing to other women, there is no biblical reason why women cannot proclaim the gospel to unsaved men as well. First Timothy 2:12 prohibits women from teaching only *Christian* men within the context of the church (1 Tim 3:15). (See Cottrell, "Priscilla," 4-5.)

16:8 Greet Ampliatus, whom I love in the Lord. We know nothing for sure about this man, other than the fact that Paul loved him in the Lord. Paul calls him (lit.) "my beloved," using exactly the same phrase the NIV translates "my dear friend" or "dear friend" in vv. 5,9,12. The point is that he was a personal friend of Paul (see v. 5) (❀ II:477).

16:9 Greet Urbanus, our fellow worker in Christ, and my dear friend Stachys. Urbanus (otherwise unknown) apparently worked with Paul somewhere before coming to Rome. Stachys, also otherwise unknown, is another of Paul's "beloved" friends (see v. 5).

16:10 Greet Apelles, tested and approved in Christ. Apelles is otherwise unknown. The interesting thing is the word Paul uses to describe him, δόκιμος (*dokimos*), translated "tested and approved." It is possible that Paul intends this in the same general sense that *all* Christians are "approved in Christ," i.e., approved by God because Christ has taken away the guilt and penalty of our sins. But this term is part of a word group that speaks of being put to the test and thus being approved as the result of specific testing. Whatever the nature of his test or trial, he proved to be faithful; and Paul commends him for it.

Greet those who belong to the household of Aristobulus. This greeting is not sent to Aristobulus himself, which means either that he was dead, or that he himself was not a believer. In any case a good portion of his household (family and servants) were Christians; these are the ones Paul greets (❥ II:478).

16:11 Greet Herodion, my relative, i.e., "my kinsman, my fellow Jew" (see v. 7). The name indicates most likely a slave or freedman in the service of someone in the Herod family, possibly a prominent member of the household of Aristobulus.

Greet those in the household of Narcissus who are in the Lord. Narcissus, like Aristobulus, must have been either dead or an unbeliever; the greeting goes to his household, or more precisely, to those of his household who are "in the Lord," i.e., Christians (❥ II:478).

16:12 Greet Tryphena and Tryphosa, those women who work hard in the Lord. The similarity of these names indicates that these women were probably sisters. Both names are based on the noun τρυφή (*tryphē*, "softness, delicacy, daintiness"). Some think they may be twins, and that their names would be equivalent to "Delicate" and "Dainty." It is ironic that women with such names would be praised for their hard work!

Greet my dear friend Persis, another woman who has worked very hard in the Lord. The name "Persis" indicates a woman from Persia, possibly a slave or freedwoman who came from that region (Moo, 925). She is otherwise unknown to us. Paul calls her "the beloved" (see v. 5), indicating again a possible personal friendship between them.

16:13 Greet Rufus, chosen in the Lord, and his mother, who has been a mother to me, too. (See ❥ II:478.) Paul declares that Rufus is "chosen" (elect) in the Lord. This might be just a general "commendatory expression" that could apply to any Christian, since all Christians are among "the elect" (so Cranfield, 2:794). But most of the things Paul says about the Christians on this list seem to refer to something extraordinary about their lives and service. Thus it is likely that "chosen" here means something more specific. Some say it means he was chosen for a particular task of some importance (Dunn, 2:897). Others say the term should be taken in the sense of "choice." I.e., Rufus was an outstanding, choice, distinguished Christian servant.

Paul also sends greetings to Rufus's mother, who, he says, was his mother, too. He surely does not mean this literally. All we can say is that "on some occasion Rufus's mother had befriended Paul in a motherly way" (Cranfield, 2:794).

16:14 Greet Asyncritus, Phlegon, Hermes, Patrobas, Hermas and the brothers with them. These men are simply not known to us. It may be, since Paul says nothing about them, that he himself did not know them personally but only by reputation. The "brothers with them" may refer to a house church to which they all belonged.

16:15 Greet Philologus, Julia, Nereus and his sister, and Olympas and all

the saints with them. This group, again unknown to us, may have constituted another house church. Some speculate that the first two were husband and wife, and the next two were their children; but there is no way to verify this.

16:16a Greet one another with a holy kiss. A chaste kiss as a form of greeting — the "osculatory salutation" (MP, 548) — and also parting, was simply a part of the culture of the ancient world in general, including Judaism (see Luke 7:45; 22:47; Acts 20:37). Ordinarily Paul would not have to exhort Christians to greet one another with a kiss, since that was the normal practice. A kiss of greeting was given to anyone for whom there was fondness or affection or even respect, and was not intended to be romantic or erotic.

The emphasis in Paul's exhortation thus must be upon the word "holy." Paul may be telling the Christians at Rome not to be afraid to use the kiss of greeting, but to make sure that it is given (and received) in a holy (i.e., chaste, nonerotic) manner (❡ II:480-481).

But is there more to it than this? This verse is not the only place where Paul exhorts the church to "greet one another with a holy kiss"; see also 1 Cor 16:20; 2 Cor 13:12; 1 Thess 5:26 (cf. 1 Pet 5:14). Does the frequency with which this exhortation appears suggest that the holy kiss was instituted by the apostles as an obligatory part of public worship? My answer is, yes, but not as a kiss as such.

Though the holy kiss was incorporated into Christian liturgy over the next few centuries (Stählin, "φιλέω," 142-145), in my judgment its culture-relative character puts it into the same category as foot-washing as a Christian practice. That is, its essence, not its form, is what is binding upon us. Its essence is that of fellowship and brotherhood; it is a concrete expression of the familial bond that exists among all Christians. Other cultural expressions of affection, fellowship, and brotherhood will serve the same purpose, e.g., a warm handshake or a hug (❡ II:481).

16:16b All the churches of Christ send greetings. Even as Paul writes, he is about to embark for Jerusalem with these Gentile churches' offering for the poor in Jerusalem, and he has a whole company of representatives of some of these churches with him (Acts 20:3-4). Speaking on behalf of their churches, these men are no doubt sending greetings to Rome through Paul (❡ II:482).

By sending this general greeting from all the eastern churches, Paul identifies himself with them and them with himself, indicating to the Roman Christians that he has the backing of these churches in his general work and in his upcoming mission to Spain. This is another subtle way of recommending himself to the congregation in Rome and winning their support for his mission.

C. WARNINGS AGAINST FALSE TEACHERS (16:17-20)

Contrary to the understanding of some, Paul is in no sense here reproving or rebuking the Roman Christians for internal and personal sins or weaknesses (in contrast with, e.g., 1 Cor). Rather, he is giving them a serious yet loving warning of dangers from without (❧ II:482).

Some think it is odd that Paul would interrupt his section on greetings and interject this warning about false doctrine, which seems so completely unrelated to the context. But this paragraph is not as unrelated as it may seem at first. For one thing, the greetings which it separates are of two different kinds. Verses 3-16 focus on the Christians in Rome to whom greetings are being sent, while vv. 21-23 name those with Paul who are sending greetings. Also, there *is* a definite connection between this paragraph and the previous verse. In v. 16 the references to the holy kiss and to "all the churches" call attention to the unity, harmony, and love that are God's ideal for his churches; and Paul knew that false teachers and their false doctrines were one of the greatest threats to this unity (Lenski, 914-915; Hendriksen, 2:510).

In summary, Paul knew from experience that false teachers could devastate a church, and he did not want this to happen to Rome. He was always conscious of this problem. Since he has not yet in this letter said anything about this danger, he sees this as an opportune moment to insert this warning.

16:17 I urge you, brothers, to watch out for those who cause divisions and put obstacles in your way that are contrary to the teaching you have learned. Keep away from them. "I urge you, brothers" is identical with 15:30, which is a personal plea. It is also similar to 12:1, where "urge" has the double sense of personal appeal and authoritative command. The latter is the case here also; Paul is invoking his apostolic authority (❧ II:483-484).

Paul exhorts the church to "watch out for" false teachers. This could mean "keep your eye on" such teachers as may already be among you and "mark them" (KJV) so as to avoid them. More likely, though, it means "be on the lookout for, keep your eyes open for" such teachers, so that you will be sure to spot them if and when they show up (in Rome). Paul's unqualified praise for the Roman congregation suggests that these false teachers were not yet present within it (1:8; 16:19a).

It is significant that Paul does not refer directly to the false teaching propagated by these false teachers, but speaks of the "divisions" and "obstacles" they cause in the church. "Divisions" are a work of the flesh according to Gal 5:20, where the word is translated "dissensions." It refers to anything that separates one group of brethren from another group. "Obstacles" is hardly a strong enough translation for the Greek word σκάνδαλον (*skandalon*) (see 9:33; 14:13), which is an occasion not just for stumbling, but for falling into ruin and destruction (see Lenski, 915).

What, then, is this potential danger, one so serious that it is able to separate brother from brother, and to lead them to destruction? The answer is *false doctrine*. How do we know this? Because Paul specifically says that what these outsiders may bring into the church is "contrary to the teaching [διδαχή, *didachē*, "doctrine"] you have learned." This implies that the Roman Christians have already learned good solid teaching, not just from Paul himself but from those leaders who started the church in Rome. Thus he warns them to be on the lookout for anyone who teaches something contrary to basic Christian belief, because false doctrine leads to division and destruction (see Moo, 930).

What Paul says here is directly opposed to the "peace at any price" approach to Christian unity, which often maligns all emphasis on sound doctrine as being divisive. But Paul is very clear. It is not *doctrine* that divides the church, but *false* doctrine. We do not have to choose between doctrinal truth and unity. Rather, we must pursue unity through sound doctrine, and "watch out for" the false doctrine that causes divisions and destruction. In and of itself, standing for the truth is not divisive in any negative sense; error is the true cause of division (see MacArthur, 2:372).

What shall we do with such false teachers, if we spot them? "Keep away from them," says Paul. Shun them, avoid them, stay out of their way. Since these men were probably not in Rome at this time, Paul is probably not talking about withdrawal of fellowship (as he seems to be in 1 Cor 5:11) but about refusing to give them any opportunity to spread their false teachings (2 John 7-11). The elders of the church should not allow them access to the congregation but should themselves expose and refute their false teaching (Titus 1:9-11).

16:18 For such people are not serving our Lord Christ, but their own appetites. By smooth talk and flattery they deceive the minds of naive people. In this verse Paul says all that he wants to say about the false teachers of v. 17. The main question is whether he has any particular false teaching in mind or whether this verse is just a generic description of false teachers of all kinds.

For those who take the former view, the next question is whether we can tell from v. 18 *which* false teaching he has in mind. Several possibilities have been suggested, with no one view gaining a consensus. The one thing we have to go on is Paul's statement that "such people" do not serve Christ but "their own appetites." "Serve" is δουλεύω (*douleuō*), which means to serve as a slave, to be a slave. We are supposed to be slaves of Christ (14:18), but these false teachers are slaves (lit.) to their own bellies or stomachs (❂ II:485-486).

In the most general sense "belly" stands for the self as such. Being a slave to one's belly thus has the sense of serving oneself, or satisfying one's own desires and ego. In this sense it could refer to almost any kind of false teaching.

Probably the best approach is to take the phrase in this most general sense, and to acknowledge that we simply are not sure if Paul had any specific group in mind, or to acknowledge that, if he did, we cannot identify it with any certainty. In this case we may take the warning as speaking generically about all false teachers, who by definition are no longer serving Christ but are slaves to their own egos. (See Cranfield, 2:802; Dunn, 2:903-904.)

One reason Paul issues such a strong warning about these false teachers, whoever they may have been, was their ability to teach and defend their false doctrines with such fluent and persuasive speech. They used "smooth talk," speech that sounds so good and plausible and beneficial, speech that creates the illusion of truth based on its form alone, regardless of its content. The Apostle thus reminds us that many a lie is hidden behind eloquence and personal charisma. We must never accept teaching as true just because of the packaging it comes in, but must "search the Scriptures" daily to see if the content of what we are being taught is indeed true (Acts 17:11). We must discipline ourselves to remember that form and style are secondary to content.

Those who are especially vulnerable to being taken in by fancy talk and flattery are described as ἄκακος (*akakos*), "innocent, simple, unsuspecting, unwary, naïve." While a certain kind of simple innocence is good (v. 19), that of which Paul speaks here is not necessarily so. In Christian infancy it may be excusable, but we are supposed to outgrow it as we mature in Christ (Heb 5:11-14). To be called simple-minded in the sense of being easy prey for false teachers is by no means a compliment.

16:19 Everyone has heard about your obedience, so I am full of joy over you; . . . In this verse Paul lets the Roman Christians know that he is not implying that their congregation is itself the origin of these false teachers. He speaks again of their universal reputation for faithfulness (see 1:8), and declares that they are the source of much joy for him personally.

But, he says, this universal good reputation is the very reason why he must warn them about the false teachers. The NIV does not translate the word γάρ (*gar*), with which this verse begins. It means "for, because." It connects with v. 17: "I urge you to watch out for false teachers, because (*gar*) you have a widespread reputation for being a strong and obedient church (❧ II:487).

How may Christians guard against false teachers? Paul gives this instruction: **but I want you to be wise about what is good, and innocent about what is evil.** Being "wise about what is good" presupposes a *knowledge* of what is good, i.e., being thoroughly familiar with sound doctrine with regard to both theology and ethics. But wisdom is more than just knowing these truths; wisdom is knowing how to use them and apply them to life. It is knowing how to live by them, and especially how to distinguish between truth and falsehood and between good and evil. It means to know all about the good, not just in terms of book knowledge but by experience as well.

At the same time, says Paul, the Christian must retain a real innocence with respect to what is evil (including both false beliefs and immoral deeds). The adjective for "innocent" here is ἀκέραιος (*akeraios*), not *akakos* as in v. 18. *Akeraios* literally means "unmixed, untainted," and thus "pure, innocent, guileless." I.e., keep your doctrine (the teaching you believe to be true) unmixed with false teachings; do not let yourself get "all mixed up" in your thinking (see Eph 4:14). Also, keep your moral life unmixed with sin and even the appearance of sin; stay as far away from evil as possible. Be so sensitive to it that the moment you suspect something is evil, flee from it at once.

16:20 The God of peace will soon crush Satan under your feet. This promise is still connected with vv. 17-19. The implication is that Satan is the ultimate source of all lies and false doctrines (John 8:44; 1 Tim 4:1) and thus is the "author of discord" (Bruce, 278). Paul does not hesitate to say that "false teachers are under the influence of Satan, as in 2 Cor 11:14-15" (Fitzmyer, 746-747; see Godet, 489-499).

But Paul's promise is that if we follow his instructions in vv. 17-19, Satan will not ensnare us with false doctrine but will instead be defeated by the power of God and the power of his truth.

The imagery here seems to be taken from Gen 3:15 (Hebrew text), where God promised that the seed of the woman (Jesus) would crush the head of the serpent (Satan). This refers to the work of Jesus in his death and resurrection, by which the Devil was decisively defeated (Heb 2:14, NASB; 1 John 3:8). Paul's point is that the followers of Christ in every way will share in the Messiah's victory over the Devil. The power that wins this victory is God's power; he is the one who actually crushes Satan. But the enemy is crushed *under our feet*, i.e., in our own experience. The word for "crush" (συντρίβω, *syntribō*) is very strong; it means "shatter, smash, crush" (BAGD, 793), leaving no doubt as to who is the winner in this battle.

This *will* happen; it is God's promise. But *when* will it happen? Many think this refers to "the final, eschatological victory of God over Satan" at the Second Coming (Hendriksen, 2:512-513; see Cranfield, 2:803; Dunn, 2:905). Such a victory is certainly assured, but that is probably not Paul's main point here. "Under your feet" does not fit very well with the eschatological defeat of the Devil, which is altogether God's doing. But it does fit the daily victories we experience in the battles of truth against falsehood, and good against evil. Such victories are won by the power of God's Word in inspired Scripture (John 8:32; Rom 1:16; Heb 4:12), and the power of God's Spirit indwelling our bodies (8:13).

The word "soon" is not the best translation of ἐν τάχει (*en tachei*), which is better rendered "quickly, swiftly, speedily, rapidly." Even if this promise referred to the Second Coming, it would not imply that this event was supposed to happen "soon" after Paul wrote. It would only mean that Christ's coming would occur quickly, "in a flash, in the twinkling of an eye" (1 Cor 15:52); see Rev 22:20 (NASB). But the promise refers mainly to our present battle against the Devil, and Paul is assuring us that the victory is not only certain but swift.

It is somewhat paradoxical to say that the God *of peace* (see 15:33; Heb 13:20) will quickly *crush* Satan under our feet. God is truly a God of peace and will establish peace, but he will not do so until his enemies have been defeated in decisive battle. True peace cannot exist in the presence of falsehood and evil. As in the case of Melchizedek (Heb 7:2), the Lord God is first of all King of

Righteousness, and then King of Peace. He does not want "just peace," but "a just and righteous peace."

The grace of our Lord Jesus be with you. This is Paul's standard way of concluding his letters, with the same or a similar blessing appearing at the end of every one of them. In every other letter except 1 Corinthians, it is or is part of the last verse; in 1 Corinthians it is the next to the last verse. Here in Romans it is not at the very end because Paul has a few more greetings to add, and because he wants to conclude this magnificent epistle with a more majestic doxology (❂II:490).

For the grace of Jesus to "be with" us means that we are existing within the shelter of his goodness and are enjoying the gifts of his love, especially the gifts of salvation (❂II:490).

D. GREETINGS FROM PAUL'S COMPANIONS (16:21-24)

16:21 At this point Paul adds greetings from those who are with him in Corinth, beginning with Timothy. **Timothy, my fellow worker, sends his greetings to you, as do Lucius, Jason and Sosipater, my relatives.** Timothy joined Paul on the latter's second missionary journey (Acts 16:1-3) and apparently had been his traveling assistant for about eight years. He was very close to Paul (1 Cor 4:17), and Paul praised him as his most unselfish and dependable worker (Phil 2:19-23). Here Paul calls him his "fellow worker" (see 16:3). He was with Paul in Corinth at this time (Acts 20:4).

Paul refers to the next three men as his "relatives," by which he does not mean close family members but fellow Jews (see 16:7). We cannot with any certainty identify these men with anyone else mentioned in the NT, though possibilities exist and speculations abound.

Most agree that the Lucius named here is not the one mentioned in Acts 13:1 (❂II:491); thus we consider this one to be otherwise unknown. Although we cannot be sure, it is possible that the Jason mentioned here is the same as Paul's harrassed host in the city of Thessalonica (Acts 17:6-9). Some think Sosipater is the same as Sopater in Acts 20:4, since the latter was probably with Paul when he wrote Romans. Morris doubts it, though, since Sosipater is Paul's fellow Jew, and the Sopater in Acts 20:4 would more likely be a Gentile since he was helping to transport the collection from the Gentile churches to the church in Jerusalem (543).

16:22 I, Tertius, who wrote down this letter, greet you in the Lord. Tertius is otherwise unknown, but we know from this verse that he was Paul's amanuensis or scribe, the one who was actually writing down the words of this epistle as Paul dictated them. Comments made by Paul in other letters suggest that he usually used a scribe (1 Cor 16:21; Gal 6:11; Col 4:18; 2 Thess 3:17), but this is the only one who is named.

Having a scribe take down his words by dictation compromises neither the integrity of Paul's authorship of this letter, nor the Holy Spirit's inspiration of it. We can reasonably assume that Paul read the finished product and gave it his apostolic "seal of approval." This one verse, though, was obviously not dictated by Paul, but was Tertius's own greeting to the Romans, perhaps at Paul's suggestion.

Tertius greeted them "in the Lord," i.e., in the name of the Lord Jesus, as a fellow Christian.

16:23 Gaius, whose hospitality I and the whole church here enjoy, sends you his greetings. Though this was a very common name, it is generally agreed that this Gaius is probably the same one listed in 1 Cor 1:14 as one of the few converts Paul personally baptized. Not quite as certain, but still possible, is Gaius's identification with Titius Justus in Acts 18:7. There is reason to think that Titius Justus was not his complete name; Gaius would have been his "first name." Also, this Titius Justus is mentioned along with Crispus (Acts 18:8), who is also linked with Gaius in 1 Cor 1:14. Finally, the Titius Justus in Acts 18:7 opened his house up to Paul and his company when they were run out of the nearby synagogue; here in 16:23 Paul speaks of Gaius's hospitality.

In any case the Gaius named here had a house in Corinth, which he was sharing at this time not only with Paul but with "the whole church." This may mean that he had a large house and allowed it to be used by the entire church *in Corinth* when they wanted to have a combined gathering of the smaller house churches in the city. Or it may mean that he provided hospitality for any Christians who were traveling through Corinth. Moo says it could have been either, but more likely the latter (935).

Erastus, who is the city's director of public works, and our brother Quartus send you their greetings. There was an Erastus who traveled with Paul (Acts 19:22; 2 Tim 4:20); for this reason some assume the one mentioned here cannot be the same person, since this one was a city official in Corinth and could hardly have traveled at will. Not everyone agrees with this, however. Fitzmyer says the two are "almost certainly" the same (750; see Moo, 935). Again, we cannot be sure.

Nor can we say one way or the other whether this Erastus is the same as a city official whose name (Erastus) appears on an inscription in Corinth from this very period. Everything fits except the fact that the title on the inscription (something like "commissioner of public works," says Bruce, 280) is not the same as the title given here, i.e., "city treasurer" (NASB; the NIV translation is imprecise and presumptuous). It is possible that Erastus held both positions at different times, holding one office when Paul wrote and another when the inscription was made.

The last name is Quartus, called "the brother" (NASB), which probably just means that he was a fellow Christian. Nothing else is known about him.

16:24 As stated earlier, this verse as it appears in the Textus Receptus, from which the KJV was translated, was probably not in the original text of Romans and thus is not included in most modern translations, including the NIV. (See Moo, 933, n. 1, for the textual data.) Its content is the same as v. 20b.

III. CONCLUDING DOXOLOGY (16:25-27)

The textual evidence regarding the integrity of this passage (i.e., whether it should be accepted as part of the original Roman letter) is mixed (❧II:493). Moo says, "A decision is very difficult; but we are slightly inclined to include the doxology as part of Paul's original letter" (936-937, n. 2).

I agree with this conclusion and will proceed with the assumption that this is Paul's own inspired conclusion to his letter. It is unthinkable that he would have ended this awe-inspiring composition with nothing more than "and Quartus, the brother" (16:23, NASB; see Godet, 502). Also, the themes which appear in these closing verses echo the themes of the opening verses, 1:1-16 (see Moo, 937-938).

One problem with this passage is that its syntax is not easily decipherable, especially since it appears to be "one long incomplete sentence" (Moo, 938; see v. 27). It may be helpful to set forth at this point a schematic of these verses, showing how the parts are related to the whole. (In what follows, the order of the words and phrases does not always follow the Greek, nor do the order and wording always conform to the NIV.)

I. Now to him who is able to establish you
   A. By my gospel, yea,
   B. [By] the proclamation of Jesus Christ —
     1. [Which is] according to the revelation of the mystery
       a. [Which was] hidden for long ages past,
       b. But now [is]
         (1) Manifested, and
         (2) Made known —
           (a) Unto all the Gentiles,
           (b) Through the prophetic writings,
           (c) By the command of the eternal God,
           (d) For the purpose of obedience of faith;
II. To the only wise God;
III. To him [I say]
   — BE GLORY FOREVER, THROUGH JESUS CHRIST! AMEN!

16:25 Now to him who is able to establish you by my gospel and the proclamation of Jesus Christ, ... As a doxology these words constitute an act of worship and praise offered up to God, but they are not addressed directly to God. They are formulated in third person, not second person. The actual declaration of praise is in v. 27b, "[To him] be glory forever through Jesus Christ!" The verses which precede these words (vv. 25-27a) are identifying the one who is being praised, and explaining (in part) why he should be praised.

That one, of course, is God; and here he is described as the one who is able (δύναμαι, *dynamai*, has the power) "to establish you." One reason Paul wanted to visit the Roman Christians was to impart to them a spiritual gift that would "make [them] strong" (1:11). The word used here and in 1:11 is the same.

As explained earlier (❷I:94-95), the spiritual gift Paul wanted to give the Romans, the gift that would establish them, was the gospel itself. Now that he has completed this epistle, he has in effect given them the gift of the gospel. Thus he can say here in 16:25 that God has the power "to establish you *by my gospel*," i.e., the gospel that was revealed and entrusted to him (1 Cor 15:1-4; Gal 1:11-12) and the gospel which he has just proclaimed in the words of this grand epistle.

"The proclamation of Jesus Christ" is not different from "my gospel," but is an explanation of it. "Proclamation" is κήρυγμα (*kērygma*), which can be either the act of preaching (Matt 12:41) or the message preached (2 Tim 4:17; Titus 1:3). Here it is the latter, and thus identifies the content of the gospel, namely, Jesus Christ (see 1 Cor 15:1-4).

Paul now describes this gospel further. The gospel by which God establishes us, he says, is **according to the revelation of the mystery hidden for long ages past, . . .** This phrase could be taken as parallel with "by my gospel," and thus as giving a second means by which God establishes us. More likely, though, it introduces a more complete description of the gospel. My gospel, says Paul, is in accordance with or in conformity with the revelation of the mystery. Everything from here through the end of v. 26 is part of one long description of this mystery.

Paul says his gospel is in accord with "the revelation of the mystery." In biblical terminology a "mystery" is a truth hidden in the mind of God and undiscoverable by human reason, and thus known only through divine revelation (see 11:25). Thus the word can apply to many things, but for Paul the mystery that seemed to awe him the most was God's plan to include Jews and Gentiles together in the church of Jesus Christ in this New Covenant age (see 11:25 again). This is the mystery that has now been revealed especially to Paul, the Apostle to the Gentiles (Eph 3:3-11); it is the mystery according to which his gospel took shape.

Paul now says three main things about this mystery. First, it was "hidden for long ages past." "Hidden" is σιγάω (*sigaō*), "keep silent, keep secret." I.e., for a long time God kept this a secret; it truly was a mystery. What are these "long ages past"? Some think this refers only to the time preceding the OT prophets (Lard, 467) since the next verse says the mystery is made known "through the prophetic writings." Another view, which I accept, is that these "long ages past" include the OT dispensation and came to an end only with the first coming of

Christ and the proclamation of New Covenant revelation. How, then, could this mystery still have been a *mystery* in OT times if it was made known through the prophetic writings? This is explained in the next verse.

16:26 [B]ut now, says Paul, this mystery is **revealed and made known through the prophetic writings by the command of the eternal God, so that all nations might believe and obey him—** Here is the second fact about the mystery: it is "now revealed" or "manifested" (NASB). "Now" refers to this New Covenant era. "Revealed" is φανερόω (*phaneroō*), the word which is also used in 3:21: "But now a righteousness from God . . . has been made known." The initial and decisive revelation of the mystery was accomplished through the incarnation, ministry, and saving work of Jesus Christ (Morris, 547). But further explanation was necessary. Thus, following Jesus' ascension into heaven, the full meaning of "the mystery of Christ . . . has now been revealed by the Spirit to God's holy apostles and prophets" (Eph 3:4b-5; see 1 Cor 2:6-16). Their revealed and inspired message is given to us in the form of the NT writings.

The third thing about the mystery is that it has been "made known" (γνωρίζω, *gnōrizō*). In Ephesians Paul uses this word five times in referring to the mystery (1:9; 3:3,5,10; 6:19). Here it could be a simple synonym for *phaneroō*, but its placement at the opposite end of the verse (in the Greek) suggests a different connotation. The mystery of Christ has now not only been revealed inwardly to the prophets and apostles, but has been and is being outwardly and publicly made known through the preaching of the gospel to all the world (Godet, 504). See Eph 6:19.

The rest of this verse consists of four prepositional phrases that modify "made known" and thus describe the preaching of the gospel, especially the essence of Paul's ministry as the Apostle to the Gentiles. First, the mystery is made known "to all the nations" (NASB), i.e., to the Gentiles. The unveiled mystery is not a secret to be jealously guarded by an inner circle of gnostic priests, but is a message meant to be proclaimed to everyone.

Second, the mystery is made known "through the prophetic writings." This presents a problem. If the mystery was not revealed and made known until the New Covenant era, how could it be made known *through the prophets*? Does this not imply that it was "made known" even in the OT era? Some say the "prophetic writings" are those of the *New* Covenant prophets mentioned in Eph 2:20; 3:5 (Godet, 505), but most rightly agree that the OT prophets are in view here. How may we explain this?

The answer is simple. Many things revealed to the OT prophets were not capable of being fully understood until the first coming of Christ (1 Pet 1:10-12). But now that Christ has come, the full meaning of these prophetic writings has been made clear. Until Jesus came, the prophecies were there, but their meaning was veiled. Now they are being properly interpreted and clarified in relation to Jesus Christ and his saving work. See 3:21.

Romans Part Six

Paul's point, though, is that the prophetic writings, now understood as applying to Christ and his church, are a *means* of making the mystery known to all the nations. Early Christian preaching was thus heavily dependent upon the OT, and modern preaching could no doubt make better and more frequent use of the "prophetic writings."

Third, the mystery is made known "by the command of the eternal God." This refers first of all to the Great Commission (Matt 28:18-20; Luke 24:47; Acts 1:8), but also refers to Paul's singular commission to be the Apostle to the Gentiles (Murray, 2:242-243). It is the express will and command of God that the now-explained mystery be made known to all.

Finally, the purpose of proclaiming the mystery of Jesus Christ is to bring about "obedience of faith." Paul used this same phrase in 1:5 to explain the ultimate purpose of his apostleship (❧I:78-82). It is fitting that he should refer to it again here at the end of his epistle. The goal of all Christian preaching and witnessing, including the goal of this very letter to the Romans, is to bring about heartfelt obedience that springs from faith in Jesus as Savior and Lord.

16:27 [T]o the only wise God be glory forever through Jesus Christ! Amen. Paul began this doxology by referring to God as the one who is able to establish and strengthen us by the gospel, and then he went into detail about this gospel and the marvelous plan by which God has made it known. Here in v. 27 he catches his breath, so to speak, and refers once more to the God whom he is about to bless. But now he refers to him as "the only wise God."

One question is whether Paul is emphasizing two things about God — his singularity ("the only God") and his wisdom ("the wise God") — or whether he is simply emphasizing the uniqueness of his wisdom. Most agree that the latter is the case. Paul has already blessed God for his wisdom in an earlier doxology (11:33). Elsewhere he declares that the message of the cross of Christ is the epitome of God's wisdom (1 Cor 1:18-25,30), and in Eph 3:10 he refers to the unveiled mystery as "the manifold wisdom of God."

His point here, then, is that the God who has devised such a marvelous plan of salvation has worked it out in the arena of history, has in this present age accomplished it through Jesus Christ, and has made it all known through the gospel — such a God is truly the essence of wisdom! Everything that Paul has written up to this point in this awesome letter causes him to praise and adore God for his wisdom. This is truly a fitting theme with which to close the epistle.

The very last phrase presents a translation problem. As noted earlier, this whole doxology is an incomplete sentence. As is typical of doxologies, it lacks a main verb. Most translations, including the NIV, simply and appropriately add the verb "be." The more difficult problem, though, is the presence in the Greek text of the relative pronoun ᾧ (*hō*, "to whom"), which makes the text read literally, "to the only wise God, through Jesus Christ, *to whom* [be] the glory forever." Grammatically "to whom" could refer to Jesus Christ, which would be doctrinally appropriate, to be sure. Most agree, though, that it refers to God, who has twice been designated as the object of this statement of praise (vv. 25a, 27a). The relative pronoun *hō* would then serve what is called a "resumptive" purpose and would be translated, "To him, I say" (Lenski, 933). The NIV and the NASB simply ignore this pronoun, but they retain the proper meaning.

The phrase "through Jesus Christ" immediately follows "to the only wise God," but is properly interpreted by the NIV as modifying "be glory forever." The eternal glory that we creatures must ascribe to God is obviously warranted by his mighty works of creation and providence, which are distinct from the redemptive work of the incarnate Christ (*GRe*, 27-43). But the glory that surpasses all other, and elicits from God's saints the highest possible praise, is the glory that is due him for what he has done through our Lord and Savior, Jesus Christ. Amen!

All in all these words of praise magnify and glorify the God of grace. It is only fitting that a doxology so "elaborate and grand in thought and in form" should close this great epistle (Lenski, 927).